Handbook of Biodiversity Methods

Biodiversity is recognised to be of global importance, yet species and habitats continue to be under increasing pressure from human-induced influences, whether in urban, rural or wilderness settings. Environmental concerns have never before been so high on the political agenda, driving increased legislation which places major emphasis on individual, public and corporate responsibility for conserving biodiversity and for managing development in an environmentally sensitive and sustainable way. The starting point for assessing legal compliance is the requirement for a comprehensive biodiversity audit. For those needing to undertake such audits, this *Handbook* provides standard procedures for planning and conducting a survey of any terrestrial or freshwater species or habitat and for evaluating the data so as to determine its local, national and international significance.

Organised in three parts, the *Handbook* first addresses planning, providing a pragmatic approach to method selection, sampling strategy, and data analysis and evaluation. The second part is devoted to habitats, describing survey, evaluation and monitoring methods for a broad range of habitats. Part III considers species and provides information on general methods before addressing specific methods of survey and monitoring for the major taxonomic groups (lower plants, fungi, vascular plants, invertebrates, fish, amphibians, reptiles, birds and mammals).

The *Handbook* provides an invaluable compendium for ecologists, wildlife managers, nature conservation professionals, local and national authorities, environmental managers, corporate bodies and companies, government conservation agencies and regulators involved in auditing ecological resources. It will enable practitioners to better monitor the condition of the biodiversity resource, resulting in improved data upon which to base future conservation, management, development and policy decisions and actions.

David Hill is Director of Ecology for RPS Group plc, a leading environmental consultancy.

Matthew Fasham is a Principal Consultant for RPS Group plc.

Graham Tucker is a freelance ecologist with Ecological Solutions.

Michael Shewry is an environmental statistician with Scottish Natural Heritage.

Philip Shaw is an environmental audit specialist with the Advisory Services of Scottish Natural Heritage.

Any opinions expressed are those of the authors and do not necessarily represent the views of RPS or Scottish Natural Heritage.

Handbook of Biodiversity Methods

Survey, Evaluation and Monitoring

Edited by
David Hill
Matthew Fasham
Graham Tucker
Michael Shewry
Philip Shaw

CAMBRIDGE
UNIVERSITY PRESS

CAMBRIDGE
UNIVERSITY PRESS

University Printing House, Cambridge CB2 8BS, United Kingdom

Published in the United States of America by Cambridge University Press, New York

Cambridge University Press is part of the University of Cambridge.

It furthers the University's mission by disseminating knowledge in the pursuit of
education, learning and research at the highest international levels of excellence.

www.cambridge.org
Information on this title: www.cambridge.org/9780521823685

First published 2005
6th printing 2012

A catalogue record for this publication is available from the British Library

ISBN 978-0-521-82368-5 Hardback

In memory of Colin J. Bibby,
an outstanding conservation scientist

Contents

Preface

This generation is living at a time when the world's biodiversity resources have never been so impoverished. If we take the UK as an example of what has happened across many parts of the planet, since 1945, largely as a result of agricultural intensification, we have lost over 50% of our ancient lowland woodlands, 150 000 miles of hedgerow, 95% of traditional hay meadows, 80% of chalk downland and 80% of wetland fens and mires. This has given rise to massive losses in some, once very common, farmland birds: in the past 30 years 40% of Song Thrushes, 54% of Yellowhammers, a staggering 87% of Starlings and 90% of Corn Buntings have disappeared.

In addition to agricultural intensification, development pressure as a result of industrialisation, human population expansion and resultant increases in the 'ecological footprint' of our own species through, for example, house building, airports, seaports, road infrastructure, water supply, energy generation, waste management, freight distribution and extraction of raw materials, has taken its toll on biodiversity. The UK government's sustainable development commission recently announced that the country has a very long way to go before existing developments, and the way we manage environmental resources, can be deemed to be 'sustainable'. This is without any consideration of the impending threat from climate change.

But it would be wrong to focus entirely on the negatives. There are signs that our attitudes to our environment are changing and there are a growing number of examples where the primary focus of governments, companies and individuals is towards the stitching back of the fabric of the environment and countryside. A range of agri-environment schemes is attempting to redress the damage caused to farmland biodiversity by the Common Agricultural Policy, reforming subsidies away from production and into environmental benefits. Organisations such as the RSPB continue to expand their reserve network and extend new habitats near existing ones by means of novel techniques based on scientific understanding. There is large-scale restoration of contaminated land sites. Coastal managed realignment offers opportunities to create massive areas of wet grassland, saltmarsh and reedbed habitat, which will provide substantial benefits to wildfowl and waders. Industry, too, is working with organisations to create large-scale reserves in currently uninteresting farmland, a prime example being the Great Fenland Project in the Cambridgeshire Fens of the UK.

As biodiversity has dwindled in the past 50 years, so policies and laws aimed at turning the tide have flourished. There are now over 200 legal instruments aimed at protecting the environment and which have an impact on countries such as the UK. The greatest successes have been achieved where there has been government regulation: we now have the best air and water quality in Britain for about 200 years, almost entirely as a result of regulation. Key instruments for biodiversity conservation in the UK are the Wildlife & Countryside Act, the Countryside and Rights of Way Act, The Nature Conservation (Scotland) Act EU Birds and Habitats Directives, the Habitats Regulations, the EIA Directive and EIA Regulations, the Hedgerow Regulations, Bonn Convention, Ramsar Convention, Bern Convention, European and National Red Lists of species of conservation concern, and Biodiversity Action Plans. A whole industry has developed to support biodiversity conservation, to save what we have and improve upon it. In parallel there has been increased site-based protection: the designation of local wildlife sites, green corridors, County Wildlife Sites, Sites of Special Scientific Interest, National Nature Reserves, Special Protection Areas, Special Areas of Conservation, Biosphere Reserves and World Heritage Sites.

During this recent period we have moved from a natural history mentality to an accountancy mentality, where numbers and targets are the order of the day. Government has set out some ambitious targets for biodiversity: by 2010, for example, it wants 95% of all SSSIs in England to be in a Favourable Condition. We have a long way to go. Currently about 42% of the one million or so hectares of SSSIs in England fail to make the grade of 'Favourable Condition'. The percentages in unfavourable condition in England, according to selected habitats, are: rivers and streams 69%, upland grasslands and heaths *c.* 65%, fen, marsh and swamp 35%, and lowland broadleaved woodland 33%. This gives an idea of the widespread losses in quality that have taken place in addition to losses in habitat quantity. Changes to quality are being addressed by a plethora of site or conservation management plans, and similar mechanisms are being used to mitigate for development impacts, including Section 106 agreements, unilateral undertakings and mitigation plans.

So, against this background of biodiversity decline and a commitment to rebuild it, there are three observations I would make. First, ecology has a vital part to play in delivering a better quality environment and better quality of life for people. Second, environmental quality improvements are increasingly being seen as solutions rather than as costly problems at the levels of both the corporate entity and society at large. Third, there is a need for high-quality information on which to base decisions. We have written this *Handbook* in order to enable biodiversity data to be collected and evaluated according to standard procedures. Future decisions on policy reforms, land management, development impacts and biodiversity conservation initiatives at a range of spatial scales can then be based on fact rather than on conjecture.

The *Handbook* consists of three parts. The first (Part I) addresses planning and describes how to set objectives, what is it you actually want to do, selecting the appropriate method, how to design a survey and/or monitoring programme, sampling strategy and data analysis. There is then a section which describes generically how to evaluate the data collected: what does it mean at different spatial scales?

Part II is devoted to habitat survey, evaluation and monitoring, describing approaches for the full range of habitats in the UK but with direct relevance to many countries. For each habitat type the potential attributes that indicate condition are defined, together with appropriate and commonly used methods for surveying them and establishing a monitoring scheme for the habitat concerned. Based on structural similarities the methods can be applied to the full range of habitat types found in Europe and, indeed, in other parts of the world. Evaluation criteria are developed and defined for each habitat.

Part III is devoted to the survey, evaluation and monitoring of species. General methods applicable to a range of taxa are first described, such as total counts, timed searches, use of quadrats, distance sampling, line transects, point counts, etc. Each taxonomic group is then addressed, from fungi to mammals. For each group, the attributes for assessing condition are described, followed by survey and monitoring methods that can be applied, and then details of particular methods for species of conservation importance as appropriate. Finally, for each group there is a section that describes the currently applicable conservation evaluation criteria.

I hope that the approaches and methods described in this *Handbook* will stand the test of time and enable us to better monitor the condition of the biodiversity resource. We should then be able to plan improved biodiversity conservation and measure how well we are doing towards meeting targets in the years ahead.

David Hill

Acknowledgements

The writing of the *Handbook* has been a mammoth task. However, we have been very fortunate to have been able to assemble a highly competent team of authors who not only eased the task but were able to take the text to greater depths of detail than any one of the editors could possibly have achieved. Their wisdom, knowledge and experience shines through. We therefore thank our contributing authors for their superb support and hard work.

We were also fortunate to have had to hand a long list of experts who kindly commented on the original version. Our sincere thanks go to Helen Armstrong, Sally Blyth, Phil Boon, Mairi Cole, Andrew Coupar, Louise Cox, Andy Douse, Kathy Duncan, Willie Duncan, Lynne Farrell, Vin Fleming, Stuart Gardner, Martin Gaywood, Doug Gilbert, Dave Horsfield, Keith Kirby, John Kupiec, Kate Holl, Philip Immirzi, Ross Johnstone, Ed Mackey, Jane Mackintosh, Jill Matthews, Angus MacDonald, Ed Mountford, John Orr, Brigid Primrose, Deborah Procter, Geeta Puri, Rob Raynor, Terry Rowell, Pamela Strachan, Chris Sydes, Neale Taylor, Gavin Tudor, Stephen Ward, Christine Welch, Peter Wortham and the late David Phillips.

RPS provided time and logistical support to the whole project which enabled us to meet deadlines and to see the whole project through to a fruitful conclusion. We are most grateful to them. Alan Crowden of Cambridge University Press and Michael Usher, then Chief Scientist for Scottish Natural Heritage, were convinced that the project was worthwhile and gave much encouragement and support.

Finally, we thank the many professionals who are striving to ensure we stitch back together the fabric of the countryside, both in the UK and abroad, to secure a future environment in which it is worth living. We hope this book plays some small part in assessing how well we are doing in the years to come.

Part I • Planning

1 • Introduction to planning

1.1 THE PURPOSE OF SURVEYING AND MONITORING

The development of a successful programme is dependent upon being clear about what you want to do and why, i.e. your objectives. It is therefore important to define what monitoring is and how surveys relate to monitoring. Survey and monitoring is undertaken for a wide range of objectives: for example, to measure a site's quality, or a species' abundance, to assess species and habitat trends, for Environmental Impact Assessment (EIA) studies, for corporate reporting, or to assess compliance with international conservation agreements. These operate at many different spatial scales and therefore necessitate targeted methods for different applications, objectives and deliverables. The significance and global importance of monitoring nature conservation is aptly summarised in Appendix 1, which describes the monitoring and reporting obligations under international conservation agreements as an example of the far-reaching implications of the need to use adequate methods.

1.1.1 General objectives of surveying and monitoring

For the purposes of Environmental Impact Assessment (EIA) studies, the term 'survey' defines the collection of spatial and/or temporal data about a species, a community or a habitat. The information provides a snapshot of presence, absence and, dependent on its design and sophistication, abundance and spatial distribution. In EIA studies the survey data are used to evaluate the ecological resource on a site, which is then assessed or evaluated against set agreed criteria. Impacts are considered in respect of this resource and assessed for significance. Parts II and III of this *Handbook* describe specific survey methods for habitats and the full range of species from lower plants to mammals. However, for some studies, particularly in relation to testing the effects of macro-environmental policy changes at a large spatial scale, actual monitoring is performed. The emphasis in Part I of this *Handbook* is the design of data collection and the analytical treatment of the data collected. Much of Part I therefore considers the planning, design and implementation of survey and monitoring, the latter often comprising a series of replicated surveys using standard methods.

Once the data have been collected they will need to be used for a specific purpose. One of the most important uses is to evaluate a site, species, community, habitat, region, etc. Part I therefore includes a section on generic approaches to evaluation of biodiversity data, with more specific treatment for habitats and species given in the relevant sections of Parts II and III.

As with monitoring, it is essential at the outset of a survey to define objectives. A project may not meet its full potential unless the aims are properly understood and researched before data collection begins. Before planning your survey methods, consider the variety of possible scenarios that could dictate your project's fieldwork techniques. Do the results need to apply to one site or to a wide geographical area? Are many species involved or just one? Are accurate counts needed (spatially referenced) or will relative counts or presence–absence data suffice? Answers to these questions will determine the time commitments required and hence cost. In general terms, surveys conducted for EIA studies should aim to provide information on the following.

- What species and habitats occur (= the resource)?
- Where do they occur?
- How many of them are there or how much of the habitat is there?
- How does this amount of the resource relate to that existing in the wider area/biogeographical region?
- What are the seasonal changes and when is the most susceptible or sensitive period for these species/habitats?

Monitoring is often loosely regarded as a programme of repeated surveys in which qualitative or quantitative observations are made, usually by means of a standardised procedure. However, by itself this is merely surveillance as there is no preconception of what the findings ought to be. Monitoring can be more rigorously defined as 'intermittent (regular or irregular) surveillance undertaken to determine the extent of compliance with a predetermined standard or the degree of deviation from an expected norm' (Hellawell, 1991) . In this context, a standard can be a baseline position (e.g. maintenance of the existing area of a particular habitat or population of a particular species) or a position set as an objective (e.g. maintenance of more than 200 ha of a desired habitat or more than 200 individuals of a desired species).

Thus, whereas surveys and surveillance are to a large extent open-ended, a monitoring programme has a specific purpose that requires the standard to be defined or formulated in advance. This requires the identification of interest *features* (e.g. various habitats and species), their *attributes* (e.g. area, numbers, structure and reproductive success) and their target state, i.e. the *standard* that is to be monitored (see Glossary for detailed definitions of monitoring terms). Monitoring for conservation purposes should be closely linked to site management and should test whether conservation and management objectives have been achieved, as outlined in Figure 1.1.

The monitoring programme and methods chosen must be *focused and fit for their purpose* and should not attempt to describe the general ecology of a site. Unfortunately, monitoring schemes often resort to measuring a wide variety of variables, which may or may not be related to the questions that need to be addressed. As a result, resources may be spent collecting unnecessary data. Even worse, it may be found that key questions cannot be answered with the information obtained. This is because monitoring is often planned backwards, on a 'collect-now (data), think-later (of a useful question)' basis (Roberts, 1991).

Strictly speaking, the minimum requirement of monitoring is an assessment of adherence to, or deviation from, formulated standards. However, it is clearly desirable to collect data in such a way that gradual change can be detected to assist management decision-making. Management adjustments (at both field and policy level) require knowledge of the dynamic situation, i.e. whether the feature is moving towards or away from the standard, from which direction, and whether the change is expected, acceptable or otherwise (Rowell, 1993).

Monitoring should not be confused with research aimed at investigating ecological processes. Nevertheless, data collected for monitoring purposes can sometimes also be used to examine possible causes of change and to investigate the relationship between features of interest and environmental variables and pressures. Such information can then be used to formulate appropriate responses. For example, comparison of sward composition with stocking density may predict optimal management regimes. Further monitoring of the vegetation and stocking rates can then confirm whether management and habitat objectives are being met.

Thus, in summary, monitoring can:

- establish whether standards are being met;
- detect change and trigger responses if any of the changes are undesirable;
- contribute to the diagnosis of the causes of change; and
- assess the success of actions taken to maintain standards or to reverse undesirable changes, and, where necessary, contribute to their improvement.

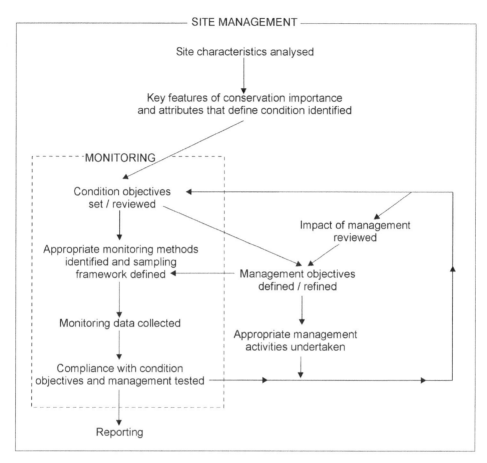

Figure 1.1. A schematic representation of the relationship between site management and monitoring.

Monitoring should therefore be an integral part of all conservation programmes.

1.1.2   Common Standards Monitoring in the UK

The UK statutory conservation agencies (the Countryside Council for Wales, English Nature, the Environment and Heritage Service in Northern Ireland, and Scottish Natural Heritage) have undertaken to monitor statutory protected sites to determine whether the features of interest for which each site has been designated are being maintained in a *favourable condition*. To provide a basic framework that will ensure consistent monitoring throughout the UK, a *Statement of Common Standards for Monitoring*

Designated Sites (JNCC, 1997) has been adopted by the agencies and the Joint Nature Conservation Committee (JNCC). This formalises the monitoring principles outlined above and provides standards for the setting of objectives, judging the condition of site features, recording activities and management measures, and monitoring and reporting within an agreed time-frame.

For further information on the Common Standards approach see Rowell (1993, 1997) and Brown (1994). See Shaw & Wind (1997) for a discussion of monitoring European conservation sites. Detailed guidance on the interpretation and application of Common Standards Monitoring has been prepared by the statutory agencies and is available from them.

2 • Planning a programme

The major steps involved in planning and executing a monitoring programme are illustrated in Figure 2.1. Many of the aspects are relevant to planning and executing a survey. A list of key considerations that must be addressed when planning a monitoring programme is given in Box 2.1 with the relevant section numbers. All of these issues should be carefully considered in a step-by-step process before any fieldwork is started.

2.1 SETTING THE OBJECTIVES FOR THE MONITORING PROGRAMME

Clearly and explicitly defining your objectives is probably the most important single step of any monitoring programme. Failure to do so may render any results gained inappropriate to the question you wished to address, and therefore useless. Carefully defining your objectives will also allow you to select the most appropriate methodology. In particular it is essential that you ask yourself: What do I really need to know? The process of defining objectives underpins good site management principles and the development of management plans (see, for example, CCW, 1996) of which monitoring should be an integral part (Figure 1.1). Guidance on establishing clearly defined objectives is provided below.

2.1.1 What features of conservation interest are to be monitored?

The first step in defining the objectives of any ecological monitoring programme must be the identification of features of interest on the site. Biological features may be habitats, species or species assemblages.

As there is clearly a link between habitat and species features, there is often likely to be some overlap between their monitoring requirements. Species, particularly plants, are often essential components that define a habitat (e.g. ericoid shrubs on heathlands). Individual species or species assemblages may therefore often be monitored as attributes of a habitat feature.

In addition to monitoring species for which sites have been designated, it is important to monitor the area and quality of suitable habitat for such species. There may also be other species that, although not necessarily of conservation concern in themselves, may require monitoring by virtue of association with a species that is a feature of interest (for example, the food plant of a particular animal species). Monitoring such habitats and associated species can give extra information about the condition of species features that may prove useful for formulating management options for the site.

Some sites may be important for the presence of a species assemblage (e.g. a diverse community of insects or a good example of a particular vegetation community). For these assemblages, it may be possible to monitor one or more indicator species, which can be used to infer the presence or status of other associated species, rather than monitoring each individual species. However, the use of indicator species should be approached with care, and in particular should only be relied on when the relationship between the condition of the indicator and that of the interest feature has been proven and quantified. If this is not the case, then all relevant species will need to be monitored. See Rowell (1994) for further guidance on the use of indicators.

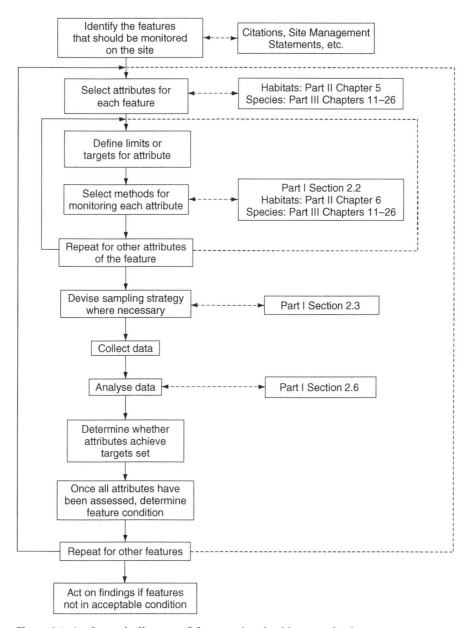

Figure 2.1. A schematic diagram of the steps involved in a monitoring programme.

The monitoring of assemblages presents some problems. On a site important for its diverse beetle community, for example, does the loss of one species constitute serious damage, or do several species need to decline before the assemblage is considered to be in an unacceptable condition? Assemblages can be assessed by using species richness or diversity indices; judgement will be required to decide how to set limits for these.

In general, an essential part of monitoring a species of conservation concern will be to monitor the area of suitable habitat, and an essential part of

Box 2.1   A checklist of considerations during the preparation of a monitoring programme

SETTING OBJECTIVES FOR THE MONITORING PROGRAMME (2.1)

What features of conservation interest are to be monitored? (2.1.1)

What is the objective for each feature? (2.1.2)

What attributes define condition in these features and what are likely to be their acceptable limits? (2.1.2)

How often should monitoring be carried out? (2.1.3)

What are the operational and/or management objectives for the site? (2.1.4)

Are there external factors that may have significant impacts on the site? (2.1.5)

What monitoring has been undertaken, and are baseline surveys required? (2.1.6)

Should the site be subdivided into monitoring units? (2.1.7)

SELECTION OF METHODS FOR MONITORING EACH ATTRIBUTE (2.2)

Is the method likely to damage the environment? (2.2.1)

Are samples required? (2.2.2)

Will the method provide the appropriate type of measurement? (2.2.3)

Can the method measure the attribute across an appropriate range of conditions? (2.2.4)

Is the method prone to substantial measurement error? (2.2.5)

DESIGNING A SAMPLING STRATEGY (2.3)

Has the method been thoroughly tested and are preliminary field trials necessary? (2.3.1)

Is the method sufficiently precise? (2.3.2)

Should sample locations be permanent or not? (2.3.3)

When should the data be collected? (2.3.6)

How will consistency be assured? (2.3.7)

REVIEWING THE MONITORING PROGRAMME (2.4)

Are there sufficient long-term resources available? (2.4.1)

Are personnel sufficiently trained and experienced? (2.4.2)

Are licences required? (2.4.3)

Is specialist equipment required and available? (2.4.4)

Are there health and safety issues to consider? (2.4.5)

DATA RECORDING AND STORAGE (2.5)

How will data be recorded in the field? (2.5.1)

How will the data be stored? (2.5.2)

Who will hold and manage the data? (2.5.3)

DATA ANALYSIS, INTERPRETATION AND REVIEW (2.6)

Who will carry out the analysis and when? (2.6.1)

How will the data be analysed? (2.6.2)

What statistical tests are appropriate to analyse the data? (2.6.4)

Is transformation of the data necessary before statistical analysis? (2.6.4)

What statistical packages are available for the analysis of data? (2.6.6)

---

monitoring a habitat will involve the monitoring of its constituent species.

Identifying notified features should be straightforward for Special Areas of Conservation (SACs) and Special Protection Areas (SPAs), as a list of features is drawn up during the designation process. Identification of notified features may be more difficult on Sites of Special Scientific Interest (SSSIs) for which the citation may be imprecise or based on an early version of the selection guidelines. For clarification, refer to the guidelines for the selection of biological SSSIs (NCC, 1989; Hodgetts, 1992; JNCC, 1994) and contact the relevant country agency.

2.1.2   What is the objective for each feature?

For each interest feature to be monitored, an objective should be defined that identifies appropriate attributes of the feature and, where possible, sets a target for each one. Each target may include an upper and a lower limit, within which the feature is considered to be in acceptable condition.

Attributes of a habitat may reflect a number of properties of the feature, including aspects of quantity (e.g. size or number of individuals),

Box 2.2 Examples of attributes that may be used to define the condition of habitats and species

HABITAT ATTRIBUTES
Quantity
area

Quality: physical attributes
geological (e.g. presence of bare rock or deep peat)
water (e.g. presence of open water or depth of water table)

Quality: composition
communities
richness or diversity
typical, keystone or indicator species
presence–absence
frequency
number or density
cover
biomass

Quality: structure
inter-habitat (landscape) scale (e.g. fragmentation, habitat mosaics)
intra-habitat scale
macro-scale
    horizontal (e.g. plant community mosaics)
    vertical (e.g. ground-, shrub- and tree-layer topography)
micro-scale
    horizontal (e.g. patches of short and tall vegetation)
    vertical (e.g. within-layer topography)

Quality: dynamics
succession
reproduction or regeneration
cyclic change and patch dynamics

Quality: function
physical and biochemical (e.g. soil stabilisation, carbon sinks)
ecosystem (e.g. net producer)

SPECIES ATTRIBUTES
Quantity
presence/absence
range
population size
frequency
number/density
cover

Population dynamics
recruitment
mortality
emigration
immigration

Population structure
age
sex ratio
fragmentation or isolation
genetic diversity

Habitat requirements

composition (presence of particular species, overall diversity, etc.), structure, function or dynamics (Box 2.2). These principles are outlined below. There is further discussion of attributes that define the condition of specific habitat types in Chapter 5.

Species attributes for which targets may be set include range, abundance, population dynamics and habitat requirements. Part III describes methods for monitoring range (presence–absence across a site), abundance (population density) and dynamics

(e.g. breeding success and population structure) (see Box 2.2). In most cases, direct monitoring of species will generally be targeted towards measuring range and abundance; more detailed studies may be constrained by a lack of resources or appropriate skills. The costs involved in monitoring population structure, for example, can be particularly high. It should be borne in mind that in some cases (for example, monitoring bryophytes in fragile habitats), quantitative monitoring may damage the habitat and hence the species, and is therefore not feasible.

The setting of targets and limits for attributes is outside the scope of this *Handbook* as these are dependent on local site conditions. The UK statutory agencies have produced guidance on this for the purposes of Common Standards Monitoring.

Habitat attributes
Quantity

Quantity may be the simplest attribute of a habitat in terms of indicating its condition. However, in many situations habitats and communities are not objectively or precisely definable and there is consequently some doubt about where boundaries lie. This can make habitat quantification and interpretation of change difficult. None the less, especially for EIA studies, this is important if habitat area is to be lost and needs to be replaced according to some criteria.

Quality: physical attributes

Certain physical attributes of a habitat can be considered to be essential or desirable in their own right. For example, the presence of peat is an essential attribute of blanket bog. Similarly, the presence of grikes is a characteristic attribute of limestone pavements.

It is often difficult to decide whether physical properties are direct attributes of a habitat or factors that may influence it. For example, are the chemical characteristics of river water (e.g. nutrient status and pH) attributes or factors that influence other aspects of the habitat such as macrophytic communities? In principle, in habitats in which such distinctions are difficult, key factors that may influence the habitat should be monitored.

Quantity: composition

The composition of a habitat in terms of its communities and species is a fundamental attribute of habitat condition. Many statutory sites are notified because of the presence of particular vegetation communities and therefore monitoring should ensure that targets for these are being met.

Monitoring all species is clearly not feasible in all but the simplest habitats. Therefore, the most commonly used species-based attributes of habitat composition are species richness and the presence or abundance of typical species or vegetation communities.

Typical species are hard to define, but Shaw & Wind (1997) suggest the following:

- species on which the identification of the habitat is founded;
- species that are inseparable from the habitat;
- characteristic species;
- species that are consistently present but not restricted;
- species that are an integral part of the habitat; and
- keystone species (Jermy *et al.*, 1996), which significantly influence the habitat's structure and function. (Note: such species may include animals as well as plants.)

Diversity indices (Magurran, 1983) are not normally recommended for habitat condition monitoring as the setting of targets and interpretation of changes in these indices is difficult.

In some cases it may be appropriate to monitor 'indicator species'. The presence and/or abundance of such species may be used to indicate favourable or unfavourable ecological conditions that may be difficult or costly to detect by other means. For example, aquatic plants can be used as indicators of overall water quality (Palmer *et al.*, 1992). Care should be taken with the use of indicator species, however, as they may not always be reliable (Rowell, 1994).

There are a number of parameters that may be appropriate for target setting and measurement when monitoring the abundance of typical (or other) species. These are described below.

Presence or absence

The simplest target for a species is that its presence at the site, or at a defined location within it, is maintained. This is normally straightforward to monitor, but there are occasions when difficulties may arise: for example, for species that are inconspicuous, difficult to identify or rare, or those that inhabit inaccessible areas.

The distribution (range) of a species across a site can be monitored by assessing presence–absence across a number of locations (e.g. grid squares), and distribution maps can be drawn up for such surveys. Repeat presence–absence surveys can indicate expansions or contractions in range.

Frequency

Frequency is the proportion of quadrats (or other sample units) examined in which the species is present. Frequency is a simple, quantitative measure, and has been widely used to describe relative abundance. With a large number of sampling units of sufficiently small size, frequency estimates of plant species can approximate to cover (see below). For plants, there are two measures of frequency: shoot frequency (the presence of any foliage within the quadrat) and root frequency (the presence of rooted individuals only). Frequency estimates depend on the size of the quadrats and of individual plant species (large plants may be over-represented compared with small plants) and the spatial distribution of individuals of a species (clustered species may be under-represented compared with more widely spaced ones). Frequency measures may also exaggerate the apparent biomass of small species and hence overestimate their functional significance.

Changes in frequency are relatively insensitive to seasonal or management changes, and therefore a large sample size is required to be effective for monitoring change in the short term. However, frequency estimates are relatively free of observer error and hence are particularly useful for general habitat condition monitoring purposes.

A useful extension of the simple frequency measure is to record presence–absence within subdivisions of each plot. For example, a plot may be divided into a 5 × 5 grid giving 25 subdivisions. The measure recorded is the proportion of subdivisions containing the species of interest. This will be more sensitive to change than simple frequency and is often quicker to record than cover. Within this *Handbook*, this measure is referred to as *sub-plot frequency*.

Density

Density is the number of individuals per unit area (e.g. plants within the habitat). Counts of numbers of individuals in quadrats have been widely used for demographic studies, but less so for vegetation monitoring because of the difficulties of defining individuals of clonal or rhizomatous plants (White, 1979) and the amount of time required to count numbers accurately in large sample sizes. However, sub-plot frequency is often used as a quicker alternative. Densities depend on reproduction, dispersal, population ages, etc., which may vary from year to year. These annual variations in population sizes mean that samples have to be recorded regularly to separate normal fluctuations from directional change.

Density estimates can be converted to total population size estimates by multiplying the density by the area of similar habitat. Alternatively, total population counts over an area may be used to derive density. Extrapolating density estimates from a smaller area to a larger one is only meaningful if the larger area has the same characteristics as the area from which the density was originally estimated. When making such extrapolations you need to be sure that all individuals are detected or that a detectability function can be estimated: see Section 10.6 for more details.

Cover

Cover is a measure of the area covered by the above-ground stems and foliage of a plant species when viewed from above. Greig-Smith (1983) defined cover as 'the proportion of ground occupied by a perpendicular projection onto it of the aerial parts of individuals of the species'. The sum of cover values from all species in layered vegetation often totals more than 100%. Cover is usually described as a percentage, or by using one of the numerous categorical indices available (see Shimwell, 1971). The most widely used of these is the Domin scale as used in the National Vegetation Classification (NVC) methodology (Rodwell, 1991 *et seq.*). (Box 2.3) Cover estimates provide a good description of the contributions of each species to the vegetation; as long as measurements are accurate, they are sensitive to short-term fluctuations in season or management. However, cover estimates, whether percentages or scales, are prone to bias and considerable care is required to ensure accuracy and consistency.

Box 2.3   The Domin scale

Domin scale	Equivalent percentage cover		
		5	11%–25%
		4	4%–10%
10	91%–100%	3	<4% – frequent
9	76%–90%	2	<4% – occasional
8	51%–75%	1	<4% – rare
7	34%–50%	+	Insignificant: normally 1–2 individuals
6	26%–33%		with no measurable cover

Biomass

Biomass is the contribution of each species measured by weight (both fresh weight or dry weight can be measured). Biomass estimates are useful for assessing productivity, but normally require destructive sampling where vegetation is concerned. Usually, only aerial parts of plants are collected.

Quality: structure

Structure is an important attribute of a habitat that can be measured at a variety of scales. Inter-habitat or landscape-scale structure may be important where, for example, fragmentation alters habitat structure and ecological processes and thereby reduces the suitability of an area of habitat for typical species. In contrast, some ecological processes and species may require mosaics of differing habitats.

Intra-habitat structure is also often a fundamental attribute of habitat condition, which itself occurs at a variety of scales. At the larger scale, vegetation community mosaics may be a distinctive feature of a habitat (e.g. bog pool and hummock communities in some blanket bogs). Vertical structure is also important, especially in woodlands, where three or more layers of ground flora, shrubs and canopy vegetation may be found.

There is probably no practical lower limit to the size of significant structural variation within habitats, as micro-scale variations in vegetation cover, height and layering may be important components of habitat condition, especially for species with specific habitat requirements. However, as the potential variety of structural attributes and their

complexity increases with decreasing scale, the setting of meaningful targets and their measurement becomes increasingly difficult. The inclusion of microstructural attributes of habitats is therefore beyond the scope of most monitoring programmes.

Quantity: dynamics

Habitats are never static and therefore monitoring must ensure that essential dynamic processes are functioning adequately. For example, vegetation surveys can indicate insufficient regeneration in individual species or whole vegetation communities. Some habitats will require areas that are temporarily altered, for example by fire or storms, to allow regrowth of young vegetation. This is particularly important in woodlands, where gap dynamics affect the species composition and structure of stands.

In some cases it is important to ensure that successional habitats change in specific directions and at desirable rates.

Quantity: function

Processes (e.g. peat formation or dune formation) are highly important ecosystem functions. However, such processes are difficult to define and even harder to monitor and assess. Thus, although these are important attributes, it is frequently impracticable to use them for monitoring habitat condition.

Species attributes
Quantity

Species may have *minimum viable population* sizes (Soulé, 1987): the number of individuals below which the population cannot persist. Minimum viable populations should therefore provide the basis for establishing minimum quantities (lower limits) for species. Unfortunately it is widely felt that there are usually too many unknowns (in terms of both theory and data) to make judgements on what those lower limits might be. Furthermore, the use of the concept is complicated by the fact that sites will not normally hold discrete and isolated populations.

Minimum *desirable* populations (the minimum population that is considered to be safely above the minimum viable population) for species are identified by judgement and consensus. Because they are normally based on estimates it is advisable to adopt the precautionary principle, so they should always be well above the likely range of any minimum viable population.

Trends in population size and range are therefore central to the conservation status of a species and are also relatively simple to monitor. Species that are decreasing as a result of habitat changes may become rarer by two means:

1. restriction of their geographical range;
2. reduction in their density.

In an ideal situation, a species' condition on a site would be judged by determining whether it had achieved targets set for its population size, rate of change, and levels of recruitment and mortality (Davies & Yost, 1998). However, there are generally insufficient data or resources to allow measurement of recruitment or mortality, and too little information on 'acceptable' rates of population change to be able to use this as part of an objective. Natural variation in populations is also poorly documented and therefore difficult to incorporate into definitions of condition for many species. One example in which population change rates are being used at the site level, however, is in the application of 'alert limits' for wildfowl populations (Atkinson *et al.*, 2000).

Measures for directly or indirectly assessing the population size of a species are:

- presence–absence
- range
- frequency

- number or density
- cover (for plants)

These are discussed under the assessment of habitat composition above. The choice of which measurement to use will depend on the characteristics of the target species (see Part III).

It should be remembered when setting objectives for the abundance of a species at a site that it is often very difficult and time-consuming to establish absolute population numbers, whether by total counts or by sampling (see Section 2.3). Objectives for abundance should be based on simple and efficient population index-based measures if such assessments are adequate for defining condition.

Population dynamics

The dynamics of, and overall trends in, population size depend on the balance between recruitment, mortality, emigration and immigration. Recruitment and mortality are of particular importance to the condition of the population. These must at least balance if the population is to remain stable and hence in acceptable condition. However, the population at a site may appear stable, yet may be dependent on immigration to offset poor productivity. As such, if deaths are greater than productivity the population acts as a 'sink' and this can be regarded as being in an unacceptable condition (but see Figure 2.3). Conversely, a population may act as a 'source' if more young are produced than are able to breed at the natal site. When considering the balance of recruitment and mortality, source and sink populations therefore need to be taken into account. To ensure a long-term underlying favourable population trend (i.e. stable or increasing) and to ensure that populations are self-sustaining, it is desirable to measure recruitment and mortality.

The following variables may have a bearing on the population dynamics of a species, and can be used as measurable attributes of species condition where appropriate:

- number of offspring produced by parent(s), e.g. seedling germination for trees or the number of young fledged per pair for birds;

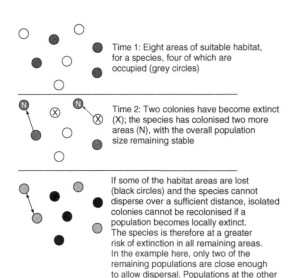

Time 1: Eight areas of suitable habitat, for a species, four of which are occupied (grey circles)

Time 2: Two colonies have become extinct (X); the species has colonised two more areas (N), with the overall population size remaining stable

If some of the habitat areas are lost (black circles) and the species cannot disperse over a sufficient distance, isolated colonies cannot be recolonised if a population becomes locally extinct. The species is therefore at a greater risk of extinction in all remaining areas. In the example here, only two of the remaining populations are close enough to allow dispersal. Populations at the other two areas cannot be replaced if they die out.

Figure 2.2. Metapopulation structure and the effects of habitat fragmentation.

- longevity; and
- mortality rates (these may vary at different life stages: mortality of young is often higher than that of adults).

Population structure

Age and sex

The ratio of different age classes of a population may be an attribute that defines condition. For example, if the mean age of a population is increasing, it indicates that recruitment is probably failing; if such a trend persists, the population may go into decline (if it is not already doing so). The sex ratio can also be important, particularly if mortality rates vary between the sexes. This is often the case for species that exhibit marked behavioural differences between males and females. For example, female bats are more at risk of catastrophic mortality when they gather in maternity roosts.

Fragmentation or isolation

Many populations are composed of a number of partly isolated sub-populations, often as a result of

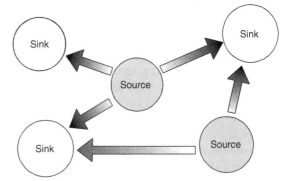

Figure 2.3. Source and sink populations. The source–sink model, (Pulliam, 1988) is an elaboration of the metapopulation model, in which habitat patches vary in their quality and hence their ability to support populations. Patches of good-quality habitat, known as sources, have a net positive population growth. Patches of poorer habitat, known as sinks, have a net negative population growth. Source populations increase until their carrying capacity is reached, whereupon individuals disperse to sink habitats. Without this dispersal, the sink populations would die out. However, sinks provide habitat for surplus individuals from sources, and these individuals can recolonise sources in the event of extinctions of source populations. The existence of sinks therefore increases total population size and the persistence of both source and sink populations.

habitat fragmentation. Such small sub-populations have a much greater chance of extinction because of random demographic accidents and local environmental variations. Therefore, persistence of such sub-populations may be dependent on other viable breeding sub-populations occurring within the effective dispersal distances undertaken by immigrating and emigrating individuals. Thus, the population as a whole exhibits a metapopulation structure (see Figure 2.2).

Although some species such as the Marsh Fritillary butterfly *Eurodryas aurinia* are thought to exhibit metapopulation structures, understanding of the processes within such populations is generally poor. It is therefore not normally possible to define condition reliably with respect to metapopulation structure attributes in such species.

Instead, the general aim should be to ensure that wherever feasible all sub-populations are 'source' populations, through provision of 'optimal' habitat conditions, as opposed to 'sink' populations (Figure 2.3).

Genetic diversity

Conservation strategies should be aimed at conserving genetic variability within species as well as conserving the species themselves. The assessment of genetic diversity in detail is a scientifically complex procedure, which is beyond the scope of a general species monitoring programme. However, genetic diversity can be conserved by ensuring that separate populations or races of species are conserved. For some species, morphologically distinct races can be identified without the need for complex analyses (e.g. the Fair Isle Wren *Troglodytes troglodytes fridariensis*); conservation and monitoring can be targeted towards these. For the majority of species, genetic diversity does not often manifest itself physically between populations, but conservation of separate populations will help to conserve within-species diversity. The introduction of individuals from outside the natural range of a species should generally be avoided, as this can reduce the genetic distinctions between populations (for example, many lowland chalk streams formerly contained endemic races of Brown Trout *Salmo trutta*, most of which have been lost through the interbreeding of races following re-stocking with and competition from introduced Rainbow Trout *Oncorhynchus mykiss*). However, it could also be argued that isolated and inbred populations may benefit from the introduction of genes from other populations.

Habitat requirements

The EU Habitats Directive recognises that favourable conservation status is dependent on the availability of sufficient habitat. Although these are not strictly attributes of a species, habitat quality and quantity should therefore also be taken into account and monitored when defining condition of a species. General aspects of habitat condition monitoring, such as physical vegetation type and structural attributes, are covered in Part II. The availability of suitable micro-habitats is important for many invertebrates, lichens, fungi and other species. Guidance for monitoring micro-habitats is not specifically provided in Part II; however, provided the characteristics of the micro-habitat are known, it should be possible to adapt the methods in Part II for monitoring some aspects of these. The abundance and availability of prey species are also components of habitat quality: guidance on monitoring these may be obtained in Part III.

2.1.3 How often should monitoring be carried out?

The frequency with which monitoring should be carried out should be established at an early stage in the development of a monitoring programme. Although, within the conservation agencies' Common Standards framework, notified features need only be assessed once every six years, it is highly desirable that monitoring be carried out with sufficient frequency to detect changes before they result in a feature's condition becoming unacceptable. At the very least, it is clearly essential that monitoring be frequent enough to ensure that changes are detected before they become irreversible.

The timescale over which changes are likely to occur and be detectable will vary according to the feature in question. In particular, the intrinsic rate of change is of fundamental importance. For example, major structural changes may normally be very slow in a woodland but potentially rapid in sand dunes. Long-lived species (e.g. perennial plants such as trees) will exhibit changes in abundance over a much longer period than will short-lived species or species that live in ephemeral habitats. Attributes also vary according to their likely rate of change. For example, the extent of a habitat may change very slowly, whereas typical species of conservation importance may decline rapidly as a result of inappropriate management. General indications of the optimum timescale for monitoring various attributes of specific habitats according to their intrinsic rate of change are provided in Chapter 5. Recommended frequencies of species monitoring are given in the sections on individual species.

Extrinsic factors may also influence a feature; monitoring programmes should therefore incorporate sufficient flexibility to deal with unforeseen and potentially rapid and catastrophic events (e.g. storms and fires). Additional monitoring may be required to establish the condition of a site after such events. More extensive and detailed surveys to establish new baseline conditions may be necessary if damage has been extensive and features have been partly or wholly destroyed.

In addition to these biological considerations, determination of the frequency of assessment should also take into account the minimum required reporting frequency and available financial resources. Therefore, an appropriate procedure for determining surveillance frequency might be as follows,

1. Select an interval consistent with:
   - the intrinsic rate of change of the feature, taking into account the precision with which that change can be measured (see Sections 2.2.3 and 2.2.4);
   - the timescale dictated by reporting requirements; and
   - the availability of funds for surveillance.
2. Aim to make a *detailed assessment* of the attribute at the required interval (for example, for woodland area, aerial photography may be required at intervals of 10 years).
3. Assess the risk of change from external factors.

Aim to make a *basic inspection* of the attribute more frequently for signs of abrupt change due to extrinsic factors (for example, for woodland area, a basic inspection at intervals of three years may be appropriate).

2.1.4 What are the management objectives for the site?

In addition to directly assessing the condition of features of interest, monitoring should, where resources permit, establish whether management objectives are being met. Ongoing management objectives and associated actions should therefore be identified and appropriate monitoring methods selected. Monitoring of management impacts is briefly covered in Chapter 5.

Habitats and species likely to change over time as a result of planned management actions should be identified, as well as the likely timescale of change in years. For example, it may be a management objective to coppice a woodland area for invertebrates and ground flora. Ideally, the two groups should be sample-surveyed before and after management, and for a series of years up to canopy closure again. Monitoring of habitats and species should tie in directly with the management objectives and actions. This is important if the cost-effectiveness of management is to be maximised and objectives achieved.

2.1.5 Are there external factors that may have significant impacts on the site?

Habitat and species condition may also be affected by external factors, such as airborne pollution or climatic change. These may therefore also require monitoring. However, because of the large scale of some of these processes, monitoring may only be feasible at a selection of sites. Data from existing monitoring schemes (e.g. Meteorological Office weather stations) may also be suitable. The availability of existing data on such factors should therefore be carefully investigated before including them in monitoring programmes.

Detailed descriptions of methods for monitoring management actions and external impacts are beyond the scope of this *Handbook*. However, brief summaries of key management measures and external factors influencing habitats are provided in Chapter 5, together with sources of further information.

2.1.6 What monitoring has been undertaken and are baseline surveys required?

A baseline survey is carried out to determine the habitats and species present on a site and their current condition. If a baseline survey of features and their attributes has not been undertaken, this will be required before a detailed monitoring programme can be planned. It is necessary to establish the baseline levels of the various attributes so that any subsequent changes in these levels can be identified.

It is therefore important to establish from the outset whether monitoring has previously been undertaken at the site, including the attributes covered, the methods used, the timescale and frequency over which it took place and whether or not it is ongoing. It is not unusual for the results of monitoring studies to be forgotten, especially if they are unpublished and the members of staff responsible have moved on. A careful and detailed investigation may therefore often be worthwhile.

Available data from previous monitoring programmes or *ad hoc* surveys should be used to review the appropriateness of methods and sampling strategies employed (see Section 2.3.1). Previous monitoring programmes should not be followed without careful consideration of their suitability, as they may have been established to meet different objectives. However, if existing monitoring programmes are likely to contribute to current monitoring objectives they should be continued. Where appropriate, existing methodologies should also be followed to maintain the validity of long-term datasets. It may also be useful to use existing fixed marker systems or permanent quadrats.

Take care over the use and interpretation of historical data that have not been properly documented. Grid references may be unreliable, and maps sometimes differ between editions and scales. Round numbers (e.g. 100 plants) are usually highly indicative of estimates. Similarly, national distribution maps are very poor indicators of the real status or change in a species (see Rich & Smith (1996) for a detailed review).

2.1.7 Should the site be subdivided into monitoring units?

For ease of assessment it may sometimes be advantageous to divide habitat features into 'monitoring units'. This may be useful if:

- features are too extensive or too fragmented to be surveyed adequately in one visit;
- you wish to assess the effects of management practices that apply only to certain parts of the feature;

- one part of a feature is in particularly poor condition and you wish to track its recovery.

Unit boundaries must not cross feature boundaries; each unit should only encompass part of **one** feature and each objective must apply to the feature as a whole.

A general discussion of monitoring complex sites is provided by Stone (1997).

2.2 SELECTION OF METHODS FOR MONITORING EACH ATTRIBUTE

Once you have defined your objectives for the monitoring programme and decided which feature attributes are important, you should then decide on the most appropriate methods for monitoring *each attribute that defines condition for each feature*. Monitoring methods for habitat attributes are listed in the tables for each habitat in Chapter 5 and described in Chapter 6. Survey and monitoring methods for species attributes are listed in the general methods tables for each species in Chapters 11–26. The methods described in these sections are often specific to one particular group of species. Chapter 10 gives a general introduction to population monitoring and describes the theory behind the sampling methods most commonly used. Although not comprehensive, the methods given for both habitats and species are likely to be the most appropriate and efficient tried and tested methods currently available.

Clearly, to maximise the efficient use of monitoring resources the most cost-effective method appropriate to the monitoring objective should be used. Thus, quick and cheap subjective methods should be used if they are adequate. It is unacceptable to use cheap methods, however, if they cannot detect all degrees of undesirable change. Such methods may be a false economy, as in the long term the financial cost of repairing damage to a feature is likely to exceed by far the costs of monitoring and of early management intervention. It should be remembered that the closer an attribute is to the limits that define condition, the more precise the chosen method must be to determine whether it is above or below the limit.

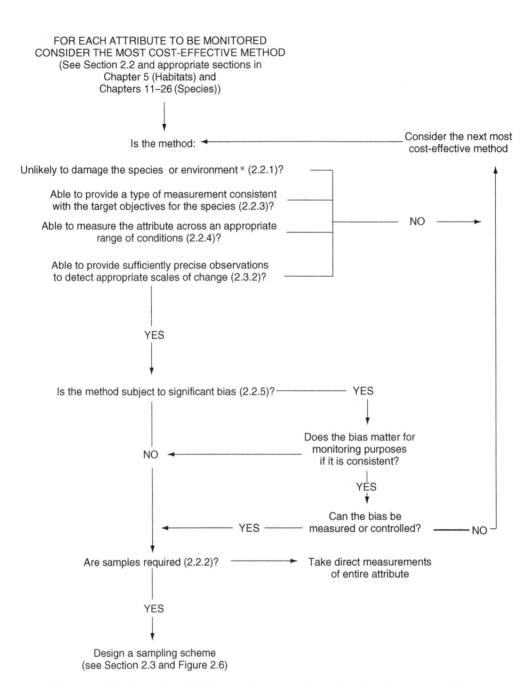

FOR EACH ATTRIBUTE TO BE MONITORED
CONSIDER THE MOST COST-EFFECTIVE METHOD
(See Section 2.2 and appropriate sections in
Chapter 5 (Habitats) and
Chapters 11–26 (Species))

Is the method: ← Consider the next most cost-effective method

Unlikely to damage the species or environment * (2.2.1)?

Able to provide a type of measurement consistent with the target objectives for the species (2.2.3)?

Able to measure the attribute across an appropriate range of conditions (2.2.4)?

Able to provide sufficiently precise observations to detect appropriate scales of change (2.3.2)?

NO →

YES

Is the method subject to significant bias (2.2.5)? ——— YES

Does the bias matter for monitoring purposes if it is consistent?

NO ←

YES

Can the bias be measured or controlled? ——— NO

← YES ———

Are samples required (2.2.2)? ——→ Take direct measurements of entire attribute

YES

Design a sampling scheme
(see Section 2.3 and Figure 2.6)

Figure 2.4. Selection of methods for monitoring each attribute (see the relevant chapter or section for further information.)
*This may depend on whether sampling uses permanent or temporary plots (see Section 2.3.3).

Selecting the most appropriate method is therefore an important step and needs to take into account the key considerations described below (summarised in Figure 2.4). If the most cost-effective method fails any of these considerations, the next most cost-effective method should be assessed.

2.2.1   Is the method likely to damage the environment?

It is clearly essential that monitoring activities do not damage features of conservation interest on a site. However, there are unfortunately numerous examples in which research and monitoring programmes have merely measured and recorded the damage caused by their own activities. Therefore, great care should be taken to ensure that the methods chosen will not cause any damage. In particular the following precautions should be strictly observed:

- Ensure that the target attributes are not damaged during sampling (e.g. by trampling) and that disturbance to other habitats and species is minimised.
- Be aware of other species or groups of conservation importance in the area and take care not to cause disturbance to them.
- Do not use vehicles on the site unless particular tracks have been identified and impacts can be avoided.
- Do not use destructive sampling methods unless absolutely necessary. If they are used, minimise impacts and understand the extent and importance of the impact to the ecological community and the attribute being monitored.
- Be able to relocate fixed quadrats and sampling locations easily in successive years or sampling periods to minimise the need for walking over the site and potentially damaging the habitats you are going to monitor (see Section 2.3.3 and Appendix 5 for further discussions).
- Position fixed sampling locations sensitively and avoid or minimise damage during their establishment.
- Avoid excessive revisiting of sites and sampling locations.

2.2.2   Are samples required?

It is sometimes possible to make complete assessments of an attribute of a feature of interest at a site (e.g. by aerial photography if complete site coverage exists, by Phase I mapping, or by counting the total number of an easily detectable species). In this case, complete measurements can be taken, although the accuracy of the method will still need to be considered when presenting the results. However, it is seldom possible, or even necessary, to do a complete count. Unless species are very rare, very conspicuous, or very localised, total counts (Section 10.1) can prove too expensive or be prone to under- or overcounting. This is particularly true when counting mobile species such as birds, or animals and plants that have a large range and inhabit remote sites where counting is either impossible or impracticable.

More commonly, it is only practicable to study a *sample* (i.e. part of a feature), and to generalise from observations made in the sample to the whole feature. Using sampling methods allows the researcher to invest more time in avoiding the problems with measurement error (see Section 2.2.5). Although there are a number of standard methods for certain species, when designing a new study it is advisable to tailor monitoring to achieve the most efficient and appropriate means of data collection. Some methods are designed to standardise data collection by time (i.e. counting species for a set length of time) and some by space (i.e. counting within a set area such as a quadrat). Choosing a method will also rely heavily on the ecology of the species or habitat concerned. Sampling is covered in some detail in the next section.

2.2.3   Will the method provide the appropriate type of measurement?

The type of measurement produced by a method is particularly important and must be consistent with the objective for each attribute. For example, the target for dead wood volume may be expressed as 'one or two large (>50 cm diameter) fallen trees or trunks visible with plenty of 5–50 cm pieces in view at each sample point'. This would require only that a subjective assessment is made at surveyed locations. If, however, the target is expressed as 'a mean of at least $10\,m^3\,ha^{-1}$ of dead wood across the site', quantitative estimates based on density measurements at survey locations would be required.

The type of data being collected will also have a significant impact on the survey design and range of analyses that can be carried out. The most commonly collected types of data are as follows.

Nominal

Each survey location is assigned to a predefined category. For example, a species may be recorded as being *present* or *absent* at a location, or a habitat may be classified as a particular type of grassland.

Ordinal

An extension of nominal data in which the categories are ordered. Thus, for example, the abundance of a plant species at a location may be classified in an ordered scale such as 'rare', 'occasional', 'frequent', 'abundant' or 'dominant' (the so-called DAFOR scale). This clearly provides more information than a nominal measure such as presence–absence, but may take longer to assess.

Quantitative

To measure abundance we may instead actually count the number of plants present or, alternatively, what area of ground they cover. This provides a quantitative measure. Other examples are the height of vegetation, the mass of an animal and the number of species at a site. These provide finer, more sensitive measures than ordinal data but may take longer to collect and may be prone to measurement error. If necessary, quantitative data can always be converted to ordinal data by grouping the data into categories, e.g. 0–2 plants, 3–5 plants, etc.

Further information on data types can be found in Fowler *et al.* (1998).

If the site is to be sampled, there is usually a trade-off between the type of data collected at each sample location and the number of locations that have to be visited. Presence–absence data are quick to collect but provide little information about each location. Thus, large numbers of locations may have to be visited to build up a picture of the quantity and condition of a feature at a site. Quantitative data can provide much more information and usually require fewer locations to be visited. However each measurement will take rather longer to collect. Section 2.3 provides more information on the design requirements for different measurement types.

Data collected for monitoring will be either a direct or an indirect measure of the attribute. A direct measure involves making measurements of the attribute itself. An indirect measure involves measuring a related variable, which is used to infer the status of the attribute being monitored (for example, using counts of otter spraints as an index of the number of otters present on a site). Such measurements are described as population indices. An index of population size is also obtained from direct sampling of a subset of a total population. For example, male moth population size can be estimated by using pheromone traps. These data are treated as an index of total population size, since one cannot be sure of the numbers of females.

2.2.4 Can the method measure the attribute across an appropriate range of conditions?

The method needs to be able to measure the attribute fully across the range of states over which condition is defined. It is essential that the method has appropriate limits of detection (i.e. the level beyond which it is not possible to measure or distinguish between presence or absence). This is most relevant to measurements of chemical concentrations, but may also affect other attributes of habitats and species. For example, the use of satellite-based remote sensing may be inappropriate for measuring changes in habitat at the site level because of the limited spatial resolution obtainable.

As another example, grapnel trawl surveys can be used to detect presence–absence of most aquatic

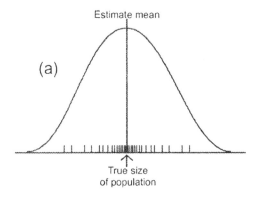 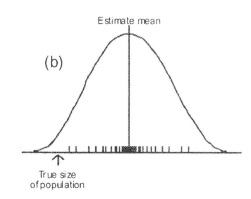

Figure 2.5. Bias in measurement. (a) Measurements are unbiased: estimates are distributed around the true value. (b) Measurements are biased: they tend to overestimate the true population.

macrophyte species but cannot be certain of detecting some small, fine-leaved or rare species. If data are required for such species, an alternative method may have to be used.

On the other hand, for simple monitoring purposes there is little point in using a technique that measures an attribute well beyond its range of acceptable condition. For example, it is not necessary to measure sub-surface water levels (e.g. by dipwells) if condition is merely dependent on water levels always being well above the surface.

2.2.5   Is the method prone to substantial measurement error?

Some measurement error is almost always unavoidable in ecological studies and it is important to consider whether such error is likely to affect the value and validity of the study. An example should help make this clear.

Suppose the population of Capercaillie *Tetrao urogallus* at a site is estimated by several observers independently. Each observer comes up with a different estimate because it is impossible to count the numbers without error. Figure 2.5 illustrates two possible sets of results. In the first (Figure 2.5a), the counts are all spread fairly evenly around the true population and so on average the observers get it about right. The error in each observer's estimate may or may not be important, depending on how good an estimate is required. To be able to judge

this, it is important to know something about how much error can be expected.

In the second set of results (Figure 2.5b) the observers tend to overestimate the true population: these estimates are said to be *biased*. Bias is clearly of concern if we think the population is much larger than it really is; if such error is present, we need to know about it. Bias is a systematic source of error that results in under- or overestimation of the attribute being measured. It causes estimates to be inaccurate. Methods free of bias are said to be *accurate*.

Of course, some observers may produce unbiased results in a given situation, whereas others may be biased. This possibility needs to be considered if successive surveys are likely to be carried out by different people and accurate measurement of change is important.

Bias may arise from several sources in a study, including:

Observer
- Incorrect identification of species.
- Failing to detect and count all individuals of a particular species being surveyed.
- Different observers recording identical observations in dissimilar ways.
- Different observers having expertise in different areas, which may affect their interpretation of the observations they record.
- Variation in observer effort (e.g. speed of assessment).

Location

- Studying a species only where it is common; if areas in which it is rare have been ignored the full dispersion of the species will not be understood. Estimates of total extent across the whole site cannot therefore be made.
- Using a small subjectively selected sample area when the site being studied is not homogeneous.

Habitat differences

- Species of plant may be more easily detected in some habitats than in others. For example, soil type and moisture content can affect the growth patterns of plants.
- Some habitats may be more accessible to survey than others.

Species differences

- Some species may be more easily identifiable than others.

Temporal sources

- The time of year (or day) when a survey is carried out can affect the results. Season is particularly important for vegetation monitoring; survey times must be standardised.

Weather

- Inclement weather affects observers' concentration and the time they will willingly spend in the field. Variation between different observers' capacity for working under difficult conditions can introduce bias.
- It may be more difficult to distinguish species in wet vegetation than in dry vegetation.
- Many species are less active under inclement weather conditions.

By being aware of potential sources of bias these problems can be reduced, measured or otherwise taken into account. For example, each time vegetation is measured, it is inevitable that there will be some recording bias, even with trained observers; numerous studies document this (for example, see Hope-Simpson, 1940; Smith, 1944; Lamacraft, 1978; Sykes *et al.*, 1983; Nilsson & Nilsson, 1985; Kirby *et al.*, 1986; Rich & Woodruff, 1990; West &

Hatton, 1990; Rich & Smith, 1996). These investigations show that:

- recorders are better at repeating their own work than that of others;
- results from small areas intensively searched are more repeatable than those from larger areas less intensively searched;
- large, broad-leaved or clumped taxa are better recorded than small, well-dispersed or fine-leaved taxa (Clymo, 1980; Sykes *et al.*, 1983); and
- quantitative work involving fully objective measurements is more repeatable than work that uses subjective qualitative or semi-quantitative measurements; visual cover estimates, in particular, are often inconsistent.

Whether bias matters to your monitoring programme depends on the accuracy of the estimates required. If the bias remains consistent and an accurate estimate is not required then the bias is less important, because it will not affect your ability to detect change. However, determining whether the bias remains consistent or not is likely to be very difficult. There are three ways of combating bias:

1. If the likely sources are anticipated, steps can be taken to minimise bias for a particular project. Bias can be reduced or controlled in a number of ways:
   - Always record as much detail in your monitoring as possible and use the same methods, approach, analysis, etc., across years, observers and sites; that way any observer bias can be kept fairly consistent. If effort cannot be kept constant, the next best thing is to measure it.
   - When choosing a monitoring method, check whether its assumptions (see individual habitat and species chapters in Parts II and III) will hold for the habitat or species you wish to study and for the period of time over which it is to be studied.
   - Record relevant weather conditions when surveying. Agree and record beforehand at what point weather conditions should postpone work.
   - Agree and record definitions (e.g. sample size, type, population unit, etc.) beforehand.
   - Calibrate observers against each other before, and during, monitoring. Introduce a system for

quality assurance to verify the data (perhaps by using a person unconnected with the study or by observers checking each other's work).

2. With careful design it is possible to avoid the problem by confining comparisons of results to attributes that have the same bias.

3. It is possible, though difficult, to measure the bias. Measuring bias can be done only if the true value can be occasionally ascertained; normally this is unachievable. A separate experiment may be helpful: for example, you could compare the results obtained by different observers measuring the same population.

If the bias may affect the monitoring and cannot be adequately measured, controlled for or reduced, then an alternative method should be used. If it is not possible to find one method that provides an apparently unbiased estimate, use a number of different methods and compare the results, or change the objectives to match what is achievable.

2.3   DESIGNING A SAMPLING STRATEGY

First and foremost the design of a sampling strategy must take into account the objectives of the monitoring study, to ensure these are met. These objectives might be defined in terms of

- how 'good' the estimate of the attribute, for the whole site, needs to be;
- what level of change between surveys needs to be detected; and
- which sections of the site are of particular interest or most likely to change.

Some other factors influencing the design are

- the type of attribute being measured;
- the method being used;
- the variability of the attribute across the site (if known); and
- the time and costs of sampling.

Figure 2.6 summarises the steps that should be considered. The steps are described in greater detail in the following sections.

In this account of sampling design we use the term *sampling unit* to mean the unit from which

measurements are taken. For example, this may be a quadrat in a habitat survey or a bird's nest in a study of breeding success. The term *population* is used to mean the set of all possible sample units across the site under study. Thus the population of $1\,m \times 1\,m$ quadrats is the total area of the site divided up into a $1\,m \times 1\,m$ grid. A *sample* is a particular set of sampling units and associated measurements.

The object of sampling is to avoid having to study an attribute across the whole site but to still be able to *estimate* what is happening across the whole site. As Samuel Johnson said, 'You don't have to eat the whole ox to know that it is tough.' Thus we make an *inference* about the whole based on an examination of only a part. For these inferences to be valid, sampling must follow certain principles:

- samples must be as representative of the whole as possible;
- more than one sampling unit is required. This is known as *replication*.

The first principle enables reliable estimation of an attribute's value for the population and is usually achieved by randomly locating the sample units. The second principle enables the variation between samples to be calculated and can be used to estimate the uncertainty in the estimate due to having only studied part of the population. For example, the area of a site covered by Heather *Calluna vulgaris* may be estimated by calculating the *mean* area of Heather in a sample of $1\,m \times 1\,m$ quadrats and multiplying this figure by the size of the site in square metres. The uncertainty in this estimate may be measured by the *standard deviation* of the estimate. An account of these important statistics is given in Box 2.4, below. See also the Glossary for further definitions of statistical terms.

A key feature of sampling is that as the number of samples taken increases, so our uncertainty over how closely the sample estimate reflects the true population value decreases. The greater the sample size, the greater the amount of survey time required, and so a balance is needed between ensuring that the estimate is 'good enough' and not expending unnecessary effort. Often, defining what is 'good enough' is not easy but will depend on

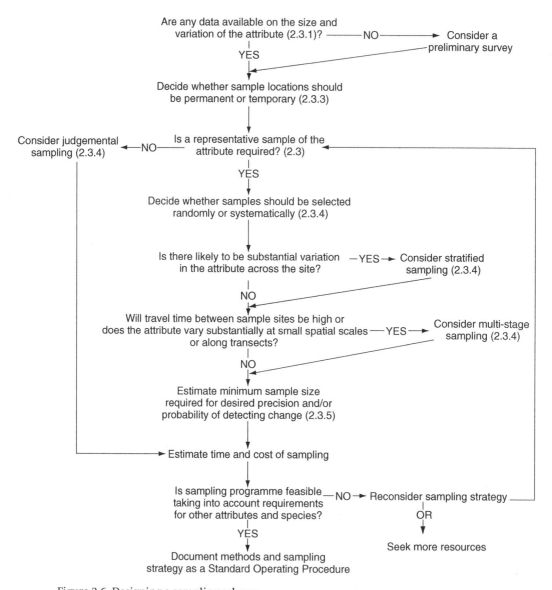

Figure 2.6. Designing a sampling scheme.

the quality of information required for the particular feature under study and the use to which the results will be put. For example, if a species of interest is important and its population is believed to be close to the limit of what is viable, then a good, or *precise*, population estimate is likely to be required. In other situations only a quick check may be needed to confirm that a population is still doing well. Further guidance on establishing the number of sample units required is given in Section 2.3.5.

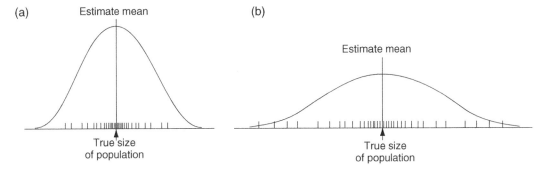

Figure 2.7. Precision of measurements taken from a sample. In (a) the measurements are fairly precise: they are closely spread around the mean value. In (b), however, measurements are imprecise: they are widely spread around the mean.

The size of sample unit chosen will depend on the species or habitat being sampled, the type of measurements being made and the method used for sampling. This aspect of a sampling scheme is therefore considered in the individual method sections in Part II, Chapter 6, and Part III, Chapters 11–26.

Sample units for monitoring habitats and many species, particularly plants, will usually be quadrats (Section 6.4.2) or transects (Section 6.4.6). Appropriate quadrat size for habitat monitoring is discussed in the sections on the use of the National Vegetation Classification (NVC) for monitoring (Section 6.1.6) and is treated in more detail in Appendix 4. Transect length for habitat monitoring is discussed in Section 6.4.6.

Sample units for species can be varied. The use of total counts, timed counts, quadrats and transects, and some other generic monitoring methods for species are discussed in Chapter 10. Other methods for particular species groups are discussed in Part III (Chapters 11–26).

2.3.1 Has the method been thoroughly tested and are preliminary field trials necessary?

Preliminary field trials can be extremely valuable and are often overlooked. They are particularly important if:

- the methodology has not been used before in similar circumstances;

- the surveyor is unfamiliar with the site and/or method; or
- there are no existing data available for the site that may help formulate a good sampling design.

Data from preliminary trials can provide an initial assessment of how close feature attributes are to their targets and limits, and an estimate of the variation in these attributes between sampling units. This information can be an invaluable aid when deciding how best to distribute the sampling units across the site and how many samples are required. Although such a preliminary trial may be time-consuming, it is likely to save time and resources in the long term, particularly where sites and their features are poorly known.

Preliminary field trials also enable the surveyor to:

- become familiar with the characteristics of habitat or study species on the site;
- become familiar with the geography of the site; and
- iron out any problems applying the method.

Larger sites tend to be more complex, with more variables influencing the habitats, and so the larger the site, the greater will be the benefits of using a field trial.

2.3.2 Will the appropriate level of precision be achieved?

Precision is a measure of the closeness of repeated measurements to each other and provides a measure of the uncertainty due to sampling (see Figure 2.7). Intuitively, if the sample measurements are all very close to each other then it is likely that the site is very uniform and so, provided there is no bias in the measurements, the sample mean is likely to be close to the population mean. Conversely, if the measurements vary a lot then the site is very variable and we have less confidence that the sample has pinned down the population mean.

Because the sample mean is our estimate of the population mean, we are usually more interested in its precision rather than that of the individual measurements. Regardless of the precision of individual measurements, we would expect that, as we increase

---

Box 2.4 Descriptive statistics: some important definitions

Mean: The sum (Σ) of all individual values (x) divided by the number (n) of observations: $(\Sigma x)/n$. See figure below.
Median: The middle observation in a set of observations that have been ranked in magnitude.
Mode: The most common value of a set of observations.
Standard deviation: A measure of the variability of a dataset in terms of the deviation of observations, x_i ($i = 1$ to n), from the mean. When monitoring, we are generally sampling a subset of the population. In this case, the *sample standard deviation, s*, is given by:

$$s = \sqrt{\frac{\sum(x_i - \bar{x})^2}{n-1}},$$

where $\bar{x}$ is the sample mean.

Variance: the square of the sample standard deviation (s^2). This is another commonly used measure of data variability but, unlike the standard deviation, it is not measured in the same units as the observations.
Standard error (SE): the standard deviation of the sample mean, given by:

$$SE = \frac{s}{\sqrt{n}}.$$

This is a more informative statistic than the standard deviation when the main interest is in the sample mean. It will decrease as the sample size increases.
Coefficient of variation: Another useful measure of the relative variability in the data, which can be compared between different attributes regardless of the units in which they are measured. Relative variability is measured by calculating the coefficient of variation (%cv), which is the standard deviation expressed as a percentage of the sample mean:

$$\%\mathrm{cv} = 100s/\bar{x}.$$

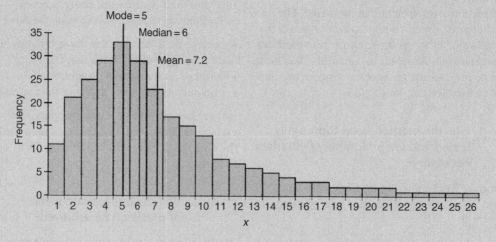

Figure B2.4. An example of a distribution showing mean, median and mode.

the number of measurements, so the sample means from repeated samples will tend to become closer and closer to one another and so each sample will tend to be closer to the population mean.

Precision in the sample mean is often measured by its *standard error* (Box 2.4), which becomes smaller as the sample size is increased (Figure 2.8). Thus precision improves as the standard error decreases.

This is not quite the whole story. As the sample size increases, so we would expect that the sample means from repeat samples will tend to become closer and closer to one another. However, the sample size (n) cannot be larger than the population size (N). When this limit is reached, the sample is of the whole population, and there is then no uncertainty remaining as to the value of the population mean. So for the standard error to be a good measure of precision it should be zero when $n = N$, which is not the case for the formula given in Box 2.4. For a finite population a more exact formula for the standard error of the sample mean is

$$SE = \sqrt{\frac{s^2}{n}\left(1 - \frac{n}{N}\right)}.$$

The quantity n/N is often termed the *finite population correction* (fpc) and it is only when its value is greater than around 0.1 that it has much effect on the value of the standard error. If less than 10% of a feature is to be sampled, as will often be the case, the fpc can be safely ignored.

Larger sample sizes require more time; precision, as measured by the standard error, typically increases only in proportion to the square root of the sample size. Hence, to reduce by half the standard error obtained from 10 sample units requires about 40 units.

What precision is needed depends on the use to which the results will be put. Two key uses for survey data are as follows.

1. Determining whether the population value of the attribute being measured is above or below a limit. If this value is close to this limit it may require a large sample size to be certain which side of the limit it really is.

2. Detecting changes between one survey and the next. If small changes need to be detected then a precise estimate of change will be needed, which will usually depend on having a precise estimate of the attribute's value from each survey.

Further guidance on establishing the number of sample units required is given in Section 2.3.5.

Finally, it should be remembered that simple monitoring methods may actually be extremely time-consuming overall because they produce relatively imprecise results and therefore require more intensive sampling. On the other hand, although some sampling methods appear daunting because they use a complicated methodology, the quality of data collected per unit time may be much higher.

2.3.3   Should sample locations be permanent or not?

Permanent sample locations can provide a good approach for improving precision when detecting changes over time is of prime importance. There are, however, a number of significant disadvantages to using permanent locations. See Appendix 5 for further information on establishing permanent sample locations.

Permanent locations should only be used if:

- Maximising change detection is of prime importance and some consistency is expected in how the attribute changes across the site; or information is needed on turnover and species dynamics; or the feature being monitored is a rare sessile species, which is confined to precisely known location(s).
- There is sufficient fieldwork time available for marking and relocating permanent sampling locations, and this time cannot be more efficiently used for collecting data from a greater number of temporary sample locations.
- Sample locations are representative of the site (see Section 2.3.4 for further discussion) and sufficient samples are taken to minimise the risk of chance events reducing representativeness.
- Provision has been made for the unexpected loss of sample locations.

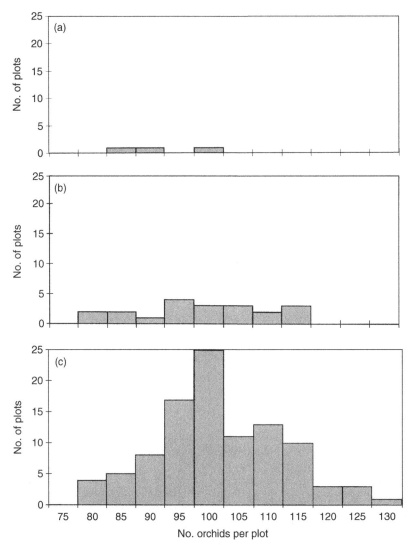

Figure 2.8. The effect of increased sample size on the precision of sample means. The data for the graphs above are taken from a hypothetical population of orchids distributed in a uniform habitat. The true population density is 100 orchids per plot (our hypothetical sampling unit), with a standard deviation (SD) of 10. This density is estimated by the mean (or average) number of orchids in the sample plots. (a) Three randomly selected plots give the mean number of orchids per plot as 94.3, with a high standard error (SE) and no clear picture of how the data are distributed. Estimates of means based on only three samples are likely to vary considerably and would therefore be imprecise. (b) The mean of 20 random plots gives a closer approximation (96.4 orchids per plot) to the true density, and has a lower standard error (2.65). (c) The mean of 100 plots (99.4 orchids per plot) is very close to the true density, with a correspondingly lower standard error (1.07). Thus estimates of means based on this high number of samples are likely to be very close to the true mean, i.e. precise. However, the cost and effort of taking 100 samples may not be worth the extra increase in precision. This will depend on available resources. Note also that the number of orchids per plot is now revealed to be approximately normally distributed (see Box 2.7).

• The feature being monitored and the surrounding environment will not be significantly altered or damaged.

Advantages of permanent locations

If permanent locations tend to change with some consistency, we are more likely to be able to detect change than when using the same number of temporary locations. This is because the estimate of change is based on the mean change within sampling units rather than the change in the mean of different sampling units. The standard error of this mean change will tend to be small when the units tend to change by the same amount.

For example, suppose that mean species richness over 20 quadrats is 15 in one year and 10 in a subsequent survey and that the decline is fairly consistent across the site. If permanent quadrats are used this consistency of change is apparent from the way the quadrats change. However, if new quadrats are selected for the second survey we only have the change in mean richness in the two sets of quadrats to go on, and there is a greater possibility that the change is due to the chance location of quadrats in the first survey being in richer parts of the site. Thus, with temporary quadrats, a change would need to be larger for us to be confident it indicated a real change across the whole site, than if permanent quadrats were used.

Permanent plots can also be particularly useful for monitoring sparse sessile species, such as some lichens, which may be confined to a small part of a site and do not spread. In this case randomly located plots would be very inefficient as most would miss the species altogether.

Disadvantages of permanent locations

Marking and relocating permanent sample locations can be difficult and time-consuming. This may offset any advantage from additional precision if observations from non-permanent samples can be obtained much more quickly.

Surveying at permanent locations may alter or damage the attribute being monitored or its surroundings, e.g. by trampling. Apart from the potential unacceptability of such damage for conservation reasons, it may also cause the samples to become unrepresentative of the site as a whole.

Permanent sample locations may become unrepresentative of the whole study area (assuming that they were representative initially) as a result of chance events that affect the locations disproportionately. Such events may also have permanent or long-lasting effects, as successive changes at one point tend to be correlated. Therefore, any recorded changes will not reflect the true pattern of change over the site and may be significantly biased. This difficulty can usually be overcome by avoiding small sample sizes. Alternatively, record a second set of samples at the end of the first monitoring period, which are used to estimate changes in the second period and so on, i.e. samples A are enumerated on the first occasion, samples A and B on the second, samples B and C on the third, and so on (Greig-Smith, 1983).

Permanent sample locations may be effectively lost as a result of unforeseeable events, such as permanent or long-term flooding of part of the site, or the growth of trees over long time periods. This problem can be alleviated by recording 'spare' samples.

2.3.4   Should the samples be located randomly, systematically or by judgement?

The arrangement, number, and size of samples has a critical influence on the results obtained and how they can be interpreted. Not surprisingly, there have been numerous investigations into this issue (see Greig-Smith (1983) and Shimwell (1971) for reviews of plant surveying techniques). Various techniques have been used to position the samples. These are summarised in Table 2.1, with various options relating to random and systematic methods described further in Table 2.2.

An illustration of the different random and systematic sampling strategies described in this *Handbook* is given in Figure 2.9.

Locating samples by judgement

Sampling units that are located by judgement cannot reliably be regarded as being representative

Table 2.1. *Summary of the advantages and disadvantages of different approaches to sample selection*

Sample location method	Advantages	Disadvantages
Judgement	Can be quick and simple if knowledge of habitat/species is sufficient	Extrapolation of results to the whole feature or site is not valid without strong justification
	Samples can be deliberately taken around e.g. a rare species or feature of particular importance; useful when all locations of a rare species are known	Comprehensive knowledge of the site is required
		Statistical analysis is not valid and errors cannot be quantified
Random	Requires minimum knowledge of the population	Collection of sample observations can be time-consuming
	Easy to analyse data and compute variability	Can result in larger errors for a given sample size compared with systematic sampling
Systematic (regular)	If the attribute is ordered spatially, there is a stratification effect, which reduces variability compared with random sampling	If sampling interval matches a periodic feature in the habitat (e.g. regular ditches), significant bias may be introduced
	Determining sample locations is easy	Strictly speaking, statistical tests are not valid, although in most cases conclusions are unlikely to be substantially affected
	Provides an efficient means of mapping distribution and calculating abundance at the same time	

of the entire study area. Consequently, observations cannot be extrapolated across the site as a whole without strong justification, and it is not valid to calculate summary statistics or perform statistical tests on such data. Such samples therefore only yield information on their own particular location. This may not matter when selecting sites for monitoring rare and/or sessile species with known locations or habitat preferences.

Temporary sampling locations are rarely placed by judgement except during NVC surveys (Section 6.1.6), in which quadrats are placed on 'representative' stands of vegetation to assist with the identification of NVC types. Data from such samples should not be used for monitoring purposes.

It is fairly common practice to locate permanent plots by judgement, particularly when monitoring rare species that are likely to be missed by random or systematic surveys. Data collected from such plots can be informative and useful

for demonstrating typical changes. However, for the reasons described above, such data should generally not be extrapolated to the whole feature or site.

Judgement sampling can, however, be informative if carried out by surveyors who use a thorough knowledge of the site and of the processes acting on the site to describe the site in an intelligent way. The usefulness of the results can be increased if the surveyors record as much detail as possible about what they did, and take photographs. If this is done well it may be possible to repeat a survey quite closely. However, it is preferable not to rely on subjective techniques such as this.

Random sampling

When the goal of sampling is to provide an indication of what is happening across the whole site, random sampling designs are generally recommended. Random sampling is usually designed to

Table 2.2. *Summary of the advantages and disadvantages of different random sampling designs*

Type of structure	Advantages	Disadvantages
Simple random	Selecting sample units is quicker and easier than for other random designs	Estimates will be less precise on heterogeneous sites than with stratified sampling
	Statistical analysis of data is straightforward	Travel time between sample units can be high
Stratified	Ensures that all the main habitat types present on a site will be sampled (if defined as strata)	If strata have not been identified prior to monitoring, preparation can be time-consuming
	Characteristics of each stratum can be measured and comparisons between them can be made	The most appropriate stratification for a site at one time may have changed when repeat surveys are carried out; monitoring efficiency may therefore also change
	Greater precision is obtained for each stratum and for overall mean estimates if strata are homogeneous	
Multi-stage or cluster	Can reduce sampling times, thus increasing efficiency	When calculating overall means, etc., larger errors are obtained than with a
	Useful for sites that are heterogeneous at small spatial scales and for studying gradients along transects	simple random sample of comparable size if sample units within major units are highly correlated

ensure that each of the population of sampling units has an equal chance of being selected. Standard statistical methods can then be used to analyse the data (see Section 2.6). Plot location should not in any way be influenced by any prior knowledge. Randomly located plots are picked from a numbered list of all plots that could be surveyed, by using random numbers generated by a computer or from tables. Locating plots by eye does not yield randomness, because samples are usually spaced too evenly. Throwing quadrats to obtain locations, although better than locating by eye, does not achieve true randomness either (this is known as *haphazard* sampling). Random samples can, however, be time-consuming to locate in the field.

Figure 2.10 shows a method for choosing sampling units randomly. Units that are found to fall outside the area are ignored.

Transect lines may also be located by utilising these points. Transects are essentially long, thin

quadrats, and many of the same considerations apply. The direction of fixed-length transect lines should usually be randomly allocated. However, it may be desirable to select a direction that allows samples to be taken along a perceived environmental gradient (e.g. a transition from acid to calcareous grassland). This has the effect of reducing variation *between* transects, thereby improving precision.

Sometimes it is impossible not to deviate from randomness when sampling, for instance if access to a particular area is not possible. If the inaccessible area is small this may not matter, but if significant bias is possible, the issue should be documented and population estimates may need adjustment.

Systematic sampling
It is often convenient to take samples at regular intervals, for instance at fixed distances along a river. However, this method creates one main problem: if

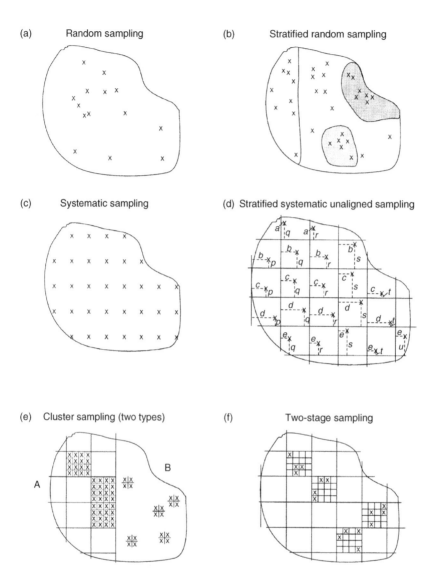

Figure 2.9. Different types of sampling strategy. (a) Random sampling: samples taken randomly from the whole study area. (b) Stratified random sampling: study area divided into strata and random samples taken in each stratum. (c) Systematic sampling: samples taken at regular intervals. (d) Stratified systematic unaligned sampling: study area subdivided into equal blocks and x co-ordinates (a–e) and y co-ordinates (p–u) generated randomly. Distance a is used in every block in the first row, b in the second row, etc. Distance p is used in every block in the first column, q in the second column, etc. (e) Two types of cluster sampling. In type A cluster areas (large squares) are chosen randomly and all sample units (x) sampled in each. In type B points are chosen randomly and samples taken in a fixed pattern relative to each point. (f) Two-stage sampling: major units (large squares) chosen randomly and minor units (x) sampled randomly from each. Major units may also be transects.

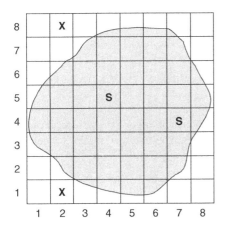

Figure 2.10. Choosing sample units from a two-dimensional map. As an example, consider choosing 1 ha sample units from a woodland. The shaded area in the diagram represents the woodland; the lines superimposed on it are 100 m apart. Number the grid rows and columns (as above). Select pairs of random numbers by using a random number generator. The first number defines the column in the grid; the second defines the row. Reject any grid squares that fall outwith the study area. This procedure can be carried out within a spreadsheet or Geographical Information System (GIS). An obvious advantage of using a GIS is that it can produce a map of the sample locations. On the ground, sample units are most easily located by using a Global Positioning System (GPS). Small errors inherent in GPS readings are not important provided these are random.

the sampling interval constantly coincides with a particular regularity in a species or habitat being monitored, the results will be biased. For example, if you are sampling vegetation at 10 m intervals, and this interval coincides with the raised parts of a hummock–hollow microtopography (perhaps stretching the example!), the vegetation in the hollows (which may be different) will not be sampled. The results will therefore give a biased picture of the vegetation. Systematic samples are not placed independently of each other (unlike random samples) so, strictly, statistical analysis is not valid. However, if a large number of samples are taken, systematic samples can usually be treated as random samples (Schaeffer

et al., 1990; Watt, 1997) without causing substantial problems, unless a systematic bias such as that outlined above occurs. Sophisticated statistical techniques have been developed for spatial analysis of both systematic and random samples (Cressie, 1993; Webster & Oliver, 2001), which enable distribution and density maps to be developed as well as providing alternative estimation methods.

Systematic sampling can be useful because sample sites are relatively easy to select and relocate, and the approach is often more appealing and straightforward to surveyors. A particular use may be when trying to map both distribution and total abundance of an organism across a study area. The advantages of a regular distribution of sample sites might then outweigh the population estimation disadvantages, for example, if a distribution map based on a regular grid were the objective of the study. Grid surveys repeated regularly can provide excellent comparative data to identify potential causes and influences of change.

What are the advantages of stratified, cluster and multi-stage sampling?
Stratified sampling

Stratified sampling is very commonly used in environmental monitoring as a way of improving the precision of estimates. Very often there is substantial variation across the site in the feature attributes being measured. This may be due to environmental gradients or differences in management, for example. In this situation it makes sense to divide the site into sub-units (strata) that relate to the different values of the attributes being monitored (e.g. different densities of a particular species) and sample each sub-unit separately (see Figure 2.9). Separate estimates are then made for each stratum, which are then combined to provide an estimate for the whole site. Stratification has a number of potential advantages:

- An attribute can be estimated with greater precision, provided that the value of the attribute differs substantially between strata and there is more variation in the attribute between strata than within strata.

Box 2.5 Optimal allocation of sampling effort for stratified sampling

First we require:

n = total number of sampling units required (e.g. quadrats).

For each stratum (h) we require:

$n_{h(opt)}$ = optimum number of units to be sampled in stratum h;

N_h = total number of possible sampling units in stratum h (the stratum area can be used instead);

s_h = estimated standard deviation of measured variable per sampling unit in stratum h;

c_h = relative cost of taking one sample in stratum h (e.g. $c_1 = 1$, $c_2 = 1.5$, $c_3 = 2$)

It is important to note that an estimate of standard deviation of the variable being measured must be made in advance *for each stratum*. This can be done either by making an educated guess or by conducting a preliminary survey. In the absence of better information, costs are often all assumed to be the same.

The proportion of sampling effort that should optimally be made in the hth stratum (considering variability and cost) is given by:

$$\frac{n_{h(opt)}}{n} = \frac{N_h s_h / \sqrt{c_h}}{\sum \left(N_h s_h / \sqrt{c_h} \right)}.$$

If the measurement is a proportion (e.g. the proportion of quadrats containing a species), this formula can be written as

$$\frac{n_{h(opt)}}{n} = \frac{N_h \sqrt{p_h q_h / c_h}}{\sum \left(N_h \sqrt{p_h q_h / c_h} \right)},$$

where

p_h = estimate of the proportion being measured, in stratum h;

$q_h = 1 - p_h$.

As a rule of thumb, for quantitative data no fewer than five samples should be allocated to each strata. For proportions rather more are advisable as, otherwise, the estimation of the standard deviation becomes very unreliable.

For further detail consult Cochran (1977).

- Separate estimates can be made for each stratum if these are of interest in their own right.
- Stratification slightly reduces the time taken to randomly locate samples.

To maximise the benefits of stratification the site should be subdivided in such a way that it minimises the within-stratum variability in the attribute being measured (i.e. strata should be as uniform, or homogeneous, as possible). This normally requires previous survey data or a preliminary survey to be carried out.

Alternatively, you can stratify according to known site variations in habitat or ecological factors, which are believed to influence the feature attributes (e.g. a sudden change in soil type). Although these divisions are not going to be as accurate, as long as there is lower variability within strata this sampling method will provide better results than simple sampling across the whole site.

If the cost of sampling varies, or the within-stratum variance in each stratum differs, sampling should be more intensive in the strata in which the costs of sampling are lower or which are more variable. Sample size should be proportional to the size of the strata if the costs and variances of each stratum are similar, or in the absence of such information. A formula for the optimal allocation of sampling effort between strata is provided in Box 2.5. Methods for calculating overall means and confidence intervals are provided in Box 2.13.

Multi-stage and cluster sampling

In many situations a site may be so large that a high proportion of time is spent travelling between sample sites. In this instance cluster or multi-stage sampling could be considered as a means of increasing sampling efficiency and in some instances can improve precision for a given sample size. Multi-stage sampling is also known as multi-level sampling or subsampling. With multi-stage and cluster sampling a *major* sample unit is selected, which is divided up into *minor* units. Data are then collected from some or all of the minor units (see Figure 2.9). With cluster sampling all the minor units are sampled, but with multi-stage sampling a random or systematic sample of minor units is selected. In some cases the minor units are themselves sampled (three-stage sampling) but two-stage sampling is the most common technique.

A common example is one in which the major units are transects and the minor units are quadrats along each transect. If all quadrats are sampled this is known as a belt transect.

The main consideration with this technique is that sample units within each major unit are unlikely to be independent of one another since spatial correlation may occur (i.e. sample units are likely to be more similar the closer they are to each other). Unless the minor units are sufficiently far apart to avoid this, overall precision is likely to be mainly determined by the variation between the major units. In cluster sampling, the minor units are usually combined and analysis is reduced to simple random sampling of the major units. This may still be advantageous, compared with simple random sampling of minor units, if there is a significant reduction in the variation between sampling units as these units get larger.

Thus, cluster and multi-stage sampling are likely to be most useful when the area being sampled is relatively uniform at large spatial scales and most of the variance occurs at small spatial scales (but at scales larger than the size of the sample unit). Transects will be most effective if oriented along a gradient in the attribute being measured. For example, in a study of tree regeneration around woodland, the transects may be oriented away from the woodland, assuming regeneration will decline with distance.

The precision of the overall estimate is primarily affected by the variance between the mean values for major units and, to a lesser extent, by the variance between minor units within each major unit. Precision is also affected by the number of units sampled at each level. In order to determine the optimum number of major and minor units to sample, some knowledge of the two variances and of the relative cost of sampling at the two stages is required. This may be obtained through a preliminary survey, or estimated based on available knowledge of the habitat in question. A preliminary survey may also be designed to investigate the optimal size of the major units as there will be a trade-off between the benefit of having a large sample of major units and increasing their size to reduce between-unit variation. Formulae for estimating the optimal number of minor and major units are provided in Box 2.6.

Methods for calculating means and confidence limits for two-stage sampling are given in Box 2.13. These methods assume that all minor units are of equal size and that each major unit contains the same number of minor units. Table 2.2 summarises the advantages and disadvantages of the different random sampling designs. For further information and detail on these see, for example, Cochran (1977) or Yates (1981).

Some other approaches
Stratified systematic unaligned sampling
This is a variation of stratified sampling that combines the advantages of random and systematic sampling. The area to be sampled is first stratified into equally sized blocks (not strata based on habitat characteristics as in stratified random sampling). Samples are placed in each block by using different *x* co-ordinates for each column of blocks but the same *x* co-ordinate within one column, and different *y* co-ordinates for each row of blocks but the same *y* co-ordinate within one row (see Figure 2.9). This technique can be an improvement on stratified random sampling because the systematic misalignment is not subject to localised clustering. This technique does not appear to have been widely used. The time taken to position samples is similar to that for stratified random sampling.

Smartt & Grainger (1974) compared the techniques discussed above. They found that stratified techniques exhibited greater overall comparative precision than random or systematic techniques, especially at low sample densities with clustered distributions. In this situation, the sampling strategies ranked in increasing order of relative precision were: random, systematic (regular), stratified random, stratified systematic unaligned.

Box 2.6   Optimal allocation of sampling effort for two-stage sampling

The following quantities need to be determined during the preliminary survey:

N = number of major units available for sampling;

n = number of major units sampled;

U = number of minor units within each major unit;

u = number of minor units sampled within each major unit;

u' = number of minor units in preliminary study;

t_m = time taken to locate each major unit;

t_u = time taken to sample each minor unit.

We then require the means and variances of each major unit. These are used to calculate the following:

$\bar{x}$ = overall mean, i.e. the mean of the major unit means;

s_x^2 = variance of the major unit means;

m_s = mean of the variances for each major unit.

The optimum number of minor units to be sampled, u_{opt}, is calculated thus:

$$u_{opt} = \sqrt{\frac{t_m/t_u}{\left(\frac{s_x^2}{m_s} - \frac{1}{u'}\right)}}.$$

It can be seen from this equation that u_{opt} increases as t_m/t_u increases and as the variance within units (m_s) increases relative to the variance between units (s_x^2).

If either $u_{opt} > U$ or $s_x^2 m_s < 1/u'$, then you should sample all of the minor units within each major unit, thereby simplifying the sampling strategy to basic cluster sampling.

If we assume that the mean approximately follows a normal distribution (Box 2.7), the number of major units to be sampled, n_p, required to give a confidence interval that extends no more than $P\%$ either side of the mean (Section 2.3.5), is roughly calculated by using the following equation:

$$n_p = \frac{s_x^2}{\frac{1}{N}\left(s_x^2 + m_s\left(\frac{1}{u} - \frac{1}{U}\right)\right) + \left(\frac{\bar{x}}{200}P\right)^2}.$$

These two equations can therefore be used to calculate the optimum number of minor units to sample within each major unit and the optimum number of major units to sample for a required precision, once initial estimates have been made of the variability of the data and the relative costs of sampling major and minor units.

Adaptive sampling

Another approach to consider for features that have very clustered distributions is adaptive sampling (Thompson and Seber, 1996). This involves selecting an initial random or systematic sample. If the target species is found in a given sampling unit, the adjacent sampling units are also included on the basis that there is a good chance these will also contain the species. Potential advantages include:

- although specialised formulae are required for estimation, adaptive sampling can provide better precision for a given amount of effort than simple random sampling;
- the method is more satisfying for surveyors, as they do not have to ignore sightings that fall just outside a sampling unit;
- a better picture of the species' spatial distribution is obtained.

One disadvantage is that the sample size cannot be determined in advance; it will depend on what is encountered in the initial sample.

Some other sampling techniques for species, such as distance sampling, are discussed in Chapter 10.

2.3.5   How many samples will be required?

As previously mentioned, increasing sample size increases precision (see Figure 2.8) as well as the cost of monitoring. Preliminary field trials or pilot surveys enable the distribution of the species or habitat to be assessed and the amount of variation in each attribute to be estimated. This can be of enormous value in helping to optimise the sampling design and in establishing the number of samples required. Without a pilot survey or some data from a previous survey, sample size estimates are usually down to guesswork.

Box 2.7   Probability distributions

The probability distribution for a particular measurement shows the probability that an individual drawn at random from a population takes a particular value, or lies within a range of values. The true distribution of a measurement across a study area is usually unknown and has to be approximated by using measurements taken from a sample. For quantitative measures, such as vegetation height or counts of plants in a quadrat, the distribution can be illustrated by plotting a histogram, such as those shown in Figure 2.8, but unless sample sizes are fairly large this may be a poor representation of the population distribution. For presence–absence data the distribution is defined by the probability that a sample unit will contain the species of interest.

A lot of statistical analysis relies on assuming that the distribution of a measure can be described, at least approximately, by a particular mathematical function. This enables us to estimate the probability that the measure is less than, or greater than, some value of interest.

By far the most common theoretical distributions that arise in monitoring are the *normal* and *binomial* distributions. These are described below.

THE NORMAL DISTRIBUTION

The normal distribution is the most commonly used function to describe the distribution of continuous data. It is one of the easiest distributions to handle in terms of statistical computation. This distribution is determined by two parameters, μ, the mean value of the population, and σ, the standard deviation. Because μ and σ relate to the population we must estimate their values by using the sample mean and standard deviation.

A normal curve is symmetrical, with the axis of symmetry passing through the mean. About 68% of all observations drawn at random from a normal distribution will fall within one standard deviation of the mean; about 95% will fall within two standard deviations. See Figure B2.7.

The normal distribution has some very desirable mathematical properties. Very often, rather than being interested in the distribution of the measurements themselves, we want to be able to say something about the mean of those measurements. This mean also has a probability distribution. An important result, the Central Limit theorem, states that as sample size increases the distribution of means of samples will almost always converge towards a normal distribution, regardless of the shape of the distribution of the original measurements. Of course, the more non-normal (e.g. asymmetrical) the parent distribution is, the larger the sample size will have to be for this to hold.

In addition, although the normal distribution is continuous it can often be used to approximate the distribution of count and binary data. This simplifies the calculations of probability for these data.

In some cases a transformation, such as log or square root, can be used to make data fit a normal distribution more closely and therefore facilitate the use of statistical methods that rely on this assumption (see Section 2.6.4).

For data that are normally distributed, the probability that a measurement is less than a specified value does not have a simple mathematical formula. However, it can be found in statistical tables or is readily calculated in most spreadsheet or statistical software.

As mentioned above we are often more interested in the distribution of the sample mean rather than that of the original data. The mean of normally distributed data has parameters μ and $\sigma/\sqrt{n}$, where n is the sample size. It is convenient to *standardise* normally distributed data so that the standardised data follow a normal distribution with a mean of zero and a variance of one. The standardised mean is calculated as

$$\frac{(\bar{x} - \mu)}{\frac{\sigma}{\sqrt{n}}}.$$

Usually, we do not know what the value of σ is: it has to be estimated by s, from the sample. If we replace σ by s in the above equation the distribution ceases to be exactly normal. In fact the standardised mean follows what is called the *t-distribution*. This distribution is dependent on the sample size n, and is referred to as having n-1 *degrees of freedom*. For sample sizes greater than about 30 the *t*-distribution is almost the same as the equivalent normal distribution and this can be used as an approximation.

The *t*-distribution is widely used in calculating confidence intervals (Box 2.8) and in statistical tests (see Section 2.6). For *t*-distributed data, as with normally distributed data, the probability that a measurement is less than a specified value can be found in statistical tables or is readily calculated in most spreadsheet or statistical software.

THE BINOMIAL DISTRIBUTION

Observations that are binary (can take one of two values) such as presence–absence often conform to the binomial distribution. Individuals may possess a certain character with the probability p or fail to exhibit it with the probability $1 - p = q$. The probability P that, in a sample of size n, x individuals possess the character is given by:

$$P = \frac{n!}{x!(n-x)!} p^x q^{(n-x)},$$

where ! = factorial (e.g. 5! = 5 × 4 × 3 × 2 × 1).

The mean and variance of the distribution are given by np and $np(1 - p)$, respectively. These quantities can be used to approximate the binomial distribution by an equivalent normal distribution provided n is large and p is not close to 0 or 1. This can facilitate the calculation of confidence intervals for p (see Box 2.8) and the use of standard statistical tests (see Section 2.6).

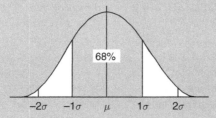

Figure B2.7. The normal distribution curve showing one (shaded) and two (unshaded) standard deviations.

How many samples are required depends very much on the individual sampling method, the type of attribute being measured, the degree of variability in the attribute being sampled and the desired precision or the degree of change that must be detected. A method for establishing the number of samples required to provide a desired level of precision is outlined below and methods for detecting change in Box 2.10.

Both approaches require some understanding of *probability distributions* and how these are applied to different types of measurement. This is outlined in Box 2.7, but a fuller account can be found in most introductory statistics texts (see, for example, Fowler *et al.*, 1998; Sokal & Rohlf, 1996).

Achieving a desired level of precision

The first question to be answered is how we specify how good we want our population estimate to be.

This will typically be in terms of the amount of error or uncertainty we are prepared to tolerate. For example, suppose we are estimating the percentage of a raised bog that is covered by sphagnum moss, and this is thought to be around 70%. We might be content for our sample of the bog to tell us that this percentage is somewhere between 60% and 80%. So, in this case, an uncertainty of 10% is acceptable. What error is acceptable will depend on the objectives for the monitoring. In some cases a rough and ready estimate may be acceptable if a feature is believed to be well within acceptable limits, but where the feature is of particular importance or is the subject of some concern, a very precise estimate may be desirable.

This approach suggests choosing a sample size that will give us enough measurements so we can be confident that the value of the attribute lies between l and u, where the range $u - l$ is sufficiently small for our purposes. The range $u - l$ is termed a

Box 2.8   Confidence intervals

If a population parameter such as the mean is estimated from a sample, there will always be uncertainty as to the whole-population value of the mean. *Confidence intervals* derived from our estimates indicate a range of values within which we have some confidence the true mean lies.

A 95% confidence interval that ranges from 10 to 30 indicates that we are 95% confident that the true population mean lies between 10 and 30. Suppose the sample has yet to be selected, then we define upper and lower 95% confidence limits, L and U, for the population mean, μ, so that

$$p\,(L < \mu < U) = 0.95,$$

or equivalently

$$p(\mu < L) + p\,(\mu > U) = 0.05,$$

where p stands for probability. L and U are functions of the mean of the sample to be selected. Once we have our sample data we can calculate particular values of L and U; let us call them l and u. If it were possible to select many different samples then each would result in different values of l and u, but 95% of the confidence intervals calculated from these samples would contain the true mean.

To calculate l and u for a particular sample we need to know something about its probability distribution. For example, for a mean that is normally distributed the standardised mean will follow a t-distribution with $n-1$ degrees of freedom, where n is the sample size, and 95% confidence limits are calculated as follows:

$$l = \bar{x} - (t_{n-1} \times SE) \text{ and } u = \bar{x} + (t_{n-1} \times SE),$$

where t_{n-1} is the value of a t-distribution, T, with $n-1$ degrees of freedom such that $p(T < t_{n-1}) = 0.025$. This value is used because we want a confidence interval that is symmetric around the mean and so we set both $p\,(\mu < L)$ and $p\,(\mu > U)$ to be 0.025.

For example, suppose we have counts of the number of bramble shoots for a simple random sample of ten quadrats. The sample mean is 6.2 and the standard deviation is 4.08. Assuming the population of potential quadrats is large, the standard error is therefore

$4.08/\sqrt{10} = 1.29$. Assuming the mean count is approximately normally distributed, the 95% confidence limits are

$$l = 6.2 - (2.26 \times 1.29) = 3.3 \text{ and}$$
$$u = 6.2 + (2.26 \times 1.29) = 9.1,$$

since, from statistical tables, for a t-distribution with $10 - 1 = 9$ degrees of freedom, $p(T < 2.26) = 0.025$. That is, we are 95% confident that the true mean density of bramble shoots lies between 3.3 and 9.1 shoots per quadrat.

Formulae for calculating standard errors for stratified and two-stage sampling are provided in Box 2.13.

The value of 95% is by far the most common confidence level used, although in some circumstances a higher or lower level of confidence may be appropriate.

Presence–absence data generally conform to the binomial distribution (see Box 2.7). In this case, the number of samples required to provide a given level of precision depends solely on the proportion of all quadrats containing the species, which is unknown. This will also depend on the size of quadrat chosen (Appendix 4). For large sample sizes and proportions greater than 0.1 and less than 0.9 the methods described above for normally distributed data are probably sufficient (see Table 2.5). Otherwise, exact binomial confidence intervals can be calculated in a spreadsheet by using the method described at, for example, www.itl.nist.gov/div898/handbook/prc/section2/prc241.htm.

For quantitative measurements that have a very non-normal distribution it is probably best to use a data transformation so that the transformed data are approximately normally distributed. Common transformations are covered in Section 2.6.4, but it is important to note here that, if a transformation is used, the mean of the transformed data will not usually be the same as the transformed mean of the original data. Thus the resulting confidence interval will be for the reverse transformed mean of the transformed data. See Section 2.6.4 for an example of this.

confidence interval for the attribute we are estimating and its calculation depends on the nature of the measurements collected and their probability distribution (see Box 2.8 for more information).

Being able to estimate the confidence interval one would expect requires some knowledge about the mean and standard deviation of the measurement of interest. This is usually obtained from a pilot survey or from a previous, similarly designed, survey. Suppose the pilot study suggests the mean is $\bar{x}$ and the standard deviation is s. If the data are approximately normally distributed then, for the main study, we would expect the 95% confidence interval that would result from a sample size of n to be:

$$\bar{x} \pm t_{n-1}s/\sqrt{n}.$$

Thus if we want the main study to provide a confidence interval that extends no more than $p\%$ either side of the estimated mean, n should be such that

$$n > (100\,t_{n-1}s/p\bar{x})^2.$$

For sample sizes greater than about 30, t_{n-1} can be replaced by 2.

Power analysis

Power analysis is a method for establishing the number of samples required to detect a given change with a given level of statistical certainty. Before continuing we need to introduce the idea of *hypothesis testing*, which, among other things, provides a framework for deciding whether a change is likely to have taken place. Box 2.9 provides the necessary introduction, an understanding of which will also be important for the account of data analysis in Section 2.6.

2.3.6   When should data be collected?

It is important that repeat sampling is carried out at approximately the same time of year each year unless seasonal cycles are being investigated. The time of sampling will depend on the attribute being measured (e.g. winter populations of migratory birds or juvenile population size of newts after breeding). The best times to survey particular vegetation types are shown in Box 6.13. It is inevitable that some surveys will have to be carried out outside these times, but it is particularly important that repeat sampling of habitats for monitoring purposes is carried out within about two weeks of the day of the year that the original survey was carried out. Serious bias may occur if surveys are carried out at different times of year.

The timing also depends on what is being monitored; the best time to monitor floristic components may differ from the best time to monitor grazing impact. For example, in heathlands, the best time to assess grazing impact is March–May, but this is probably not a good time to assess floristic composition. The effect of detectability on data is important. In some cases, plants are best counted after flowering; this avoids the possibility of being attracted to flowering plants only.

2.3.7   How will consistency be assured?

For reliable monitoring it is essential that the methods used for assessing attributes are constant between surveys. Therefore, before the first survey is carried out a standard operating procedure (SOP), otherwise known as a monitoring protocol, should be written, describing in detail the methods to be used, so that everyone understands what is required and the methods are kept consistent between observers and years. Any modifications that are found to be necessary during the execution of the survey should be noted down immediately afterwards and the SOP amended accordingly. The SOP should then be followed as closely as possible in all subsequent surveys. However, if deviations from the SOP are necessary, then these should be recorded. Monitoring reports should ensure that the SOPs are written out in full in the methods section or placed in an appendix. Deviations from SOPs should also be reported in the monitoring report, and the implications for the results and interpretation of the monitoring should be discussed.

When designing a SOP, consultation with the appropriate government agency specialist is important in case a standard procedure is already

Box 2.9   Hypothesis testing

Once data have been collected we are typically interested in using them to test some hypothesis about the population under study: for example, that the population of birds at a site is above some preset level, or that the percentage of a raised bog covered by sphagnum moss is higher in year 2 than in year 1. Because our measurements are from a sample of the site or population, we cannot test these hypotheses with certainty, but provided measurements are from a statistically representative sample we can estimate how confident we are that the hypothesis holds.

Hypothesis testing involves comparing two hypotheses, a *null* and an *alternative hypothesis*. Typically, we want to test whether the data from the sample provide any evidence for rejecting the null hypothesis (usually denoted H_0) and accepting the alternative hypothesis (usually denoted H_1). Thus for example, H_0 might be that sphagnum cover has not changed across the site and H_1 that it has. Has there been a sufficiently large change in the sample measurements of cover that it is unlikely that H_0 is true and that it can be rejected?

To see whether the collected data are consistent with the null hypothesis of no change, we need to estimate the likelihood of observing such a large change in a sample given that the null hypothesis is true. If this likelihood is small then the null hypothesis is unlikely to be true, and it is likely that a real change has taken place. This likelihood is termed the *significance level* of the test and is frequently set at 5%. This would mean that if the null hypothesis is true only 1 in 20 samples would be expected to show such a large change, suggesting that the null hypothesis is false.

TYPES OF ERROR

Whatever the significance level used there is always a chance of incorrectly rejecting the null hypothesis, and this is termed a Type I error. In addition, there is always a chance of incorrectly accepting the null hypothesis when it is false, and this is called a Type II error. After all, just because a test is not significant, it does not necessarily follow that the null hypothesis is true. For example, it is possible that the change in sphagnum cover is quite small and that insufficient data have been collected to detect it.

In a monitoring study a Type II error amounts to concluding that no change is taking place when in fact it is. In many situations it is preferable to err on the side of caution and try to limit Type I errors. However, Type II errors may have profound consequences in monitoring studies because real changes in the condition of a feature may not be detected. For monitoring studies it may therefore be prudent to follow the precautionary principle and specify significance levels above 5% at least as a trigger for further studies.

CHOOSING A TEST

Performing a test involves calculating an appropriate *test statistic* and deciding whether its value is extreme enough to warrant rejecting the null hypothesis. The type of test chosen will depend on the type of data being analysed and the assumptions that we make about the distribution of the data (see Section 2.6.4 and Figure 2.11). For example, one class of statistical test, known as *parametric* tests, assumes that the data are drawn from a particular distribution. The normal distribution is the one most commonly used; if continuous data are not normally distributed, they can often be transformed into a closer approximation of a normal distribution (see Section 2.6.4). Alternatively, *nonparametric* or *resampling* methods can be employed, which do not make assumptions about the underlying distribution of the data.

The *test statistic* is compared with tables of values derived from the appropriate statistical distribution for the required level of significance. If the test statistic is greater (or, for a few tests, smaller) than the tabulated value for the chosen significance level, then we can conclude that the null hypothesis (no difference) can be rejected. By convention, 5% is frequently used as the significance level, but it is useful to present the actual level of significance at which the null hypothesis would be rejected. A very small value would give strong evidence for rejection, but a value around, say, 10% would still raise doubts that the null hypothesis is correct.

For example, suppose that the null hypothesis is true and the test statistic is normally distributed. If its value under this hypothesis lies in either of the 2.5% tails, there is a 95% chance that the data come from a different distribution, and so there is evidence for rejecting the null hypothesis. See Figure B2.9.

ONE- OR TWO-SIDED TESTS

In the example above, the statistical test is *two-sided*: H_0 is rejected if the test statistic falls in either tail of the distribution. These are the norm and arise, for example, if the alternative hypothesis is that there has been a change, without specifying the direction of change. This is normal because we do not usually know the direction of change in advance. A *one-sided* test is appropriate if a one-sided hypothesis is specified in advance. This arises, for example, if we want to test whether an attribute is below a specified value.

The power of a statistical hypothesis test is the probability of rejecting the null hypothesis given that the alternative hypothesis is true, and, in the case of monitoring, is therefore a measure of the likelihood of correctly deciding that a change has taken place. Conversely, the significance level of a test is the probability of rejecting the null hypothesis when it is true. Thus it measures the likelihood of incorrectly deciding that a change has taken place. This is illustrated, with an example for normally distributed data, in Box 2.10.

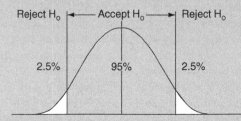

Reject H_0 |← Accept H_0 →| Reject H_0

2.5%   95%   2.5%

Figure B2.9. Accepting and rejecting the null hypothesis. See text for details.

used for the species or habitat and to check the suitability of the proposed monitoring method.

It is important to check the repeatability of the method used. This can be tested by having one observer repeat a survey immediately after another observer, or by the same observer conducting duplicate counts. The results of quality control are useful for several reasons. Apart from highlighting the occurrence of any differences that may be present due to the ability of a surveyor, such as in species identification, plant cover estimates, interpreting maps or using a compass, it may be possible to incorporate the results into statistical tests. Confidence limits and standard errors can be calculated based on the variation in total counts or mean values in order to break down the variation caused by observer bias compared with the variation due to other reasons. If major discrepancies are found between two surveys, the underlying cause should be identified and corrected if possible. If this is not achievable, the results for the survey on which quality control was carried out may need to be taken as the average of the two repeats. Alternatively, the site may have to be resurveyed for a third time, or one set of results may have to be discounted. The final decision should be accurately recorded so that the same remedy can be applied in the event of the problem recurring (see p. 21).

There is no doubt that the accuracy of interpretation is considerably enhanced when one recorder is involved in repeating work on one site for a long period of time.

2.4   REVIEWING THE MONITORING PROGRAMME

2.4.1   Are there sufficient long-term resources available?

It is important that the long-term future of the monitoring programme be considered from the outset; monitoring of some species and habitats has to be a long-term undertaking. However, many projects start off being too ambitious. Therefore, before embarking on the detailed design of a monitoring

Box 2.10 Power analysis

When testing a hypothesis we calculate the appropriate test statistic T, and if that statistic exceeds a critical value t, the *null hypothesis*, that no change has occurred between time 1 and time 2 (H_0: $\mu_2 - \mu_1 = 0$) is rejected in favour of the alternative hypothesis (H_1: $\mu_2 - \mu_1 \neq 0$), where μ_1 and μ_2 are the population values at times 1 and 2, respectively.

The 'power' of the test is therefore $p(T > t \setminus \mu_2 - \mu_1 \neq 0)$, where '$\setminus$' means 'given that'. Thus the power is the probability that the test statistic exceeds the critical value when the means of samples from time 1 and time 2 are different (the test reaches the correct conclusion).

Plotting this probability against $\mu_2 - \mu_1$ shows how the power increases as μ_2 and μ_1 become further apart, i.e. we are much more likely to detect a change if that change is large (see Figure B2.10).

When $\mu_2 - \mu_1 = 0$ the probability that $T > t$ is the probability α of rejecting H_0 when H_0 is true: the significance level, or the probability of a Type I error.

When $\mu_2 - \mu_1 \neq 0$ the probability that $T \leq t$ is the probability of not rejecting H_0 when H_1 is true (β) – a Type II error – and the power is $1 - \beta$.

A power analysis consists of calculating the number of samples required to detect a given level of change for chosen values of α and β.

NORMALLY DISTRIBUTED DATA

The example presented here is suitable for equally sized, normally distributed samples (software is available for this and other distributions; see below). A pilot survey is required to obtain an initial estimate of the variance of the data.

We need to decide what we consider to be the acceptable probability of concluding that no change is taking place when in fact it is, and of concluding that change is taking place when in fact it is not. The null hypothesis, H_0, is that no change has occurred. The alternative, H_1, is that change has occurred.

We define:

$\alpha = P(T > z_{\alpha/2}$ or $T < -z_{\alpha/2} \setminus H_0$ is true) = chance of Type I error (the significance level);

$\beta = P(-z_{\alpha/2} < T < z_{\alpha/2} \setminus H_1$ is true) = chance of Type II error;

$1 - \beta = P(T > z_{\alpha/2}$ when H_1 is true) = chance of correctly deciding a change has occurred (the power of the test);

where T is a test statistic that follows a standard normal distribution and will be calculated after the data have been collected, and $z_{\alpha/2}$ is the value from tables from the normal distribution for the chosen significance level, α. For example, if $\alpha = 0.05$ then $z_\alpha = 1.645$ and $z_{\alpha/2} = 1.96$.

The power, $1 - \beta$, for a given sample size can be found from the following equation:

$$z_\beta = d/s_d - z_{\alpha/2},$$

where s_d is the estimated standard error of a level of change, d, for the given sample size. For non-permanent plots, this is usually calculated by first estimating the sample standard deviation, s, from the pilot data. For reasonably large sample sizes, s_d is then usually estimated as

$$s_d = \sqrt{(2s^2/n)} .$$

Trying different values of n will give an indication of the sample size required to achieve a given power. Permanent plots are more problematic in that s_d will depend on how consistently the plots change, which is difficult to predict.

If plots are non-permanent and simple random sampling has been used (i.e. without stratification, etc.), these formulae can be solved for n:

$$n = \frac{2(z_{\alpha/2} + z_\beta)^2 s^2}{d^2}$$

or

$$n = \frac{2(z_{\alpha/2} + z_\beta)^2 P_{\text{cov}}^2}{C^2}$$

where s^2 is the sample variance from the preliminary survey, P_{cov} is the percentage coefficient of variation (see Glossary) of the preliminary sample, and C is the change to be detected expressed as a percentage.

It can be seen from these equations that the number of samples required to detect change will increase as the significance level of the test increases (i.e. as the chance of making a Type I error decreases), the power of the test increases (i.e. the test is more likely to be correct) and the variance of the data increases. The number of samples required decreases as the level of change required to be detected increases.

EXAMPLE

Let us assume that we are monitoring the number of orchids flowering in a meadow by using simple random sampling. The change to be detected is set at a mean decrease of flowers per 4 m^2 quadrat of 10%. We will use the conventional significance level of 5% for α and we will arbitrarily set the power of the test as 60% (i.e. there is a 40% chance that the test will wrongly accept the null hypothesis).

A preliminary study was carried out, and the percentage coefficient of variation of the number of orchids in the quadrats was estimated to be 36.21. Using tables we obtain $z_{0.2} = z_{0.025} = 1.96$ and $z_\beta = z_{0.4} = 0.25$. The number of samples required is therefore:

$$n = \frac{2(1.96 + 0.25)^2 36.21^2}{10^2} = \frac{12807.7}{100};$$

$$t = 128.08 \approx 128.$$

So roughly 128 quadrats would be needed to detect a change of 10% in orchid numbers per quadrat at the 95% significance level with a power of 60%.

Statistical power depends on the type of statistical test chosen. One test is said to be more powerful than another if it is more likely to reject the null hypothesis when the null hypothesis is false.

Power analysis is most useful when planning a study, at which point it is used to calculate the number of samples needed to detect a given change with a predetermined power and significance level (e.g. to detect a 10% change in cover with a power of 80% at the 5% significance level). When selecting a suitable significance level and statistical power, the precautionary principle should be considered (i.e. is it better to conclude that change is taking place when in fact it is not than to conclude that no change is taking place when in fact it is?).

A retrospective power analysis can be carried out after the study, which can be useful if a non-significant result is obtained (see, for example, Thomas & Juanes, 1996). In this case, sample size and significance level are known; these, and the estimate of variance obtained from the study, can be used to calculate the size of change that was detectable with the desired level of statistical power.

Power analysis is useful because it can provide an indication of what is achievable for a given amount of effort. Thus it may become apparent that only very large changes are detectable with current resources and that to detect small amounts of change, particularly in variable populations, requires a lot of effort. If this is considered at the planning stage of a monitoring

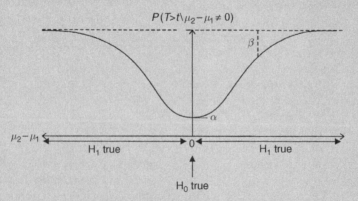

Figure B2.10. The increase in the power of detecting change as the change increases in extent.

programme it will help to avoid the possibility that the monitoring will fail to achieve its objectives.

Performing a power analysis requires data from a pilot or previous survey that provides an indication of variability in the measurement across the population. Software is usually needed to do the necessary calculations and there are a number of programs freely available. An example is DSTPLAN, which is available at odin.mdacc.tmc.edu/anonftp/. The program MONITOR can be used to estimate the number and intensity of surveys needed to achieve a given power for detecting trends over time. This program can be downloaded from www.mp1-pwrc.usgs.gov/

powcase/monitor.html, but some care is needed to ensure that the assumptions made by MONITOR are likely to be met. For an introduction to power analysis, a software review and details of where to obtain power analysis programs see the Internet site www.interchg.ubo.ca/cacb/ power and the US Geological Survey web page www.mp1-pwrc.usgs.gov/powcase/powcase.html; see also Thomas & Krebs (1997).

Further information on this subject is also available in Rotenberry & Wiens (1985), Lipsey (1990), Peterman (1990a,b), Muller & Benignus (1992) and Taylor & Gerrodette (1993).

programme, it is vital to assess the resources available, including funding, staff time, staff expertise and existing equipment. This should then be taken into account in the selection of features and attributes to be monitored (see Sections 2.1.1 and 2.1.2) and the frequency of monitoring (see Section 2.1.3). However, as a minimum, resources should be sufficient to provide an adequate standard and frequency of monitoring for all the features and their attributes for which monitoring is mandatory.

Following this initial assessment, the full study requirements should be assessed after establishing the optimum methods. Monitoring costs should be based on the most cost-effective method that meets the objectives for monitoring each attribute and the required standards of precision and accuracy, etc., as described in Section 2.2.

The assessment should take a long-term view of the requirements for monitoring and available resources, including likely year-to-year variations in monitoring needs and budgets. A poor monitoring design is one in which the monitoring effort changes from year to year, or in which monitoring is dropped in one year because of a lack of resources. This variability introduces yet another confounding factor, which will cloud the interpretation of the results obtained.

If the resources needed for a full monitoring programme exceed those available, the two options are: (i) to seek more funds; or (ii) to trim the monitoring programme in the least damaging way, e.g. by monitoring less frequently or by

excluding attributes for which monitoring is discretionary. However, it should be remembered that excluding other features and attributes from monitoring may be a false economy. In the long term, the costs of restoring habitats or species populations may far exceed the costs of monitoring and early management intervention.

At the outset it is important to work out how much time the optimum monitoring protocol will take to achieve. Then determine whether sufficient resources (especially suitably qualified staff) will be consistently available when required.

2.4.2   Are personnel sufficiently trained and experienced?

Consideration of staff resources available for monitoring must include an assessment of the expertise and experience necessary for the chosen methodology and, if necessary, the acquisition of a licence (see below). As a minimum, it is essential to be familiar with the habitat, study species and survey methods required. The correct identification of target species may require specialist personnel even if the methods themselves are straightforward. Alternatively, the method itself (e.g. electrofishing or bird ringing) may require specialist training and/or licensing. If the monitoring involves several people they should all be trained to a minimum standard and recording techniques should be standardised; this can be done as part of a preliminary study.

Monitoring work may well be contracted out to staff from outside agencies. These people must also be suitably trained and experienced to carry out the work to a sufficient standard.

2.4.3   Are licences required, and are there animal welfare issues to consider?

An important consideration when surveying and monitoring species (particularly for rare species) is that staff may need to hold a licence. For example, under the 1981 Wildlife & Countryside Act, licences are required from the relevant government department or agency to enter bat roosts, trap protected species such as Great Crested Newts, and survey many rare breeding birds. Invasive mark–recapture methods such as toe-clipping for amphibians may require a Home Office licence under the Animals (Scientific Procedure) Act 1986. It is therefore necessary before a method is selected and used that the need for a licence be investigated. If one is required, staff should obtain the licence and any necessary training in advance.

Animal welfare issues may need to be considered: certain survey and monitoring techniques may have unacceptable effects on the animals being surveyed, or on other groups (for example, small mammals may be killed in invertebrate or amphibian pitfall traps). Apart from the obvious point that humans are morally obliged not to cause unnecessary suffering to wildlife in the cause of surveying, there are other reasons for considering animal welfare. Many scientific journals such as the *Journal of Zoology* are now asking authors and referees specifically to address whether animal welfare issues have been taken into consideration. In addition, public (and political) support for monitoring activities may be affected by the impact of survey methods on wildlife and the environment in general.

2.4.4   Is specialist equipment required and available?

All equipment needed for the monitoring study should be made available for its duration so that standardised methods are employed. A scoping exercise prior to starting the formal monitoring may be valuable in determining what equipment is necessary. Going into the field and realising that a piece of equipment is required halfway through getting to the site, or once on it, is disorganised and may waste considerable time and money. On the other hand going into the field laden with excessive gear will slow you down and is unnecessary.

2.4.5   Are there health and safety issues to consider?

Fieldwork can be a dangerous activity and so before carrying out any such work, a careful risk assessment should be undertaken to identify potential risks and minimise these by ensuring that safety precautions are strictly followed. Recommended precautions for general fieldwork are given in Box 2.11, but these are not intended to be comprehensive. Fieldwork involving the use of specialist equipment or activities, such as diving, will certainly need additional safety measures and may well require staff to be suitably qualified.

2.5   DATA RECORDING AND STORAGE

2.5.1   How will data be recorded in the field?

Once the sampling protocol has been defined, the field data sheets can be designed. Specially designed forms encourage consistency and reduce unnecessary writing. Where lots of data are being recorded relatively quickly it may be advantageous to type the data directly into a hand-held datalogger. A database structure should be written, which prompts the observer to enter the appropriate record. The advantage of this method is that a large dataset can be downloaded directly to a computer.

Some remote sampling in which continuous recording of environmental variables is required as part of the habitat condition assessment can also be achieved with automatic dataloggers. It is unlikely that automatic datalogging will be essential or cost-effective for the majority of methods of assessing habitat condition.

Box 2.11   General health and safety considerations for working in the field

- Before undertaking monitoring, survey work, etc., discuss the proposed activity and terrain with your line manager and others with relevant knowledge and experience. This will help in deciding the relevance of the items below and those elsewhere in this *Handbook*.
- Lone working procedures should be followed. The minimum requirements, whether alone or as a party, are that you leave details of your itinerary with a responsible person; you make arrangements to contact a responsible person at least every eight hours and at the end of the working day; and you ensure that your contact knows what to do if you fail to make scheduled contact.
- Always have suitable clothing for the activity, terrain and weather conditions. Principles of good clothing concern insulation, and protection from precipitation and wind. Although it should be recognised that survival in exposed winter mountain environments can be extremely difficult without improvising an effective shelter, a fair test of your clothing and equipment is the answer to the question: could I survive, be it very uncomfortably, if I were immobilised for 24 hours? High-visibility clothing is desirable in many situations, both to prevent accidental injury and, more importantly, to be located in an emergency. Boots provide protection and grip. In general, choose the lightest pair that will do the job: the requirement for a rigid-soled heavier boot increases if you will be travelling in steep, rocky and winter terrain.
- Carry a map and compass. Know how to use the compass to take a bearing, set a course and walk on a compass bearing.
- Consider whether a survival bag might be necessary in remote and/or upland or/mountainous situations. Spare blankets are not recommended.
- Take spare warm clothing.
- Have with you some high-sustenance food such as sweets, chocolate, glucose tablets or biscuits.
- Always carry some means of raising alarm. A whistle and torch are essential items and other items such as flares, electronic devices and air/- or gas-pressured alarms should be considered.
- The International Alpine Distress Signal is six long whistle blasts or torch flashes in succession, repeated at 1 min intervals. The reply is three long whistle blasts or torch flashes repeated at 1 min intervals.
- Always carry a first aid kit and know how to use it. Emergency first aid training is available for those not in possession of full certificates.
- Inoculation against tetanus is strongly recommended for all staff engaged in fieldwork.
- Staff receiving special medical treatment, such as a course of injections, or suffering from medical conditions, such as diabetes, allergies, rare blood groups, etc., are reminded of the advisability of carrying a card or some other indication of special medical requirements.
- Where applicable, sufficient additional medicines, etc., should also be carried on field trips to ensure that no medical complications arise owing to lack of treatment. In an emergency the carrying of such items can save a lot of time and perhaps save your life.
- Staff visiting hazardous areas should inform those based at the location of any special medical condition, e.g. diabetes. This, in the event of an accident or the person becoming lost, is of great value to the rescue services. If a party is well equipped and it is overdue, no great concern may be shown for several hours. However, if a member of the group requires regular treatment, a search may be speeded up; for example, instead of a preliminary foot search being undertaken, a helicopter could be called for immediately.
- If you are new to an area, ask the area staff about any hazards.
- Do not fail to inform visiting members of staff of any dangers in the area they intend to work in.
- Staff about to embark on a rigorous period of fieldwork, especially after a period of relative inactivity, are reminded that some attention given to physical fitness beforehand can make the job more enjoyable as well as being a positive contribution to safety.

- Always move carefully over rough, rocky or vegetation-covered ground, avoiding any loose boulders, etc. Care should be taken on wet ground such as bogs, mud or fens.
- Never run down scree slopes or steep hills, and take care not to dislodge loose rocks or other objects.
- Before setting out on a field trip check the local weather forecast. This could save a wasted journey or prevent you or your party encountering adverse weather conditions, which could put your lives at risk. Be aware of weather conditions around you while outside, for example distant storms, which may change direction and come towards you.
- Avoid machinery, whether in use or not.
- Enquire about and avoid potentially dangerous animals.

- Take care to avoid hazardous substances such as herbicides and pesticides.
- Exercise extreme caution in areas of landfill, tips and spoil heaps, which could be unstable, especially in wet weather. Look out for weakness resulting from underground combustion and for any toxic substance, including gas, that may be present.
- Identify areas where game shooting may take place. Find out when and where this is taking place and take appropriate measures, including wearing high-visibility clothing.
- Note that care of general health while doing fieldwork is essential, as exhaustion can lead to careless mistakes and lower resistance to diseases.

Source: extract from SNH Health and Safety Manual.

2.5.2   How will the data be stored?

Storage directly on to a computer or interface in the field saves time but machines are prone to breaking down and may be expensive to back up. Work out a standard procedure for storing the data with understandable file names if on a computer, or filed by project or site name if in map form. Maps can also be scanned in and stored on computer hard drives, or CD-ROM as a security measure. Collecting data in the field is laborious, expensive and difficult to repeat, so good computer and digital storage of information is sensible. The information storage needs to take account of software and hardware obsolescence: data will need to be retrieved several decades from now. Consider also the requirements of data analysis software, which may only read data organised in a particular format.

Databases, such as Microsoft Access®, enable easy manipulation of data for various methods of analysis. They are also useful for holding textual data, such as descriptions of sites, changes to vegetation, etc., which are non-numeric. However, spreadsheets offer better capacity for analysing numerical data and are easier to use, especially for beginners. If the data are entered into a spreadsheet they can usually be imported into a variety of statistical packages for analysis.

Back-ups of all data files should be kept on disks or different computers, preferably in different buildings. Logs of existing data, with descriptive details and locations, should be kept for all sites. Hard copies of all data should also be kept. Although much of this is common sense and generally accepted good practice, it is surprisingly often ignored.

2.5.3   Who will hold and manage the data?

It is usually valuable to make one person responsible for databases and for managing them, i.e. updating, upgrading, producing reports from them, and so forth. Some databases, such as Microsoft Access®, allow the manager to design standard reporting forms and outputs, which anyone responsible for a site, or an aspect of the habitat, or, for example, policy factors affecting it can use to produce standard outputs. This limits individual bias in interpretation and presentation. Such databases can be made read-only prior to entering a password, which prevents data from being changed by unauthorised personnel. However, the data should be made available for use throughout an organisation and beyond, depending on commercial confidentiality or other constraints, so it is important to make sure that people know of its existence and the name of the contact person or data manager so that they can gain access to it should they need to.

2.5.4 Will the data be integrated with other datasets and if so, how?

If data are held in a program suite, such as that containing Microsoft Access® or Excel®, they can be integrated with data collected by someone else quite easily. If stored on a compartment basis (i.e. a management compartment for a site, as used in the standardised Countryside Management System (CMS)), integration with species-based data can be achieved in relation to compartment-based management projects. This is an essential part of project planning as part of the Conservation Management Plan for a site. For example, data for a site may be held on a compartment-by-compartment basis, corresponding to management units listed as projects in the Conservation Management Plan for the site. As such, both textual and numerical data can be held in the same file. In addition, there could be a number of fields that describe other data held for the site, which have been collected elsewhere. This information should consist of type of information, e.g. habitat survey data, year(s), compartments, whether material has been published, and perhaps compatibility of these data with those held in the monitoring database. Links to research projects could similarly be made.

Spatially referenced data can be integrated into a geographical information system (GIS) such as ArcGIS®. GIS systems are becoming increasingly widely used; they can add value to the analysis of spatially referenced data by enabling other datasets held for the site to be overlaid and compared (for example, data on soil type can be overlaid and correlated with data on vegetation communities). The examination of spatial trends in the range of a species can also be carried out with a GIS program. In addition, the ability to generate visual representations of your data can greatly enhance the ease with which it can be interpreted and understood. For example, a map of a site showing changes in the extent of a particular habitat type will lend weight to a description of the statistical analysis used to demonstrate that such a change is occurring.

2.6 DATA ANALYSIS, INTERPRETATION AND REVIEW

2.6.1 Who will carry out the analysis and when?

Data should be collected, stored and filed in such a way that anyone with the required skills should be able to analyse it. It is always important to describe through written SOPs:

- how and when the data were collected;
- what problems and/or issues arose and how they might affect the interpretation of the data;
- the sampling design together with clearly labelled maps of site and stratum boundaries;
- the notation and codes for species; and
- the format, location and file names of computer datasets or hard copies.

In addition it is important that monitoring programmes should identify the resources required for data analysis and the writing of reports, who should be responsible for this, and when it should be undertaken. Often this is overlooked and data accumulate that are never properly analysed and presented.

The data analysis should be carried out by someone with a good understanding of statistics and, in particular, an awareness of when particular analytical methods are appropriate and the potential pitfalls associated with their use. Misapplied tests or poorly presented data can lead to misinterpretation and poor management decisions.

2.6.2 What are the steps in analysing data?

A comprehensive account of statistical methods for data analysis would take up most of this book and there are already numerous books devoted to this (see the suggested references at the end of this section). The sections that follow simply outline the approach to take with some common methods and the pitfalls to look out for.

Further information on statistical techniques

BOOKS
See References for full details.
   Bailey (1981)
   Dytham (2003)
   Fowler *et al.* (1998)
   Kent & Coker (1992)
   Krebs (1999)
   Manly (1997)
   Mead *et al.* (1993)

   Sokal & Rohlf (1996)
   Young & Young (1998)
   Zar (1984)

INTERNET SITES
www.ltsn.gla.ac.uk (a good starting point for online statistical resources)
www.anu.edu.au/nceph/surfstat/surfstat-home/surfstat.html (an online text in introductory statistics)
www.stats.gla.ac.uk/steps/glossary/index.html (detailed statistical glossary)

Three distinct stages in the analysis of survey and monitoring data can be identified, as follows.

1. Description and presentation of data
2. Making inferences about the site or population
3. Interpretation and presentation of findings

Each of these stages is discussed in turn and together they provide a framework for ensuring that appropriate methods are used and that the findings are communicated successfully.

2.6.3   Description and presentation of data

The importance of exploring and summarising data, before launching into anything more complex, cannot be overstated. The dangers of missing out this step include the following.

- Inappropriate analyses are used or the assumptions for these do not hold.
- Peculiar or erroneous data values, which may exert a strong influence on how the data are interpreted, are not detected. These 'outliers' may be caused by measurement or recording error or mistakes during data entry. Alternatively, they may be valid measurements that just happen to be rather extreme. In the latter case, it may be decided to include these values in the analysis, but it is important to be aware of the extent to which conclusions are influenced by one or two outliers.
- Clear patterns and other features of the data are missed. Graphical and tabular display of data can reveal important aspects of the distribution of

data values or how different measurements are related. These can affect how the data are then analysed and interpreted. For example, are the measurements of vegetation height normally distributed or are there distinct vegetation types on the site, resulting in a more complex distribution? Alternatively, is there an association between the abundance of one species and another? Spatial patterns are only likely to be revealed by mapping; if these can be combined with other local datasets, additional relationships may become apparent.

- The main features of the data are poorly presented. Interpretation and presentation of findings is covered in Section 2.6.5, but it is worth noting here that graphical displays are often the most powerful way of communicating what the data show and it is worth taking time to find the best way of achieving this.

The best way of summarising and displaying data depends on the following.

- The type of data available. Whether the data are nominal, ordinal or quantitative will affect what descriptive statistics and displays make sense.
- The amount of data available. With a sample size of 10 it will not be possible to say much about the underlying probability distribution the data follow, but with 100, a histogram, or similar, should be informative.
- The objectives for the analysis. If interest centres on whether a measurement has changed over

time, examination of changes in some summary measure, such as the sample mean, is appropriate. If relationships between measures are of interest a scatterplot or cross-tabulation can be helpful.

Nominal and ordinal data

Nominal and ordinal data are summarised by calculating the proportion of sampling units that fall within each category: for example, the proportion for which the species was present or the proportion of quadrats in a particular vegetation height class. Such data can be displayed in bar charts, and shifts in the distribution of values in each class may be apparent by plotting the results of two or more surveys together. For ordinal data this might take the form of a series of stacked bar charts.

Relations between two such categorical variables can be investigated through cross-tabulation or bar charts with one variable grouped within the other.

Quantitative data

A much greater range of possibilities is available for quantitative variables. If data from sufficient sampling units are available, the distribution of each variable can be investigated by using graphs such as histograms, box plots and dot plots. The latter two are particularly useful for revealing outliers. Histograms, box plots and normal-probability plots can reveal peculiarities in the shape of the distribution (e.g. skewness) and indicate whether a data transformation (Section 2.6.4) might be required prior to using hypothesis tests, as for example in Box 2.12.

Descriptive statistics such as the mean and standard deviation of the dataset (Box 2.4) can be useful summaries, providing a central, middle value and a measure of variability, at least for data that are not too non-normal. Formulae for calculating mean and standard deviations for data collected by using stratified or two-stage sampling are provided in Box 2.13.

The mean will not be a very informative summary if the variable has a distribution with a cluster of low values and another of high values, for example. In this case the distribution is said to be bimodal and this could happen if the site covers two very different habitats or the population contains distinct sub-populations.

In addition, the mean is sensitive to outliers, so if, for example, the variable has a distribution where most of the values are fairly small but a few are fairly large, changes in the mean over time will be very sensitive to the values from a small number of sampling units. In this case the median, which does not suffer from this problem, may be a better summary statistic.

Changes between surveys can be viewed by plotting summary measures, such as means, as a time series. The addition of error bars to such charts, which may show confidence intervals or standard errors, can illustrate changes in the variables' variability. Displaying the individual values, perhaps as a series of box plots or dot plots, can reveal changes in the distribution as well as in the mean or median.

Scatter plots can help explore relations between quantitative variables; and the extent of *linear* association can be measured by calculating correlation coefficients.

2.6.4 Making inferences about the site or population

In general, we want to use data collected from a sample of a population to be able to say something about the population as a whole. That is, we want to make an *inference* about the population. For example: has sphagnum cover changed and by how much; has the abundance of species x declined; or is the breeding success rate of species y at a satisfactory level?

Thus the reason for analysing survey and monitoring data will usually be either:

- to compare data from a single sampling occasion against a pre-defined limit (for example, the limit below which a population should not fall); or
- to compare data from two or more sampling occasions to determine what changes have occurred.

Both of these objectives will usually involve the use of hypothesis tests (Box 2.9) and or confidence intervals (Box 2.8). Hypothesis tests enable us to say, for example, whether there is evidence that

Box 2.12 Histograms, box plots and normal probability plots

The data presented are percentage cover measurements for Heather *Calluna vulgaris* from 120 quadrats.

(A)   HISTOGRAM
The area of each bar represents the proportion of measurements falling in the interval shown by the horizontal axis. In most cases, where all bars have the same width, the height of each bar is the number of measurements in that interval. In this example (Figure B2.12a) the distribution is clearly skewed and a transformation is likely to be needed prior to analysis.

(B)   BOX PLOT
The box (Figure B2.12b) extends to the lower and upper quartiles, with a line indicating the median. The lines outwith the box extend 1.5 times the width of the interquartile range or to the lowest or highest value. Values outside this range are indicated as outliers. For normally distributed data we would expect a fairly symmetrical plot around the median. This is not the case here; a number of outliers are indicated.

(C)   NORMAL PROBABILITY PLOT
This plots the cumulative proportion of data values against that expected for normally distributed data (Figure B2.12c). Departures from the straight line indicate departures from normality. Again the data are clearly non-normal and transformation is required if parametric methods are to be applied.

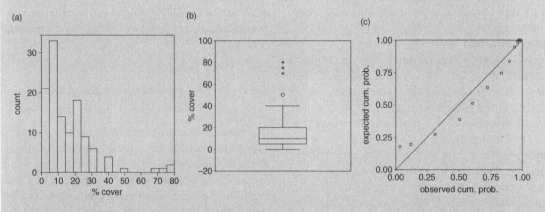

Figure B2.12. Examples of (a) histogram, (b) box plot and (c) normal probability plot. See text for details.

change in some population measure has taken place. However, this of itself may be of limited interest. Often we know that some change is likely because populations and habitats are naturally dynamic. Rather, we want to know how much change there has been so that the ecological significance of this change can be evaluated. This is where confidence intervals, or similar, are useful in providing a range in which we have some confidence that it contains the true level of change. See Eberhardt (2003) for a discussion of this and other issues surrounding hypothesis testing.

Statistical methods will usually make some assumptions about the distribution of the data, or more specifically about the *test statistic*. This is the summary measure for which we want to calculate confidence intervals or form hypotheses. Most commonly this will be the mean value or the proportion falling in a particular class. This summary measure will also have a sampling distribution, because different samples will result in a different value for the summary measure, but its distribution may be very different from that of the original data.

Box 2.13   Estimating means and standard deviations for stratified and two-stage sampling

STRATIFIED SAMPLING

For each stratum (h) and for a measurement x, we define:

n = total number of units (e.g. quadrats, individuals, etc.) sampled in all strata;

n_h = number of units sampled in stratum h;

N_h = total number of possible sampling units in stratum h;

$\bar{x}_h$ = mean of x in stratum h;

s_h = standard deviation of x in stratum h.

Then if we calculate

W_h = stratum weight for stratum $h = N_h/N_{total}$ where $N_{total} = \sum N_h$,

the estimate of the overall mean is calculated as

$$\sum W_h \bar{x}_h.$$

If we define

$$f_h = n_h/N_h$$

then the standard error of the overall mean is

$$SE_x = \sqrt{\left(\sum W_h^2 s_h^2 (1 - f_h)/n_h\right)}.$$

If this mean is approximately normally distributed then we can calculate confidence intervals in the usual way (Box 2.8). The number of degrees of freedom (df) for calculating the required t-statistic is

$$df = \frac{\left(\sum g_h s_h^2\right)^2}{\sum(g_h^2 s_h^4/(n_h - 1))},$$

where $g_h = N_h(N_h - n_h)/n_h$.

TWO-STAGE SAMPLING

We assume that the same number of minor units are sampled within each major unit. If we define the following:

N = number of major units available for sampling;

n = number of major units sampled;

U = number of minor units within each major unit;

u = number of minor units sampled within each major unit;

then the overall mean is estimated as

$\bar{x}$ = mean over the major units of the minor unit means.

Defining

s_x^2 = variance of the minor unit means;

m_s = mean of the variances within minor units;

the standard error for $\bar{x}$ is calculated as

$$SE_x = \sqrt{\left(1 - \frac{n}{N}\right)\left(\frac{s_x^2}{n}\right) + \left(1 - \frac{u}{U}\right)\left(\frac{m_s}{un}\right)}.$$

As introduced in Box 2.7, a key result (the *Central Limit theorem*) states, in essence, that as the sample size increases the distribution of the mean of a variable from a random sample will converge to being normally distributed. As many of the standard methods in statistical inference assume that the test statistic is normally distributed, this result is of huge significance. It means that, provided the number of samples is *sufficiently large*, we can assume that the mean of the variable of interest is approximately normal. What we mean by sufficiently large will depend on the distribution of the underlying data. For example, data that exhibit a very skewed or otherwise non-normal distribution will require a large sample size before their mean can be regarded as normal.

An outline of the stages of data analysis is shown in Figure 2.11. This illustrates that selecting an appropriate statistical method depends crucially on the distribution of the test statistic. The sections that follow describe the various methods available. Methods primarily aimed at quantitative data are split into three broad classes: parametric methods, methods based on ranks and resampling methods. The analysis of category data is considered separately. A rather different approach, Bayesian inference, is also briefly described.

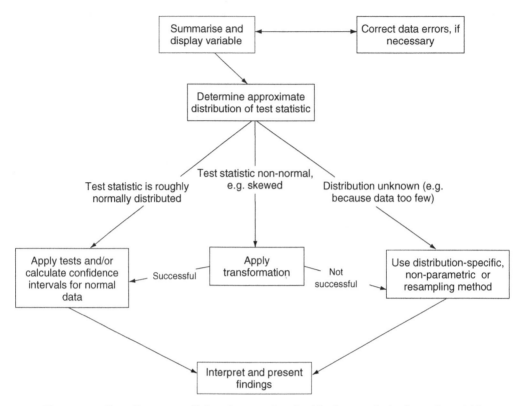

Figure 2.11. Flow diagram outlining the steps involved in data analysis, for each variable of interest.

The choice of test also depends on whether data for more than one survey are *paired* or *unpaired*. Paired data arise from permanent plots in which the measurement taken in a given plot during one survey can be compared directly with the measurement taken during another survey. If a new sample is selected for each survey the two samples cannot be paired in this way. Tests for paired samples are usually more powerful than those for unpaired, or independent, samples.

Parametric methods
Parametric methods assume that the test statistic follows a particular distribution, usually the normal distribution. If the underlying data are very non-normal and/or sample sizes are small it will be necessary either to transform the data prior to

analysis (see p. 61) or to use a non-parametric or resampling method.

For quantitative data that are not very skewed in distribution, 25–30 samples are usually sufficient for assuming that the sample mean is approximately normal. If the distribution is very skewed, for example because of a large number of zero counts, rather more samples are needed. An alternative is outlined on p. 60.

Table 2.3 lists some parametric tests to consider for different situations. Although these cannot be detailed here, accounts are readily found in most statistical textbooks or in the documentation for statistical software.

T-tests
The *t*-test compares the mean values from two groups and is by far the most commonly applied

Table 2.3. *Some parametric statistical tests appropriate for analysing survey and monitoring data*

Number of samples	Paired or unpaired data	Some tests to consider
One	n/a	One-sample *t*-test
Two	Paired	Paired *t*-test
	Unpaired	Independent sample *t*-test
More than two	Paired	Repeated measures analysis of variance
		Route regression
		Generalised additive models
	Unpaired	Analysis of variance
		Linear or polynomial regression
		Generalised additive models
		Time-series analysis

test. It is worth summarising a few of the considerations needed for using it appropriately.

- *T*-tests are reasonably robust to minor departures from the assumption that the data are normally distributed.
- The independent sample *t*-test would be used to compare results from two surveys using non-permanent plots. This test assumes that the data from the two samples have similar variances. Although the test is also robust to small departures from this assumption, provided the two samples are of similar size, the variances should be compared. Most statistical packages include a test for comparing variances. Some packages will provide a modified *t*-test to be used when the variances are different.
- A paired *t*-test should be used for data from permanent plots and will be more powerful than an independent sample test provided there is some correlation between the data from the two surveys.
- Tests can be one-sided or two-sided. Use two-sided tests unless a one-sided hypothesis test has been specified in advance of the survey or there is an *a priori* reason for change being in only one direction.

When data from more than two surveys are available, the class of methods called Analysis of Variance (ANOVA) can be used to look for differences across the surveys. Repeated measures ANOVA is used for data from permanent plots. ANOVA can be used to look for trends, but as more data become available the methods for detecting trends outlined on p. 59 can be considered.

Methods based on ranks

When there are insufficient data to be able to apply parametric methods with confidence, or when there are other concerns over the applicability of such methods, then non-parametric methods based on ranking the data provide an alternative. If the measurement of interest is ordinal then methods based on ranks are often appropriate. In general, such non-parametric methods are less powerful than the parametric equivalent, so the applicability of parametric or resampling methods should be considered first.

The two most commonly used tests are the Mann–Whitney rank-sum test and the equivalent for paired data, the Wilcoxon signed rank test. These and some other rank-based tests are listed in Table 2.4.

Table 2.4. *Some rank-based tests appropriate for analysing survey and monitoring data*

Number of samples	Paired or unpaired data	Some tests to consider
One	n/a	Sign test
		Wilcoxon test
Two	Paired	Wilcoxon signed rank test
		Sign test
	Unpaired	Mann–Whitney test
More than two	Paired	Friedman test
	Unpaired	Kruskal–Wallis test

Mann–Whitney test

Sometimes called the Mann–Whitney *U*-test or Wilcoxon's rank-sum test, this compares the distributions of two independent samples. Unlike the *t*-test, which specifically compares the mean from the two samples, the Mann–Whitney test simply tests whether the two distributions are identical or whether one tends to have larger values than the other.

The two samples are combined and numbered according to their rank, from smallest to largest. The sum of these ranks for one of the samples is then selected as the test statistic with particularly small or large values indicating that the selected sample comes from a distribution that is shifted to the left or right of the other one. Whether the test provides evidence for rejecting the hypothesis that the groups have the same distribution is determined from statistical tables or, more commonly, by the software performing the test. Such software will also make allowance for any ties in the rankings.

Wilcoxon's signed rank test

For paired data this tests whether one group tends to have larger, or smaller, values than the other. For each pair the difference in values is calculated and then these differences are ranked from smallest to largest without regard for sign. The sum of the ranks for the negative differences and for the positive differences are calculated separately. The test statistic is the smaller of these two sums; particularly small or large values will indicate that one or other group tends to take larger values than the other. As for the Mann–Whitney test, the Wilcoxon test is usually performed by using statistical software, which will also take account of ties.

Resampling methods

The advent of fast computers has made possible the development of another class of methods that derive distributional properties of summary statistics by generating large numbers of new samples from the original data. Primarily used for quantitative data, such methods enable the calculation of confidence intervals and the use of hypothesis tests without making assumptions about the distribution of the data and are usually more powerful than nonparametric methods that make use of data rankings rather than the data values themselves. Two particular methods in common use are the bootstrap and randomisation tests. A good reference for further detail is Manly (1997).

Bootstrapping

The idea behind bootstrapping is that if it is difficult to make distributional assumptions about a summary measure then the data themselves are the best guide to what that distribution is. To approximate what would happen if new samples were selected from the population under study, bootstrapping involves selecting new samples (resamples) from the sample data themselves. Such resamples are selected with replacement, that is each sample value can occur more than once in each resample. Large numbers of resamples (typically around 1000) are drawn and for each one a new estimate of the summary measure is calculated. In its simplest form a bootstrap 95% confidence interval is then estimated by reordering the resampled estimates from smallest to largest and selecting the 2.5 and 97.5 percentile values as the interval limits. This simple form of the bootstrap is relatively easy to implement in a spreadsheet, although many general-purpose statistics packages provide a range of bootstrapping methods.

Bootstrapping can also be used for hypothesis testing but the above method can be adapted if interest centres on the likelihood of change in a mean value between two surveys. If permanent plots were used then simply calculate the change for each plot and bootstrap these change values using the mean as the summary measure. If the resulting confidence interval does not extend across zero we can be reasonably confident that there has been a change. For non-permanent plots the two samples have to be bootstrapped separately. Each resample from the two samples is paired and the difference in means calculated. These can then be used to estimate a confidence interval for the difference in means.

Bootstrapping has gained in popularity in recent years and will often be recommended by journal referees if there is any doubt over the distribution for quantitative data.

Randomisation tests

Another class of methods that are primarily used for testing differences between two or more groups are randomisation tests. This is essentially a resampling method without replacement where the observed difference between groups is compared with what would be obtained by randomly allocating the data to the groups. In theory all possible allocations could be considered and a distribution of possible differences generated. Under a null hypothesis that there is no difference between the groups it seems

reasonable to suppose that the observed difference will not be particularly large when compared with this distribution. The null hypothesis is rejected if less than 2.5% of the randomised differences are greater than the observed difference (two-sided test). In practice it is usually impracticable to generate all possible allocations and so a large random sample of allocations is more commonly used.

Randomisation tests are used for detecting change and trends where the data are extremely non-normal. They are also used in multivariate analysis, for example to test the significance of relationships between species and environmental variables.

Categorical data

For presence–absence data or where interest centres on the proportion of samples falling into a particular category, parametric methods can sometimes be applied but rather more samples are likely to be needed than for quantitative data. Table 2.5, adapted from Cochran (1977), gives minimum sample sizes for a confidence interval based on a normal approximation to be applicable.

Calculation of confidence intervals is outlined in Box 2.8. For proportions, the formula to use for the standard error is

$$SE = \sqrt{\frac{\hat{p}(1 - \hat{p})}{n - 1}\left(1 - \frac{n}{N}\right)},$$

where $\hat{p}$ is the sample estimate of the proportion of interest.

Table 2.5. *Smallest sample sizes needed to use a normal approximation when calculating confidence intervals for proportions*

Proportion of plots in category of interest	Required sample size
0.5	30
0.4	50
0.3	80
0.2	200
0.1	600
0.05	1400

Table 2.6. *Some tests appropriate for analysing categorical data.*

Number of samples	Paired or unpaired data	Some tests to consider
One[a]	n/a	Exact binomial confidence interval Normal approximation Binomial test
Two[b]	Paired	McNemar's test
	Unpaired	Chi-squared test Fisher's exact test Normal approximation
More than two	Paired	Cochran Q test
	Unpaired	Chi-squared test

[a] For ordinal data the ranking methods described in *Methods based on ranks* (p. 56) may be appropriate.
[b] Note that the parametric regression and modelling methods may also be appropriate.

Table 2.7. *Example data for chi-squared test*

Year	No of quadrats with species present (O)	Expected number of quadrats with species (E)	Total number of quadrats taken
1	40	25	50
2	30	25	50
3	50	50	100
4	30	50	100
Total	150	150	300

To compare two samples to see, for example, whether a change has taken place in the proportion of the site falling within a category interest, the most commonly used tests are chi-squared (χ^2) tests and, for paired data, McNemar's test. These and some other tests for categorical data are listed in Table 2.6.

Chi-squared tests
These are a class of tests for examining hypotheses for category data. For example, suppose presence–absence data are available from four surveys and interest centres on whether the proportion of plots containing a species has changed. The data can be presented in the form of a table (Table 2.7) whose cells show the number of sample plots for which the species was present and absent for each survey. In this example new plots have been used for each survey.

To test the null hypothesis that the proportion of quadrats in which a species is present is the same in each year, we compare the observed data with that which would be expected if no change had taken place. The chi-squared test is then used to see whether the observed and expected values are sufficiently different for it to be unlikely that no change has occurred. The chi-squared statistic is calculated from the equation:

$$\chi^2 = \sum \frac{(O_i - E_i)^2}{E_i},$$

where O_i is the observed frequency of the species in question in a given year i and E_i is the expected frequency if the species is not changing.

Expected values are calculated by:

$E(\text{one year})$

$$= \frac{\text{total quadrats in which species present}}{\text{total number of quadrats overall}}$$
$$\times \text{ total quadrats taken in that year}.$$

This value is compared with values of χ^2 from statistical tables. We need the degrees of freedom, which is given by the number of years minus 1; in this case 3.

Bayesian inference

Bayesian inference differs from the *classical* methods described so far in that it makes use of prior information about the population measure of interest. Rather than treating this measure as being fixed, Bayesian methods give it a probability distribution, which is determined by the nature of the measure and the extent of prior knowledge. This *prior distribution* is then combined with information provided by the survey data, using Bayes' theorem, to derive a *posterior distribution* for the measure. This posterior distribution tells us what we know about the population measure given the data and our prior knowledge and can be used to provide an estimate of the measure and a Bayesian equivalent of the confidence interval, often called the *credible interval*.

Prior information comes from expert knowledge about the site or population, from previous surveys and/or from surveys on similar sites or species. The prior distribution is defined according to the quality of this information, so, for example, a normally distributed prior will have a large variance if the prior information is rather vague and uncertain, and a small variance if the population measure is fairly well known.

The chief advantages in this approach are that

- all available information is made use of;
- the interpretation of credible intervals and Bayesian hypothesis tests is more straightforward than for classical methods; and
- recent developments mean that complex models, including spatial structure, can be analysed.

The disadvantage, for some, is that specification of the prior distribution is inevitably partly subjective. However the effect the prior has on the final estimates can be controlled: vague prior distribution will have relatively little effect and the more data that are collected, the greater will be the relative influence of the data compared to the prior.

The basic principles behind Bayesian inference are straightforward, but its implementation can quickly become complicated. Although fast computers have made complex Bayesian models feasible, keeping things relatively simple depends on careful choice of prior and data distributions.

The availability of software tools, such as WinBUGS (www.mrc-bsu.cam.ac.uk/bugs), have raised the profile and popularity of Bayesian methods. For an introduction see Lee (1987) or Marin *et al.* (2003).

Detecting trends

When a monitoring scheme has been running for some years the question is likely to arise as to whether there are discernible trends in the size of a population of interest or in the extent of a habitat, for example. It is unlikely to be worth investigating this until five or more repeat surveys have been carried out.

The first step, as always, is to plot the data as a time series, i.e. the summary measure on the vertical axis against time on the horizontal axis. Are any trends apparent? Are they linear or more complex? Are cyclical patterns apparent?

Testing for trends is most straightforward if the measure used comes from complete counts rather than from sample surveys and the trend appears to be reasonably linear. The most common approach is to then fit a regression line through the values, with time as the explanatory variable. The gradient in the regression line is then tested to see whether it is significantly different from zero. If so, a trend is indicated.

There is one complication with this method. Standard regression analysis assumes that the values of the measurement variable are independent of each other. In effect this means they are uncorrelated. However, the results of successive surveys are very commonly correlated because the size of a population or habitat in Year 1 will have an effect on its size in Year 2. The effect of this *autocorrelation* is that the statistical significance of the gradient will be overestimated. This is unlikely to be an issue if the gradient is very highly significant, but in some cases positively autocorrelated data can give the appearance of a trend.

There is no easy way of getting around this problem. One approach is to use bootstrapping of the regression model parameters. An alternative is to include a term in the regression for the previous year's count, to remove some of the autocorrelation effect. However, the correct method to use will depend on the nature of the autocorrelation; a fairly large number of surveys are likely to be needed before it can be studied in detail. Perhaps the simplest way forward is to consider whether autocorrelation is likely given the ecology of the species or habitat under study and, if so, to interpret borderline trends with caution.

If the trend is clearly non-linear, and sufficient data are available, more complex models such as polynomial regression or generalised additive models can be fitted.

Where the survey data comprise sample measurements then this should be allowed for in the trend analysis. The simplest way is to include each measurement in the model so that uncertainty in the true population mean is taken into account. One alternative for permanent plots is to model each plot separately and combine the resulting trend estimates to get a picture of the overall trend. This is the approach taken by route regression (Geissler and Sauer, 1990) which is very widely used in North America. Generalised additive models have been proposed as a more flexible alternative (see, for example, Fewster *et al.*, 2000).

Long time series are fairly uncommon in ecology but there is a substantial literature for methods

concerned with modelling, studying autocorrelation structure, detecting cyclical behaviour and forecasting. A good introduction is provided by Chatfield (1996).

Some particular issues
The following sections provide a discussion of two common scenarios that arise.

Data with many zeros
This situation frequently arises when the species of interest is often absent from sample plots. Measures such as counts of individuals or percentage cover often exhibit a preponderance of zeros. For example, Figure 2.12 shows the distribution of counts of occupied Manx Shearwater *Puffinus puffinus* burrows from a sample of 20 m² plots. Because this distribution is so skewed the distribution of any summary statistic is also likely to be skewed, despite the relatively large sample size. For this example, either of two approaches will probably work well.

1. Given the large sample size it is reasonable to assume that the mean count per plot will approximately follow a log-normal distribution (a skewed

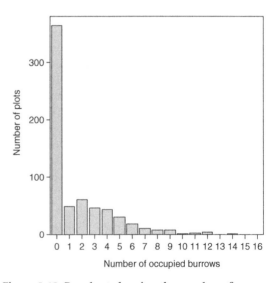

Figure 2.12. Bar chart showing the number of occupied Manx Shearwater burrows. See text for futher details.

distribution whose logarithm would be normally distributed). Confidence intervals for the mean can then be calculated by using the methods described in the next section. Change in this mean could probably be assumed to be approximately normally distributed.

2. To avoid any distributional assumptions, bootstrapping of the counts can be used to generate confidence intervals, etc. In this particular example this was complicated by the fact that a stratified random sampling scheme was used and so each stratum had to be resampled separately. Results were very similar to those obtained by using the first approach.

Small sample sizes

When sample sizes are small it is likely to be difficult to determine the distribution of the data with any confidence. See Figure 2.8 for an example of how the true distribution only emerges as sample size increases. In this situation it may be difficult to justify applying parametric methods. Exceptions occur where there are theoretical grounds for assuming a particular distribution or there is evidence from other, similar, data.

An example of the former is presence–absence data, where the proportion of plots where the species is present may be assumed to follow a binomial distribution. In this case the sample size may be too small to be able to use a normal approximation but exact confidence intervals can be calculated for binomial data. Many statistical packages can do this, but an Internet search should also reveal a number of relevant tools and methods.

In many cases non-parametric methods may be the only alternative. Resampling may also be suspect if there are insufficient data to adequately regenerate the underlying distribution.

Is transformation of the data necessary before statistical analysis?

Many examples of count or frequency data are drawn from distributions that are strongly skewed (i.e. asymmetrical) and therefore do not nearly approximate to a normal distribution. In addition, the distribution's variance may depend on the mean

(as it does for the Poisson distribution, for example). Most parametric tests assume that the data are normally distributed, which also implies that the variance is independent of the mean. Applying a transformation to the data can often help to rectify these problems by 'stabilising' the variance and making the distribution more symmetrical.

If the distribution of the transformed variable is not exactly normal, this is probably not critical, provided that the sample size is moderately large. Often it is more important to choose a transformation that stabilises the variance. However, transformations may not work for data with a sophisticated or complex structure.

The effect of different transformations should be examined to see which gives the best approximation to the normal curve. Histograms or normal probability plots can be used for this purpose and the goodness-of-fit of your data to a normal distribution can be tested by using a chi-squared test (see above, p. 58).

Data are usually transformed to make parametric analysis possible. Any confidence interval, or similar, obtained through transformed data should be back-transformed into the original units. This is because an answer expressed in terms of angular degree units or square roots will not be intuitively meaningful when considering estimates of counts of species, etc. Note, however, that the back-transformed mean of the transformed data will not usually be the same as the mean of the untransformed data, and so the back-transformed confidence interval will be for a different summary measure. For example, if the log transformation is used, so that

$y_i = \log(x_i)$ where x_i are the original measurements then

$$\bar{y} = \Sigma \log(x_i)/n = \log(\text{product of the } x_i)/n$$
$$= \log (\text{geometric mean of the } x_i).$$

Thus the reversed transformed value of $\bar{y}$ is the geometric mean of the x_i and reverse transformed confidence intervals will be for the geometric mean, not the usual arithmetic mean.

For the above example there is an alternative approach that provides confidence intervals for the arithmetic mean. If the logarithm of the mean of a measurement, x, is normally distributed, x

itself is said to follow a log-normal distribution. An approximate 95% confidence interval for $\bar{x}$ is

$$\left(\frac{\bar{x}}{K}, \bar{x}K\right)$$

where

$$K = \exp[1.96 \times \sqrt{var(\log_e \bar{x})}]$$

and

$$var(\log_e \bar{x}) = \log_e \left[1 + \frac{var(\bar{x})}{\bar{x}^2}\right].$$

A transformed distribution may not look vastly different from the original; the transformation is also acting on the variance of the data, which may be more important. For example, the mean of a Poisson distribution is equal to the variance and the variance thus increases with the mean; the variance is dependent on the mean. In this case a square root transformation helps make the variance independent of the mean, allowing tests based on the normal distribution to be used.

Some commonly used transformations are given below.

- log x: This is appropriate for clumped count data in which the variance of the sample is greater than the mean, or for variables that always take positive values such as area (such distributions are often skewed to the left). Each observation is replaced by the logarithm of itself.
- log $(x + 1)$: This is appropriate for count data containing zeros. Log $(x + 1)$ is used because log (0) is undefined and hence meaningless. Adding 1 to each observation avoids this problem.
- $\sqrt{x}$: The square root transformation for count data, which follows a Poisson distribution (randomly distributed), or for regularly distributed data, is appropriate when the variance of a sample is roughly equal to the mean.
- arcsin($\sqrt{x}$): The arcsin ($\sin^{-1}$ or inverse sine) transformation is appropriate for observations that are proportions or percentages, or for frequency measures (e.g. presence–absence within sub-quadrats).

First, take the square root of each observation. Then find the angle in degrees whose sine equals this value. Percentage observations should first be converted to proportions (divide by 100). The arcsin transformation is also useful for cover data that have been converted to proportions.

Analysing more than one variable at a time

More complex statistical analyses, such as multivariate techniques (e.g. principal components analysis and correspondence analysis) for more than one variable, can be employed to examine community composition or the relation between community composition and environmental variables. These techniques are mainly exploratory in nature. There are also various analytical techniques for examining relations between variables, such as correlation and multiple regression, which might be appropriate for more in-depth analysis of data. These are beyond the scope of this *Handbook* but see, for example, Jongman *et al.* (1995) for more information.

2.6.5   Interpretation and presentation of findings

Once the data have been described and analysed, the results have to be interpreted and presented. This is often the longest and most difficult part of the process. Great care should be taken to ensure that appropriate conclusions are drawn and that results are successfully communicated. A study is only as good as the ability of people to understand its findings. After all, the key aim of such presentations is to influence the management of a site or species and effect change where needed.

Interpreting analyses

Analyses should be geared towards satisfying the objectives for which a survey or monitoring study was set up. Typically this involves determining the status of a site or species and, possibly, whether the site or species is in acceptable condition. In addition, it is often desirable to examine whether existing survey work is adequate and what improvements are needed. For example:

- Are sample sizes sufficient to give adequate precision and/or to detect small enough changes? If not, then either more effort is required for future surveys or expectations will have to be reduced.
- Are the measurements adequate and can they be taken with sufficient accuracy? It may, for example, become apparent that measurements are too error-prone for analysis to be reliable.
- Is the sample design adequate or could improvements to the stratification, for example, be made?

Some other points to bear in mind when drawing conclusions from analyses include the following.

- If the statistical test is non-significant this does not mean that the null hypothesis is true, just that there is insufficient evidence to reject it.
- If a significance level of 5% is used then bear in mind that 1 result in 20 will be significant purely by chance. This may not be important for single tests, but if many tests are performed there is an increasing likelihood that one will be significant by chance. This frequently arises in ANOVA when multiple comparisons between groups are being made. Most statistical textbooks will suggest strategies for dealing with this problem.
- Where possible, check that a test's assumptions are satisfied. Many tests are fairly insensitive to mild departures from their assumptions, e.g. t-tests and the assumption that the data are normally distributed.

Presenting results

The key to successful presentation is to decide what are the main messages you what to get across and how to convey them bearing in mind the nature of the audience you are aiming at. The type of audience will affect the level of detail included and the level of technical expertise that can be assumed. In most cases a survey or monitoring report would be expected to include the following.

1. The rationale for the study together with any required ecological background.
2. A statement of the study objectives.
3. An account of the methodology used: the sampling design, field methods, measurements and analysis methods as well as the rationale for these. If necessary, some technical detail may be consigned to an annex.
4. The results of the study. Full data tables, if required, may be consigned to an annex.
5. A discussion of the findings together with the management implications.
6. An assessment of the study and its adequacy together with recommendations for future improvement.

Most results will be presented in the form of tables and/or charts. Charts can provide a very powerful way of conveying information, and appropriate displays should be considered wherever possible. However, they are open to misuse. In particular:

- Ensure charts are clearly labelled with units of measurement and avoid unnecessary clutter (e.g. gridlines and non-essential annotations). Clutter can detract from the message a chart is intended to convey.
- Avoid exaggerating trends, for example by only displaying the observed range of data. The axes for measurements that can take any positive value should normally start at zero. It is easy to make a trend look very substantial by starting axes at the minimum observed value.
- Include error bars, such as confidence intervals, around graph values that are derived from a sample. This avoids giving the false impression that the exact population values are shown and hence that any change is a real change.

Tables should also be clearly labelled and uncluttered. For clarity:

- Data values should be right-justified and separated for ease of reading. Comma separators can be used to make large values clearer.
- When the results for statistical tests are presented, show p-values rather than just whether or not the result was significant. Levels for determining significance are to some extent arbitrary, so results that do not quite achieve significance may still be of interest.
- Show the criteria used to determine the significance or otherwise of tests.

- Confidence intervals for estimates are also often useful, not only to convey uncertainty but to show the range within which the true value is likely to lie in relation to a target value, for example.

2.6.6   What statistical software is available for the analysis of data?

Most spreadsheet programs, such as Microsoft Excel, have functions for simple statistics and a reasonable range of tailor-made analytical routines and graphics. However the range of statistical analysis that can be carried is usually limited; non-parametric tests, for example, are generally absent. Statistical add-ons for Excel are available and these provide an inexpensive way of gaining access to most of the commonly used tests. Examples of these are Berk & Carey (2000), Analyse-it (www. analyse-it.com), and XLStat (www.xlstat.com).

However, dedicated statistics programs are best for most statistical analyses, not only for their analytical capabilities but for the ease with which they can be used to present data and check assumptions. These are recommended if a regular requirement for statistical analysis can be identified. Systat (www.systat.com), Minitab (www.minitab.com), SPSS (www.spss.com), STATA (www.stata.com), SAS (www.sas.com) and Genstat (www.nag.co.uk) are all examples that can cope with most of the statistical tests and models in common use and rather more besides. STATA and SPSS are specifically able to analyse data from stratified and other survey designs.

Some resampling methods are available in many general-purpose statistics packages. An example of a dedicated package can be found at www. resample.com.

More specialised software may be required for certain types of ecological data and analyses. CANOCO, for example, provides a good range of ordination and clustering techniques for multivariate environmental data (www.canoco.com; ter Braak & Smilauer, 1998). DECORANA is another well-established program for ordination and TWINSPAN is widely used for the classification of species and sites according to similarity (both available from the Centre for Ecology and Hydrology in the UK: www.ceh.ac.uk). MVSP is another popular multivariate analysis package that also enables calculation of a range of diversity indices (www.kovcomp.co.uk/mvsp). Finally, a good online resource with links to many free and commercial software sites can be found at www.statistics.com.

3 • Biodiversity evaluation methods

3.1 BIODIVERSITY VALUES AND EVALUATION PURPOSES

In general terms, biodiversity evaluation is the process of measuring the value (ideally quantitatively) of biodiversity components, such as the number of species present, the population of a species, a habitat (usually meaning a vegetation community) or the sum of all such components within a given area or site. Such evaluations may be carried out for a variety of reasons, e.g. for conservation priority setting, as part of Biodiversity Action Plan (BAP) development, for the selection of Protected Areas, for the identification of a site's features of conservation interest, as part of conservation objective setting, management planning and monitoring processes, and as part of an EIA or other statement to comply with planning procedures for a proposed development.

Evaluations may be carried out on various components of biodiversity (i.e. from genetic variation within species, to individual species, species assemblages, biotopes and biomes) and at a variety of scales, from specific sites, to counties, regions, countries, biogeographical areas (although these may be smaller than countries) and global. A wide range of potential biodiversity values may be considered, including intrinsic and socio-cultural values (Daily, 1997; Posey, 2000), and more direct socio-economic benefits (Daily, 1997), such as food, building resources, medicines and waste decomposition, etc. (Spellerberg & Hardes, 1992).

As this *Handbook* concentrates on site surveys and monitoring, rather than on regional- or national-scale studies, this chapter focuses on site evaluations. We do not consider socio-economic and socio-cultural values; the reader is referred to texts such as Usher (1986), Smith & Theberge (1986), Spellerberg (1991) and Treweek (1999).

3.2 A FRAMEWORK FOR ECOLOGICAL EVALUATIONS

Appropriate approaches and criteria for biodiversity evaluations vary considerably depending upon their purpose, their scale and the biodiversity components in question. As stated previously, it is vital that objectives be clearly defined and the work planned through to its conclusion.

Spellerberg (1991) identifies the following six general best practices that should be included in any evaluation framework.

1. Evaluation objectives should be defined.
2. Criteria should be quantifiable, rather than subjective.
3. Evaluations should be repeatable.
4. Evaluations should be based on biological principles.
5. The methods, results and analysis should be explained so that they can be understood by everyone who has an interest in the area being evaluated.
6. Costs in time and money should take into account the depth and integrity of underlying surveys.

We have incorporated such concepts into a proposed generic framework for conducting site-based biodiversity evaluations, as outlined in Figure 3.1.

3.3 IDENTIFICATION OF VALUABLE ECOSYSTEM COMPONENTS

A key step in any evaluation is the identification of biodiversity components or functions that are considered to be important or valuable. These are

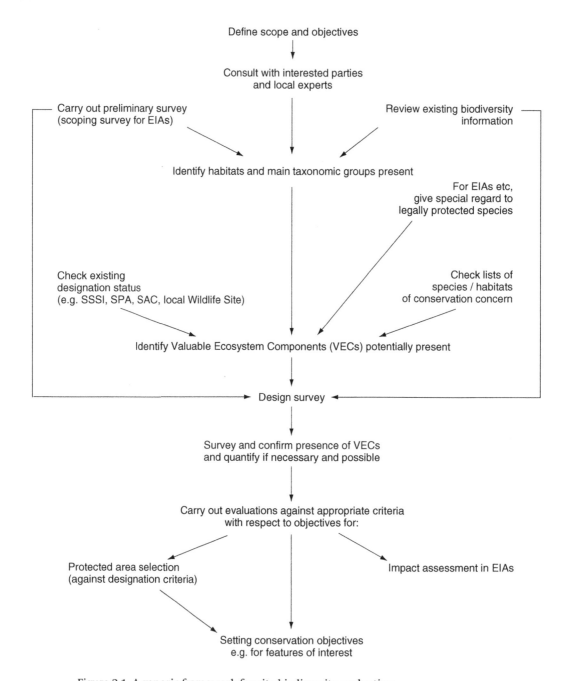

Figure 3.1. A generic framework for site biodiversity evaluation.

called Valuable Ecosystem Components (VECs) by Treweek (1999) and are sometimes referred to elsewhere as Valued Ecological Receptors or Valued Ecological Resources. In SSSI and UK statutory conservation agency terminology, VECs would at least include notified features of interest.

The identification of VECs has a major and obvious bearing on the outcome of any evaluation exercise, as an ecosystem, habitat or site will not be regarded as important if interest features are over-looked. Indeed, one of the main underlying causes of biodiversity loss is the lack of appreciation of the value of its properties and functions.

It may not be practical to identify and use all VECs in an evaluation, even in the most simple habitats, as too many species and other components and functions will have some value. It is thus normal to base evaluations on a sub-set of selected VECs of particular value. For EIAs, however, it is necessary to identify all VECs that are of more than negligible value and which will receive impacts. The criteria used to select or identify such VECs should be objective, consistent, transparent and defensible (Treweek, 1999). Ecosystem attributes that may be selected as VECs at a site may include distinct genetic populations of a species, species popula-tions, species assemblages, vegetation communities, habitats and ecosystem functions.

In practice, species and habitats of particular conservation importance are the most commonly identified VECs as these are easiest to define objec-tively and to measure quantitatively. In contrast, ecosystem functions, though perhaps of as great an importance as VECs, are difficult to define and describe in terms that allow objective evaluations to be made of their importance. Nevertheless, this should be attempted as far as possible when it is considered that a site is likely to provide an impor-tant ecological function.

There are a variety of species attributes that may be used as criteria for their selection as VECs. These include commercial value, rarity, endanger-ment, their role as flagship or umbrella species (i.e. ability to provide benefit to others through their conservation), their importance for ecosystem function (i.e. keystone species) and their value as indicator species (See, for example, Eberhardt, 1976; Treweek, 1999).

The US Fish and Wildlife Service Habitat Evaluation Procedure (HEP) (USFWS, 1980), for example, identifies four categories of 'evaluation species':

- species with public interest, economic value or both;

- species known to be sensitive to specific land use actions that may serve as 'early warning' or indi-cator species for an affected wildlife community;
- species that perform a key role in a community because, for example, of their role in nutrient cycling or energy flows; and
- species that represent groups of species that uti-lise a common environmental resource (guilds).

In the UK and elsewhere in Europe, the presence of species or habitats of high conservation priority is one of the most commonly used criteria for pro-tected area designation and consideration in EIAs. The presence of particularly high numbers or high proportions of species (irrespective of their conser-vation status) is also a frequently used criterion for the selection of sites for protection for nature con-servation purposes. For example, the internation-ally recognised criteria for the designation of Ramsar Sites (see Section 3.7.6) include thresholds for the proportion of biogeographic waterfowl populations (e.g. more than 1% of the flyway popu-lation) and total waterfowl numbers (e.g. more than 20 000 individuals).

The evaluation framework (See Figure 3.1) iden-tifies a number of activities that will assist in iden-tifying VECs. These include reviewing existing biodiversity information, consulting with local experts (e.g. county recorders, biological records centres, Wildlife Trusts) and conducting prelimin-ary surveys. Even brief surveys are likely to be valuable. They can establish the range of VECs that may be present, and this can help considerably in the subsequent design of full surveys (or mon-itoring). Although preliminary surveys will not be able to adequately establish the presence of all species VECs, they should identify habitats that are present. This information may be used to iden-tify potential species VECs, which may then be verified by subsequent surveys. For example, a brief site visit might establish that ponds are pre-sent that are suitable for, and within the vicinity of known populations of, Great Crested Newts *Triturus cristatus*. A specific newt survey may then be planned and carried out at a suitable time.

Evaluation of sites on the basis of species- and habitat-based VECs requires some assessment to have been made of the conservation status of the individual habitats and species in question. The following sections therefore describe key principles underlying the assessment of species and habitat conservation priorities. Specific details and guidance on assessments and legislation affecting current species and habitat conservation priorities within the UK are then provided in Section 3.5.

3.4   PRINCIPLES UNDERLYING THE SETTING OF CONSERVATION PRIORITIES

3.4.1   Conservation objectives

Conservation priorities depend in the first instance on conservation objectives. In terms of global objectives, there is reasonable agreement that the prevention of global extinction should be the focus of activity, in which case the degree of threat (i.e. risk of extinction) is of primary concern in setting priorities. This is reflected in the production of IUCN Red Lists of species that are considered to be at risk of global extinction according to various categories of threat. Beyond this, there are many different views on global biodiversity conservation priorities; such diversity of opinion is not surprising as there is no single feasible way of measuring or valuing biodiversity overall (Purvis & Hector, 2000).

The risk of extinction at national level is also probably the commonest basis for national species conservation priority setting. However, at national or sub-national levels biodiversity conservation is increasingly incorporating broader multiple objectives. In the UK, for example, bird conservation objectives have traditionally focused on rare species, but in recent years greater attention has been given to species that occur in internationally important numbers, despite many of these being highly abundant (e.g. many species of wintering waterbird). There is also increasing concern for species that are common and widespread but declining rapidly, as rapid declines of common species may involve the loss of many millions of individuals from the environment. This is clearly a substantial biodiversity impact even if the species are not immediately threatened with extinction. As a result, a suite of common but rapidly declining farmland birds, such as Turtle Dove *Streptopelia turtur*, Skylark *Alauda arvensis*, Starling *Sturnus vulgaris* and Yellowhammer *Emberiza citrinella*, are now on the UK Red List (Gregory *et al.*, 2002) and are a focus of considerable conservation action. Priority-setting under the UK Biodiversity Action Plan (BAP) process has also used broader criteria than just extinction risk in its selection of Priority Species.

3.4.2   The importance of rarity

Rarity has often been considered to be one of the most important factors influencing the risk of extinction of a species, and many Red Data lists have focused on this. Rarity has also often been used as a secondary criterion whereby, for example, a declining species is not considered to be threatened unless it is has also crossed a rarity threshold. However, rarity is not a straightforward concept: there may be a variety of circumstances under which species may be rare (Rabinowitz, 1981). Species may have small (or large) total ranges, occupy few (or many) habitat types, and be scarce or abundant where they do occur. As indicated in the brief examples in Table 3.1, seven of the combinations of these factors (the shaded boxes) would qualify as rare within the possible range of meanings of the term. It is therefore evident that rarity embraces both a spatial and a numerical dimension. For any particular species some aspects of rarity may be an evolutionary property, such as habitat specificity, small natural range or low natural densities. Such species may always be rare and therefore unlikely to respond to conservation measures. On the other hand, small range or low densities may be the result of human impact, which may be reversible.

Inclusion of rarity factors in an evaluation requires data on the range or number of individuals of a species (or habitats, communities, or abiotic features), not only at the site in question, but at wider scales. Important elements of rarity are also scale-dependent. A locally rare species may also be regionally or globally rare, or it may simply

Table 3.1. *The seven forms of rarity based on a species' geographical range, habitat specificity and local population size* Indicative bird species have been added for each category in relation to range, population size and habitat use in the UK.

| Local population size | Geographical range | | | |
| | Large | | Small | |
	Wide habitat use	Narrow habitat use	Wide habitat use	Narrow habitat use
Large, dominant somewhere	Common and locally abundant over a large range in several habitats	Locally abundant over a large range in a specific habitat	Locally abundant in several habitats over a small range	Locally abundant over a small range in a specific habitat
Example birds	Blackbird *Turdus merula*	Reed Warbler *Acrocephalus scirpaceous*	Pink-footed Goose *Anser brachyrhynchus* (wintering)	Great Skua *Stercorarius skua*
Small non-dominant	Constantly sparse over a large range in several habitats	Constantly sparse over a large range in a specific habitat	Constantly sparse over a small range in several habitats	Constantly sparse over a small range in a specific habitat
Example birds	Long-eared Owl *Asio otus*	Garganey *Anas querquedula*	Montagu's Harrier *Circus pygargus*	Capercaillie *Tetrao urogallus*

Source: Rabinowitz (1981).

be rare because it is at the edge of its range (e.g. breeding Golden Orioles *Oriolus oriolus* or Redwings *Turdus iliacus* in the UK). Normally, increased importance should be given to species that are rare on a global scale. Some locally abundant species may also be of high conservation importance if the species in question is rare at a global or wide geographical scale (e.g. Great Skua *Stercorarius skua* and Great Crested Newt).

3.4.3   Levels and scales of threat and population importance

Whichever criteria are used for threat evaluations, a hierarchical level of importance should be established according to the scale of the assessment, so that the highest priority for conservation and/or protection is given to species or habitats that are globally threatened. However, it is also necessary to take into account their local status to assess the necessity for taking action at a local scale. This enables the principle of 'thinking globally and acting locally' to be put into practice. The highest priority should be given to species and habitats that are both globally and locally threatened.

Assessments below global scales should also refer to appropriate biogeographical populations. In practice, however, assessments of populations are more often based on national or regional (e.g. European) populations for political and administrative reasons. This is because some species could otherwise have more than one conservation status within a country, which would send confusing and mixed messages to policy makers and the general public. Some steps towards defining conservation status on the basis of biogeographic populations have, however, been made for migratory water birds. Different waterfowl flyway populations have been defined (Rose & Scott, 1997) to enable identification of important waterbird populations under the Ramsar Convention. These flyway populations have in turn been used to define threatened waterbird populations for the African–Eurasian Waterfowl Agreement, an agreement under the Convention on Migratory Species of Wild Animals.

Any evaluation of conservation priorities for a species (or habitat) should also take into account

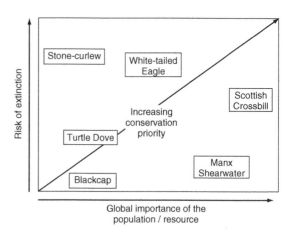

Figure 3.2. Key factors defining the conservation status of a species' population or area of habitat. (Scientific names of species: Stone-curlew *Burhinus oedicnemus*, White-tailed Eagle *Haliaeetus albicilla*, Turtle Dove *Streptopelia turtur*, Blackcap *Sylvia atricapilla*, Manx Shearwater *Puffinus puffinus*, Scottish Crossbill *Loxia scotica*.)

the importance of the population or resource being considered. Thus, the evaluation of a species' population conservation status should consider two key independent factors: the risk of extinction of the population in question (i.e. its threat status) and its biogeographical importance, i.e. the proportion it represents of the appropriate biogeographical (or national or regional) population (Figure 3.2). The same conservation evaluation principles may be applied to an area of habitat.

Thus, for example, a very high priority should be given to a species' population that is endemic and is at a high risk of extinction. However, it is important to note that a population may be a high priority nationally because the species is highly threatened nationally, irrespective of its numbers in relation to international or global populations (e.g. Stone-curlew in Figure 3.2). This is because the maintenance of a species' range (and potential genetic variation associated with this) can also be an important conservation aim after prevention of complete extinction. On the other hand, a population of a species may be very important because it is a large proportion of the biogeographical population, irrespective of its conservation status (e.g. Manx

Shearwater in Figure 3.2). In these circumstances a country has a particular responsibility for the species and should at least take appropriate measures to monitor the status of the species and guard against potential events (e.g. an oil spill) that could affect the population suddenly and catastrophically, or gradually over a longer period of time. Such species are often the subject of national and local Biodiversity Action Plans (BAPs).

This concept of assessing both the risk of extinction and the importance of the population can be applied at a variety of scales. For example, for bird species, the status and importance of a population on a site can be compared with that of the county, country or biogeographic region (e.g. flyway). A hypothetical example of national priority setting according to a species' biogeographical range is depicted in Figure 3.3.

Although consideration of the biogeographical importance of populations is not normally explicitly carried out in the preparation of Red Data Books (RDBs), this approach was developed by BirdLife International in its assessment of the conservation status of European birds (Tucker & Heath, 1994; BirdLife International, 2004). The highest of four categories of Species of Conservation Concern (SPECs) was given to species that were globally threatened, irrespective of the proportion present in Europe, because it was felt that these species should be a high priority wherever they occur regularly. However, the second highest priority (SPEC 2) was given to those species that were considered to have an Unfavourable Conservation Status in Europe and populations that are concentrated (i.e. more than 50%) in Europe. Other species with an Unfavourable Conservation Status were placed in the SPEC 3 category.

This approach has been taken further in the UK. The first RDB for birds in the UK (Batten *et al.*, 1990) included the international importance of populations as one of its qualifying criteria. However, this concept was expanded with revised criteria in the subsequent reassessments and publication of *Birds of Conservation Concern* by UK non-governmental organisations (NGOs) (Gibbons *et al.*, 1996), *Birds of Conservation Importance* by the UK Statutory agencies (JNCC, 1996) and the

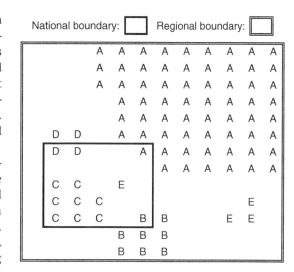

Figure 3.3. National priority setting, based on a species' regional (e.g. European) range size and the proportion of its range occurring within the country in question. Each species' geographical range is represented by an array of letters. Species A is widespread within the region, but rare within the country. Species B and E are equally rare within the country, but much less widespread within the region as a whole. Species D has half of its range within the country, whereas species C is endemic (and relatively widespread) within the country. If conservation status were to be assessed solely on the basis of national range size, species A, B and E would be of high priority for conservation action or protection, and species D and C less so. Alternatively, if regional range size is the sole criterion used, species D and E would be accorded the highest priority, followed by B and C, then A. Finally, a national assessment based on the proportion of each species' range occurring within the country would select C, then D, followed by E, B and A. Ideally, national priority setting should attempt to balance all three measures: national conservation status, wider conservation status (regional or global) and degree of endemism.

combined NGO and Agency Red and Amber-listed birds (Gregory *et al.*, 2002). These lists included the BirdLife International SPEC categories 1–3 as well as species with internationally important populations.

Table 3.2. *Species traits other than population status that have been used for ranking between-species conservation priorities*

Trait	Priority given to	Example references
Evolutionary uniqueness	Species with most unique characters	Vane-Wright *et al.* (1991)
	Species with greatest genetic diversity	Crozier (1992, Nee and May (1997)
	Species in clades[a] undergoing evolutionary radiations	Erwin (1991)
Phenotypic traits	Maximising diversity of phenotypic traits	Owens & Bennett (2000)
Protection status	Species poorly represented in protected areas	Scott *et al.* (1993), Cassidy *et al.* (2001)
Land use change	Species in areas susceptible to destruction	Menon *et al.* (2001)
Ecosystem role	Species important in ecosystems (e.g. pollinators)	Allen-Wardell *et al.* (1998)
Multi-species interactions	Maximal phylogenetic diversity within a set of interacting species	Witting *et al.* (2000)

[a] A group of species (in this instance) sharing a closer common ancestry with one another than with members of any other clade.
Source: (Mace & Collar, 2002).

3.4.4   Other factors affecting species conservation priorities

Factors other than population status or range size may influence the overall conservation priority ranking for a species or habitat, examples of which are listed in Table 3.2. Most of these have rarely been applied. However, genetic diversity is increasingly being incorporated into decision-making in relation to rare and/or threatened species. A species distributed across a number of isolated sites, e.g. Pollan *Coregonus autumnalis pollan* in lakes in Ireland, has a potentially high genetic biodiversity; and each isolated population contributes to the diversity within the species and hence its overall ability to survive. In the case of Floating Water-plantain *Luronium natans*, much of the population in the UK is found in the canal network and is thought to derive from vegetative reproduction from a single population in Wales. If this is the case, the canal plants have relatively low genetic diversity compared with that of isolated lake populations and would rank low in an evaluation.

3.5   SPECIES AND HABITAT CONSERVATION PRIORITY LISTS

There are a large number of conservation assessments and legislative instruments that should be taken into account in any evaluation of a species' or habitat's conservation priority. In the UK ecological evaluations should take special note of:

- IUCN global Red Lists
- Convention on Migratory Species Appendices
- Bern Convention Appendices 1, 2 and 3
- European Red Lists or lists of species of conservation concern
- Wild Birds Directive Annex I
- Habitats Directive Annex I and 2
- Wildlife & Countryside Act Schedules 1, 5 and 8
- CROW Act 2000 list of habitats and species under Article 74 (for England and Wales only)
- Nature Conservation Act 2004 (Scotland)
- UK Red Lists and birds of conservation concern
- UK BAP listed species and habitats

Background information on the derivation of each of these lists is outlined below. Further information and accounts of other lists referring to specific species groups are provided in each species chapter.

3.5.1   IUCN Red Lists

The IUCN Red Lists and Red Data Books (RDBs) were first conceived in 1963 to draw attention to the conservation needs of globally endangered species. In particular, the identification of endangered species was carried out to assist with defining conservation priorities and the drafting of species protection legislation. The Red Lists were prepared under the auspices of the Species Survival Commission (SSC), one of the commissions of IUCN (The International Union for the Conservation of Nature). The selection of species for inclusion was carried out by using standard data sheets and largely subjective assessments. Species were categorized according to threat: Endangered, Vulnerable, Rare, Out Of Danger or Indeterminate.

This simple priority classification set a global standard for conservation assessment for more than 30 years. By the late 1980s discussions were taking place on how the criteria could be quantified to make the selection process more objective (Fitter & Fitter, 1987). After an extensive period of preparation and consultation, IUCN adopted more precise and quantitative Red List Categories in 1994 (IUCN, 1994). These criteria (referred to as Version 2.3) were used for the *1996 IUCN Red List of Threatened Animals* (Baillie & Groombridge, 1996), *The World List of Threatened Trees* (Oldfield *et al.*, 1998) and the *2000 IUCN Red List of Threatened Species* (Hilton-Taylor, 2000).

Then, in 1996, IUCN members called for a further review to ensure that the criteria were applicable to a wide range of organisms, especially long-lived species and species under intensive management. As a result a further revised set of threat categories and criteria was adopted by IUCN Council in 2000 and published in 2001 as Criteria Version 3.1 following further refinement (IUCN, 2001). The aim has been to develop a method and set of criteria that provide a more objective assessment of extinction risk, which can also be consistently applied by different people across the full range of taxa. All new assessments and reassessments of IUCN Red Lists use this system. Some assessments from 1996 to 2000 have also been converted to follow the revised categories and criteria. It is now intended that SSC will leave this system unchanged for a sufficient period to allow genuine changes in conservation status to be monitored.

The current categories of threat are listed below and a diagrammatic summary of the relationships between these categories is shown in Figure 3.4. The assessments may be made either by relating simple population status attributes to numerical thresholds or by a more complex Population Viability Analysis (PVA). PVAs use demographic models to predict the probability that a given population will become extinct (or decline to a specified level) within a given time period (see Beissinger & Westphal (1998) for review).

- **Extinct (EX):** A taxon is Extinct when there is no reasonable doubt that the last individual has died. A taxon is presumed Extinct when exhaustive surveys in known and/or expected habitat, at appropriate times (diurnal, seasonal, annual), throughout its historic range have failed to record an individual. Surveys should be over a time frame appropriate to the taxon's life cycle and life form.
- **Extinct in the wild (EW):** A taxon is Extinct in the Wild when it is known to survive only in cultivation, in captivity or as a naturalised population (or populations) well outside the past range. A taxon is presumed Extinct in the Wild when exhaustive surveys in known and/or expected habitat, at appropriate times (diurnal, seasonal, annual), throughout its historic range have failed to record an individual. Surveys should be over a time frame appropriate to the taxon's life cycle and life form.
- **Critically Endangered (CR):** A taxon is Critically Endangered when the best available evidence indicates that it meets any of the criteria A to E for Critically Endangered, and it is therefore considered to be facing an extremely high risk of extinction in the wild. Criteria A to D relate to

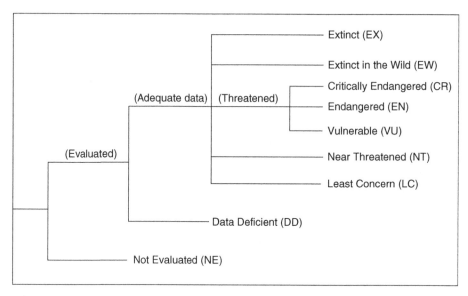

Figure 3.4. Current IUCN Red List threat categories (IUCN, 2001).

numerical thresholds for species in rapid decline, with small, fragmented, declining or fluctuating ranges, or with very small populations or ranges. Criterion E is an unfavourable PVA indicating a probability of extinction of more than 50% within ten years or three generations (whichever is longer).

- **Endangered (EN):** A taxon is Endangered when the best available evidence indicates that it meets any of the criteria A to D for Endangered, and it is therefore considered to be facing a very high risk of extinction in the wild, or if under Criterion E it has a PVA indicating a probability of extinction of more than 20% within 20 years or five generations.
- **Vulnerable (VU):** A taxon is Vulnerable when the best available evidence indicates that it meets any of the criteria A to D for Vulnerable, and it is therefore considered to be facing a high risk of extinction in the wild, or if under Criterion E it has a PVA indicating a probability of extinction of more than 10% within 100 years.
- **Near Threatened (NT):** A taxon is Near Threatened when it has been evaluated against the criteria but does not qualify for Critically Endangered, Endangered or Vulnerable now, but is close to

qualifying or likely to qualify for a threatened category in the near future.
- **Least Concern (LC):** A taxon is Least Concern when it has been evaluated against the criteria and does not qualify for Critically Endangered, Endangered, Vulnerable or Near Threatened. Widespread and abundant taxa are included in this category.
- **Data Deficient (DD):** A taxon is Data Deficient when there is inadequate information to make a direct or indirect assessment of its risk of extinction based on its distribution and/or population status. A taxon in this category may be well studied, and its biology well known, but appropriate data on abundance and/or distribution are lacking. Data Deficient is therefore not a category of threat. Listing of taxa in this category indicates that more information is required and acknowledges the possibility that future research will show that threatened classification is appropriate. It is important to make positive use of whatever data are available. In many cases great care should be exercised in choosing between DD and a threatened status (CR, EN or VU). If the range of a taxon is suspected to be relatively circumscribed, and a considerable period of time has elapsed

since the last record of the taxon, threatened status may well be justified.

- **Not Evaluated (NE):** A taxon is Not Evaluated when it has not yet been evaluated against the criteria.

Full details of the current IUCN Red List Categories and criteria are provided in IUCN (2001). They can also be obtained together with guidelines on their use at http://www.redlist.org/info/categories_criteria.html.

The most recent published list of globally threatened species is in 2004 *IUCN Red List of Threatened Species* (Baillie *et al.*, 2004). An updated list of threatened taxa is maintained in a searchable database by the SSC Red List Programme accessible at www.redlist.org/. However, the only taxonomic groups that have been comprehensively assessed are the birds and mammals. The vast majority of plant taxa listed in the 1997 IUCN Red List of Threatened Plants (Walter & Gillett 1998) have not yet been evaluated against the revised Red List Criteria and are therefore not included. Instead, the conservation status of plants may be ascertained by searching the SSC database and the UNEP-WCMC Threatened Plants database at http://www.wcmc.org.uk/species/plants/red_list.htm.

Most Red List assessments are carried out by the members of the IUCN Species Survival Commission. All the birds are assessed by BirdLife International and its partners. Other assessments and much taxonomic and distribution information have been provided by various partner organisations.

3.5.2   The Bonn Convention

The Convention on the Conservation of Migratory Species of Wild Animals, more often known as the Bonn Convention (or CMS), aims to conserve terrestrial, marine and avian migratory species throughout their range. It is one of a small number of intergovernmental treaties concerned with the conservation of wildlife and wildlife habitats on a global scale.

Parties to the CMS work together to conserve migratory species and their habitats by providing strict protection for the endangered migratory species listed in Appendix I of the Convention and by concluding multilateral Agreements for the conservation and management of migratory species listed in Appendix II. The Bonn Agreements of direct relevance to terrestrial and freshwater habitats and species in the UK at the moment are the African-Eurasian Migratory Waterbird Agreement and the Agreement on the Conservation of Populations of European Bats (EUROBATS).

The CMS is typically implemented legally through the legislation of any given country and/or the European Union, for example in the UK, the Wildlife & Countryside Act, the EU Birds Directive (79/409/EEC) and the EU Habitats Directive (92/43/EEC).

3.5.3   Bern Convention

The Convention on the Conservation of European Wildlife and Natural Habitats, also known as the Bern Convention, was adopted on September 1979 in Bern (Switzerland) and came into force on 1 June 1982. It now has 45 Contracting Parties including 39 Member States of the Council of Europe as well as the European Community, Monaco and four African states.

The aim of the Convention is to:

- conserve wild flora and fauna and their natural habitats;
- promote co-operation between states; and
- give particular emphasis to endangered and vulnerable species, including endangered and vulnerable migratory species.

The contracting parties have undertaken, *inter alia*, to protect the habitats of wild flora and fauna species, and to give special attention to the conservation of the species listed in:

- **Appendix I:** strictly protected flora species.
- **Appendix II:** strictly protected fauna species.
- **Appendix III:** protected fauna species.

This Convention has greatly influenced the development of EU nature conservation legislation, being the inspiration for the EU Birds and Habitats Directives. It has also had an important influence on the UK's main conservation legislation, the Wildlife & Countryside Act 1981. See http://www.nature.coe.int/english/cadres/bern.htm for more information on the Bern Convention and lists of species on the various Appendices.

3.5.4   European Red Lists and lists of Species of Conservation Concern

European Red Lists or their equivalent have been produced for some taxa. For example, BirdLife International has produced lists of Species of Conservation Concern (SPECs) in Europe (Tucker & Heath, 1994; BirdLife International, 2004). As described above, this does not use IUCN criteria but develops these and includes assessments of the importance of European populations as well as their threat status. Further information on the categories and criteria used for SPECs is given in Part III, Chapter 24 on birds.

A European Red List has also been produced by the Council of Europe for butterflies (http://www.vlinderstichting.nl/en/randc/rdb.htm).

3.5.5   European Union Birds and Habitats Directives

In 1979, the European Community adopted Council Directive 79/409/EEC on the conservation of wild birds in response to the 1979 Bern Convention. This Directive, usually referred to as the Birds Directive, provides for the protection, management and control of naturally occurring wild birds within the European Union through a range of mechanisms. One of the key provisions (under Article 4) is the establishment of an internationally co-ordinated network of protected areas, known as Special Protection Areas (SPAs) for 182 species listed in Annex I of the Directive. These are species that are considered to be in danger of extinction, vulnerable to specific changes in their habitat, rare, or requiring particular attention by reason of the specific nature of their habitat. Within SPAs, Member States are obliged to take necessary steps to avoid deterioration of natural habitats and disturbance of the species, where this disturbance would be significant in terms of the objectives of the Directive.

In 1992 the then European Community adopted Council Directive 92/43/EEC on the Conservation of Natural Habitats and of Wild Fauna and Flora, known as the Habitats Directive. This international wildlife legislation is intended to provide EU Member States with a mechanism to meet their obligations under the 1979 Bern Convention (see above) and to complement the provisions of the 1979 Birds Directive. The main aim of the Habitats Directive is:

. . . to contribute towards ensuring biodiversity through the conservation of natural habitats and of wild fauna and flora in the European territory of the Member States to which the Treaty applies (Article 2).

The 24 articles of the Directive specify a range of measures, including conservation of features in the landscape that are important for wildlife, the protection of species listed in the annexes from damage, destruction or over-exploitation, the surveillance of natural habitats and species, and ensuring that introductions of non-native species are not detrimental to naturally occurring habitats and species. One of the most stringent obligations (under Article 3) is to select, designate and protect a series of sites, to be called Special Areas of Conservation (SACs), for 169 natural Habitats of Community Interest listed in Annex I of the Directive and 623 Species of Community Interest listed in Annex II[1].

Habitat types of Community Interest are, within the EU territory[2]:

1. in danger of disappearance in their natural range; or

2. have a small natural range following their regression or by reason of their intrinsically restricted area; or

3. present outstanding examples of typical characteristics of one or more of the five following biogeographical regions: Alpine, Atlantic, Continental, Macronesian and Mediterranean.

---

[1] Birds are not included because they are listed in Annex I of the Birds Directive.

[2] Within EU territory: i.e. within the European territory of the Member States to which the Treaty establishing the European Economic Community applies.

Some of these Habitats of Community Interest are given priority status because the Community has a particular responsibility for their conservation in view of the proportion of their natural range which falls within the EU territory. The importance of these Priority Habitat types is emphasised at several places in the Directive (Articles 4 and 5 and Annex III), not only in terms of the selection of sites, but also in the measures required for site protection (Article 6) and surveillance (Article 11). Definitions and interpretations of the Habitats of Community Interest have been provided by the European Commission Environment Directorate (European Commission, 1999) and further information on their occurrence in the UK is given by McLeod *et al.* (2002). Of these Habitats of Community Interest, 76 are believed to occur in the UK, of which 22 are Priority Habitat types.

Species of Community Interest (listed in Annex II of the Directive) are those that, within the EU territory are:

1. endangered, except those species whose natural range is marginal in that territory and which are not endangered or vulnerable in the Western Palaearctic region;
2. vulnerable, i.e. believed likely to move into the endangered category in the near future if the causal factors continue operating; or
3. rare, i.e. with small populations that are not at present endangered or vulnerable, but are at risk. The species are located within restricted geographical areas or are thinly scattered over a more extensive range; or
4. endemic and requiring particular attention by reason of the specific nature of their habitat and/or the potential impact of their exploitation on their habitat and/or the potential impact of their exploitation on their conservation status.

A number of Species of Community Interest are also given priority status because the Community has particular responsibility in view of the proportion of their natural range which falls within the EU territory.

In recent times 51 Species of Community Interest have been recorded in the UK, but only one Priority Species currently occurs as a native

species, the liverwort Western Rustwort *Marsupella profunda*. Further information on their occurrence is given in McLeod *et al.* (2002).

Together the SACs and SPAs are known as the Natura 2000 network. This network will provide the most stringent protection mechanism for many habitats and species with restricted ranges or small populations. However, for other more dispersed species (e.g. those associated with many farmland habitats), site designation is unlikely to protect more than a small portion of the total resource. The Habitats Directive therefore also specifies that the conservation status of flora and fauna should be maintained throughout their range.

In the UK, the Directives have been transposed into legislation by The Conservation (Natural Habitats, & c.) Regulations 1994 and The Conservation (Natural Habitats, &c.) (Northern Ireland) Regulations 1995, as amended (informally known as 'The Habitats Regulations'). Under British law all SACs and SPAs will be underpinned by SSSI designations.

The UK submitted its first report to the European Commission summarising the implementation of the Habitats Directive in the UK from 1994 to December 2000 (Salmon, 2001). As of June 2003 there were 242 SPAs in the UK, covering some 1 470 000 ha. As of January 2004, 605 sites covering some 2 500 000 ha had been proposed as candidate SACs, and a further ten as proposed SACs covering some 290 000 ha. As a matter of policy for planning and all other consent regimes, the UK Government and the devolved administrations already treat candidate SACs as though they were fully designated.

3.5.6   Wildlife & Countryside Act

The Wildlife & Countryside Act 1981 was introduced as the principal mechanism for the legislative protection of wildlife in Great Britain. It does not extend to Northern Ireland, the Channel Islands or the Isle of Man. It has been subsequently amended with significant changes relating specifically to Scotland and England and Wales. This legislation is the chief means by which the Convention on the Conservation of European

Wildlife and Natural Habitats (the 'Bern Convention') and the European Union Directives on the Conservation of Wild Birds and Natural Habitats and Wild Fauna and Flora are implemented in Great Britain. The Act is divided into four parts.

- Part I is concerned with the protection of wildlife.
- Part II relates to the countryside and national parks (and the designation of protected areas).
- Part III covers public rights of way.
- Part IV deals with miscellaneous provisions of the Act.

Sections 1–8 of Part 1 relate to the protection of birds. Section 1 prohibits the intentional killing, injuring or taking of any wild bird and the taking, damaging or destroying of the nest (while being built or in use) or eggs. It prohibits possession of wild birds (dead or alive) or their eggs. There are additional penalties for offences relating to birds on Schedule 1, and it is also an offence to disturb Schedule 1 birds at the nest or the dependent young of Schedule 1 birds. Section 2 outlines exceptions to Section 1: notably, it identifies quarry and pest species.

Section 9 prohibits the intentional killing, injuring or taking of, the possession of and the trade in wild animals listed on Schedule 5. In addition, places used for shelter and protection are safeguarded against intentional damage, destruction and obstruction; animals protected under the relevant part of Section 9 must not intentionally be disturbed whilst occupying those places.

Section 13 identifies measures for the protection of wild plants. It prohibits the unauthorised intentional uprooting of any wild plant species and forbids any picking, uprooting or destruction of plants listed on Schedule 8. It also prohibits the sale, or possession for the purpose of sale, of any plants on Schedule 8 or parts or derivatives of Schedule 8 plants.

3.5.7   The CROW Act 2000

The Countryside and Rights of Way Act 2000 (CROW Act) strengthens the legal protection for threatened species and brings the Wildlife &

Countryside Act 1981 in England and Wales up to date. The importance of biodiversity conservation is also given a statutory basis, requiring government departments to have regard for biodiversity in carrying out their functions, and to take positive steps to further the conservation of listed species and habitats.

Section 74 of the CROW Act requires the Secretary of State for England and the National Assembly for Wales each to publish a list of species and habitat types that are of principal importance for the conservation of biological diversity in England and Wales, respectively. The Section 74 list for England can be viewed on the DEFRA web page http://www.defra.gov.uk/wildlife-countryside/cl/habitats/habitats-list.pdf. The equivalent list for Wales can be viewed on the National Assembly for Wales website: http://www.wales.gov.uk/subienvironment/content/guidance/species-statement-e.htm. These two lists are based on UK Biodiversity Action Plan (UK BAP) Priority Habitats and Species lists.

In England, *The England Biodiversity Strategy* (DEFRA, 2002), developed under the UK BAP process, is the principal means by which the Government complies with its duties to conserve, and promote the conservation of, habitats and species listed under Section 74 of the Act. The list will be kept under review and a report on any necessary revisions will be made as part of the first report on progress on the Biodiversity Strategy for England.

3.5.8   Nature Conservation (Scotland) Act 2004

In a similar way the Nature Conservation (Scotland) Act 2004 overhauls the current legislation concerning SSSIs and the protection of wildlife in Scotland and gives a statutory basis for the Scottish Biodiversity Strategy (SBS). It aims to make the SSSI system more adaptable and efficient and strengthens the legal protection of specified species of plant and animal. The Act imposes a new duty on public bodies 'in exercising any functions, to further the conservation of biodiversity so far as is consistent with the proper exercise of those functions'. The Act refers them to the SBS, which elaborates on what this duty may involve.

The SBS is underpinned by a series of five implementation plans, a research strategy and a set of biodiversity indicators. Details can be found at www.scotland.gov.uk/biodiversity. The Scottish Executive is also publishing lists of those habitats and species considered to be of principal importance in respect of the new responsibilities placed on public bodies.

3.5.9   National Red Lists and lists of species of conservation concern

A wealth of Red Lists have been produced in the UK, and elsewhere, on species that are considered to be at risk of national extinction (as described in Part III of this *Handbook*). These have typically adapted the early IUCN criteria and used the same largely subjective categories of threat (see Section 3.5.1). This has tended to produce lists that are dominated by rare species, many of which are likely to be at the edge of their range, and hence these lists undervalue global priorities. Application of the new quantitative IUCN (2001) criteria is also problematical at regional or national levels, as conspecific populations (i.e. populations of the same species) may support the population of interest. IUCN (2003) have therefore produced guidelines for the regional and national application of the IUCN (2001) Red List criteria that go some way to overcoming the problems described above. It should also lead to greater standardisation of criteria, which will aid comparisons between countries.

According to the IUCN guidelines, regional and national assessments should be carried out in a two-step process, which differs slightly for breeding and non-breeding populations. In Step 1, the IUCN 2001 Red List criteria are applied to the population in question, resulting in a preliminary categorisation. In Step 2, the existence and status of any conspecific populations outside the region that may affect extinction risks is taken into account. For example, preliminary categories should be downgraded (i.e. to a lower threat status) if immigration from outside the region is likely to reduce

extinction risks within the region. Less often, upgrading may occur where the population within the region is a demographic sink, such that it is unable to sustain itself, and where the extra-regional source is expected to decrease. To date these guidelines and the IUCN (2001) criteria have not been applied in any UK Red Lists, but have been used elsewhere, e.g. for birds in Sweden, Finland and Switzerland.

However, the IUCN criteria still only focus on establishing extinction probabilities and do not prioritise species according to the importance of the biogeographical populations in question. This lack of a 'big-picture' view can result in some important priorities being missed (Mace & Collar, 2002). In the UK, and other developed countries with relatively low levels of biodiversity, there is also justification for giving attention to species that remain relatively common (and thus are currently at a very low risk of extinction) but are nevertheless declining. Consequently, some recent assessments of the conservation status of species in the UK have moved away from the narrower Red Listing of threatened species to more inclusive lists of species of conservation concern, which, for example, include species with internationally important populations and common but declining species. Such an approach has been taken for birds in the UK (Gregory *et al.*, 2002) and all species under the UK BAP.

Red Lists and other lists of species of conservation concern should therefore be taken into account in evaluations as appropriate to their underlying objectives and particular assessment criteria. Detailed descriptions of such UK lists for each species group are given later in the appropriate chapters of this *Handbook*.

3.5.10   UK Biodiversity Action Plan listed habitats and species

The Biodiversity Convention was ratified by the UK Government in June 1994. However, even before this, the Government had committed itself to produce a consultative national action plan, *Biodiversity: the UK Action Plan* (Anon., 1994) based on the principles of the Biodiversity

Convention. This plan was launched with the overall goal: 'to conserve and enhance biodiversity within the UK and to contribute to the conservation of global biodiversity through all appropriate mechanisms'.

The plan stated that this is to be achieved through the conservation and, where practicable, enhancement of:

- the overall populations and natural ranges of native species and the quality and range of wildlife habitats and ecosystems;
- internationally important and threatened species, habitats and ecosystems;
- species, habitats and natural and managed ecosystems that are characteristic of local areas;
- the biodiversity of natural and semi-natural habitats where this has been diminished over recent decades.

By October 1999, three hundred and ninety-one Species Action Plans (SAPs) and 45 Habitat Action Plans (HAPs) had been published in reports produced by the UK Steering Group (UKSG, 1995a,b; UKBG, 1998a,b,c, 1999a,b,c).

As part of the development of the UK BAP, lists were produced of Priority Habitats and Species requiring conservation actions. Priority Habitats were defined[3] as:

- Habitats for which the UK has international obligations;
- Habitats at risk, such as those with a high rate of decline, especially over the past 20 years, or which are rare;
- Habitats that may be functionally critical (i.e. areas that are part of a wider ecosystem but provide reproductive or feeding areas for particular species); and
- Habitats that are important for UK BAP Priority Species (see below).

All EU Habitats of Community Interest (Annex I) occurring within the UK are included as UK BAP Priority Habitats. A full list of UK BAP Priority Habitats, indicating their relationship to EU

habitats of community importance, is provided in Appendix 2.

Species that qualify under one or more of the following criteria should be considered as Species of Conservation Concern (SoCC) :

- Threatened endemic and other globally threatened species;
- Species where the UK has more than 25% of the world or appropriate biogeographical population;
- Species where numbers or ranges have declined by more than 25% in the last 25 years;
- In some instances, where a species is found in fewer than fifteen 10 km squares in the UK; and
- Species listed in the EU Birds or Habitats Directives, the Bern, Bonn or CITES Conventions, or under the Wildlife & Countryside Act 1981 and the Wildlife Order (Northern Ireland) 1985.

Species that qualify for one or both of the following categories should be considered as Priority Species:

- Species that are globally threatened;
- Species that are rapidly declining in the UK, i.e. by more than 50% in the past 25 years.

The intention is that all Priority Species should be the subject of conservation action through the development of SAPs. A full list of UK BAP Priority Habitats, SoCCs, further notes on their selection criteria and current versions of HAPs and SAPs are available from the UK BAP website library at www.ukbap.org.uk/Library.

The UK BAP listing of species is primarily for guiding strategic conservation priorities and therefore reference to SoCC lists with respect to site evaluations is not always appropriate. Implementation of necessary actions for SoCC species will be largely through the SAPs and country strategies such as the England and Scottish Biodiversity Strategies. Many SoCC species are also common and widespread, such as the Song Thrush *Turdus philomelos* (a Priority Species), and site-based actions may not be of significant benefit for such species. Reference should therefore be made to individual SAPs to assess the importance of site-based measures for SoCC species.

---

[3] Two additional categories were identified and adopted for marine habitats.

3.6   SITE EVALUATIONS AND SELECTION OF PROTECTED AREAS

3.6.1   General principles and criteria

One of the commonest reasons for undertaking ecological evaluations is to assess the importance of a site in relation to potential designation as some form of protected area. Evaluations may also be carried out at a later stage for management planning or related purposes to identify, or confirm, the important features (such as species or habitats) that are present and that qualify the site for a particular designation status.

The approaches and methods used for identifying areas that should receive some form of protection vary widely and depend on the overall objectives for individual sites and the series of protected areas within a given territory (Williams, 1998; Margules & Pressey, 2000). However, an overall set of principles for protected area selection is given by Ratcliffe (1977), who suggests that priority should be given to sites and features that:

- are intrinsically most fragile and sensitive to human impact;
- have already been reduced in area or quality through human impact;
- are predictably most vulnerable to further damage and loss through a combination of fragility, sensitivity and probable expansion of impact;
- would represent the greatest loss to nature conservation if they were damaged or destroyed; and
- would be the most difficult to restore or re-create if they were damaged or destroyed.

A variety of approaches have been developed for identifying sites that should be included in a protected area series, most of which focus on the fourth point above, i.e. evaluations of a site's ecological importance.

Threshold criteria versus target-led approaches
The selection of protected areas is essentially based on a process of comparison, usually with certain selection criteria. These can be broadly categorised as simple criterion-led approaches, selection methods based on targets, and selection strategies incorporating complementarity considerations. Simple criterion-led approaches typically define a standard (e.g. area of a particular habitat of conservation importance, or threshold number of individuals of a species of conservation importance) such that all sites exceeding this standard are included in the protected area series.

An important advantage of this approach is that it is simple and can be applied gradually, with sites added sequentially to the series as data become available. The conservation importance of features, habitats and species needs to be reasonably well known, but the location of all habitats and species of conservation importance within the territory being considered does not need to be known in advance.

One of the problems with a criterion-led approach is that it is open-ended, such that sites are added no matter how much of a resource has been given protection. Thus, overall representation targets for species or habitats in a protected area series are not explicitly stated beforehand. This may be acceptable if the aim is to protect all sites above a defined value, but may result in problems if criteria turn out to be too inclusive or too restrictive. To overcome such problems, the idea of setting objectives for a protected area network as a whole has emerged and is receiving increasing support.

Target-setting can also explicitly ensure that the series of sites contains adequate representation of the total territory range of habitats, vegetation communities, species assemblages and individual species that are considered to require protection. However, this needs to be carried out against a classification of the range of variation in habitats, communities and species, which the series of sites is intended to represent. The minimum aim of the representative principle would therefore be to select a series of sites that complement one another in terms of the habitats or species present. Ideally, each habitat or species should be represented by at least one, and preferably the best, example. However, in the face of existing threats to sites this approach is unlikely to be sufficient to maintain the representative set of habitats and their characteristic features. An important principle of site selection should therefore be that as rarity, threat or other ecological values increase, then so does the need to ensure that a larger proportion of the habitat or species' population is under protection.

In practice, most protected area series have been selected by using simple criterion-based systems within an overall representation target framework. This is probably because it is easier to make relative judgements about the conservation value of habitats and species than it is to make difficult *a priori* decisions on how much should be protected. Protection targets also often tend to be arbitrary and unless widespread consultation is undertaken they will have little ownership or acceptance outside the conservation community.

Complementarity considerations

Criterion-led approaches (which, as described below, often focus on species rarity and diversity) tend to result in selection of sites that are similar in terms of their range of habitats and species. Such approaches are therefore inefficient in the selection of sites where objectives focus on representation across a network of sites. Instead, an evaluation of the degree to which species communities complement each other may help identify a minimum set of sites or area of land required to safeguard all species within a particular group (Vane-Wright *et al.*, 1991; Howard *et al.*, 1997; Balmford & Gaston, 1999). This involves identifying a series of sites whose habitats or species lists largely complement each other.

The majority of protected area selection techniques incorporating complementarity do so by using iterative steps; at each step all sites are compared to test how well they complement areas that have already been chosen. The most straightforward approach, which uses a so-called 'greedy' algorithm (i.e. rule-based calculation), first selects the area that is richest in the selected feature of interest (e.g. threatened species), then selects the area that adds the highest number of features that are not in the first. It then selects the area that adds the highest number of features that are not present in either of the first two, and so on.

Alternatives include various weighted algorithms, including ones that consider a site's level of irreplaceability (Pressey *et al.*, 1994). This allows the degree of flexibility in the series and irreplaceability of individual sites to be evaluated. Irreplaceability is particularly important because the loss of the more irreplaceable sites in a series closes options of ever achieving a representative protected area system. Irreplaceability provides a single measure of conservation value of a site that is defensible (Bibby, 1998). Thus, some algorithms give a high priority to sites that contain species or habitats that are not found elsewhere. Some algorithms also check back to ensure that early choices remain appropriate after the inclusion of others.

Using such an approach, Williams *et al.* (1996) identified a set of twenty-seven 10 km × 10 km grid squares in which all British breeding birds were represented at least once. Similarly, Hacker *et al.* (1998) showed that all African primate species occur within a set of grid squares that cover just 3.8% of the area sampled.

However, despite a great deal of research being carried out into protected area selection techniques, selection algorithms and other computerized approaches have been used only infrequently by those involved in making decisions on the establishment of protected area networks (Prendergast *et al.*, 1999). This appears to be mainly because decision-makers are unaware of the sophisticated computer tools for reserve selection. Where this is not the case, there have been problems with funding and with understanding of the tools, and a general antipathy towards what is seen as a prescriptive approach to conservation. There are also common methodological limitations to its application, including the following:

- *Inadequate data on species and habitat distributions.* Selection algorithms can only be fully applied when species distributions are well known and the contents of potential nature reserves deduced. Consequently, as noted by Sutherland (2000), where there are sufficient data for carrying out such analyses, protected area networks are usually already well established.
- *Differences in scale.* There is often a substantial mismatch between the resolution at which distribution data are available and the scale at which protected areas are designated. Indeed, data

resolution is often close to one order of magnitude greater than the average size of protected areas (Hopkins *et al.*, 2000).

- *Dependence on presence–absence data.* A species' presence at a site does not necessarily mean that it has a viable population there. Areas selected by using complementarity may miss the best examples of certain species' populations, particularly of those associated with species-poor areas. Some selection algorithms have therefore been refined to take account of species abundance rather than mere presence–absence (Turpie, 1995).

- *Political and economic considerations.* Sites selected through complementarity analysis may not necessarily offer the best opportunities for successful long-term conservation. In practice, the selection of protected areas is usually strongly influenced by political considerations, opportunities, land prices (Ando *et al.*, 1998), the threat of local development (Margules & Usher, 1981), or proximity to existing reserves. Accordingly, reserve selection algorithms have recently been developed that incorporate rules for including mandatory areas, forcing adjacency and excluding undesirable areas (Lombard *et al.*, 1997).

3.6.2   Evaluation and selection criteria

Although no standard set of criteria has emerged for the purpose of site evaluations, assessment criteria have commonly focused on the presence of certain rare (or otherwise threatened) species or habitats, diversity, size and naturalness. Other criteria have included fragility, degree of threat, educational, scientific, recreational and cultural value, ecological or geographical location, the presence of potential buffer areas, shape, accessibility and potential conservation effectiveness (see Smith & Theberge (1986) for review).

Whichever criteria are used, to be defensible they need to be objective, explicit, based on widely accepted ecological scientific principles and the best available data, and (ideally) quantifiable. However, criteria have varied widely in this respect.

It is also important to remember that criteria will not be meaningful if applied across a wide range of sites and habitats that differ considerably in their ecological characteristics. Thresholds of significance, for instance size or species diversity, might differ significantly between habitat types or biogeographical regions. It is therefore advisable to group sites for evaluation into similar types before comparisons are carried out.

More detailed consideration is given below to five of the most widely used criteria.

Rare or abundant species

Many protected areas have been selected and designated purely on the basis of the occurrence of species. This is largely because species provide the simplest quantifiable and most objective currency of conservation value. Most species-based selection criteria assess a site's importance for particular rare species or other species of conservation importance and/or the abundance of species.

Such approaches have been frequently used for the selection of protected areas for birds. For example, the Ramsar Convention includes a criterion for designating Ramsar sites on the basis of the presence of 20 000 waterfowl or more than 1% of a flyway population (see Section 3.7.6 below). BirdLife International has taken this type of approach and developed it to create a standard set of global criteria and regionally specific criteria for identifying Important Bird Areas (IBAs), which BirdLife recommend should receive appropriate statutory protection (Heath & Evans, 2000).

The species occurrence approach is also increasingly being applied to other taxa. For example, PlantLife International has developed criteria for Important Plant Areas for Europe (Anderson, 2002), which include thresholds for the presence of rare species (as well as rare habitats).

Diversity

Species and habitat diversity has been one of the most frequently used evaluation measures for biotic communities. Selection of diverse sites tends to be favoured because they are believed to contain more of the variety of natural resources within a given area; however, problems may arise if complementarity is not taken into account. There are also less tangible aesthetic values in diversity and it has often been suggested that diversity is a factor promoting ecosystem stability, but this idea is not well founded in observation or theory (Bibby, 1998).

Species or habitat richness (measured in numbers of species occurring) are the most intuitively simple measures of diversity. However, if population sizes or areas are measured, they can be combined into more sophisticated diversity indices (Magurran, 1983). Two commonly used indices are Shannon's Index, $\sum(p_i \ln p_i)$, and Simpson's index, $1 - \sum p_i^2$. Here, p_i is the proportion of individuals in the population belonging to species i. In each case, a high value indicates a large number of species with similar abundances, whereas a low number indicates domination by a few species. The requirement for abundance information makes the measurement of diversity more time-consuming, however, and indices are more difficult to interpret than species or habitat numbers.

Species richness measurements also depend on the scale at which they are measured; richness invariably increases with the increasing size of the area surveyed (MacArthur & Wilson, 1967; Rosenzweig, 1995). Such species–area relations are likely to occur as a result of environmental heterogeneity. Increasing the area will include additional habitat types, or variations within these, depending on how habitats are defined. However, at large scales biogeographic and historic factors may be important contributors. Species–area effects can be examined and corrected by regression analysis. Richness estimates may also vary according to sampling effort (for instance the number of quadrats measured). This can also be corrected for (although it is more complex) by rarefaction, which resamples the data to estimate the number of species for a fixed (smaller) sampling effort (Simberloff, 1972).

Particular care must be taken in interpreting the results of richness and diversity assessments. For example, some semi-natural habitats of high ecological value are characteristically species poor. Indeed, Bibby (1998) suggests that the appeal of diversity as an indicator has almost certainly led to under-representation of inherently less diverse habitats in many protected area systems.

Consequently, habitat richness indicators need to be related to expected levels of species richness for habitats and, ideally, ecological regions. Degradation of natural habitats can also actually result in an increase in overall biodiversity even though species of conservation importance may decline. Thus, species richness and diversity measurements should also focus on those species that are characteristic of the habitat, and not on the overall richness of the habitat.

In practice, diversity scores have been little used for protected-area selection. However, some evaluation scoring systems have been developed that combine abundance, species conservation value and species richness data. For example, in the UK this approach has been used for selecting SSSIs (NCC, 1989) for birds and amphibians (see Part III).

The Environment Agency (EA) have also developed a Community Conservation Index (CCI) for evaluating the conservation importance of riverine macro-invertebrate communities. Although this has not been introduced into full use yet by EA, it has been used in a number of Environmental Impact Assessments. A CCI score is calculated by first assigning tabulated Conservation Scores to each species in the sample based on their national conservation status. An overall CCI score is then derived by calculating the mean Conservation Score and multiplying this by a tabulated Community Score, which reflects either species richness or the rarest taxon present (depending on whichever gives the highest score). A high CCI score indicates a site with high conservation value for its rare taxa or species richness. CCI scores can vary from 1.0 (no conservation interest) to 30.0+ (high conservation interest).

Size (extent)

The size of a site, typically its area but sometimes its length (linear habitats), depth or volume (e.g. lakes), is important in modified environments where natural communities are fragmented and isolated. In more extensive habitats, it is less obvious because the boundaries may be difficult to define.

Of foremost importance is the attainment of a minimum size, which will vary according to the protection objectives. In a fragmented landscape large blocks may be necessary to contain viable populations of particular species (especially wide-ranging predators, such as large raptors or, outside the UK, Wolves *Canis lupus*, Lynx *Lynx lynx*, etc.). Large sites may also be more likely to support interior species, which are intolerant of habitat edges.

Larger sites may also be valued beyond the minimum viable size, because large areas of habitat typically contain a greater diversity of habitats and species. Size may also influence the management options available, such as the ability to resolve usage conflicts or to enable natural vegetation succession and landscape-scale dynamics.

Related to the issue of size is that of shape, and a site's proximity and linkage to other similar habitat blocks, as these factors may influence species occurrences through emigration and immigration. Based on biogeographical studies, some basic rules of thumb have been proposed, and widely referred to, for the selection of nature reserves (Diamond, 1975). These are simply that:

- larger areas are better than smaller areas;
- one large area is better than separated areas of the same total area;
- adjacent areas are better than isolated areas;
- linkages ('corridors') between areas are better than completely isolated areas;
- clusters of areas are better than areas in a line; and
- compact areas are better than linear areas.

However, there have been many erroneous and inappropriate applications of these island-biogeography-based theories to site evaluation and the selection of protected areas. Other factors need to be taken into account in considering the optimal size, distribution and shape of nature reserves. Indeed, in many cases these other factors will be more important. For example, in some circumstances, very small reserves might be appropriate, for instance in safeguarding plants with minute ranges. In linear habitats, such as rivers, other properties such as length and continuity become important. These typically relate to their corridor function, their value rising with the number or areas of sites they are able to connect.

Naturalness

Naturalness is a criterion that is difficult to define objectively, yet it is highly valued in conservation assessment. The principal reason for valuing naturalness as a criterion for identifying sites for protection is that there is often a close relationship between the naturalness of a habitat and its biodiversity value. For example, research on river invertebrate communities in England has starkly shown that diverse physical river reaches, as found in more natural rivers, support invertebrate communities of much greater diversity than highly modified or uniform ones (Smith *et al.*, 1991). Perhaps most importantly, a high proportion of rare species are often associated with natural or near-natural habitats, primarily because such habitats now tend to be rare in developed countries.

The application of the naturalness criterion is particularly relevant to habitats such as rivers (Boon *et al.*, 1996a) and other wetlands. It is also consistent with developments under the Water Framework Directive where the condition of riverine habitats will be related to definitions of pristine habitat. Application of the naturalness criterion to other habitats needs some care and qualification as many that are of conservation value (such as moorlands, heathlands, and flower-rich grasslands) are plagioclimax habitats that have been maintained by centuries of human intervention. Determining naturalness therefore requires considerable knowledge of individual habitats, the effects of long-term natural process on them, and their response to human intervention.

Other reasons for favouring natural habitats and ecosystems have included the scientific need for sites at which to study natural ecological processes. There are also emotional and aesthetic factors at play in the greater perceived value of wilderness and ecosystems less tainted by humans (McCloskey & Spalding, 1989).

Representativeness

This criterion (also occasionally referred to as typicalness) aims to select sites that best represent a particular habitat of interest and which possess as many desirable habitat characteristics and special features as possible. On closer analysis, however, it is clear that this selection criterion involves a mixture of desirable attributes that are best separated. In other words, the concept of representativeness is made up of other separate commonly used ecological evaluation criteria of diversity in particular, but also to some extent of size and rarity. It may therefore be more appropriate to regard representativeness as an underlying principle, which site selection processes aim to satisfy, both within a single site and through the totality of all sites, and then to satisfy this principle by the application of criteria relating to it.

3.6.3   Nature Conservation Review criteria

The use of multiple criteria that take into account the presence of species, habitat quality and other ecological factors gives a better integrated assessment of the overall value of a site than does concentration on selected attributes or species groups. However, the broad range of information that must be taken into account makes evaluation more complex and subjective. One set of criteria that have been particularly frequently used are those developed by Ratcliffe (1977) for the UK Nature Conservation Review (NCR). These are summarized in Table 3.3.

Although now over 25 years old, the NCR criteria have been widely adopted and adapted in the UK and abroad. In particular, they formed the basis for the UK SSSI selection criteria (NCC, 1989). They have also been frequently used as the basis for ecological evaluations for management planning purposes and many ecological impact assessments in the UK. However, Treweek (1999) points out that these criteria have their drawbacks; notably the lack of criteria relating to recoverability or the replaceability of natural resources of particular importance when assessing impacts and mitigating for them. In addition, not all of the criteria (e.g. intrinsic appeal) are measurable by using defensible, consistent and objective techniques.

3.6.4   Scoring systems

A frequently cited problem with ecological evaluations is that assessments are subjective and therefore comparisons among sites may be difficult or misleading. Some multiple-criterion scoring systems have therefore been established to produce indices of habitat or species assemblage value, in an attempt to provide more quantifiable and objective assessments.

Several authors have proposed the use of multiple evaluation criteria, which are then given weights or priorities by using scoring systems. Scoring enables abstract evaluation criteria to be expressed numerically and hence they can be used more readily in decision-making. Various scoring procedures have been developed and have been reviewed by Margules & Usher (1981), Smith & Theberge (1986) and Usher (1986). Westman (1985) summarises the four main types of scale and associated permissible mathematical and statistical operations associated with scoring procedures.

Although a wide variety of systems have been developed for evaluating habitats, few have been widely accepted or used for protected area selection in the UK or internationally. However, one system that has been widely used is SERCON (System for Evaluating Rivers for CONservation), which was developed in the mid-1990s as a technique for assessing the conservation value of rivers in the UK (Boon *et al.*, 1996a,b). It aims to provide a more comprehensive, rigorous, and repeatable method for conservation evaluation of rivers than had hitherto been available. SERCON evaluations first involve gathering all available information about the physical character of a river system, from Environment Agency River Habitat Corridor Surveys (Environment Agency, 2003), which then guides the user into determining the size of the assessment unit (the Evaluated Corridor Site). Data on other physical, chemical and biological features of the river corridor are then gathered together from all relevant sources. Finally the collated data are translated into a series of scores for specific attributes on a scale of 0–5. Scores are weighted and combined to give separate indices of conservation value for six criteria (Physical Diversity; Naturalness; Representativeness; Rarity; Species Richness; Special Features). Scores can be combined to give an overall assessment on an A–E scale, with A representing the highest-quality band.

A scoring procedure may also be used for selecting SSSIs on the basis of their breeding bird

Table 3.3. *The NCR criteria developed by Ratcliffe (1977) for evaluating nature conservation importance*

	Application / notes
Primary criteria	
Size	Including both area of vegetation types and population sizes for individual species.
Diversity	Applied either as simple species richness, or by giving different weightings to species according to their 'interest'.
Rarity	Applied either to habitats or to species. The latter most commonly tested by comparisons with national or county population size or distribution by 10 km squares.
Naturalness	Habitats that are least intensively modified by humans are generally more highly regarded.
Representativeness or typicalness	A measure of how well the study area represents habitats or vegetation types on a wider scale.
Fragility	Some habitats or species are especially vulnerable or sensitive to anthropogenic change. Those with restricted area or ranges are generally held to be more vulnerable.
Secondary criteria	
Recorded history	Can be useful in confirming that a site has been 'important' for some time. Sites with a long history of study may contribute significantly to our understanding of ecological processes.
Potential value	Relates to the likelihood that appropriate management could restore or enhance an area's ecological value.
Position in geographical or ecological unit	Some areas of fairly low 'intrinsic value' may be more important because they form successional stages between more important areas. In addition, nationally common habitats or species might be very rare locally.
Intrinsic appeal	Habitats or species with public appeal promote the cause of nature conservation and can attract funds. This criterion can also be interpreted to include estimates of public use, access and amenity value.

Source: Treweek (1999).

assemblage (NCC, 1989). This 'BTO index' is largely derived from a study of bird communities in different habitats in Britain (Fuller, 1982). The index for a site is calculated by summing the scores across all species that are regularly present according to a habitat-specific list. Each habitat list includes all the characteristic species of the habitat that have a total British population of fewer than 1 000 pairs (at the time) and all other more abundant species that are primarily associated with the habitat, or which are particularly threatened by habitat change. All species with a British population of more than one million birds are excluded. Each species score is based on its British population size, such that species with fewer than 10 pairs score 6, whereas species with a population of 100 000–1 000 000 pairs score 1. The site index may then be compared with the stated site selection threshold score, which is based on the theoretical maximum score for each habitat for species with more than 100 pairs. For most habitats, the threshold for qualification as an SSSI is taken as 50% of the theoretical maximum.

Treweek (1999) notes that there has been some debate over the efficiency and validity of scoring methods for ecological evaluations (van der Ploeg & Vlijm, 1978; Gotmark et al., 1986; Usher, 1986; Anselin et al., 1989). In particular, difficulties have arisen over the combination of quantitative and qualitative criteria.

As in the examples described above, weighting is often used to convert different systems of measurement to common formats and to increase the influence of criteria related to particularly important ecological factors. However, there is rarely any biological rationale for weightings. For example, there is no clear basis for deciding that birds with British populations of 1–10 pairs should be given a weighting six times that of a species with a population of 100 000 – 1 000 000 pairs. Weightings therefore often tend to be arbitrary and based on the subjective opinion of a few experts. To solve this problem some methods use consultation approaches to provide weighting values. For example, the Environmental Evaluation System (Dee et al., 1973) uses a combined scoring and weighting method that attempts to combine scientific measurements of 'value function' with selected indicator variables with weightings based on values allocated by members of the public chosen to represent relevant interest groups.

When scoring systems are used they should ensure that all criteria and weightings are explicitly defined. Care should also be taken to ensure that the use of single, numerical indices based on combined scoring and weighting systems does not create a false impression of precision and conceal uncertainties in the underlying evaluation data.

3.7   SITE CONSERVATION DESIGNATIONS

As indicated in Figure 3.1, any evaluation of a site's conservation priority should establish its protected area status and, whether or not it is designated as such, assess its compliance with appropriate designation criteria. Ecological evaluations in the UK should take into account the following Protected Area categories and associated designation criteria.

- World Heritage Sites
- Biosphere Reserves
- Biogenetic Sites
- Wild Birds Directive SPAs
- Habitats Directive SACs
- Ramsar sites
- National Nature Reserves
- Site of Special Scientific Interest (Wildlife & Countryside Act, CROW Act, Nature Conservation (Scotland) Act)
- Local Nature Reserves
- Wildlife Sites

The background to these designations and, where appropriate, their selection criteria are provided below.

3.7.1   World Heritage Sites

World Heritage Sites are areas of global natural and/or cultural significance, and are nominated by the state within which they are situated. The nominations are then considered by a World Heritage Committee of Party States. Sites that are accepted are placed on the World Heritage List. World Heritage Sites must have strict legal protection and any management of the site must ensure that this continues. Further information on the Convention and a list of World Heritage Sites can be found at http://whc.unesco.org/nwhc/pages/home/pages/homepage.htm.

3.7.2   Biosphere Reserves

Biosphere Reserves represent globally significant examples of biomes (biological communities) for both terrestrial and coastal environments. They have particular value as benchmarks or standards for the measurement of long-term changes in the biosphere as a whole. They were devised by UNESCO under Project No. 8 of their Man and the Biosphere (MAB) programme, and were launched in 1970. Criteria and guidelines for selection of sites were produced by a UNESCO task force in 1974. Although Biosphere Reserves are not always statutorily protected areas, all British sites are also National Nature Reserves. Further information on the MAB Programme and a list of Biosphere Reserves can be found at http://www.unesco.org/mab/index.htm.

3.7.3   Biogenetic Reserves

In 1973, the European Ministerial Conference on the Environment recommended that a European network of reserves to conserve representative examples of European flora, fauna and natural areas be established. Their selection is generally based on two criteria.

- Their value in terms of nature conservation: they must contain specimens of flora or fauna that are typical, unique, rare or endangered.
- The effectiveness of their protective status: this must be sufficient to ensure the long-term conservation or management of a site according to the objectives set, as defined in Council of Europe Resolution (76) 17.

All sites in the UK are existing Sites of Special Scientific Interest (SSSIs), and most are also National Nature Reserves (NNRs).

3.7.4   Special Protection Areas (SPAs)

The 1979 EC Directive on the Conservation of Wild Birds requires member states to take conservation measures particularly for certain rare or vulnerable species and for regularly occurring migratory species of bird. In part this is achieved through the designation of statutory Special Protection Areas (SPAs) by the UK government on the advice of the statutory conservation agencies. All SPAs, apart from those that are proposed for designation at sea, have first to be notified as Sites of Special Scientific Interest (SSSIs).

Further information on SPA designation procedures and criteria is provided in Chapter 24.

3.7.5   Special Areas of Conservation (SACs)

SACs are designated under the EU Habitats Directive and are defined as areas with outstanding examples of selected habitat types (listed in Annex I of the Directive) or areas important for the continued well-being or survival of selected non-bird species (listed in Annex II) in a European context. The process for the selection and designation of SACs is set out in Article 4 and its application in the UK is summarised in McLeod *et al.* (2002). SACs are identified, initially as Sites of Community Importance (SCIs), by a two-stage process according to criteria provided principally in Annex III of the Directive. Sites that are adopted by the Commission as SCIs must then be designated by the member state as SACs as soon as possible, and at the latest within six years.

Stage 1 is an assessment of the relative importance of sites containing examples of the individual Annex I habitat types and Annex II species in each member state, against the following summarised Annex III criteria:

- Habitats:
  (a) degree of representativeness;
  (b) area;
  (c) degree of conservation of habitat structure and functions and restoration possibilities; and
  (d) global assessment of conservation value (i.e. an overall assessment, based on (a–c) above).
- Species:
  (a) population size and density;
  (b) degree of conservation of the features of the habitat that are important for the species, and restoration possibilities;
  (c) degree of isolation of the population in relation to the species' natural range; and
  (d) global assessment of conservation value (i.e. an overall assessment, based on (a–c) above).

Further guidance on the assessment of the Annex III Stage 1 criteria is given in the EC guidance document for the Natura 2000 Standard Data Form (European Commission DGXI, 1995).

The global assessment referred to in the Annex III criteria is an assessment of the overall value of the site for the conservation of the relevant Annex I habitat or Annex II species. Particular attention is paid to the global assessment as an overall index of a site's conservation value. Following the European Commission DGXI (1995) guidance, sites are graded A, B or C, which in the UK has been interpreted as follows.

(A) Sites holding outstanding examples of the habitat or populations of the species in a European context.

(B) Sites holding excellent stands of the habitat, or populations of the species significantly above the threshold for SSSI or ASSI[4] notification but of somewhat lower value than grade A sites.

(C) Examples of the habitat or populations of the species that are of at least national interest (i.e. usually above the threshold for SSSI or ASSI notification on terrestrial sites) but not significantly above this. These habitats or species are not the primary reason for SACs being selected.

Although there is a distinction between the principal features for which sites have been selected (those graded A or B) and those that are only of secondary interest (those graded C), it is important to note that all three grades are qualifying SAC interest features and hence all such sites are afforded protection at the European level.

Stage 2, which is also known as the 'moderation' stage, is an assessment of the overall importance of the sites in the context of the appropriate biogeographical region and the EU as a whole. All the sites identified by member states in Stage 1 which contain Priority Habitat types and/or Priority Species are adopted as SCIs. Other sites listed by Member States are assessed in relation to their contribution to maintaining or re-establishing, at a Favourable Conservation Status, a natural habitat in Annex I or a species in Annex II and/or to the coherence of Natura 2000 according to the following summarised Annex III criteria.

- the relative value of the site at a national level;
- the relationship of the site to migration routes;
- the total area of the site;
- the diversity of habitats and species present on the site; and
- the overall quality of the site in the context of the biogeographical region and/or the European Union.

The text of the Directive also includes other site selection requirements or qualifications and these

need to be taken into account in assessments of sites against the Annex III criteria. These include:

1. restrictions on the site selection obligations in respect of widely dispersed and aquatic species (Article 4.1);
2. the requirement to contribute towards the maintenance of Favourable Conservation Status (Article 2.2 and Article 3.1); and
3. the obligation on each Member State to select a series of sites that reflects the proportion of the EU resource of a given habitat or species within their national territory (Article 3.2).

Further selection principles and guidance on the interpretation of the Annex III Stage 1 criteria were produced at a meeting between Member States of the Atlantic Biogeographical region and the European Commission in 1994 (Hopkins & Buck, 1995), as follows.

Provision of information

Acknowledging that the quality and extent of information about habitat types and species varies within the Region, Member States will provide information to the Commission in the Natura 2000 data entry form using the best scientific information available at the time according to the format agreed by the Habitats Committee.

Balancing the national lists

1. Acknowledging that outstanding single interest sites in terms of quality, extent or range make an important contribution to the Natura 2000 network, special emphasis will be given to identifying and delimiting sites containing complexes of interests on Annexes I and II as valuable ecological functional units.
2. Member States will give significant additional emphasis in number and area to sites containing priority habitat types and species.
3. In considering the degree of representativeness of Annex I habitat types on individual sites, Member States will take account of the best examples in extent and quality of the main type (which is most characteristic of the Member State) and its main variants, having regard to geographical range.
4. Acknowledging that sites containing Annex I habitat types and Annex II species at the centre of their

---

[4] Areas of Special Scientific Interest as designated in Northern Ireland.

range will make an important contribution to Natura 2000, Member States will take responsibility for proposing sites containing habitats and species that are particularly rare in that Member State, with a view to preserving the range.

5. It is acknowledged that certain habitat types and species listed in Annexes I and II are relatively common and extensive in certain Member States. These Member States will have particular responsibility for proposing a proportion of the resource that is sufficient to contribute significantly to the maintenance of the habitat types and species at a favourable conservation status.

6. Where Annex II species' populations are too small to be naturally viable, or where the species occur only as vagrants or reintroductions, Member States may exclude them from consideration for site selection.

7. Artificial areas need not be excluded from site selection if they have spontaneously given rise to Annex I habitat types or host Annex II species and if it is considered that they have exceptional value.

Defining boundaries

It is acknowledged that different Member States will have different approaches to the definition of boundaries (e.g. the inclusion of buffer zones within the site), according to the habitat type or species concerned and the legal and management measures necessary to protect and extend the landscape context.

A summary list of the selection criteria and additional principles used for site selection in the UK are shown in Table 3.4.

The various Annex III criteria and additional guidelines listed above are principles that should be taken into account when assessing sites for potential inclusion in the SAC network. They do not include qualitative thresholds or standards against which site attributes (e.g. area) can be measured. Measurable thresholds could be set for some criteria, such as area, but SAC selection requires an assessment of multiple criteria, many of which (e.g. conservation structure and function) cannot easily be quantified. There is also no straightforward or non-arbitrary way of combining and weighting the relative importance of the various criteria. The assessment of sites against the criteria and principles in Table 3.4 has therefore

been carried out in the UK by expert judgement (McLeod *et al.*, 2002), which is in accordance with the European Commission view that 'best expert judgement is an appropriate means of ranking sites' (European Commission DGXI, 1995).

This does, however, mean that it is difficult for others outside the expert group of assessors to establish whether or not a particular site should qualify as an SAC. Evaluations of sites with respect to their potential qualification as SACs can therefore only be judged against the general principles described above, their interpretation in the UK (as documented in McLeod *et al.* 2002) and the precedent set by sites that have been proposed as candidate SACs (i.e. SCIs).

All Annex I habitats and Annex II species considered to be of European importance that occur in candidate SACs are identified as qualifying features. However, habitat fragments, small populations of species, and habitats and species occurring outside their natural range are generally treated as 'non-significant presences'. Although these habitats and species are listed on the Natura 2000 standard data forms, they do not require conservation objectives and are not protected under the Directive (as stated in the EC guidance document *Managing Natura 2000 sites* (European Commission, 2000)). In the UK, the criteria and associated thresholds used for SSSI selection have generally been used to distinguish between non-significant presences and qualifying interest features.

For further information on the SAC selection process see McLeod *et al.* (2002) and www.jncc.gov.uk/ProtectedSites/SACselection/default.htm. This site also includes up-to-date details of candidate SACs and the Annex I habitats and Annex II species represented within them.

3.7.6   The Convention on Wetlands (Ramsar Convention)

The Convention on Wetlands of International Importance especially as Waterfowl Habitat, more popularly known as the 'Ramsar Convention', was the first of the modern global intergovernmental treaties on conservation and wise use of natural resources, and came into force in 1975. Compared

Table 3.4. *Summary of criteria and additional principles used for SAC selection in the UK*

	Reference
Site assessment criteria: Annex II species	
(i) Representativeness	Annex III Stage 1A(a); Article 1e; Conclusions of 1994 Atlantic Biogeographical Region Meeting (para. 4).
(ii) Relative surface area of habitat	Annex III Stage 1A(b); Article 1e; Conclusions of 1994 Atlantic Biogeographical Region Meeting (para. 4).
(iii) Conservation of structure and function	Annex III Stage 1A(c); Article 1e.
(iv) Global assessment	Annex III Stage 1A(d).
Site assessment criteria: Annex II species	
(v) Proportion of UK population	Annex III Stage 1B(a); Article 1l; Conclusions of 1994 Atlantic Biogeographical Region Meeting (para. 7).
(vi) Conservation of features important for species survival	Annex III Stage 1B(b); Article 1i.
(vii) Isolation of species populations	Annex III Stage 1B(c); Conclusions of 1994 Atlantic Biogeographical Region Meeting (para. 7).
(viii) Global assessment	Annex III Stage 1B(d).
Additional principles	
(ix) Priority/non-priority status	Annex III Stage 1D; Article 1d; Conclusions of 1994 Atlantic Biogeographical Region Meeting (para. 3).
(x) Geographical range	Article 1e.
(xi) Special UK responsibilities	Article 3.2; Conclusions of 1994 Atlantic Biogeographical Region (para. 6).
(xii) Multiple interest	Annex III Stage 2.2(d); Conclusions of 1994 Atlantic Biogeographical Region Meeting (para. 2).
(xiii) Rarity	Conclusions of 1994 Atlantic Biogeographical Region Meeting (para. 5).

Source: McLeod *et al.* (2002).

with more recent ones, its provisions are relatively straightforward and general. The official name of the treaty reflects its original emphasis on the conservation and wise use of wetlands primarily to provide habitat for waterbirds. Over the years, however, the Convention has broadened its scope to cover all aspects of wetland conservation and wise use, recognising wetlands as ecosystems that are extremely important for biodiversity conservation and for the well-being of human communities.

The treaty requires Contracting Parties to designate Ramsar sites, promote the wise use of wetlands, establish Nature Reserves, initiate training and undertake international co-operation in the conservation of wetlands. The first obligation under the Convention is to designate at least one wetland for inclusion in the List of Wetlands of International Importance (the 'Ramsar List') and to promote its conservation. Selection for the Ramsar List should be based on the wetland's significance in terms of ecology, botany, zoology, limnology or hydrology. As of March 2004 the Convention had 138 Contracting Parties, who have designated 1369 wetlands (amounting to nearly 120 million hectares) as Ramsar sites.

The Contracting Parties have adopted specific criteria for identifying Ramsar sites, the most recent of which were adopted by the 7th

Conference of Parties (CoP7) in 1999. However, these should be used in conjunction with the *strategic Framework and Guidelines for the Future Development of the List of Wetlands of International Importance*, as also adopted by CoP7. The current criteria are listed below and can be obtained, together with the Strategic Framework document, from the Ramsar website at www.ramsar.org.

Group A of the Criteria. Sites containing representative, rare or unique wetland types
  Criterion 1: A wetland should be considered internationally important if it contains a representative, rare, or unique example of a natural or near-natural wetland type found within the appropriate biogeographic region.
Group B of the Criteria. Sites of international importance for conserving biological diversity
  Criteria based on species and ecological communities
  Criterion 2: A wetland should be considered internationally important if it supports vulnerable, endangered, or critically endangered species or threatened ecological communities.
  Criterion 3: A wetland should be considered internationally important if it supports populations of plant and/or animal species important for maintaining the biological diversity of a particular biogeographic region.
  Criterion 4: A wetland should be considered internationally important if it supports plant and/or animal species at a critical stage in their life cycles, or provides refuge during adverse conditions.
Specific criteria based on waterbirds
  Criterion 5: A wetland should be considered internationally important if it regularly supports 20,000 or more waterbirds.
  Criterion 6: A wetland should be considered internationally important if it regularly supports 1% of the individuals in a population of one species or subspecies of waterbird.
Specific criteria based on fish
  Criterion 7: A wetland should be considered internationally important if it supports a significant proportion of indigenous fish subspecies, species or families, life-history stages, species interactions and/or populations that are representative of wetland benefits and/or values and thereby contributes to global biological diversity.
  Criterion 8: A wetland should be considered internationally important if it is an important source of food for

fishes, spawning ground, nursery and/or migration path on which fish stocks, either within the wetland or elsewhere, depend.

3.7.7   National Nature Reserves

National Nature Reserves (NNRs) are nationally important sites that are protected and managed for wildlife. They were initially established under Sections 16–29 of the National Parks and Access to the Countryside Act (1949) to protect the most important areas of wildlife habitat and geological formations in Britain, and as places for scientific research. All are therefore nationally important. These provisions were strengthened by the Wildlife & Countryside Act (1981). NNRs are either owned or managed by the UK Statutory Agencies or by approved bodies such as Wildlife Trusts.

3.7.8   Sites of Special Scientific Interest

The first SSSIs were designated under The National Parks and Access to the Countryside Act (1949). Further SSSIs were subsequently designated and SSSI protection measures enhanced under the Wildlife & Countryside Act (1981) and the Wildlife & Countryside Amendment Act (1985). The protection of SSSIs was further strengthened by the Nature Conservation (Scotland) Act 2004 and, in England and Wales, by the Countryside and Rights of Way Act 2000. Both Acts amend the 1981 Act's provisions; they contain measures to increase protection of SSSIs and to provide additional powers for the prosecution of perpetrators of wildlife crime. This includes enabling the conservation agencies to refuse consent for damaging activities; providing new powers to combat neglect; increasing penalties for deliberate damage; a new court power to order restoration; improving powers to act against cases of third-party damage; and placing a duty on public bodies to further the conservation and enhancement of SSSIs. The new measures for SSSIs came into force on 30 January 2001.

SSSIs form the basic unit of UK protected area legislation; most higher designations are superimposed onto existing SSSIs. As legally defined, an SSSI is an areas which, in the opinion of the Nature Conservancy Council (NCC) and its successor bodies, is 'of special interest by reason of any of its flora, fauna, or geological or physiographical interest'. Coastal SSSIs do not extend beyond the mean low water mark and therefore do not cover marine habitats.

The criteria for selection have been steadily refined over the years. The rationale for site selection was originally based primarily on habitat types, recognizing six major habitat 'formations': (1) coastlands, (2) woodlands, (3) lowland grassland, heath and scrub, (4) open water, (5) peatlands and (6) upland grassland, moor and mountaintops. In each case, the best known examples were selected according to a range of criteria, as described previously. In the 1960s and 1970s the sites were graded as of International, National, Regional and County importance, and the first two categories became known as 'key sites'.

In 1989 NCC published a standard set of Guidelines for selection of biological SSSIs (NCC, 1989). However, the criteria have been reviewed at intervals, and refined in the light of new surveys. The approaches and criteria used to select SSSIs differ considerably between habitats and species groups. Details of the 1989 criteria and updates are therefore not discussed here, but are provided in Parts II and III for habitats and species, respectively. Since 1991 the Joint Nature Conservation Committee (JNCC) has been the focus for the production and revision of the guidelines, which can be viewed on the following JNCC webpage: http://www.jncc.gov.uk/Publications/sssi/sssi_content.htm.

As described previously, the condition of SSSIs in the UK is monitored under a Common Standards Monitoring (CSM) framework agreed between the UK statutory conservation agencies and the JNCC (JNCC, 1998). The key element of CSM is that the condition of each site is assessed with respect to site-specific conservation objectives for the interest feature(s) for which the site was notified or, in the case of SPAs, cSACs (Natura 2000 sites) and Ramsar sites, the features for which the site was designated.

3.7.9 Local Nature Reserves

A local authority can declare a site that it owns, leases or of which it controls the management as a Local Nature Reserve (LNR) under Section 21 of the National Parks and Access to the Countryside Act 1949. Sites are of local interest but not necessarily national interest. Under the Act local authorities have the power to issue bylaws to protect their LNRs; although there is no obligation to manage an LNR to any set standard, management agreements are often put in place.

3.7.10 Wildlife Sites

In an attempt to give further protection to wildlife, particularly at a local level, the Wildlife Trusts and others have designated a series of some 40 000 Wildlife Sites[5] across Britain over the past 25 years (Everitt et al., 2002). The designation of Wildlife Sites complements the protection afforded by statutory sites (SSSIs), primarily by identifying other areas that have substantive wildlife interest and therefore merit some form of protection. They may also play an important role in protecting and enhancing the value of SSSIs, by maintaining wildlife corridors (and thereby linking sites) and by providing buffer areas (which may reduce impacts on SSSIs).

The *Wildlife Sites Handbook* (The Wildlife Trusts, 1997) states that:

Wildlife Sites, identified by locally-developed criteria, are the most important places for wildlife outside legally protected land such as SSSIs and ASSIs.

The DETR Local Sites Review Group defined the purpose of Wildlife Sites[6] in March 2000 as follows:

The series of non-statutory Wildlife Sites seek to ensure, in the public interest, the conservation, maintenance and enhancement of species, habitats, geological and geomorphological

---

[5] The term 'Wildlife Sites' is used here in accordance with national recommendations of the Wildlife Trusts and equates to County Wildlife Sites, Local Wildlife Sites, Sites of County Biological Importance, Sites of Nature Conservation Importance (SINCs) and other similar terms.

[6] Originally referred to as Local Sites by the Group.

features of substantive nature conservation value. Wildlife Site systems should select all areas of substantive value including both the most important and the most distinctive species, habitats, geological and geomorphological features within a national, regional and local context. Sites within the series may also have an important role in contributing to the public enjoyment of nature conservation.

Wildlife Sites are seen as complementary to SSSIs, while differing in two key respects.

- Wildlife Sites are not statutorily designated, but many receive statutory protection through the planning system.
- The Wildlife Site system aims to select all sites that meet the given selection criteria, not just a sample of these sites.

It has been recognised by the Wildlife Trusts and DETR (now DEFRA) that a wide range of approaches and criteria have been used to identify Wildlife Sites. For example, an assessment of Wildlife Site identification systems found that although some 68% used quantifiable written criteria, 7% selected sites on professional judgements alone (Everitt *et al.*, 2002). In most cases Wildlife Site criteria are based on the Ratcliffe (1977) criteria, or in some cases adapted SSSI criteria (NCC, 1989). These criteria are typically used to review habitat types in each county and to identify those that are of substantive value and require conservation. Criteria are then listed which define habitat types that qualify as Wildlife Sites. These may be very simple, e.g. 'semi-improved grasslands which retain a significant element of unimproved grassland'. However, most criteria provide some form of quantity threshold for each habitat, sometimes in relation to NVC communities, e.g. 'neutral grasslands supporting good examples of at least 0.2 ha in size (either in a block or as a number of smaller areas) of one of the following NVC communities: (i) MG4 (Meadow Foxtail – Great Burnet flood meadow); (ii) MG5 (Crested Dog's-tail – Common Knapweed meadow and pasture)'.

However, one of the limitations of such criteria is that they do not define 'significant elements' or 'good examples', and this can lead to inconsistencies in designation and difficulties with recording justifications for designation. More sophisticated criteria therefore also define quality thresholds for

habitats. This is often by setting a threshold for richness of listed indicator species (i.e. characteristic species of the habitat that are associated with habitats that are considered to be of high ecological quality). Some criteria systems allocate scores to the indicator species to reflect the quality of the habitat with which they are associated, and/or the conservation importance of the indicator species. However, it is not always clear how these scores are set. Habitat quality may also be defined by physical or chemical properties or features, such as water quality, or the presence of riffle and pool systems on rivers. The advantage of using such criteria is that they can be applied where comprehensive species data are unavailable. However, they are indirect measures of wildlife value and should therefore be based on good scientific evidence of associations between the features and biodiversity value.

Species-based criteria for Wildlife Sites tend to be simpler, with sites qualifying if they are species-rich, or if they hold viable or significant populations of particular species of conservation importance, sometimes referred to as notable species. Such notable species typically include species that are protected under the Wildlife & Countryside Act, the Wild Birds Directive or the Habitats Directive, or listed as a UK BAP Priority species, or nationally rare, or scarce or rare at a county level.

Evaluations of particular sites with respect to county Wildlife Site standards need to be made in relation to the specific criteria for the county in question. These can normally be readily obtained from the appropriate Wildlife Trust.

3.8 SITE EVALUATIONS FOR MANAGEMENT PLANNING

An ecological evaluation is usually an essential component of any site management plan, as this identifies, or confirms (if a prior evaluation was conducted), the VECs, or features of interest, that are present and assesses their overall importance. This assessment forms the basis for setting the overall objectives for the site and conservation objectives for each feature, the most important function of the management planning process. As stated in the Ramsar Management Planning Guidelines:

It is essential that management objectives be defined for each important feature of the ecological character of the site and for all other important features related to the functions and values of the site, including socio-economic, cultural and educational values. In other words, those responsible for developing the management plan must be clear about what they are trying to achieve.

A variety of formats and structures have been developed and adopted for site management planning purposes, but many of these are similar and recommend the Ratcliffe (1977) criteria as a basis for evaluations, e.g. Ramsar Management Planning Guidelines (Ramsar Bureau, 2002), the RSPB (Hirons et al., 1995) and the Countryside Council for Wales (CCW, 1996). Further information on ecological evaluations for management planning is provided in these publications.

3.9 SITE EVALUATIONS FOR ENVIRONMENTAL IMPACT ASSESSMENTS (EIAs)

Biodiversity evaluations for an EIA can be considered to have two purposes. The first is to establish whether a proposed development will have any legal biodiversity protection requirements. This requirement applies to all developments that could affect legally protected sites (e.g. SSSIs), habitats (e.g. ancient hedgerows), species (i.e. those protected under the Wildlife & Countryside Act), or other biological features (e.g. individual trees), irrespective of the size, scale or location of the development. It is also worth noting that legal protection does not necessarily reflect biodiversity value (e.g. Badgers *Meles meles* under the 1992 Protection of Badgers Act, Foxes *Vulpes vulpes* and other mammals under the Wild Mammals Protection Act, trees protected under Tree Preservation Orders and hedges protected under the Hedgerow Regulations 1997).

With respect to legal protection of species, the EIA must set out what steps will be taken to ensure that the law is not contravened. In this sense, the results of the assessment must be 'absolute': there is no requirement for an assessment of the degree

of significance of the impact on these species. The protection afforded to legally designated sites is in some cases specified with respect to ecological impacts (e.g. SACs). In these instances, legal and other guidance should be followed to determine whether a proposal will cause any contravention of legal status or protection, or have a significant effect on the integrity of a system, resource or feature. However, more often the requirements relating to legally protected sites are not so clear-cut, as the law enables decision-makers to permit development on such sites if a good case can be made or where impacts can be successfully mitigated or compensated. To inform this decision-making process, it is therefore necessary to demonstrate the degree of significance of impacts.

The second purpose is to identify, document and quantify as far as possible all potentially valuable ecological components (VECs) that may be affected by the development. VECs should include those that may be affected by off-site impacts such as those from emissions or effluents, waste material dumping, production of material to be used on site, road construction, water supplies and building material. Thus it is essential that all species of conservation concern (see Section 3.5), important habitats (3.6), designated sites (3.7) and other potential VECs are identified within an appropriate zone of potential impact for the species or habitat in question. For example, a zone of impact for an area of heathland that may suffer from atmospheric pollution from a proposed road development may be much larger than, and entirely separate from, the road footprint.

Potential impacts should first be identified as part of a scoping exercise, involving consultations with interested parties (e.g. statutory conservation agencies and local conservation NGOs), interrogating biological records centres, an appraisal of existing information and a preliminary site visit by experienced ecologists to identify the main habitats and species groups that are present. This should then be followed up by full surveys of appropriate groups to verify and quantify as necessary the presence of VECs identified in the scoping exercise. Further information on these aspects of the EIA process can be found in PPG9, the UK government's planning policy guidance on nature conservation currently being reviewed as Strategic Planning Guidance (www.defra.gov.uk).

3.9.1   EIA evaluation criteria

The collected information on each valued ecological component within its potential impact zone is then typically assessed against a range of biodiversity evaluation criteria, such as the Nature Conservation Review (Ratcliffe, 1977) criteria described above (see Section 3.6.3). However, a wide range of approaches and criteria have been developed and used, some of which are reviewed by English Nature (1994), DoE (1995b), Treweek (1999) and Byron (2000).

One important strategic-level appraisal framework in the UK is contained within the *New Approach to Appraisal* (NATA) developed by the Department for Transport and the Regions (DETR, 1998). This was initially formulated to provide a clear and open framework for the appraisal and prioritisation of trunk road investment proposals. Subsequently the NATA approach has been further developed into *Guidance on the Methodology for Multi-Modal Studies* (GOMMMS) for use in general transport planning (DETR, 2000). The GOMMMS approach continues to be seen by the Department for Transport as the primary source of guidance for the development and appraisal of strategies and plans for surface transport. In 2003 the advice originally set out in GOMMMS and its key supporting documents was fully incorporated into the Transport Analysis Guidance (TAG) website (www.webtag.org.uk).

The approach has four stages:

- Stage 1: Describing biodiversity features.
- Stage 2: Appraisal of environmental capital.
- Stage 3: Appraisal of the proposal's impact.
- Stage 4: Derivation of an overall assessment score: large/moderate/slight beneficial and adverse, neutral.

The appraisal stage (2) uses the concept of defining environmental capital, which has been developed by the statutory environmental bodies (Countryside Agency, English Nature, English Heritage and the Environment Agency) in

co-operation with the Department for Transport. This approach is used to assess which biodiversity VECs (termed 'features' in GOMMMS) matter, why they are important now and how that may change over time in the absence of the proposal. This provides a base level of environmental capital against which the impact of the proposal on that level of capital can be appraised. VECs are categorized according to five levels of value: negligible, lower, medium, high and very high. However, interpretation of these categories is difficult as the assessment criteria are not clearly explained. Furthermore, there are insufficient categories to allow for distinction of biodiversity components of regional or local values. This results in rather subjective broad-brush assessments that can be acceptable for initial strategic assessments but are inappropriate for EIAs.

Nevertheless, the approach can be used as a basis for a more detailed and clearly defined assessment framework, as for example outlined in Table 3.5, where VECs are classified into six categories from Parish/Neighbourhood Importance to International Importance. As with the application of other frameworks, where a VEC can be valued at a number of levels, the highest value should be used.

Use of this framework will unavoidably require some decisions to be made by judgement, for example on what constitutes a viable area of habitat and significant populations etc. These decisions should be made by informed expert judgement, based on the best available data and in close consultation with statutory conservation bodies and other relevant consultees. Further guidance may also be obtained from The Institute of Ecology and Environmental Management (IEEM) guidelines for ecological assessment (www.ieem.org.uk) (currently under revision at time of going to press).

It is also important to note that a distinction needs to be made between significant and important populations or habitat areas. Significant populations relate to species that are in some way threatened or otherwise of conservation importance and that are substantial enough to warrant conservation. For example, six pairs of Hen Harrier *Circus cyaneus* would be significant, but six pairs of a common and widespread species such as Song Thrush would not; both of these species are Red

Table 3.5. *A potential framework for defining the ecological value of Valued Ecosystem Components (VECs)*

Level of value	Examples of qualifying VECs
International	• Valuable biological features within sites of international importance, i.e. World Heritage Sites, Biosphere Reserves and Biogenetic Reserves. • Designated or qualifying features within a Ramsar site or site of EU importance, i.e. designated or candidate Natura 2000 site (SAC or SPA), or features that qualify an area for such designations. • Internationally significant and viable areas of a habitat type listed in Annex I of the Habitats Directive. • Regularly occurring globally threatened species (i.e. IUCN Red Listed) or species listed on Annex I of the Bonn Convention. • Internationally important populations of a species (e.g. more than 1% of a flyway population of birds). • Nationally significant populations of an internationally important species (i.e. listed on Annex II of the Habitats Directive, or Annex I of the Birds Directive, or with an unfavourable status in Europe). • Regularly occurring populations of internationally important species that are threatened or rare in the UK or of uncertain conservation status.
National	• Designated or qualifying features within nationally designated sites (SSSIs, ASSIs, NNRs, Marine Nature Reserves), or features that meet the published selection criteria for national designation. • Nationally significant and viable areas of UK BAP Priority Habitats identified as requiring site protection (see HAPs). • Nationally important populations of a species (e.g more than 1% of national population for birds). • Significant populations of nationally important species, i.e. listed on Schedules 5 and 8 of the 1981 Wildlife & Countryside Act (as amended) and UK Red Data Book species (excluding scarce species) or, if not a non-Red Data Book species, listed as occurring in 15 or fewer 10 km squares in the UK. • UK BAP Priority Species requiring protection of all nationally important sites. • Any regularly occurring population of a nationally important species that is threatened or rare in the region or county.
Regional (i.e. government regions)	• Regionally significant and viable areas of key habitat identified in a Regional BAP. • Regionally significant and viable areas of key habitat identified as being of regional value in the appropriate English Nature Natural Area. • Regionally important populations of a species. • Significant populations of a regionally important species. • Regularly occurring, locally significant populations of species listed as being nationally scarce (i.e. which occur in 16–100 10 km squares in the UK), or in a Regional BAP or relevant Natural Area on account of their regional rarity or localisation.

Table 3.5. (*cont*)

Level of value	Examples of qualifying VECs
County/ Metropolitan	• Designated or qualifying features within Local Nature Reserves or Wildlife Sites, selected on county/metropolitan criteria, or features that meet the published selection criteria for designation. • Semi-natural ancient woodland greater than 0.25 ha in area. • Significant and viable areas of habitat identified in County BAPs as requiring site protection. • Species populations of county/metropolitan importance. • Significant populations of a county/metropolitan important species (i.e. listed in a County/Metropolitan Red Data Book or BAP on account of their regional rarity or localisation).
• **District/Borough**	• Biological features within Local Nature Reserves, etc., selected on District/Borough ecological criteria. • Areas of habitat identified in a sub-County (District/Borough) BAP or in the relevant Natural Area profile, and other features that are scarce within the District/Borough or that appreciably enrich the District/Borough habitat resource. • Diverse and/or ecologically valuable hedgerow networks. • Semi-natural ancient woodland smaller than 0.25 ha in area. • Species populations of District/Borough importance. • Significant populations of a District/Borough important species (i.e. listed in a local BAP on account of their local rarity or localisation).
Parish/Neighbourhood	Areas of habitat considered to appreciably enrich the habitat resource within the context of the Parish or Neighbourhood, e.g. species-rich hedgerows. Valuable biological features within Local Nature Reserves selected on Parish ecological criteria.

Source: Based on draft IEEM guidelines for EIAs, currently under review at the time of going to press.
Notes: See Section 3.7 for details on designations.
The **viability** of an area of habitat is defined by NCC (1989), paragraph 2.10.3, as 'Given that the intrinsic vegetational quality of the habitat is acceptable, its area must be big enough to be viable, in respect of the resistance of the habitat and its flora and fauna to edge effects, loss of species and colonisation by unwanted species.'
Unless defined in appropriate publications, **significant** numbers of species or habitat areas (internationally, nationally, etc.) should be agreed in consultation with statutory conservation agencies and other relevant consultees.

Listed in the UK (Gregory *et al.*, 2002). Important populations are those that are sufficiently abundant to warrant conservation irrespective of the conservation status of the species in question (e.g. a wintering population of Tufted Duck *Aythya fuligula* that is more than 1% of its flyway population).

Care should also be taken in assessing the importance of individual sites for species, particularly with regard to widespread Red List and BAP listed species.

Box 3.1 An evaluation of Valued Ecosystem Components (VECs) potentially affected by a hypothetical development

This example relates to the proposed development of a marina on an estuary in East Anglia, which may directly affect some 120 ha of mudflats, sand dunes, saltmarsh, mixed farmland and a small brackish lagoon. The development site partially overlaps with an SAC, SPA, SSSI and a County Wildlife Site. Example VECs are listed in the table (according to their highest ecological value), but for simplicity many are omitted, and VECs that may be affected by off-site impacts are not considered. HD, Habitats Directive; WBD, Wild Birds Directive.

Value (see Table 3.5)	Example VECs	Rationale
International	108 ha of estuary habitat	Designated SAC feature (HD Annex I habitat)
	80 ha mudflat	Qualifying SAC feature (HD Annex I habitat)
	22 ha Atlantic salt meadows (Glauco-Puccinellietalia maritimae)	Qualifying SAC feature (HD Annex I habitat)
	Important wintering population of Wigeon *Anas penelope* (>2% of NW European flyway population)	Designated SPA feature
	Petalwort *Petalophyllum ralfsii*	Qualifying SAC feature (Annex II species)
National	1.8 ha coastal lagoon	SSSI Notified feature (HD Annex I habitat, but not SAC qualifying feature)
	Nationally important wintering population of Lapwing *Vanellus vanellus*	Notified SSSI feature
	Small wintering population of Short-eared Owl *Asio fammeus*	WBD Annex I species, population not nationally significant, but species is regionally rare
	Stinking Goosefoot *Chenopodium vulvaria*	Schedule 8 of Wildlife and Countryside Act 1981 as amended 1988, Nationally vulnerable
Regional	Otter *Lutra lutra*: regular reports, population unknown	HD Annex II spp, but dispersed species and population not of international or national significance, but spp rare in East England
	Regular breeding population of Redshank *Tringa totanus*	Regionally significant population of Amber listed species (see Chapter 24)
	Small-flowered Catchfly *Silene gallica*	Nationally scarce, UK BAP priority species and County BAP species
County / Metropolitan	3 ha of mobile foredune and yellow dune	Small area of degraded dunes does not conform with HD Annex I habitats or SSSI criteria; qualifies as Wildlife Site (but not designated)

Value (see Table 3.5)	Example VECs	Rationale
	0.8 ha reedbed	County Wildlife Site feature
	Breeding Reed Bunting *Emberica schoeniceus*	UK BAP Priority Species and Red List species but dispersed and site protection not proposed in SAP. Listed as target species in County BAP
	Sharp Rush *Juncus acutus*	Nationally scarce, locally rare and diminishing
Parish	200 m of ancient hedgerow, with some mature oaks	Rare habitat in parish
	Farm pond	Artificial pond, but frog spawning site. Would be an issue if lost and contained Great Crested Newt
	Breeding Linnet *Carduelis cannabina*	UK BAP Priority species and Red List species but dispersed and site protection not proposed in SAP. Only breeding colony in parish

It is inappropriate to give all UK BAP Priority Species a 'national' level of importance within EIA evaluations. Instead, evaluation levels should be dependent on the 'Policy and Legislation' and 'Site Safeguard' measures that are given in the BAP or corresponding Species Action Plan (SAP) for the species in question. Thus, species for which the national SAP recommends the safeguard of all sites are afforded national importance. The level of importance that is attached to other species should then reflect the recommendations in sub-national BAPs. For example, if a regional BAP identifies a requirement to protect all populations of a particular species (where there is no similar recommendation in the UK BAP) each population should be considered to be of regional importance. Similarly, if a sub-national BAP identifies the need to protect all populations above a certain size, these populations should be considered to be of importance at the relevant scale.

Some example evaluations of VECs according to the framework and categories outlined in Table 3.5 are presented in Box 3.1 for a hypothetical site.

Part II • Habitats

4 • Introduction to habitat evaluation

4.1 HOW TO USE THE *HANDBOOK*: A RECAP

Part II of the *Handbook* is intended as a general-purpose source of detailed, practical information on study design, sampling and analysis as well as on the most commonly used methods for surveying and monitoring terrestrial and freshwater habitats.

The development and successful implementation of a survey and monitoring programme involves making a series of crucial decisions. Part II of the *Handbook* is therefore designed to provide a step-by-step guide through the process of planning and executing a survey and monitoring programme. However, the design and implementation of a programme is not a linear process, but often involves iterative steps that depend on the outcome of other decisions. Because monitoring is largely defined by a series of surveys, the term 'survey' is usually also implied where the term 'monitoring' is used throughout this *Handbook*. The main topics covered in Part II are listed below.

4.2 HABITAT SURVEY AND MONITORING

This chapter identifies the attributes of major habitat types that provide an indication of their condition. These should be the focus of habitat condition monitoring programmes. For each habitat a summary table lists these attributes and provides cross-references to descriptions of the recommended methods for monitoring them (provided in Chapter 5). Reference should also be made to generic guidelines on defining Condition Objectives for statutory sites that are being developed by the UK conservation agencies (visit their websites for latest information). Condition monitoring has gained acceptance as a cost-effective way of assessing the quality of designated sites. Depending on the objectives of the study, the range of methods described in this chapter will be useful for different situations.

Chapter 5 provides detailed information on the most commonly used habitat survey and monitoring methods. Qualitative as well as quantitative methods are included to cover situations in which resources are limited or sophisticated methods are unnecessary. The descriptions also aim to provide sufficient practical information for most of the techniques to be applied in the field. More specialised techniques are summarised and key sources of further information listed. Specialised monitoring techniques carried out in collaboration with other bodies are also summarised and the reader is referred to appropriate specialist documentation.

Each section on methods, dealt with fully in Chapter 6, starts with a table summarising the information covered in that section. The following points are considered:

- the recommended uses of the method;
- the efficiency of the method, i.e. the combined quantity and quality of data produced in relation to cost and effort;
- the objectivity of the method;
- the precision obtainable;
- the likely nature of any inherent bias;
- the expertise and equipment required;
- field methods; and
- data storage and analysis.

Chapter 7 briefly describes monitoring methods for management practices (such as grazing and burning) and other environmental processes, such

Topic		Where to find it	
		Part	**Chapter or Section**
Planning a monitoring programme	General monitoring theory	I	1.1
	Setting objectives for monitoring	I	2.1
	Selection of monitoring methods	I	2.2
	Designing a sampling strategy	I	2.3
	Reviewing a monitoring programme	I	2.4
	Data recording and storage	I	2.5
	Data analysis	I	2.6
Habitat monitoring	Attributes of major habitat types	II	5
	Habitat monitoring methods	II	6
	Management monitoring methods	II	7
Species monitoring	General species monitoring theory	III	10
	Species attributes and monitoring methods	III	11–26

as erosion, all of which may influence the features of interest on a site. It is important that monitoring programmes, where necessary, include monitoring of management practices; although it is beyond the scope of this *Handbook* to deal with these in detail, further sources of information on these subjects are listed.

When using this *Handbook* as a guide for selecting habitat monitoring methods and designing sampling schemes, the reader should first look up the habitat type that is to be monitored in Chapter 5. The habitat tables in each of the sections in that chapter list the appropriate methods for monitoring each attribute of the habitat. Consult the relevant sections in Chapter 6, and then return to Part I to follow the remaining steps for designing a monitoring programme and sampling scheme (if the appropriate method requires it).

5 • Habitat requirements and issues

The primary purpose of this section is to identify, for each broad habitat type, the potential attributes that indicate the condition of the habitat and to recommend methods that may be used for monitoring each of these. These recommended methods are described individually in Chapter 6, or in Part III (species) for methods that are more often applicable to surveying and monitoring individual species. The section also identifies key management actions and other environmental factors that may have impacts on the habitat and may therefore require monitoring. Finally, any specific monitoring issues (e.g. practical implementation, health and safety and the frequency of monitoring) that may influence the design of a survey or monitoring programme in the habitat are briefly described. Habitats have been divided according to UK Biodiversity Action Plan (BAP) Broad Habitat types. Based on structural similarities the methods can be applied to the full range of habitat types found in Europe and, indeed, other parts of the world.

Within the UK, JNCC have recently published online guidelines on Common Standards Monitoring. This provides guidance on setting and assessing conservation objectives for the range of species and habitat features which occur on UK protected sites. The process is now well advanced, with guidance available on conservation objectives and assessment methodologies for about 75% of the features of designated sites. At the time of writing, guidance was available for coastal, lowland grassland, lowland heathland, upland and woodland habitat features. Guidance on lowland wetlands and freshwater habitats is being developed.

These guidelines are available online at www.jncc.gov.uk/csm/guidance/default.htmintroductory and should be consulted when devising monitoring programmes for habitats on designated sites, as there may be additional attributes that require monitoring listed in the JNCC guidelines which are not covered in the habitats sections in this *Handbook*.

5.1 WOODLAND AND SCRUB

5.1.1 Survey and monitoring requirements and methods

Attributes for assessing habitat condition

Woodlands can exist under a great range of environmental conditions, from tree line to floodplain, on virtually all soil and rock types, from dry rock outcrops to permanently waterlogged marshland, and from coastal dunes to inland mesic loams. Inevitably, when presenting guidance for the full range of woodland types, there will be a large number of methodologies, some of which will be required in only one woodland type.

Woodlands also vary greatly in structure. Although they are generally defined by the prevalence of trees, the trees can vary in stature and degree of cover. For example, acid oak woodland may occur as tree-line scrub, and coastal scrub woodland may be no taller than a person; on the other hand, towering groves of single-stemmed trees, spreading pollards from old parkland and multi-stemmed coppices growing out from past felling are all included in the term 'woodlands'. Furthermore, the aims of treatment vary within any one structure, so that, for example, a formerly coppiced stand may be re-coppiced, allowed to grow naturally, or converted to wood-pasture. The attributes that should be monitored within one particular structure may not be appropriate for another. The implications of what is observed will vary according to management intentions.

Change within woodland varies in kind, spatial scale and timescale. It can be broadly classified as follows:

1. Natural expression of the growth, mortality and regeneration of trees and shrubs, which changes stand structure and composition and influences other components of the woodland. This is usually measurable over decades: *significant* trends are rarely detectable in less than 10 years.
2. Disturbances created by natural forces or by managers. These may be abrupt events (e.g. fire, blow-down, felling) or slow changes (e.g. as a result of drought, change in deer culling regime), the effects of which will require monitoring over many years.
3. Responses by ground vegetation (open-space vegetation and field layer under trees) to 1 and 2, combined with the internal dynamics of these assemblages. Response rates, and thus monitoring frequencies, vary according to the character of the changes to which the assemblages are responding.
4. Responses of fauna to 1–3; internal dynamics of animal species and interactions; direct influences on fauna, e.g. by pest management or deer hunting. Rapid changes from year to year are characteristic, especially of small animals. Monitoring should be an annual process, but the problem is to distinguish between long-term trends and short-term fluctuations.
5. Changes in site condition as a consequence of (i) 1–4; (ii) physical processes acting directly, and thus factors in 1–4; (iii) long-term maturation, e.g. of soils; and (iv) pollution uptake.

Recently proposed monitoring frameworks for woodland habitats (Kirby, 1994; Kupiec, 1997) accept that anything more than a quick site inspection by an experienced observer is time-consuming and thus expensive. In practice, monitoring in woodlands is a choice of strategies:

- Recording events (i.e. abrupt changes in the status quo) when they occur, with their immediate consequences. The record forms a basis for assessing change at a later date.

- Subjective observations by an experienced observer, interpreted in terms of trends and factors. For example, the adequacy of regeneration can be assessed in a single, short visit by an observer, who can make experienced judgements on the opportunities for, and state of, present regeneration, and on its future prospects. The results are not normally valid statistically, but assessments are immediate, are useful for management planning, and help to identify issues for more detailed investigation.
- Detailed, precise observation, which enables any change to be quantified and validated by statistical tests. This requires careful design, long-term data storage and a capacity to analyse the data. It thus requires substantial resources and effort, and must be carried out to a high standard.

The principal questions for most woodland stand monitoring are (i) is it regenerating? (ii) is it changing in composition? and (iii) is it changing in structure? Of these, regeneration is both the most difficult question to answer and the question most often asked. Woods must regenerate to persist, but regeneration is often patchy and episodic. Woods have survived even where regeneration has been absent from much of the wood for much of the time. The more pertinent issue is whether a wood is regenerating when it should, i.e. when it would do so naturally, or should do so under management.

Recognising when adequate regeneration is taking place is also problematical. The presence of seedlings and saplings does not guarantee that there will be recruitment to the canopy. The presence of a thicket of saplings may be no more effective in the long term than a sparse scatter: there is only so much room for canopy trees. On average, one large oak needs to generate only one other large oak in 300–500 years to sustain the species and the wood. Even in natural woods, the regeneration of a particular species is likely to be extremely irregular in space and time.

Against this background the critical question is: are enough individual saplings of the right mix of species developing beyond the reach of grazing and browsing when and where circumstances are right for regeneration? 'Right' for canopy trees would be defined by availability of canopy space, plus an 'extension' to cover advance regeneration of shade-bearing species. 'Right' for structure would be defined by cover and stratification that normally allows enough light through to permit an understorey to develop.

Regeneration relates to the continued existence and future character of the woodland. Other attributes relate to its condition.

A description of attributes indicating the condition of woodland and scrub habitats is presented below and summarised in Table 5.1.

Shape and size

Shape and size is a particular issue for upland woodland types, floodplain woodland and bog woodland. It is rarely an issue in lowland woods, where most boundaries are sharply defined and static, but may be significant where the wood abuts semi-natural non-woodland habitats. Defining what counts as woodland is problematical in wood-pasture and regenerating woodland.

Monitoring requires delimitation of the woodland boundary. This is generally straightforward in high-definition lowland farmland, but often difficult in upland pastoral environments. Delimiting woodland requires a decision on the minimum size of feature to be heeded (a fractal issue). Even on rapidly changing boundaries, repeating observations at intervals of 10 years would be sufficient from the point of view of the woodland.

Soil

Forest soils change naturally, but profile development is usually very slow. Erosion is rarely severe, and soil creep on slopes is very slow. Rapid change occurs very locally when trees fall over. A change in the dominant trees and shrubs may also change humus characteristics. Forest operations can also change soils. When drainage ditches are dug, profile character and microtopography are altered in the immediate vicinity. Felling and extraction can alter natural microtopography and mobilise soil nutrients.

Pollution inputs are likely to be the major concern at the present time. Throughout Europe there is concern about acid rain, nitrate deposition and

the lateral spread of fertilisers from nearby fields through drift and leaching.

Measurement of natural changes would be extremely laborious, and would certainly not be cost-effective. Measurement of most soil changes due to forestry operations is best done directly, e.g. flow in drainage ditches, extent of rutting and distribution of surface disturbance during forestry operations. Measurement of change in nutrient status due to pollution inputs or forestry operations can be achieved by:

1. repeated samples from the same points (i.e. the equivalent of permanent plots); and
2. analysis of chemicals in run-off.

Of these, the latter is expensive but offers the possibility of constructing nutrient budgets. The former should be far less expensive, especially if the initial observations are repeated only when there is a need to know.

Observations of change due to forest operations should be made before and after operations. Baseline soil nutrient observations should be repeated on a need-to-know basis, but there is a case for repeating them after 25 years, even if no particular need has arisen in the meantime.

Hydrology

This is particularly important for floodplain woodland and bog woodland, but it can also be an issue in any wood where streams, flushing zones and water tables influence condition. Monitoring needs differ greatly between woodland types.

In floodplain woodland, channel configuration can be tracked by a combination of aerial photographs and on-site observation of areas of erosion and deposition. Location of bank erosion and shoal deposition can be noted annually on site maps. The flooding regime is best followed from flow records of river managers, combined with on-site observation of main floods. The assessment of water quality would also normally depend on information from river managers (see Section 5.10). In bog woodland, the need is to assess water table fluctuation and water quality.

In most woods there is a need to monitor any streams and springs that may be present. In some

Table 5.1. *A summary of the quality attributes providing an indication of the condition of woodland habitats, and their recommended monitoring techniques*

Attribute	Habitat properties	Monitoring technique
Size and shape	Area of individual wood and configuration of boundaries	Aerial photographs (Section 6.1.3) Phase I mapping (6.1.5) Comparison with historical maps (not described)
Soil	Structure Nutrient status	Soil cores (6.2.2) Chemical analysis (not covered) or run-off chemistry (not covered)
Hydrology	Watercourse configuration Flooding regime Water chemistry Water table fluctuations	Mapping River flow data/visual inspection Chemical analysis (not covered) Dipwells (6.2.1)
Composition	Stand pattern in managed forests: • extent of old, mid- and young growth • extent and configuration of felling patches and canopy gaps • rotation of managed stands • stock of particular size classes • thinning extent and degree	Stock mapping (6.5.1): covers all aspects of stand pattern monitoring
	Communities	Quadrats (6.4.2) or transects (6.4.6), with NVC analysis (6.1.6) where NVC communities are Notified Features or important attributes
	Species composition, richness and diversity	Species lists Temporary plots (6.5.3) Plotless sampling (6.5.4)
Structure	Age class diversity Horizontal and vertical structural diversity Retentions to natural death Thinning extent and degree	Enumeration by permanent plots (6.5.2), temporary plots (6.5.3), plotless sampling (6.5.4), mapping individual trees (Part III, Section 15.2.4)
	Deadwood: standing and fallen • volume • size distribution • spatial pattern	Enumeration (see above), measurement of fallen wood and decay condition (6.5.5)
Dynamics	Open spaces • Extent and location	Stock maps (6.5.1) Fixed-point photography (6.1.4) Aerial photography (6.1.3)

Table 5.1. (*cont.*)

Attribute	Habitat properties	Monitoring technique
	Seedling regeneration; composition, number and distribution Renewal of coppice stools Amount and distribution of planting Provenance of planted stock and natural regeneration	Enumeration (see above) Ground vegetation condition (6.4)

forms of wet woodland (e.g. alder woods) the water table is another important factor. One can also envisage the degree of flushing in slope woods becoming an issue, but it rarely if ever arises.

An annual check of springs and watercourses should be sufficient to alert managers to significant changes, supplemented by checks after extremely wet periods (or major floods) and after severe droughts. More detailed hydrological monitoring is, however, more difficult (see Section 6.2.1).

Stand extent and structure

This is the core of forest monitoring, and in forests managed for timber production this links standard forestry monitoring with environmental monitoring. In such cases, two classes of observations are normally required:

1. stock maps (Section 6.5.1), which show the patchwork of stands; and
2. enumerations of trees and shrubs (Sections 6.4 and 6.5), which show composition and stand structure.

Stock maps partition the stands according to age of canopy and main species, show felling coupes, and give information on patch size and configuration. They are simplifications that convey whole-site structure and work well in woods managed on a moderate- to large-scale felling pattern and with coupe shapes. They show little or nothing of vertical stand structure, or of fine detail.

Enumerations of individual trees and shrubs give information on size-class distributions, stand composition and how these are related. It is by this

method that recent recruitment can be assessed and prospective long-term changes in stand composition picked up. Here, too, past irregularities in recruitment can be identified, subject to the limitation that only the survivors provide information. Enumerations also provide an opportunity to record the condition of individual trees, e.g. crown vigour, degree of damage by squirrels, etc.

The pattern of sampling determines what information can be gathered on distributions of species and size classes. A regular grid of plots can give distribution information. Plotless sampling (Section 6.5.4) does not, but it can be more refined if samples are confined to units recognised on stock maps. Transects (Section 6.4.6) give information on small-scale patterns, such as groups and zonation. Plots and transects can be used to map canopy gaps; aerial photographs can also be used.

Rare features, e.g. pollard trees or large coppice stools, are best mapped individually.

Photographs record a great deal of detail in a non-quantitative and unedited fashion. They are best for giving a general impression of change, demonstrating change to others and monitoring features that were not initially thought to be important. Fixed-point photographs (Section 6.1.4) can be a cheap but effective method of revealing the main features of long-term change, provided that enough care is taken to select a representative set of points and to record location and conditions accurately.

Changes can be identified by repeating an observation. Permanent plots and transects have to be marked and re-found. In return for the extra effort involved, they can provide detailed insights into stand dynamics, population changes and the fate of individual trees. Repeated enumerations in temporary plots give information on net change, but the fate of individuals is not known; this restricts the analysis of factors underlying change. However, it is not essential to have permanent plots unless it is necessary to track the progress of individual trees. A well-structured temporary sample will generally be sufficient to monitor the progress of a population.

In a managed semi-natural woodland it may be sufficient to generate a stock map. Rare and special features can be mapped on to a stock map base. Age-class distribution can be expressed in terms of areas. If particular species are dominant in parts of a wood, age class can also be expressed in terms of species. Patch size and shape can be measured from maps. This approach is appropriate in woods in which:

1. felling is done in well-defined patches; and
2. operations within a patch are relatively simple, such as clear-cut felling.

In semi-natural woods managed on an irregular basis, e.g. group felling or irregular thinning without clear felling, enumerations should form the basis of monitoring. Likewise, in non-intervention woodland, it will be necessary to enumerate and/or record permanent or temporary plots. Canopy gaps should be defined and delimited.

Monitoring dead wood is important, especially because of its biodiversity value to fungi, invertebrates, birds, etc. Dead wood can be partly recorded in ordinary enumerations, i.e. snags and stumps. Other dead wood elements (e.g. fallen wood, dead branches on living trees, decay columns) have to be separately recorded. The transect method (Section 6.5.5) permits this for patches of 1 ha or more. A quicker alternative, based on indices for each dead wood element, is promising, but has not been adequately tested (Peterken, 1996). One can also map the categorical quantities of dead wood on a defined grid for the site.

Change in features recorded on stock maps (Section 6.5.1) is determined mainly by the plan of management, but catastrophic natural events may also intervene, and you cannot assume that the plan will be carried out to the letter. An annual record of management operations that affect the stock map (and major natural events) should be made, i.e. the stock map should be updated annually, and old stock maps should be retained as part of the record.

Change in stands is generally slow, but rapid change may occur unpredictably. In undisturbed stands general records need not be repeated at intervals of less than 10 years. When stand-changing events occur (e.g. windthrow, drought, disease), a record should be made immediately after the event. If such an event takes place, it would be advantageous to have observations shortly before the event, so routine observations should not be too far apart. The optimal interval would probably be routine general recording every 10 years, or thereabouts, combined with small subsampling at 5 year intervals and recording immediately after a major disturbance.

Regeneration

Seedlings and saplings are part of both the stand and the ground vegetation. They are considered separately because regeneration is a key indicator of the state of a wood.

Estimates of seedling density and distribution rarely provide useful information on the progress of regeneration. However, if regeneration of a particular species is failing, observation of seedlings may indicate whether the failure is in seed production or post-germination survival. In woods in which regeneration is not taking place, a seedling survey will indicate the potential. However, observations over several years will be necessary to allow for the 'mast year' phenomenon (years in which trees produce an unusually large volume of seed).

Estimates of the distribution and density of small saplings (less than 1.3 m in height) are far more meaningful. Saplings are established individuals that have the capacity to grow into trees, but almost all fail to become trees because they are killed by competition, browsing, breakage, drought, etc. It is quite possible for a substantial population of saplings to be permanently present, yet for no regeneration to be occurring, i.e. there is no recruitment to the canopy.

Large saplings (taller than 1.3 m) should be monitored as part of stand enumeration.

Permanent plots in which individual saplings are mapped allow the population dynamics of regeneration to be understood. It is possible to follow the fate of individuals (merely counting the number of seedlings present in a plot may conceal the fact that none of them lives longer than three years). The ability to find the remains of saplings that were recorded on a previous occasion commonly allows population turnover to be determined and the cause of death to be identified. This is only possible if monitoring occurs regularly. If more than 5 years elapse between samples, the chances are that the remains of saplings will not be visible.

Temporary plots and plotless sampling allow the density, composition and distribution of seedlings and saplings to be quantified, and to demonstrate changes from previous observations, but the interpretation of these observations may be equivocal. In general, if there is a need to observe small saplings (i.e. those missed by ordinary stand enumerations), it should be done by a method that allows the processes to be understood, i.e. by recording at the level of individuals in permanent plots.

If regeneration takes the form of regrowth from stumps, the simplest and most useful measure of any individual would be the height above ground of the tallest sprout. In many cases, such regrowth exceeds 1.3 m in the first or second season, and would thus be recorded as part of ordinary stand enumeration. In woods in which regeneration takes the form of planting, one assumes that the manager will keep a record of what is planted and where. If saplings are protected by tubes or sticks, it is simple to record their survival and growth.

If one is observing naturally regenerating individuals in permanent plots, observations should be at least annual. The optimum is probably two observations each year, at the start of the growing season and at its end.

Ground vegetation

Ground vegetation changes continually. In addition to the seasonal cycle, the small-scale pattern of species changes from year to year as individuals grow, spread, decay and die. Variations in soil moisture content due to periods of heavy rain or drought generate perpetual adjustments in the balance between species. Superimposed on these changes are responses to changes in the structure and composition of the stand, both natural and due to management.

The ground vegetation component of National Vegetation Classification (NVC) types may change (e.g. as a result of fire or grazing), but site characteristics are the main control. If a different tree species colonises the wood, there could be a change of NVC type without any change in the species composition of the ground flora. However, a map of NVC types has value in monitoring as a basis for stratifying sample points. Exact delineation of boundaries between types is not necessary to design the pattern of sampling, and will rarely be sufficiently exact to detect slight shifts in boundaries.

Change in ground vegetation diversity happens at various scales. Change is inevitable at the scale of $1 \, m^2$, and species turnover can be high in $10 \, m \times 10 \, m$ plots (more than 40% of species over 15–20 years). Change at larger scales is less, and change at the whole-site scale (i.e. colonisation and extinction) is rare. Any assessment of ground vegetation change must take account of scale.

Whole-site monitoring requires a species list for the site. This will include those localised species not detected in the aggregate of sample plots. The total number of species in all sample plots does, however, provide an alternative measure of whole-site species richness. Sample plots provide an opportunity to measure small-scale change and vegetation height, to map distributions, and to take fixed-point photographs. The capacity to map changes may be important if there is reason to suspect patchy change, e.g. due to lateral fertiliser drift.

Sample plot recording of ground flora is normally worth repeating at 10 year intervals, so that a reasonably recent record is available for comparisons when a substantial change is suspected, e.g. after change in grazing pressure.

Open spaces

These are the 'permanent' open spaces, i.e. mainly glades in upland woods and rides in lowland woods. For some species groups, the biodiversity of open spaces may exceed that of tree-covered ground. Most take the form of grassland and tall herb communities (Section 5.4). A map showing the exact configuration of 'permanent' open spaces is required as a baseline, which is part of – or a supplement to – the stock map. The degree of shading of rides and boundary characteristics should also be recorded.

Newly created permanent open spaces should be recorded as part of the annual updating of a stock map. Boundary conditions may be best recorded by fixed-point photography at 5 year intervals.

Management requirements and external impacts
Management and external impacts that require monitoring include forestry practices and natural disturbances, grazing and browsing intensity, fire, pollution (particularly atmospheric inputs) and public access and disturbance.

Forestry practices are typically monitored by stock maps. Stock maps can also record large-scale natural disturbances; small-scale impacts can be detected by routine enumerations. See Chapter 7 for more details on monitoring other impacts.

5.1.2   Specific issues affecting the monitoring of the habitat

Woodlands generally change slowly, but major rapid change can happen as a result of natural events, changes in grazing/browsing regimes, and forestry operations. Annual recording is very rarely justified, except at the level of an annual inspection. Rather, monitoring is most efficiently undertaken by:

1. establishing baselines; and
2. recording events.

Baselines describe the condition at a particular date. The record can be repeated when there is a need to assess change. Rigid adherence to a predetermined recording interval is rarely necessary. However, if the interval between recordings is large, there is an increased risk that no recent record will be available before a major change. For example, with a recording interval of 20 years,

there is a possibility that the most recent record of condition before a major blowdown (which is unpredictable) will be 19 years before the event. Accordingly, the best tactic is to repeat records at suitable intervals for each attribute, or after major events. Subsamples can be recorded between main recordings, or to determine whether a full re-recording is worthwhile.

Recording of ground vegetation should be undertaken in the growing season. Strong seasonal changes require that plots be recorded during a particular season. Lists should be compiled at two points in the season, to cover spring and summer aspects. Enumeration of stand condition is best avoided during the peak of the growing season (May to July). Winter recording is best for stand structure. Thus, there can be a degree of complementarity in the annual monitoring programme.

Compartmentalisation of monitoring may be desirable in larger and heterogeneous woods. Different monitoring programmes may be necessary in areas undergoing different treatments (i.e. in what foresters used to call working circles).

Care should be taken to ensure that the monitoring programme does not itself affect the condition of the wood. Recording of permanent plots (including transects) can damage vegetation and alter the browsing patterns of deer. Marker posts can influence both deer and forestry contractors.

5.2   LOWLAND WOOD-PASTURES AND PARKLAND

5.2.1   Survey and monitoring requirements and methods

Attributes for assessing habitat condition
Some wood-pastures require separate treatment from woodlands. Those that do are defined as consisting of an open scatter of trees in a matrix of pasture (i.e. parkland), and also include very open parts of mature woodlands (pine (*Pinus* spp.) woods, oak (*Quercus* spp.) woods and birch (*Betula* spp.) woods). Although many woodlands sustain such a high pressure of grazing and browsing that they may eventually become wood-pastures, they should be regarded as woodland for present purposes.

The trees in parklands are generally large and/or old. They are isolated from each other or distributed in small groups. Either way, the trees should be regarded as individuals and recorded as such. The ground vegetation can be regarded as grassland or heathland (see Sections 5.4 and 5.6, respectively). A description of attributes indicating the condition of wood-pasture and parkland habitats is presented below and summarised in Table 5.2.

Shape and size

The extent of parkland is extremely difficult to measure, principally because its boundaries are vague. Boundaries may be roughly delimited on a map, but a precise delimitation requires decisions on minimum density of trees and minimum mappable patch size. Change is better assessed in terms of individual trees. Patches of closed woodland within wood-pastures should be monitored as woodland.

Stands

The special feature of monitoring parkland is the treatment of the stand as a population of individual trees. Change can be quantified in terms of numbers and distribution of trees of a particular class. Each tree can be mapped and numbered, aided by a recent vertical aerial photograph (Section 6.1.3).

A baseline record of individual trees is required. This can be supplemented by photographs from recorded points of a sub-sample of trees (Section 6.1.4). The record will be a mixture of precise quantities (e.g. girth) and classes (e.g. crown condition).

Dead wood is commonly an important component. Most takes the form of decay columns and dead branches on living trees. A supplementary record of fallen dead wood and stumps is desirable, based on the transect method (Section 6.5.5).

Once a baseline is established there is rarely any justification for repeating monitoring assessments at less than 10 year intervals. A sub-sample of trees can be checked between main recordings.

Regeneration

Regeneration is commonly a critical issue in parklands. Unlike in woodland, however, regeneration is generally achieved by planting with protection from grazing, or by protecting naturally set saplings. Monitoring regeneration can thus be a matter of recording the survival of marked samples of individuals.

In open woodlands, which have effectively been pastures with trees for at least decades, the aim may be to regenerate woodland by removal of, or reduction in, grazing animals. The initial stages of this process can be successfully monitored by fixed quadrats or transects (Section 6.5.2).

An annual inspection is desirable, preferably at the end of the growing season, or before animals are admitted to pasture. Height and growth of important individuals may be worth recording annually but, as growth during each of the past 5 years or so can generally be assessed by inspection of individuals, any more general recording is only worthwhile at this interval. Likewise, an annual inspection is desirable during the early stages of restoration of grazed woodland.

Management requirements and external impacts

Management and external impacts that require monitoring are similar to those for woodland and scrub and include forestry practices and natural disturbances, grazing and browsing intensity, fire, pollution (particularly atmospheric inputs) and public access and disturbance. Disturbance caused by public access and grazing are often of particular concern in wood-pastures.

Forestry practices are typically monitored by stock maps. Stock maps can also record large-scale natural disturbances; small-scale impacts can be detected by routine enumerations. See Chapter 7 for more details on other impacts.

5.2.2   Specific issues affecting the monitoring of the habitat

The critical features of parklands are generally:

1. the mortality rate of existing trees, particularly the largest and oldest;
2. the amount and growth of recruitment;
3. the amount and condition of dead wood; and
4. the condition of ground vegetation.

The peculiar character of parklands emphasises the need for monitoring at the level of individual

Table 5.2. *A summary of the quality attributes providing an indication of the condition of wood-pasture habitats, and their recommended monitoring techniques*

Attribute	Habitat properties	Monitoring technique
Size and shape	Area of individual wood and configuration of boundaries	Aerial photographs (Section 6.1.3)
		Phase I mapping (6.1.5)
		Comparison with historical maps (not described)
Soil	Structure	Soil cores (6.2.2)
	Nutrient status	Chemical analysis (not covered) or run-off chemistry (not covered)
Hydrology	Watercourse configuration	Mapping
	Flooding regime	River flow data/visual inspection
	Water chemistry	Chemical analysis (not covered)
	Water table fluctuations	Dipwells (6.2.1)
Composition	Stand pattern in managed forests: • extent of old, mid- and young growth • extent and configuration of felling patches and canopy gaps • rotation of managed stands • stock of particular size classes • thinning extent and degree	Stock mapping (6.5.1): covers all aspects of stand pattern monitoring
	Communities	Quadrats (6.4.2) or transects (6.4.6), with NVC analysis (6.1.6) where NVC communities are Notified Features or important attributes
	Species composition, richness and diversity	Species lists Temporary plots (6.5.3) Plotless sampling (6.5.4)
Structure	Age class diversity Horizontal and vertical structural diversity Retentions to natural death Thinning extent and degree	Enumeration by permanent plots (6.5.2), temporary plots (6.5.3), plotless sampling (6.5.4), mapping individual trees (Part III, Section 15.2.4)
	Deadwood: standing and fallen • volume • size distribution • spatial pattern	Enumeration (see above); measurement of fallen wood and decay condition (6.5.5)
Dynamics	Open spaces Extent and location	Stock maps (6.5.1) Fixed-point photography (6.1.4) Aerial photography (6.1.3)
	Seedling regeneration; composition, number and distribution Renewal of coppice stools Amount and distribution of planting Provenance of planted stock and natural regeneration	Enumeration (see above) Ground vegetation condition (6.4)

trees. It also offers excellent opportunities for retrospective monitoring, by using old maps, ground photographs and aerial photographs.

5.3 FARMLAND BOUNDARY FEATURES

5.3.1 Survey and monitoring requirements and methods

Attributes for assessing habitat condition

Farmland and field boundaries commonly consist of fences, ditches, grassy banks, walls or hedges, or various combinations of these. Fences by themselves hold little of interest for biodiversity. However, the other features may be of considerable conservation importance and may be the prime source of biodiversity within artificial farmland landscapes.

Ditches may hold important aquatic, floating and emergent plants, invertebrates and amphibians, particularly where they occur alongside semi-natural farmland habitats and are unpolluted by fertilisers, manure or pesticides. They may also provide important feeding and breeding habitats for birds. Attributes used in assessing the condition of such habitats are water quality (in particular, avoidance of eutrophication), water quantity, ditch structure, vegetation structure and composition (i.e. avoidance of overgrazing or excessive cutting and dredging). Water quality attributes are covered in detail in Sections 5.9 and 5.10.

Where possible, water should be maintained in the ditch all year. If ditches regularly dry out, they have little value for aquatic plants and animals, although the ditch bed may contain some wetland plants. Deep ditches can hold permanent pools of water without interfering with field drainage. As a minimum, ditches or pools should hold 30 cm of water (ideally 1 m) in stretches at least 3 m long (Andrews & Rebane, 1994). The structure of the ditch is also important for other reasons. In particular, shallow margins provide favourable conditions for wetland plants, invertebrates and amphibians. Poached margins provide particularly good conditions for many invertebrates (P. Kirby, 1992), as well as feeding areas for birds. In narrow, deep ditches, the bottom is often shaded by overhanging vegetation and high banks. This will inhibit aquatic vegetation but may provide good cover for animals. In contrast, wide drains with sunlit water will favour the growth of vegetation. Overall, therefore, it is generally advantageous to aim for a variety of structures along stretches of ditch. This can be achieved by rotational management.

In general, the condition of ditches is dependent on vegetation structure and composition, which is in turn dependent on water quality and quantity (including seasonality), ditch structure and management. These attributes and influencing factors should therefore be monitored. Vegetation can be simply monitored by transects, with overall condition simply related to the number of submerged, floating and emergent wet bank species per 20 m (see NCC, 1989). For further information on monitoring ditch vegetation see Alcock & Palmer (1985). Other attributes will normally be dependent on specific site conditions.

Grassland banks and strips adjoining fields are also important sources of biodiversity in the farmland landscape. Under favourable conditions they may have relatively rich plant assemblages and hold scarce or rare farmland species. They may also provide suitable habitats for invertebrates (especially overwintering insects), small mammals and nesting birds. However, their quality is highly dependent on their plant species composition and the soil nutrient status. Sown grasslands, which are dominated by species-poor seed mixes and/or are subject to fertiliser applications, are generally of low conservation interest. Further details on the attributes of grassland habitats and their monitoring methods are provided in Section 5.4.

At first sight walls may appear to be devoid of biological interest. However, old walls may harbour rich lichen assemblages and potentially some rare or scarce species. They may also provide suitable habitats for some plants (especially mosses, liverworts and ferns), invertebrates, amphibians, reptiles, small mammals and birds. In general their quality is primarily dependent upon their age (especially in the case of lichens, as these are extremely slow-growing) and the presence of micro-habitats (such as crevices). Particular species inhabiting walls may also be dependent on specific conditions, such as a damp or shady environment with a particular aspect.

Hedgerows are well known for their conservation importance in a wide range of farmland habitats. Although they seldom hold rare species or plant communities, they may hold relatively high diversities of plants and provide important sources of food and cover for a wide variety of animals, especially insects and birds. Over 600 species of plant (including some endemic species such as the Whitebeam *Sorbus devoniensis*), 1500 insect species, 65 bird species and 20 species of mammal have been recorded at some time living or breeding in hedgerows (Anon., 1995). They may also provide an important function in linking habitats in open farmland landscapes, thereby providing dispersal routes for species that cannot cross large open spaces (see, for example, Simberloff & Cox, 1987; Bennett, 1990).

Attributes providing an indication of the overall quality of a hedgerow are species composition, structure, whether it contains trees, and its relationship to other habitats (Andrews & Rebane,1994). Older hedges in England tend to have a greater plant species richness and associated structural diversity (Pollard *et al.*, 1974), as well as more mature trees and dead wood. These attributes, in turn, support rich communities of invertebrates and other animals. In contrast, recently planted hedges tend to have low plant species diversity, often being dominated by Hawthorn *Crataegus monogyna* or Blackthorn *Prunus spinosa*. Proximity to woodland has also been shown to be important for species diversity (Wilmott, 1980). Another important aspect of species composition is the presence of native species. Low numbers of non-native plants will not be a problem (unless they are particularly invasive), but hedges that are dominated by native species will hold more insects (Kennedy & Southwood, 1984). Old hedges are also more likely to be linked to non-farmed habitats and may be extremely valuable if they are, for example, connected to ancient woodlands or other habitats of high conservation importance.

In general, tall, dense and broad hedges are richest in biodiversity. Plant, invertebrate and bird species richness may be affected by structure (Pollard *et al.*, 1974; P. Kirby,1992; Green *et al.*, 1994, Parish *et al.*, 1994, 1995; MacDonald & Johnson, 1995; Lewis *et al.*, 1999). Structure is profoundly affected by management, and probably also by age. The complexity of a laid hedge provides better habitats for invertebrates and birds than does a simple line of bushes managed by cutting or coppicing. Hedge-laying also maintains more dead wood, which is particularly important for invertebrates.

The external form of the hedge is an important attribute of hedgerow quality: trimming reduces structural diversity and flowering and fruit production. Severe trimming will also reduce a hedge's suitability for nesting birds (Lack, 1987). A hedge that is trimmed into an 'A' shape with a wide base may also shade out ground vegetation and become less suitable for associated animals. In contrast, a hedge that has become leggy, perhaps as a result of browsing on lower growth by livestock, is poor for scrub-nesting birds but is more likely to have a well-developed and richer herbaceous ground flora. However, the actual shape of a trimmed hedge may be less important for wildlife than is often claimed (Hill *et al.*, 1995). The development of ground flora and associated animal communities is much more likely to be influenced by accidental fertiliser applications and pesticide drift.

Numerous methods have been used to describe hedges, but they may not be the most applicable for monitoring. A summary of attributes giving an indication of habitat condition in hedgerows and recommended methods for monitoring them is provided below. This takes into account recommendations for a standard method for local Biodiversity Action Plan (BAP) surveys of hedges, which has been proposed by the UK Steering Group for the Species-rich Hedgerow Biodiversity Action Plan.

For monitoring hedgerow extent it is necessary to adopt a consistent definition that can be readily applied during field surveys. In this respect the proposed UK Steering Group definition of a hedgerow is 'any boundary line of trees or shrubs less than 5 metres wide, provided that at one time the trees or shrubs were more or less continuous'. This broad definition is proposed because it avoids the need to distinguish between lines of trees and rows of bushes. Earth or stone banks or walls are not included, in accordance with the Species-rich Hedgerow BAP. However, if these features occur in association with a line of trees or shrubs, they are considered to form part of the hedgerow. A length of hedge between connections with other hedges or other linear features (i.e. inter-nodal length) is counted as a separate hedge. A hedgerow with a gap of more than 20 m is con-sidered to be two separate hedges.

Although the survey methodology proposed by the Steering Group is meant to be for species-rich hedges, it could be applied to others. However, monitoring all hedges could be onerous and is unlikely to be a priority of a monitoring programme. It may be appropriate in many cases to target species-rich hedges for monitoring beyond the simple assessment of extent. Species-rich hedges are defined in the Species-rich Hedgerow BAP as 'any hedge that has 5 or more native woody species on average in a 30 metre length, or 4 or more in north-ern England, upland Wales and Scotland'. The BAP also recommends that hedges that contain fewer woody species but have a rich basal flora should be included if possible, although no practical criteria have as yet been agreed for defining them on this basis. Table 5.3 summarises the attributes indicat-ing the condition of hedgerows, along with their recommended monitoring techniques.

Rich *et al.* (2000) compared four different hedge survey techniques on the same hedgerows: stand-ard 30 m lengths, 10 m plots, the Hedgerow Evaluation and Grading System (HEGS), and features of importance as defined in the UK Government's Hedgerows Regulations 1997. All methods identified variation between hedgerows which could differentiate between hedgerow types (e.g. parish/community boundaries, new hedgerows), or compare hedgerows in different areas (e.g. communities). The number of species in 10 m lengths, 30 m lengths and the whole hedge-row were highly correlated; surveys of sections can thus indicate overall species richness, although 30 m lengths gave better results than 10 m lengths. In general a good relationship between the HEGS value and the 'importance' as defined by the

Hedgerows Regulations was found, but it was not predictive for middle-ranking hedgerows, and the HEGS method cannot be used as a proxy for the Hedgerows Regulations or vice versa. General sur-veys can be carried out with these two methods together to maximise both ecological and context-ual information collected during surveys.

Management requirements and external impacts

Farmland boundary features are profoundly affected by agricultural management practices (see Barr *et al.* (1995) for hedges) and therefore these, as well as habitat quality, should be thoroughly monitored.

Stocking density and grazing or browsing inten-sity can have serious impacts on the vegetation of ditch margins, grassy banks and hedges. Stocking density can be easily monitored by regular stock head counts or by inspection of farm management records obtained directly from the landowner. However, stock will preferentially graze some vegetation. Monitoring grazing intensity, e.g. by marking hedgerow branches and recording damage or by excluding grazing from banks and ditch margins, may therefore be a more reliable indicator of impacts, but it is more difficult.

The accidental or intentional application of fer-tilisers, pesticides and other agrochemicals (e.g. plant growth regulators) to farmland boundary fea-tures can have major direct and indirect effects on vegetation and animal communities. Farm records can again provide basic data on their use, but these will be of little value in predicting impacts unless such agrochemicals are not used or are applied infrequently. Such data may also be unreliable.

Where fertilisers, pesticides, etc. are applied fre-quently, impacts can only be assessed by more sophis-ticated procedures. Detecting fertiliser application may require chemical analysis of soils (Section 6.2.2) or water (Section 5.9.) Herbicide and other pesticide applications may be detected by chemical analysis of soil and/or plants or indirectly from quadrats (Sections 6.4.2–6.4.5) if there are marked changes in botanical composition (e.g. a marked decrease in the broadleaved herb component). Liming can be detected from soil pH analysis (Section 6.2.2.) These monitoring methods are, however, likely to be time-consuming, complex and difficult to interpret, and

Table 5.3. *A summary of the quality attributes providing an indication of the condition of hedgerows, and their recommended monitoring techniques*

Attribute	Habitat properties	Monitoring technique
Physical properties	Extent	Phase I survey (Section 6.1.5) or aerial photography (6.1.3)
Composition	Presence/frequency of indicator species	Species listings over defined hedgerow lengths, line transects (6.4.6), or quadrats (6.4.2–6.4.4) for hedge bottoms
	Species richness (woody species and ground flora)	Line transects (6.4.6) or quadrats (6.4.2–6.4.4) for hedge bottoms
Structure	General structure and shape, including: • length of gaps at top of hedge • length of gaps in woody plants • coverage at base of hedge • shape of hedge (e.g. 'A', box, etc.)	Subjective visual assessment for major changes (e.g. trimming) or fixed-point photography (6.1.4)
	Average height	Sample measurements with a graduated pole, or fixed-point photography (Section 6.1.4)
	Width: • average hedge width • width of rough herbage composed of native species at hedge base	Sample measurements with a graduated pole
	Density	Subjective assessment or chequered board (see, for example, Fuller *et al.* (1989))
	Dead wood	Transect and subjective assessment of part (6.5.5)
	Presence of trees (live and dead)	Include as target notes in Phase I surveys (6.1.5)

are therefore probably beyond the resources of most monitoring programmes.

As described above, the structure of hedgerows is primarily controlled by their management. Laying or coppicing is carried out to reinvigorate the hedge and is best done on 8–12 year rotations. Trimming is routinely done to avoid excessive shading of crops, to maintain access and to retain the general shape of a hedge. To be most beneficial for biodiversity, trimming is best carried out on rotations of 2–3 years or longer (Andrews & Rebane, 1994; Hill *et al.*,1995). These management practices can normally be easily monitored from farm records or simple visual inspections every couple of years (as the effects of trimming are visible for several years).

5.3.2   Specific issues affecting the survey and monitoring of habitat

As there is the possibility of agricultural practices having a major impact on farmland boundary features, monitoring should be carried out frequently. In particular, it is prudent to carry out routine site visits annually to make simple visual inspections of features and to monitor management practices. More detailed quantitative assessments of features should be carried out at no more than 3 year intervals, or immediately if annual inspections reveal apparent impacts or detrimental management activities.

Some monitoring data can often be obtained directly from landowners' or managers' farm records. However, as explained above, such general data may

Table 5.4. *Native woody species that occur in hedgerows in the UK*
These are typical species, not an exhaustive list.

Trees		Shrubs	
Common name	**Scientific name**	**Common name**	**Scientific name**
Alder	*Alnus glutinosa*	Blackthorn	*Prunus spinosa*
Crab Apple	*Malus sylvestris*	Broom	*Cytisus scoparius*
Ash	*Fraxinus excelsior*	Elder	*Sambucus nigra*
Aspen	*Populus tremula*	Gorse	*Ulex europaeus*
Downy Birch	*Betula pubescens*	Gooseberry	*Ribes uva-crispa*
Silver Birch	*Betula pendula*	Guelder Rose	*Viburnum opulus*
Bird Cherry	*Prunus padus*	Hawthorn	*Crataegus monogyna*
Wych Elm	*Ulmus glabra*	Hazel	*Corylus avellana*
Elm species	*Ulmus* spp.		
Gean (Wild Cherry)	*Prunus avium*	Juniper	*Juniperus communis*
Wild Plum	*Prunus domestica*	Dog Rose	*Rosa canina*
Holly	*Ilex aquifolium*		
Pedunculate Oak	*Quercus robur*	Wild Rose	*Rosa* spp.
Sessile Oak	*Quercus petraea*	Spindle	*Euonymus europaeus*
Scots Pine	*Pinus sylvestris*	Bay Willow	*Salix pentandra*
Rowan (Mountain Ash)	*Sorbus aucuparia*	Eared Willow	*Salix aurita*
Crack Willow	*Salix fragilis*	Grey Willow	*Salix cinerea*
Goat Willow	*Salix caprea*	Osier	*Salix viminalis*
White Willow	*Salix alba*	Purple Willow	*Salix purpurea*
Whitebeam	*Sorbus aria*		

Sources: NCC (1988) and Stace (1997)

not be an accurate indicator of the actual impacts of management practices. Furthermore, such data may not be reliable, for example as a result of inconsistent record-keeping. It is also possible that some activities (intentional or accidental) may be concealed if they contravene management agreements or general codes of good environmental practice.

Most general field monitoring of vegetation can be carried out between May and September, but should be carried out within the same 2 week period of the year as the original survey when repeating monitoring of ditches, grassy banks or hedgerow ground flora.

Hedgerow shrubs and trees are normally fairly easily identified and can therefore be monitored by most biologists with general field training (see Table 5.4). However, vegetative identification of grasses and sedges is usually critical for monitoring hedgerow ground floras, ditches and banks, and it may be necessary to use a specialist botanist for such detailed work.

5.4   GRASSLAND AND HERBACEOUS COMMUNITIES

5.4.1   Survey and monitoring requirements and methods

Attributes for assessing habitat condition

Grassland and herbaceous NVC communities are designated features or attributes of broader habitats of many SSSIs. A key requirement is therefore to monitor their continued presence, extent and quality. This can be carried out by repeat NVC surveys incorporating properly replicated quadrat sampling (see Sections 6.1.6 and 6.4.2 for detailed discussions) or by using appropriate mapping techniques. Simple repeat NVC mapping is not considered to be appropriate for monitoring purposes.

Many lowland sites are in enclosed areas on farms, and defining their extent is relatively simple. On larger upland sites the grasslands may form part of a much larger complex, including blanket bog and heathland, and sampling is therefore required to determine changes in extent and distribution. As grassland composition is often strongly related to soils and topography in such sites, careful stratification may be required to ensure that sampling designs are effective and efficient, and cover the full range of vegetation types present.

In addition, various aspects of the vegetation, such as species richness, presence of particular typical or indicator species, sward height and cover, soil nutrient status, etc., may be needed to assess whether the quality of the vegetation is being maintained. Species richness is an easily understood and measured variable, which can indicate grassland quality. In general, the more species-rich a grassland, the more valuable it is for nature conservation. The diversity should be of species characteristic of that community, and not extraneous species (e.g. non-native species or trees invading from adjacent woodland); some grasslands are inherently more species-rich than others. One way to clarify that richness is an intrinsic function of the community concerned would be to assess the ratio of species listed in the appropriate NVC table in Rodwell (1991 et seq.) to other species, or to assess the ratio of constants, differentials and preferentials to associates and other species (Rodwell, 1991 et seq.). Bear in mind that oversampling a local community will result in a number of constants higher than that indicated in the NVC tables.

The presence and/or abundance of particular species may often be considered useful in helping to define condition in many grassland and other vegetation communities. These most often relate to desirable species that are of conservation importance or species that are indicators of favourable ecological condition. Undesirable species, such as exotic or invasive species, or indicators of poor condition may also need to be monitored. For example, in species-rich *Nardus* grasslands, an absence or sparse cover of Crested Dog's-tail *Cynosurus cristatus* and Perennial Ryegrass *Lolium perenne* is considered to be necessary for acceptable condition (Davies & Yost, 1998).

If it is only necessary to establish the presence or minimum approximate population of a species that is likely to be reasonably common and detectable, then simple look–see or count methods may be adequate (see Part III, Sections 15.2.1 and 15.2.2.) However, if species are rare or difficult to detect, or if accurate quantitative assessments (e.g. of cover) are needed, sampling procedures such as quadrat or transect techniques will probably be required (Section 6.4.)

The dispersal of species within a grassland can be of use when determining quality. When many rare species or typical indicators are dispersed throughout the grassland at medium to high frequency rather than being in single isolated clumps at low frequency, grasslands are often old and of high quality with a long history of the same management.

Sward height, cover and litter are valuable indicators that should be monitored as a matter of course when collecting quadrat data or surveying sites. When swards are ungrazed, height, cover and litter all increase, resulting in decreased reproduction of many species and a decrease in the proportion of small, short-lived species. The presence of associated grassland features, such as anthills, often adds diversity and they may also be worth monitoring in their own right.

Table 5.5 summarises the attributes that indicate the condition of grasslands and gives recommended techniques for monitoring them. Detailed methods and reviews of monitoring grasslands are outlined by Byrne (1991), Hodgson et al. (1995) and Robertson (1999).

Management requirements and external impacts
Monitoring of management practices (Sections 7.1–7.3) may be as important as monitoring the quality of the habitat. It should perhaps be carried out as part of a site monitoring programme.

Table 5.5. *A summary of the quality attributes providing an indication of the condition of grasslands, and their recommended monitoring techniques*

Attribute	Habitat properties	Monitoring technique
Physical properties	Extent and distribution	Phase I mapping (Section 6.1.5) with aerial photography (6.1.3) for basic long-term monitoring NVC surveys with quadrat sampling (6.1.6) for NVC vegetation types
	Soil nutrients	Chemical analysis (not covered)
Composition	Characteristic communities	Quadrats (6.4.2) or transects (6.4.6), with NVC analysis (6.1.6) where NVC communities are Notified Features or important attributes
	Functional components of vegetation	FIBS (6.4.4)
	Species composition and richness	Mini-quadrats (6.4.3)
	Presence/absence of typical/indicator species	Look−see or total counts (Part III, Sections 15.2.1 and 15.2.2,) quadrats (6.4.2, 6.4.3) or transects (6.4.6)
Structure	Sward height	Drop-disc, ruler
	Cover	Conventional quadrats (6.4.2) or point quadrats (6.4.5) if precise measurements are required
	Litter	Quadrats (6.4.2)

Most grassland and herbaceous communities need to be managed by mowing, burning or grazing to maintain their quality. There are often severe practical difficulties in ensuring that these operations are carried out at the right time each year, and therefore monitoring of such activities will often be needed to establish a long-term view of the stability of the community.

Grasslands vary in their sensitivity to changes in management and subsequent recovery. For instance, application of fertiliser to nutrient-poor grassland may result in rapid and irreversible changes, yet effects due to the absence of grazing can be reversed after even a decade. In setting the timescale for monitoring, any threats to, and the sensitivity of, each site and community will therefore need to be considered.

Monitoring stocking density may require regular stock head counts, although stock will often graze some types of grassland in preference to others. When stock are absent, previous use can be assessed from dung. As stock selectively graze some vegetation types in preference to others, monitoring the stocking density alone for a site may not reflect the true grazing pressure on valuable vegetation. Here, more detailed methods, such as counting the proportion of grazed shoots or leaves, may be required.

Detecting fertiliser application may require chemical analysis of soils (Section 6.2.2). Herbicide application may be detected by chemical analysis of plants and/or soil or indirectly from quadrats (Sections 6.4.2–6.4.4) where there are marked changes in sward composition (e.g. a marked decrease in the broadleaved herb component). Liming can be detected from soil pH analysis (Section 6.2.2.) Some management monitoring data can often be obtained from the landowners' or managers' farm records. However, such data may not be reliable, for example as a result of inconsistent record-keeping. It is also possible that some actions (intentional or accidental) may be concealed if they contravene management agreements or general codes of good environmental practice.

On upland grasslands the impacts of grazing and burning can be monitored by using the method developed by MacDonald *et al.* (1998a,b) for SNH.

5.4.2 Specific issues affecting the survey and monitoring of habitat

Grasslands and herbaceous communities should be monitored at 3 or 6 year intervals. Hay meadows should be surveyed before they are cut. Most general monitoring can be done between May and September but should be carried out within the same 2 week period of the year as the original survey when repeat monitoring.

Vegetative identification of grasses and sedges is usually critical for monitoring grasslands, so the work will need to be carried out by a specialist botanist.

When carrying out assessments of grasslands it should be remembered that it can be difficult to record quadrats safely and effectively if inquisitive stock are present. Trampling by stock can also affect tall herb vegetation, and lodging (vegetation falling over as a result of excessive growth, wind or rain) has marked effects on the ease and accuracy of recording quadrats.

5.5   LIMESTONE PAVEMENT

5.5.1 Survey and monitoring requirements and methods

Attributes for assessing habitat condition

In Europe, limestone pavements are restricted to Britain and Ireland, and internationally they are a rare habitat. Most pavements are quite small and extend over only a few hectares. All examples are important irrespective of size, and extent should be monitored to check for damage and encroachment. From a national study only 3% of pavements in Britain were found to be undamaged and only 13% were 95% or more intact (Ward & Evans, 1976).

The biological interest is provided by a variety of microclimates, which results in a mosaic of different plant communities. The development of vegetation over pavements ranges from sparse,

scattered vegetation to pastures, woodland clearings and closed woodland canopies. The resulting diversity and unusual combinations of plants of woodland, rocky habitats and grassland growing together on a pavement are key attributes, resulting in a range of NVC types. Ward & Evans (1976) regarded open pavements as the most important floristically. Open pavements with a good 'view' are also important from an earth science perspective, but the maintenance of existing woody cover is often necessary to maintain overall diversity.

Ward & Evans (1975, 1976) documented all the limestone pavements in Scotland and England and included species lists for all sites, with a crude estimate of frequency. They limited floristic recording to grikes more than twice as deep as they were wide, and this method should be followed for consistency. Species lists were used to create a floristic index, which was used to rank pavements, and deviations from this figure can be used to monitor maintenance of diversity. Most surveys took about one hour by two botanists, and it is suggested that this should be repeated as closely as possible and at a similar time of year. Repeat botanical surveys will vary depending on the botanist and the amount of effort, so measures should be taken to standardise surveys (Rich & Smith, 1996). As site-based surveys return generally similar but rarely identical species lists, the floristic index from repeat surveys should be within ±20% of the Ward & Evans (1975) baseline figure to account for sampling error and indicate maintenance of the floristic index.

The earth science interest centres on maintenance of the key physical features for which each site is selected (such as the grikes), and their visibility (i.e. they should not be covered by excessive vegetation). The variation in structure of grikes and other typical karst geomorphological features, such as solution basins, erratics, runnels, etc., is also important for the biological features of the pavements as it adds a diversity of habitats. Physical structure is unlikely to change except by damage, although perched erratics tend to get pushed off by vandals.

During the botanical survey, notes can be kept of damage by geologists (these are typically small

Table 5.6. *A summary of the quality attributes providing an indication of the condition of limestone pavements, and their recommended monitoring techniques*

Attribute	Habitat properties	Monitoring technique
Physical properties	Extent	Phase I or NVC survey (Sections 6.1.5 and 6.1.6), aerial or fixed-point photography (6.1.3 and 6.1.4)
	Removal of limestone, damage by geologists	Field surveys
Composition	Floristic index	See text and Ward & Evans (1975, 1976)
	Characteristic communities	Quadrats (6.4.2) or transects (6.4.6), with NVC analysis (6.1.6) where NVC communities are Notified Features or important attributes
Structure	Cover of wood and scrub	Aerial or fixed-point photography (6.1.3 and 6.1.4)

chips taken off edges of grikes, often obvious because of their lack of lichen or algae cover). Existing damage can be marked with a small spot of enamel paint so that new damage can be assessed, but this is usually a relatively minor problem. Table 5.6 gives a summary of attributes useful when assessing the condition of limestone pavements and the methods recommended for monitoring them.

Management requirements and external impacts

Variation in woody cover of pavements is important for the diversity of the habitat in its own right; in cases in which biological sites have been selected to include this, maintenance of the existing woody cover is regarded as desirable. If sites have been selected for their earth science importance, the requirement for open views should be taken into account.

In the past limestone pavements have been widely damaged by removal of limestone for rockeries, walls and building materials, and minor damage still occurs from geological sampling.

Because of the difficulty of stock grazing on limestone pavements, most sites are unlikely to be under threat from an increase in cattle grazing pressure but there may be a gradual impoverishment associated with sheep grazing. Some open pavements that support rarities should continue to be lightly grazed to prevent scrub encroachment.

On pavements with deep grikes, low-intensity grazing may be tolerated. Some improvements may be achieved locally if grazing is reduced or removed.

Air pollution and acid deposition could well be damaging the geomorphological features as a result of an increased rate of erosion, although this is a slow process and a long-term problem. Lichens may have some role in protecting the pavements from weathering.

The amount of public pressure, and hence the amount of monitoring of damage required, will vary depending on catchment area. For example, some sites in Scotland do not appear to be under the same public pressure as those in England, and there seems to be little point in monitoring erosion or other damage from visitors unless it is identified as a potential problem.

5.5.2 Specific issues affecting the survey and monitoring of habitat

It is recommended that these sites are monitored at 3–6 year intervals. This should be carried out between June and September when the flora is fully developed.

The boundary of the limestone pavement should be taken as the edge of the exposed limestone. The small size and relative accessibility of most pavements, and the existence of a standard method (Ward & Evans, 1975), will not impose significant logistical limitations on surveys.

Fixed-point photography has worked well as a monitoring tool at a number of sites, and is useful for assessing changes in woody cover or limestone extraction. Aerial photographs are also useful for spotting limestone removal on larger pavements.

NVC surveys with quadrat sampling of each grike are unlikely to be worth while, and may be difficult because of the patchy nature of the vegetation. A broad overview of the vegetation types should be taken. Quadrats (Section 6.4.2) or transects (Section 6.4.6) may be useful for assessing changes in vegetation related to grazing.

Particular care should be taken when undertaking fieldwork because of the risks of falling on slippery pavements in wet weather. Monitoring should be carried out by two people, and other appropriate safety measures outlined in Box 2.11 should be followed.

5.6   LOWLAND AND UPLAND HEATHLAND

5.6.1   Survey and monitoring requirements and methods

Attributes for assessing habitat condition
Heathlands are subject to significant reclamation pressure, at least in the lowlands. Most heathland types occur as part of habitat mosaics in which they exhibit gradations into other communities (e.g. grassland, blanket bogs). They show strong edge effects and are vulnerable to fragmentation. It is therefore important to monitor their extent and distribution.

Soils are a key feature determining the nature of the heathland vegetation. They tend to be acidic, nutrient-poor podzols and shallow peat. Soil pH may not always be low; in The Netherlands the rarer heathland plant species are often associated with soils of pH greater than 5 (Roem & Berendse, 2000). Nutrient enrichment is usually very damaging. Heathlands may be freely drained or more or less permanently waterlogged. Wet heath types may depend on a high water table, which may require monitoring.

In general the more diverse the heathland in terms of characteristic heathland species and structure the better. Heathlands are usually defined as having a cover of 25% or more of the main ericaceous species (*Calluna*, *Empetrum*, *Vaccinium* or *Erica* spp.) (NCC, 1990a,b), and cover of these species is therefore an essential indicator of condition. Gorse (*Ulex* spp.) may also be important on lowland heaths. Much of the vegetation is naturally species-poor but no one plant species should cover more than 90% of the ground. This will allow the development of diversity within the limits characteristic of the habitat. In the west, heathland may be very important for oceanic bryophytes and lichens. Heavy grazing and excessive burning (or poor burning practices) may result in reduced cover of ericaceous and other species.

In general, mixed-age stands of ericaceous species on heathlands are more valuable than homogeneous stands, as the former tend to have more microhabitats for invertebrates, lichens, bryophytes and higher plants, and they also indicate that regeneration conditions are suitable. Bare ground may vary from large areas in recently burnt stands to virtually none in closed mature stands; this is quite natural, but some bare ground is usually desirable.

Scrub (birch, pine) and Bracken *Pteridium* invasion is often a problem on both lowland and upland heaths and may not be desirable, although it is an integral part of the habitat.

A summary of attributes useful when assessing the condition of heathlands is provided in Table 5.7 together with recommended monitoring methods. An additional method for monitoring Heather *Calluna vulgaris* cover is given in MacDonald & Armstrong (1989).

Management requirements and external impacts
Heathlands are semi-natural habitats, and require management techniques such as grazing, burning or cutting (with the possible exception of some maritime heaths) to maintain structural and species diversity and prevent scrub encroachment.

Low-intensity grazing is often valuable in creating diverse microhabitats and is the preferred management, although it is not always practicable (Gimingham, 1992). Grazing regimes need to be adapted to local situations. Many upland heaths are managed as grouse moors by patchwork

Table 5.7. *A summary of the attributes providing an indication of the condition of heathlands, and their recommended monitoring techniques*

Attribute	Habitat properties	Monitoring technique
Physical properties	Extent and distribution	Phase I mapping (Section 6.1.5) with aerial photography (6.1.3) for basic long-term monitoring NVC surveys with quadrat sampling (6.1.6) for NVC vegetation types
	Soil pH and nutrients	Soil analysis (6.2.2)
	Bare ground	Conventional quadrats (6.4.2)
	Water table	Dipwells or WALRAGS (6.2.1)
Composition	Characteristic communities	Quadrats (6.4.2) or transects (6.4.6), with NVC analysis (6.1.6) where NVC communities are Notified Features or important attributes
	Ericaceous and other keystone species cover	Conventional quadrats (6.4.2), aerial photographs (6.1.3)
	Species composition and richness	Conventional quadrats (6.4.2) or line/point intercept transects (6.4.6)
	Presence/abundance of typical/indicator species	Look–see or total counts (Part III, Sections 15.2.1 and 15.2.2) quadrats (6.4.2 and 6.4.3) or transects (6.4.6).
Structure	Occurrence and scale of horizontal and vertical structure (patchiness)	Transects (6.4.6) and fixed-point photography (6.1.4) Drop-disc or ruler for height
	Age/physical structure of ericaceous shrubs	Plant size and demographic techniques (Part III, Sections 15.2.3 and 15.2.4)
	Scrub invasion	Fixed-point (6.1.4) or aerial photography (6.1.3)

burning, or as sheep walks. Overgrazing can occur, normally near supplementary feeding locations or around the lower margins of moors close to better-quality pastures. Grazing and burning are key factors on many heaths, and much impact monitoring will be directed towards this (Sections 7.1–7.2) A method for monitoring the impacts of upland land management practices has been developed by MacDonald *et al.* (1998a,b) for SNH.

Air pollution should be below the critical concentrations required to maintain the low nutrient status of the heaths (SO_2 10 $\mu g\,m^{-3}$, NO_2 30 $\mu g\,m^{-3}$, NH_3 8 $\mu g\,m^{-3}$) (English Nature, 1993). In recent years concentrations of SO_2 have declined as a result of effective drives to remove such emissions from power stations across Europe, whereas pollution from NO_x remains a problem.

5.6.2 Specific issues affecting the survey and monitoring of habitat

It is recommended that heathlands are monitored at 6 year intervals. Late summer is an appropriate time for monitoring floristic parameters, as the weather is likely to be better and the plants fully developed, but work can be carried out for most of the growing season (April–October) in these essentially evergreen communities. Early spring is the best time to monitor heather browsing, after winter browsing has finished but before new growth occurs. Access may be difficult late in the season because of deer stalking or grouse shooting.

Sites containing heathlands are often very large and complex, with other related vegetation types such as blanket bogs intermixed. Monitoring may therefore have to be integrated with that of other habitats. The large scale can make access difficult if vehicle tracks are absent, and walking though tall heather can be extremely tiring.

The large size of many heathland sites also means that sampling will be essential, as it will not be possible to monitor the whole site. As heathland composition is often strongly related to soils and topography in such sites, careful stratification may be required to ensure that all communities and subcommunities are adequately and efficiently sampled. Stratification according to ownership or management may also be appropriate because this is likely to be the major factor determining the condition of the vegetation. In large areas of uniform moorland it may also be efficient to carry out sampling using a multi-level strategy (Part I, Section 2.3.3.)

Accurately determining location can be difficult when mapping. Boundaries between communities can be ecotonal in nature, and different surveyors may not be consistent in their interpretation of boundary locations.

Heather damage may be caused by invertebrates, especially certain moth species (e.g. Winter Moth *Operophtera brumata* caterpillars) and the Heather Beetle *Lochmaea suturalis*. Damage can also be due to other factors, such as weather and fungal diseases.

5.7   FENS, CARR, MARSH, SWAMP AND REEDBED

5.7.1   Survey and monitoring requirements and methods

Attributes for assessing habitat condition
This group includes a range of habitats, each of which presents its own problems for monitoring. Carr is essentially swampy woodland; monitoring techniques appropriate for woodlands will therefore be important (Section 5.1.) Marsh monitoring will include techniques appropriate for grasslands and herbaceous vegetation (Section 5.4).

Fens may vary from small areas around a calcareous spring to large sites (e.g. the 300 ha Insh Marshes near Kingussie); size is critical. Most examples are small and widely scattered, often occurring as isolated, fragmented sites in the lowlands, and this fragmentation imposes significant limitations on their potential for recovery after damage. Fens are among the habitats that have undergone the most serious declines across Europe. Swamps and reedbeds often occur around the margins of lakes, lochs, pools and rivers (Sections 5.9 and 5.10).

These habitats are wetlands, and the rise and fall of the water table and movement of water are important factors in determining the plants and communities that occur. The height of the water table, typically at or slightly above or below that of the substrate, appears to be especially important in controlling zonation and succession to other vegetation types. Hydrological regimes should therefore be monitored, but this is a complex subject that cannot be covered here (see Section 6.2.1.) Similarly, water chemistry has a profound influence on wetland vegetation and should be carefully monitored. Further information on this subject is provided in Section 5.9.

Fen vegetation is variable but very distinctive and contains many species that are rare or scarce. The type of vegetation and its richness are key indicators of habitat quality. Wheeler (1989) proposed that two botanical indices based on richness indicators and rare species could be used for rapid evaluation of sites; a similar approach could also be used for monitoring.

There is often some variation in topography across a fen, which can be important for maintaining diversity. The vegetation itself often forms small mounds with wetter areas between (and sometimes shallow pools), allowing species of wet and dry ground to grow adjacent to each other. Variations in topography may also be associated with old peat cuttings. Natural transitions to non-fen habitats are rare features and can be of high value.

A summary of attributes that are useful in providing an indication of the condition of wetlands is provided in Table 5.8 together with recommended monitoring methods. Rowell (1988) provides practical advice on monitoring peatlands including fens.

Table 5.8. *A summary of the quality attributes providing an indication of the condition of wetlands, and their recommended monitoring techniques*

Attribute	Habitat properties	Monitoring technique
Physical properties	Extent	Phase I mapping (Section 6.1.5) with aerial photography (6.1.3) for basic long-term monitoring
		NVC surveys with quadrat sampling (6.1.6) for NVC vegetation types
	Soil pH and nutrients	Soil analysis (6.2.2)
	Hydrological regime	Piezometer, dipwells or WALRAGS (6.2.1)
	Water chemistry	Macrophyte indicators for standing waters or chemical analysis (not covered)
Composition	Characteristic communities	Quadrats (6.4.2) or transects (6.4.6), with NVC analysis (6.1.6) where NVC communities are Notified Features or important attributes
	Species composition and richness	Conventional quadrats (6.4.2) or line/point intercept transects (6.4.6)
	Presence/abundance of typical/indicator species	Look–see or total counts (Part III, Sections 15.2.1 and 15.2.2) quadrats (6.4.2 and 6.4.3) or transects (6.4.6).
Structure	Vegetation height	Drop-disc or ruler
	Scrub invasion	Fixed-point (6.1.4) or aerial photography (6.1.3)

Management requirements and external impacts

The main threats to fens are reclamation, drainage and abstraction from aquifers, cessation of traditional management practices such as grazing and turf cutting, overgrazing, eutrophication, development of scrub, and flood defences. Some of these may require off-site monitoring, and large-scale catchment protection may be required for fens because of their dependence on the flow of ground or surface water of an appropriate quality.

Management of fen vegetation varies. Some short fens are maintained by light grazing and its associated trampling, the low nutrient concentrations and scouring by water erosion. Reedbeds should not be grazed. These and others, such as *Cladium* (sedge) beds, may require regular cutting. Peat cutting and scrub clearance are also required in some sites.

Minerotrophic or topogenous fens develop under the influence of ground water, the nutrient content of which is critically important in determining species composition. High species richness is strongly related to low nutrient status. Nutrient enrichment by agricultural fertiliser run-off or sewage is therefore highly damaging. Rivers tend to have high nutrients in their sediments, although fens can occur in floodplain situations.

5.7.2 Specific issues affecting the survey and monitoring of the habitat

These habitats should be monitored every 3 years. The vegetation of wetlands is most developed late in the summer (July–September) and is best monitored in August when water levels are at their lowest. The presence of breeding birds may also restrict access at other times of year.

A high level of botanical skill is needed for NVC surveys of fens and similar habitats because of the range of difficult groups, such as grasses, sedges and bryophytes, which form important parts of the vegetation.

It may be very difficult to place quadrats in tall swamp without damaging the vegetation; transects may be easier to record. If largish areas of uniform vegetation are picked to minimise edge effects, quadrats can be crudely delimited by placing ranging poles sideways through the vegetation. Rowell (1988) suggests the use of circular quadrats, which can be threaded through the vegetation. In either case it can be difficult to see both sides of the quadrats clearly without trampling vegetation all around.

Fens are difficult habitats to survey. Tall swamp vegetation is disorienting and difficult to walk through; there may be sudden changes to open water and the surface may be unstable because of floating vegetation. Aerial photographs may be invaluable for mapping inaccessible areas at a gross scale. Some access by boat can help with surveying. Chest waders are more useful than wellington boots. Eye protection may be needed in reedbeds.

Permanent markers may be difficult to relocate under water, in deep peat or in tall vegetation, but are unlikely to be interfered with because of their location. Birds may perch on them, resulting in localised nutrient enrichment from droppings. Vegetation can be quite heterogeneous, and is amenable to investigation through transects and by stratified sampling.

5.8   LOWLAND RAISED BOG

5.8.1   Surveying and monitoring requirements and methods

Attributes for assessing habitat condition

Raised bogs have been officially recognised as one of Europe's rarest and most threatened habitats. Since 1840 the area of primary, active lowland raised bog in the UK has decreased from around 95 000 ha to 6000 ha, a decline of 95%. Only about 3800 ha of this remains intact, some 800 ha of which are in Scotland. Extent is thus the first important attribute to monitor. The most common causes of loss have been peat extraction or conversion to agriculture or forestry. Mineral extraction, built developments and neglect probably account for most of the recent losses.

Topography is a second attribute. Lowland raised bogs form deep peat deposits of variable depth (5–10 m) with a flat or gently sloping topography and sometimes a steeper edge. Most natural undisturbed bog surfaces usually show distinctive fine-scale variation with small drier hummocks and wetter hollows related to growth of *Sphagnum* and other plants.

A third attribute is the water table. The water table may be maintained by both rainwater and ground water (Lamers *et al.*, 1999). It is higher than the surrounding land and is therefore very susceptible to drainage. Invasion by birch or willow may indicate surface flushing or that the bog is drying out. Transects of dipwells may therefore be valuable to provide hydrological information but, as there are long-term natural cycles of drying and wetting related to natural variations in climate, dipwell data may need to be correlated with rainfall.

A fourth attribute is the presence of (and preferably active formation of) the peat itself. Assessments of whether peat growth is active or not can be made by measuring peat depth and rates of peat accumulation directly, although if decomposition in the catotelm equals accumulation in the acrotelm, the net result is no peat accumulation, despite the fact that peat is actively being laid down. Strictly speaking, active growth of peat is therefore a feature of peat formation, not of peat accumulation. Peat shrinkage is usually caused by drainage or other disturbance. The characteristic vegetation is dominated by *Sphagnum* spp. (especially *S. papillosum*, and sometimes *S. magellanicum*), and it is important that a healthy growth is maintained in wet conditions. To a large extent, if the *Sphagnum* is healthy and growing, the remainder of the habitat should be in good condition.

A summary of attributes that provide an indication of the condition of lowland raised bogs is provided in Table 5.9 together with recommended monitoring methods. Stoneman & Brooks (1997) and Rowell (1988) provide practical advice on monitoring bogs.

Management requirements and external impacts

The management of bogs can markedly affect the quality of the site. Grazing, burning, drainage,

Table 5.9. *A summary of the quality attributes providing an indication of the condition of lowland raised bog, and their recommended monitoring techniques*

Attribute	Habitat properties	Monitoring technique
Physical properties	Extent	Phase I mapping (Section 6.1.5) with aerial photography (6.1.3) for basic long-term monitoring NVC surveys with quadrat sampling (6.1.6) for NVC vegetation types
	Water table	Dipwells or WALRAGS (6.2.1)
	Peat depth	Soil cores (6.2.2)
Composition	Characteristic communities	Quadrats (6.4.2) or transects (6.4.6), with NVC analysis (6.1.6) where NVC communities are Notified Features or important attributes
	Species composition and richness	Quadrats (6.4.2–6.4.4) or transects (6.4.6)
	Presence/abundance of typical/indicator species	Look–see or total counts (Part III, Sections 15.2.1 and 15.2.2) quadrats (6.4.2 and 6.4.3) or transects (6.4.6)
	Sphagnum cover	Conventional quadrats (6.4.2) or transects (6.4.6)
Structure	Pattern (hummock/hollow, bog pools, etc.)	Quadrats (6.4.2–6.4.4), transects (6.4.6), or fixed-point (6.1.4) or aerial (6.1.3) photography for large-scale surveys
	Scrub invasion	Fixed-point (6.1.4) or aerial photography (6.1.3)
Dynamics	Peat formation	Growth of *Sphagnum*

forestry and scrub invasion can all damage the vegetation. Under natural conditions raised bogs may have been lightly grazed or ungrazed (unlikely), and most will survive by themselves if the water table and air pollution regimes are satisfactory.

5.8.2   Specific issues affecting the survey and monitoring of habitat

It is recommended that bogs are monitored at intervals of not less than 3 years. They should ideally be surveyed in June–October when their vegetation is fully developed, but as they support few annual or deciduous species it is possible to survey them in all seasons.

Air pollution (especially sulphur-based pollution) is known to damage *Sphagnum* communities, so favourable conditions in the long term will require pollution climates below the critical thresholds (SO_2 10 µg m^{-3}, NO_2 30 µg m^{-3}, NH_3 8 µg m^{-3}) (English Nature, 1993). Ground water quality can also affect bog communities (Lamers *et al.*, 1999).

Maps are usually too small in scale to show the detailed minor topographical variations, and finding your location on a bog may be a significant problem. Furthermore, as there are fine gradations between many bog communities, there is likely to be significant variation in the boundaries drawn by different surveyors; monitoring such boundaries is unlikely to be reliable. Aerial photographs may be really helpful for both location and boundary delimitation. Careful stratification may be required to ensure that the range of bog communities and sub-communities is adequately covered and sampling is carried out efficiently.

Vehicular access is always undesirable and in any case is usually impossible. Trampling can affect *Sphagnum* cover on some bogs, with footprints remaining for 20–30 months. It is very easy to damage bog vegetation during a survey, and damage by trampling around permanent quadrats is often excessive (Rowell, 1988). Duckboards, ladders or inflatable mattresses can help to spread the weight of the surveyor. Permanent markers may be difficult to relocate or may become overgrown by

Sphagnum; the sensitivity of the vegetation to trampling means that non-permanent techniques should be used wherever possible. These effects, coupled with small-scale variations from year to year, can make comparisons problematic.

Ideally, the peat moss should be intact, but most bogs have been damaged in one or more ways by cutting, drainage, burning, grazing, agriculture, forestry and other developments. If these activities are still continuing, specific monitoring of their effects may be required (see Chapter 7).

Bogs can be dangerous and should be surveyed with care. Safety guidelines outlined in Part I, Box 2.11 should be followed.

5.9   STANDING OPEN WATER

5.9.1   Surveying and monitoring requirements and methods

Attributes for assessing habitat condition

This habitat class includes both natural and artificial standing fresh waters, ranging in size from a few square metres upwards, and therefore encompasses a large variety of habitats in Britain, including freshwater lochs, meres, reservoirs, gravel pits, ponds, canals and temporary pools. As a result of this variety and the special character of these habitats, their attributes and the monitoring methods can only be outlined in this *Handbook*. Further information is available on these topics in the recommended reference sources listed at the end of the book. Lagoons and other marine habitats are not covered by this volume. Ditches were discussed in Section 5.3.

Palmer *et al.* (1992) found that their plant community classification closely followed classifications based on water chemistry (see, for example, Vollenweider, 1968; Ratcliffe, 1977). Submerged and floating macrophytes form the primary basis for the classification and selection of SSSIs for freshwater habitats (NCC, 1989). For standing waters, representative sites are selected for each of ten types of macrophyte community identified from a detailed study of water bodies throughout Britain (Palmer, 1989; Palmer *et al.*, 1992). The characteristic macrophyte communities of these types

Table 5.10. *The trophic categories of waters in terms of nitrogen and phosphorus*

Status	Total P (mg^{-1})	Inorganic N (mg^{-1})
Ultra-oligotrophic	<0.005	<0.02
Oligo-mesotrophic	0.005–0.01	0.2–0.4
Meso-eutrophic	0.01–0.03	0.30–0.65
Eu-polytrophic	0.03–0.1	0.5–1.5
Polytrophic	>0.10	>1.5

Source: From Vollenweider (1968).

are therefore fundamental to assessing condition and must therefore be monitored and maintained. Other important plant-related attributes include NVC community species richness, taking into account the level of richness expected for the type of water body. A rich assemblage of *Potamogeton* spp. in particular is also a good indicator of high botanical quality. An extensive fringe of emergent vegetation is also a desirable attribute of an open water site, even if its intrinsic value as fen habitat is not high.

The abundance and availability of phosphorus (Table 5.10) normally limits and therefore determines the growth of phytoplankton and macrophytes (Mainstone *et al.*, 1993). Under certain circumstances, nitrogen can be the limiting nutrient for aquatic plants, particularly if phosphorus concentrations are very high as a result of enrichment from sewage treatment works or internal loading.

However, the availability of plant nutrients changes with the seasons as a result of a variety of influences. Therefore, a more constant measure of productivity is provided by alkalinity (Table 5.11). According to this scheme, water bodies are conventionally classed as dystrophic, oligotrophic, mesotrophic and eutrophic in increasing order of calcium carbonate concentration and productivity. A fifth class is marl lakes, which have the highest levels of alkalinity but in which productivity is limited because phosphate is bound to the sediment and therefore unavailable for plant growth.

Dystrophic waters include the small waterbodies and pool systems commonly found on peat bogs. They are solely rain-fed and thus receive

Table 5.11. *Alkalinity characteristics of different types of freshwater body*

| | Alkalinity | | |
Status	CaCO$_3$ (mg l^{-1})	mequiv. l^{-1}	pH
Dystrophic	0–2	0.00–0.04	<6
Oligotrophic	0–10	0.0–0.2	6–7
Mesotrophic	10–30	0.2–0.6	*c.* 7
Eutrophic	>30	>0.6	>7
Marl	>100	>2.0	>7.4

Source: From Ratcliffe (1977).

water that contains no mineral salts dissolved from the underlying rocks (Andrews, 1995). Peat staining also reduces light penetration and macrophyte growth. Consequently, productivity is low and they support a restricted range of flora and fauna. The water is also often too acidic to support fish. However, the absence of fish and low numbers of other predators such as birds provides favourable conditions for dragonflies, water bugs, midges and other invertebrates.

Oligotrophic waters are typically upland lakes in areas with hard, nutrient-poor rock types. They have a low biodiversity and biomass of plants and animals; fish are principally salmonids. Mesotrophic waters have the highest biodiversity of standing fresh waters, often combining elements of oligotrophic and mesotrophic systems, and also support rich and abundant macrophyte communities. Furthermore, relative to other types of lake, they contain a high proportion of nationally rare and scarce species of aquatic plants (Anon., 1995). Macro-invertebrates are also particularly well represented. Eutrophic waters are more typical of lowland areas of Britain and support a high biomass of vegetation (including plankton and macrophytes), and high numbers of fish (usually coarse species such as cyprinids, Perch *Perca fluviatilis* and Pike *Esox lucius*) and birds, particularly in winter.

Nutrient status is therefore normally regarded as a key attribute of water bodies, as it is an inherent and inseparable characteristic of such features (see Part II, Section 2.1.2 and Glossary). Consequently, a common requirement of monitoring standing waters is to measure their characteristic nutrient and pH properties to ensure that these are being maintained within natural fluctuations. Direct measurement of such chemical properties can be undertaken but interpretation may not always be straightforward. However, as macrophytes are highly influenced by water chemistry, monitoring information on their distribution and abundance can provide information on water chemistry conditions. Macrophytes have been widely used for pollution monitoring of rivers in Europe and the UK, but less so for standing waters. Palmer *et al.* (1992) used the results of their analysis of macrophytes (as described above) for the development of a 'trophic ranking score' system that allows assessment of changes in trophic status over time. See Palmer (1989) and Palmer *et al.* (1992) for further details.

Advantages of using macrophytes to monitor water chemistry include the fact that they are generally large and easy to identify with the naked eye, can be sampled rapidly, are present throughout the summer months, and can act as accurate reflectors of overall conditions at a fixed point within a water body (Bell, 1996). The disadvantages of using macrophytes are their seasonality, the lack of knowledge about their natural population fluctuations and difficulties with the identification of some species.

A standard method for surveying aquatic macrophytes was developed by the Nature Conservancy Council (NCC) and has been used since 1975 to record aquatic information on standing water bodies throughout Britain. This has been used as the basis for the botanical classification of standing waters described above (Palmer, 1989; Palmer *et al.*, 1992). The method entails walking the perimeter of the water body to record shoreline and shallow-water vegetation. Deeper water is sampled by means of a grapnel thrown from the bank at frequent intervals during the perimeter walk. Where possible, a boat is used, and grapnel samples are obtained from the bottom during transects of the lake and passages parallel to the shore. The cover of all aquatic plants is recorded on a subjective DAFOR scale of abundance: dominant, abundant, frequent, occasional, rare. Although this technique is suitable for the classification and conservation evaluation of standing water bodies it is too subjective and insensitive to be adequate for all but the most basic monitoring purposes. The DAFOR scale in particular is highly subjective and prone to considerable interpretative variation between observers (see Section 6.4.2.)

A variety of methods have been used for monitoring macrophytes, including satellite imagery and aerial photography, grab and rake sampling, subaqua diving and the use of sonar and remotely operated vehicles (ROVs); see Bell (1996) for a review. However, none of these methods has been developed to a stage of wide application and there are no accepted standard protocols. Nevertheless, a suggested technique for the use of grapnel samples to obtain semi-quantitative data on macrophyte presence and frequency is provided in Section 6.3.2. Other methods for monitoring attributes of open water bodies are given in Table 5.12.

Other important aspects of water chemistry that influence the quality of standing water habitats include the concentrations of dissolved oxygen, ammonia, toxic substances such as heavy metals (some of which may occur naturally, e.g. in acidic waters), and pesticides. These cannot, however, be regarded as direct attributes of standing water bodies, but are rather influencing factors that are, in turn, primarily influenced by external factors (e.g. pollution). They should nevertheless be monitored as they can have significant impacts on the condition of interest features. The monitoring of these water chemistry attributes is, however, a specialised activity and the interpretation of results is complex (see Parr (1994) and Hellawell (1997) for reviews). It is therefore recommended that specialist advice be obtained on such chemical analyses.

Water clarity is also an important factor, determining underwater light intensities and hence the occurrence and vertical zonation of aquatic plants. A simple relative measure of this can be obtained by using a Secchi disc. Secchi discs are about 30 cm in diameter with alternating black and white or yellow quarters. The disc is lowered slowly on a calibrated line until the disc is no longer visible, at which point the depth is recorded. The disc is then lowered further and raised until it reappears, at which point a second depth reading is taken. The average of these depths is the final Secchi disc visibility reading. This reading provides a relative measure of water clarity, but can also be used to calculate the depth to which photosynthetic organisms can occur. This is termed the euphotic zone (Z_{eu}) and is between 1.2 and 2.7 times the Secchi disc depth (Moss, 1998). Secchi disc measurements should be made under consistent light conditions and in calm water. Even then, measurements tend to differ according to conditions and variation between observers. For more accurate measurements, underwater light meters should be used, or turbidity (the concentration of suspended particulate matter) can be measured by using a turbidity meter or a suspended solids monitor.

In addition to the primary influence of water quality, other relevant physical attributes of standing waters include the depth and profile of the water body and its substrate type. Maintenance of these conditions and an overall diversity of the physical forms is important.

The vegetation of water bodies can change relatively rapidly as a result of changes in water quality, which in turn can be very rapid as a result of pollution incidents. Vegetation monitoring should therefore be carried out fairly frequently, probably at intervals of no more than 3 years. Sampling of appropriate water-quality determinants should be carried out at least annually, with replicate samples collected on a number of occasions during the peak growing season and preferably at other times as well, especially for water bodies known to be subject to pollution. Phosphorus concentration measurements during the growing season should include total phosphorus as well as soluble reactive phosphorus (SRP), as most SRP will be taken up by growing phytoplankton and macrophytes. Water-quality monitoring is carried out by the regulatory authorities on water bodies over 1 km^2 in size (and a small number of others); these authorities should therefore be contacted when such monitoring is required, to establish what data are routinely collected for the water body in question.

Table 5.12. *A summary of the quality attributes providing an indication of the condition of open water bodies, and their recommended monitoring techniques*

Attribute	Habitat properties	Monitoring technique
Physical properties	Extent	Aerial photography (Section 6.1.3) or satellite-based remote sensing (6.1.2)
Structure	Depth and profile	Physical surveys with echosounders or depth lines (not covered)
	Substrate type	Grab samples, subaqua or ROV inspections (not covered)
Water chemistry	Nutrient status, pH, dissolved oxygen, toxic substances, etc.	Trophic ranking score system (see text) or chemical analysis (see text)
	Turbidity/underwater light	Secchi disc or light meter (see text)
Composition	Community type	NCC method (see text) or NVC for detailed surveys (6.1.6)
	Macrophyte abundance or species richness	Quadrat or transect surveys by subaqua diving (Part III, Section 14.2.1) Grapnel surveys (6.3.2 or 14.2.1)
	Emergent vegetation	Fixed-point photography (6.1.4), quadrat surveys (6.4.2 and 6.4.3) or transects (6.4.6)

Physical attributes are unlikely to change rapidly and therefore monitoring may only need to be carried out at 5–10 year intervals, depending on local circumstances. Additional and immediate monitoring may, however, be required if physical changes are known to occur at a site. See Table 5.12 for a summary of the attributes indicating the condition of open water bodies and recommended techniques for monitoring them.

Management requirements and external impacts

Many standing water bodies require no, or relatively little, management to maintain their conservation interest. However, standing water bodies are increasingly subject to a number of detrimental external impacts.

Pollution is probably the main impact on standing waters but tends to differ between lowland and upland water bodies (Alexander *et al.*, 1997). Nutrient enrichment (eutrophication) from pollution is the main impact on standing waters in the lowlands because of the proximity of intensive agricultural activities and higher densities of human settlements. As described above, under most circumstances aquatic plant productivity in freshwater systems tends to be limited by phosphorus availability. Phosphorus-rich pollutants, such as run-off from cereal fields, farmyard slurry, manure and silage seepage, and effluent from sewage treatment works, are therefore the major causes of freshwater eutrophication (Klapper, 1991). However, nitrogen can become limiting in waters in which phosphorus concentrations are very high. An increase in nitrate concentrations, resulting from agricultural run-off following fertiliser application or the ploughing of old grasslands, may therefore contribute to eutrophication in such circumstances.

The effects of eutrophication may also be exacerbated by excessive water abstraction upstream leading to a reduction in the quantity of water reaching a water body. This may increase nutrient concentrations in the incoming water and increase residence time in the water body, thereby increasing the available time for nutrient uptake by plants.

Eutrophication is less of a problem in the uplands because of the absence of intensive farming and the low human population density. Instead, oligotrophic lakes are prone to acidification from pollutants in rain on account of their naturally low pH and poor buffering capacity.

Other threats include siltation, as a result of ploughing (for agriculture or forestry) or peat cutting on surrounding land, the introduction of alien species of fish, and disturbance of waterbirds and otters resulting from the use of water bodies for leisure activities.

These external factors should therefore be monitored where appropriate, but in many cases these are likely to be the responsibility of the regulatory authorities and may already be covered by ongoing monitoring programmes.

5.9.2   Specific issues affecting the monitoring of the habitat

The monitoring of freshwater habitats is a specialised subject and cannot be dealt with comprehensively here. In particular, assessments of water chemistry can be difficult and require specialised equipment. The interpretation of results in relation to the condition of and impacts on features of interest is also complex. It is therefore recommended that specialist advice be obtained on these subjects. Further information on these can also be obtained from some of the recommended sources listed at the end of the book.

As described above, general assessments of water quality by using macrophyte indicators are easier than chemical analyses. A method for monitoring macrophyte presence and frequency is described in Section 6.3.2.

There are a number of specific practical considerations to take into account when selecting appropriate methods for monitoring water bodies. In particular, the size of the water body will considerably influence the efficiency of different techniques and the resources required to sample it. Access is also an important consideration. Detailed and quantitative techniques may be difficult or impossible to carry out along deep tree-lined water bodies or on large shallow lakes. The distance from a road or navigable watercourse may also restrict the use of some survey methods; ROVs, boats, diving equipment, etc. are difficult to transport on foot. Tables summarising

the suitability of various methods in relation to these and other considerations (such as the macrophyte growth form) are provided in Bell (1996).

Safety is clearly a key consideration when carrying out fieldwork at large water bodies. Key safety measures that should always be followed include proper training of personnel in safety aspects of aquatic monitoring (especially in the use of boats); the correct use of appropriate safety equipment (e.g. life jackets when working over or alongside deep water); working in pairs or teams (never alone); and proper emergency planning (including notifying others of routes and expected return times when working in remote locations). Other safety precautions listed in Part I, Box 2.11, should also be followed where appropriate.

5.10   RIVERS AND STREAMS

5.10.1   Surveying and monitoring requirements and methods

Attributes for assessing habitat condition

As with standing waters, river habitats exhibit a wide range of physical and biological variation, from headwater streams to mature reaches and estuaries. As a result of this variety and the special character of these habitats, their attributes and monitoring methods can only be outlined in this *Handbook*. Further information is available on these topics in the recommended reference sources listed at the end of the book.

Ten major types of river have been identified and used as a basis for SSSI selection (NCC, 1989). This classification was initially based on a Two-Way INdicator SPecies ANalysis (TWINSPAN) of macrophyte data from 1055 sites on over 100 rivers throughout Britain, which identified 54 subdivisions (Holmes, 1983). This has since been recently updated following a re-analysis and the addition of data from a further 459 sites to the original dataset (Holmes *et al.*, 1998, 1999a). The overall structure of the new classification is the same as that of the first version. The highest level consists of four broad groups (A–D) representing an environmental gradient from lowland eutrophic rivers to those that are essentially upland, torrential and oligotrophic.

Group	RCT	Description
A	I	Lowland, low-gradient rivers
	II	Lowland, clay-dominated rivers
	III	Chalk rivers and other base-rich rivers with stable flows
	IV	Impoverished lowland rivers
B	V	Sandstone, mudstone and hard limestone rivers of England and Wales
	VI	Sandstone, mudstone and hard limestone rivers of Scotland and northern England
C	VII	Mesotrophic rivers dominated by gravels, pebbles and cobbles
	VIII	Oligo-mesotrophic rivers
D	IX	Oligotrophic, low-altitude rivers
	X	Ultra-oligotrophic rivers

These four sub-groups are divided into 10 River Community Types (RCTs) with subdivisions into 38 sub-types (see later).

Macrophyte communities are highly influenced by water-flow regimes, water nutrient status and substrate type. These factors tend to vary across the stages of a river as it flows from source to mouth. Consequently, the classification, as described below, reflects the different stages of a river as well as its geology, water chemistry, substrate and characteristic macrophyte communities.

Thus, although macrophyte communities may be the designated features of conservation interest within an SSSI or other site, other attributes of nutrient status, pH and substrate should also be monitored (where feasible) as these are inherent and inseparable characteristics of each River Community Type. Similarly, underlying geology is also an inherent and inseparable characteristic, but this does not need monitoring as it is not expected to change.

The principal factor in controlling the nutrient status of freshwater ecosystems is the abundance and availability of phosphorus, as this normally limits the growth of phytoplankton (free-floating unicellular algae) and macrophytes (other aquatic plants) (Mainstone *et al.*, 1993). Under certain circumstances, nitrogen can be the limiting nutrient for aquatic plants, particularly if phosphorus concentrations are very high as a result of enrichment from sewage treatment works. However, the availability of plant nutrients changes with the season.

A more constant measure of productivity is provided by alkalinity, as indicated by the amount of calcium carbonate dissolved in the water. Definitions of the various trophic categories according to nutrient status (Vollenweider, 1968) and alkalinity (Ratcliffe, 1977) are given in Section 5.9.

Other important aspects of water chemistry that influence the quality of river habitats include dissolved oxygen concentrations, ammonia concentration, turbidity, and concentrations of toxic substances such as heavy metals (some of which may occur naturally, e.g. in acidic waters), and pesticides. These cannot, however, be regarded as direct attributes of river habitats, but they are influencing factors, which are in turn influenced by external factors (e.g. pollution). They should nevertheless be monitored as they can have significant impacts on the condition of interest features.

The monitoring of water chemistry is a specialised activity and the interpretation of results can be difficult (see Parr (1994) and Hellawell (1997) for reviews). It is therefore recommended that specialist advice on such chemical analyses be obtained. Required data may also be collected by the environmental protection authorities as part of their routine water quality monitoring programmes.

Alternatively, water quality can be assessed through macroinvertebrate indicators. This is, however, a specialised technique and cannot be described here. A useful summary of the subject can be found in RSPB/NRA/RSNC (1994); recent reviews of the subject have been carried out by

Metcalfe-Smith (1994), Hellawell (1986, 1997) and Wright *et al.* (1994). Information on techniques can be found in Part III, Chapter 20; see also Hellawell (1978) and HMSO (1978, 1980, 1983). Macrophyte identification guides are available in Croft (1986) and various Institute of Freshwater Ecology publications (www.ceh.nerc.ac.uk). Again, the environmental protection authorities should be contacted, as such data may be available as part of their monitoring programmes.

As with standing waters, macrophytes may be monitored to assess overall water quality (see Section 5.9 for advantages and disadvantages) as well as their own condition as features of conservation interest. Consequently, macrophytes have been widely used for monitoring the water quality of rivers in Europe and the UK. The current technique for this purpose being used in the UK is the mean trophic rank (MTR) system (Holmes *et al.*, 1999b) which develops the earlier plant score system developed by the Standing Committee of Analysts (1987).

The MTR system is based on surveys of selected (usually common) aquatic macrophytes. These are assigned a number from 1 to 10 according to their tolerance/preference for enriched or clean waters: this is the species trophic rank (STR). Depending on the species cover value of listed taxa within a 100 m reach (recorded on a nine-point scale), a mean trophic rank can be assigned. The method is applied by surveying a 100 m length of river, preferably by wading or a combination of wading and walking along the banks in narrow rivers. Where rivers are wadeable, or a boat can be used safely and effectively, the whole channel width should be surveyed. For wide and deep rivers in which the central channel is devoid of vegetation or cannot be accurately surveyed because of its depth, turbidity, etc., a strip 5 m wide down one side (ideally with little shading from trees) should be surveyed. If water clarity is poor, a glass-bottomed bucket or an underwater video camera should be used.

Surveys should be carried out once or twice a year between June and September. From the standard list of species, cover values are estimated on a nine-point scale, with 1 being less than 0.1% cover and 9 being more than 75% cover. MTR calculations have three suffixes of confidence to assess the reliability of the results: I–III indicate whether paired sites being compared were physically comparable; A–C indicate whether results may have been affected by poor survey conditions or the effects of management; and a–c identify how many macrophyte species on the recording sheet were present. The greater the number, the better the confidence in the results.

The MTR system has been used for monitoring water quality around effluent discharge points. Reviews of survey results have shown that the method is effective and efficient. It performed best on river systems that were not already enriched prior to the discharge being monitored and worst on extremely enriched river systems in which one more discharge makes very little difference. Scores are distorted if two sites being compared are not similar in physical character and when few species that are used to calculate scores are present. The method has given good results from clean oligotrophic rivers in south-west England and the Lake District.

A brief review of general monitoring methods for macrophytes is provided in Bell (1996). At its simplest, monitoring may focus on confirmation of the presence of a particular River Community Type. This can be easily carried out by using the standard method for river macrophyte surveys developed by the NCC for its national survey of river communities. Full details of this are given in Holmes (1983) and Boon *et al.* (1996a,b, 2002). In essence, the survey method involves recording macrophytes at sites 1 km long (formed from two contiguous 500 m lengths), situated 5–7 km apart. Surveys include the entire channel and lower slopes of the banks, with separate records being made for macrophytes that are more or less permanently submerged and those that are typically subject to alternate inundation and exposure with the rise and fall of river levels. Terrestrial plants with no special affinity for rivers are excluded from the survey; although rare aquatic plants are recorded, these are not used in the classification process. At each site an estimate is made of the relative macrophyte abundance by using a simplified DAFOR-type scale (1, rare; 2, occasional or frequent; 3, abundant or dominant) and a simple percentage cover scale

(1, <0.1%; 2, 0.1–5.0%; 3, >5%). Surveys are carried out by walking the banks and wading, or by boat for deeper rivers. However, the repeatability of this technique and resulting consistency of classification is unknown, and it may be inadequate for all but the most basic monitoring purposes. Certainly, the abundance and percentage assessments for each species are too subjective and crude for monitoring purposes. Vegetation composition monitoring should instead be carried out by the appropriate adaptation of quadrat and transect techniques (see Section 6.3 for bankside vegetation and Part III, section 14.2.1, for aquatic vegetation).

A method for monitoring aquatic plant assemblages by rake or grapnel samples in deep, slow-flowing rivers is outlined in Section 6.3.2. Maps of the cover of individual species may be appropriate for small stretches of shallow rivers. Mapping may be time-consuming, but it provides detailed and reproducible results that can justify the effort. Further information on this technique is provided in Standing Committee of Analysts (1987) and Wright *et al.* (1981).

Other key features of river habitats include important morphological and hydrological attributes, such as channel width, depth, slope, capacity, substrate type, flow velocity and flow rate (and its seasonality) and the presence of various important habitat features, such as riffles and pool sequences, bars, meanders and waterfalls, etc. The effects of such attributes on river ecology are complex but these, together with biological data, have been recently incorporated in a model that provides a comprehensive and integrated assessment of river conservation value: SERCON (System for Evaluating Rivers for CONservation). SERCON utilises existing habitat and species data for a range of river corridor attributes to apply classic conservation assessment criteria, such as diversity, naturalness, representativeness and rarity, but in a more rigorous manner than has been done in the past (Boon *et al.*, 1996a,b).

For the assessment of many river corridor attributes SERCON depends on outputs from River Habitat Surveys (Environment Agency, 2003) or, rarely, River Corridor Surveys (NRA, 1992) unless similar data are available from other sources. Generally, SERCON is intended to work at large scales, i.e. catchment or sub-catchment scale. It is therefore primarily used as a broad-scale conservation evaluation tool, although evaluations are carried out by dividing rivers into a series of evaluated catchment sections (ECSs). Monitoring of each ECS may be carried out on the basis of scores from the model or individual SERCON attributes. However, assessments of these attributes are to some extent subjective and therefore variation between repeat surveys by different people may limit its value for monitoring compared with more objective and quantitative methods. A full SERCON assessment is also time-consuming, but SERCON is currently being revised; it is expected that version 2 will have a slimmer variant as well as the full version. However, some SERCON attributes could form a useful suite for monitoring.

General monitoring of morphological attributes of rivers can be carried out by using River Habitat Survey methods (see Section 6.3.1.) More detailed and accurate monitoring of the extent of these attributes will probably need to be carried out by the adaptation of other methods such as fixed-point photography (Section 6.1.4), quadrats and transects (Section 6.4 and Part III, Section 14.2.1) or by specialised monitoring techniques that cannot be described here.

Monitoring the hydrological attributes of a river, such as flow rates, is complex, time-consuming and expensive. However, sufficient information necessary for basic conservation monitoring purposes is likely to be available from the environmental protection authorities.

A summary of river attributes that require monitoring is provided in Table 5.13, together with recommended methods for monitoring each. These are described more fully in Chapter 6.

Management requirements and external impacts

High human population density and the presence of intensive agriculture directly affects river condition and water quality. The frequency of rivers affected by, or at risk from, organic and chemical pollution from agriculture, domestic wastes and industry generally increases in the lowlands (and in some areas towards the coast) as the land is more densely populated, agriculture is more intensive and industry is

Table 5.13. *A summary of the quality attributes providing an indication of the condition of rivers, and their recommended monitoring techniques*

Attribute	Habitat properties	Monitoring technique
Physical properties	Extent	Aerial photography (Section 6.1.3) or satellite-based remote sensing (6.1.2)
River morphology	Channel width (bank, full and low flows), shape, substrate type, presence of riffles, pools, meanders, water control structures, etc.	River habitat surveys (6.3.1) or fixed-point photography (6.1.4) for general surveys, quadrats (6.4.2 and 6.4.3) or transects (6.4.6) for detailed studies
Hydrology	e.g. water flow rates and depth	Obtain from environmental protection authorities
Water chemistry	Nutrient status, pH, BOD, dissolved oxygen, toxic substances, etc.	Obtain from environmental protection authorities or use mean trophic rank system (see text) or macroinvertebrate indicators (see text)
Vegetation extent and structure	Coverage of banks and watercourse Vegetation height	Fixed-point photography (6.1.4), line transects or quadrat methods (6.4 or 14.2.1) for detailed studies
Vegetation composition	River community type	NCC method (see text) or NVC surveys (6.1.6) for detailed studies
	Bankside and emergent vegetation species abundance or richness	Line transects (6.4.6) or quadrat methods (6.4.2 and 6.4.3)
	Aquatic macrophyte species abundance or richness	Grapnel surveys in slow moving deep water (6.3.2), quadrat or transect surveys (14.2.1) or mapping for detailed studies in shallow water (see text)

more common. This may also be exacerbated by water abstraction as this may lead to low flows, which can contribute to high pollutant concentrations and reduced dissolved oxygen concentrations. Overall pollution impacts may, however, be less in downstream sections on account of the dilution of pollutants by large volumes of water.

In the upstream reaches and headwaters, pollution may occur from various types of discharge and domestic waste. The ploughing and/or drainage of moorland for forestry and agriculture can lead to high levels of silt and peat run-off, which increases the turbidity levels of the water. Oligotrophic and acid waters are also particularly susceptible to acidification from acid deposition.

In addition to pollution and abstraction problems, management actions may have detrimental effects on the conservation interest of rivers. In particular, flood defence measures such as bank strengthening and canalisation, removal of riparian vegetation, dredging, and the installation of water control structures such as weirs, can have profound impacts on river morphology and in turn on their biological interest. Fisheries management and recreational activities can also have impacts through habitat modifications, disturbance and, in the former case, the introduction of alien species or artificially increased populations of native fish.

5.10.2 Specific issues affecting the survey and monitoring of habitat

As with standing waters, the monitoring of rivers is a specialised subject and therefore it is recommended that specialist advice be obtained before planning and implementing a monitoring programme for these habitats. See Section 5.9 for a discussion of practical considerations regarding monitoring of water bodies. As described above, routine monitoring of water quality and various hydrological factors is carried out on many rivers by the environmental protection authorities. Relevant data may therefore be available for some sites.

Safety is clearly a key consideration when carrying out fieldwork on rivers. Key safety measures that should always be followed include proper training of personnel in safety aspects of aquatic

monitoring (especially in the use of boats), the correct use of safety equipment (e.g. life jackets when working over or alongside deep water) and working in pairs or teams and never alone. Other safety aspects listed in Part I, Box 2.11, should also be followed where appropriate.

Special care should be taken when working on rivers that are liable to rapid changes in flow.

5.11   MONTANE HABITATS

5.11.1   Surveying and monitoring requirements and methods

Attributes for assessing habitat condition

Montane sites include a range of habitats above the natural tree line. Ninety per cent of the UK resource occurs in Scotland. Information on the monitoring of many of the habitats present in the uplands is covered elsewhere (scrub in Section 5.1; grasslands in Section 5.4; heathlands in Section 5.6; wetlands in Section 5.7; streams and pools in Sections 5.9 and 5.10; and blanket bogs in Section 5.12). Only a brief account is therefore provided here.

Key attributes of importance to montane habitats are physical features such as bare cliffs, rocks, scree and soil and the prolonged presence of snow patches. Montane vegetation types are rather distinct and often rare in the UK, such as alpine calcareous grassland. Montane habitats commonly occur in mosaics to form habitat complexes of particular collective importance for their flora. Species composition can be very important, with many relict Arctic–alpine and endemic species occurring. A summary of the key attributes that require monitoring is provided in Table 5.14, together with recommended methods for monitoring each.

Management requirements and external impacts

Montane vegetation is particularly vulnerable to heavy grazing (Section 7.1), accidental burning (Section 7.2), erosion (Section 7.3) and air pollution. Montane habitats are known to be sensitive to air pollution and acidification, so maintaining an acceptable condition in the long term will require pollution climates below the critical concentrations (SO_2 $10\,\mu g\,m^{-3}$, NO_2 $30\,\mu g\,m^{-3}$, NH_3 $8\,\mu g\,m^{-3}$)

Table 5.14. *A summary of the quality attributes providing an indication of the condition of montane habitats, and their recommended monitoring techniques*

Attribute	Habitat properties	Monitoring technique
Physical properties	Extent	Phase I mapping (Section 6.1.5) with aerial photography (6.1.3) for basic long-term monitoring NVC surveys with quadrat sampling (6.1.6) for NVC vegetation types
	Exposed rock, scree and bare soil, and snow lie	Aerial (6.1.3) or fixed-point (6.1.4) photography, quadrats (6.4.2) or transects (6.4.6)
	Soil nutrients	6.2.2
Composition	Characteristic communities	Quadrats (6.4.2) or transects (6.4.6), with NVC analysis (6.1.6) where NVC communities are Notified Features or important attributes
	Species composition and richness	Mini-quadrats (6.4.3)
	Presence/absence of typical/indicator species	Look–see or total counts (Part III, sections 15.2.1 and 15.2.2,) quadrats (6.4.2 and 6.4.3) or transects (6.4.6)

(English Nature, 1993). These aspects should therefore also be monitored though, as it may be difficult to monitor air pollution directly, data may need to be drawn from wider-scale models.

5.11.2   Specific issues affecting the surveying and monitoring of habitat

It is recommended that uplands are monitored at 3 or 6 year intervals. They are almost always best surveyed in July and August when the weather is better and the vegetation fully developed. Access may be difficult late in the season because of deer stalking or grouse shooting.

When planning surveys allow at least 1 day lost to bad weather for each survey day. The logistics of getting equipment into place can be very difficult; often, cursory surveillance may be the best option. Aerial photography (Section 6.1.3) may be cost-effective for large areas.

Determining your location may be very difficult in wet weather, and especially on large uniform upland areas is virtually impossible from maps. Global positioning systems (GPS) have distinct advantages, despite their inaccuracies (although these are substantially improving over time).

The complexity of some sites means that stratified sampling will be required and will have to be carefully designed to efficiently cover the range of habitats and their localised variations. On account of the large size of sites and the time required to move between samples, multi-level sampling may be appropriate (Part I, Section 2.3.)

If permanent quadrats are to be used, frost heave may result in loss of markers. Using good location features, such as large boulders, and making detailed measurements may be very helpful for relocating quadrats. Rock climbing bolts have been used as markers but are now considered unsightly. Scree slopes are often mobile; permanent quadrats are therefore inadvisable on this habitat.

For assessing changes in many features of the vegetation, such as species richness and sward height and cover, the techniques outlined in Section 5.4 can be applied. The hanging quadrat technique may be useful for recording quadrats on vertical surfaces (Rich & Matcham, 1995).

Unfortunately, the NVC does not cover lichen and bryophyte vegetation, and there is no workable account of these vegetation types available. James *et al.* (1977) give a preliminary conspectus of lichen communities, which may be of some use for some communities. The specialist upland bryophytes and lichens also require expert botanists.

The persistence of snow patches varies from year to year, but snow cover has usually gone by late July. The snow often acts to catch nutrients from wind-blown vegetation, and snow patches are thus often relatively nutrient-rich compared with surrounding ground.

Alpine cliffs and rocks can support rich plant communities. These habitats are dangerous to work on and often unstable. Roped-access work may be required for critical areas, but is very time-consuming. Particular care should be taken when working in montane areas; all relevant safety recommendations outlined in Part I, Box 2.11, should be strictly followed where appropriate.

5.12   BLANKET BOG

5.12.1   Surveying and monitoring requirements and methods

Attributes for assessing habitat condition

Under a number of conditions (such as suitable rainfall–evapotranspiration regime and topography), blanket bogs often occur as the dominant habitat type within extensive landscapes, and may form mosaics with other vegetation types; such extensive blanket bog landscapes are of particular importance. Habitat extent is therefore a key attribute.

The physical structure of bogs is also considered to define their condition and therefore there are several structural attributes that should be monitored. It has been suggested that blanket bogs require at least 0.5 m of peat (NCC, 1990a) to separate the vegetation communities from the underlying substrate and provide the appropriate hydrological and chemical conditions for *Sphagnum* growth, although many have on average 2–3 m of peat. Some blanket bogs may also have shallower peat areas because of their topography. Ideally, the peat mass should be intact, but most bogs have been damaged to some extent by cutting, drainage, burning, grazing, erosion, afforestation or agricultural improvement (see below).

High water tables are essential for bogs to be active (i.e. forming peat); most bogs have water tables near the surface except in drought conditions. However, monitoring water tables alone is not sufficient, even if it could be achieved in a meaningful way, and assessments of whether the bog is forming peat are also important. On account of the slow rate of peat accumulation (in the region of 10 cm over 100 years), it is not practicable to assess this by measuring peat depth and rates of peat accumulation. Instead, it is normally assumed from the active growth of *Sphagnum*. The presence of characteristic *Sphagnum* species can be used to infer the occurrence of active peat formation. In general, if the *Sphagnum* is healthy and growing, the habitat should be in good condition. Other typical species indicative of peat formation capability are often locally important on blanket bogs, and appropriate species may be selected on a site basis. For example, in the north and west *Racomitrium* often replaces *Sphagnum* as the dominant bryophyte, and Cotton Grass *Eriophorum vaginatum* is an important peat-forming species on many high-altitude bogs.

In wet, humid climates the vegetation may be dominated by *Sphagnum*, but in drier conditions there is usually more Heather *Calluna*, Cross-leaved Heath *Erica tetralix*, *Eriophorum* spp. and Deer Grass *Trichophorum* spp.. The significance of different species varies with altitude, longitude and latitude. A significant proportion (perhaps more than 10%) of *Sphagnum* in the main bog communities is considered to indicate active peat formation. Locally determined cover proportions should be derived from analysis of existing quadrat data and other historical observations. Similarly, proportions of other species may be derived from existing data.

Certain NVC bog communities can also indicate good, relatively undisturbed blanket bogs, depending to some extent on geographical location (Rodwell, 1991, vol. 2). The M17 *Scirpus cespitosus-Eriophorum vaginatum* blanket mire, often associated with the M1 *Sphagnum auriculatum* bog pool community in the pools or wettest areas, is the characteristic blanket bog type in oceanic parts of Britain, generally at low altitudes. The M18 *Erica tetralix–Sphagnum papillosum* raised and blanket mire occurs over large areas in Caithness (A. Coupar, personal communication) on cols and in depressions (Rodwell, 1991) and has associated areas of the M2 *Sphagnum cuspidatum/recurvum* bog pool community. The M15 *Scirpus cespitosus–Erica tetralix* wet heath may occur in naturally better drained areas at the bog margin. The M19 *Calluna vulgaris–Eriophorum vaginatum* blanket mire is dominant on high-level blanket bog. NVC-based survey and monitoring is, however, by itself too general to differentiate between good and poor bog communities (such as M18), being particularly insensitive to changes in structural attributes (e.g. as a result of grazing). Interpretation of the presence of so-called 'degraded' communities should also be undertaken with care.

Woody species (except *Salix repens*, *Betula nana*, *Vaccinium* spp. and Bog Myrtle *Myrica gale*) are generally not considered to be natural components of blanket bogs. Therefore, invasion by other birch, willow or other woody species should be monitored, although this may indicate surface flushing (unlikely) and the absence of grazing and burning, rather than a drying out of the bog.

Lastly, structure is very important in blanket bogs in determining hydrological functioning and the presence of different features and niches. At a large scale, individual blanket bog units (mesotopes) occur in a range of topographical positions such as watersheds, valley sides, spurs and saddle mires. These often form inter-related complexes (macrotopes) of greater interest than individual mesotopes.

Within each mesotope it is also natural to have variation in the communities present related to variations in topography, hydrology and substrate features, including transitions to vegetation on mineral soils. Pool and ridge patterning in some of the northern bogs is of particular interest. All bogs display some form of surface patterning, which represents an important source of biodiversity.

Most relatively undisturbed bog surfaces usually show distinctive fine-scale variation (microtopes) with small drier hummocks and wetter hollows related to growth of *Sphagnum* and other plants, although the large-scale features may be highly restricted or locally frequent.

A summary of attributes providing an indication of the condition of bog habitats and their recommended monitoring methods is given in Table 5.15.

It is recommended that bogs be monitored at 3 to 6 year intervals.

Management requirements and external impacts

The management of bogs can markedly affect their quality. Grazing, burning and drainage can all damage the vegetation, and even trampling can affect *Sphagnum* cover. Under natural conditions the blanket bogs are likely to have been lightly grazed. Information on indicators of drying, burning, grazing and trampling are given in MacDonald *et al.* (1998a,b).

Air pollution (especially sulphur-based pollution) is known to damage *Sphagnum* communities so maintaining an acceptable condition in the long term will require pollution regimes below the critical concentrations (SO_2 10 µg m^{-3}, NO_2 30 µg m^{-3}, NH_3 8 µg m^{-3}) (English Nature, 1993).

Stoneman & Brooks (1997) provide management advice for blanket bogs.

5.12.2   Specific issues affecting the survey and monitoring of habitat

Bogs should be surveyed from July to September when their vegetation is fully developed, although all attributes other than those pertaining to deciduous species can be monitored at other times of year.

Wet bog habitats can be very sensitive to trampling and there is therefore a considerable risk of damage from monitoring activities. Methods should be chosen appropriately, according to local conditions. In general, permanent quadrat or transect methods should be avoided and disturbance of the bog surface kept to a minimum. In particular, on vulnerable habitats, automated or remote monitoring techniques should be used where appropriate. The number of sampling locations should also be kept to the minimum necessary and the interval between sampling occasions should be as long as possible.

As mentioned above, bog habitats can be very extensive and this raises a number of problems. In

Table 5.15. *A summary of the quality attributes providing an indication of the condition of blanket bog,
and their recommended monitoring techniques*

Attribute	Habitat properties	Monitoring technique
Physical properties	Extent	Phase I mapping (Section 6.1.5) with aerial photography (6.1.3) (or satellite-based remote sensing (6.1.2) for very large sites). NVC surveys with quadrat sampling (6.1.6) for detailed studies
	Water table	Dipwells or WALRAGS (6.2.1)
	Bare peat	Aerial photography (6.1.3), quadrats (6.4.2 and 6.4.3) or transects (6.4.6)
	Peat depth	Soil augers or levels from mineral ground
Composition	Characteristic communities	Quadrats (6.4.2) or transects (6.4.6), with NVC analysis (6.1.6) where NVC communities are Notified Features or important attributes
	Species composition and richness	Mini-quadrats (6.4.3) (quadrat size depending on scale of vegetation)
	Presence–absence of typical or indicator species	Look–see or total counts (Part III, Sections 15.2.1 and 15.2.2), quadrats (6.4.2 and 6.4.3) or transects (6.4.6).
Structure	Landscape and habitat mosaics	Aerial or fixed-point photography (6.1.3 and 6.1.4)
	Structural features (pool and hummock, and/or hollow and ridge as appropriate)	Conventional quadrats (6.4.2) or transects (6.4.6). Photographs from vantage points may be useful (6.1.3 and 6.1.4)
Dynamics	Peat formation	Quadrat- (6.4.2 and 6.4.3) or transect- (6.4.6) based assessment of indicator species

particular, vehicular access is likely to be impossible, and is in any case undesirable because of the potential for lasting, if local, damage. A considerable amount of time is likely to be spent walking to monitoring locations. Sampling strategies should therefore be designed with this in mind, using techniques such as multi-stage sampling (Part I, Section 2.3.4). Automated monitoring techniques (e.g. for water levels) may also be cost-effective but should only be used in very specific circumstances, e.g. the monitoring of a consented, but potentially damaging activity. Similarly, expensive remote methods such as aerial photography (or for very large sites, satellite-based sensing) may be financially viable.

Variations in topography, hydrology and other physical properties can lead to considerable heterogeneity in bog habitats. As a result, it may often be necessary to subdivide large and complex sites into compartments for monitoring purposes (Part I, Section 2.1.7.)

The size, remoteness and extreme weather conditions of many bog sites also raise potentially significant safety problems. Safety protocols (see Part I, Box 2.11) should therefore be strictly followed. In particular, personnel should not carry out monitoring alone at remote sites and should be properly equipped and trained.

5.13   MARITIME BOULDERS, ROCKS, CLIFFS AND SLOPES

5.13.1   Surveying and monitoring requirements and methods

Attributes for assessing habitat condition
The 4000 km of sea cliffs in the UK are a major nature conservation resource of international

importance. They are important as extensive areas of natural habitat, which is often relatively little affected by human activity. Some cliffs have important geological exposures, but the geological, botanical and zoological interests may not coincide. Cliff habitat, as defined here, includes all the vegetation types in the NVC sea cliff vegetation chapter of Rodwell (2000, vol. 5), from the vegetation of vertical sections at the base of a cliff to the flatter top parts.

The extent of the sea cliff habitat is not easy to measure because vertical projections are not represented well on maps, although in practice often the upper parts of cliffs are slopes and only the lower parts are vertical. Natural erosion of cliffs results in regular loss of area. Rather than monitoring loss of material to the seaward side (which could be monitored by photographs from the sea), it may be best to concentrate on monitoring loss to agriculture, etc. on the inland side.

Coastal sea cliff vegetation and species composition are important factors to monitor, as they are the basis of this unique habitat. The vegetation often shows marked zonation depending on geology, erosion, geographical location and especially the degree of exposure to wind and salt spray. The lowest zones are primarily occupied by lichens and some bryophytes, which grade into higher plant vegetation above. In some exposed sites the clifftop vegetation grades into maritime heath, grassland and scrub, which form an integral part of the cliff habitat, but in many cases they are truncated by agriculture or development inland. Soft cliffs often display a much wider range of vegetation than that included in the NVC maritime cliffs section, and much of it is of nature conservation interest.

The most important influence on the habitat is the amount of salt spray, which is strongly influenced by situation and exposure. On the accessible upper parts of the cliff top, where salt deposition is weakest, structure and composition may be strongly affected by management, especially grazing. The soil sodium : organic content ratio is a useful yardstick for assessing the influence of spray (Rodwell, 2000). Table 5.16 gives a summary of the attributes providing an indication of the condition of maritime habitats and their recommended monitoring methods.

Management requirements and external impacts

An account of sea cliffs and their management has been presented by Mitchley & Malloch (1991). The main management tools are grazing, mowing and burning, although much of the lower parts of cliffs are inaccessible and do not need to be managed.

The main problem in maintaining the area of sea cliff is that the upper edge is usually valuable farmland, which is expensive to use as a replacement for areas lost to erosion. The most practical measure to maintain area may be to ensure that no further truncation of the inland margin of the cliff vegetation occurs, and accept loss on the seaward side.

The main threats to sea cliffs are agricultural activities, tourism, and coastal development and protection. Coastal protection works or uncontrolled dumping may prevent erosion and affect coastal processes, leading to loss of interest. There may be some risk from accidental fires, although this has probably decreased with the cessation of stubble burning. Oil pollution may be a serious risk in some places close to shipping lanes; the lower cliff communities may be seriously affected by oil deposition.

5.13.2   Specific issues affecting the survey and monitoring of habitat

It is recommended that cliffs be monitored at 3 or 6 year intervals. They can be surveyed between May and October, although if annual species are important they should be surveyed in early summer. This may conflict with the bird nesting season.

Salt deposition during summer storms may have a dominant influence on the zonation of the vegetation and cause the death of some areas. It may be worth monitoring salt deposition if damage is also expected from herbicides etc. used on adjacent farmland.

Unfortunately, the NVC does not cover lichen and bryophyte vegetation, which is predominant at the lowest levels on cliffs; the best available account of these vegetation types available is James et al. (1977). The specialist maritime bryophytes and lichens also require expert survey.

As vegetation composition is often strongly related to soils and topography, careful stratification

Table 5.16. *A summary of the quality attributes providing an indication of the condition of maritime habitats, and their recommended monitoring techniques*

Attribute	Habitat properties	Monitoring technique
Physical properties	Extent	Phase I mapping (Section 6.1.5) with aerial photography (6.1.3) for broad long-term changes NVC surveys with quadrat sampling (6.1.6) for detailed studies
	Soil salinity	Soil analysis (6.2.2)
Composition	Characteristic communities	Quadrats (6.4.2) or transects (6.4.6), with NVC analysis (6.1.6) where NVC communities are Notified Features or important attributes
	Species composition and richness	Mini-quadrats (6.4.3)
	Presence–absence of typical or indicator species	Look–see or total counts (Part III, Sections 15.2.1 and 15.2.2), quadrats (6.4.2 and 6.4.3) or transects (6.4.6)
Structure	Zonation between vegetation types	Transects (6.4.6), fixed-point (6.1.4) or aerial photography (6.1.3)
	Pattern within vegetation types	Quadrat sampling (6.4.2 and 6.4.3), fixed-point photography (6.1.4)

may be required to ensure that the range of quality and extent is adequately covered.

Generally, the upper limit of cliff vegetation is marked by a change to agriculture or development, but in some localities there may be natural transitions to moorland. The influence of the sea and salt declines with increasing distance from the sea and decreasing exposure, and it may be difficult to define the inland edges. If permanent markers are required, these are best established at the landward edge on sites with significant erosion.

Safety considerations may prevent detailed mapping of vegetation for monitoring. There are severe practical difficulties in mapping vertical cliffs, especially on crumbly rocks. Rope work may be required and this must be carried out by adequately trained personnel using appropriate equipment. The hanging quadrat technique may be useful for recording quadrats on vertical surfaces (Rich & Matcham, 1995). For assessing changes in many features of the vegetation, such as species richness and sward height and cover, the techniques outlined in Section 5.4 can be applied. For dwarf shrub heath, see Section 5.6.

5.14   SHINGLE ABOVE HIGH TIDE

5.14.1   Surveying and monitoring requirements and methods

Attributes for assessing habitat condition

The major vegetated shingle structures of Britain have been reviewed in detail by Randall (1989) and Sneddon & Ranwell (1993, 1994). There are estimated to be 6115 ha in the UK. These may be of considerable interest for their geomorphology in addition to their distinctive plant and animal communities.

In general the extent of shingle should be relatively easy to monitor on the inland edge, though the shore edge may be more dynamic. The development of a shingle beach is dependent on a supply of sediment and waves, winds and tidal currents. Much material may be lost or supplied naturally during storm episodes, but some loss may also occur through shingle extraction or indirectly as a result of coastal protection elsewhere. The supply of shingle to the site by natural processes is best monitored from continued measurements of erosion or accretion at fixed points and may need to be assessed over decades. Mass movement of shingle to or from a site is very difficult to quantify.

The vegetation types present are key attributes. Shingle habitats include open pioneer stages close to the sea, and grassland, heaths, scrub and moss- and lichen-dominated vegetation on very old, stable shingle further inland. Near the shore the vegetation is typically open with many maritime species. These decrease in abundance away from the shore as inland species increase. The NVC types have been revised by Sneddon & Ranwell (1993), whose classification provides more detail than the NVC but requires rationalisation. Some sites may be important for lichens; undisturbed shingles may have their own distinctive communities (James *et al.*, 1977), which may require monitoring in their own right.

Salinity, hydrology, and the stability, morphology and composition of the shingle are principal factors determining vegetation composition. Strong patterning within the vegetation may occur related to shingle ridge structure, with distinct lines of *Crambe* or *Glaucium* on the shingle ridges. These patterns may become blurred as humus builds up in the shingle and is colonised by additional plants. For invertebrates this structuring of the vegetation and small-scale mosaics are more important than its composition.

There may be strong zonation from the shore to the inland edge that is of considerable interest. The vegetation of the foreshore is strongly controlled by the environment and only physical damage will markedly affect it. Chance determines which species colonise the foreshore. Transitions to inland communities are often truncated by anthropogenic activities, or shingle communities may grade into rocky or sandy habitats. Sites with a range of communities, including pioneer communities, are especially valuable.

Shingle sites are often associated with other special interest habitats, such as lagoons, sand dunes and saltmarshes, and the transitions between them can be of interest. The hydrology is often important for lagoons and saltmarshes. Table 5.17 summarises the attributes indicating the condition of shingle, together with recommended techniques for their monitoring.

Management requirements and external impacts

Most shingle sites do not require management. However, human pressures such as coastal defence works, development, shingle extraction and recreational activities may need some monitoring.

Shingle extraction has affected some sites and is probably the single most damaging activity. Military and tourism activity has also damaged some sites. Grazing may result in the loss of some sensitive taxa, but most sites are ungrazed. Oil pollution may occur at some sites.

Shingle banks may be coastal defence features in their own right, and they are often maintained by supplies of shingle from further up the coast. Coastal defence works elsewhere may therefore starve some sites of their supplies.

5.14.2   Specific issues affecting the survey and monitoring of habitat

It is recommended that shingle sites be monitored every 3 years. Measurements of growth or loss of shingle should be made every decade. Sites are best monitored between May and October, but nesting birds may restrict access. Mapping can be difficult in uniform shingle structures, but is often relatively traightforward provided details of topography are available. Aerial photographs can be invaluable.

5.15   SAND DUNES AND STRANDLINE VEGETATION

5.15.1   Surveying and monitoring requirements and methods

Attributes for assessing habitat condition

Sand dune vegetation includes strandlines, dunes, dune slacks, dune heath and scrub. The different types form a complex, dynamic, sensitive ecosystem capable of rapid change, and each part creates its own problems for monitoring. Because of the dynamic nature of sand dunes and their associated vegetation, long-term (10 year) views on the amount of each habitat and natural succession between them should be taken.

There is a significant amount of information available on the extent and composition of sand

Table 5.17. *A summary of the quality attributes providing an indication of the condition of shingle, and their recommended monitoring techniques*

Attribute	Habitat properties	Monitoring technique
Physical properties	Extent	Phase I (Section 6.1.5), NVC surveys with quadrat sampling (6.1.6), fixed-point (6.1.4) or aerial photography (6.1.3)
	Hydrology	Piezometers, dipwells or WALRAGS (6.2.1)
	Salinity	Soil analysis (6.2.2) and water chemistry analysis (not covered)
	Topography and land loss	Level surveying or fixed-point height surveys (not covered), aerial photography (6.1.3)
Composition	Characteristic communities	Quadrats (6.4.2) or transects (6.4.6), with NVC analysis (6.1.6) where NVC communities are Notified Features or important attributes (see also Sneddon & Ranwell (1993) community types)
	Species composition and richness	Mini-quadrats (6.4.3)
	Presence/absence of typical/indicator species	Look–see or total counts (Sections 15.2.1 and 15.2.2), quadrats (6.4.2 and 6.4.3) or transects (6.4.6)
	Zonation between vegetation types	Transects (6.4.6), fixed-point (6.1.4) or aerial photography (6.1.3)
Structure	Pattern within vegetation types	Quadrat sampling (6.4.2 and 6.4.3), fixed-point photography (6.1.4)

dunes (see, for example, Dargie, 1993). Although the overall extent is relatively easy to monitor, the proportions of NVC types within each system can be very difficult to follow reliably as a result of the intrinsic difficulties of surveying a complex habitat, the natural rate of change and the natural continual gradation between the dune communities. The typical standardised succession from strandline to yellow dune to grey dune to fixed dune, and to dune heath in some sites, can be used as a framework for understanding the dynamics of the system, but the whole sequence is rarely seen in practice. Typically the vegetation patterns are strongly related to topography, soil pH, water table, nutrient availability and grazing. There are usually extensive mosaics forming complex patterns across the dunes, and within each part there may also be mosaics of vegetation. These complexities mean that a very clear set of requirements must be set out before attributes are selected for monitoring, and different attributes will be required for different parts of the dune system.

The percentage cover of vegetation usually increases inland and the extent of bare sand decreases. Bare sand can give a good indication of the likely stability of dunes and indicate grazing or public pressure, but occasional erosion of stabilised dunes may occur naturally and is central to long-term maintenance of slacks.

Sand dunes decrease in salinity and pH and increase in organic content with increasing distance from the sea. Nutrients are usually low throughout except on the strandline. Soil analysis can therefore provide valuable information directly relevant to the vegetation types. The water table is also very important for determining the distribution of slacks and their associated vegetation, and may be worth monitoring if water abstraction is increasing. Water will vary in salinity depending on the local hydrology.

Given the importance of grazing to dune systems, it is worthwhile monitoring some aspects of grazing, such as stocking densities, at the same time as other features (see Section 7.1). A summary of attributes giving an indication of the condition of sand dune and strandline habitats and their recommended monitoring methods is provided in Table 5.18.

Management requirements and external impacts
The main management tools on dunes are grazing and scrub clearance. The structure of individual stands is largely determined by grazing, the intensity of which is site-specific and requires careful adjustment. Undergrazing results in rank grassland and development of scrub, whereas heavy grazing results in few flowers, poaching, erosion and uniform turf. Both Rabbit *Oryctolagus cuniculus* grazing and low nutrient concentrations are important for the maintenance of diversity on some dune systems.

Oil pollution episodes can have dramatic effects on strandlines on account of both the toxic effects of the oil and the effects of the clean-up operation. Tidy beach campaigns (for the prestigious 'Blue Flag' awards) can also significantly damage strandline habitats if cleaning is carried out mechanically, but some cleaning of human rubbish by hand must be made acceptable in some sensitive areas: unsightly rubbish needs to be removed in order to improve habitat condition (Llewellyn & Shackley, 1996).

The major threats to dune systems are coastal protection, tourism, golf courses, afforestation, land claim for agriculture, sand extraction, military use and access roads (Ranwell, 1972; Doody, 1985). The major causes of erosion on many dune systems are human feet and vehicles. Coastal defence works may also affect the supply of sediments and alter coastlines, with knock-on effects for the occurrence of these habitats. All these may require monitoring.

5.15.2 Specific issues affecting the survey and monitoring of habitat

It is recommended that dune systems be monitored at 3 or 6 year intervals. The strandline communities act as metapopulations, with repeated recolonisation from a few permanent major donor sites or as a patchwork mosaic of extinction and recolonisation, and may require monitoring annually (a long-term view of the occurrence of these must also be taken, such as over 25 years). Different parts of the dune systems may need to be monitored at different times of year; for example, slacks and strandlines are best monitored in July and August, whereas yellow dunes are best monitored in May and June while annual plant species are still present.

As the composition of dune vegetation is often strongly related to soils and topography, careful sampling stratification may be required to ensure that the full range of communities is adequately and efficiently covered. For assessing changes in many features of the vegetation, such as species richness and sward height and cover, the techniques outlined in Section 5.4 can be applied. For dwarf shrub vegetation see Section 5.6, and for slacks much of the fen section (5.7) will be relevant.

Orientation on dune systems while monitoring can be extremely difficult, even with good topographic maps. Permanent markers are notoriously difficult to re-find and frequently become undermined or buried by sand.

5.16   SALTMARSH

5.16.1   Surveying and monitoring requirements and methods

Attributes for assessing habitat condition
There are estimated to be about 44 370 ha of saltmarsh in Britain, occupying about 10% of the coastline (Burd, 1989).

Saltmarshes are dynamic habitats; natural change in extent is to be expected. They may be subject to periods of sediment erosion or accretion. Sediment movement patterns may be quite complex. Larger saltmarshes are intrinsically more valuable than smaller ones because of the increased range of habitats within them and the lesser disturbance occurring at the upper edges. The development of small steps or edges at the outer margin of the marsh is usually an obvious sign of erosion. Accretion can be monitored by

Table 5.18. *A summary of the quality attributes providing an indication of the condition of sand dunes and strandline vegetation, and their recommended monitoring techniques*

Attribute	Habitat properties	Monitoring technique
Physical properties	Extent	Phase I mapping (Section 6.1.5) with aerial photography (6.1.3) NVC surveys (6.1.6) with quadrat (6.4.2) or belt transect (6.4.6) sampling or fixed-point (6.1.4) photography
	Topography and sand accumulation/erosion	Level surveying or fixed-point height surveys (not covered), aerial or fixed-point photographs (6.1.3, 6.1.4)
	pH and nutrient content of sand	Soil analysis (6.2.2)
	Water table	Dipwells (6.2.1)
	Ground-water salinity	Conductivity meters (6.2.2)
Composition	Characteristic communities	Quadrats (6.4.2) or transects (6.4.6), with NVC analysis (6.1.6) where NVC communities are Notified Features or important attributes
	Species composition and richness	Mini-quadrats (6.4.3)
	Presence–absence of typical or indicator species	Look–see or total counts (15.2.1, 15.2.2), quadrats (6.4.2, 6.4.3) or transects (6.4.6)
Structure	Percentage bare sand	Quadrats (6.4.2–6.4.4), transects (6.4.6) or aerial photography (6.1.3)
	Tidal litter	Quadrats (6.4.2–6.4.4) or transects (6.4.6)
Dynamics	Zonation	Transects (6.4.6), fixed-point (6.1.4) or aerial (6.1.3) photography

measuring the increased height of a marsh relative to fixed points, or the extension of its outer edge. Extent is thus a key factor in monitoring but is subject to long-term natural changes.

Saltmarshes are quite complex habitats and provide a range of attributes that can be measured, depending on the monitoring objectives. Natural changes in species and vegetation may occur, coupled with changes in the sediments. It should be possible to monitor the range of vegetation types present on saltmarshes fairly simply; most sites have been mapped by using a simplified vegetation survey (Burd, 1989). Species composition can also be surveyed for selected species.

A key attribute is the vegetation zonation, determined by tidal submergence. The zonation is usually simple to observe and map by using transects. Transitions to freshwater swamps at the inland end of coastal-linked lakes, lochs and estuaries and natural communities inland are valuable, but sites have often been truncated by sea walls, land reclamation or agriculture.

Many saltmarshes are dissected by small creeks and channels, which provide microhabitats within more uniform areas of marsh. The upper levels of ungrazed or lightly grazed marshes are usually relatively rich in species, at least partly as a result of the range of microhabitats present, but lower marshes are intrinsically relatively species-poor. Some inland species may also occur near the top of weakly saline marshes. Salt pans and small pools within the marsh are an intrinsic part of many marshes and also add diversity. Structural diversity within the vegetation may be very important for invertebrates. Variation in the salinity of the sediments adds to the floristic diversity.

Table 5.19. *A summary of the quality attributes providing an indication of the condition of saltmarshes, and their recommended monitoring techniques*

Attribute	Habitat properties	Monitoring technique
Physical properties	Extent	Phase I mapping (Section 6.1.5) with aerial photography (6.1.3) NVC surveys (6.1.6) with quadrat (6.4.2) or belt transect (6.4.6) sampling or fixed-point (6.1.4) photography
	Saline sediments or water	Conductivity meters, soil analysis (6.2.2)
	Physiography (salt pans, creeks, etc.)	Physical mapping, aerial or fixed-point photographs (6.1.3, 6.1.4)
	Organic litter	Physical mapping, aerial or fixed-point photographs (6.1.3, 6.1.4)
Composition	Characteristic communities	Quadrats (6.4.2) or transects (6.4.6), with NVC analysis (6.1.6) where NVC communities are Notified Features or important attributes
	Species composition and richness	Mini-quadrats (6.4.3)
	Presence–absence of typical or indicator species	Look–see or total counts (Part III, Sections 15.2.1 and Section 15.2.2), quadrats (6.4.2 and 6.4.3) or transects (6.4.6)
Structure	Zonation	Transects (6.4.6)
Dynamics	Accretion on existing marsh	Level surveying (not covered)
	Tidal inundation	Observation at peak high tides, water level monitoring

Deposits of organic litter from vegetation are typical of the strandline on the upper shore, and indeed contribute to the nutrient balance of some upper-shore communities (e.g. SM24 *Elytrigia atherica* saltmarsh). These deposits are of natural occurrence, but are now often supplemented with much human-generated rubbish and flotsam. A summary of the attributes providing an indication of the condition of saltmarshes and their recommended monitoring methods is given in Table 5.19.

Management requirements and external impacts

In general, management of saltmarshes is restricted to grazing, which can greatly modify the vegetation structure and species richness. Saltmarshes important for plants are probably best left ungrazed or lightly grazed, but those that are of interest for birds may be grazed more heavily. Heavy grazing tends to result in poor vegetation zonation. A historical view of the grazing regime should be taken.

The main threats are erosion and land reclamation, which can be monitored from changes in extent, heavy grazing, which can be monitored from the vegetation, and pollution. Turf cutting may cause damage locally but is generally sustainable. Oil pollution is generally damaging to saltmarshes, at least in the short term, although some species are surprisingly tolerant. Natural degradation of oil is preferable to removal, as it may cause less damage to the marshes. The implementation of managed retreat for coast protection works may result in increased areas of upper marsh in the future.

5.16.2   Specific issues affecting the survey and monitoring of habitat

It is recommended that saltmarshes be monitored at 6 year intervals. Longer-term studies may be needed to assess loss and gain due to natural changes in the coastline. They can be monitored throughout the season, although if identification of some species such as *Atriplex* and *Salicornia* is required this is best done in August to September.

As saltmarsh composition is variable, careful sampling stratification may be required to ensure that the full range of communities is adequately and efficiently covered. If permanent markers are to be used, it should be remembered that relocation can be difficult because of mud deposition. For assessing changes in many features of the vegetation, such as species richness and sward height and cover, the techniques outlined in Section 5.4 can be applied.

Changes in the sea level, coupled with isobatic rebound, may cause longer-term changes in salt-marshes. Local monitoring data may therefore need to be interpreted against these changes, which will have to be extrapolated from the few sea-level monitoring sites.

As a result of the tidal nature of saltmarshes and the presence of creeks (which are often deep, muddy and complex), particular care must be taken to observe safety procedures when monitoring. Refer to Part I, Box 2.11, for details of the safety precautions that should be followed.

6 • Methods for surveying habitats

6.1 GENERAL HABITAT SURVEY AND MONITORING METHODS

The methods described in Section 6.1 may be applied to the surveying and monitoring of most habitat types. Section 6.1.1 provides an overview of remote sensing technology, which includes both satellite-based remote sensing (Section 6.1.2) and aerial photography (Section 6.1.3). Remote sensing, Phase I habitat mapping (Section 6.1.5) and National Vegetation Classification (NVC) surveys (Section 6.1.6) are principally survey techniques for mapping and/or quantifying the extent of different habitats at a variety of scales. This may be carried out for a number of different purposes:

- audits of habitat resources;
- the production of maps for management plans; and
- general recording of changes in landscapes and habitats, e.g. to document the result of land-use changes or management practices.

Such methods may also be used for basic monitoring of the presence, extent and distribution of habitats. Knowledge of the distribution and extent of habitats and vegetation types is useful for identifying site features and their approximate boundaries, defining monitoring units, defining homogeneous strata for stratified random sampling and locating samples within defined habitats of strata.

6.1.1 Remote sensing principles

The term 'environmental remote sensing' covers all means of detecting and measuring environmental conditions from a distance. There is a huge variety of remote sensing instruments currently available, which cover both imaging and non-imaging systems. This section covers only imaging systems. The principal differences between these systems relate to their:

- modes of data collection (e.g cameras, scanners, radars etc.);
- storage media (film or digital); and the
- platforms from which the instrument operates (aircraft or satellite).

The optimum data source for any project will depend upon the user's requirements. To assess the suitability of different sources of imagery, the general principles that govern their operation are outlined below.

Data collection

All remote sensing systems depend upon differences in the way in which ground objects interact with solar radiation. We can tell the difference between one object and another, and also infer something about an object's properties by the way in which it reflects, transmits or radiates this radiation across different parts of the electromagnetic spectrum. Recording these variations in the visible parts of the spectrum can be achieved photographically or electronically; however, variations at non-visible wavelengths require the use of electronic sensor technology.

Photography uses chemical reactions on the surface of a light-sensitive film to record energy variations within a scene. Most other remote sensing instruments use sensors to detect these energy variations, which are then converted to a digital reading. Whereas a camera records an instantaneous image across a whole field of view, most airborne or satellite-borne scanning systems depend upon the forward motion of the platform to build up an image from a series of scanned lines (these instruments are often called line scanners). As the instrument moves over the ground, the sensor readings vary according to the amount of light reflected back from the ground and an image is built up line by line. Through geometrically controlling these readings it is possible to build up an image of light variation over a geometric grid. Each grid cell, called a pixel (picture element), has a digital number that corresponds to the amount of light reflected from the area on the ground covered by the pixel within a specified part of the light spectrum. These digital numbers can either be displayed on a computer screen or by using a specialised film recorder to produce a photographic image.

The size of the pixel determines the spatial resolution of digital imagery. This is in turn driven by the height of the instrument above the ground and the focal length of its lens system. Satellite-borne instruments tend to provide digital imagery with a spatial resolution greater than 5 m (i.e. objects smaller than 5 m can be distinguished). Airborne systems have a much higher potential resolution but they tend to provide one-off coverage. With all remote sensing systems there is the trade-off between spatial resolution and frequency of coverage: no system provides high spatial resolution with frequent coverage, although the most recent Earth observation systems such as SPOT 5 do provide coverage of less than 10 m resolution over Europe with repeat coverage every three days.

From data to information

Remotely sensed images can be used to map vegetation. Visual interpretation of aerial photography is a long-established procedure whereby the interpreter is able to discriminate and outline different vegetation types on the basis of size, shape, tone, texture, context and shadows. It is possible to interpret all imagery in this way. However, most digital imaging devices have the ability to record reflectance properties across many wavebands. Many of these contain valuable information, which helps to discriminate between vegetation types. The amount of radiation reflected at different spectral wavelengths varies for each vegetation type. If the 'spectral signature' for a particular vegetation type is known, then it is possible to identify all other areas of the image with the same properties. This is called digital image classification and there is a wide range of statistical pattern recognition techniques that support this type of digital image analysis. However, the effectiveness of these techniques always depends upon the extent to which objects can be differentiated on the basis of spectral and textural properties. Often it is not possible to distinguish between different species of plant, for example. Again the user must be aware that it may not be possible to use remotely sensed imagery to interpret traditional ecological classification systems (e.g. those based on plant types, cover and abundance).

Resolution trade-offs

One very important advantage of satellite-borne sensing systems over airborne ones is that they provide the opportunity for regular coverage of an area at relatively low cost. They are, therefore, potentially attractive for monitoring purposes. The resolution and frequency of coverage is set by the satellite orbit and the viewing geometry of the instrument (e.g. wide-angled or telephoto).

Geostationary satellites (e.g. Meteosat) are positioned over the equator at altitudes of around 36 000 km and therefore proceed at the same speed as the Earth rotates. They can provide imagery on an hourly basis over very large areas and are ideally suited for use by meteorological agencies for weather forecasting and climate analysis. Typical pixel sizes are 4 km (i.e. a square of side length 4 km) at the equator; such imagery is therefore unlikely to be of any practical value for habitat analysis at a local level. Higher-resolution imagery can be obtained by bringing the satellite nearer to the ground. However, this requires the satellite to be in a polar orbit and although the spatial resolution of the imagery is improved (e.g. pixel size of 1 km) the temporal resolution is reduced (e.g. 12 hours). The most common medium-resolution satellite-imaging systems are also meteorological ones, such as the NOAA AVHRR, which are commonly used in television weather broadcasts. These medium-resolution systems are still too coarse for most land applications. As a consequence, there is a growing family of high-resolution Earth-observing satellite systems. These achieve coverage at a resolution that can be measured in metres by the use of long focal length lenses, but in so doing reduce temporal coverage still further (i.e. from hours to days).

The Landsat series (seven since 1972) is perhaps the most well established of the 'Earth-observing satellites'. The existing instrumentation on Landsat 7, the Enhanced Thematic Mapper (ETM), records in eight spectral bands across the visible, near middle and into the thermal infrared. The panchromatic (black and white) band has a pixel size or a spatial resolution of 15 m. All the remaining bands have a pixel size of 30 m, except the thermal channel, which has a poorer ground resolution of 60 m. The satellite orbits at an altitude of 705 km and the time between repeat coverages is 16–18 days, depending upon latitude. A standard scene covers an area of 185 km × 170 km (approx. 31 000 km^2). The French SPOT satellite series (five since 1986) offers similar capabilities to the Landsat series but provides the added enhancement of simultaneous acquisition of stereo pairs of images (600 km × 120 km) from the SPOT 5 platform. Stereo coverage allows for the derivation of height information directly from the imagery by using digital photogrammetric techniques. The elevation accuracy from the High Resolution Stereoscopic (HRS) instrument on SPOT 5 is quoted as 10 m.

The first of a new generation of commercial, high-resolution satellite systems was launched in 1999. Through reducing orbital altitude to 680 km and increasing the focal length of the camera, Space Imaging's IKONOS satellite is able to provide imagery with ground resolutions of 1 m in panchromatic mode and 4 m in multi-spectral mode. This spatial resolving power is comparable to that of high-altitude aerial photography. IKONOS has been followed by two other high-resolution spaceborne systems: Quickbird (launched 2001) and OrbView (launched 2003). Information on all of these systems is available from a number of websites but the most useful UK site at the time of writing is that hosted by infoterra, formerly the UK National Remote Sensing Centre (www.infoterra-global.com).

As introduced above, a key issue with these different satellite-borne systems is the trade-off between temporal and spatial resolution (Table 6.1). This has implications for their application in habitat monitoring. Generally speaking, systems such as AVHRR are used for monitoring global vegetation changes on a seasonal basis, whereas LANDSAT and SPOT imagery is used for national land cover surveys such as the DETR Countryside Survey 2000. It is likely that the new high-resolution systems such as IKONOS will be applicable to site-level assessments. A major restriction to the practical application of satellite imagery in the UK is the difficulty of obtaining cloud-free imagery. The opportunities for acquiring cloud-free imagery are greater for satellites with shorter revisit periods. This highlights one of the major advantages of aircraft surveys over satellite methods. Not only can aerial surveys provide data with vastly improved spatial resolution, but the operator is also able to restrict flying sorties to those days with clear conditions. As the technology develops, airborne remote sensing may become more capable of supplementing field survey information on widespread habitats and landscape features.

Aerial film camera systems are mature technologies that have been used successfully for many years. Digital camera technology is now also finding its way into the airborne imaging marketplace. Not only is processing time reduced (because film development is no longer necessary) but also, unlike scanning systems, each frame of imagery is captured in a single exposure, which facilitates geometric restitution. One problem, however, is that each frame must be downloaded between each acquisition and so ultimately a limit is reached at which it is not possible to download quickly enough. Even with the fast pace of technology advancement, it is likely to be some time before airborne digital sensors will be able to compete with conventional film cameras in terms of image quality and efficiency.

New airborne scanning instruments, such as the Compact Airborne Spectrographic Imager (CASI), also have considerable potential for habitat evaluation. One particular advantage of the CASI system is that its configuration is programmable and the

Table 6.1. *Specifications of some current Earth-observing satellite sensors*

Sensor name	Year of first launch	No. of spectral bands	Nominal spatial resolution (m)	Revisit period[a]	Image frame (km × km)	Cost of digital data (based on 2000 prices)[b]	
						£ per scene	£ per square km[c]
IKONOS	1999			2.9 days	13 × 13	3042	18
Pan		1	1				
XS		4	4				
SPOT	1986			26 days[d]	60 × 60		
Pan		1	10			800–1700	0.25–0.50
XS		3	20			800–1350	0.25–0.40
LANDSAT				16–18 days	185 × 170[e]		
ETM	1999	7	15–60			400	0.01
TM	1982	4	30–60			160–2200	0.005–0.070
MSS	1972	4	80			120–600	0.003–0.020
AVHRR	1979	5	1100	12 h	2400 × 2400	80	negligible
KFA	—	Film		—			
1000			5		80 × 80	1800–2250	0.30–0.35
3000		Camera[f]	2–3		21 × 21	2250–3000	5–7

[a] For polar-orbiting satellites, the exact revisit period will depend on latitude.
[b] Hard-copy imagery will be cheaper than digital data. The lower price ranges relate to older imagery.
[c] These costs are given for comparative purposes only. It may not be possible to buy imagery on a per km² basis.
[d] The SPOT satellite is actually steerable and thereby can obtain, by request, more frequent coverage.
[e] 'Quarter scenes' of LANDSAT imagery may also be purchased.
[f] Costs here are based on scanned photography but it is also possible to purchase prints.

precise number of spectral bands, their locations and bandwidths can be selected in flight. A spatial resolution of between 0.5 m and 10 m can be achieved, depending on the flying altitude.

LIDAR (a light detection and ranging instrument) is often flown in combination with the CASI system. LIDAR is a laser range-finder that measures the time of flight of a laser beam from the aircraft to the ground and back. The information provides elevation data, which can be used for vegetation measurement and mapping and is particularly useful for providing textural definition. Other systems, such as synthetic aperture radar (SAR), offer similar specialist facilities. For further information on such instrumentation refer to a standard remote-sensing textbook (e.g. Lillesand & Kiefer, 1994).

Satellite specifications and cost

The major commercial sources of satellite data in the UK are the National Remote Sensing Centre (now Infoterra) and NPA Group (see Box 6.1 for contact information). Table 6.1 provides an indication of the relative costs of imagery. Since satellite data can be expensive (particularly as it is usually necessary to purchase a whole scene even if the study site is only a fraction of the area), it is worth contacting your local university's geography and or environmental sciences department before purchasing data, because they may know of existing images that may be bought at a much lower cost. Again the major centres of remote sensing expertise are readily found on the Internet.

Aerial photographs can be obtained from a variety of sources. If it is necessary to commission a special survey to meet the data requirements, then the costs of flying will have to be included. Monitoring will necessitate several repeat surveys over time. Generally, there are no cost savings when multiple aerial surveys are done, but time series of satellite data can often be purchased with major discounts.

Applications of remote sensing

Satellite or aerial imagery can be used in a wide range of applications, but selecting appropriate solutions from the growing range of technical options can be difficult.

Table 6.2 presents some common land cover and landscape features and poses three questions:

1. What is the minimum ground resolution required to detect or measure them?
2. What scale of imagery will provide data at this resolution?
3. What instrument platform is most commonly used to provide this imagery?

From Table 6.2, it is possible to identify the technical solutions most appropriate to particular mapping tasks. Some key points are:

- No single type of imagery suits all purposes.
- The requirements for detection are less demanding than those for measurement.
- Users wanting to identify or measure several different land cover features from the same imagery will have to accept that some will be more prone to errors than others.
- Remotely sensed imagery generally cannot provide information that is directly comparable to botanical classifications (e.g. Phase I habitat survey and NVC).

One way of ensuring high mapping accuracies would be to use large-scale imagery, but as photo scale increases, the number of images required to cover any given area increases geometrically. Scale and cost are therefore inter-related.

'Fitness for purpose' can only be established by being very clear about the trade-offs and inter-linkages between the following.

- *Purpose:* what do you *need* to know?
- *Method:* what technical options do you have?
- *Economy:* what can you afford?
- *Error:* what types and level of error can you tolerate?

Sections 6.1.2 and 6.1.3 describe the applications of satellite-based remote sensing and aerial photography in habitat mapping and monitoring.

6.1.2   Satellite-based remote sensing

Applications of satellite remote sensing

The early LANDSAT satellites were principally employed for expansive crop inventory projects.

Table 6.2. *Data users' requirements and recommendations*

| Data requirement | Ground resolution (m) | Image recommendations | | Platform[a] |
| | | Smallest scale for: | | |
		Detection	Measurement	
Land cover classification and mapping				
Forestry				
Species	0.1	1:5 000	1:2 500	LAA
Isolated trees	0.3	1:12 000 to 1:20 000	1:6 400 to 1:9 600	LAA
Forest strips < 20 m wide	30	1:1 500 000	1:750 000	SAT
Groups of trees (< 0.25 ha) (mainly broadleaved/conifers/mixed)	1.0	1:64 000 to 1:125 000	1:32 000 to 1:64 000	HAA
Mature forest stand (broadleaved/conifers/mixed)	30	1:1 500 000	1:750 000	SAT
Felling	10	1:500 000	1:250 000	SAT
Non-forest				
Scrub (species)	0.3	1:12 000	1:6 400	LAA
Scrub (stand)	3	1:184 000	1:92 000	HAA
Grasses (species)	0.1	1:3 200	1:1 600	LAA
Grasses (stands)	3	1:184 000	1:92 000	HAA
Peatland	3	1:184 000	1:92 000	HAA
Blanket bog	3	1:184 000	1:92 000	HAA
Non-vegetated surfaces				
Rocks and cliffs	3	1:184 000	1:92 000	HAA
Dunes	3	1:184 000	1:92 000	HAA
Built-up land	3	1:184 000	1:92 000	HAA
Urban open space (e.g. cemeteries)	3	1:184 000	1:92 000	HAA
Derelict land	3	1:184 000	1:92 000	HAA
Bare soil	0.3	1:12 000	1:6 400	LAA
Extensive bare soil	10	1:500 000	1:250 000	SAT
Transport routes	3	1:184 000	1:184 000	HAA
Water				
Coastal water/estuaries	10	1:500 000	1:250 000	SAT
Inland open water	3	1:184 000	1:92 000	HAA

Table 6.2. (cont.)

Data requirement	Ground resolution (m)	Image recommendations		Platform[a]
		Smallest scale for:		
		Detection	Measurement	
Marsh	3	1 : 184 000	1 : 92 000	HAA
Saltmarsh	3	1 : 184 000	1 : 92 000	HAA
Canals	5	1 : 310 000	1 : 155 000	HAA
Hydrological condition	10	1 : 500 000	1 : 250 000	SAT
Interpretative information				
Habitat mapping				
Forest edge	30	1 : 1 500 000	1 : 750 000	SAT
Forest–agriculture edge	30	1 : 1 500 000	1 : 750 000	SAT
Forest–water edge	10	1 : 500 000	1 : 250 000	SAT
Forest–abandoned land edge	10	1 : 500 000	1 : 92 000	SAT
Fire breaks	3	1 : 184 000	1 : 92 000	HAA
Vegetative condition				
Insect effect	0.3	1 : 12 000	1 : 6 400	LAA
Disease	80.0	1 : 3 900 000	1 : 2 100 000	SAT
Pollution effect	0.3	1 : 12 000 to 1 : 20 000	1 : 6 400 to 1 : 9 600	LAA
Phenological stage	0.3	1 : 12 000	1 : 6 400	LAA
Resource parameter measurement				
Tree dimensions (height, basal area, crown diameter)	0.3	1 : 20 000	1 : 9 600	L–MAA
Biomass statistics (annual production, plant density)	0.3	1 : 12 000	1 : 6 400	LAA
Animal counts	0.3	1 : 20 000	1 : 9 600	L–MAA
Nesting trees	1.0	1 : 40 000	1 : 20 600	MAA

[a] LAA, low-altitude aircraft (150–3660 m); MAA, medium-altitude aircraft (3660–9150 m); HAA, high-altitude aircraft (9150–19 820 m); SAT, satellite (over 190 km).
Source: Adapted from Aldrich (1979).

Box 6.1 Contact information for obtaining remote sensing data

(correct at time of writing)

Infoterra Ltd (formerly the National Remote Sensing Centre)
Atlas House, 41 Wembley Road, Leicester, LE3 1UT
Tel: 0116 2732300
Fax: 0116 2732400
www.infoterra-global.com

Nigel Press Associates Group
Crockham Park, Edenbridge, Kent,
TN8 6SR
Tel: 01732 865023
Fax: 01732 866521
www.npagroup.co.uk

English Heritage
National Monuments Record
PO Box 569
Swindon SN2 2XP
Tel: 01793 414600

Fax: 01793 414606
www.english-heritage.org.uk
Air Photographs Unit
National Assembly for Wales
Cathays Park
Cardiff CF10 3NQ
Tel: 02920 823819
Royal Commission on the Ancient and Historical Monuments of Scotland
John Sinclair House
16 Bernard Terrace
Edinburgh EH8 9NX
Tel: 0131 662 1456
Fax: 0131 662 1499/1477
www.rcahms.gov.uk
Public Records Office of Northern Ireland
66 Balmoral Avenue
Belfast BT9 6NY
Tel: 02890 255905
Fax: 02890 255999
www.proni.nics.gov.uk

This agricultural monitoring role has continued with the later satellites (e.g. the Monitoring Agriculture by Remote Sensing (MARS) project run by the Joint Research Centre on behalf of EUROSTAT). The higher spatial resolutions (*c.* 30 m) provided by these later satellites, particularly the Thematic Mapper (TM), have provided the opportunity for pan-European and national land-cover mapping programmes.

At the European level, the principal initiative has been in connection with the development of a co-ordinated information network on the environment (CORINE). As part of this, each EU member state has been requested to provide a 1 : 100 000 scale land-cover map for their national area. Although most member states have obtained this through manual interpretation of appropriately scaled hard copy LANDSAT TM images, the UK was able to take advantage of a national mapping initiative, the Land Cover Map of Great Britain (Fuller *et al.*, 1994).

The production of the 1990 Land Cover Map of Great Britain was achieved using Landsat TM imagery. To improve classification accuracy, both summer and winter imagery was used. Geometric errors were controlled by geometrically correcting the summer images to the Ordnance Survey National Grid and then resampling the winter images to fit. A land-cover classification system was developed, which was appropriate both to user requirements and to the 'fitness for purpose' of such medium-resolution imagery. However, some of these classes (e.g. bracken) still had standard errors of around 33% (Pakeman *et al.*, 2000).

The 1990 Land Cover Map methodology has been refined for a new land-cover map of Great Britain (LCM2000). The main reporting structure is based on the Broad Habitats identified in the UK Biodiversity Action Plan. The relationships between these Broad Habitats and the LCM2000 Target Classes and Sub-Classes are given in Table 6.3.

At an individual country level, similar satellite image-based land-cover mapping initiatives have been conducted by MLURI (the Macaulay Land Use Research Institute) (Wright & Birnie, 1986;

Satellite-based remote sensing: summary of key points

Recommended uses   Satellite-based remote sensing may be used for measuring Broad Habitat extent, but is not currently recommended for detailed site monitoring because the spatial resolutions are too poor. However, in conjunction with ground surveys and aerial photography, satellite imagery can be a useful additional data source.

The method also has some potential for monitoring habitat quality through measurement of vegetation change (e.g. heather cover on a moorland) if a change from a 'desirable' to a 'less desirable' state can be defined in terms of vegetation change that can be monitored with remote sensors.

The potential of the most recent generation of high-spatial-resolution satellite sensors has yet to be fully explored but may be applicable for some site-level assessments.

Efficiency   Remotely sensed data are generally cheaper to obtain than data obtained by field survey, although the size of the study area will affect the cost and efficiency. Satellite imagery is available at different costs, according to the level of pre-processing that the data have undergone. Some corrections will still be necessary in order to remove, for example, geometric and atmospheric distortions.

Field survey is still essential for ground truthing and calibration. This will probably be required for each separate image.

Objectivity   Automated habitat classifications may be objective in the sense that classification is carried out by computer. However, analysis based on spectral signatures alone does not benefit from additional knowledge of size, shape, context, etc.

Precision   Satellite-based sensors commonly achieve a resolution of 10–30 m. The most recent generation of satellite sensors have an improved spatial resolution of 1–4 m.

Bias   The reflectance properties of areas of vegetation can vary from image to image, owing to factors such as cloud, moisture and season. These variations must be considered for successful application of automated classification procedures.

Expertise required   An understanding of the computer hardware and software for image processing and interpretation is essential. Experience in recognising ecological and land-cover classes is also required.

Equipment required   Contact information for the major UK satellite data re-sellers can be found in Box 6.1. To view and interpret remotely sensed data, a computer capable of handling large quantities of data and with a good quality printer is required. A GIS (see Glossary) such as ArcInfo is also useful for manipulating and comparing images and adding extra information.

Key methodological points to consider   At present, satellite-based remote sensing does not provide a reliable method for monitoring changes in semi-natural habitats.

Satellite imagery can be used for site mapping but does not achieve the level of detail obtained from either Phase I surveys or aerial photography.

Airborne remote sensors are capable of producing detail comparable with that of Phase I Habitat Survey.

Data analysis   Calculation of habitat extent is achieved with computer software. If data are input into a GIS, information derived from other sources, such as ground survey, can be included.

Wright & Morris, 1997; G. G. Wright *et al.*, 1997). SNH has also demonstrated the value of satellite imagery in several applications:

- primary stratification in relation to the choice of sample areas for the National Countryside Monitoring Scheme (NCMS);

- mapping the extent and condition of blanket bogs (Box 6.2); and
- woodland monitoring under the Earth Observation Network 2000 (Box 6.3).

In many of these applications, satellite imagery was used in combination with both aerial imagery

Table 6.3. *The relationship between terrestrial Broad Habitats and LCM2000 Classes*

Broad Habitats	LCM2000 Target Class	LCM2000 Sub-classes and variants
Broadleaved, mixed and yew woodland	Broadleaved and mixed woodland	Trees
		deciduous
		evergreen
		Scrub/shrub
		deciduous
		evergreen
Coniferous woodland	Coniferous woodland	Standing
Boundary and linear features	(Not identified in LCM2000)	Felled
Arable and horticulture	Arable and horticulture	Wheat
		Barley
		Oats
		Maize
		Oilseed rape
		Peas
		Field beans
		Linseed
		Sugarbeet
		Potatoes
		Unknown arable
		Horticulture
		Perennial crops
		Set-aside (bare)
Improved grassland	Improved grassland	Agricultural/managed grass
		mown/grazed
		hay/silage
		Grass, semi-improved, reverting
		Grazing marsh
		Set-aside with grass or weeds
		Rough
Neutral grassland	Natural and semi-natural grasslands and bracken	Neutral – unimproved/neutral

Table 6.3. (cont.)

Broad Habitats	LCM2000 Target Class	LCM2000 Sub-classes and variants
Calcareous grassland		Calcareous
Acid grassland		Acid *Nardus* with rushes
Bracken		Bracken
Dwarf shrub heath	Dwarf shrub heath	Closed heath
		'wet' heath
		'dry' heath
		gorse
		Open heath
Fen, marsh and swamp	Fen, marsh and swamp	Swamp
		Fen/marsh
Bog	Bog	Bog
		shrub
		grass (*Molinia*) or herbaceous
Standing open water and canals		Water (inland)
Rivers and streams		
Montane habitats	Montane (bare/heath)	
Inland rock	Inland bare ground	Natural
		Despoiled
Built-up areas and gardens	Built-up areas and gardens	Suburban/rural developed
		Continuous urban residential/commercial industrial
Supralittoral rock	Supralittoral rock and sediment	Rock/shingle
Supralittoral sediment		Dune – with/without shrubs
Littoral rock	Littoral rock and sediment	Rock, mud and sand
Littoral sediment		Saltmarsh, grazed and ungrazed
Oceanic seas	Sea/estuary	
Sublittoral categories		

164

and ground data. Such integrated approaches – combining census data with sample data – are increasingly used. So the question is not whether one source of data is better than another, but how they can best be used together.

6.1.3   Aerial photography

Recommended uses

There is a wide range of potential uses for aerial photography. The relationships between resolving power and photo scale (Table 6.2) hold true, and aerial photos are generally best employed to identify and classify structural components in the landscape. They are not generally suited to species-based classifications.

Aerial photography has been widely used in ecological applications. It has been used for both inventory and monitoring at national to local levels, especially as an adjunct to Phase I habitat surveys. Whereas in the 1970s it could be said that the interpretation of aerial photos was a well-developed area technically, recent developments in the use of digital image acquisition and analysis techniques have opened up a whole new range of approaches including the advent of digital camera systems, on-screen interpretation and the linkages with GIS technology for analysis and presentation.

There are many examples of national surveys in the UK that employ aerial photography. Some are specifically related to baseline audit, others use historical aerial photography to provide either a

---

Box 6.2   Scottish Blanket Bog Inventory

The Scottish Blanket Bog Inventory (SBBI) is an example of the use of remote sensing for characterising extensive biotopes more consistently, repeatably and cost-effectively than can be achieved by any other means. Undertaken by Scottish Natural Heritage, the SBBI maps the extent, distribution and condition of blanket bog vegetation throughout Scotland.

The method employs an unsupervised classification of Landsat 5 Thematic Mapper 30 m imagery, which is validated by National Vegetation Classification (NVC) ground survey. The classified image products will provide improved information on the vegetation communities and hydrological status of blanket bogs throughout Scotland.

For further information, see Reid & Quarmby (2000).

Box 6.3   Earth Observation for Natura 2000 (EON2000)

Habitat inventory and land-cover change information is required across Europe to support the Natura 2000 scheme. Developing a method for routine data collection over such a wide area presents obvious difficulties. Designated sites in Scotland, Austria and Finland were selected to test the possibility of using imagery from space-borne sensors to derive forest habitat inventories.

Landsat TM, IRS, LISS, SPOT Pan and IRS Pan images (Table 6.1) were used for the inventories, and historic Landsat TM images were used to validate and demonstrate methods of change detection. An Internet-based system was designed and implemented to facilitate the

use of Earth Observation images and techniques for environmental monitoring applications.

Although the spatial resolution was found to be insufficient to generate the more detailed inventories required, the potential of basic classification for baseline inventories at a national level was acknowledged. Change detection approaches successfully flagged up ecological change and the method was recognised by conservation organisations as being of practical application in targeting ground survey resources. Lack of available satellite sensor data to evaluate ecological change was flagged up as a major issue for an operational system.

For further information see http://geospace.co.at/EON2000.html.

Aerial photography: summary of key points

Recommended uses

- Rapidly assessing the nature conservation resource in an area
- Establishing a framework of data for a monitoring baseline
- Monitoring broad-scale changes in habitat extent

Efficiency   Six days maximum AQE are required to evaluate each 5 km × 5 km square (including one day field checking).

Objectivity   Reasonable as long as standard methods are used for distinguishing between habitat types and field checking is used to assess accuracy. A problem arises in areas where few distinctive boundaries occur and a line has to be drawn between two habitats that grade into each other. This problem derives from a fundamental problem of using a map to represent natural variation and will lead to variations between interpretations by different people.

Precision   The errors involved in measuring habitat areas on 1 : 10 000 scale maps are generally well below 5%, although some habitat types are more prone to errors than others.

Bias   Sources of bias arise from misidentification of habitat types from photographs and inaccurate mapping of boundaries. Unless slopes are included when calculating areas with a planimeter or digitising equipment, areas on slopes will be underestimated and areas of high relief will be overestimated relative to areas of low relief.

Expertise required   Mappers should be trained in the recognition of different habitat types from photographs, and in the use of stereoscopes. The ability to use a planimeter or digitising equipment is necessary if these items are used to process images. It is helpful if the people analysing the photographs have on-the-ground experience of the area involved and either have general ecological and land-cover experience or have been trained in Phase I habitat surveying (see Section 6.1.5).

Equipment required   Overlapping aerial photographs, stereoscope, digitising equipment, pens, pencils, rulers, light table, etc. for map-making.

Key methodological points to consider   Good-quality overlapping vertical aerial photographs are essential. Colour photographs are preferred, if available. For monitoring, two matching sets of photographs are required, taken at the same time of year for the area being monitored. The time of year the photographs were taken is important; some habitats are hard to identify at certain times of year. Some field checking will be necessary, particularly for habitats that are hard to recognise accurately from photographs.

Data analysis   Areas of habitat can be measured via digitisation and analysis with a GIS package such as Arc View.

census of land cover change (e.g. *Landscape Change in the National Parks*; Countryside Commission, 1991) or a sample of change (e.g. the NCMS; Mackey *et al.*, 1998). There is a growing body of knowledge concerning the use of aerial photography for monitoring change. In general terms, the following hold true.

- Changes can be divided into those relating to quantity (i.e. changes in area or stock) and those relating to quality (i.e. changes in composition or condition).
- Rapid changes in quantity or stock (e.g. major afforestation in the period from *c.* 1946 to *c.* 1988) can be reliably identified by using historical aerial photography.

- Slow changes in quantity, often associated with minor shifts in boundaries of the order of 1–5 m, over 20–30 years are poorly identified (i.e. they lie within the bounds of line positioning errors).
- Changes in quality are poorly or seldom identified by using conventional point, line and area interpretations or mapping conventions. (This type of change is most amenable to the use of digital imagery.)
- Changes in semi-natural communities that involve complex interdigitating boundaries, which are often transitional rather than discrete, are extremely difficult to detect and quantify reliably.

Time series of medium-scale photography (i.e. around 1 : 25 000 scale) can provide the most reliable information on major transfers of stock, particularly in managed areas such as woodland and arable land. They provide least reliable information on changes in the quality or composition of land cover types or in complex and slow changes (e.g. in semi-natural cover types). To maximise the potential for detecting changes in these situations, it is recommended that longer time intervals between photographs be used.

Expertise required

Interpretation of aerial photographs is a skill acquired largely through experience. Anyone undertaking analysis of aerial photographs should be trained to a consistent standard in the recognition of features on photographs. Previous ground knowledge of the area can make it easier to recognise and interpret features on the photographs (although this might introduce some bias).

Interpreters will need to be familiar with the use of stereoscopes and digitising equipment. If on-screen interpretation and digitising is to be attempted, interpreters must be confident that they can distinguish the same level of detail from the screen as from traditional stereoscopic analysis. Some additional training may be necessary; on-screen stereo-interpretation facilities represent a new technology, and experience of best practice is limited. A comprehensive background to aerial photograph interpretation is provided by Lillesand & Kiefer (1994).

Equipment required

Good-quality aerial photographs are essential (Appendix 6). A 60% forward overlap is required to provide stereo coverage for use with a stereoscope. The choice between colour and black-and-white photography will depend on the availability, season of acquisition and quality of photographs, the habitat type of interest and the preference and experience of the individual interpreter. The Ordnance Survey (OS) hold and provide records for the past 10 years, before passing these on to national organisations. The English Heritage National Monuments Record office in Swindon holds older OS photos, their own, and RAF records

(from the period 1940–60). The contact addresses are given in Box 6.1. Other more recent sources include the company 'getmapping' (www.getmapping.co.uk). In addition, airborne scanning systems (e.g. CASI) can be hired from independent organisations. These images can be either digital or analogue and can in some cases achieve a level of detail similar to that obtained with Phase I Habitat Surveys. A fuller review of this technique is given in Pooley & Jones (1996).

A stereoscope provides a three-dimensional image from overlapping pairs of photographs. This facilitates the identification of habitat types, as the height and texture of vegetation becomes more obvious. There are two sizes of stereoscope that are useful: a small portable set is easily employed for mapping but can only be used on a small part of a 22 cm $\times$ 22 cm photograph at a time, whereas a large desktop mirror stereoscope allows the viewing of the whole overlapping area.

For mapping, a set of coloured pens and pencils plus drawing equipment is required. Crude area estimates can be obtained by using a Romer dot grid (a transparent overlay with a given density of dots per square unit) or a planimeter. However, a low-cost digitising tablet will provide more reliable measures and will enable maps to be digitised and manipulated with a GIS package such as ArcView.

Some field checking is recommended when analysing aerial photographs; the equipment required for this is similar to that required for Phase I habitat surveys (Section 6.1.5). The design of appropriate field checks may require some statistical advice to ensure appropriate methods that avoid biasing the results and ensure cost-effectiveness.

Methods
Selection of photography

If the available sources of photographs are inadequate, commissioning photography may be required. Some operators provide low-cost small-format aerial photographs (e.g. 35 or 70 mm). These can be useful, providing the equipment to analyse them is available (for example, many older stereo-plotters are set up to deal only with large-format photographs).

Outline methods

Overlapping matched pairs of aerial photographs are examined under a stereoscope, and blocks of distinct habitat types are identified. It is possible to mark outlines and calculate areas directly on the photographs. However, it is generally preferable to transfer habitat boundaries to Ordnance Survey base maps (usually 1 : 10 000 scale) by using an optical device such as a Sketchmaster and standard colour codes. This mapping process allows for the correction of relief distortion and camera effects. An easily interpretable map that can be stored and copied as required is also produced. Alternatively, a planimeter, a photogrammetric plotting instrument or a digital photogrammetric device can be used to map vegetation directly from the photographs once the boundaries have been identified.

Field checking is recommended to verify that habitat classifications are accurate.

Habitat classification and identification

The NCMS (Mackey *et al.*, 1998) used the land classification developed by the Institute for Terrestrial Ecology (ITE) for Cumbria (now CEH), based on an estimation of the environmental factors responsible for making up the landscape, supplemented by satellite data (Box 6.4). The classification is hierarchical, split initially into linear features (e.g. hedgerows and tracks) and area features (eg. woodland, scrub).

As an example at a country level, the Land Cover Map of Scotland (carried out by the MLURI) was more ambitious. It was a complete survey of Scotland and identified many more habitat types than did the previous surveys (Box 6.5).

Although most studies have recommended that a standardised habitat classification is desirable, they generally have created their own variants. Comparisons between surveys are made harder and an agreed standard classification has not been formalised across the UK (but see Gilbert & Gibbons (1996) for a comparison of different survey classifications). The introduction of the UK Biodiversity Action Plan and its recognition of Broad Habitats (Table 6.3) may stimulate harmonisation of UK habitat classification systems. Classifications should be decided upon with the reasons for the study in mind. The quality of photographs available will also affect the choice

---

Box 6.4   National Countryside Monitoring Scheme (NCMS)

The NCMS is a Scotland-wide sample survey of land-cover change. Utilising aerial photography from *c.* 1947, *c.* 1973 and *c.* 1988, the NCMS has quantified the magnitude, rate and geographical variation in change over the second half of the twentieth century. During this period, considerable changes took place in Scotland's urban and rural environment, but prior to the NCMS little could be said about the overall impact of human activities on semi-natural habitats. The NCMS provides an objective account of the key changes and explains the changing relationships between land-cover features.

Aerial photography was used as the source for land-cover interpretation, but it was impracticable to map the whole of Scotland's land cover in sufficient detail. Instead, a stratified random sample of 5 km × 5 km squares (later 2.5 km × 2.5 km) was developed, covering 7.5% of Scotland's land area. Land cover was interpreted in terms of 31 areal features and five linear features. For each of the 467 sample squares, the interpreted features were mapped at a scale of 1 : 10,000. Land-cover maps for each sample square were digitised and processed on a GIS, and overlay analyses allowed the computation of land-cover change between time periods. Statistical software allowed sample square data to be extrapolated to provide estimates of extent, change and interchange for a geographical region of interest. Standard errors and confidence intervals provide a measure of the uncertainty in the estimates due to sampling.

For further information see Mackey *et al.* (1998) or www.snh org.uk/trends/landcover.

Box 6.5   Land Cover of Scotland 1988 (LCS88)

This survey, carried out by the MLURI, was a complete census of Scotland, covering 78 828 km^2. The survey was intended to be a baseline for future monitoring, for which a new land-cover classification system was devised in consultation with SNH and Ecological Advisors Unit within the then Scottish Office.

OBJECTIVES
To provide a basic land-cover inventory for the whole of Scotland, enabling studies of land-cover change, and to digitise the information for input into a GIS.

CLASSIFICATION
The habitat and land-use classification system was hierarchical and recognised summary, principal, major and main land-cover features and sub-categories. From these different levels, 23 summary features and 40 original land-cover features were identified. These were increased to 126 'single features' (i.e. land-cover types) by sub-categories created from the original 40. Area statistics were based on these 126 single features and mosaics of these features.

The use of mosaics of mixed land-cover features (defined as 'visible mixtures of two land-cover features in which the total area of each is below the minimum mapping unit for separate identification') stretched the number of categories to 1327 individual features. Although this increases the level of complexity of the classification, it allows the description and measurement of land-cover combinations that would otherwise be ignored, such as wooded bogs.

MONITORING
A ten-yearly survey with LCS88 data as a baseline was proposed. Two pilot studies have been conducted in the Central Valley and Cairngorm areas.

SURVEY METHOD
Aerial photography specifically for the project involved mainly panchromatic film, with some natural colour coverage in the Central Valley. Collection took place during 1987–9. Land-cover boundaries were identified by interpreters with extensive local knowledge before digitisation. The digitisation of the dataset and subsequent field checking took place between 1989 and 1993.

SUMMARY
The LCS88 survey is widely regarded as an accurate survey. Potential error sources included the referential error resulting from differences between people in their interpretation of land-cover features. In an assessment of this error it was found that interpretation rates depend upon classification level: overall error rates increased with increased detail. At the most detailed level, the error was estimated at around 25%. This reflects the issues relating to error and the use of one image source for all features, particularly at low levels in the classification hierarchy.

The use of mosaics, while allowing for the recognition of more habitat types, means that estimation of single cover types is difficult. The survey area covered 78 823 km^2, whereas the area covered by single cover measurements was 54 817 km^2. The remaining 24 006 km^2 is tied up in mosaics. For example, the single feature area of heather moorland in Scotland was estimated as 6882 km^2. If the areas of all mosaics containing heather moorland as the primary or secondary feature are included, the total reaches 16 922 km^2. To estimate the amount of heather present in the mosaic areas requires an assumption about the composition of the mosaics (e.g. 60 : 40). This may or may not be valid.

Sources: Gilbert & Gibbons (1996) and MLURI (1993).

of habitat types: colour photographs can allow more types to be distinguished than monochrome ones.

As an example, the guide to habitat identification given in Table 6.4 is based primarily on the study by Langdale-Brown *et al.* (1980), which used monochrome photographs. Colour photographs may be easier to interpret.

Mapping
The mapping and calculation of areas from aerial photographs requires the identification of features

Table 6.4. *Characteristics of habitat types for aerial photograph analysis by means of a stereoscope*

Habitat type	Characteristics
Deciduous woodland	Tallest vegetation with rounded crowns varying in height and diameter with irregularly spaced occasional gaps
	Light and medium tones
	Coarse, irregular texture
	Rounded shadows
	Light, feathery appearance on winter photographs
Coniferous woodland	Tall, dense stands, small-crowned trees regularly spaced
	Medium to dark tones
	Medium regular texture
	Pointed conical shadows
Mixed woodland	Tones vary from light to dark
	Irregular texture
	Variously shaped shadows
Scrub	Predominantly woody vegetation of medium height: shrubs, bushes, occasional trees often interspersed with patches of grassland
	Some distinct rounded crowns and areas of coalescing canopy
	Mottled appearance due to mixture of woody vegetation (medium and dark tones) and grasses (light tones)
Dwarf shrub heath	Low vegetation
	Very dark tones
	Fine and regular texture giving a smooth, dark appearance
Unimproved grassland	No perceptible height
	Irregular mix of light and medium tones
	Fine texture, with occasional rougher or tussocky areas
	Less regular than agricultural land
	No signs of cultivation
Improved grassland	No perceptible height
	Mixture of light and medium tones
	Finer and more regular texture than unimproved grassland
	May be signs of improvement such as drainage lines, walls and vehicle tracks
	No signs of ploughing
Wetland	Very varied appearance due to the variety of community types occurring
	Identification can be based upon local knowledge, the relief of the area or the proximity of areas of open water
Open water	Either very light or very dark tones
	No texture
Agricultural land	Low: no perceptible height
	Textureless: very fine regular texture
	Signs of cultivation such as plough lines or farm machinery tracks

on the photographs that can be pinpointed on the base map. Sometimes this is straightforward, where there are a great number of anthropogenic features, such as roads, buildings and field boundaries, which appear on maps and can also be recognised on photographs. However, there may be difficulties in areas of semi-natural habitat where there are few ground references. In such cases, it may be necessary to introduce local control, for example through use of a GPS. The identification of several points of known grid reference is also essential if photographs are to be analysed or digitised directly.

Areas of uniform habitat type can be marked on the base map with standard colour codes based on those used for the Phase I habitat survey (Section 6.1.5). Colours of maximum contrast are used to produce an easily interpretable map. If a mixture of two habitat types occurs with no uniform individual blocks (or blocks are too small to map accurately), use alternating lines of the colours for each habitat. Make the thickness of the lines proportional to the relative predominance of the habitats. Moodie (1991) used alphanumeric codes rather than colours for improved grassland and arable land in order to draw more attention to areas of unimproved semi-natural habitat on the map.

Field checking

Problems typically occur when attempting to distinguish between grasslands and agricultural land, and between improved and semi-improved grassland. Areas identified as potentially unimproved grassland in which no previous survey has recorded this habitat should be checked from the ground by a surveyor trained in Phase I habitat surveying. Local knowledge can be especially useful at this stage. Some limited field checking should be carried out for all habitats to act as a calibration for the aerial photograph analysis.

Data storage and analysis
Data storage

Good practice dictates that habitat maps created from aerial photographs should be stored in light-proof cabinets to prevent colour fading. To ensure security, separate copies should be kept in

a different location and digitised photographs and other files kept on computer should be backed up.

Sampling

Given that aerial photography offers a synoptic view of large areas, it is mostly used to provide census information. However, it can be used to provide estimates of habitat area in the same way as ground surveying. One approach is to use stratified random sampling, which can improve precision and ensure adequate representation of less common features in the sample (this is sometimes also known as 'area-frame sampling'). The estimates of habitat area obtained by this method have standard error terms that are directly related to the number of samples taken.

Two issues arise from the above: the first relates to how to stratify and the second relates to how to determine numbers of samples to obtain estimates of a desired precision. A good worked example of solutions to these issues is provided by the NCMS. This shows how lower-resolution satellite imagery can be used to provide adequate information for stratification (in this case into upland, lowland, intermediate and urban classes). Alternatively, stratifications could be provided by the ITE's (now CEH) Land Classification System, the Land Cover Map of Great Britain or, indeed, more recent classifications such as SNH's Natural Heritage Zones. The choice of sampling intensity is often a simple trade-off between cost and precision. The NCMS sample, for example, provided coverage of 7.5% of Scotland. The ITE Countryside Survey provides a sample of less than 1% of Britain. The result is that area estimates for NCMS are useful at a Scottish and local authority region level, whereas the Countryside Survey data are useful at a national level but become increasingly uncertain at sub-national or regional levels. Fitness for purpose is a critical consideration when designing sampling schemes and it is always advisable to seek statistical advice in the design of such schemes.

Calculation of habitat areas

The advent of digitising tablets has largely removed the need to rely on manual methods of calculating areas from maps. The Romer dot grid, the planimeter and a host of other ingenious methods have now been supplanted by standard functions for measuring map metrics within low-cost GIS or autocad facilities. These include not only area calculations but also a range of other metrics such as perimeter length (Wadsworth & Treweek, 1999). For those interested in fully exploiting the potential for deriving metrics from digital maps, reference should be made to the spatial analysis program FRAGSTATS, which is specifically designed for quantifying landscape structure (see, for example, Haines-Young & Chopping, 1996). The landscape indices provided by FRAGSTATS include the following.

- patch (e.g. mean patch size)
- edge (e.g. total edge)
- shape (e.g. average shape index: the patch parameter divided by the perimeter of a square of the same size)
- core area (e.g. sum of core areas of each patch)
- landscape diversity (e.g. Shannon diversity index)
- contagion and interspersion indices

Comparisons between photographs

The standard methods for change detection aim to control errors by close attention to geometric and mapping accuracy. So, for example, the NCMS methodology used high-precision stereoplotting equipment to ensure accurate location of boundaries at each image date so that when the maps were overlaid any changes observed were real rather than artefacts of the method. For 'look-back' studies conducted by the MLURI (alongside the development of the LCS88), interpretation errors were controlled by providing analysts with the 1988 interpretation and asking them to note only actual changes. This approach both reduced the opportunity for changes due to line misregistration and improved the amount of intelligence being given to the interpreters. In both the NCMS and the study of changes in the National Parks (Countryside Commission, 1991), the repeatability of the photographic interpretation was tested by having some areas examined by two different interpreters. Where many interpreters are involved, another device to aid consistency is to allocate

interpretation blocks on the basis of a checkerboard design. This forces the need for correlation around edges and acts as an internal check of consistency.

Conventional methods of change detection essentially involve map overlay procedures and hence the need for attention to detail in terms of accurate geometry and labelling. An alternative approach is borrowed from digital image processing. In this, time series of aerial photographs are scan-digitised and either co-registered (i.e. digitally superimposed) or registered to a common map base and then superimposed. The advantage of this method is that it makes no prior assumptions about the structure of the landscape. Changes are detected as differences between the images, and the interpreter has to separate these according to whether they are real changes or due to normal seasonal variations. This type of analysis is most extensively used in relation to the analysis of change from long time series of satellite imagery (e.g. to monitor tropical deforestation processes). It has only recently been applied to aerial photography, but it offers major advantages in that it enables changes in quality to be assessed and can deal with changes across gradational boundaries. Research is currently being conducted at the MLURI to develop a knowledge-based change detection system (SYMOLAC) that uses this approach combined with advanced artificial intelligence methods. For an in-depth review of methods for change detection, refer to Lunetta & Elvidge (1999).

Change detection also poses problems in validation. In general, changes are measured from a present that is known to a past that is not (i.e. historical interpretation has no equivalent ground truth information). In the absence of historical ground information with which to validate the interpretation of the historical photography, the only assumption that can be made is that the known error rates calculated for the present day apply equally to the historical dataset. It is essential to understand that, even with this assumption, the error rates attached to the change dataset (i.e. when one interpretation is subtracted from the other) may be poorer as the errors may not coincide spatially and will thus be inherited by the change dataset. An analysis of sampling systems for change detection accuracy assessment is provided in Chapter 15 of Lunetta & Elvidge (1999). Where a considerable investment is planned in developing a habitat monitoring system based upon interpretation of historical sequences of imagery, careful attention should be paid to the topic of accuracy and the method of validation.

Summary of advantages and disadvantages
Advantages

- Aerial photography provides a relatively quick assessment of extent of Broad Habitat types.
- It can be used as a monitoring baseline.
- Historical trends can be examined by using past photographs.
- The time taken for analysis compares favourably with a ground survey.
- Boundaries can generally be more quickly and accurately mapped than by a ground survey.

Disadvantages

- Fewer habitat details can be distinguished than with a Phase I habitat survey.
- If photographs are of poor quality, accurate analysis is not possible.
- Some habitats can be hard to distinguish on photographs, necessitating field checking of results. Interpretation errors increase with the level of detail that is attempted.
- Measured habitat area will be underestimated for slopes unless three co-ordinates are used to digitise maps. Likewise, high-altitude areas will be overestimated relative to low-altitude ones.
- Unknown bias is introduced if habitat extent is estimated from incomplete photographic coverage.

6.1.4 Fixed-point photography

Recommended uses
Fixed-point photography is considered to be an essential part of many monitoring programmes, as it provides a relatively simple method of recording broad changes in vegetation and habitat.

Photographic records can also provide important information on management operations and visual evidence of changes in some environmental variables, such as degree of flooding. Although not directly related to monitoring, photographs can also be useful for site familiarisation during desk studies and provision of illustrative materials for reports, etc. They can also be very useful for convincing people that change has actually occurred on a site if the timescale of change has been slow and hence not very noticeable. The main value of repeated photographs is that they provide a quick visual impression of change through time.

Fixed-point photography from ground stations is applicable to a wide range of habitats, but it must be recognised that in many more open habitats major changes in the pattern of vegetation communities will be more readily assessed by stereoscopic examination of aerial photographs (Section 6.1.3), provided the ground is not steeply sloped. On steep slopes, fixed-point photography can be more accurate than aerial photography. Photographs can also be used to record individual quadrats if taken from directly above, and these can be analysed objectively at a later date if necessary. Other alternative/additional methods to consider include Phase I mapping (Section 6.1.5) and NVC surveys (Section 6.1.6).

Fixed-point photography of permanent quadrats is often used for monitoring individual species, particularly fungi, lichens and bryophytes (see Part III).

Time efficiency
Photography is a cost-effective method for recording and monitoring change, being relatively cheap and straightforward to carry out. If the use of ranging poles is necessary for lining up repeat photographs or indicating vegetation height (see below), it will be more efficient to employ two people.

The time required to sort, document and store photographs should not be forgotten or underestimated as this is critical to the success of photographic monitoring programmes. Interpretation of changes is normally by subjective visual assessment and therefore relatively quick and easy.

Fixed-point photography: summary of key points

Recommended uses

- Monitoring broad changes in habitat extent and type, e.g. through succession and patch dynamics
- Photographic records are useful for many purposes other than monitoring, e.g. recording management operations and site familiarisation

Efficiency   Relatively quick to carry out in the field by one person; some additional time required to manage photographic records; subjective analysis is quick and easy

Objectivity   Normally subjective, although semi-objective counts or measurements can be obtained with appropriate set-ups

Precision   Not measurable, as data are usually qualitative

Bias   Not measurable, as data are usually qualitative

Expertise required   Only a basic knowledge of photography; other techniques are easily learnt

Equipment required   Basic photographic equipment and tripod (cost *c.* £500)

Key methodological points to consider

- Little need to anticipate changes that are likely to take place, especially if comprehensive coverage is attained

- Medium-speed black and white film can be used. Colour will allow greater precision when distinguishing features/boundaries. High-quality (i.e. sharp and correctly exposed) photographs are required. Avoid very bright days, when shadows create contrasting images that lack detail
- Standard methods should be used that allow photographs to be repeated with the same camera configuration at the same position at the same time of year
- It is useful to include graduated ranging poles in photographs as markers against which vegetation height or water levels can be assessed
- Linkage of photographic recording to other monitoring projects (especially aerial photography) is useful
- It is essential that photographs and details of their location, direction, timing and camera configuration, etc. are properly stored so that successive photographs can be easily retrieved and compared

Data analysis   Photographs are normally analysed subjectively. Analysis is therefore sensitive to individual interpretation

Expertise required

A basic knowledge of 35 mm single-lens reflex photography is essential. Although photographic monitoring is relatively simple, and can probably be carried out effectively by most people if they follow procedures carefully (as described below or in other methodological descriptions), training in photographic monitoring is desirable.

If the fixed-angle method described below is to be used, it is recommended that each step be learnt and rehearsed thoroughly before embarking on the actual photography at the site. The procedure is simple once mastered, but care should be taken to avoid mistakes, especially when taking and registering the first photograph in a programme.

Using the full procedure detailed below will increase the time and hence costs of monitoring, and is therefore best restricted to cases where:

- quantitative measurements are going to be made from the photographs for analysis; or
- you are working in a habitat or landscape with little in the way of distinctive permanent features with which to orientate yourself by using previous photographs in the field.

Equipment required

The equipment required (see Appendix 6) for fixed-point photographic monitoring requires a capital expenditure of about £500. However, this equipment can be used to monitor many sites and most of it is likely to be of use for other purposes.

The basic requirement of fixed-point photography is that the system must enable the precise relocation of the camera position in both the horizontal and the vertical plane. There must therefore be provision of a permanent marker, whether already existing or installed especially for the purpose (see Appendix 5 for a discussion of the use of permanent markers). The use of a firm tripod that prevents camera shake and allows the camera to be fixed at the right angle above the right spot is also recommended.

The type of tripod used is particularly important if the fixed-angle method (described below) is to be used. For this method NCC (1987) recommend the use of a Linhof Propan pan and tilt head (Model II). This can be used with many tripods, but care must be taken when purchasing to ensure that it is compatible and that any existing pan and tilt head on the tripod is removable. The use of a ball and socket head between the tripod and the pan head is also recommended to avoid the necessity for levelling the tripod.

For long-term monitoring purposes monochrome photographic prints are normally recommended as the best material (NCC, 1987) as the negatives and prints generally last longer in long-term storage than do colour equivalents, particularly if properly processed for archival storage. If monitoring is also used for informing management decisions in the short term, colour film can provide more information and better discrimination between habitat types. You can always use two film backs or camera bodies with both monochrome and colour films. If colour slide film is used, the slides can last for several decades if infrequently projected and stored in cool, dark and dry conditions.

The speed of the film used is also an important factor to consider. Fast films will yield less fine detail than will slow films because of their inherent grain size, but allow the use of faster shutter speeds and/or smaller apertures to give greater depths of field. However, as the photographs are taken from tripods, slow shutter speeds can often be used satisfactorily in suitable conditions. On balance, therefore, a medium-speed film is the best compromise.

Digital cameras are now available and allow easy computer storage and manipulation of images. Many digital cameras can now match the resolution of film. If the technology remains in long-term use, digital images are preferable to film.

Field methods
Number and layout of photographs
Perhaps the most difficult decisions to make in the planning of photographic monitoring is the number and location of positions from which photographs are to be taken. Where possible, locations should be integrated with other monitoring projects and also aim to include representative views of all the interest features on the site and all major forms of management of each. The Site Management Statement or Management Plan should therefore be consulted, together with any available survey information (particularly habitat maps) in order to identify appropriate locations. It is often useful to take photographs that show a range of scales including the subject in relation to its surrounding landscape, the subject itself and representative detailed shots of the subject.

The number of locations chosen, and the range of photographs taken at each, will clearly depend on the size and complexity of the site, but should not be allowed to become unworkable. In some cases it may be appropriate to devise a programme whereby different locations are recorded in different years and at different return intervals, depending on the speed of change anticipated in the feature or attribute (see below). However, it is preferable to take more photographs than necessary than not to take enough.

Frequency and timing of photographs
In most habitats and situations vegetation changes detectable from fixed-point photography are unlikely to be noticeable at intervals of less than 5–10 years. However, where sudden changes are believed to have occurred, e.g. as a result of management or natural events, such as storms, photographs should be taken to record changes irrespective of the time elapsed since the previous monitoring. Some habitats (e.g. sand dunes) are

notoriously dynamic and therefore prone to mostly gradual but potentially rapid changes. Photographic monitoring of features and their attributes in such habitats should therefore be more frequent. The recommended frequencies for monitoring habitat features are summarised in Chapter 5.

It is important that the time of year at which photographs are taken within any particular sequence is consistent. If possible, a date should be chosen when seasonal vegetation change is relatively stable so that the effects of annual variations in weather or vegetation are minimised. Alternatively, some phenological cue may be used, such as the flowering of a key species. Where regular management is practised (e.g. mowing), photography should be consistently before or after such activities. In woodlands, features of tree- and shrub-layer structure are best recorded during the winter. In some habitats, winter and summer records may be useful, for example for comparison of high and low water levels.

Taking initial and repeat photographs

The simplest method of taking repeat photographs is to relocate the fixed points and use previous photographs as guidance for lining up the shot. This may be adequate for many general purposes, but for systematic monitoring two systems for fixed-point photography are recommended by NCC (1987) and are described below. The first is the 'fixed-angle system' (Bignal, 1978) used to monitor Loch Lomond. This is recommended for National Nature Reserves (NNRs) and other situations in which intensive observations over a long period of time are envisaged. The alternative 'centre pole system', devised by M. J. D'Oyly, is less time-consuming in the field and is recommended where there are problems with access, topography or a shortage of resources.

The method chosen to relocate photographs will depend on the actual use to which they will be put; there is little point in precisely relocating points by using the fixed-angle system if one is using the photographs to make a simple subjective assessment of broad changes.

Fixed-angle system

All the equipment necessary for this system is described above (see Appendix 6) and should be used in strict accordance with the following NCC (1987) procedure.

A   Initial photographs

A1   Locate or install permanent marker (see Appendix 5), making sure enough information is recorded for its relocation.

A2   Set up tripod over the marker; centre with aid of a plumb bob slung from base of centre column, and adjust its height so that the camera lens will be at a standard height above ground level.

A3   Using ball and socket head: set pan head to level position (red line) on tilt scale; fit pan head to tripod, level pan head, clamp ball and socket. Without ball and socket head: set pan head to level position (red line) on tilt scale; fit pan head to tripod, level pan head by manipulating tripod.

A4   Fix camera to pan head, in horizontal configuration, positioned so that the back of the baseplate aligns with mark scribed across the head.

A5   Supporting camera, release the two locking knobs on the pan head, and move camera until a suitable view is framed. Lock knobs tight.

A6   Adjust camera settings and take photographs. NCC (1987) recommend two photographs are taken. However, given the relatively low cost of film compared with that of staff time, we recommend that bracketed exposures are taken, i.e. one photograph at the predicted ideal exposure, one underexposed by one *f*-stop, and one overexposed by one *f*-stop. Digital photography is less expensive than film.

A7   Select a feature that appears at the centre of the horizontal field of the photograph. Step back at least two paces, and take a compass bearing over the lens centre of the camera to the selected feature. (If there is no suitable feature it may be necessary to locate a ranging pole, or similar marker, in the middle view, but this is laborious unless an assistant is available.) Record the bearing.

A8   Record tilt angle from the pan head scale.

A9 Make sure that the following have been recorded: date, time of day, site, location reference, compass bearing, tilt angle, camera height, lens used and focal length, any filters used, film type, exposure details, film roll and exposure numbers. Notes on weather conditions and features shown in the view should also be recorded.

A10 Before dismantling equipment and moving on, consider whether one or more additional photographs could usefully be taken from the same point (e.g. perhaps as part of a panoramic view). Also (although not mentioned in the NCC instructions), it is recommended that a photograph of the tripod is taken before it is removed from the fixed marker. This will help relocation of the marker on future occasions.

B   Repeat photographs

B1 Locate permanent marker (see Appendix 5).

B2 Follow steps A2, A3 and A4 as described above.

B3 Holding compass, step back two paces and, sighting over the lens centre of camera, select distant feature that corresponds to the bearing recorded for the first photograph. In the absence of a suitable feature, align assistant with ranging pole in middle of view or, if single-handed, align ranging pole by taking a back bearing on the camera.

B4 Align camera so that selected distant feature or ranging pole is central in the horizontal field of view. Clamp horizontal scale of pan head. Remove ranging pole (if used), or move to most appropriate location if required in shot for scaling or estimation of vegetation height.

B5 Set tilt scale to angle recorded for first photograph. Clamp tilt scale.

B6 Check against print of first photograph that the same view is again framed. If there is clearly a discrepancy, not explained by the passage of time, check, and, if necessary adjust to correspond with the original photograph, and record new bearing and tilt angle.

B7 Adjust camera settings and photographs (see A6).

B8 As under A9, make sure that the following have been recorded: date, time of day, site, location reference, compass bearing, tilt angle, camera height, lens used and focal length, any filters used, film type, exposure details, film roll and exposure numbers. Notes on weather conditions and features shown in the view should also be recorded.

B9 Before dismantling equipment and moving on, make sure that all views from the point have been repeated.

Centre pole system

The centre pole system requires the equipment detailed in Appendix 6 except the pan head and compass, and was devised to monitor woodland cover in an area already covered with permanent transects marked by metal stakes at 100 foot (approximately 30 m) intervals (NCC, 1987). The method involves photographing forwards and backwards along the transect at each stake. This generally requires taking a large number of photographs in a limited time, and the system was designed with this in mind. This method is perhaps best used in areas in which transects or gridlines are already marked, unless it is decided to set up permanent markers before photographic monitoring takes place, which will involve additional time and expense (see Appendix 5 for advice on setting up permanent markers).

The main feature is a standard ranging pole placed at a set distance from the camera; the camera is centred on the mid-point of the pole. The procedures for first and repeat photographs are the same, and follow guidelines detailed by NCC (1987).

1. Set up camera at marker, normally in horizontal configuration (although vertical configuration can be used on steep slopes if necessary), on tripod. Centre over the marker with the lens a standard height from the ground.

2. Measure a standard distance along transect towards next marker, and plant the ranging pole (upright and carefully aligned) at this point.

3. Free the ball and socket head, and centre the aim of the camera on the mid-point of the ranging pole.

4. Clamp the tripod head, adjust camera settings and take two photographs.

5. From all but the first marker, repeat steps 2–4 with the camera directed back to the previous marker.

The type of pole and its distance from the camera should be standardised for any particular set of photographs. The pole should also be buried to a standard depth on each occasion. Alternatively, a ranging pole support can be used on all occasions so that the tip of the pole rests on the ground and the pole is held vertically.

Data storage and analysis

Films should be processed and record sheets and photographs indexed and filed as soon as possible after shots are taken. A good indexing and filing system is essential. Where possible, the slide index should be computerised and stored in a database or spreadsheet for easy search and retrieval. Duplicate sets of photographs should be stored in appropriate separate locations. Storage of digital images is simpler.

Analysis is normally by subjective comparison (by eye) of a series of photographs taken over a period of time, recording any obvious changes.

Ideally this should be done at a simple level as soon as each new set of photographs is taken.

In some instances, simple mapping of habitat changes, such as area covered by scrub, may be useful. In turn this can provide quantitative estimates of habitat area and change. Mapping is normally done by eye, although in some circumstances images can be scanned or digitised and areas, etc, calculated by computer. Aerial photographs are, however, more appropriate for such analysis techniques.

Box 6.6 outlines the problems that may be encountered with fixed-point photography, and some possible solutions.

Summary of advantages and disadvantages

The main advantage of photography for monitoring is that there is little or no scope for subjectivity in anticipating the changes that are likely to take place (NCC, 1987). In any other form of recording there is always the possibility that some critically important observation will be omitted from the record simply because of an assumption that change would affect particular attributes of the habitat or be

---

Box 6.6   Likely problems and solutions

The most likely problems to be encountered are due to inconsistent camera configurations and inaccurate relocations. These can be avoided by carefully following the prescribed methods and thorough and accurate recording of data.

Other problems can be expected to arise from the very changes that are being monitored. Tall herbage or woody growth may develop on or just in front of the camera position. This may lead to a temporary interruption in photographic records. If this is likely to be for a long time (e.g. through tree growth) or is unacceptable for other reasons, then it may be appropriate to relocate the observation point. This should be precisely recorded. Sometimes a degree of 'gardening' in the foreground may be justifiable, although in other cases it may be unacceptable disturbance to natural processes.

Difficulties may also arise on mobile habitats. On active dunes, for instance, the natural movement of dune ridges can lead to permanent markers being undercut or buried. Even if the precise horizontal location can be found, it may differ considerably in height. Similar changes can occur on saltmarshes, cliffs, and habitats prone to landslides. In such situations a regular system of photographic recording points may be inappropriate and it may be better to use carefully selected camera locations that can be reasonably expected to remain stable. In some circumstances the construction of purpose-built platforms for photographic recording may be necessary.

Weather conditions can also cause problems. Wet and misty conditions should be avoided, and very bright and sunny weather can also be problematic. Shadowing obscures useful detail and can confuse interpretation and identification of features and attributes.

Phase 1 habitat mapping: summary of key points

Recommended uses

- Providing relatively rapid records of vegetation and wildlife habitat over large areas of countryside
- Providing an objective basis for identifying sites warranting more detailed surveys (e.g. Phase II, also known as NVC) or deserving consideration for protection
- Preparation for planning a monitoring programme, including identification of features and sampling area boundaries
- Monitoring large-scale changes in the extent and distribution of distinct Broad Habitat types

Efficiency   Relatively rapid, ranging between *c.* 1 and 6 km^2 per surveyor per day

Objectivity   Reasonably objective as long as surveyors are adequately trained in surveying and mapping techniques

Precision   The errors involved in measuring habitat areas on 1:10,000 scale maps are generally likely to be well below 5%, although the original boundaries may be more variable

Bias   Estimates of habitat area can be biased by misidentification of vegetation or inaccurate mapping, especially in fragmented and mosaic habitats. The use of aerial photographs as an adjunct to boundary mapping can help to address this. Small rare habitat types can be over or underestimated if areas are calculated from maps by using sampling techniques. Habitat areas on hillsides will be underestimated if dot grids are used on two-dimensional maps. If areas are measured with a planimeter or with digitising equipment, altitude can be included from spot heights to allow some consideration of slope to be made

Expertise required   Surveyors must be able to recognise the dominant and other characteristic plant species necessary for the identification of Phase I survey habitat types. Further botanical expertise is desirable to enable extra information to be recorded in the form of target notes

Mapping skills are also necessary for surveying in the field and for the production of master maps

Equipment required   No specialist equipment required for surveying; basic requirements include Phase I manual, botanical field guides (see Appendix 3), binoculars and maps. Equipment for producing master maps and calculating habitat areas includes basic office equipment and Romer dot grids

Key methodological points to consider

- Surveyors must work to a consistent standard to ensure accuracy and compatibility between surveys
- Planning of fieldwork is necessary to ensure that the survey area is covered in the field season and habitats are visited when key species are readily identifiable
- Aerial photographs can be useful to increase the speed and efficiency of mapping, particularly in areas of difficult or restricted access
- If habitat areas are estimated by using sampling methods, care must be taken to avoid bias arising from the non-random distribution of habitats

Data analysis   Areas of different habitat types are best calculated manually by using a Romer dot grid. Maps can also be digitised, analysed and stored in a GIS. Areas can be expressed as percentage of a given area covered by each habitat type, or as total area covered by each habitat type. Data can be used as a baseline for future monitoring, but considerable care must be taken in the interpretation of changes because of potential inconsistencies between surveys

in a particular direction. Photographic recording in the field is also relatively quick and simple in comparison with other monitoring methods and provides an easily interpretable visual picture of change with time.

The main disadvantage of photographic monitoring is that it only gives broad indications of change that cannot be quantified or tested by objective statistical methods.

6.1.5   Phase I habitat mapping

Anyone carrying out a Phase I habitat survey will require the Nature Conservancy Council (NCC) publication *Handbook for Phase I Habitat Survey: A Technique for Environmental Audit* (NCC, 1990a). It is beyond the scope of this section to reproduce the specific habitat classifications and codes necessary for Phase I survey, which are contained in the NCC handbook. This section therefore presents a synopsis of the manual for general information and reference purposes. The reader is referred to the NCC handbook itself for specific definitions and procedures.

Recommended uses

Phase I habitat surveying is a standardised system developed by the NCC for classifying and mapping wildlife habitats in all parts of Britain. Phase I surveys can provide, relatively rapidly, a record of semi-natural vegetation and wildlife habitat over large areas of countryside. Habitat classification is based principally on vegetation, augmented by reference to topographic and substrate features, particularly where vegetation is not the dominant habitat component.

The information provided by a Phase I survey has many uses: it can provide an objective basis for determining whether a site merits more detailed Phase II surveys (Section 6.1.6) or whether it deserves consideration for protection as an SSSI, Local Nature Reserve, etc.

In a monitoring context, an initial Phase I survey is a useful precursor to the design of a new monitoring programme for a site. Information from a Phase I map can be used to establish feature and sampling area boundaries and on occasions to identify strata for stratified sampling, although differentiation of vegetation types may be better carried out by using Phase II (NVC) surveys. A Phase I map can also be used as a clearly defined baseline for monitoring changes. However, variations by surveyors in the identification of habitat types and boundaries are sufficiently high to significantly limit the reliability of changes deduced from repeat Phase I mapping (see Box 6.10; see also Cherrill & McClean (1999a, b), who found only *c.* 26% correspondence between maps). Therefore, data from Phase I mapping are only likely to be suitable for detecting large-scale changes in Broad Habitat types over relatively long time periods. Such broad data can be useful when collected over long

periods for illustrative and interpretative purposes, but are likely to be too insensitive and unreliable for detecting small changes. Phase I mapping may be appropriate for distinct habitat types with sharply delimited boundaries in which mapping can be carried out with the aid of aerial photography (Section 6.1.3). Under such circumstances, apparent changes in Broad Habitat extent and distribution can be treated with reasonable confidence.

Time efficiency

Surveyor fieldwork rates will depend on many factors, including the relative competence of surveyors and the topography, complexity, number of target notes recorded, and accessibility of the area to be surveyed. The scale of mapping also affects survey rates.

Phase I survey rates per surveyor have ranged from $0.8\,km^2$ to $6.4\,km^2$ per day. Assuming a total of 90 field survey days per year, a total of $81-580\,km^2$ can be covered by an individual surveyor in one field season (NCC, 1990a). In practice, the upper end of this scale is extremely ambitious and should not be used for calculating effort required to survey a site.

As a further approximate guide to the breakdown of mapping stages, the time taken to produce and analyse a $5\,km \times 5\,km$ $1:10\,000$ scale habitat map is:

- Field survey and production of fair copy 8–10 days
- Production of final copy from fair copy 1.5–2.5 days
- Analysis of final copy by using dot grid 1.0–1.5 days

Based on Phase I surveys of Cumbria and Lancashire 1983–88 from NCC (1990a).

Expertise required

Surveyors should be competent botanists with an aptitude for accurate field recording and mapping. It is essential that surveyors be adequately trained to ensure accuracy and consistency both within and between surveys. Discrepancies between surveyors can be reduced if surveyors are trained to a uniform standard. Detailed descriptions of Phase I habitat types, colour codes and alphanumeric symbols are given in the *Handbook for Phase I Habitat Survey Field Manual* (NCC, 1990b). A thorough knowledge of the major vegetation types and habitats is necessary, including their dominant and characteristic species. Further botanical skills are desirable: these allow extra information concerning species composition to be recorded by using target notes, which draw attention to particular features of interest.

Surveyors should also be trained in other fieldwork skills, including the use of binoculars in vegetation survey, mapping techniques, navigation and route finding, habitat identification, and indications of trophic status, soils and land management. Cherrill & McClean (1999a,b) recommend aerial photographs to help improve mapping.

The work is physically demanding, so surveyors should be fit and healthy.

Writing and numerical skills are required for the production of target notes and reports, and the ability to produce neat final maps is essential if cartographers are not employed.

Equipment required

Appendix 6 summarises the equipment required for Phase I habitat surveying.

Field methods
Outline method

Ideally, a trained surveyor will visit every parcel of land in the area to be surveyed. The vegetation is mapped on to Ordnance Survey maps, usually at a scale of 1 : 10 000. An area of vegetation is assigned to one of some 90 specified habitat types, identified on the map by standard colour codes or symbols. In addition, further information is recorded by the use of dominant species codes within many habitat types, and by the use of descriptive 'target notes', which give a brief account of particular areas of interest. Habitat types and codes are described in detail by NCC, (1990a,b). Only the standard colours in the Berol Verithin series should be used. These are available from stationers or from Berol Ltd, Oldmeadow Road, King's Lynn, Norfolk PE30 4JR. Marks made with these pencils, however, do not photocopy or scan into computers well.

Each distinct habitat unit is recorded in the field by using standard coloured pencils or alternative lettered/alphanumeric codes. Colours and codes should be entered directly on to copies of the large-scale Ordnance Survey maps.

There are advantages in mapping directly in colour in the field, but some surveys have chosen to use pen or pencil only, mapping habitat boundaries and using codes to identify habitat types. This method is quicker and more convenient, particularly in wet conditions and when recording uncomplicated areas. The use of colour is preferable in complex areas and where there are large amounts of semi-natural vegetation. Pencil marks can also be altered at a later date, something that should be avoided.

It is important to standardise the minimum size of habitat unit to be mapped. It is suggested that at 1 : 10 000 scale all habitat units larger than 0.1 ha should be mapped, and at 1 : 25 000 all units larger than 0.5 ha should be mapped (NCC, 1990a,b). It is possible to map smaller units such as ponds, and target notes can also be used to draw attention to small areas of noteworthy habitat. It is also important to agree protocols for mapping fragmented or mosaic habitats.

The overall aim of a target note is to give a concise picture of the nature conservation interest of a site in the context of its land use and management. They must be clear, succinct and informative; even the briefest description can enhance the usefulness of the habitat map. Target notes are used to provide extra detail in particular habitat types, or to point out areas of interest that would otherwise not be recorded by using the standard habitat codes. They are very important as they can provide an indication of areas that might require further study, as well as providing useful additional information on any other features of note identified by the surveyor, such as uncommon or rare plant species, mammal signs, bird species, etc. A target note is recorded as a red circle with an individual number on the map; explanations of the reasons for the target notes are included with the final survey report.

Dominant species in each habitat unit should be recorded wherever possible by using standard species codes given by NCC (1990b).

In practice much of the mapping can often be carried out from public rights of way, with the use of binoculars at relatively short ranges to identify the vegetation. This avoids the time-consuming process of seeking access permission, although this will be necessary in areas where no rights of way occur. However, the quality of grazed grassland can be very difficult to assess without visiting the actual site.

Aerial photographs may also be useful as an adjunct to ground surveying. Although aerial photography is no substitute for fieldwork when carrying out Phase I surveys, the availability of contemporary aerial photographs at a suitable scale can increase the speed and efficiency with which field surveys are carried out and the accuracy of mapping boundaries. Photographs can also be used to map areas with difficult or restricted access or for mapping the interiors of large woods.

Informal or fixed-point photographs may also be useful, especially for subsequent interpretation of differences that might simply be the result of surveyor variation. For large sites a large number of photographs might be required, but this may not be practicable.

Choice of scale

Phase I surveys are mapped onto either 1 : 10 000 or 1 : 25 000 scale Ordnance Survey maps. Generally, countrywide Phase I surveys have been carried out at either scale, but there has been an increasing tendency to standardise on a scale of 1 : 10 000 despite some of the advantages of the smaller scale.

There is no doubt that, for some uses, a 1 : 10 000 scale is desirable as it allows greater detail to be recorded, but it is recognised that for very large sites, such as in the Scottish Highlands, a 1 : 25 000 scale survey may be the only economically feasible option. If surveys are carried out at this scale it is recommended that full use be made of target notes to provide greater detail.

Survey preparation

A work programme should be planned carefully at the beginning of the survey to ensure that the area to be surveyed is covered in one field season. A systematic approach, completing one map at a time so that no gaps are left, has much to recommend it. However, some habitats are best surveyed at different times of year from others; woodlands in spring, grasslands in midsummer, heathlands in late summer and autumn and open waters between mid-June and September (see Box 6.9).

To survey an area one habitat at a time at the ideal time for each habitat is likely to be costly and time-consuming, involving repeated visits to each area. A suitable compromise would be to survey areas most rich in woodland in spring and early summer, areas most rich in grasslands in midsummer, and areas most rich in moorland later in the season. Within these areas all habitats should be surveyed at the same time.

The field season should be considered as starting in late March – early April in southern and central Britain and late April – early May in the north of Britain. The season generally ends about mid-October, although it may be possible to undertake some surveying in November if the weather is mild. End-of-season surveys should generally be restricted to checking previously surveyed areas; data from such surveys should be treated with caution because many plant species will no longer be apparent.

Each day's fieldwork should be carefully planned to ensure that the maximum amount of ground is covered, and to minimise back-tracking and overlap. Care should be taken to ensure that the whole area is covered; a gap may mean that another visit will be necessary.

Data storage and analysis

The field maps made by surveyors are transferred to 'fair' maps either by the surveyors themselves or by cartographers. Surveyors are likely to be more precise, because they are familiar with the areas being surveyed, whereas cartographers will generally produce more consistent and neater maps. Fair maps can be monochrome or colour, but the final objective is to produce an accurate, full-colour master habitat map, which has a high visual impact and is easy to interpret.

The procedure for the preparation of master maps has varied from survey to survey; for a summary of different methodologies see NCC, (1990a,b).

Master maps should be stored in lightproof cabinets to minimise colour fading. Colour copies should also be kept for security. Habitat maps are most easily reproduced by photocopying, either in colour or in monochrome. A monochrome copy of the master map allows black and white copies to be made as required. Habitat area measurements, completed target notes and general description sheets should be stored on paper in grid square order. Fair maps produced in drawing packages can be stored electronically.

Data analysis

For monitoring purposes, either to establish a baseline or for comparison with a previous baseline survey, the area covered by each habitat type can be measured from Phase I habitat maps. In order to simplify this task, NCC (1990a, b) suggest that the 90 or so Phase I habitat classifications be combined to give 34 categories for measurement. Consistent use of these groups will allow quick comparisons to be made between different surveys and will facilitate the compilation of regional and national statistics on habitat extent.

Measurements of the extent of each of the different types of habitat in the area covered by the survey can be made with a Romer dot grid. Planimeters are not sufficiently accurate for the measurement of small areas. A dot grid is a transparent plastic sheet covered in regularly spaced dots at a given density (e.g. 10 per cm^2). The grid is placed over the map and the numbers of dots falling in each habitat type are counted. The area of each habitat is calculated from the map scale and dot density. For example, at $1 : 10\,000$ scale with a grid dot density of 10 per cm^2, 1 cm = 100 m; $1\ cm^2 = 0.01\ km^2$; 1 dot = 0.01/10 = 0.001 km^2. So if one habitat type is covered by 125 dots, its area = $125 \times 0.001 = 0.125\ km^2$.

The advent of digitising tablets has largely removed the need to rely on manual methods of calculating areas from maps. Dot grids and planimeters have now been supplanted by standard functions for measuring map metrics within low-cost GIS or autocad facilities. These not only include area calculations but also provide a range of other metrics such as perimeter length (see Wadsworth & Treweek, 1999). The time required to digitise both the base map and the habitat overlay will be considerable but, once completed, data processing and extraction and area calculation is very quick and accurate. This also allows high-quality colour plots to be made whenever needed.

For monitoring purposes, it is recommended that areas of all habitats be measured as described above, preferably with the more accurate and sophisticated GIS technology. If only a rough idea of habitat extent is required, estimates of habitat abundance can be obtained by using sampling procedures. Refer to NCC (1990a,b) for further details of sampling strategies for area estimation.

Calculated areas should be entered into a spreadsheet for graphical and statistical analysis, and for ease of data storage and retrieval.

Summary of advantages and disadvantages
Advantages

- Provides relatively rapid record of vegetation and habitat type over large areas of countryside.
- The use of standard methods and recording procedures allows easy general comparisons between different surveys to be made.
- Habitat maps can provide valuable information for planning site monitoring programmes.
- The level of detail obtained in a Phase I survey is higher than that obtained by using aerial photography or remote sensing.
- The use of descriptive target notes can draw attention to areas that merit further study and can record additional ecological information that might be of interest.

Disadvantages

- Requires substantial amount of fieldwork before maps can be compiled and the data analysed.
- Habitat classes are relatively broad, so finer-scale variation will be missed.
- Discrepancies between individual surveyors can lead to biased area estimates.
- A problem can arise when trying to accurately map boundaries between habitat types where

there is a gradual transition between the two. This can lead to biased area estimates.

- Errors made on original survey maps cannot be checked without returning to the field.
- Areas where access is denied, or where access is problematic, such as large, dense woodlands or wetland, can be difficult to survey from the ground.
- Overall, the method is too insensitive and unreliable for most site monitoring requirements, but it is particularly useful in EIA studies.

A case study of the use of repeat Phase I habitat surveys for monitoring vegetation at three sites is presented in Box 6.7.

6.1.6   National Vegetation Classification (NVC) surveys

Recommended uses

The National Vegetation Classification (NVC), published in *British Plant Communities* (Rodwell *et al.*, 1991 *et seq.*), is the standard phytosociological classification method in Britain. It offers a reliable framework for identifying vegetation types, interpreting the ecological factors that control them, and assessing their importance in a national and local context. The NVC is also often used to describe a field technique of vegetation survey (also known as Phase II survey) derived from the protocol used in the original classification study. Thus although the NVC was not developed as a monitoring tool, it can provide a conceptual framework and practical tools for monitoring vegetation (Rodwell, 1997). As this is a rather complex subject with some potential pitfalls, the uses and misuses of NVC for monitoring are discussed in some depth below.

Perhaps the most valuable use of the NVC is as a precursor to the establishment of a monitoring programme. NVC surveys can provide inventories and maps of NVC communities and subcommunities at a site. First, these may be used as a basis for the identification and characterisation of site features (Rowell, 1993); see Part I, Section 2.1. At its simplest level, a Notified Feature (i.e. one that is listed in the designation citation) may be defined as an NVC community or subcommunity. Alternatively,

a feature may be defined as a rich diversity, distinctive mosaic or zonation of NVC types. Where vegetation features have not been clearly defined in NVC terms or other ways, a subsequent NVC survey may be used as a *post hoc* means of providing a precise definition of features on the basis of a standardised technique and classification system. Such surveys may also reveal or highlight previously unrecorded features of interest.

Where NVC types are not named as whole features, they may be important attributes of broader habitat features (see Davies & Yost, 1998). Furthermore, the presence of locally determined constant species, preferential species (i.e. those that predominantly occur in one community type) and associated species (i.e. other species that occur in the NVC type) is also a monitoring requirement for some habitat types. Thus, to some extent the NVC is often used as a basis for defining the condition of vegetation. However, great care should be taken in the use of NVC datasets from *British Plant Communities* as standards for defining 'poor' and 'good' examples of vegetation stands. Such data should not be used to normalise management of stands to become 'perfect matches' to the NVC community tables, because the maintenance of the local variation invariably present is central to the conservation of biodiversity. The NVC types are idealised summary classes, which provide reference points for classification of vegetation occurring in the field.

Where NVC types are site features or attributes that require monitoring, a logical starting point is to carry out an NVC survey if this has not been recently done. Indeed, the establishment of the NVC types present will often be a prerequisite for setting the correct objectives and limits for a site. Guidelines for identifying attributes that define condition (see, for example, SNH, 2000) will differ according to NVC type. Where NVC surveys are to be carried out, communities and sub-communities should be identified by using properly replicated quantitative quadrat-based methods (see below) rather than subjective visual assessments, even if these are done by experts.

In theory, repeat NVC mapping could be used for monitoring both the extent and the composition of habitats (in terms of NVC types present, not species

Box 6.7 A case study of the use of Phase I survey for monitoring vegetation

INTRODUCTION

This study (Dargie, 1992) examined the effectiveness of repeat Phase I survey as a monitoring data source for use at sites requiring information on habitat change. Three sites previously surveyed using Phase I were selected: Benacre Broad, Suffolk; Skipwith Common, North Yorkshire; and Hannah's Hill, Northumberland.

METHOD

The sites were resurveyed by, as far as possible, the same methods that were used in the original site survey. The two completed habitat maps for each site were produced at the same scale, and the new map was overlaid on top of the old one, with a clear acetate grid of 1 mm squares placed on top of both.

For each repeat survey map polygon, the types of first survey habitat beneath were noted, with the number of 1 mm squares that the habitat occupied. Each repeat survey habitat type had, at the end, a count of 1 mm squares for each of its underlying first survey habitat types. These data were converted into hectares and entered into a transition matrix, with repeat survey habitat codes entered along the top and the first survey codes in the left-hand column. This matrix presented a concise record of measured change, with row (first survey) and column (second survey) totals giving the quantities of each habitat at the two dates of survey.

RESULTS

(1) Benacre Broad, Suffolk

In addition to some relatively small faults in the repeat mapping, two major errors were identified. First, mudflats created by the loss of reed swamp were recorded as brackish lagoons because they had been inundated by salt water at the time of the survey. Second, local experts considered that both surveys had mistaken areas of reed swamp for inundation vegetation.

(2) Skipwith Common, North Yorkshire

The first survey was made by using field checking to place Phase I categories on to a boundary map derived from aerial photographs. The boundaries might

therefore relate to the date of aerial photography rather than of the field survey; this difference is important if accurate rates of habitat change are required. The repeat survey was based on vertical colour aerial photographs.

Errors due to tilt were noticed on both maps but comparison of fixed-point and line distances suggested that these were small. There were discrepancies in habitat definition between the two surveys. The first survey did not separate *Salix cinerea* scrub and omitted a small area of unimproved neutral grassland. More seriously, there was confusion between marsh or marshy grassland and inundation vegetation habitat types in both surveys, plus differences in the separation of wet and dry heath.

However, the maps and interpretation, suggesting an expansion of woodland and a corresponding decline in heathland, bracken and wetland, were well received by local experts, and indicated habitat losses not fully appreciated by local managers.

(3) Hannah's Hill, Northumberland

Both surveys were carried out without the use of aerial photographs, and major differences were found between them. The repeat survey had a much higher density of habitat boundaries, and few of these coincided with boundaries from the first survey. Overall it was felt that the boundary displacement represented considerable planimetric error rather than actual changes in habitat extent.

CONCLUSIONS

Perhaps the most important finding of this study was that the use of aerial photographs in conjunction with Phase I surveys considerably increases the accuracy of the surveys and the confidence placed in the results. It is essential that monitoring surveys should be accurate and perceived to be reliable if management decisions are to be based upon their findings. The accurate mapping of vegetation boundaries is therefore vital.

The correct identification of habitat types is also very important, but mistakes in identifying habitat types can be more easily corrected than can errors in determining boundaries.

If accurate measures of habitat change are required it is essential that precise field methods are used in conjunction with aerial photography and maps derived from good photographic rectification.

NVC surveys: summary of key points

Recommended uses

- Baseline descriptions and mapping of vegetation as a precursor to designing a monitoring programme
- Confirmation of NVC types present when these are features or attributes for which monitoring is required
- Interpretation of changes in vegetation

Efficiency   Fairly slow and labour-intensive

Objectivity   Reasonably objective provided trained surveyors are used, but some subjectivity over boundaries of communities and especially subcommunities

Precision   No data available

Bias   Identification of communities and vegetation may be subject to significant bias from individual surveyors

Expertise required   Competent botanist with NVC experience

Equipment required   Quadrats/tape measures, maps, floras, NVC guide, ruler, compass, spirit level with angle measuring device, coloured pencils

Key methodological points to consider

- Is an NVC survey necessary: are there more efficient means to gather the data you require?

- Time of year for survey; some communities are best surveyed in appropriate seasons (e.g. woodland in early summer) (see Box 6.9)
- Where mapping is to be carried out, follow standard mapping methods, such as Phase I overlain with standard NVC codes
- Scale of mapping: for most purposes 1 : 10 000 is probably adequate
- Boundaries of vegetation types and mosaics can be difficult to define
- Ensure representative quadrats are recorded; quadrat sizes should be selected by following the NVC guidelines
- Surveyors can cover 5–200 ha per day depending on topography and complexity of vegetation
- Comparisons of repeated simple NVC mapping cannot provide sufficiently reliable estimates of changes in extent or distribution of NVC types to be appropriate for most monitoring purposes
- There are a few vegetation types not covered in the original classification, though these are relatively rare

Data analysis   A high level of statistical analysis on properly replicated and sampled data (e.g. G-tests) is required to assess change with any degree of confidence at the community level

within a community). Given that some interest features are defined in terms of the NVC, this will be required in some instances. The extent of a selected habitat could be measured simply from the NVC maps and any changes in area assessed directly. However, monitoring data from NVC mapping are only likely to be able to detect change at a fairly crude scale (e.g. change of community, large-scale damage) and over a long time period. Furthermore, assessing changes in composition within a community from NVC mapping data alone is fraught with difficulties. It is at best very crude, and confidence can only be placed in obvious changes at a community level after inspection of historical data. The mapping data will not be sufficient for assessing management impacts such as those arising from fertiliser application, etc. (these require more

detailed techniques such as point quadrats; see Section 6.4.5) and will not detect gradual change before large changes have occurred. Measurement of structural changes may show the consequences of alterations in management regimes long before the NVC classes change.

NVC mapping is also time-consuming (see below) and therefore costly. NVC repeat mapping is therefore not recommended as a general method for monitoring. If NVC mapping is to be employed for other long-term monitoring purposes, it is advisable to have repeated all or part of the survey at the time the baseline is set up, to assess repeatability and obtain error estimates to see whether the method will give the information required.

Instead of conventional repeat mapping it is recommended that NVC communities and subcommunities be monitored by more objective and quantitative means, such as those employing quadrat- or belt-transect-based sampling methods (see Sections 6.4.2 and 6.4.6). An initial NVC survey can play a vital role in designing the optimum sampling strategy and methods for such programmes. In particular, NVC maps can identify the approximate boundaries of vegetation types. Irrespective of whether NVC vegetation types are features in their own right, or attributes of features, NVC boundaries can be used to define sampling areas and sampling strata for stratified sampling. The maps can also be used to locate transects across vegetation boundaries where changes in the extent of vegetation stands need to be monitored. Although, as mentioned above, NVC mapping can be time-consuming, the cost of a one-off initial survey may often be offset by savings obtained through the reduced sampling requirements of an optimally designed monitoring programme.

A potential role for the NVC with respect to monitoring is its use as an analytical and predictive tool (Rodwell, 1997). Each NVC vegetation type characterised can be related to particular environmental conditions, including climatic, edaphic and biotic influences, the combination of which favours the development of the vegetation type, and the continuance of which is essential to sustain it. Although available information on NVC communities and subcommunities varies, this provides a valuable predictive capacity. This can illuminate spatial contrast between vegetation types and temporal relationships in successions, regressions or lines of deflected development, where serial processes are still ongoing or where management or other environmental changes have stimulated vegetation change. Despite being incomplete, such a predictive framework of spatial and temporal relations enables the fabric of a site and its features to be related to potential conditions. The NVC can thus help to define objectives, identify possible management options and aims and provide some basis for calculating costs and benefits. Cooper & Rodwell (1995) outline a preliminary attempt at such a process for the English Nature Yorkshire Dales Natural Area.

Although such analyses may be based on data from NVC surveys, the classification framework can be used in conjunction with survey techniques that are not themselves of the NVC type.

Time efficiency

The time taken to survey an area depends on the complexity of the site, its accessibility, the scale of the survey and the skill of the surveyor. A simple 'walkover' (better defined as a 'site appraisal') survey will be quicker than one supported by quadrat data (the latter is always preferable). Quadrats in species-poor heathland may take 5 minutes to record, in species-rich hay meadows over 30 minutes, and large $50\,m \times 50\,m$ woodland quadrats over 60 minutes on top of the time taken to do the site appraisal and lay out the grid.

As a crude guide in average lowland areas, a pair of experienced surveyors (one mapping and one quadratting) can map about 25–50 ha in lowland grassland or mire (of low habitat diversity) per day, excluding travel and access permission time. In the uplands where there are large tracts of similar low diversity vegetation, experienced surveyors may be able to cover 100–150 or even 200–300 ha per day. Sites that are difficult to see over or are very complex (e.g. sand dunes, reedbed–fen complexes, mire mosaics) may take considerably longer, with less than 5 ha per day being covered.

Allow about double the survey time for typing up quadrats, drawing neat maps, analysing data and writing the report if the survey takes up to a week. The time taken to write up is proportionately smaller for larger surveys but could still take up to half as long again as the actual data collection.

Expertise required

Surveyors should be competent field botanists, able to identify the majority of species in the field. Vegetative identification of grasses, rushes and sedges may be essential for some communities, such as grasslands and mires, as will knowledge of bryophytes, such as *Sphagnum* spp. in bogs and *Drepanocladus* spp. in flushes. A list of botanical identification guides is given in Appendix 3.

Training in survey and recognition of NVC types is important to ensure consistency, especially if more than one surveyor is being used to survey a large site. Surveyors do not need to know all the NVC communities initially, but they should be familiar with those likely to be encountered in the course of the survey. There is no doubt that recognition of vegetation types improves with experience and knowledge, but it is also well known (if unquantified) that different surveyors may put boundaries between communities and especially subcommunities in different places; this limits the accuracy of the method. Although general ecologists may be able to map boundaries of communities and note some changes (e.g. encroachment of scrub into heathland), they may not have the expertise and experience to assess whether community types are changing at the same time.

Equipment required

The equipment required is listed in Appendix 6 Although photographs are not essential, they can be highly informative and will provide invaluable supplementary information about typical and atypical examples of vegetation. It may also be worth taking a trowel and a pH meter to take a brief look at soils (Section 6.2.2), which can also provide information about the vegetation type.

Field methods

There is no formal definition of what 'an NVC survey' actually comprises or what its standards or methods of quality assurance should be. However, the following field techniques, derived from the protocol used in the research carried out to develop the NVC, have been widely adopted. A series of NVC field guides is currently being prepared by the Joint Nature Conservation Committee (JNCC).

Many details of the field survey, such as the scale of mapping, will have to be decided before going into the field. As the composition of vegetation is a function of the management, soils and climate, it is useful to be aware of the influence of these factors before going into the field; very useful syntheses of each major group are given by Rodwell *et al.* (1991 *et seq.*)

NVC mapping should be seen as a more detailed form of survey than the basic NCC Phase I habitat survey (NCC, 1990a, b). Much of the advice relating to Phase I (Section 6.1.5) can be applied to NVC mapping, although the detail required means that more time is required as well as a higher level of expertise.

The general procedure for NVC mapping is given in Box 6.8. If the site already has Phase I maps, take copies into the field and work from them if no aerial photographs are available, overlaying NVC codes as appropriate and checking vegetation boundaries as you go.

In addition to these procedures, it is useful to take general photographs of the site and quadrats. These can convey an enormous amount of information not gleaned from the species listed in a quadrat. Depending on resources and time available, these may be taken by using fixed-point photography (see Section 6.1.4).

Best times for survey

The best times to survey particular vegetation types are shown in Box 6.9. These are usually determined by the time at which the vegetation is best developed. It is inevitable that some surveys will be carried out outside these times. There is little point in surveying woodland ground flora communities after July, and most wetland communities are best surveyed in late summer.

For monitoring, try to repeat the survey within two weeks of the original day of recording. Differences between seasons are most significant in spring and early summer.

Scale of base maps

In general, 1 : 10 000 maps will provide the basic background information. A 1 : 5 000 scale is usually necessary to monitor extent of habitats on most SSSIs reasonably well. Larger-scale maps (e.g. 1 : 10 000, 1 : 25 000, 1 : 50 000) are only likely to be useful for summarising data at a larger scale on a GIS.

Smaller-scale maps at 1 : 2500 or even 1 : 1250 may be more use for detailed work. The main limitations with such maps are that recent digital coverage may not be available, they may lack features visible on the ground (making location difficult to pinpoint), and large pieces of paper are hard to handle in the field, especially in wet weather.

The problems of deciding how small an area to map are discussed in Box 6.10.

Box 6.8   General procedure for NVC mapping

1. Start with boundaries and edges of sites, and work inwards if possible, working from known locations to unknown locations.

2. By eye, select areas of uniform vegetation for mapping and quadrats. Selecting 'uniform' areas does depend to some extent on experience and knowledge of the site, and is best done by walking through the areas rather than by selecting from a distance. Knowledge of key preferential species is essential for identifying homogeneous stands. Communities that differ often appear as such on the aerial photographs, so these can be used as a guide to identifying stands. However, not all communities or sub-communities will stand out on the aerial photographs; care should therefore be taken when identifying different stand types.

3. At each new known vegetation type record a quadrat of appropriate scale (see Box 6.11 below) and continue to record until at least five, and preferably ten, quadrats have been recorded from the site as a whole, deliberately selecting them to show the variation you are recording in that community or sub-community (this will be invaluable for anybody repeating your work in the future). It may be worth recording more quadrats of any particularly interesting vegetation types. Ensure that the quadrat is sampled entirely within a stand and that it does not include elements of the surrounding communities; avoid edges and transitions. Do not forget to record details of vegetation height, cover (including dwarf shrub, bryophyte, lichen and bare ground), aspect and slope with the species list. Quadrats do not need to be marked or relocatable unless so desired. Noting the most characteristic species in each vegetation type by using the DAFOR scale can provide additional information. Correct identification of the plants encountered is fundamental to the quality and accuracy of the survey methodology. They should be identified on site, or within a day or two before they deteriorate. If samples need to be kept for longer then they should be pressed and dried or, in the case of bryophytes, kept in dry paper packets to ensure the specimens do not go mouldy.

4. At each new unknown vegetation type or distinct variant, record enough quadrats to identify the NVC type from tables in the field, or to allow identification in the office. Again, record at least five, and preferably ten, quadrats. Record vegetation details, again noting the most characteristic species in each vegetation type by using the DAFOR scale.

5. Cross-reference the location of each quadrat on the map. This will allow the quadrat data to be referred back to particular stands and/or communities.

6. Colour in the areas covered by each vegetation type on the map to ensure full coverage, and mark on the appropriate NVC code (it will usually be more efficient to ensure coverage at the time than to return later to fill in gaps). The standard Phase I habitat colours (JNCC, 1993) are often useful for varied sites, although this is less useful for sites with many different communities and subcommunities of the same general type (e.g. blanket bogs). If specific colours have been used for particular communities in previous surveys it may help to use the same ones again. If time is limited, or if mapping onto aerial photographs, the areas of each vegetation type can be marked off with a fine liner pen and marked with the appropriate NVC code.

7. Draw firm lines for clear boundaries and dotted lines for less certain ones; mark mosaics of vegetation as mosaics (see also below).

8. As soon as practicable after the survey (it may be worth doing this every two days while it is fresh in the mind), draw up neat maps and work out the identity of unknown vegetation types.

Boundaries of vegetation

In the field there are often sharp changes in NVC type directly related to sharp environmental boundaries (e.g. change from blanket bog to upland heathland coinciding with the transition of peat to mineral soils). In other cases, there is a more gradual change from one NVC community to another (for example. species-rich *Nardus*

Box 6.9   The best times for NVC surveying

Woodlands: April–June (some types can be surveyed
   into October)
Scrub: April–October
Hedges/boundaries: April–October
Heaths and mires: April–October
Hay meadows: May–June or before they are cut
Upland grasslands: late May/early June – early/
   mid -September

Aquatics: July–September
Swamps and tall herb fens: July–September
Saltmarshes: August–September
Sand dunes: May–August
Sea cliffs: May–October
Shingle: May–October
Ruderals: June-October

---

grasslands merging into upland heathland). This causes problems for mapping in the field and for monitoring the extent of habitats where transitions can be related to management (for example, a relaxation of grazing may result in reversion of *Nardus* grassland to upland heathland). Other communities may form intricate mosaics (for example, springs of the alpine pioneer formations of *Caricion bicoloris-atrofuscae* occur in scattered clusters in upland heaths). Some problems of deciding on boundaries are discussed in Box 6.10.

Selection of quadrat size

Quadrat sizes should be selected as appropriate for the scale of the vegetation in the field (see Appendix 4). For linear or irregular features, quadrats of different shape but equivalent area may be required; some small stands such as bryophyte flushes may need to be sampled in their entirety. The appropriate quadrat sizes as described in the NVC are shown in Box 6.11. The advantage of using these sizes is that the data can be directly related to the NVC.

Identifying communities

In practice in the field, vegetation types are best named from the tables in *British Plant Communities* (Rodwell, 1991 *et seq.*) rather than from the keys, which do not always work well and contain relatively little information. From the quadrats recorded, establish which species are the constants (those occurring in over 60% of the quadrats),

compare these with the constants in the tables (a possible short-list may be obtained by checking the index of species in the back of each volume) and take into account the less frequent species. Always check the description of the vegetation against the text and full table. Full details of how to interpret the tables are given in each *British Plant Communities* volume. Maps of the known distributions of communities in the NVC volumes are very incomplete and should not be used to judge whether the NVC type identified is likely to be correct or not.

There are two computer programs available that can be used to help allocate quadrat data to NVC communities: MATCH and TABLEFIT (Box 6.12). Both use the basic NVC table data but differ slightly in other measures used to give a diagnosis (e.g. species richness). They give a measure of 'goodness of fit' against the defined NVC types, and must only be used as an aid to identification and not for definitive results. They are also no substitute for expert interpretation. There is little to choose between them (Palmer, 1992) and both cost about the same. A slight advantage of MATCH is that if data are being handled in VESPAN (see Box 6.12) the quadrats can be exported to MATCH singly or in groups. The results given must be taken as guidance only and must only be used as an aid to identification because odd community placements can be given. For example, vegetation with constant *Carex nigra* in inland Wales has been assigned to a dune slack community by MATCH.

Box 6.10 Common problems and solutions

SCALE

It is often difficult to decide what is the smallest area
to map; this also partly depends on the objectives of
the survey and is best judged in the field from the scale
of the mapping, the community involved and the
context. Three birch trees in the middle of a bog are
probably not worth mapping as an NVC type, but are
worth noting as present. Despite their small size it is
worth mapping all petrifying springs with active tufa
formation as they are listed in the EC Habitats
Directive and are a habitat of European importance.
One small 1 m × 1 m clump of *Typha* sp. (Bulrush) in
a *Phragmites* sp. reedbed is not a different vegetation
type as it occurs at low frequency in such vegetation,
but a 10 m × 5 m patch might be worth mapping
separately.

BOUNDARIES BETWEEN VEGETATION TYPES

Deciding on the exact boundary between communities
is often difficult. The most practical approaches are to
pick out 'good' areas, which equate to known or
recognisable vegetation types, and either mark an
approximate boundary between them as a dotted
line or mark a transition zone including the problem
vegetation. This may require quite a bit of walking to
and fro, recording quadrats if needed, until the
differences can be clarified. The variability and errors
associated with different surveyors placing boundaries
in different places have not been quantified, but are
likely to be particularly significant in sites with many
transitions between similar vegetation types. Such
variability is a major factor limiting the usefulness of
repeat NVC mapping for monitoring purposes. If
monitoring of the extent and boundaries of vegetation
is required, appropriately designed quadrat- or
transect-based sampling should be used.

MOSAICS

The traditional treatment of complex mosaics of
vegetation is to mark an area as a mosaic and estimate
what proportion is occupied by each vegetation type.

Mosaics are often very hard to map in the field; if
detailed notes of the vegetation are taken it may be
possible to map them later from a distance (e.g. the
opposite hillside) or from recent aerial photographs.
Mosaics may also occur within communities related to
the growth forms of different species, e.g. shorter grass
between large clumps of *Deschampsia cespitosa* (Tufted
Hair-grass). In these cases, if it is difficult to decide
whether this is really one vegetation type or two
forming a mosaic, look for qualitative differences in
the composition of the vegetation related to the two
components. If the *Deschampsia* simply occurs as
Deschampsia among the same species as in the shorter
grass it is probably one vegetation type; if it is
consistently associated with other species it may be
best to treat it as two communities.

COMMUNITIES THAT DO NOT FIT THE NVC

It is very difficult to describe when a vegetation type
is a variant of an NVC community and when it does
not fit properly. Dealing with communities that do
not clearly fit the NVC, which may form up to 5–10%
of the vegetation in some surveys, can be approached
in two ways. First, allocate them to the nearest-fit NVC
type and say in the report that this has been done.
However, for monitoring purposes, this could lead to
the exaggeration of change. Second, present the
quadrat data and describe them as communities in
their own right (e.g. 'hazel hedges') or give a
description relating to two or three NVC types between
which the community may lie. Given such a complex
range of communities, it is possible that some may
actually be included under different chapters of the
NVC (for example, woodland *Cardamine amara* (Large
Bittercress) flushes are included under mires rather
than woodlands). Very detailed localised sampling may
also result in many species becoming 'constants'
locally when they are not constants in the wider
national context. Contact the local survey teams such
as those from English Nature or Countryside Council
for Wales as they could have knowledge of other
vegetation types that have been recorded in the area
of survey.

Box 6.11 Sizes of quadrat for NVC surveys

Woodlands:	50 m × 50 m for canopy and shrub layers, 4 m × 4 m or 10 m × 10 m for ground layer
Scrub:	10 m × 10 m, exceptionally 50 m × 50 m in open patchy scrub
Hedges/boundaries:	30 m lengths for canopy, 10 m lengths for ground flora
Heaths and mires:	2 m × 2 m or 4 × 4 m, exceptionally 10 m × 10 m in very impoverished or grossly structured vegetation
Grasslands:	2 m × 2 m or 4 m × 4 m where large tussocky vegetation is present
Aquatics:	2 m × 2 m or 4 m × 4 m
Swamps and tall herb fens:	4 m × 4 m or 10 m × 10 m
Saltmarshes:	2 m × 2 m or 4 m × 4 m
Sand dunes:	2 m × 2 m or 4 m × 4 m
Sea cliffs:	2 m × 2 m or 4 m × 4 m
Shingle:	2 m × 2 m or 4 m × 4 m
Ruderals:	2 m × 2 m or 4 m × 4 m where large tussocky vegetation is present

Box 6.12 Computer programs for vegetation analysis

Details are correct at time of writing.

VESPAN 3 (VEgetation and SPecies ANalysis), 1997, A. J. C. Malloch

A Windows-based program for handling, presenting and analysing vegetation data including TWINSPAN and DECORANA. Available from Biological Sciences, University of Lancaster, Lancaster LA1 4YQ, price £100 + VAT; upgrades from previous versions £50 + VAT.

MATCH 2, 1997, A. J. C. Malloch

A Windows-based program for comparing vegetation data against the NVC. Available from Biological Sciences, University of Lancaster, Lancaster LA1 4YQ, price £100 + VAT; upgrades from previous versions £25 + VAT.

TABLEFIT 1.0, 1996, M. O. Hill

A DOS-based program for comparing vegetation data against the NVC and the EC CORINE types. Available from Centre for Ecology and Hydrology(CEH), Monks Wood, Abbots Ripton,

Huntingdon PE17 2LS (or under 'software' on http://mwnta.ac.uk/ite), price £80 + VAT.

TABLECORN, **DECORANA** and **TWINSPAN**, 1996, M. O. Hill

A DOS-based program for analysing vegetation data. TABLECORN converts data from TABLEFIT into DECORANA and TWINSPAN formats. Available from Centre for Ecology and Hydrology(CEH), Monks Wood, Abbots Ripton, Huntingdon PE17 2LS (or under 'software' on http://mwnta.ac.uk/ite), price £75+ VAT.

FIBS

FIBS (Functional Interpretation of Botanical Surveys) was developed by the Unit of Comparative Plant Ecology for English Nature (see Section 6.4.4).

CANOCO (CANOnical Community Ordination), 1988, C. J. F. Ter Braak

A Fortran program for canonical community ordination by correlation analysis, principal components analysis (PCA) and redundancy analysis. Available from Microcomputer Power, 111 Clover Lane, Ithaca, NY 14850, USA. Tel: (607) 272 2188.

Data storage and analysis

Storage

Quadrat data can simply be filed for later use (cross-referenced in report, stating storage location), written up with the report or held on a computer. The best computer program for handling, presenting and analysing data in a format compatible with the NVC is VESPAN (Box 6.12) but others are available. Maps can be stored on GIS or in hard-copy format.

Changes in NVC types present

A crude analysis of changes in NVC types present at particular points can be made by comparing repeat NVC survey maps. However, it is often difficult to be certain whether a change is real or simply due to a different surveyor. Change from a heathland to a grassland community is likely to be real, but a change from one heathland sub-community to the most closely related sub-community is more likely to be an artefact. The original data may need to be examined with care.

The monitoring of changes in the extent and distribution of NVC types should be carried out by using properly replicated quadrat- or belt-transect-based sampling programmes. Replicated permanent quadrats may be used, but there are problems with this approach (see Byrne, 1991; Robertson, 1999). Individual quadrats can rarely be precisely relocated to allow them to be re-recorded meaningfully (a 10 cm error in relocating a 2 m × 2 m quadrat can result in 5% error), and usually too few are taken to allow for appropriate replication. Repeated estimates of Domin cover values (see Box 2.3) by different surveyors have been found to show differences of up to five Domin scale points for the same quadrats (Leach, 1988). In addition, grazing can markedly alter vegetation structure without significantly affecting its composition.

A possible approach may be to obtain Domin cover values from at least five quadrats (see Section 6.4.2) placed in representative areas of vegetation within an approximate distance from each of a number of sampling points on a systematically placed grid. The five sets of quadrat data can then be analysed with the assistance of MATCH and TABLEFIT programs to allocate an NVC type and similarity coefficient (see below) to each systematic sampling point on the grid. The overall extent of each NVC type on a site may then be estimated as a frequency of occurrence from the combined samples, and compared between surveys by appropriate tests (e.g. G-tests or χ^2 tests). If the grid is permanent, the NVC type at each location may also be used for spatial analysis of change.

Standard multivariate ecological analytical techniques such as TWINSPAN, DECORANA and CANOCO (see Box 6.12) can also be used to analyse larger quadrat or vegetation datasets if data are collected appropriately. These are extremely powerful tools. However, quadrat data derived from NVC surveys for monitoring purposes are unlikely to be suitable for such detailed analysis. Be aware that TWINSPAN is sensitive to the order in which species are input (Tausch et al., 1995; Dirkse, 1998).

Analysis and prediction of change

As described above, the NVC provides a powerful tool for analysing and predicting change. For example, the use of MATCH or TABLEFIT similarity coefficients to look at changes in the species composition of communities over time is shown in Figure 6.1 (see also Rich et al., 1991, 1992).

As many of the communities are related, changes from one to another may occur with changes in management, soils, natural succession, etc. By understanding how the communities relate to one another the direction of change can be understood and therefore interpreted against the field situation. For example, the expected direction of changes in the MG12a Festuca arundinacea (Tall Fescue) grassland, Lolium–Holcus sub-community following changes in three different environmental factors are shown in Figure 6.2. Such changes may occur over periods ranging from a year to decades depending on the strength of the driving force. Details of many of these relationships are mentioned in the NVC volumes (Rodwell, 1991 et seq.), but these should only be regarded as indicative and there is no substitute for appropriately replicated experiments.

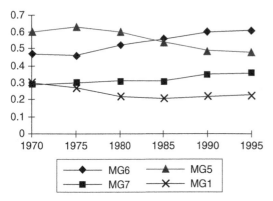

Figure 6.1. Changes in MATCH similarity coefficients for a hay meadow following introduction of grazing and fertiliser application in 1975 (hypothetical example). The changes in coefficients show a change from a hay meadow community MG5 to a grazed pasture community MG6. Coefficients for MG7 ryegrass leys (which can be derived from MG6 by applying more fertiliser and heavy grazing) and MG1 False Oatgrass (*Arrhenatherum elatius*) grassland (a rank unmanaged grassland type) are also shown.

Summary of advantages and disadvantages

The NVC can provide a conceptual framework and practical method for monitoring sites that have been selected on the basis of their vegetation communities. In particular:

- The NVC classification and survey method can be used to describe a site and is often used to identify and define features and/or attributes that require monitoring.
- The NVC classification and associated datasets can assist with the definition of objectives and the setting of limits for a feature.
- A baseline NVC mapping survey can be used to identify approximate boundaries of vegetation types as an aid to optimising the design of detailed objective and quantitative monitoring programmes.
- The NVC can be used as an analytical tool for investigating changes in vegetation and predicting the outcome of management, etc.

However, the main disadvantages are that NVC mapping can be time-consuming, it requires competent botanists, the boundaries between communities or even the identity of a community may vary with the surveyor, and it may be too crude to reveal gradual or subtle vegetation changes (e.g. as a result of management changes).

Therefore, for monitoring purposes:

- The NVC should not be used for normalising vegetation types when setting feature objectives and limits.
- Repeat NVC mapping surveys alone should not be used for monitoring the extent or distribution of vegetation communities; other supporting information is required.

MG6 *Lolium–Cynosurus* grassland
MG11 *Festuca–Agrostis–Potentilla* grassland
MG12a *Festuca arundinacea* grassland, *Lolium–Holcus* sub-community
MG12b *Festuca arundinacea* grassland, *Oenanthe* sub-community

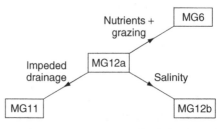

Figure 6.2. Expected directional changes in an MG12a community following changes in three environmental factors.

6.2   PHYSICAL ATTRIBUTES

The following sections give a brief overview of the physical attributes of a site that are most likely to require monitoring, namely hydrology and soils. Both of these attributes can have considerable effects upon plant and animal communities.

For the purposes of habitat monitoring, it is unlikely that detailed analyses of hydrology and soils will need to be carried out as a regular monitoring activity. However, some consideration will usually need to be given to these aspects at some point, and so the key issues involved are summarised.

6.2.1   Hydrology

Although probably the most fundamental aspect of wetlands and particularly bog ecosystems, hydrology is all too often ignored in monitoring programmes or added as an afterthought (Lindsay & Ross, 1994). One of the main reasons for this is that it is a complex subject. Although dipwells or piezometers, etc., can be easily installed, the interpretation of results in terms of impacts on features of conservation interest is often difficult. Therefore, although it is strongly recommended that appropriate hydrological monitoring be carried out where necessary, a detailed treatment of the subject is beyond the scope of this *Handbook*. It is therefore recommended that further specialist advice on the subject is obtained from appropriate experts and organisations such as SEPA, the Environment Agency, and specialists within the UK statutory conservation agencies.

6.2.2   Soil characteristics

The study and classification of soils and soil characteristics is a large subject with a considerable amount of literature devoted to it. However, for the purposes of habitat monitoring, assessments of many soil characteristics are unlikely to be required. It will generally be sufficient to restrict soil analysis to nutrient status, pH, structure, texture and moisture content, because these have the greatest effect on vegetation (for example, some plant species will

only be found on alkaline soils). For further information on these and other soil characteristics that may be of interest, such as salinity and redox potential, consult Jones & Reynolds (1996).

It should be remembered that soils are biological entities, which include vital communities of soil organisms. The health of these fungus, animal and plant populations is also an important attribute of soil condition. Soils are also influenced by the vegetation growing in them as well as by the chemical composition of the underlying substrate. For example, the decomposition of heather litter releases acids, which tend to lower the pH of the soil underneath the plants. These inter-relations between physical and biological properties of the soil and other ecosystem components are often complex but should be borne in mind when interpreting the results of simple monitoring of physical attributes.

Fertility

A broad indication of fertility can be obtained by measuring total base cations, which indicates the supply of plant macronutrients (e.g. nitrogen, potassium and phosphorus) available in soil solution. Fresh soil samples and laboratory analysis are required.

Soil pH

The pH is a measure of the acidity or alkalinity of a solution. It is measured on a logarithmic scale from 1 to 14: a pH below 7 indicates acidity, a pH of 7 indicates a neutral solution (e.g. pure distilled water) and a pH above 7 indicates alkalinity. A pH reading is a measurement of the activity of hydrogen or hydroxyl ions. Soil pH can be measured in two ways (both of which can also be used for measuring the pH of water).

Indicator strips

Strips of indicator paper that change to a particular colour when immersed in a solution of a particular pH are commercially available. Wide-range paper is available, which covers the whole range pH 1–14, but this is less accurate than using narrow-range paper.

A small amount of soil is mixed with distilled water, and the paper is immersed in the solution for several minutes before the pH is measured. Indicator paper is cheap and quick, but less precise than a pH meter.

pH meters

If available, a portable pH meter is the best way to measure pH in the field. A standard electronic pH meter has an electrode, which is inserted into a solution of one part soil mixed with two parts distilled water. Some pH meters also have a temperature probe, which, when inserted into the solution, compensates for differences in the temperature of the solution from room temperature (pH readings are affected by temperature).

Meters need to be calibrated against solutions of known pH; buffer tablets to make up solutions of pH 4, 7 and 9 are generally supplied with pH meters. At least two of these should be used to calibrate the meter before any readings are taken. It is also a good idea to check the calibration at regular intervals, because some meters have a tendency to drift after a while. Portable pH meters are accurate to within ± 0.01 pH units. Laboratory-based instruments can be accurate to ± 0.001 pH units.

If soil is being measured in the field, it is possible to take samples directly by hollowing out a small hole for the electrode, filling this with distilled water, and inserting the electrode (with the temperature electrode inserted close by). Otherwise, samples can be mixed in beakers in the field, or collected for later analysis in a laboratory. If the latter course is chosen, soil samples should be sealed in airtight bags or containers to prevent the soil from drying out before the pH is measured.

Soil profile and texture

A soil profile is a vertical cross-section down through the soil, which exposes layers or *horizons*. An examination of the profile and the type of soil horizons present can provide a valuable general indication of the chemical and physical condition of the soil. For example, the smell of hydrogen sulphide (rotten eggs) or presence of a gleyed horizon (dark grey mottled with orange-red iron oxide patches) indicates alternating wet and dry soil conditions.

Soil profiles can be examined by digging a vertical, smooth-faced pit and using a measuring tape to measure the depths of the soil horizons. Soil samples from the different horizons can be taken for chemical analysis. A less destructive and faster method is to take core samples with an *auger*, a hollow cylinder that is twisted into the ground and removes a cylindrical soil core.

Measuring the depth of peat layers may require several interlocking rods with the soil corer fixed to the end, because peat layers can be very deep. In situations in which the underlying sediments are very different from the peat, the depth of peat can be measured by using radar and seismology. However, these techniques are still partly experimental, and are expensive (Lindsay & Ross, 1994).

Soil texture is a measure of the size of the particles that make up the soil. Soil type is a continuum from clay (particle size $< 2\,\mu m$) through silt (2–$50\,\mu m$) to sand (50–$2000\,\mu m$) and gravel ($> 2000\,\mu m$) and is based on the relative proportions of different particle sizes in the soil. For most biological purposes, the coarse distinctions of sand, silt and clay soils will be sufficient, but more accurate classifications are available should they be required (e.g. the texture scale used by the United States Department of Agriculture; see Jones & Reynolds (1996)).

Field assessments of soil texture from soil profiles are likely to be sufficient for most monitoring purposes. However, if necessary particle size can be measured by passing dried soil samples through sieves of successively smaller mesh sizes, although this is less accurate for small particles than for larger ones. A better method is to separate soil particles by sedimentation. A sample of soil is mixed in a clear cylinder filled with water. Organic material will float to the top, and the soil particle types will settle according to size (larger, heavier particles will settle out to the bottom faster than small, light ones). The percentages of each particle type can be measured (Jones & Reynolds, 1996) and can be used to classify the soil texture according to the FAO classification (FAO, 1977).

Soil texture and physical properties obtained from soil profiles are important attributes of soils but change slowly. Therefore, although measurements need to be carried out over long time periods, observations are only needed infrequently.

Soil moisture

The moisture retention capacity of soil is correlated with its organic matter content and differs between soil types. For ecological purposes, soil moisture is divided into three types according to its availability to plants, as follows.

1. Free-draining water drains away or evaporates soon after rain but may be available to plants for several days, depending upon the soil type (sandy soils drain much quicker than clays) and the drainage characteristics of the site (an impermeable layer, such as an iron pan, can impede drainage and lead to soils becoming waterlogged).
2. Plant-available (capillary) water occupies the gaps between soil particles and is of most importance for plants as it remains in the soil for longer than does free-draining water.
3. Plant-unavailable (hygroscopic) water forms a thin film on the surface of soil particles, which cannot be taken up by the root systems of plants. (Most of the water in clay soils is held in plant-unavailable form, and this is why they are more prone to drying out during droughts than are silty or loamy soils, despite containing higher amounts of water.)

The plant-available water content of a soil can be estimated from the loss of weight of the soil at *field capacity* (i.e. the state attained after the soil has been saturated and allowed to drain for about two days) after being air-dried. Keep soil samples in airtight plastic bags to prevent any evaporation before analysis in the laboratory. Measure the mass of each soil sample, then allow it to dry naturally (e.g. spread it on paper for a week) before weighing it again. The difference between the two masses is approximately the amount of plant-available water held in the soil.

Electronic soil moisture meters are also available for taking measurements directly in the field.

Soil organic matter

A determination of soil organic matter content can indicate overall biological activity in a soil and the speed of turnover of nutrients. It is readily measured by igniting dried samples in a laboratory and measuring mass loss after burning.

6.3   RIVER MORPHOLOGY AND AQUATIC VEGETATION COMPOSITION

As discussed in Sections 5.9 and 5.10, survey and monitoring of aquatic habitats is a complex and specialised subject. Therefore a detailed treatment of the subject is beyond the scope of this *Handbook* and only brief accounts of survey and monitoring methods are provided below. It is recommended that further specialist advice on the subject be obtained from appropriate experts and organisations such as the Environment Agency, SEPA, Centre for Ecology and Hydrology and specialists within the UK statutory conservation agencies or key staff within consultancies.

6.3.1   River Habitat Survey

Recommended uses

The River Habitat Survey (RHS) has been developed in response to the need for a nationally applicable classification of rivers based on habitat quality. It is a logical development of the River Corridor Survey (RCS), which is principally a map-based system for surveying 500 m lengths of river (see NRA (1992) for detailed methods). The RCS provides information on the location of habitats and plant assemblages within river channels, margins, banks and the river corridor. Most information is subjective (except for some basic river channel measurements) and therefore too prone to inter-surveyor variation to be used for most monitoring purposes. However, RHS provides a more detailed and objective means of recording river habitat characteristics that can be used for broad monitoring purposes.

RHS provides four distinct but related outputs:

- a standard field survey method (which can be used, where appropriate, as a consistent framework for collecting data for general monitoring purposes);
- a computer database, containing information from a national reference network of UK sites;
- predictions of which physical features are expected to be present within an RHS site at a particular location (taking into account altitude, height of source, etc.);
- a scheme for assessing habitat quality.

River Habitat Survey: summary of key points

Recommended uses

- To survey the general physical and vegetation structure of a river
- To monitor broad changes in river structure and vegetation, e.g. as a result of pollution or river engineering works or other impacts

Efficiency   Relatively rapid: average time for surveying standard 500 m lengths of river is *c.* 60 min

Objectivity   Semi-objective through standardised forms

Precision   Tests have shown that inter-surveyor variation is low and consistent results are achieved irrespective of position of spot checks within 500 m reaches

Bias   Subjective assessments are prone to individual interpretation, but this is minimised by training and a detailed methods manual

Expertise required   Must be carried out by an accredited and trained surveyor. Training takes only 2–3 days and no expertise is required beyond a biological background and familiarity with river habitats

Equipment required   Standard recording forms, maps and a ranging pole

Key methodological points to consider

- Fieldwork is the basis of assessments, supplemented with information from maps
- The procedure is carried out on 500 m reaches, with 10 spot checks carried out within each
- The survey methods have been developed for rivers in England and Wales but have now been expanded for Scotland and Northern Ireland as well
- More detailed quantitative analysis of channels and vegetation may be required for specific monitoring requirements

Data analysis   The data are amenable for rapid transfer to the RHS database and analysis by RHS programs or SERCON (see Section 5.10.1).

RHS aims to predict, with statistical probability, those features that ought to occur in unmodified examples for the full range of river types in England and Wales (although the system has been extended to Scotland). The scheme for assessing habitat quality comprises a simple five-band classification (excellent, good, fair, poor, bad) based on a comparison of the observed features with those expected for the particular river type. Crude monitoring can therefore be carried out by reference to these broad scales, or in relation to specific targets set for attributes that are measured as part of the RHS.

Other alternative and additional methods to consider for morphological features include aerial photography (Section 6.1.3), fixed-point photography (Section 6.1.4) or adaptations of quadrat (Sections 6.4.2 and 6.4.3) or transect (Section 6.4.6) techniques. If quantitative assessments of plant abundance are required, detailed objective methods should be used, such as transect- or quadrat-based surveys for bankside vegetation or shallow rivers and grapnel samples (Section 6.3.2) for deeper, slow-moving water.

Time efficiency

The technique is relatively simple and quick. According to Raven *et al.* (1997) the time taken to survey a 500 m length of river (i.e. the standard survey unit) varies according to the complexity of the site and ease of access, i.e. inherent factors that affect any river surveying. Simple sites may take only 35–40 min to complete, whereas those of complex character may take an hour or more. The average time for a site in their study was just under 1 h.

Expertise required

The RHS survey must be carried out by an accredited surveyor. However, the training for this is relatively simple (2–3 days) and does not require specialist knowledge beyond a biological background and familiarity with rivers. Although specialist geomorphological or botanical expertise is not needed, consistent recognition of features included on the field survey form is essential.

Equipment required
No specialist equipment is required other than standard field equipment, maps and the RHS manual and standard recording forms.

Adaptation of standard recording forms on to portable data logging devices is possible and may be cost-effective for large monitoring projects.

Field methods
An illustrated manual (Environment Agency, 2003) has been produced and should be consulted for full details on field procedures.

Data storage and analysis
Data are recorded on standard recording forms and can easily be transferred to the RHS computer database, either manually or by optical reading. Data analysis programmes are included as part of the system, for example for assessment of overall habitat quality. Data may also be used for SERCON evaluations (see Section 5.10.1). Alternatively, specific attributes can be analysed separately.

Summary of advantages and disadvantages
The method provides an up-to-date, tried and tested standard means of recording the general physical and vegetation character of river reaches, which is part of a national surveying scheme. It is also relatively quick and simple. Although not designed specifically for monitoring, it can be used for monitoring the overall quality of river habitats by a simple five-point scale. The survey methods can also be used as a framework for collecting data for general monitoring of specific attributes.

However, the technique is largely qualitative and only semi-objective. It may therefore also be necessary to develop site-specific quantitative and objective monitoring methods for some key attributes (see Section 5.10.1).

6.3.2   Grapnel surveys of aquatic macrophytes

Recommended uses
The technique has been developed by George Hinton at English Nature for the semi-quantitative assessment of species presence–absence. It is a simple but fairly time-consuming technique for establishing the frequency of occurrence of individual species, which can probably be used on lakes of up to 100 ha or slow-flowing deep rivers.

The data collected can provide an accurate semi-quantitative assessment of abundance and distribution for most species, although it tends to miss some low-growing plants such as *Fontinalis* and rosette-forming species. The dominant species (in biomass terms) is consistently identified and the method picks up species contributing as little as 5% of the total biomass.

Other alternative or additional methods to consider include the use of double-headed rakes or grab samples (see Bell, 1996). Rakes may be used from the shore by throwing out on a line. Grabs are also less prone to bias against small species, which are not detectable by grapnels. However, these methods collect too much material to be used effectively for anything other than establishing presence. Rake methods may therefore be best if boat access is difficult, if the species to be sampled is very rare or localised, or if it is only necessary to establish that a species is present.

Subaqua equipment or ROVs may be used for carrying out transects or surveying quadrats etc., but these methods are very slow, expensive and require specialist equipment and expertise.

Time efficiency
Grapnel surveys are fairly slow to carry out, but can produce detailed assessments of the frequency of occurrence and distribution of species. Approximately 25 stations across four or five transects can be sampled in a day. A small water body requires at least ten transects of 25 stations and therefore such a water body would take at least two days to survey.

Grapnel surveys: summary of key points

Recommended uses

- Semi-quantitative assessments of the abundance (frequency) of aquatic macrophytes in lakes or large slow-moving rivers
- Mapping the distribution of species and aquatic macrophyte communities

Efficiency   Relatively slow, but can provide detailed results
Objectivity   Objective
Precision   Moderate
Bias   Biased against small-leaved species
Expertise required   Competence in identifying aquatic vegetation from fragments of vegetation. Boat handling and GPS experience necessary in many situations

Equipment required   Grapnel and graduated cord and a boat and compass or preferably a GPS for large water bodies; safety equipment; standard recording equipment
Key methodological points to consider

- The technique uses a grapnel on a graduated cord to take small samples of vegetation from the bottom of the water body; this is repeated 10 times at each sample location to obtain a frequency estimate of presence
- By sampling at many locations a semi-quantitative map of distribution and abundance can be developed

Data analysis   Standard data techniques for the analysis of presence–absence frequency data can be used

However, in larger water bodies, most aquatic vegetation will occur in a relatively narrow zone, with little or no vegetation growing where the water is deepest. Samples can therefore be targeted in this zone, and this will increase the efficiency of the method.

Expertise required

It is essential that surveyors be able to identify aquatic plants from fragments of vegetation. However, as the range of aquatic macrophytes is fairly limited, especially within geographical regions and certain types of water body, such techniques can be fairly rapidly learnt.

For all but the smallest lakes, samples will need to be obtained by boat. Boat-handling experience is therefore an essential requirement for the surveyor or an assistant. Experience with the use of GPS is also necessary for surveying large water bodies.

Equipment required

The equipment required is listed in Appendix 6.

Field methods

Ten samples are obtained at each sampling station, with the use of a small 7 cm grapnel on a cord.

A presence of 1 is recorded for each species detected, regardless of its apparent abundance. The method thus provides a frequency of 0–10 for each species at each sampling point.

Repeat transects at Bosherston Lakes (Hinton, 1989) showed that the mean frequency values for each species from 250 grapnel drops was within 10% of the grand mean (based on 2000 drops).

At each sample point the depth is recorded by using graduations on the grapnel cord. It is recommended that basic chemical parameters should also be recorded at the mid-point of each transect. Turbidity should be measured by using Secchi discs (Section 5.9.1) and supplemented if possible by *in situ* pH and conductivity readings (see Jones & Reynolds, 1996).

For small lakes the position of each sample point can be ascertained by compass bearings on fixed points such as church towers, jetties, etc. However, this can be time-consuming and inaccurate on large lakes. In these circumstances the use of a GPS may be appropriate. Recent work reported by Hinton (1997) found that a hand-held GPS is able to provide position fixing accurate to within 25 m. During fieldwork the GPS can be used to navigate to the selected stations (identified by ten-figure grid references) at which the boat is anchored while grab samples are carried out.

Grapnel surveys should be carried out during the period from June to September, but the precise timing will depend on the species; some species may require surveying earlier in the year. Repeat surveys should be at similar times of the year, unless seasonal variation is being investigated, and repeated at least every three years. Some rarer species may require monitoring more frequently. Initial surveys may have to be more frequent to establish how much variation occurs, both seasonally and annually, and to determine the optimum monitoring time.

Working from boats can be hazardous; suitable safety clothing should be worn. Surveyors should also be aware of the risk of catching Weil's disease. Toxic blue-green algae may also be a hazard. Consult a relevant health and safety policy (e.g. Part I, Box 2.11) for further information.

Care should be taken to clean fragments of vegetation from the grapnel when moving from site to site; some aggressive introductions can grow from fragments.

Data storage and analysis

The data can be used to calculate overall mean frequency tables for each species over the lake. In addition, geographically referenced species frequency data can be stored on a spreadsheet or database and displayed over a scanned 1 : 10 000 map by using a standard GIS such as ArcView (Hinton,1997).

It should be remembered, when using such analyses to identify trends in abundance, that some aquatic plants are annuals, and populations will fluctuate from year to year as sites are colonised and recolonised. Many species fluctuate considerably, both seasonally and annually. Five-year means of frequency may be used to remove some of this natural variation from the data.

Summary of advantages and disadvantages

The technique provides a simple method for obtaining semi-quantitative estimates of species presence– absence. Data can therefore be readily used for monitoring overall abundance and distribution targets. It is, however, time-consuming and tends to underestimate the presence of certain species. It can only be used in still or slow-flowing water.

6.4   GROUND AND SHRUB VEGETATION

6.4.1   Total counts of individuals

Recommended uses

This method is appropriate for monitoring the presence or abundance of rare and/or distinct species that are attributes of habitat quality. The target species are normally chosen because of their rarity value in order to maintain a close check on population levels and to avoid situations in which a species may disappear from a site through inappropriate management. These can include species that are typical of a particular community or habitat, or other 'indicator' species expected to respond quickly to changes in the habitat. It may also be an appropriate method to be applied to invasive weedy species such as creeping thistle, in situations in which information is needed on the degree of the potential conservation problem, again in response to management of the area.

For some situations, counts of the total number of individuals may be more appropriate than the total area covered. An additional application of this method is in the assessment of condition, which may be indicated by a minimum population of a particular species, or even a semi-quantitative threshold. For example, good condition may be defined as a particular species being dominant or merely present.

Where precise estimation of population numbers is difficult, especially if distribution is highly dispersed, then quadrat- or transect-based sampling methods should be considered (see Sections 6.4.2–6.4.5). However, total counts of individual plants are most often associated with the monitoring of particular species of conservation importance. This method is therefore treated in more detail in Part III under the look–see method (Section 15.2.1) and total counts (Section 15.2.2).

Total counts of individuals: summary of key points

Recommended uses   Accurate and absolute population counts of the changes in number of rare and/or distinct:

- 'typical' species of a habitat
- 'indicator' species of the effect of management changes on the habitat,
- 'indicator' species of the health of the habitat, including invasive species e.g. Ragwort (*Senecio jacobaea*) and Creeping Thistle (*Cirsium arvense*)

Efficiency   Relatively quick if the area is small and the species are large and/or obvious; extremely laborious and time-consuming if the site is large, the species small, or the vegetation diverse

Objectivity   Objective, but subjective variations do exist (see below)

Precision   Not relevant to a single measurement

Bias   Bias occurs at high abundance

Expertise required   Dependent on the difficulty of species identification, but characteristic features can be quickly learned if only a few species are being monitored, even if all growth stages are to be recorded

Equipment required   Basic recording equipment i.e. field notebooks, standardised recording forms, identification notes/guides and hand-held computers on occasions

Key methodological points to consider

- Select species that are suited to this method; it is not appropriate for large and complicated sites
- Search site or area systematically without damage to vegetation
- Consider other methods for estimating populations for large sites and for populations that may be large or widely distributed

6.4.2   Conventional frame quadrats: cover and density estimates

Recommended uses

Visual estimation of plant cover and abundance (or the presence–absence of species) is a common method of describing vegetation, which can be applied to the whole study area or to sample plots. There are several different approaches to the subject, but most involve the placing of conventional quadrats (i.e. not mini-quadrats as described in Section 6.4.3, nested quadrats as described in Section 6.4.4, or point quadrats as described in Section 6.4.5) and/or transects (see Section 6.4.6).

Quadrats may be permanent or temporary. Permanent quadrats have fixed positions, which are relocated at each recording period. Temporary quadrats are placed in the area to be monitored but removed after recording is done; a new set of temporary quadrats is placed in the same area at the next recording period.

The major advantages of permanent quadrats are that there is usually less variation due to the effects of sampling in the change data, and

fewer quadrats have to be recorded to detect the same level of change. Thus, changes in values (e.g. of species abundance) are more likely to be real than if a new set of quadrats is selected each time. Although measurement error can still occur (for example, through the incorrect identification of species), permanent quadrats reduce sampling variation from data and provide a clear illustration of change at a particular point.

There are, however, a number of disadvantages of permanent quadrats. Repeated recording concentrated in the same small area may itself cause changes in the vegetation through trampling or continued removal of material for identification. It is also possible that quadrats may 'naturally' become unrepresentative of the area as a whole during the course of a monitoring scheme, and this may significantly bias results if only a few are placed. (This can be overcome by recording sets A and B in year 1, B and C in year 2, C and D in year 3, etc.; see Greig-Smith, 1983.) Finally, marking and relocating quadrats can be very time-consuming, although recent developments with laser range-finders (Total Stations) are making

Frame quadrats: summary of key points

Recommended uses   Monitoring of vegetation when estimates of cover or density are required (e.g. for NVC surveys)

Efficiency   Relatively time-consuming; larger quadrats are difficult to search thoroughly; efficiency of cover estimates can be particularly poor when physical fatigue sets in

Objectivity   Cover values can be very subjective

Precision   Deriving cover values can be very imprecise, especially with large quadrats and inexperienced surveyors

Bias   More conspicuous species, such as those in flower or those forming clumps, may be given overestimated cover values

Expertise required   Considerable expertise is required to enable the accurate identification of vegetative vascular and lower plants; some (easily learnt) skills required for improving estimates of cover values

Equipment required   Quadrats; basic recording equipment, i.e. field notebooks, standardised recording forms, identification notes/guides and hand-held computer on occasions

Key methodological points to consider

- Surveyors should familiarise themselves with site and vegetation prior to survey
- Optimum quadrat size should be estimated and the number of quadrats required calculated from preliminary survey data
- Care must be taken when choosing whether to estimate cover by percentages or cover bands (e.g. the Domin scale)
- Precision and accuracy of estimates can be increased by subdividing quadrats
- Trampling of vegetation may affect the ease with which species can be seen or cover values estimated

Data analysis   Standard methods can be applied providing that the sample is representative of the site Only non-parametric tests can be applied to the analysis of non-linear cover scores

---

quadrat relocation much easier in some habitats (see Appendix 5).

The advantages and disadvantages of permanent versus temporary plots are discussed in more detail in Part I, Section 2.3.2. However, recent thoughts are that monitoring schemes based on randomly located permanent quadrats should be avoided unless minimising sampling variation is of prime importance.

Cover estimates provide a good description of the contribution that each species makes to the vegetation community, and they are sensitive to short-term fluctuations in season or management. One major advantage of cover as a quantitative measure is that different plant groupings (mosses, herbs, grasses and shrubs) can all be evaluated in comparable terms. If the vegetation has a distinct layered structure (i.e. shrubs and undergrowth), the cover of species in each layer is measured separately (Bonham, 1989). Cover is normally expressed as a fraction, percentage, or amount of cover on a scale or index basis. It must be remembered that, as vegetation is usually layered, percentage cover values can add up to more than 100%.

This method of describing the vegetation involves listing the species present within the sample area, and attaching to each species an assessment of abundance. A number of recording formats and techniques have been in place for many years; the most frequently encountered and applied include the DAFOR, Braun–Blanquet and Domin scales, which are alternatives to estimating the actual percentage cover. The Daubenmire scale is used for estimating cover alone but is not widely used. The most widely used method in recent years has been the Domin scale, which is most frequently encountered by ecologists in its use by the NVC (see Section 6.1.6).

A once widespread approach that is now rarely used for quadrats is the DAFOR scale, which combines subjective assessments of frequency and cover into five classes: dominant, abundant, frequent, occasional and rare. There are no definitions for these classes. Prefixes are also used to refine and qualify assessments by using terms such as 'very' or 'locally'. These prefixes have been widely applied but frequently misused. Some surveyors have modified the DAFOR scale with quantitative cover estimates (e.g. the ROFAD scale: < 5% rare, 6–20% occasional, 21–50% frequent, 51–90% abundant, 91–100% dominant; see Williams *et al.* (1998)).

DAFOR values are especially subjective and imprecise and therefore of limited use for monitoring. Different observers tend to have different definitions for the terms. Given the variability of DAFOR ratings they will only indicate change in species abundance (and therefore be useful as signals for action) if the change is very large, or if smaller changes are consistent over a number of years. This may be useful if monitoring only needs to detect an obvious disastrous change at a site (Byrne, 1991).

The Braun–Blanquet and Domin scales give more information than DAFOR, but are still subjective and are affected by the same over- and underestimating problems for certain species as is DAFOR. Domin values vary greatly with observer and species condition.

More recent monitoring methods have looked at the value of recording presence–absence rather than cover as a means of vegetation monitoring, with frequency as the favoured approach (Byrne, 1991; Rich *et al.* 1991; Hodgson *et al.*, 1995). These developments have aimed to produce more consistent data, and have been favoured because monitoring is comparatively quick, they reduce the amount of observer error through removing the need to record cover values, and they are less tiring to carry out. These frequency methods are described in Section 6.4.3 and are probably more appropriate for most vegetation monitoring purposes other than where estimates of cover and density are specifically required, e.g. for NVC surveys (Section 6.1.6).

Time efficiency

Considerably more time is required to estimate scores or cover values than is needed to record simple presence–absence data. This is further increased if bryophytes and lichens must be identified and scored. Time taken will be further dependent on quadrat size, vegetation diversity and surveyor experience. For example, a 2 m × 2 m quadrat on a species-poor heathland may only require 5–10 min to record, whereas an equivalent quadrat on a species-rich grassland may require up to 30 min. These times exclude that required to mark permanently or relocate the site of a quadrat if this is necessary. Time efficiency can also be increased with additional surveyors.

Recording can also be slower in wet vegetation and in very bright sunlight. It is also easier to miss species under these conditions.

Time savings can be made if certain species or groups of species are omitted (especially species that are difficult to identify quickly in the field, such as certain bryophytes or vegetative grasses) but the resultant data may be of only limited use. Savings in time can be re-allocated to recording more sites or quadrats.

Fewer quadrats are needed than for presence–absence methods (Section 6.4.3) to detect a given level of change.

Expertise required

Considerable expertise is required to be able to identify correctly the full range of plant species (including bryophytes and macrolichens) typically recorded in cover value assessments (see Appendix 3 for identification references). This skill can be especially demanding for vegetative material. Experience is further required to estimate cover values to a consistent level, although even then they are generally inaccurate.

Equipment required

Temporary quadrats require some form of delimitation to ensure accurate recording. There are many alternatives, some constructed beforehand and others constructed on site. The latter mostly consist of pegs (e.g. metal skewers or tent pegs) and wire, string or cord to link between the pegs. Hammers or mallets are sometimes required to push the pegs into hard ground. There are advantages to using thick cord or line: it is less prone to tangling and stretching and it often copes better in wet conditions. Plastic-coated cord may be preferable to string. Length should be regularly checked as it can change according to environmental conditions and stretching. It is important to maintain constancy in the shape of the quadrat; a set-square or other means of triangulation is needed for measuring right angles.

An alternative method, which is easier to use in the field (but harder to carry around between sample points), is a pre-made square (of wood, plastic or metal). These can be further subdivided into grids (by using wire or string at regular intervals along the quadrat margins), which can considerably improve the accuracy of cover assessments.

Field notebooks, clipboards or weatherwriters and specially designed recording cards are traditionally used to collect floristic data. These methods of data capture require the further stage of transferring the information to a computer-based and/or paper filing system back in the office. Much time can be spent on this, and errors in data transcription can occur during this process. To allow more time for data interpretation, records can be captured in the field by using a small hand-held computer, although it is possible that recording errors may be more difficult to check with this method of data capture. Trials in the Unit of Comparative Plant Ecology at Sheffield University showed that computers were less efficient than paper when used for direct field recording. Optical data scanners do not cope well with muddy or creased field cards. However, considerable developments are obviously occurring in this field and this form of data entry may become more common in future.

The marking and relocation of permanent quadrats is covered in Appendix 5.

Field methods

Before embarking on a quadrat survey, a number of key decisions must be made. First, a decision has to be taken on the optimum quadrat size; this is discussed in Appendix 4 (and see also Box 6.11). Quadrat sizes normally vary from $1\,m \times 1\,m$ to $4\,m \times 4\,m$, although in certain species-poor moorland habitats $10\,m \times 10\,m$ may be more appropriate. The use of smaller quadrats is normally favoured as they are quicker to set up and record, increase the

chances of detecting species, and are therefore also more likely to improve observer consistency, even though they have larger edge effects (Leach *et al.*, 1992). If the data are to be used for NVC analysis, quadrat size must be consistent with those used by NVC surveys (Box 6.11).

Second, a sampling strategy needs to be designed. This is complex and itself involves a number of key decisions (outlined in Part I, Figure 2.6) including selection of the appropriate means of locating samples (i.e. randomly or systematically), optimisation of the sampling (e.g. by stratification of the site and/or by multi-level sampling) and the calculation of the number of samples needed to provide sufficient precision to meet the monitoring objectives. These issues are described in detail in Section 2.3.

Once each quadrat has been placed, a list of species is recorded and each species assigned a value on whichever measurement scale system you are employing. To increase accuracy this normally involves placing the species in a broad category to begin with, and then refining the record if necessary later in the recording process (Bonham, 1989).

Cover estimates can be made more accurately by division of the quadrat area into smaller units; this makes estimates more objective by concentrating the area of search, but takes more time.

The range of cover values for each 'layer' is given from 0 to 100%, and possibly divided into a number of categories, with each category assigned a rating or scale. Use of a scale is optional but it recognises the low accuracy of cover measurements. Most scales have unequal class intervals, which allow easier estimation of cover-to-area relationship but are harder to analyse statistically. A finer breakdown of scale toward the lower scale values allows better estimation of less abundant species.

A more elaborate approach, again little used in recent years, is the Braun–Blanquet scale, a semi-quantitative method, which gives a combined estimate of abundance and cover. The sampling unit is called a 'relevé' and its size is based on the minimal area concept. Cover is measured on a scale based on a range of percentage cover values (see Table 6.5). A second scale that measures the grouping of a species is less widely used.

Box 6.13   Frame quadrats: likely problems and solutions

The more complex the habitat or vegetation community (particularly grasslands, which can often consist of a diverse and dense mixture of plants), the more likely it is that differences will occur between recorders. Some plants can be especially challenging to identify, particularly small non-flowering individuals of grass and sedge species. Even the same observer re-recording the same quadrat can produce different lists (Robertson, 1999).

Visual estimates of cover by means of the Domin or a related scale will not necessarily pick up small changes in abundance, particularly if the recording is not carried out at both times by the same observer (Greig-Smith, 1983). It is certainly not easy to detect, for example, a 10% change in cover from 50% to 40% for a species; both would be given the same value if the Domin scale was used. In any event, there would always be uncertainty over whether a detected change in cover was a reflection of the changed abundance of the species or was due to observer error (Hodgson *et al.*, 1995).

Even an experienced observer may assign a species to a scale value lower or higher than that actually occupied by the species. Because the mid-points of each class interval are widely spaced, there can be a large variation in data between investigators. In addition, in a species-rich herbaceous community errors of estimates are more likely with finer scale intervals

than with scales that have broad categories (Bonham, 1989).

DAFOR values are especially subjective and imprecise and therefore of limited use for monitoring. Different observers tend to have different definitions for the terms. Given the variability of DAFOR ratings, they will only indicate changes in species abundance rather than quantifying any change.

Small species tend to score lower than conspicuous ones. Similarly, a species in full flower is likely to receive a higher rating than one that is in a vegetative condition at the time of sampling. Species that form clumps are also more conspicuous than species that are more evenly scattered and would be preferentially classed in an abundance scale (Kershaw & Looney, 1983). This applies to all methods of estimating cover. Cover can be particularly difficult to estimate accurately in areas of diverse vegetation and tall vegetation.

The Braun–Blanquet and Domin methods give more information than does DAFOR, but are still subjective and are affected by the same overestimating problems for certain species as DAFOR.

Differences between surveyors can be reduced, at least to some degree, by training. More consistent results can also be achieved by defining the values or scoring terms more precisely. The use of pairs of observers will produce more consistent results (Hooper, 1992) but means that more expense will be incurred. Cover estimates made by using mini-quadrats (Section 6.4.3) or nested quadrats (Section 6.4.4) will also be less prone to error.

The Domin scale is a modified Braun–Blanquet approach, and is now the most widely used scale. The increased number of divisions (which often relate to fractions, e.g. 1/2, 3/4) (see Table 6.5) enables a more detailed assessment to be made of plant coverage; a relatively high degree of consistency can be obtained with experienced recorders. However, if you have to decide on the exact percentage cover to obtain a Domin value, more information is maintained by using percentage cover than by use of the Domin value. The use of the Domin scale within the context of the NVC is described in Section 6.1.6.

It is convenient to record species lists and ratings onto standard survey cards; the area covered by the species list should be clearly recorded (Byrne, 1991).

Many communities contain species that are able to coexist because they occupy a different temporal niche. Therefore, the vegetation should be recorded at a time of year when the majority of species are likely to be visible above ground, large enough for easy identification and before any major perturbation of the site occurs (e.g. burning, introduction of grazing or haymaking). However, this may not always be possible. Sampling in future

Table 6.5. *The Domin and Braun–Blanquet scales*

Value	Domin scale	Braun–Blanquet scale
10	91–100%	—
9	76–90%	—
8	51–75%	—
7	34–50%	—
6	26–33%	—
5	11–25%	76–100%
4	4–10%	51–75%
3	<4%–frequent	26–50%
2	<4%–occasional	6–25%
1	<4%–rare	1–5%
+	Insignificant: normally 1–2 individuals with no measurable cover	<1%

years should always be carried out at the same time of year as the initial survey, although flexibility in some years may be required to accommodate climatic variations (i.e. early or late summers). Suggested times for surveying the floristic composition of vegetation are given in Box 6.9).

Some common problems and solutions that may be encountered with frame quadrats are given in Box 6.13.

Data storage and analysis

This method will produce percentage cover or Domin scores for a large number of species in each quadrat. Some way of summarising the important changes is required. One way to gain a visual impression of changes in scores for each species would be simply to plot Domin scores on the *y* axis and time on the *x* axis. This will demonstrate any clear increases or decreases in scores, and statistical tests designed for ranked data (Section 2.6) can be used to test for significant changes over time.

Percentage cover data are not normally distributed, and either should be analysed with non-parametric tests or, more commonly, the data can be transformed (Part I, Section 2.6.3) into a closer approximation of a normal distribution and analysed with parametric statistics (e.g. *t*-tests), but

care should be taken to check that the transformed data meet the assumptions of parametric tests. Cover scales are non-linear, so values (even from randomly located quadrats) cannot be analysed by parametric statistics; non-parametric statistics based on ranks (such as the Mann–Whitney test) (see Table 2.3) can be used. There has been some work on transforming Domin values so that parametric statistical analysis is possible (Currall, 1987). However, if it is intended to collect data suitable for parametric statistical analysis, it would be preferable to collect accurate percentage cover values and use a suitable transformation, or use a linear scale. This need not be any more time-consuming and the data produced will be more detailed than Domin scores transformed to percentages (Byrne, 1991).

Another means of identifying the more important changes between years is to list for each quadrat those species that have increased or decreased by a large amount (e.g. two or more Domin points) in a consistent manner over the sampling period. A signal for action could be registered if a large consistent decrease in a species was recorded in a majority of quadrats, but several years' data would probably be needed before a signal could be registered, and only large changes could be detected by this method (Byrne, 1991).

Where Domin data are collected from quadrat sizes comparable to those used for NVC surveys, the data can be used to establish and monitor the presence of NVC communities (see Section 6.1.6).

Summary of advantages and disadvantages of cover scores
Advantages

- Cover values provide good descriptions of the contribution that each species makes to vegetation communities.
- Recording by using Domin values is widely used (e.g. by NVC surveys) and understood.

Disadvantages

- Estimation of cover can vary significantly from recorder to recorder.
- Recording all species present, including bryophytes and macrolichens, can be time-consuming.
- Inaccuracies in identification occur for difficult species.
- Domin and other cover scales are non-linear and therefore values, even from randomly located quadrats, can only be analysed by using less powerful non-parametric tests.

Summary of advantages and disadvantages of permanent quadrats
Advantages

- Reduced variation in data due to the effects of sampling means that fewer quadrats are likely to be needed to detect a given level of change.

Disadvantages

- Repeated recording may cause changes in the vegetation.
- Low numbers of plots, which were originally located within representative areas of habitat, may become unrepresentative of the whole site over time.
- Establishment and relocation of quadrats can be difficult and time-consuming.

- The inaccurate relocation of quadrats can seriously bias the monitoring.

Other measures that may be taken in frame quadrats, such as vegetation height, presence–absence and sub-plot frequency, are discussed in the section on mini-quadrats below (Section 6.4.3).

6.4.3   Mini-quadrats

Recommended uses

Frame quadrats can provide a simple, efficient and reliable way of determining the frequency of species, assessed by recording the presence or absence of species within each of a set of randomly located samples. They can also be used to monitor species composition if the total number of species in random mini-quadrats is recorded.

The most common application of the technique has been through the use of random mini-quadrats, which was developed in the late 1980s by the England Field Unit of the NCC. Their method was designed primarily to monitor a series of grassland transplants.

Temporary quadrats are located either completely randomly across the survey area or according to a stratified random sampling approach (see Part I, Section 2.3.3 for further details).

Time efficiency

Experienced recorders are usually able to record between 50–100 quadrats in a full day with the random mini-quadrat method. For planning purposes, assume a rate of ten (10 cm × 10 cm) quadrats per hour based on recording all species. The time taken to record quadrats is obviously slower in long vegetation and during periods of bad weather (Byrne, 1991).

Expertise required

Considerable expertise is required to be accurate in plant identification, especially for lower plants and certain vegetative phases of grasses, sedges and rushes (see Appendix 1 for identification references). Cover values are not estimated, so experience of their estimation is not required for this method.

Mini-quadrats: summary of key points

Recommended uses   Monitoring floristic change in relation to land management changes. Mini-quadrats are relatively quick to record. More traditional quadrat recording using cover values is less so

Efficiency   Individual quadrats are quick to record; more quadrats are needed to detect change than standard frame quadrats

Objectivity   Objective where only presence–absence data collected

Precision   Poorer than other methods but this is offset by its efficiency, and it can be quite precise if lots of quadrats are used

Bias   Frequency can be biased against species with a more clumped distribution. Shoot frequency will be biased against smaller plants, but rooted frequency does not have this problem, although it is slower to assess accurately

Expertise required   Competence required in plant identification; special expertise required if vegetative states of grasses, bryophytes and macrolichens are to be recorded

Equipment required   Quadrats, identification notes, field guides and basic recording equipment (i.e. field notebooks, standardised recording forms); hand-held computer on occasions

Key methodological points to consider

- Measuring presence–absence is very quick to record, but the estimate of frequency will be influenced by quadrat size
- Preliminary trials should be carried out if necessary to establish optimum quadrat size and the number required to achieve the desired level of precision
- Patchiness in species distribution will reduce the likelihood of a randomly placed quadrat finding the species

Data analysis   Dependent on material collected If presence–absence recorded, random mini-quadrats are commonly analysed by a χ^2 test (see Part I, Section 2.6.4); for other measures see *Data storage and analysis* below

Equipment required

Field notebook, clipboards or weatherwriters and specially designed recording cards are traditionally used to collect floristic data. These methods of data capture require the further stage of transferring the information to a computer-based or paper filing system back in the office. Much time can be spent on this, and errors in data transcription can occur during this process; see also Section 6.4.2.

Field methods

There are no simple rules for determining quadrat size for frequency surveys. The size of quadrat needed to monitor a species depends on the frequency of the species and its distribution (see Appendix 4 and Box 6.11). However, for the widely used 'mini-quadrat' system for estimating species frequency in lowland grasslands, temporary quadrats of size 10 cm × 10 cm are used. In tussocky heathland, 1 m × 1 m quadrats may be more appropriate.

Generally, for presence–absence, at least 100 mini-quadrats are required per survey area. The purpose of having a reasonably large number of quadrats is to increase precision and the likelihood of detecting change. Abundance of each species is objectively measured by its frequency (the total of its occurrences in the quadrats: for example, presence in 80 out of 100 quadrats equals 80% frequency). These frequencies can then be analysed to show relatively small changes in abundance. The point of using small quadrats is that only a small area has to be searched, and this increases the chance that different observers will record the same list of species.

Shoot frequency (which includes all species rooted within the quadrats plus any aerial shoots within or overhanging the quadrat) is generally used for ease of recording. Measurements of root frequency provide a less biased estimate of the frequency of occurrence of smaller plants and have been recommended for monitoring whereverpossible (Robertson, 1999). However, assessing root frequency can be much more time-consuming and can cause damage to vegetation. Which definition of occurrence is adopted is largely dependent on monitoring objectives. Where vegetation composition in terms of sward or canopy is the attribute of concern, defining occurrence according to shoot frequency is appropriate. If the recovery of species or species populations is of concern, root frequency should be monitored.

The random location of samples should be carried out according to the principles outlined in Section 2.3.3. Once their co-ordinates have been obtained, quadrats should be located and recorded as follows.

1. First, establish and measure axes (i.e. the boundaries of the monitoring plot) for determining random co-ordinates. Measurements may be paced out or defined more accurately with tape measures. Use random number tables or a spreadsheet package such as Excel to generate random co-ordinates for the required number of quadrats. Pairs of random co-ordinates can also be generated from the VegAn computer package (Blake, 1988). Enter random co-ordinates on the recording sheet.
2. Work along the longer axis of the plot. Find the random number pair with the lowest co-ordinate for this axis. Pace the required distance along this axis and mark the spot (e.g. with a bamboo cane).

Use the second co-ordinate of the pair to determine the number of paces taken away from the marker (at 90°) and place the quadrat at this point. Either return to the bamboo cane and continue pacing to the next co-ordinate on the long axis or else proceed directly to the next point. If the latter, it is important to return to a fixed landmark at intervals, to avoid cumulative locational errors building up. An alternative is to use a GPS. Recorders should avoid looking at the vegetation when pacing out quadrat locations, so as to avoid any possibility of 'choosing' the final location.

3. Place the quadrat on the ground once the correct position has been reached. It is important to use a standard method for this. This might be to face straight ahead and place the quadrat at arm's length, or to place the quadrat immediately in front of the right foot. The quadrat should be carefully lowered into the vegetation, avoiding pushing vegetation from outside into the quadrat area. This can be difficult with small quadrats in tall vegetation. If it proves very difficult a larger quadrat should be considered.
4. Record litter, bare ground and vegetation height (see Box 6.14), if necessary before the vegetation is disturbed by searching for species. Litter and bare ground should be assessed as amounts visible

Box 6.14 Measuring vegetation height and structure

The most usual method for measuring height is to assess average height crudely by eye, with a ruler placed upright in the vegetation.

Another widely used technique is to employ a long ruler with a light disc that is able to slide along the rule. The disc is dropped from a certain standard height and stops when it comes into contact with the vegetation. The height measured is not necessarily true vegetation height, as it is affected by the weight of the disc and the density and flexibility of the vegetation, but it is quick to record.

Other methods are to pull the vegetation straight before measuring the length or to measure the tallest

undisturbed individual at every placement of the rule. Exact protocols for this type of measurement should be decided and written down so that the method can be repeated exactly in the future.

The principle that the rule is placed randomly or systematically in the centre of the quadrat is important. The quadrats in which the vegetation is measured should either be randomly located or on a stratified (restricted) random basis.

For random samples, the results for mean height from each quadrat are compared against the results of other surveys by using t-tests or equivalent.

For stratified random samples, an overall estimatefor the site is calculated (see Part I) and changes tested by using t-tests or non-parametric equivalents.

from directly overhead. If litter or bare ground is present but at less than 50% cover, a tick is recorded. If the cover of litter or bare ground is 50% or more, the figure '50' is recorded.

5. Record all vascular plant species present within the quadrat area (according to roots or shoots), and bryophytes if required, using a tick for mature plants, a letter 'S' for a seedling, and a tick and an 'S' for mature plants and seedlings. A seedling is defined as a plant having six or fewer true leaves or any plant with cotyledon leaves. This distinction is not made for annuals such as Fairy Flax *Linum catharticum*. The species contributing most to cover (as viewed from directly overhead) is noted by a circled tick.

Other measurements that can be made are abundance (number of plants of each species in each quadrat) and sub-plot frequency. To collect sub-plot frequency data, the quadrat is divided into sub-quadrats (usually 25 or 100 divisions), and presence–absence of each species is recorded in each to give a frequency for each quadrat. This measurement is more sensitive than simple presence–absence in the whole quadrat and thus fewer quadrats will be needed to detect a given level of change.

Some likely problems and solutions that may be encountered with this method are outlined in Box 6.15.

Data storage and analysis

Simple analysis of whether changes have occurred in the proportions of species present are normally made through the preparation of contingency tables and analysed with χ^2 tests (see Part I) or G-tests (see Sokal & Rohlf, 1996). Long-term changes in species frequency (i.e. percentage of quadrats containing each species) may also be analysed with, for example, Cochran's test of linear trend.

If subdivided quadrats have been used to obtain a frequency measure for each quadrat, the proportion (p) of sub-quadrats containing each species can be transformed by using a $\sin^{-1} (\sqrt{p})$ transformation (see Part I, Section 2.6.3) and usually analysed with parametric statistics.

For further information see the statistical reference texts listed in Part I, Box 2.5.

Summary of advantages and disadvantages
Advantages

- The use of small quadrats increases species detection and recording rates.
- Presence–absence data are quick to collect.
- Different field workers are likely to achieve very similar results. There is no need to mark and relocate permanent quadrats.
- There are no problems with subjectivity and there is no need to allocate cover values, only presence or absence.

Box 6.15   Mini-quadrats: likely problems and solutions

The larger the quadrat, the higher the frequency values will be and the harder and slower it will be to search for species. You should therefore use a quadrat size appropriate for the vegetation being sampled (see Appendix 4). The appropriate quadrat size for frequency measurements varies between species; a set of nested quadrats of differing sizes may be required (see Section 6.4.4).

Some vegetation will be too coarse or too tall for very small quadrats to be used. However, once established, quadrat size should not be changed during a monitoring scheme. The England Field Unit found 10 cm × 10 cm quadrats to be suitable for monitoring the commoner species on grassland sites except where the vegetation became very coarse or tall during the monitoring period. However, if only selected species had been recorded (rather than all species), larger quadrats might also have been practical.

Although recording rooted frequency is considered to be preferable, shoot frequency was used (in the England Field Unit's study) to save time in recording, as it was felt that difficult and time-consuming decisions (particularly with grasses) would have to made in determining whether or not a species was rooted within a quadrat.

Disadvantages

- The technique requires a large number of randomly located quadrats, which are time-consuming to place.
- Tall and coarse vegetation causes difficulties with small quadrats.
- The measurement of shoot frequency can create bias in over-representation of larger species. If this is a problem for the particular vegetation type, it can be avoided by measuring root frequency but this is more time-consuming.

6.4.4   Nested quadrats for Functional Interpretation of Botanical Surveys (FIBS)

Recommended uses

This method, known by the acronym FIBS (Functional Interpretation of Botanical Surveys) is a simple method for surveying and monitoring grassland vegetation by using a nested quadrat design to assess species frequency (see Box 6.16 for information on the principles of nested quadrats). The method was developed by the Unit of Comparative Plant Ecology at Sheffield University, in conjunction with the Peak Park Planning Board and English Nature. Only herbs are recorded, to minimise the problems caused by identifying other taxonomic groups: the presence of grasses, rushes, sedges or bryophytes is usually not recorded.

This nested quadrat method employs temporary $1 m^2$ quadrats, which are located randomly within strips across a field or large plot. Each quadrat is subdivided into six nests, beginning at the bottom left-hand corner ($10 cm \times 10 cm$, $20 cm \times 20 cm$, $30 cm \times 30 cm$, $40 cm \times 40 cm$, $50 cm \times 50 cm$, $1 m \times 1 m$). The sequential examination of the nests encourages systematic searching of the quadrat;

Nested quadrats for FIBS: summary of key points

Recommended uses

- Simple method for monitoring functional changes in the floristic composition of species-rich vegetation
- From ecological theory and a database consisting of a range of simple ecological, morphological and distributional attributes for a large number of species, FIBS analysis can be used to analyse why vegetation has changed

Efficiency   Relatively quick to record as only uses a restricted range of species, and collects only presence–absence data

Objectivity   Objective as only presence–absence data are collected. Subjective in that some species are omitted from data collection

Precision   Poor, unless the recommended level of replication is increased

Bias   Frequency can be biased against species with a more clumped distribution, but nested quadrats do compensate to some degree

Expertise required   Basic competence required in plant identification, but some more difficult species are excluded from data collection

Equipment required   Quadrats, identification notes or guides and basic recording equipment, i.e. field notebooks, standardised recording forms; hand-held computer on occasions

Key methodological points to consider

- Each site will normally be subdivided into strips or sub-plots
- Quadrat size is $1 m^2$ and sampling is undertaken within different size cells nested in this quadrat
- Quadrats should be non-permanent and positioned randomly
- Recording is focused on broadleaved herbs, woody species and ferns
- Presence–absence data are collected

Data analysis   The nested quadrat method uses FIBS analyses (see *Data storage and analysis*) and plotting of cumulative frequency against cell size. Floristic change is interpreted by reference to the functional characteristics of the species present and utilises an autecological database

---

Box 6.16   Principles and uses of nested quadrats

The principle behind nested quadrats is that a quadrat is sub-divided so that the area of every subsequent 'nest' is greater than that of the previous one. Large-scale nested quadrats can be used where differently sized quadrats need to be used for different vegetation sizes and types (such as 1 m × 1 m for herbaceous vegetation, 5 m × 5 m for scrub and 10 m × 10 m for trees). The data from each quadrat are analysed separately, the principle being that larger quadrats are needed for larger vegetation in order to assess frequency and density accurately.

Small-scale nested quadrats can be used in which the largest nest is, for example, 2 m × 2 m. The smallest area is surveyed first, and species presence and/or cover is recorded. Any additional species found in the second nest are recorded, followed by additional species in the third and so on. It is usually advisable to stop only when there is a large reduction in the additional number of species for each size increase, although in general this is 0.1 m × 0.1 m for vegetation dominated by cryptogams (i.e. plants without true flowers or seeds such as ferns and lichens), 1 m × 1 m for species-poor grassland, 2 m × 2 m for rank herbs and shrubs and 4 m × 4 m for

trees (Shimwell, 1971). The ideas behind using nested quadrats are as follows.

1. The aim is to show the increase in species numbers with a corresponding increase in area.
2. An implement such as a pin with a minutely small area can be placed in each nest at random to give a value for percentage cover.
3. The numbers of individuals of each species in each nest will give a value of density and distribution and show whether a species shows a clumped or evenly spaced distribution.
4. The presence–absence of a species in each nest will give a percentage frequency within the whole quadrat.

The number of species found in a quadrat will increase as the size of the quadrat increases; plotting the number of species against quadrat area will initially show a steep slope. This relation will change quite quickly to a situation in which there is little increase in number of species for a corresponding increase in quadrat size; at this point, the optimum quadrat size can be determined for that vegetation type for the Braun–Blanquet method. Sometimes the change in slope is unclear, and the point of change can depend on the axis scale.

---

the different scales of the nests allows less common species to be picked up in the larger nests. Frequency is again used to measure relative abundance and changes over time. A reduced list of species, which excludes those difficult to identify, has been drawn up (Robertson, 1999).

A similar nested approach has also been developed from this original application for the monitoring of Environmentally Sensitive Areas (ESAs) in England, which comprises a fixed unit (stand): a rectangular area of 32 square sub-units (nests) in an 8 × 4 grid. Each holds a series of cells of increasing size. The size is chosen to reflect the overall scale of the vegetation and is usually a compromise between being large enough to encompass the majority of species present and small enough to be managed within available resources (Critchley, 1997).

Time efficiency

When recording a reduced list of species, 40–80 quadrats per day can be completed. If all vascular plants are listed then 20–40 quadrats can be recorded per day, depending on the richness of the vegetation.

In studies to date, a total number of 40 quadrats per survey area have typically been recorded (but see *Field methods* below).

Expertise required

Some expertise is required to ensure accurate plant identification, but as many of the difficult species are omitted from data collection, less expertise is required compared with alternative recording methods. On certain occasions more expertise is required for certain grasses, sedges and rushes (see Appendix 3 for identification references). Cover values are not estimated, so experience in their estimation is not required.

Equipment required

Field notebooks, clipboards or weatherwriters and specially designed recording cards are used to collect floristic data. These methods of data capture require a further stage of transferring the information to a computer or to a paper filing system back in the office. This can be time-consuming, and errors in data transcription can occur during this process. A bar code reader could be used. Species lists, together with their bar codes, are produced on a laser printer and copied on a high-grade photocopier (Hodgson *et al.*, 1995).

Field methods
Subdivision of the site

Provided that the site is greater than 1 ha and less than 3 ha, the area should be subdivided into five more or less equal strips, with boundaries delimited as far as possible by the use of existing features (e.g. walls or vegetation boundaries) and marked on to site plans. Compass bearings and permanent markers can be further used to delimit strips. If there is more than one management unit, each must be monitored separately. Further subdivisions may be required to take into account variations in topography and vegetation (see Hodgson *et al.*, 1995).

The simplest situation is a homogeneous site, which can be subdivided into five equal strips. If the site is sloping, factors such as soil depth, nutrient status and hydrology are likely to vary along the slope, so the site may need to be subdivided along contour lines. Where there is a mosaic of plant communities it is sometimes difficult to agree on exact boundaries, but where distinct vegetation types are separated by a natural boundary a modification of the sampling method may be feasible and desirable.

Where no natural boundaries exist, effects of management on vegetation should still be monitored by aligning the strips in such a way that the chances of detecting differences in the intensity of grazing or other site management practices are maximised. However, environmental gradients need to be taken into account.

Shape and size of the site

Even if the site is irregular in shape, the strips should still be approximately equal in size. If a site is greater than 2 ha in size, it may be inappropriate to subdivide the whole area into five strips, because quadrats will have to be placed at very low densities. This poses no problem if the vegetation is relatively homogeneous; however, this may not always be the case.

Choice of species

A reduced list of species should be considered; for most sites, grasses, sedges, rushes and bryophytes should not be recorded. Exceptions include agricultural weeds and certain easily identified monocotyledonous dominants. The latter group can contribute greatly to the structure of the vegetation.

The monocotyledons that it may sometimes be appropriate to record include: *Brachypodium pinnatum*,[1] *Bromus erectus*,[1] *Calamagrostis* spp.,[1] *Carex acutiformis/riparia*,[1] *C. paniculata*,[1] *Deschampsia cespitosa*,[1] *Glyceria maxima*,[1] *Juncus acutiflorus*,[2] *J. conglomeratus/effusus*,[2] *J. inflexus*,[2] *J. squarrosus*,[2] *J. subnodulosus*,[2] *Luzula sylvatica*,[1] *Molinia caerulea*,[1] *Nardus stricta*,[1] *Phalaris arundinacea*[1] and *Phragmites australis*.[1] (The number beside each name identifies the method by which the species should be surveyed and monitored, as detailed below.)

Amongst the bryophytes, *Sphagnum* spp.[2] should be included, but all other species should be ignored.

Method of recording

Eight randomly placed quadrats should be recorded from each strip or sub-plot, making a total of 40 quadrats for the complete site, except for smaller sites, where the number of quadrats would be 8 × the number of strips. However, it should be noted that if analysis of the frequency of individual species over time is required, then a change would need to be quite large (perhaps around 30%) before it would be found to be statistically significant, depending on the confidence level required (Robertson, 1999).

> **Box 6.17** Nested quadrats: likely problems and solutions
>
> One major problem with very small quadrats is that they will provide useful data for only the very commonest species. Species of lesser abundance will be recorded too infrequently to be included in the monitoring exercise. Equally, if a larger quadrat size, which is more suitable for the less abundant taxa, is employed, the most abundant species will be present in such a high proportion of the quadrats sampled and at such high population densities within each quadrat that it is unlikely that any change in their abundance will be detected.
>
> This problem of quadrat size is overcome with the nested quadrat approach in which, if a species is not found in the smallest cell of the quadrat, it is then looked for in a succession of progressively larger cells within the quadrat.
>
> The method assumes that dicotyledons and monocotyledons are equivalent groups. They are not: there are a few monocotyledonous annuals and many more wetland monocotyledons. Initial tests suggest that, provided monocotyledonous dominants are included, the method is defensible. However, it must be emphasised that it is recommended only when the resources available for monitoring work are not sufficient to carry out more detailed surveys (Hodgson *et al.*, 1995).

Where two or more recorders are involved, they should all record quadrats from all five strips on the site to:

- assist in discussions and facilitate agreement on taxonomic problems; and
- prevent systematic sampling errors between areas that might arise due to different recorders.

For each $1\,m^2$ quadrat the species present in the bottom left cell are noted. Subsequently, records are made of the additional species present when the cell size is increased successively to $20\,cm \times 20\,cm$, $30\,cm \times 30\,cm$, $40\,cm \times 40\,cm$, $50\,cm \times 50\,cm$ and $100\,cm \times 100\,cm$.

The very smallest seedlings should be ignored because of identification problems, but larger ones with cotyledons and at least three true leaves should be included. Herbaceous species are recorded only if they are rooted in the cell, but woody species are included if a living stem is in the cell.

The additional monocot species should be recorded by one of the two following procedures.

1. In the case of tufted or stand-forming species that are obviously apparent in unmanaged habitats but which may be harder to see in shorter vegetation (identified by superscript[1] above), the number of $50 \times 50\,cm^2$ cells within the $1\,m^2$ quadrat in which patches occupy at least $10\,cm^2$ should be recorded. These species will therefore be scored on a scale from 0 to 4.

2. Taller, easily identified, ecologically important, highly visible species (identified with superscript[2] above, i.e. rush species) should be recorded as for herbs (see above).

In addition, simple habitat information (amount of bare soil, litter, bryophytes, etc.) can also be collected by using procedure (1). When $50\,cm \times 50\,cm$ quadrats are used for this procedure, they should be placed sequentially in a clockwise order. This will prevent recorders being uncertain about where to place the next quadrat. Refer to Box 6.17 for some potential problems with nested quadrats, and their possible solutions.

Follow-up survey

Follow-up surveying is recommended every 2, 3 or 5 years depending on the habitat. The procedure is basically identical to that of the initial baseline survey except for the following.

- Monitoring should be restricted to herbs and to the important grasses, sedges and rushes present in at least 10 quadrats in the baseline survey.
- Important agricultural weeds should be monitored on each occasion irrespective of their frequency to obtain information on the effect of management on adjacent farmland.

- The list of species for monitoring should be updated on every third visit, as species that were initially rare may become sufficiently widespread for inclusion.
- Repeat surveys should be recorded at the same time of year as in the original survey. This will help to ensure that contrasted phenological patterns of growth among the species present do not distort the results.

Data storage and analysis

Analysis of FIBS data is complex, and cannot be described in detail here. For the full method, refer to Hodgson *et al.* (1995). A brief discussion is presented here.

The first stage of analysis is to identify whether there has been any change in the abundance of the monitored species. Two procedures may be employed.

1. An 'exact' method involves curve fitting, in which cumulative frequency is plotted against cell size. It is then possible to identify whether a species has increased or decreased, and whether change has occurred over the whole site or in only part of it. The differences between the curves at different times can be statistically assessed.
2. A simpler method can be used to calculate a value for changed abundance for each species in each cell size, although this is a less satisfactory method of data analysis.

Floristic change is interpreted by reference to the functional characteristics of the species present, and utilises an autecological database (see Hodgson *et al.*, 1995). Briefly, the ecological characteristics of declining species are compared to see if trends can be identified and attributed to changes in grazing, succession, etc. For example, if annual species that require moist conditions appear to be declining, this could be linked to periods of drought or increased drainage.

FIBS analyses should be carried out on:

1. the characteristics of the initial vegetation (for reference, for deciding frequency of monitoring and for comparing different sites);
2. a comparison of the characteristics of 'increased' and 'decreased' species (the main part of the analysis for detecting and interpreting floristic change); and
3. a comparison of the characteristics of the different strips or sub-plots (to examine whether the site is heterogeneous and whether floristic change is occurring across the whole site or is restricted to certain areas).

Summary of advantages and disadvantages
Advantages

- Smaller quadrats are quicker to record, improve inter-observer consistency, and increase species detection rates.
- Presence–absence data are quick to collect.
- Different field workers are likely to achieve very similar results.
- The use of nested quadrats circumvents problems related to the optimal quadrat size in relation to plant abundance.
- There is no need to mark and relocate permanent quadrats.
- There are no problems with subjectivity; there is no need to allocate arbitrary cover values.
- Recording concentrates on broadleaved herbs, woody species and ferns to minimise taxonomic errors.
- Sites are subdivided to maximise the chances of detecting the localised incidence of vegetational change.
- The FIBS method of data analysis can aid interpretation of floristic change.

Disadvantages

- The method involves a low level of replication and precision, and hence only large changes are detectable.
- The plant species used for monitoring are restricted, and this may not be appropriate for some monitoring purposes and habitats.
- Analyses are complex and will only become user-friendly once a final protocol has been agreed and appropriate computer programs written.
- The method is only really suitable for the more species-rich vegetational types (i.e. mesotrophic and calcareous grasslands).

6.4.5   Point quadrats

Recommended uses

Point quadrats are used in short vegetation when very accurate estimates of cover are required, particularly in the short term. Vegetation is recorded by passing long needles or pins down through vegetation and noting either the first or all species touched. The method can be applied to single pins repeated many times, but more often pins are grouped into frames to make recording easier. If ten pins are used in a frame, percentage cover is estimated at 10% intervals. Point quadrats can also be used for recording canopy structure, which is often important in grazing studies (Bullock, 1996).

Point quadrats can give precise estimates of cover, although the estimation of percentage cover for different species can vary with the pin diameter (Goodall, 1953). They are best used on simple, short and unlayered vegetation; tall, tussocky or layered vegetation is harder to record because of the large number of touches (Goodall, 1953). Point quadrats are very sensitive to changes in structure and composition of the vegetation and are best used for analysing short-term effects. They are of less use for long-term studies.

Time efficiency

The recording of point quadrats is very time-consuming and laborious. The technique can be very slow and requires considerable dexterity, especially in dense vegetation.

Expertise required

Expertise and skill are required, both to identify the species of plant touched by the points, and also to operate the point quadrat equipment. It is difficult to free-handedly lower a pin steadily and vertically through the vegetation while also noting touches and identifying species.

Equipment required

A point-frequency frame consists of a wooden or a metallic frame with two legs and two cross-arms (see Levy & Madden, 1933). The cross-arms have ten or more perpendicular equidistant holes. Steel rods or wire pins are slid through the holes. You can use the same pin for each observation or use a separate pin for each hole. However, working with a single pin is slower than using multiple pins. The size of the frame can be designed to suit local vegetation

---

Point quadrats: summary of key points

Recommended uses

- Estimation of cover in short vegetation (< 20 cm), in which a high level of precision is required

Efficiency   Very time-consuming

Objectivity   One of the most objective methods of estimating cover

Precision   Precise in short vegetation in still conditions

Bias   Generally low

Expertise required   Skill required to operate equipment and identify every leaf touched, particularly for grasses and sedges

Equipment required   Point frame quadrat and standard field recording equipment

Key methodological points to consider

- Location chosen in similar manner as for frequency quadrats (Section 6.4.2)
- Decide beforehand whether to record first hit or all hits
- Choose pin spacing to suit vegetation pattern
- Care is required when lowering pins
- Avoid windy days to minimise plant movements
- Repeat monitoring must use pins of the same diameter

Data analysis   Single pins are analysed as for presence–absence data, but pins grouped in quadrats are analysed in the same way as sub-plot frequency data (Section 6.4.3)

conditions, such as sward height and vegetation patterns, which will determine the spacing of pins and height of the frame.

Field methods

Samples should be taken at an appropriate number of locations as described in Part I, Section 2.3.

Lowering pins steadily through vegetation is difficult; it is generally easier either to push the point into the soil and note touches along its length (in this case the point diameter must be as small as possible), or to use a point frame that supports ten points. The supporting rod is pushed into the ground, and readings are taken at each hole in the crossbar. A record is made of each species touched by the point of each pin as it descends.

A decision also needs to be made over whether to record first hits only or to record all hits. Recording first hits only is quicker and easier, particularly in taller vegetation, and is sufficient to provide data on presence or absence of species. Recording all hits on a species gives a measure of 'total cover' of a species, a measure that reflects the size of plants as well as their abundance in the vegetation (Bullock, 1996).

If canopy structure is being measured, inclined point quadrats are often used. These are simply point quadrats that are lowered through the vegetation at an angle (usually 32.5° to the vertical) (Warren-Wilson, 1960). In this case, as well as recording all the hits of the point quadrat, the height of each hit is also noted.

Box 6.18 highlights the main problems, and their solutions, when using this technique.

Data storage and analysis

Data from single-pin frames equate to frequency data and can be analysed by a χ^2 test for fully randomised samples (see Part I).

If pin frames have been grouped to form 'quadrats', the data can also be analysed in the same way as sub-plot frequency data: see Section 6.4.3 and Byrne (1991).

Summary of advantages and disadvantages
Advantages

- Point quadrats are considered to be the most objective way to estimate cover. Points can be considered as plots with a very small area, and there is minimal error or personal bias when points are used: either the point contacts a part of a plant, or it does not.
- The canopy structure of short vegetation cannot be sampled in any other way.
- Small changes in plant cover can be detected accurately.

Disadvantages

- Point quadrats tend to underestimate the overall contribution to the vegetation of erect-leaved species and overestimate the cover of species with nearly horizontal leaves. The attitude of the leaves of most species varies with environmental conditions (Bonham, 1989).
- The area sampled is very small, so large numbers of samples are needed to detect the rarest species.
- Direct measures of cover by point quadrats are too laborious and time-consuming to be appropriate for most monitoring purposes.

Box 6.18   Point quadrats: likely problems and solutions

Point quadrats are time-consuming to record and every leaf touched needs to be identified: this is often difficult. Errors can occur from other sources such as movement of plants by wind or improper lowering of the pins by the observer. This can be rectified by training and experience and choosing to record only on windless days.

Because the total area sampled is small, only the more frequent species can be sampled by using pin frames. It would be easy to increase the number of samples if only a few target species were to be recorded, but this may still be insufficient for some species.

6.4.6   Transects

Recommended uses

There are a variety of different types of transect, each used for a different purpose. These are summarised in Part III, Section 10.1, Figure 10.1. For habitat monitoring, the most commonly used transects are line intercept transects, point intercept transects and belt transects. Other transect types are used for species monitoring and therefore may be required for monitoring species attributes of habitat features. Refer to Part III for details of these methods.

A line intercept transect, sometimes called a 'one-dimensional transect', is used for making continuous observations along a line. The method consists of measuring the intercept of each plant along a line, which is usually placed on the ground, to give a measure related to the density of plants. For longer transects, plants are only recorded that touch the tape at standard distances (e.g. every 10 m) or randomly allocated distances along the transect. Alternatively, percentage cover can be estimated by measuring the length of transect line occupied by each species and using this to calculate the percentage of the length of the transect that is 'covered' by the species.

A point intercept transect involves recording presence–absence of species at set points along the line. This can be used to estimate frequency.

Line transects can be used to measure density by recording the perpendicular distance of plants from the transect line. For further information see Bonham (1989) and the discussion of distance sampling methods in Part III, Section 10.4.

Belt transects are normally used to monitor changes in vegetation along a gradient or across a community boundary. They consist of frame quadrats of any size laid contiguously along the length

---

Transects: summary of key points

Recommended uses

- Line intercept and point intercept transects can be used for measurements of cover and frequency in tall or sparse vegetation
- Belt transects are particularly useful for monitoring vegetation changes along environmental gradients or across vegetation boundaries

Efficiency   Line intercept and point intercept transects can be efficient in areas of sparse vegetation; belt transects are time-consuming if all species are to be recorded

Objectivity   Subjective if the belt transect approach is adopted with the use of cover values; objective if presence–absence is recorded

Precision   Line intercept and point intercept transects are precise; for the precision of belt transects, see frame quadrats

Bias   Counts of touches or estimates of cover will often depend on the height of the line transect; for other biases relating to belt transects, see frame quadrats

Expertise required   Comprehensive plant identification skills normally required (unless only selected indicator species are being monitored). The line intercept method is easily learnt. Additional belt transect expertise required is dependent on the vegetation measures being collected

Equipment required   Measuring tapes (or another form of marking distance); permanent markers at each end if transects are permanent; frame quadrats for use with belt transects; standard field recording equipment

Key methodological points to consider

- Randomly or systematically locate line transect locations
- Determine appropriate length of transect(s) and mark each end (perhaps permanently)
- Place line or tape at an appropriate height to the vegetation (including ground level as an option)
- Belt transects are often permanent and located across environmental gradients or community boundaries in question; follow other principles for frame quadrats

Data analysis   Data analysis depends on the transect method and sampling strategy used

of the transect. Cover, local frequency or other vegetation attributes can be estimated for each quadrat, and the variation in attibutes along the transect can be determined. This information can be compared between sampling occasions (for example, to see whether the extent of a plant community has changed).

As for frame quadrats, transects may be permanent or temporary. For general monitoring purposes it is recommended that permanent transects are not used unless minimising sampling variation is of prime importance (see Section 6.4.2 or Part I, Section 2.3.2 for a detailed discussion). An exception to this is where belt transects are deliberately placed across vegetation boundaries, for example to monitor changes in the extent of an NVC community. In such situations, permanent transects provide a precise and efficient means of monitoring such changes, but steps should be taken to ensure that transects are, and remain, representative, and that sufficient transects are allocated to allow for lost samples.

When randomising the location of fixed-length temporary transects, it is not necessary to randomise the direction of the transect; it is recommended that all transects lie in the same direction (Greenwood, 1996). However, it is important that all points within the study area are equally likely to be sampled. To achieve this, an area of one complete transect length surrounding the study area must be included when start points are selected (Part I, Section 2.3.3); parts of transects that fall outside the study area are ignored, but any fragment that falls within the study area should be surveyed.

Time efficiency
Line transects are particularly efficient in areas of sparse vegetation, although time needs to be set aside to mark out the transect prior to recording data. However, if the vegetation is dense, then recording all touches can be time-consuming, in which case point transects are more efficient. Cover estimates will also be more difficult where plants are small, indistinct and intermingled.

Belt transects are time-consuming if all species are to be recorded and many quadrats are used, but they can provide detailed information on vegetation changes.

Expertise required
Transect methods are not complicated; surveyors will find the techniques straightforward once the technique has been used in the field. Botanical identification skills are required (see Appendix 3 for a list of field guides).

Equipment required
Equipment includes some type of line (wire, rope or tape), two pegs for securing the line tightly at either end, and a hammer for driving in the pegs. Measuring tape will be needed to mark out distances along the transect. Frame quadrats are required for use with belt transects (see Section 6.4.2). See Sections 6.4.2–6.4.4 for further details depending on whether standard cover or frequency data are required or FIBS methods are to be used. Standard field recording equipment (notebook, pens, field guides, etc.) will be needed. A compass may be required to orient transect lines.

Field methods
Before carrying out the transects, a sampling programme must be devised. This is a complex and critical process and is discussed in detail in Part I, Section 2.3.

For line intercept and point intercept transects the line or tape is stretched taut at a height at which it will make contact with the vegetation canopy. If basal cover is being estimated, the line is placed at ground level. The length of each intercepted plant part is measured. The total length of the transect line and the total length intercepted by vegetation are used to estimate percentage cover.

Tapes are often used for lines; intercepts should be recorded on one edge only. The location of the start and end of the transect line can be marked with permanent stakes if monitoring is to be repeated with permanent transects. The length of transect used will depend on the type of vegetation being sampled. In general, cover in herbaceous

Box 6.19   Transects: likely problems and solutions

Parker & Savage (1944) tested the reliability of the line intercept method. The data were reproducible by the same observer but differed among observers. The entire plant should be used for the unit of measurement to simplify data collection.

See Sections 6.4.2–6.4.4 for information on problems relating to frame quadrats if used as part of a belt transect system.

communities can be estimated with short transects (less than 50 m), whereas long transects (50 m or greater) should be used in some shrub communities. Transects do not necessarily have to follow a straight line (Bonham, 1989).

If belt transects are used with frame quadrats, then see Sections 6.4.2–6.4.4 for details on recording quadrats. Problems with using transects, and their solutions, are presented in Box 6.19.

Data analysis

There are a number of approaches that can be taken, depending on the exact transect method used and sampling design.

Point intercept presence–absence data can be analysed by using χ^2 tests. If presence–absence is measured at points along the transect, data can be analysed in the same way as sub-plot frequency data for quadrats (Section 6.4.3).

A simple quantitative approach in which temporary belt transects are used is to sum the cover-abundance or frequency values for each species across all the individual squares for all the transects, thus obtaining a form of cover-abundance value for each species for each year of monitoring. Changes in cover-abundance values from year to year indicate overall shifts in species, although they provide little information about the spatial character of these changes. Thus all the change may be due to the changes on a single transect, or it may be a more widespread phenomenon, but the drawing out of such information requires more sophisticated analysis.

It should be remembered that if cover-abundance totals are increasing, it is not evident from these totals whether species are spreading by expansion from small foci of living vegetation, or whether the increase in abundance values is caused by a more widespread but thinly scattered increase (Lindsay & Ross, 1994).

For permanent transects, a second approach, which is less quantitative but provides a clearer picture of the changes between transects for individual species, involves the simple mapping out of each year's data for a species. By comparing the 'species transect maps' from consecutive years and, particularly, comparing those for the baseline year with the most recent data, it is possible to obtain a good visual impression of spatial changes over time.

Summary of advantages and disadvantages
Advantages

- In certain vegetation types it may be simpler to use line transects than quadrats; they can provide more productive sampling in sparse vegetation and can be more practical in tall vegetation. They may also be easier to search more thoroughly than quadrats of the same total area.
- Line transects are quicker to record than are quadrats.
- Belt transects can produce very detailed data, for example for monitoring changes across vegetation boundaries.
- Line point transects are useful for measuring changes in total vegetation cover, although accuracy depends on the length of line and number of points used per line.

Disadvantages

- Transects intentionally directed along environmental gradients or across habitat boundaries only sample restricted areas; all areas of the site will not have an equal chance of being sampled, and this makes the extrapolation of results across the whole site problematic.
- Transects are often not suitable for measuring the cover of individual species in habitats where plants are closely intermingled and vegetation-type boundaries are not distinct.

- Long transect lines produce underestimates of species cover when points are widely spaced, because several patterns of species may be crossed. However, estimates of total cover are unaffected by the length of line (Bonham, 1989).
- Belt transects can be very time-consuming to record.

6.5   TREES AND WOODLAND STANDS

6.5.1   Stock maps

Recommended uses

Many attributes of woodland can be monitored by an adaptation of the standard forestry technique of stock mapping. This involves mapping the configuration of stands defined by (i) age; (ii) structure; and (iii) dominant tree species. This is simple enough in even-aged monocultures, in which boundaries are usually sharply defined, but requires more elaborate procedures in semi-natural woods, mixtures and stands of a more complex structure. The result is a map showing the pattern of compartments and sub-compartments, the latter being stands that are reasonably uniform with respect to stand age, structure and dominant species.

Time efficiency

The time taken to complete a stock map will depend upon the complexity of the wood being mapped and the level of detail required. It should be possible to map 20–50 ha per day with well-equipped and competent surveyors if not every detail is being recorded.

Expertise required

The identification of the dominant tree species is necessary (including the identification of deciduous trees in winter if required). Surveyors also need to be able to estimate stand age. This is easier for some species than for others, but a degree of experience will be necessary for making this assessment.

Surveying and cartographical skills are also required.

Equipment required

Appendix 6 summarises the equipment required for stock mapping.

Stock maps: summary of key points

Recommended uses

- Mapping compartments of woodland delineated by similar stand characteristics
- Monitoring species composition in terms of dominants
- Monitoring age-class distributions at larger scales
- Monitoring rotational management and open space patterns
- Monitoring large-scale effects of natural disturbance

Efficiency   Time taken will depend of the character of the wood

Objectivity   Reasonable once classification is decided

Precision   Will depend on the scale of mapping chosen (usually 1 : 10 000 or more detailed) and the sharpness of boundaries between compartments

Bias   Accurate identification of boundaries and species essential

Expertise required   The ability to identify tree species in all seasons is essential. Surveying and cartographical skills are also required

Equipment required   Basic surveying equipment such as ranging poles and tape measures if detail and precision is required; otherwise, distances can be measured by pacing (see below for details). OS base map and vertical aerial photographs are necessary

Key methodological points to consider

- Need to classify stands by age of dominant species
- Consideration should be given to the size of the smallest unit that will be recorded

Data analysis   Data are presented in the form of maps; areas can be estimated from these maps by using the methods applicable for aerial photography (Section 6.1.3) and Phase I survey (6.1.5)

Field methods

To begin with, if good-quality aerial photographs are available for the wood, these can be used to delineate obvious boundaries of different stand types (for example, patches of conifers can be readily distinguished from deciduous trees; see Section 6.1.3). These can be mapped on to a base OS map at the required scale (usually 1 : 10 000).

However, to obtain finer detail, some ground survey work will be required, particularly for estimates of stand age. Survey techniques for woodland are described in greater detail by Kirby (1988).

Briefly, sharp discontinuities in canopy composition, age or stand structure should be identified. In managed woods these are commonly correlated, whereas in woods in which there has been little management intervention there will probably not be abrupt changes (except perhaps in areas that have at some point been cleared by natural disturbance). Open spaces should also be treated as 'stands'. Where boundaries are poorly defined or follow tortuous configurations, arbitrary boundaries should be accepted if there is significant variation in stand characteristics. Well-defined tracks should generally be accepted as boundaries, even when the stands on either side are identical. This process is best initiated with aerial photographs and subsequently refined and verified on the ground.

One basic method for mapping is to lay out a grid system in the woodland based on 100 m × 100 m squares (or whichever size is most appropriate for the woodland), identified by using compass bearings, and record the dominant species and age (or stand type; see Kirby (1988) and Peterken (1980, 1981) for details of stand-type classification systems) at each grid point. Lines can then be drawn on the map around clusters of points with similar stand types, giving an approximation of compartment boundaries.

Most forestry stock maps include glades as separate sub-compartments, but treat rides and roads as boundaries. Monitoring for nature conservation, however, requires that track, ride and road characteristics be monitored. It should be possible to devise a classification appropriate to the size, based on usage, width and degree of shade from adjacent stands, and to map rides and roads on this basis.

Estimates of age can either be made on the basis of the surveyor's experience (to do this for many tree species will require considerable expertise), or by using an increment borer to take a core sample from a representative sample of trees in each stand to obtain an average ring count.

The level of detail recorded for stand structure will depend on the monitoring objectives. Briefly, if precise ages are not required, trees can be classed as seedlings, saplings, young trees, mid-aged trees, mature trees, over-mature trees and dead trees. The precise point at which, for example, a sapling becomes a young tree involves a degree of subjectivity, so the classifications should be decided in advance of the survey (based on measurements such as girth and height) and adhered to throughout the survey. It should be borne in mind that different species have different speeds of growth, and so criteria for classifying different species may alter.

The growth form of the dominant trees in each stand should be recorded as: maiden, coppice stool, tree singled from coppice, shrub, pollard or climber. Finally, estimates of height can be used to partition vertical structure (ground layer, understorey layer, subcanopy layer, canopy layer); stands can be differentiated on the basis of subcanopy features as well as dominant canopy features.

Data storage and analysis

The stock map is a reference document, which shows the patterns of habitats, the pattern of stand dominants and the pattern of age classes at the canopy level. The map can be revised after each forestry operation (if appropriate) or natural disturbance. If the wood is treated as non-intervention, the stock map may be revised every 10 years or so.

Stock maps should be stored as for Phase I survey maps (Section 6.1.5). The stock map is used to examine age-class distribution at the larger scales, rotations and open space patterns. Comparisons of successive maps can be made by eye to gain a visual impression of trends in the data. However, for more rigorous analysis, the areas of each stand type can be estimated by using the same procedures described for aerial photography (Section 6.1.3) and Phase I mapping (Section 6.1.5).

Summary of advantages and disadvantages
Advantages

- An easily interpretable map of compartments, rides, glades, etc. is produced, which can be used for monitoring purposes in itself or as a guide for choosing areas for further investigation.
- Stock mapping could be carried out as part of a more detailed survey, thus reducing the time taken to carry out two separate surveys.
- Stock maps are reasonably quick to complete, provided that a fairly coarse level of detail is being recorded.

Disadvantages

- The level of detail is restricted to age, species and structure of only the dominant tree species in each compartment.
- Mapping entire woodland areas may be problematic and time-consuming, particularly when dense scrub is present and there are no sharp boundaries between different stands.

6.5.2   Permanent plots

Recommended uses
The use of permanent plots (either in the form of quadrats or transects) in which individual trees are mapped and measured is the most detailed form of stand monitoring. They can be used for monitoring changes in woodland composition and structure down to the scale of individual stems. Changes recorded in several permanent plots can be averaged and extrapolated to give an indication of the changes taking place over the entire woodland area. If plots are sufficiently numerous and distributed in a suitable manner, statistical interpretations can be made.

Permanent plots are samples which are marked in such a way that the record can be repeated exactly on the same ground. Permanence has the advantage that any change observed is real within the limits of the plot and can be related to the performance of individual trees and shrubs. Permanent plots can also be illustrated with fixed-point photographs (Section 6.1.4) and used to visually demonstrate and appreciate change. Permanent plots also allow the performance of individual trees to be monitored. The disadvantage is the extra work required to mark plots and archive the data. A further, though usually insignificant, disadvantage is that the plot markers on the ground may actually influence what happens within the plot.

Time efficiency
Permanent plots require a significant initial investment to generate the first record, but subsequent recordings usually take far less time to complete. Field recording is best done with two (or perhaps three) people. A person working alone cannot readily move tapes, nor transfer repeatedly from measuring to recording and back. Even after the plots are clearly delimited for recording, it is usually most efficient to have one bookkeeper in control.

The time taken to record data depends on the structure of the stand. Old growth lacking an understorey can be recorded quite quickly. Young growth containing many multi-stemmed trees and/or groves of saplings can be very time-consuming to record. In an average stand being recorded by three people, it should be possible to lay out and record six $20\,m \times 30\,m$ transect sections in a day. Re-recording a transect is quicker if the amount of change has been small. Separate plots will take longer if precise relocation is required.

Expertise required
Surveyors must be able to identify all tree species and assess their condition in terms of age, health, height, girth, etc. It is usually necessary to make decisions about what to record and the degree of detail required before the monitoring work commences. An understanding of woodland succession is therefore needed. In addition, familiarity with the techniques for quadrat or transect sampling and data collection is necessary.

Permanent plots: summary of key points

Recommended uses

- Monitoring changes in woodland composition and structure down to the scale of individual trees (including fallen dead logs)
- Providing a time series of data on successional or other changes taking place
- Monitoring the amount of regeneration occurring

Efficiency   Three people working together should record six 20 m × 30 m transect sections per day (see main text for details)

Objectivity   Good, as long as classifications (e.g. amount of canopy cover) and field methods are rigorously defined and adhered to

Precision   Good, providing plots are accurately relocated on return visits and measurements of tree location, height, etc. are accurate. Precision of estimates of change extrapolated over whole woodland will depend on the number of plots and the percentage of the total area covered

Bias   Care must be taken when using permanent plots to estimate wider-scale changes. Unrepresentative plots, or too few plots, will give unreliable estimates of compositional and structural change occurring through the whole woodland. Since trees are generally non-randomly distributed, biased estimates of relative density can be obtained

Expertise required   The ability to identify tree species in all seasons, and to assess their condition, is essential. Familiarity with transect and quadrat sampling methods and techniques is also necessary

Equipment required   Basic surveying equipment such as ranging poles and tape measures (see below for details)

Key methodological points to consider

- Recording permanent plots can be time-consuming, especially when setting up new ones. The density of trees in the plots and the distance between plots should be taken into account when deciding how many plots to sample and what size they should be
- It is essential that permanent plots can be accurately relocated on subsequent visits. The plot markings must be durable and interference-proof
- The size and shape chosen for permanent plots will affect the type of change that they are capable of monitoring; long transect belts will record grouping and zonation changes more clearly than small square plots. However, small plots can provide a better representation of the wood as a whole

Data analysis   Data can be held and processed by using a spreadsheet package. For analysis, a time series of changes in single plots can be produced, or changes in average plot composition, structure, etc. over time can be estimated and tested for statistical significance

The technique of fixed-point photography (Section 6.1.4) is useful to provide a visual record of changes in the composition or structure of particular plots over time.

Equipment required
The equipment required is fairly basic surveying equipment (Appendix 6). It should be borne in mind that permanent plot markers should remain in place for many years; it is advisable to use long-lasting materials, and to fix them securely in place. Galvanised metal posts are most commonly used.

A compass is required to measure the locations of trees if circular plots are being used. A hypsometer such as an Abney level can be used if accurate measurements of canopy height are desired.

Field methods
Plot shape
Plots can be circular or rectilinear in shape. Circular plots require one central marker, whereas rectilinear plots generally require a marker in each corner. Markers themselves are subject to decay, destruction and vandalism, so four markers should

be more secure than one, but this increases costs and the time taken to set up the plots. The usual compromise is to have two central posts marking the mid-line of the plot. The location of individuals within plots can be simply defined with both plot shapes (bearing and distance for circular plots, x and y co-ordinates for rectilinear plots), but is somewhat easier with rectilinear plots, because compass bearings take longer to determine than do x and y co-ordinates and are usually less precise.

The choice between using square plots and rectangular belt transects depends on circumstances and the overall pattern of sampling.

- A large number of small (e.g. 20 m × 20 m) square plots is a statistically superior representation of the wood as a whole, which also allows whole-site distributions to be assessed at the scale of the distance between plots. However, the effort required to position and mark plots is substantial, and individual plots are easy to mislay over long intervals between recordings. Groups and transitions are difficult to detect and monitor. In addition, edge effects in small plots may be large.

- Transects laid out across the main directions of variation allow groups and zonations to be detected and monitored. They require much less effort to position and mark. They are also proof against neglect and vandalism, for transects can be re-established even if only two markers remain in position. Location of individual trees is easy to record by co-ordinates. However, single transects may not contain a valid subsample of the whole wood and do not allow whole-site distributions to be assessed. The dynamics of stands within the transect may be strongly influenced by events and conditions in the stand outside the transect.

- Single large (at least 100 m × 100 m) square plots may allow groups and zonations to be detected and monitored, but are more likely to represent a single woodland type. They require a grid of markers, partly as security, but mainly to facilitate accurate recording. The dynamics of stands within a large square plot are less influenced than transects by events and conditions in the stand outside the plot (the centre of the plot being much further from unrecorded stands). Recording accurate co-ordinates in large plots is difficult unless the ground is nearly level.

Data measurements

Individual trees can be mapped by recording the co-ordinates of their centres to the nearest 10 cm. Greater accuracy is rarely required, but may be necessary in dense groups of saplings. Large, multi-stemmed trees are best annotated to show individual stems. Dense clusters of stems from stools (e.g. hazel coppice) may not be worth mapping individually, although each stem should be recorded. Although all individuals attaining 1.3 m in height should be recorded, a minimum threshold for recording stems is usually 2–5 cm diameter at 1.3 m height.

The features that might be recorded for each tree or trunk of a tree during routine enumerations are: species, height, trunk circumference (girth) or diameter at breast height (gbh or dbh), canopy position, origin (e.g. coppice), health measurements, and individual characteristics (e.g. height of lowest branch on large trees, distinctive shapes). Where large and veteran trees are of special interest, some estimate of dead wood (Section 6.5.5) may be needed.

- *Girth and diameter.* Conventionally measured at 1.3 m (breast height), taken by standing above the tree if on sloping ground (a small nail driven into the base of the tree allows precise relocation of 1.3 m height on subsequent surveys). If this falls on an atypical section (e.g. a fork or rot hole), measure immediately below. Calipers are available to measure diameter, but they are heavy, inaccurate on irregular shapes and awkward in semi-natural thickets; tapes are generally better all round. Although tapes are available that read directly into diameters from a girth, these do not give the accuracy necessary to study the growth of individual trees.
- *Canopy position and crown size.* Useful for detailed analysis of change. Best recorded at a somewhat coarse level of canopy, subcanopy, tall underwood, short underwood; and large, medium or small.
- *Height.* Not always useful for monitoring, and best avoided if unnecessary on cost–benefit considerations. Where height measurements are

useful (e.g. when monitoring young regenerating woodland), it can be estimated by standing back and counting approximate 2 m steps from bottom to top (the scout method). Use a hypsometer for more time-consuming but more accurate measurement.

- *Origin.* Recorded by using a simple classification, which will generally take the form: coppice, pollard, maiden, planted, naturally regenerated.
- *Health.* For general use, a simple classification suffices, usually a four-point scale from healthy and vigorous to crown dead/alive only at base, which recognises increasingly severe symptoms of ill health or stress. Bark stripping by grey squirrels, ponies, deer, etc. can be similarly recorded (i.e. severely debarked, partly debarked, not debarked).

Where individual large and veteran trees are being recorded, a more complex codification may be necessary. Surveyors will have to devise codes that are appropriate to the site and as objective and quantitative as possible, e.g. number of live crown branches; proportion of circumference at 1.3 m with live bark.

Photographs of important or sample trees are helpful. They allow unforeseen characteristics to be assessed, and they can be used to explain any conventions used for classifying health, canopy position, etc.

Canopy gaps can be rapidly recorded and provide valuable information on gap-phase regeneration opportunities and canopy disturbance rates. In simply stratified stands they are easily defined, but in overlapping, multi-layered stands they need to be carefully defined and will take longer to record.

Separating areas in which the ground is open or partly shaded is important. Gaps can be easily mapped on to scale charts of the plot by using individual trees as reference points and pacing out the edges of gaps viewed vertically from the ground.

Canopy spread of individual trees can be estimated by vertical projection of the canopy margins on to the ground, taking two diameters at right angles. The greatest difficulty arises with tall, narrow-crowned trees, for which the proportionate error when projecting spread vertically on to the ground is high and the canopy spread is small, but as these trees will often be in closed canopy stands the position of neighbouring trees and their canopy form can be used as a guide.

Estimating the cover of each species in a plot is based on the convention that a tree wholly occupies the area within its canopy spread, even though the foliage is thinly spread. Two approaches are possible:

1. to record cover within equal cover bands of e.g. 10%; and
2. to recognise unequal cover bands, which are more discriminating at low cover values (Table 6.6).

The latter is generally most useful, even though it does not allow cover to be averaged over a number of plots; most species occur at low cover, so making distinctions within the lowest cover bands conveys more information.

Permanent plots can be used to monitor regeneration by assessing the numbers and population dynamics of seedlings and small saplings, and the associated state of ground vegetation.

Table 6.6. *Example of a canopy spread classification*

Scale	Description	Scale	Description
10	Complete cover	4	Below 5% cover
9	Above 75% cover	3	One large individual
8	50–75% cover	2	One small individual
7	33–50% cover	1	Saplings only
6	15–33% cover	X	Seedlings only
5	5–15% cover	D	Dead plants only

Record species, numbers and condition according to a standard procedure to estimate density of regenerants. Condition can be measured by height, degree of grazing/browsing damage, etc. Such records can be repeated on an annual basis at the same time of year if responses to a change in grazing pressure must be measured. Analysis of changes and the underlying factors causing the changes is restricted by the lack of information on turnover. Recording of this kind is relatively quick, so it is practicable to use long permanent transects as a basis and thus obtain information on large-scale patterns. SNH has used very long transects of this kind in large sites by recording every 10 m in 100 m, counting saplings, etc., within 1 m of the line (see Box 6.21).

Recording individuals precisely means that survival, mortality and recruitment can be measured. This requires mapping individual seedlings and saplings, which is only practicable on a small scale (e.g. 5 m × 5 m). The scale of practicable recording decreases as the density of regenerants increases. If the issue is the survival of seedlings through the first year, recording will be necessary at intervals of 3 months. If the issue is the survival of established seedlings, recording at annual intervals at a constant time during the growing season may be sufficient. Remains of regenerants that have died can often be found, and these help to explain mortality factors. Analysis of these observations is time-consuming. In all cases, supplementary notes describing the stand and points of interest are useful.

Key field method elements

1. Select plot positions or transect lines according to pre-determined criteria.
2. Lay out plot approximately with ranging poles and pacing.
3. Establish baseline, then lay out accurately with tapes and adjust ranging poles.
4. Record with tapes in position.
5. Photograph from a position that is itself accurately recorded.
6. Replace ranging poles with permanent markers.

See Peterken & Backmeroff (1988) for full details of the use of transects. See Mountford & Peterken (1998) for an example of results obtained from detailed recording of permanent transects.

Data storage and analysis
Data storage
Field records should be placed on to scale charts drawn on graph paper, showing the location and size of each stem. Additional notes can be referenced from these. Original field records should be retained and kept on file, even after data have been transferred onto a computer. This will allow checks to be made and will permit future workers to examine the original data for other purposes if required.

Hard copies of computer databases and spreadsheets should also be filed, and backup computer files made for security. The basic data and records of methods should be stored in separate locations, again for security purposes. The locations and contents of files should be kept on record, so that any successor staff will be made aware of the existence of the records and where they can be accessed.

Data analysis
Analysis with a computer spreadsheet program such as Microsoft Excel or Lotus 1-2-3 has proved satisfactory. Input the data so that each line of the spreadsheet represents one stem, which is given a code number. Each column represents an attribute of a stem (e.g. height, girth, etc.) at each recording date. Separate stems on single individuals have separate rows, but they are linked through code numbers.

Further information, such as the number of individuals of each species per plot, can also be entered into a computer package.

Thus, the changes over time of particular attributes of individual trees can be displayed graphically and analysed statistically. Average changes for particular plots, groups of trees or particular species can also be calculated and analysed to examine trends in the growth, regeneration, age structure, distribution and relative abundance of species.

Box 6.20   Permanent plots: likely problems and solutions

The precise relocation of permanent plots is likely to be the most problematic aspect of monitoring by using this method. To ensure that plots can be relocated it is essential that plot markers be sturdy. It should also be borne in mind that permanent plots are vulnerable to vandalism; locate the markers out of harm's way if possible. If fixed-point photographs are taken of the markers, it may be possible to relocate plots even if the markers are destroyed. The fixed-point photographs will in any case be a useful part of a monitoring programme.

See Part I, Sections 2.3.2 and 3.4.2 for further discussion of the problems encountered with permanent plots.

Likely problems with this technique, and their solutions, are summarised in Box 6.20.

Summary of advantages and disadvantages
Advantages

- Relocation of plots allows precise measurements of change to be made down to the scale of individual trees.
- Any change observed is real (within the confines of the plot and subject to measurement error), not estimated, and can be related to the performance of individual trees.
- If required, a large number of data on many aspects of the distribution, condition and performance of trees can be collected. The amount of data gathered can be tailored specifically to the needs of the monitoring programme.
- With sufficient numbers of plots, changes can be statistically extrapolated to estimate changes that have occurred in the woodland as a whole.
- Permanent plots can be recorded with fixed-point photography to provide an additional visual record of changes.
- Surveys of other species (e.g. birds, lichens) can be related to the permanent plot.

Disadvantages

- Extra work is required to mark and relocate plots and to store individual plot records.
- Changes within plots may be very slow; there is a risk that over the timescales required to monitor changes, especially in well-developed climax woodland, plot locations could be lost or even destroyed.
- Changes within plots may not be representative of changes occurring at the whole woodland level, particularly if small numbers of plots are used.
- Maintaining long-term studies is notoriously problematic and requires particular dedication.

Box 6.21 describes a case study of a method for monitoring tree regeneration and browsing damage by using permanent plots.

6.5.3   Temporary plots

Recommended uses

Temporary plots are plots that are marked out and recorded only once. They can be useful for providing a snapshot of the age structure and composition of a wood for general survey purposes; for example, as releves for later classification such as the NVC (Section 6.1.6).

For the purposes of monitoring change, enough randomly distributed plots must be recorded on each occasion to give a representative sample of the woodland. A quantification of stand characteristics with standard errors can be made, which can be compared (by using statistical tests) with later surveys to see whether any significant changes have occurred. One or two plots recorded as samples on surveys and not permanently marked will not be useful for monitoring change, because the error involved if data are extrapolated over a larger area will be too large for any meaningful conclusions to be drawn.

The method for recording temporary plots is the same as for permanent plots (Section 6.5.2). However, fewer data can be compared between survey dates, because the progress of individual trees cannot be tracked. It may, therefore, not be useful to record as much information on the characteristics of individual trees as one does for permanent plots.

Box 6.21 Case study: a method for monitoring tree regeneration and red deer damage using permanent plots

This method was developed by the ITE for monitoring woodland regeneration in areas in which deer grazing pressure was causing concern. It can easily be adapted to other monitoring requirements.

The monitoring system is based on a series of permanent 1000 m line transects incorporating five 10 m × 2 m quadrat sites at 200 m intervals. The lines are marked every 100 m with conspicuous markers.

At least one transect should be established for every 2 km² of study area. The starts of transects should be located at easily recognisable features such as bridges, track divides, etc. Each transect is 1000 m × 2 m oriented along a fixed arbitrary compass bearing. Re-recording of established transects should be carried out within 2 weeks either side of the time of year when first recorded. Repeat recording should be carried out

every 5 years for conifer woodland and every 2 years for broadleaved woodland.

RECORDING ALONG TRANSECT

1. Along the entire length of the transect a count is made of all trees (of each species) between ground flora height and 3 m. The use of a 1 m or 2 m measuring pole is helpful for determining whether trees fall within the 2 m transect corridor, and whether small trees are above or below the surrounding vegetation layer. String is tied between the marker posts to mark out the line.
2. The state of the leader (largest tree) in each 100 m section is recorded.
3. Sections of transect between quadrats are described as (a) entirely open (no trees within 200 m), (b) entirely wooded (>20 trees per 100 m² per section) or (c) scattered trees (0–20 trees per 100 m² per section).

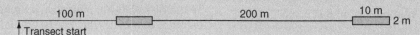

RECORDING QUADRATS

1. Mark the corners of each quadrat with marker pegs. String can be tied around these.
2. Record the ground vegetation species or types where this occupies more than 25% of the quadrat.
3. Count all trees from emerging seedlings below vegetation layer to 3 m in height.
4. Record state of leading tree.
5. Count deer dropping groups.

6. Take four fixed-point photographs of each quadrat at 90° intervals.

TIME EFFICIENCY
No more than 5 minutes should be spent assessing each quadrat unless there are difficult circumstances such as a large number of seedlings or difficult terrain.

Normally a transect can be set up and recorded in half a day providing the ground is reasonable.
Source: Sykes *et al.* (1985).

One advantage of temporary plots, provided that a sufficient number are taken, is that a sample representative of the entire wood can be taken each time. A permanent plot, although it provides excellent data on changes within the plot itself, is not necessarily representative of the woodland as a whole, especially if chance events affect the area containing a permanent plot more than elsewhere.

Time efficiency
The time taken to record temporary plots themselves will be similar to that needed for permanent plots (Section 6.5.2), although the time taken overall will be generally less as there is no need to set up permanent markers at the start of the monitoring programme or relocate plots with precision on subsequent surveys. In addition, it is

Temporary plots: summary of key points

Recommended uses

- Recording sample plots for surveys
- Estimating changes in community structure and species distribution/abundance over large scales

Efficiency   Temporary plots should generally be quicker to record than permanent plots (see main text for details)

Objectivity   Good, as long as classifications (e.g. amount of canopy cover) and field methods are rigorously defined and adhered to

Precision   Good, providing measurements of tree location, height, etc. are accurate. Precision of estimates of change extrapolated over whole woodland will depend on the number of plots

Bias   Too few plots will give unreliable estimates of compositional and structural change occurring through the whole woodland. Because trees are generally non-randomly distributed, biased estimates of relative density can be obtained

Expertise required   The ability to identify tree species in all seasons, and to assess their condition, is essential. Familiarity with transect and quadrat sampling methods and techniques is also necessary

Equipment required   Basic surveying equipment such as ranging poles and tape measures (see below for details)

Key methodological points to consider   A sufficient number of plots must be taken to ensure that a representative sample of woodland is obtained. The size and shape of plots will affect the type of change that they are capable of monitoring; long transect belts will record grouping and zonation more clearly than small square plots

Data analysis   Data can be held and processed using a spreadsheet program. For analysis, a time series of changes in single plots can be produced, or changes in average plot composition, structure, etc. over time can be estimated and tested for statistical significance

likely that less information will be recorded on temporary plots, though this may not necessarily be the case.

Expertise required
Refer to Section 6.5.2.

Equipment required
The equipment required for recording temporary plots is listed in Appendix 6.

Field methods
The method for recording temporary plots is the same as for permanent plots. Refer to Section 6.5.2 for details.

Data storage and analysis
Data storage
Refer to Section 6.5.2.

Data analysis
Analysis of data is performed by using a spreadsheet program, as for permanent plots (Section 6.5.2). However, because the performance of individual trees is not measured, the analysis of change over time is restricted to the comparisons of averaged quantities such as height, girth, approximate age, etc., or changes in the average density, relative abundance or other attributes of species.

Summary of advantages and disadvantages
Advantages

- Temporary plots are quicker to locate and record than are permanent plots.
- A sufficient number of randomly distributed plots provides a representative sample for monitoring changes on the scale of the whole woodland.
- The location of samples can be varied to ensure that they are always representative of the entire woodland at the time of each survey.

- The analysis and storage of data is quicker and simpler than for permanent plots.

Disadvantages

- Information on the progress of individual trees cannot be collected.
- If not enough plots are recorded, the results cannot be used for monitoring changes and are not representative of the woodland as a whole.

6.5.4   Plotless sampling

Recommended uses

Plotless sampling is a relatively quick method for estimating density, average height, girth, canopy spread, etc. of trees. The method is most commonly used for estimating density, but any other information that can be recorded about individual trees can be measured and averaged (see Section 6.5.2).

Repeating surveys and comparing the results with those of previous surveys gives an estimate of changes in density, etc. over time.

There are several methods for estimating density, etc. by using plotless samples. These are described in *Field methods* below.

Time efficiency

Plotless sampling is generally a much faster method for estimating tree density (or other characteristics) than quadrat or transect plots in woods, because the plots must be large to give a representative sample of the community (Bullock, 1996).

The time necessary to record a suitable number of samples will also depend on the method of sampling chosen (see *Field methods* below). The point-centred quarter and T-square methods will take longer than the nearest-individual method.

Expertise required

Plotless sampling is not a specialist technique. Obviously, surveyors must be able to identify tree species (including during winter if necessary) and be competent at making accurate measurements and recordings in the field. The use of a hypsometer

---

Plotless sampling: summary of key points

Recommended uses

- Estimating the density, height, girth, etc. of trees in a woodland
- Estimating changes in these quantities

Efficiency   Generally a much faster method for estimating attributes than using permanent or temporary plots

Objectivity   Little room for subjectivity if method is properly followed. Some subjectivity arises if deciding not to include saplings; at what point does a sapling become a tree?

Precision   Depends on the particular method used and the number of samples taken

Bias   Serious bias can result if the distribution of species is not random (either clumped or uniformly distributed). If different species have different spatial distributions, a biased estimate of relative density will be obtained. This method does not select a totally random sample of trees

Expertise required   The ability to identify tree species and competence at field measurements and recording is necessary

Equipment required   Little equipment necessary (tape measure, field recording equipment); see main text for details

Key methodological points to consider

- If measuring density of separate species, decide in advance which ones to look at: scarce species may be time-consuming to study because the distance between individuals can be large
- The core area in which random points are located should be smaller than the entire study area to allow for the possibility that the nearest individual trees to some points may lie outside the study area
- Ensure that enough points are taken to allow a representative sample to be obtained

Data analysis   Generally very simple and quick to perform; see main text for details

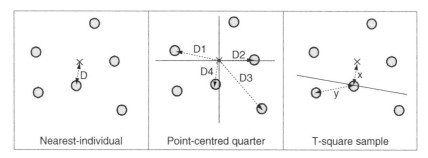

Figure 6.3. Plotless sampling methods. See text for details.

or Abney level may be necessary if an accurate measure of height is desired.

Equipment required

Very little equipment is required for plotless sampling (Appendix 6). Tape measures are necessary for recording distance, girth, etc. A compass is useful for the point-centred quarter method (see below) but not essential. A relascope can be used to estimate mean basal area of trees at a given point (Horsfall & Kirby, 1985); whether or not this measurement is needed will depend on the monitoring requirements being met.

Field methods

A number of plotless sampling methods are possible. The three most commonly used for trees are described here.

These methods are generally used for estimating density. However, other information about trees selected by using any plotless sampling method can also be recorded (e.g. height, girth, condition, etc.). For details concerning the recording of these observations refer to Section 6.5.2. The remainder of this section deals with estimating density.

All the methods require the locating of a certain number of randomly selected sample points. If you are estimating density etc. for each species separately, the same set of points can be used for all species. This will be quicker than locating a different set of points for different species.

The minimum number of sample points necessary will depend on the variations in tree distribution, but at least 50 should be taken (Bullock, 1996). If there is considerable variation in the data it may be preferable to stratify the wood into reasonably distinct stands (see Sections 6.5.1 and 2.3.3) and take separate sets of measurements in each.

All methods involve the assumption that distance is measured to the centre of the tree, which must be estimated.

The methods are illustrated in Figure 6.1.

Nearest-individual method

The tree nearest to the sample point is located, and the distance between it and the sample point is measured. The density is calculated thus:

$$Density = 1/(2D_{\mathrm{m}})^2$$

where D_{m} = mean distance for all samples.

Point-centred quarter method

Two perpendicular straight lines, which cross each other at the sample point, are measured out, creating four quadrants centred on the sample point. The orientation of these lines should be the same for all points. A compass bearing can be used for this, or if a transect is being used to locate sample points, the transect line can be used for orientation.

In each quadrant the distance to the nearest tree is measured. These four distances are averaged, and density is calculated thus:

$$Density = 1/D_{\mathrm{m}}{}^2$$

where D_{m} = mean of average distances.

T-square sample method

Because trees are rarely randomly distributed (they tend to be either clumped, or if in plantations, regular), the above methods give biased results. T-square sampling overcomes some of this bias because it combines two methods (nearest-neighbour and point-to-object) that are biased in opposite directions. If species are aggregated, nearest-neighbour overestimates density, whereas point-to-object underestimates it; if species are regular the opposite is true (Greenwood, 1996). Therefore some of each bias will cancel the other out.

From each random point the distance (x) is measured to the nearest individual of each species in question. A line at right angles to the line from the point to the tree is laid out, and the distance (y) is measured from the tree to its nearest neighbour on the opposite side of the line from the original point. Density is calculated thus:

$$Density = n^2/(2.2828 \sum x \sum y),$$

where n = number of points.

Data storage and analysis
Data storage
See Section 6.5.2.

Data analysis
Density calculations are given in the field methods section (above).

It is worth noting that the bias arising from the non-random distribution of species has led some ecologists to state that plotless methods should not be used for estimating density. Even if trees are randomly distributed (which is unlikely), a random sample of trees is not obtained by using plotless sampling, because the method ensures that isolated trees are more likely to be sampled (Bullock, 1996).

The T-square method is reasonably robust when used on non-random distributions, but it is worthwhile applying a test of randomness to the data in order that possible biases are not overlooked (Greenwood, 1996).

Density estimates and other information recorded can be compared between surveys on different dates by using statistical tests to monitor changes over time as long as enough samples are taken on each survey, the bias is not too severe and the direction of bias is understood.

Summary of advantages and disadvantages
Advantages

- Plotless sampling is generally a much faster method than quadrats or transects.
- Little equipment is required.

Disadvantages

- If species are at very low density it may take a long time to locate the nearest individual.
- When surveying an area with high species diversity, the time taken to measure separate species will be greater.
- The method contains inherent bias due to the non-random selection of trees even if trees are approximately randomly distributed.

6.5.5   Dead wood surveying and monitoring

Recommended uses
Surveying and monitoring the amount of dead wood present in a woodland is a useful measure of habitat quality. Dead wood is a vital part of the woodland ecosystem, providing habitat and food for numerous organisms including invertebrates and fungi.

Overmanaged woods may contain less dead wood than they should, because dead trees are sometimes removed. Monitoring the amount of dead wood present is useful in this context. See Section 5.1 for more details.

Time efficiency
This will depend upon the precise method chosen for survey and the amount of dead wood present.

Once the method is understood, dead wood in a compartment can be quantified in 2.0–2.5 hours on site and 1.0–1.5 hours of calculations.

Dead wood: summary of key points

Recommended uses

- Surveying and monitoring dead wood is useful for assessing the habitat quality of a woodland, because dead wood provides niches for a wide variety of flora and fauna

Efficiency   Takes 2–4 hours to assess and analyse dead wood content in a compartment (see main text for details)

Objectivity   As it is impracticable to include every dead twig in a woodland, some arbitrary criteria for exclusion must be applied

Precision   Estimates of dead wood volume are based on the assumption of cylindrical shape; this is an approximation, but is likely to be sufficiently accurate for monitoring purposes

Bias   Overgrown dead wood is easily overlooked, leading to an underestimation of dead wood content. Dead wood on living trees is difficult to measure

Expertise required   No specialist expertise necessary

Equipment required   Basic woodland surveying equipment

Key methodological points to consider

- Dead wood is easily overlooked
- For monitoring purposes, a statistically sufficient sample must be taken each time a survey is carried out
- Safety should be considered when monitoring dead wood, particularly if assessing dead branches above head height or whole standing dead trees

Data analysis   Straightforward and reasonably quick to do; see main text for details

Expertise required

Basic field recording and transect or quadrat mapping techniques are necessary.

Equipment required

The equipment requirements for monitoring dead wood are summarised in Appendix 6.

Field methods

Fallen wood can be mapped and measured in representative plots. The plots should be at least 20 m wide. Select a convenient minimum size of dead wood to be recorded: a useful convention is all fallen stems attaining 1 m in length and 15 cm mid-diameter (those smaller than this are hard to find and only comprise a small proportion of the total volume). Each qualifying piece is then recorded by:

1. approximately mapping by locating its end points (for permanent plots);
2. measuring its length and mid-girth (or diameter if the log is partly buried); and
3. recording degree of decay on a four- or five-point scale.

Monitoring is achieved by repeating the survey. The volume of each piece can be calculated by assuming that it is a cylinder with the diameter of the mid-point. The time taken for each recording of each plot depends on the density of small pieces of dead wood. The time taken to compute results is facilitated by a spreadsheet. Transect sections (see Section 6.5.3) can conveniently be used as plots. In this instance, the stand data can be related to the dead wood data. A convenient assay of dead wood can be achieved by measuring the diameter of all pieces intersected by the boundaries between sections of the transect.

An alternative approach, the line transect method, has been developed from techniques for measuring logging waste. This is applicable to measuring all forms of dead wood in a compartment. Within the area to be assessed, ten 25 m transects are randomly located. Randomisation is achieved by locating initial points regularly by pacing, then selecting a compass direction for the transect by using random numbers, ensuring that each transect stays within the area to be assessed. Fallen wood is assessed by measuring the diameter of all pieces intersected by the tape marking the transect lines.

Box 6.22   Likely problems and solutions

The variation in size between large pieces of dead wood is high. These should probably be individually counted rather than averaged to avoid large amounts of variability in the data.

Stumps and snags can be assessed by measuring height and diameter of all those whose centres fall within 2 m of the transect line (i.e. within a belt 4 m wide). Likewise, dead wood in living trees can be assessed in all trees whose centres stand within the 4 m wide belts. Formulae are available for converting basic observations into length and volume per hectare. The principal difficulty lies in sampling the large logs, which are few, but important, and easily missed. Logs above 20 cm diameter may have to be individually assessed.

Rapid assessment of dead wood by using fixed-point photographs has proved to be impracticable. Even large logs can be lost in ground vegetation.

Data storage and analysis
Data storage
See Section 6.5.2.

Data analysis
Rapid assessment of the main dead wood elements at a compartment scale can be achieved by means of indices for each element. A five-point scale of quantity can be devised for each element, and the compartment being assessed can then be scored for each element. The sum of the indices gives a site dead wood index, which can be calibrated against actual estimates of volume. Speed of assessment is bought at the cost of accuracy. The method has yet to be fully developed.

Repeat surveys will give data for comparison with earlier surveys to monitor changes in the amount and type of dead wood present. The standard errors in this system may be large, so significant measurements of change may be difficult to achieve (see Box 6.22).

Summary of advantages and disadvantages
Advantages

• Measuring dead wood content gives extra information about habitat quality, which would otherwise not be recorded. This can be very useful when assessing the potential habitat for species that require some dead wood at some stage of their life cycle.

Disadvantages

• The standard errors in this method may be large, so significant measurements of change may be difficult to achieve.
• Dead wood is often easy to overlook, especially if overgrown by vegetation. This leads to biased results.

7 • Surveying and monitoring management or environmental impacts

As well as surveying and monitoring the condition of features of interest on a site, it is also often necessary to monitor the effects of management practices or environmental impacts. Management is usually carried out with the aim of achieving a particular target condition for a feature; for example, grazing might be introduced to maintain the species richness of a grassland, or burning might be carried out to rejuvenate a patch of moorland. It therefore follows that the impacts of management need to be monitored to ensure that management practices are having the desired effect. If management appears to be ineffective or has adverse effects, then the management regime can be appropriately adjusted. Records of past management practices and changes resulting from these are therefore vital if interventionist site management is to be more than a hit or miss affair. Building up a body of knowledge on the effects of different levels of grazing, burning, etc. on different habitats will enable management regimes to be sensitively designed. Monitoring non-management impacts such as those caused by erosion or unplanned fires is also important. Erosion is a naturally occurring process in some habitats, but may also be caused or exacerbated by management practices. Surveying and monitoring the effects of, for example, developments such as ports, marinas, airports, built development and associated infrastructure is now the norm, and yet few such studies exist to show the effects of such environmental impacts. Standardisation of the methods of data collection, as provided in this *Handbook*, and an increased importance placed on the publication of results in association with developments, will hopefully redress the balance in the coming years.

This section presents a summary of the management and environmental impacts that are most likely to be of concern when monitoring. An overview of the issues involved and a brief discussion of the key features that should be monitored, together with some pointers for monitoring techniques, is given. References are provided should any further details be required.

Recreational impact monitoring is not covered, but a useful review of the monitoring of trampling impacts can be found in Legg (2000).

7.1 GRAZING AND BROWSING

7.1.1 Background

Grazing and browsing are vital management requirements for many habitats, including heathlands, peatlands and grasslands. Grazing by domestic and wild animals can also influence the species composition and structure of most habitats.

Different herbivores have different plant preferences, feeding habits and dunging habits. The plant preferences of grazing animals can profoundly affect vegetation structure and composition. Stocking levels and seasonal grazing regimes have further impacts on a site, as do the inter-relationships between different herbivores that may be present on one site, including domestic stock such as sheep and cattle and wild animals such as deer, rabbits and voles. When monitoring the impact of grazing it may be necessary, in some situations, to be able to assess the relative importance of different grazers in determining the condition of the site. Supplementary feeding and shepherding influence ranging behaviour and hence affect the site and might also need to be monitored.

7.1.2   The effects of grazing and browsing

Digestibility and palatability of plants are important in determining the grazing influences of livestock. For example, areas of vegetation associated with flushes, or areas of vegetation on calcareous pockets within a site, are often relatively more attractive to grazing animals than are the surrounding habitats. Some species, particularly many grasses, sedges and rushes, are more resistant to grazing than others, and therefore may become more abundant in heavily grazed sites. These factors, as well as the feeding preferences of individual animals, can create a very varied pattern of vegetation throughout the whole site. Considerable differences in species composition, vegetation structure and height, amount of open and bare ground, and degree of damage to trees and shrubs through bark stripping can occur.

Undergrazing can allow rank grasses and unpalatable plants such as ragwort to spread (although under very low grazing pressure unpalatable plants may decline relative to competitive palatable species, which are no longer held in check by grazing). For example, the spread of trees and scrub onto heathland and grassland areas, particularly in lowland regions, has been linked with the decline of livestock grazing. It is also known that overgrazing of heathland can lead to the replacement of heather with grasses (Bardgett & Marsden,1992). Overgrazing can also lead to excessive poaching and weed invasion. Excessive browsing can completely prevent tree regeneration in woodlands. Patterns of damage to plants and the resulting growth responses can be distinctive and especially pronounced in trees and shrubs. These have been well described for heather: 'drumstick' growth occurs when mature heather is overgrazed, and 'topiary' growth (domed bushes) occurs when building-phase heather is overgrazed (MacDonald et al.,1998a,b).

The effects of grazing animals are, however, not limited to the direct effects of grazing on the plants themselves; they can also be very important for habitat attributes required by associated fauna (for example, heavy browsing of dwarf shrubs on moorland edges and in the field layer of pine woods has considerable detrimental effects on Black Grouse *Tetrao tetrix* and Capercaillie *Tetrao urogallus*). Larger animals, such as cattle and Red Deer *Cervus elaphus*, can open up vegetation through trampling and create bare areas, which can act as regeneration sites for plants. If this is particularly severe it can lead to soil erosion or the spread of undesirable species on to the site. Dunging can affect nutrient cycling, especially when it is concentrated in parts of a site, and again can cause problems if severe, for example through soil eutrophication. All of these elements need to be borne in mind when designing a monitoring programme for a site.

An important aspect of grazing and browsing impacts, from the point of view of monitoring design, is that they are always 'patchy' over a range of spatial scales, and rarely constant throughout the whole site.

7.1.3   Monitoring methods

Aerial photographs (Section 6.1.3) can be of use for the identification of historical changes in habitat (e.g. the spread or decline of trees or heathland). These changes can sometimes be linked to alterations in management regimes. If records of historical grazing regimes are available, the information gained from the study of past aerial photographs could be used to predict the results of future changes in grazing levels (although reversion to previous grazing regimes does not always lead to the recovery of the previous vegetation). However, it is very difficult to pick up from aerial photographs any subtle changes caused by grazing.

The majority of the monitoring of grazing will normally focus on grassland and heathland habitats. Tall herb communities, scrub (e.g. sub-Arctic willow scrub) and flushes can also be very sensitive to grazing and are likely to require monitoring in respect of this if they are features of interest on a site. The monitoring of wild grazing animals such as deer may also be very important in woodland and scrub habitats. In general, estimates of vegetation height, plant species richness, cover or frequency collected by using quadrats (Sections 6.4.2–6.4.5) or transects (Section 6.4.6) will be sufficient for most monitoring purposes. Vegetation height is a useful measurement of grazing intensity and is often under-recorded, even though it can be an important factor (for example, sward height of grazed grasslands can be of particular importance for the success of some butterfly species). Additional information on vegetation structure and amount of bare ground may also be of interest and should be collected if deemed necessary.

Depending on the reasons for monitoring, a number of aspects of grazing and associated land management activities may need to be noted. These may include:

- stocking rates and grazing periods;
- supplementary feeding;
- type of stock and breed;
- timing and rates of applications such as farmyard manure or lime;
- details of rolling, chain harrowing and burning;
- numbers and species of wild grazing and browsing animals; and
- control of pest species such as Rabbits *Oryctolagus cuniculus* and weeds such as Ragwort *Senecio jacobaea*.

It is probably best to record this information separately from any assessment of grazing impacts to avoid the possibility of biasing an observer's assessment.

An additional piece of information that can be useful is the pattern of use of the ground by stock. However, this information can be extremely time-consuming to obtain, and involves a number of site visits at different times of day and on different days. A simpler way of obtaining this information is from the assessment of impacts on the vegetation and/or patterns of dung distribution.

Approaches to monitoring grazing have been developed by MacDonald *et al.* (1998a,b) for SNH and by English Nature (1995). Although the former only covers upland habitats, the principles can be applied to lowland situations. The latter covers heather moorland. These two methods are described below.

SNH guide to surveying land management impacts in upland habitats (MacDonald *et al.*, 1998a,b)

Assessments are made of the condition of vegetation and ground features to determine whether land is heavily, moderately or lightly grazed. You should look for direct evidence of grazing impacts and base assessments only on this evidence, relying as little as possible on supposition (although you can use well-established knowledge of animal behaviour and ecological processes in order to interpret this evidence).

A detailed guide to the assessment method has been developed, which cannot be described here. However, the following features should be recorded:

Effects on soil:

- amount of bare ground, including trampled bare peat and sparseness of the vegetation;
- bare peat exposed by trampling, wallowing and rubbing by livestock and wild animals;
- percentage of poached ground;
- amount of dung deposited by different species of grazing animals; and
- extent of sheep, deer or cattle paths.

Effects on vegetation composition and community structure:

- sward height and structure;
- sward height of dwarf shrubs in associated grass patches;
- presence of seedlings and saplings above a certain height;
- presence of 'weedy' species in dense extensive patches;
- patches of taller vegetation, including tall herbs, ferns or tussocky grass; and
- cover and frequency of small, rosette-forming, creeping or mat-forming herbs.

Effects on plant growth and reproduction:

- the presence of topiary growth forms caused by the close grazing or browsing of saplings and bushes;
- browsing of seedlings or saplings;
- evidence of bark stripping;

- uprooted bundles of grass tillers;
- disruption of moss and liverwort carpets;
- accumulation of dead plant litter in the sward;
- amount of flowering of indicator species (e.g. cotton grass);
- signs of grazing on indicator species; and
- degree of flowering and vegetative state of potentially taller herbs.

Additional information on features such as the form of clipping of plants, the characteristics of severed shoots, and the height at which most signs of grazing or browsing occur can suggest which animals may be having the most impact.

Grazing index (English Nature, 1995)

The grazing index is a systematic and easy method of assessing the vegetation condition of heather moorland. It provides a rapid field assessment of the grazing level on a moorland and indicates if the area is likely to be under threat from heavy grazing pressure.

The heather moorland is divided into blocks of 10–50 ha; within each of these blocks an assessment is made by scoring three vegetation indicators while walking the land. Little botanical knowledge is required and a 50 ha block can be assessed in under 2 hours.

A 'W' or representative walk is conducted across the whole of the 'index unit' to make an assessment of the percentage of grasses and dwarf shrubs, and to identify the area of heather to be assessed at the next stage. Once the areas of heather have been identified, another 'W' or representative walk is made. This time, an assessment is made within each quadrat (size can be between 25×25 m^2 and 2×2 m^2) of the percentage cover of *Calluna vulgaris* and other ericoid shrubs. While walking this heather area, the surveyor also assesses the age structure and growth forms of heather. Guidance should be given on the recognition of features that indicate heavy grazing (e.g. lack of regenerating heather, or drumstick and topiary growth forms).

A score is calculated for each block of heathland surveyed (see English Nature (1995) for details). The grazing index score is the sum of the scores for each of the component blocks, which is then compared to a graduated scale, which in turn indicates the intensity of grazing.

Although relatively simple, the grazing index method has a number of limitations. First, it relies on only a relatively small number of grazing indicators. Second, no distinction is made between past and current grazing intensity; some sites will have become grass-dominated a long time ago and have little prospect of reverting to heather in the foreseeable future even if current grazing pressure is low. Third, the percentage of grass to heather is used as an indicator, but very recent heavy grazing may cause a significant detrimental impact on heather without immediately having much effect on the heather–grass balance. Finally, the grazing index is an average, which can be misleading as heather areas often shrink from the edge where grazing is high, whereas grazing intensity in the centre of heather stands is much lower. Such averages are of limited use unless the grazing pressure is extremely high, as it is in many parts of England and Wales. In regions or habitats where grazing levels are generally low the use of the grazing index is not recommended.

7.2   BURNING

7.2.1   Background

Burning is practised frequently and widely over a wide range of vegetation types. It is most commonly employed as a management technique in the uplands, mainly for the maintenance of grouse moors. The burning of heather stimulates new growth and rejuvenates the heather sward, although if large areas are burned it will result in the loss of age-structure diversity. Burning is also widely practised on sheep walks and deer forest.

Burning is also employed to improve the grazing quality of hill land by stimulating a new flush of grass growth, and can also be used to bring rough grassland back into condition before the reintroduction of grazing. Unplanned fires often occur in a range of habitats, but dwarf-shrub heathlands are particularly vulnerable.

7.2.2   The impact of burning

The degree of the impact caused by burning will depend on a number of factors but it is primarily influenced by the amount and distribution of fuel material on the site and weather conditions at the time of the fire. This is influenced by the habitat type, vegetation composition and structure, and also by the current management regime operating on the site.

The impact of the fire will be further influenced by the amount of moisture present in the surface layers of soil or peat, the wetness of the vegetation and the amount of litter on the site. Fire impact is also affected by the ability of species either to avoid fire damage or to recover from it. Resilience to burning varies between species and according to the age and size of the plant. Flowering and seed production of some plant species is often enhanced after burning, which can help to promote rapid recovery through the establishment of seedlings even if vegetative recovery is slow. Burning can also remove the litter layer and thereby create gaps, which offer further opportunities for the establishment of new plants.

Monitoring of intentional, accidental and 'wild' fires should be carried out to determine:

- the geographical extent and intensity of burns, and to evaluate the immediate effect of a fire on vegetation and ground condition, particularly peat and litter;
- the recovery of vegetation following a burn;
- the cumulative impacts of repeated fires; and
- beneficial changes to future management practices (e.g. the identification of suitable areas of mature vegetation that might be protected from burning, or the identification of areas that might benefit from regular burning).

7.2.3   Monitoring methods

Monitoring requirements will vary from site to site; most of the techniques for monitoring of vegetation changes have already been described in previous sections. Fires often have sharply defined boundaries, which can make the monitoring of extent more straightforward. The features to be monitored listed below are taken from the method developed by MacDonald *et al.* (1998a,b) for SNH. Although this guide specifically covers uplands, most of the principles also apply to the lowland situation.

Although the sampling techniques described are not principally designed for monitoring, the indicators of burn intensity can form a measurement basis for quantitative monitoring if used in conjunction with quadrats (Section 6.4.2) or transects (Section 6.4.6). Photographs can also be used to make methods more repeatable. The impact assessment methods described are relatively quick to undertake but some are not tightly defined. Some judgement is required, and this makes the assessment more difficult to repeat exactly.

It is important to note that information on other management activities that may also occur on the site following a burn will also need to be collected, especially grazing regimes, mowing cycles and pollution. These activities will considerably affect the recovery of vegetation and will possibly influence decisions taken on the future management of the site.

Monitoring the geographical extent of burns

The best method for measuring the extent of a burn, particularly large-scale burns, is the use of aerial photographs (Section 6.1.3). However, these will usually have to be specially obtained for this purpose as soon as possible after the burn, thus increasing the costs of monitoring. Burns on dwarf-shrub-dominated heathland should be discernible on aerial photographs for at least 5 years.

Existing aerial photographs can be helpful in identifying the extent of past burns. This will enable the impacts of fires over a longer time period to be examined. Fixed-point photography (Section 6.1.4) can also be used, although markers will have to be selected after a burn has occurred and will not therefore yield any data on the effects of the fire.

Simply walking across the site to record impacts will yield useful information, and will probably be required in any case to record additional information other than the extent of burns. This is best undertaken with annotated aerial photographs to aid orientation and accurate mapping, and needs to be systematic if the impact on the entire site is to be described.

In heath vegetation with a high proportion of graminoids (especially Purple Moor-grass *Molinia caerulea*) it can be very difficult to identify burnt areas on aerial photographs after the year in which the fire occurs. There is much less contrast in colour and structure between burnt patches and the surrounding area than there is in vegetation dominated by heather. This is because *Molinia* regenerates rapidly after burning; burnt areas in this type of vegetation can be hard to identify even from the ground.

Fires can also be hard to identify on aerial photographs where they have burned in an irregular pattern (light and/or fast-moving fires often burn patchily) or have burned through patchy vegetation. However, these fires can usually be readily identified on the ground for several years after they occur.

To determine burn intensity and evaluate the immediate effects of a fire on vegetation and ground condition, the following checklist gives some of the main factors that need to be recorded to categorise the intensity and frequency of burns (adapted from MacDonald *et al.* (1998a,b)):

- pattern of fire advance;
- colour of burnt patches immediately after burning;
- extent of bare peat, erosion and exposed mineral soils;
- degree of combustion or 'cooking' of the surface and upper layers of peat;
- solidity and texture of the upper peat layers;
- amount of ash, and amount and size of charcoal fragments, immediately after burning;
- damage and degree of combustion of loose moss mats, lichens, plant litter, grass tussocks and woody material;
- effects of fire on any bushes and trees; and
- survival of clubmosses and ferns.

These points mostly relate to blanket bog and upland heath, where burning is most frequently encountered. However, some of these features can

also be used to monitor the impact of fire on other habitats.

Monitoring the recovery of vegetation following a burn

This is best achieved through the use of quadrats (Section 6.4.2) or transects (Section 6.4.6). Changes in cover of plant species or groups should be recorded at regular intervals to examine the changes that take place before and after a burn. Alternatively, presence–absence or frequency of key species can be recorded in the same way.

Bryophytes and lichens can be important groups to record; for example, the recovery of *Sphagnum* mosses is particularly important in bog and other mire habitats. Other important indicators of the speed of recovery of vegetation are the amount of bare ground present after the burn and the speed at which it is colonised by plants.

If permanent plots are used for monitoring, then the use of metal posts or buried markers is recommended, as wooden posts can easily be lost if further fires occur at the site. A range of burned areas may need to be examined to cover the variety of impacts caused by variation in fire intensity, vegetation type, soil type, etc.

Particular features that may be worth recording include:

- pattern of colonisation and regrowth after burning;
- occurrence of indicator species (normally lichens and mosses) that appear after a burn;
- amount of regeneration, and whether this occurs from seed or from sprouting stems;
- extent, diversity and luxuriance of mosses, including *Sphagnum* mosses;
- relative structural dominance of dwarf shrubs compared with certain grasses;
- abundance of certain grasses and vascular plants;
- abundance and luxuriance of certain *Cladonia* lichens;
- relative abundance of different dwarf-shrub species;
- abundance of dwarf-shrub seedlings in years after burning; and
- average density of vascular plant species.

7.3   EROSION

7.3.1   Background

Erosion can occur on a wide range of scales, from localised bank erosion caused by cattle poaching or stream flow to the large-scale loss of vegetation and topsoil resulting in the loss of large areas of habitat.

Peat soils, in particular, can be particularly susceptible to erosion once their protective vegetative cover is removed. Consequently erosion is most widespread, and is often most severe, on blanket bog habitats (Section 5.12). Some types of friable upland soils found on a number of mountains in north-west Scotland are also very vulnerable to erosion once the overlying vegetation mat is disrupted.

Erosion can also occur on steep slopes if the underlying substrate is susceptible (e.g. very friable soils with low shear strength, on account of a low clay content). Exceptional weather conditions, such as heavy rainstorms, can produce unusually high hydrological loading of the soil, which further weakens its cohesion. Heavy grazing, trampling, and frequent or high-intensity burning may further weaken and destabilise the soil. This type of erosion most commonly occurs on valley sides and cliff faces. Poor drainage can be another cause of erosion. Gullying can be caused by artificial drains if they lead into, and overload, an existing water track.

Sand dune habitats are also susceptible to erosion, but dunes are naturally dynamic, particularly in the earlier stages of dune succession, so erosion is not inherently a problem. Problems with erosion on sand dunes tend to be correlated with areas subject to high visitor pressure.

7.3.2   The impacts of erosion

At its most destructive, erosion can cause the loss of not just vegetation but entire soil profiles and rock faces. Following the initial onset of erosion, the affected area can increase in size substantially until a natural equilibrium is reached or management is undertaken to stabilise the erosion. Whole vegetation communities can disappear and species can be threatened. Structures such as paths and tracks, stock fences and interpretative features can all be swept away or undermined.

However, some species rely on ground disturbance for survival and cannot persist in more stable habitats. Some species of conservation concern can therefore benefit from certain erosion events (for example, many plant species in the East Anglian Brecklands are dependent on vegetation disturbance by intensive rabbit burrowing or rotavation to keep their ecological niches open).

The monitoring of erosion should therefore be carried out to:

- monitor the spread of the problem, or the degree of stabilisation, so that appropriate action can be taken (e.g. the construction of stabilisation structures);
- determine the rate of vegetation recovery so that any further work that may be required can be identified (e.g. vegetation establishment);
- identify possible future threats to adjacent habitats and species; and
- identify dangerous areas where access by members of the public and others may need to be restricted.

7.3.3   Monitoring methods

This is best achieved by referring to some of the methods outlined in Chapter 6. Aerial (Section 6.1.3) and fixed-point (Section 6.1.4) photography can be particularly useful for delimiting areas affected by erosion in the first instance and for monitoring the spread or stabilisation of eroding areas over time.

For more precise recording of the speed of erosion it may be worth considering placing markers along some or all of the erosion fronts. At the most basic level, these can be simple wooden posts spaced at regular intervals, but more sophisticated calibrated measuring devices can be used to measure loss of soil or peat from the ground surface. Problems can arise, however, if the substrate is in danger of further erosion or slippage, and the potential dangers of firstly placing the markers and subsequently reading them should be borne in mind.

The risks may be potentially too great for monitoring erosion from the ground, particularly on steep slopes. Binoculars may be useful to take measurements from calibrated markers at a safe distance.

Another monitoring method that is normally worth considering is the recording of vegetation recovery on eroded ground. This is most frequently undertaken through the use of quadrats (Section 6.4.2) or transects (Section 6.4.6), although this can also be dangerous in certain circumstances and should not be attempted on dangerous terrain. If the eroded ground is stable enough for work to be carried out safely, cover estimates or presence–absence of certain species can be made (see Sections 6.4.2 and 6.4.3) to gain some idea of the speed of vegetation recovery and the successional relationships between the plant communities that colonise the disturbed areas.

7.4   VEGETATION SURVEYS IN RELATION TO DEVELOPMENTS

There are a number of reasons why vegetation surveys are required in relation to development proposals as part of the planning and development control process. Most development proposals that have the potential to affect habitats, either voluntarily or as a planning application requirement under domestic or European conservation legislation, will need a vegetation survey. The survey is normally included as part of an ecology chapter of the Environmental Statement (ES) or Environmental Impact Assessment (EIA). If the planning application for the development is successful there will then often be the need to:

(a) survey the development site (and off-site areas if potential off-site impacts have been identified at the ES survey stage), prior to the development and during it to prevent encroachment of the development footprint and construction activities into areas of habitat identified by the ES as being of conservation or ecological interest (with habitat evaluated at local, regional, national and international scales);

(b) survey particular areas prior to the writing and implementing of a plan for the translocation of specific species, communities or habitats of noted value;

(c) provide data on successive changes in habitat areas and condition during the course of development;

(d) monitor habitat areas and condition for a period after construction;

(e) monitor habitat mitigation and/or creation.

It is usual for such survey and monitoring work to be made a 'planning condition' associated with a planning permission, often being legally binding through a Section 106 Agreement or Unilateral Undertaking.

The majority of the survey work outlined in (a–e) above takes the form of a map of the habitats, communities or specific target species on the site and any off-site areas to which impacts from the development may be exported through, for example, habitat fragmentation, diffuse pollution, dust, etc. An extended Phase I survey with target notes and condition assessment would be the usual approach for development related impact assessment. In addition, it may be necessary and appropriate to measure vegetation attributes such as cover, height, soil moisture, etc., as a development progresses in order to determine whether pervasive impacts are taking place. The relevant chapters and sections of the *Handbook* should be consulted for the specific objectives and focus of the impact assessment work.

8.1 KEY EVALUATION CONSIDERATIONS

The conservation importance of habitats occurring in the UK has generally been assessed in terms of the threat status of each habitat type, where attributes such as rarity and rate of decline (of overall area) have been taken into account. In terms of evaluating the conservation importance of any particular habitat type, reference must be made to international and national conservation legislation and initiatives such as the UK Biodiversity Action Plan (UK BAP) process, described further below.

The key considerations with regards to evaluating habitats are listed below.

1. Check lists of habitats of conservation importance (see below for information on which lists to check and where to obtain the relevant information).
2. Check existing designation status: for EIAs (see Box 8.1), the search area should extend to 2 km from the boundary of the site. This will inform the results of the Phase 1 survey and highlight areas of habitat on or near the site that are within the boundaries of statutory or non-statutory designations.
3. Carry out a preliminary (scoping) survey for habitats. This will normally be a Phase I habitat survey (see Section 6.1.5) to identify the broad habitat types present on site.

These three steps should enable the determination of Valuable Ecosystem Components (VECs) (in terms of habitat types) that may *potentially* be present. To establish the *actual* presence or absence of a VEC, further survey may be necessary; for habitats, a National Vegetation Classification (NVC) survey (Rodwell, 1991) is recommended. Habitats listed in European legislation have been interpreted in terms of the NVC classification; the definitions of priority habitats for conservation in the UK also use this system.

Habitats can often be of value to particular species, rare or otherwise, for example because an area of habitat supports a viable population of the species. However, this chapter is concerned with the intrinsic value of habitat types, rather than with their value for species.

8.2 PROTECTION STATUS IN THE UK AND EU

With regards to the protection of habitats, the following legislation is relevant:

- EU Directive 92/43/EEC on the Conservation of Natural Habitats and of Wild Flora and Fauna (the Habitats Directive);
- Wildlife & Countryside Act 1981;
- Countryside & Rights of Way Act 2000 (Section 74); and
- Nature Conservation (Scotland) Act 2004.

The criteria for listing habitats on Annex I of the EU Habitats Directive are summarised in Part I of this Handbook, as are the site designation criteria for SACs. The full text of the Habitats Directive can be viewed on www.ecnc.nl/doc/europe/legislat/habidire.html, which gives the list of Annex I habitats. Similarly, the rationale for the selection of SSSIs under the Wildlife & Countryside Act (1981, as amended) is also relevant; the Guidelines for the Selection of Biological SSSIs can be viewed on the JNCC website at www.jncc.gov.uk/Publications/sssi/sssi_content.htm.

Section 74 of the CROW Act requires the Secretary of State for England and the National

Assembly for Wales to each publish a list of species and habitat types that are of principal importance for the conservation of biological diversity in England and Wales, respectively. The Section 74 list for England can be viewed on the DEFRA webpage www.defra.gov.uk/wildlife-countryside/cl/habitats/habitats-list.pdf. The equivalent list for Wales can be viewed on the National Assembly for Wales website on the following webpage: www.wales.gov.uk/subienvironment/content/guidance/species-statement-e.htm.

These two lists are based on UK Biodiversity Action Plan (UK BAP) Priority Habitats and Species lists. In England, the list of Section 74 Habitats consists of the full list of UK BAP Priority Habitats with two additions ('Lowland Mixed Deciduous Woodland' and 'Upland Birch Woodland'). In Wales, the list of Section 74 Habitats comprises the UK BAP Priority Habitats list with the same two additions ('Lowland Mixed Deciduous Woodland' and 'Upland Birch Woodland') but also seven deletions (reflecting the fact these habitat types do not occur in Wales): 'Chalk Rivers', 'Upland Hay Meadows', Littoral and Sublittoral Chalk', 'Lophelia pertusa Reefs', 'Serpulid Reefs', 'Machair' and 'Native Pine Woodlands'. There is currently no equivalent legislation for other countries within the UK.

8.3   CONSERVATION STATUS IN THE UK

The evaluation of Valued Ecosystem Components (VECs) (both habitats and species) for EIAs should ideally follow the approach outlined in Part I of this *Handbook*, based on IEEM guidelines (2002), which recommend grading the importance of sites or components thereof against the following levels of value:

1. International;
2. National;
3. Regional;
4. County/Metropolitan;
5. District/Borough;
6. Parish/Neighbourhood.

The generic evaluation section in Part I provides examples, at each level of value for both habitats and species, which take into account the size (and

therefore viability) of areas of habitat when attempting to rank examples of different habitat types against each other. Box 8.2 provides a real example of the use of Ratcliffe criteria to assess a range of vegetation types as part of an EIA.

Habitats found on a site should be evaluated in relation to the habitat types listed on Annex 1 of the EU Habitats Directive and the UK BAP (Section 74) Priority Habitats lists. Local biodiversity partnerships may also have published, through the production of local BAPs, lists of habitats of local conservation importance that, if available, should also be used for evaluation purposes. Guidelines for the selection of sites of conservation importance at a County level may also be available from the Local Authority or Wildlife Trust.

Habitat types found on a site that are listed as habitats of conservation importance will generally rank higher than types that are not, and habitats of international conservation concern will rank higher than those of national concern or local concern. However, a small patch of an otherwise nationally or internationally important habitat type may not be a viable area of habitat, and as such may rank lower than a large, ecologically viable area of a locally important habitat type. Reference should also be made to the Ratcliffe criteria (size, diversity, naturalness, rarity, fragility and typicalness as primary criteria, and recorded history, position in an ecological/geographical unit, potential value and intrinsic value as secondary criteria) when considering the value of areas of habitat.

Habitat types to be valued as being of international importance include:

- An internationally designated site or candidate site (SAC, cSAC, etc);
- A viable area of a habitat type listed in Annex I of the Habitats Directive, or a smaller area of such habitat which is essential to maintain the viability of a larger whole.

Habitats of national value include:

- A nationally designated site (SSSI, ASSI, NNR etc) or a discrete area, which the country conservation agency has determined meets the published selection criteria for national designation, irrespective of whether or not it has yet been notified;

- A viable area of a priority habitat identified in the UK BAP (or Section 74 for England or Wales), or of smaller areas of such habitat which are essential to maintain the viability of a larger whole.

Habitats deemed to be of regional importance would include the following:

- Viable areas of key habitat identified in the Regional BAP or smaller areas of such habitat which are essential to maintain the viability of a larger whole;
- Viable areas of key habitat identified as being of Regional value in the appropriate Natural Area profile;
- Sites which exceed the County-level designations but fall short of SSSI selection guidelines, where these occur.

Habitats of county/metropolitan importance include:

- Semi-natural ancient woodland greater than 0.25 ha;
- County/metropolitan sites and other sites that the designating authority has determined meet the published criteria for designation, including Local Nature Reserves selected on county/metropolitan criteria (these will often have been identified in local plans);
- A viable area of a habitat type identified in a county BAP.

Areas of habitat with district/borough importance include the following examples:

- Semi-natural ancient woodland smaller than 0.25 ha;
- Areas of habitat identified in a sub-county (district/borough) BAP or in the relevant EN Natural Area profile;
- District sites that the designating authority has determined meet the published criteria for designation, including Local Nature Reserves selected on district/borough criteria;
- A diverse and/or ecologically valuable hedgerow network.

Habitats of parish/neighbourhood value include areas of habitats considered to appreciably enrich the habitat resource within the context of the parish or neighbourhood, such as species-rich hedgerows. Note that species-rich hedgerows may come under the Hedgerow Regulations, requiring their removal to be approved through the planning process.

Unlike for species, the above list does not mention the IUCN Red Data Books. Part I of this *Handbook* provides an overview of the programme for species, which are assessed in terms of their threat status. Currently, there is no direct equivalent for habitats. However, the feasibility of a Red Data Book for NVC vegetation types is currently being researched, with the aim of providing information on the rarity or otherwise of different NVC communities. In the meantime, the NVC books themselves (Rodwell *et al.*, 1991 *et seq.*) can be consulted as a guide to the extent of different communities. However, the 'distribution maps' associated with each community are very incomplete and the text gives a better guide. For example, compare the distribution map for U20 (*Pteridium aquilinum – Galium saxatile*) on page 498 of NVC Volume 3 (Grasslands and Montane Communities) with the text on the distribution of the community on page 495. The SSSI selection guidelines also give an indication of the rarity of different NVC communities, stipulating in some cases that all occurrences of a particular community type are eligible for SSSI selection, for example S24 *Phragmites australis – Peucedanum palustre* fen.

Using Annex I of the EU Habitats Directive for habitat evaluation

In the UK, these habitat types have been interpreted in terms of the National Vegetation Classification (NVC) (Rodwell 1991 *et seq*). The JNCC Report by Jackson & McLeod (2002), provides an overview of current knowledge on aspects of the conservation status in the UK of habitats (in terms of range and extent) and species (in terms of distribution and estimated population size) that are listed on Annex I and II of the EU Habitats Directive. For habitats, it also provides guidelines on the relationship between NVC types and Annex I habitat types. This report is also currently available on the JNCC website: www.jncc.gov.uk/Publications/JNCC312/default.htm.

As noted above, in order to fully evaluate the habitat types found on a site in relation to the EU Habitats Directive, an NVC survey is required. Therefore, if the Phase I habitat survey carried out as part of a scoping survey for a site suggests that an Annex I habitat may be present, an NVC survey should be conducted as part of the evaluation, to determine the presence or absence of habitats of European conservation importance. For example, a Phase I survey may show the presence of Wet Dwarf Shrub Heath on a site situated on the north Cornwall coast. This heathland may be one of the NVC community types M14, M15, M16 or H5, in which case the heathland may be the EU habitat type 'Temperate Atlantic wet heaths with *Erica ciliaris* and *Erica tetralix*'.

Using the UK BAP Priority Habitats (Section 74 Habitats) for evaluating habitats

The UK BAP Priority Habitats list, from which the Section 74 habitat lists for England and Wales are derived, are defined within a wider framework of Broad Habitat types that are largely comparable with the Phase I Survey habitat categories (NCC, 1990a,b). Within each Broad Habitat type are one or more Priority Habitat types (i.e. habitats of UK conservation importance), some of which are extensively defined and some of which are very narrowly defined. For example, 'Lowland Calcareous Grassland' is classified as the first nine calcareous grassland NVC communities (CG1 – CG9) and in essence includes all types of calcareous grassland that occur in the lowlands. In contrast, 'Upland Hay Meadows' comprises the single NVC community MG3 *Anthoxanthum odoratum – Geranium sylvaticum* grassland. As such, UK BAP Broad and Priority Habitats can often be identified through a Phase I Survey. However, for some Priority Habitats, an NVC survey will be needed to determine the presence or absence of a particular UK BAP Priority Habitat type. The JNCC has recently published an updated version of its 'Phase I Habitat Survey' methodology, which includes an appendix giving the relationship between Phase I habitat categories and NVC communities (JNCC, 1993). This may help in the assessment of habitats against UK BAP and Annex I lists.

The criteria used to list UK BAP Priority Habitats can be found in Part I of this *Handbook*. A full list of UK BAP Priority Habitats is provided in Appendix 2. The list of UK BAP Broad and Priority Habitats can be found at www.ukbap.org.uk/habitats.htm.

Using the local BAP process to evaluate habitats

The local BAP process was developed as part of the UK BAP to implement habitat and species action plans at a local level. In addition to setting targets for the implementation of action plans for UK BAP Priority Habitats, many local BAP groups have listed and produced action plans for habitats deemed to be of conservation importance at a local level. These lists, if available, should be used to evaluate habitat types that do not fall within the national or international levels of value, as illustrated above. However, it must be noted that at the local level, habitats are often included in local BAPs on the basis of their value for species, rather than their intrinsic value. For example, the Merthyr Tydfil Biodiversity Action Plan (South Wales) includes an action plan for Coniferous Woodland because it often supports important populations of Crossbill *Loxia curvirostra*, Nightjar *Caprimulgus europaeus*, Siskin and various birds of prey such as Goshawk *Accipiter gentilis*, each of which has a particular level of conservation significance in the UK.

The definitions of these local habitat types are usually based on the UK BAP Broad Habitat types. As such, a Phase I Habitat Survey should identify the presence of these habitats on a site.

Box 8.1 Suggested methodology for checking existing designations

The MAGIC project (Multi-Agency Geographical Information for the Countryside) is a one-stop shop for rural and countryside information from the partner organisations (e.g. conservation agencies). It brings together definitive rural designation boundaries and information about rural land-based schemes into one place and can be used as the starting point for checking the presence or absence of statutory sites of nature conservation interest. The website (http://www.magic.gov.uk/) can provide information about statutory designations on or near a particular site, as well as other countryside information, such as English Nature Natural Areas.

Currently, the procedure for obtaining information pertaining to a particular site is as follows (from the MAGIC website homepage).

1. Click on 'Site Map'.
2. Click on 'Interactive Map'.
3. Under Step 1, highlight 'Design my own topic'.
4. Tick layers to be viewed: these should include all statutory designations at a minimum: National Nature Reserves, National Parks (including provisional), Ramsar Sites (for birds), Sites of Special Scientific Interest, Special Areas of Conservation and Special Protection Areas (for birds). Other layers may be useful for the evaluation of particular species or groups of species, for example RSPB Reserves.
5. When the layers have been selected, click on 'Save Selection, then 'Done'.

6. Under Step 2, select (for example) 'Grid Ref' and enter the grid reference for the site in question, then click on 'Open Map'.
7. Wait for the map to load: this may take a while depending on how many layers have been selected.
8. Information about the various layers can be found by clicking on the 'i' symbol at the top of the map, selecting the layer required and then clicking on the feature on the map. For example, the name of a SSSI can be obtained by selecting 'Sites of Special Scientific Interest' and clicking within the SSSI boundary shown on the interactive map.

When carrying out an evaluation for an EIA, statutory designations within 2 km of the site boundary should be considered. SSSI citations can be obtained from the country agencies (for some agencies, this information is available on their website). By clicking on 'Protected Sites' on the JNCC website (http://www.jncc.gov.uk/), further information about international designations such as SACs can similarly be obtained.

Non-statutory designations, such as County Wildlife Sites (CWS, also known as Sites of Interest for Nature Conservation, SINC, and Sites of Nature Conservation Interest, SNCI) are not currently available online. Therefore the local Wildlife Trust will need to be consulted regarding the presence or absence of local wildlife sites on or near a site (up to 2 km from the site boundary for EIAs). The local Trust should also be able to provide the criteria for selecting local wildlife sites and the reasons for selecting individual sites. Once again, this information will inform the evaluation of the importance of various habitat types in a local context.

Box 8.2   Examples of assessment of vegetation types

The following examples, modified from a real EIA, show how the Ratcliffe criteria can be used to place vegetation and habitats in context.

The meadows present in the EIA study area were assessed for nature conservation importance by using the standard criteria (Ratcliffe, 1977).

In addition, reference was made to the survey of unimproved neutral grasslands in East Sussex (Steven, 1990) to give local context. This survey mainly concentrated on the Weald, often by a field-by-field search; wet meadows were poorly covered. No meadows in the EIA study area were included in the register.

MG1 *ARRHENATHERUM ELATIUS* GRASSLAND

Arrhenatherum elatius grasslands are characterised by dominant *Arrhenatherum*, *Dactylis glomerata*, *Holcus lanatus* and *Heracleum sphondylium*. They occur on freely draining to seasonally moist soils which are weakly acidic to calcareous, and which are often moderately or strongly nutrient-rich. They are usually ungrazed, but may be mown. They are widespread in lowland Britain on roadsides, banks, neglected pastures, etc. (Rodwell *et al.*, 1991 *et seq.*). Although they are a fairly natural vegetation type and are often fairly species-rich, they are thought to be a considerably modified NVC type, with generally low botanical interest (NCC, 1989). They are common in Britain.

In the study area, these grasslands occurred mainly on the roadsides and in a few neglected fields. No species-rich examples or areas of large extent occur. They are considered to be of Parish/Neighbourhood value.

MG5 *CYNOSURUS CRISTATUS – CENTAUREA NIGRA* MEADOW AND PASTURE

These grasslands are characterised by *Festuca rubra*, *Cynosurus cristatus*, *Lotus corniculatus*, *Plantago lanceolata*, *Dactylis glomerata*, *Holcus lanatus*, *Trifolium repens*, *Centaurea nigra*, *Agrostis stolonifera*, *Anthoxanthum odoratum* and *Trifolium pratense*. They are typically species-rich pastures but can be quite variable in composition. They occur on soils that are not high in nutrients, neither acid nor alkaline, and which are freely drained.

They have usually not been sprayed with herbicide, and they receive either little or no fertiliser. They are usually cut for hay, and are ungrazed in summer but may be grazed in winter (Rodwell *et al.*, 1991 *et seq.*). They are still locally frequent nationally but have declined dramatically owing to agricultural intensification.

These are the commonest of the unimproved meadows in East Sussex (Steven, 1990); there were many hay meadows of this type in the study area. Most examples were of the widespread MG5a *Lathyrus pratensis* sub-community. These ranged from species-poor to more species-rich. Most examples were small and partly improved and were of Parish/Neighbourhood value only, but the more species-rich, probably unimproved examples may be of County/Metropolitan importance. The best example at Home Farm, Ambridge, is designated a SSSI as a hay meadow and is of National Importance.

One example of the less common type, MG5c *Danthonia decumbens* sub-community, was found. This is known from at least nine other sites (total 29.8 ha) in East Sussex. The meadow found was a moderate area (5 ha) on a steep slope within a large, partly improved MG5a example, and was assessed as of District/Borough value.

MG7 *LOLIUM PERENNE* LEYS

Lolium perenne leys are characterised by dominant *Lolium perenne* associated variably with *Phleum pratense*, *Poa trivialis*, *Trifolium repens*, *Dactylis glomerata*, *Alopecurus pratensis*, *Plantago* species, *Taraxacum* species and other nitrophilous herbaceous plants. They are typically very species-poor communities characteristic of the more nutrient-rich and heavily improved soils of medium pH, which are usually well-drained. They are either heavily grazed or are cut for hay or silage. They are the predominant, modern agricultural pasture in lowland Britain (Rodwell *et al.*, 1991 *et seq.*). They are generally highly improved, species-poor, and intensively managed. This is considered to be a considerably modified NVC type, with generally low botanical interest (NCC, 1989).

The examples in the study are of very low interest and therefore classified as being of negligible conservation interest.

Part III • Species

9 • Introduction to species assessment

9.1 SPECIES SURVEYING AND MONITORING

Chapter 10 of this part gives an introduction to the theory and principles of population survey and monitoring and describes the general methods used to estimate population size. These methods will often need to be tailored to suit the requirements of the species being studied; this information is provided in the sections on species groups.

Chapters 11–26 contain details of the standard methods used to survey each group of species, from fungi to mammals. Attributes that provide an indication of the condition of species in each group are identified at the start of each chapter, and methodologies for monitoring these attributes are described; references for further information are listed at the end of the book. Specific recommendations and current survey and monitoring protocols for selected species that occur in the UK and appear on Annex II of the EU Habitats and Species Directive (apart from vagrant and introduced species) are described at the ends of these chapters.

Each section contains a table summarising the methods covered. A brief summary of the following points is given:

- the recommended groups for which the method is appropriate;
- the type of data that the method provides (i.e. presence/absence, population size, etc.);
- the efficiency of the method, i.e. the combined quantity and quality of data produced in relation to cost and effort;
- the precision obtainable;
- the likely nature of any inherent bias; and
- advantages and disadvantages.

Each method is then described in three sections: (1) principles; (2) field methods; and (3) data analysis and interpretation. Data analysis is covered in Part I, Section 2.6, and Appendix 2. The data analysis sections in this part therefore refer to these sections unless other analysis specific to the method is required. However, it should be remembered that other tests may be appropriate; the reader should refer to Section 2.6 for a fuller discussion of data analysis.

The availability of suitable habitat is a key attribute defining the condition of a species. Species monitoring will therefore require the monitoring of the condition of their habitats: refer to Part II for general habitat monitoring methods. This attribute is generally not dealt with in this part, although it is referred to for species that are very sensitive to small changes in habitat condition, such as many lichens. In such cases, regular monitoring of habitat condition is of critical importance, but it may not necessarily require the use of techniques described in Part II.

When using this *Handbook* as a guide for selecting survey and monitoring methods and designing sampling schemes, you should look up the species that are to be surveyed in Chapters 11–26. The tables at the start of these chapters list the appropriate methods for surveying them. Consult the relevant sections, and then return to Part I to follow the steps for designing a survey and monitoring programme and sampling scheme (if the appropriate method requires it).

Having described the survey and monitoring methods available for each species group there is then a section describing how data collected can be used in the conservation evaluation of the species group, whether for site evaluation for EIA or conservation status assessment. A generic description of evaluation is given in Part I of this *Handbook*.

10.1 INTRODUCTION

This section describes some general principles and methods that are applicable to many of the species groups covered in Chapters 11–26. Methods have been divided into several broad groups. These include total counts and methods that sample species over defined areas or periods of time or both. There is, however, some overlap between them. For example, quadrats may be sampled along a transect; fixed-radius point counts can be construed as circular quadrats. Where necessary, the reader will be referred to the relevant chapters.

Methods may be loosely divided into those for sedentary species and those for mobile species. Sedentary species are often easier to sample. Quadrats may be used because, given enough time, all the individuals in a sample area can be counted. In contrast, mobile species may flee from observers.

When sampling an area for mobile species, it is necessary to obtain a 'snapshot' of how many individuals exist in that area before they move significantly, or react to the presence of the observer. For a strip transect, density can be estimated by dividing the number of individuals seen by the area of the transect. However, this estimate will be biased downwards if you are more likely to miss individuals that are further away from you as you make the observations.

If it is likely that individuals are being missed then it is worth considering distance sampling methods. Distance sampling is a generic method of estimating density, commonly applied to mobile animals, which takes into account the fact that individuals are often less detectable when they are further away from the observer. Distances to individuals are estimated from a fixed line (line transects) or a point (point counts). Estimates of density can be calculated by adjusting for the fall-off in detection with distance from the line or point. Software has been developed to allow relatively simple analysis of sophisticated distance sampling methods (see Section 10.6).

In many cases, it is possible to employ a range of different methods simultaneously to maximise available data collection. For example, all quadrat and transect methods can be applied to several species at once.

The other methods covered in this chapter are trapping webs, the removal method (used mainly for estimating fish populations sampled with electrofishing), and mark–recapture techniques.

10.2 TERMINOLOGY

There are some inconsistencies in the names given to different point and transect methods in the literature. To clarify and standardise these terms, an illustration of the different transect and point methods and a summary of the nomenclature used in this *Handbook* is provided in Figure 10.1. We have chosen to differentiate one-dimensional transects, in which contacts are only recorded on the line, continuously or intermittently, as line intercept and point intercept transects, respectively. Belt transects are lines of contiguous or spaced-frame quadrats, whereas strip transects are very long, thin quadrats. 'Line transect' refers only to transects in which distances are measured from the line to objects (either exactly or by grouping them into bands). Point counts, in which objects are counted from a fixed point, are also referred to as 'point transects' in the context of distance sampling.

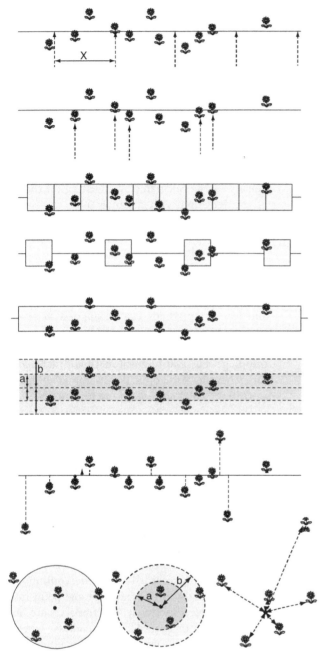

Point intercept transect
Recording presence/absence of species
at set distances (x) along a line.
Measures frequency.

Line intercept transect
Continuous measurements of intercepts
along a line. Normally used for estimating
vegetation cover.

Belt transect
Contiguous (above) or spaced (below) frame
quadrats laid along a line. Each quadrat
is recorded separately. Measures frequency,
cover, density or other variables. Normally
used to study changes along an environmental
gradient or across vegetation boundaries.

Strip transect
Essentially a very long and thin quadrat of fixed
width; individuals are counted within this strip.
Estimates density.

Line transect
A line walked by the surveyor who either
places each individual within several
distance bands (above) or estimates
perpendicular distance to each individual
(below). Estimates density and detectability.

Point transect/point count
A count made within a fixed radius (left),
within several distance bands (middle) or
exact distance estimation from a
point (right). Estimates density and
detectability. Referred to as 'point transects'
by Buckland *et al.* (1993) as they can be
considered as transects of zero length.
The right-hand example is also known
as a Variable Circular Plot (VCP).

Figure 10.1. Types of transect and point count.

10.3   TOTAL COUNTS

10.3.1   Principles and methods

If you are surveying a conspicuous species in a small area, or an aggregating species, it may be possible to count the entire population and arrive at an accurate assessment of population size. However, it is unlikely that you will be able to make total counts with confidence very often.

An example in which total counts may be appropriate is when the number of orchids in a meadow needs to be established; if the sward is short and the orchids are very conspicuous, then counts will be accurate. Total counts of plant species are covered in more detail in Sections 15.2.1 and 15.2.2.

Counting breeding seabirds is another situation in which total counts are often employed. However, if you cannot be certain that the whole population has been counted, data should be presented as a minimum population estimate. This may well be sufficient if you only need to check that the population is above a lower limit.

If the species is mobile and widespread, several surveyors will be needed to make simultaneous counts at different sites to ensure that individuals are not counted more than once. This is the method used for surveying wading birds: surveys are synchronised to minimise the chance of a flock of birds moving from one site to another between counts (Section 24.2.1).

10.3.2   Analysis

In principle, a total count is the total population, so if counts change over time no analysis is needed to demonstrate a change between years. Regression analysis or time-series analysis may, however, be necessary to establish whether there are significant trends over a number of years, particularly if the population exhibits cyclical changes.

10.4   TIMED SEARCHES

10.4.1   Principles

Timed searches (also termed timed counts, direct counts or direct searches) can be used to standardise the surveying of cryptic species, or species spread over a wide area, which cannot easily be sampled by using transects or point counts. For example, timed counts provide a simple and efficient means of obtaining estimates of relative abundance of Odonata (the order of insects including dragonflies and damselflies) in wetlands where the terrain would make transects problematic (Section 16.2.4). Another example would be counting birds flying past a headland; in this case the area of search cannot be easily quantified. In both cases, searching for a set amount of time introduces an element of standardisation, which can be repeated in subsequent surveys.

10.4.2   Methods

Timed searches are often used when surveying for presence–absence of a species; the surveyor walks around a site looking for the target species, and if nothing is found after a set time an absence is recorded for that visit. If several such surveys fail to register a presence, it can usually be concluded that the species is absent (although this will depend on the intensity of the search; absence is hard to demonstrate conclusively).

It is usual to further standardise timed search surveys by searching only within a delineated area; this enables a minimum density to be estimated. If the site is so large that a surveyor cannot cover the whole area adequately within the time allotted for the survey, it should be subdivided into sample areas, and a random sample of these selected for searching. The size of search area chosen will depend upon the size of the site and the ecology of the target species. Presence–absence searches for scarce and/or widely dispersed species will generally need to be undertaken over a large area. For quantitative repeat monitoring surveys, numerous smaller sample areas should be searched for a shorter time in order to generate more data from each survey. Quadrats (Section 10.5) may be appropriate to select such areas for searching. This is particularly appropriate for smaller species with high population densities.

10.4.3   Analysis

The analysis of presence–absence surveys is obviously straightforward if the species is found. Confirming an absence is more problematic. Unless a species is sufficiently conspicuous and identifiable to guarantee detection, and the site has been comprehensively searched (which will rarely be the case), then it cannot be said for certain that the species is absent. Several thorough surveys with negative results will be needed before it may be reliably assumed that a species is absent.

Presence–absence data from different areas can be used to build up a distribution map of the species, which can be updated periodically to detect changes in range.

Data from timed searches that involve counts can be expressed as numbers found per unit time (divide total number found by duration of survey). A mean figure and confidence limits can be calculated if an appropriate sampling method has been used. Such data can be treated as an index of population; results from different years can be compared statistically to look for trends in the data, provided consistency can be assured. Analysis can be in the form of *t*-tests, analysis of variance or regression, although non-parametric analyses may be required if distributional assumptions cannot be satisfied (see Part I, Section 2.6.4).

Data from timed searches in a set area can be used to estimate a minimum density in that area (as well as numbers per unit time as above). Again, this should be treated as an index (or a minimum density), because it is unlikely that all individuals will be found. This estimate can be extrapolated across areas of similar habitat to obtain a total population index. It might also be possible to calibrate timed search results by carrying out a timed search in one area for the standard length of time, and then continuing the search intensively until you are reasonably confident that all individuals have been found. The ratio of individuals found in the timed search to total individuals found can be used to derive a multiplier, which can be applied to other timed searches to estimate total numbers. This calibration should be carried out more than once to obtain a better estimate of the multiplier and to enable

calculation of the precision in this estimate. Results from different years can be compared statistically by using the methods outlined above.

It should be remembered that timed counts will vary according to the efficiency of surveyors and the nature of the terrain. Methods should therefore be standardised and documented with as much detail as possible to ensure comparability.

10.5   QUADRATS

10.5.1   Principles

Quadrats are used to define sample areas within which measurements of some sort are taken. The selection of quadrat locations can be made by judgement, systematically, or randomly. This subject is covered in detail in Part I, Sections 2.3.3 and 2.3.4, and is not repeated here.

The measurements taken within quadrats will depend on the species being surveyed and the objectives of the study or monitoring programme. The simplest measurement is presence–absence of a species within the quadrat. If repeated in many quadrats an estimate of overall percentage frequency can be obtained. Alternatively, if a quadrat with subdivisions is used, presence–absence in each subdivision can be recorded and an overall percentage of subdivisions containing the species can be calculated per quadrat (referred to here as sub-plot frequency). Other measurements commonly recorded are density (number of individuals within the quadrat) and cover (of plants: a measurement of the area of substrate covered by a perpendicular projection of foliage and stems). These are described in more detail in Part I, Section 2.1.2.

The size of quadrat will affect measures of frequency (Appendix 4). It is obvious that a larger quadrat will have a greater chance of recording presence of a particular species than a smaller one. Quadrat size therefore needs to be such that extreme percentage frequencies are avoided (i.e. the species is neither nearly always present nor nearly always absent). Once selected, it is of course vital that quadrat size be kept constant between repeat surveys. Nevertheless, where possible, small quadrats should be used for frequency hnps in top right mis

estimates as these are more easily and accurately searched. When counting individuals to obtain density estimates, quadrat size does not affect the measurement in principle, although the larger the quadrat the more likely it is that some individuals will be missed. Quadrat size should be such that samples can be gathered efficiently; if quadrats are too large, they will take too long to record. If they are too small, the target species may not be sampled even if it is present, especially if it is rare. A fuller discussion of the selection of appropriate quadrat size and a list of commonly used sizes for different plant species is given in Appendix 4.

10.5.2   Permanent quadrats

Permanent quadrat locations provide a good way of reducing between-quadrat variability when changes over time are being monitored. If changes are fairly consistent across the site, permanent plots will detect change more efficiently than will temporary plots. They can therefore give a more precise measure of change. They are also appropriate when monitoring rare sedentary species that occur in a few known locations. For example, the health of specific lichen colonies is often monitored by using permanent quadrats that are deliberately placed over them (Section 12.2.2). In such circumstances, random temporary quadrats would be highly inefficient and imprecise; such quadrats may not coincide with colonies at all. However, permanent quadrats that are placed by judgement cannot provide a reliable assessment of trends over the whole site unless they cover the whole of the population. Therefore, if information is needed on whether other colonies are being established, numerous randomly or systematically located quadrats will be required.

Another advantage of permanent quadrats is that more data can be collected on the survival and growth of individual organisms (especially plants) within the quadrat. However, there is a risk that permanent quadrats, particularly if located in fragile habitats such as peat bogs, might damage the species being monitored. Quadrats should never be left *in situ* because they

may affect the species being monitored; they must be relocated from markers such as posts or transponders. See Appendix 5 for instructions on the installation of permanent markers.

10.5.3   Temporary quadrats

Temporary quadrats have the advantages of being quicker to locate, less damaging to the surrounding environment and, if located correctly, always representative of the habitat as a whole (permanent quadrats may become unrepresentative as a result of chance events or successional change). However, they usually produce less precise estimates of change for a given sample size.

Temporary quadrat locations are particularly appropriate for ephemeral plant species or short-distance mobile species such as ground beetles or benthic invertebrates.

Many of these advantages and disadvantages of permanent and temporary quadrats apply equally to some types of transect (Section 10.7). Further discussion of the advantages and disadvantages of permanent and temporary quadrats is provided in Part I, Section 2.3.3.

10.5.4   Methods and analysis

Quadrat methodology and analysis for plant species is covered in detail in Part II, Sections 6.4.2–6.4.5, 6.5.2 and 6.5.3. For other species, the precise methodology may vary depending upon the nature of the species being surveyed, but in general the species will simply be counted within the quadrat, either for frequency data or for density (and hence population size) estimation. For species that are difficult to identify in the field, collecting equipment will be necessary; see the relevant chapters on the species groups for the equipment required. It is important that samples be labelled clearly so that the location from which they were taken can be ascertained for later analysis.

Analysis of quadrat data can be straightforward for monitoring purposes; the most important analysis will be the examination of trends in the range, frequency and abundance of the target species.

Frequency data can be analysed by using a χ^2 test. Cover and density (or abundance) can usually be analysed by using t-tests, analysis of variance or regression. Non-parametric statistics may be more appropriate, depending on the distribution of the data; for a fuller discussion of data analysis refer to Part I, Section 2.6.

10.6   DISTANCE SAMPLING

10.6.1   General principles

Distance sampling is a method of obtaining density estimates for species, based on estimating distances to individuals from a line or a point. The major advantage of this approach is that detection does not have to be complete, as the method provides a means of estimating the number of missed individuals within a given distance from the observer. The method is most commonly applied to mobile species such as mammals and birds, but is also well suited to many slow-moving or stationary organisms (Buckland et al., 2001).

The number of objects recorded will always decrease with distance from the observer. Unless species are sedentary and it can be guaranteed that they are obvious enough not to be overlooked, it is safest to assume that the observer will fail to detect all individuals. Analysis of distance data involves modelling the decline in detectability with distance from the observer and using this to calculate a corrected density estimate.

The choice of whether to sample with line transects or at points (point transects) will depend on several factors, including the time available to collect data, the mobility or elusiveness of the species in question, the density of the species, whether more than one species is being studied, and the nature and variability of the habitat (see Section 10.6.2). There are a number of important assumptions that need to be met if either of these distance sampling methods are to produce reliable density estimates.

1. Objects must be distributed randomly with respect to the sample lines or points.
2. Objects exactly on the line or point must be detected with certainty.
3. Objects must be detected before they move appreciably in response to the approach of an observer.
4. Distances must be measured accurately.

Assumption 1 is addressed by positioning lines or points systematically or randomly so that they provide a representative sample of the area being studied. Lines or points should not be located along footpaths, roads or field boundaries; this introduces unknown bias into the sample as these are likely to be atypical in terms of species density.

Assumption 2 may be difficult to achieve in ship-based surveys, for example, or if individuals are often hidden in undergrowth. Careful design can often overcome this difficulty, for example by using multiple observers, but in extreme cases it may be necessary to estimate the percentage detected on the line and adjust density estimates accordingly.

Assumption 3 is a problem if it is possible that individuals will move appreciably towards or away from the observer prior to detection. Movement of objects towards the observer (a common behaviour among some passerine birds, for example) could increase the density estimate. Alternatively, objects may flee the observer, which will bias the results in the opposite direction. Bias of this kind is further exacerbated if the object moves and is recorded twice from the same point or line. The principle of distance sampling is that each count provides a 'snapshot' of objects occurring around the point or line. As long as the speed of objects moving before and up to the time of detection is appreciably slower (less than one third) than that of the observer, random movement of objects is not likely to be a concern when using line transects. The methods cannot be used to count rapidly moving objects such as most birds in flight. Random movement is more of a concern with point counts, as bias arising from errors increases with the square of distance for points but only linearly for lines.

Counting the same object twice from a different line or point does not violate any of the assumptions made by distance sampling methods. If double counting is commonplace, however, it may be due to a weakness in the method. For example, when carrying out flush counts of grouse by using dogs and multiple observers, it is important that birds are not flushed from one transect to the next.

Assumption 4 is important and it is worth investing some time into training observers to measure distances accurately. A better option is to use a laser range-finder. These are very accurate and affordable and greatly improve the reliability of distance measurement and therefore of density estimates. A high-quality compass is also needed, as distance from the line is usually measured by using distance from the observer and the angle between a line from the observer to the individual and the transect (see Box 10.1).

If it is impracticable to measure distance accurately, it may be useful to group distances at intervals into bands. If only two intervals are used an assumption has to be made about the way in which detectability declines with distance, and it is not possible to compare different models to find which one fits best. Hence, three intervals or more are recommended. This method is often used in multiple species projects, such as the national BTO/RSPB/JNCC Breeding Bird Survey (BBS). This method is favoured for such projects because it would take a considerable amount of time to measure exact distances for the large number of species involved, and it provides a reasonably robust way of dealing with detectability problems. However, for more species-specific work it may be useful to consider taking exact measurements.

10.6.2   Line and point transects

The assumptions for distance estimation from points are the same as for line transects (Section 10.6.1). Line transects have a number of advantages over point methods when carrying out distance sampling. They are more efficient at collecting large sample sizes and less prone to bias from measurement errors. Line transects are also less biased by species mobility and are more suitable than point counts for open habitats in which species can be detected at long distances.

Point transects are often used in habitats such as woodland, where line transects may be difficult to follow and dense vegetation makes disturbance and detection problems significant. It is also easier to locate points randomly in habitats where access is a problem. They also allow an observer more time to locate individuals in habitats where they may miss them while concentrating on walking a line.

The time spent at a point is critical. The aim is to spend the minimum amount of time that is necessary to detect all individuals present at the beginning of the count period, in order to minimise the probability of animals entering or leaving the area during the count period. As a rule, somewhere between five and ten minutes is probably long enough to record all the individuals of a species in the vicinity of the point. Any longer and random movement of objects may cause an increased or decreased density estimate.

When conducting point counts, it is much more important to be aware of bias associated with clusters (herds of animals or flocks of birds), although this is also a consideration with line transects. There are a number of reasons for detectability varying with cluster size. For instance, larger groups may be more vocal and therefore recorded more often at greater distances. On the other hand, large groups may be more alert and less likely to be recorded, particularly in dense vegetation. The calls of some bird species may also trigger others to respond. This may be a particular problem when surveying songbirds. Sometimes it may be better to measure the distance to clusters, rather than to each individual, and estimate the size of the cluster. Distance analysis software (Section 10.6.4) can analyse clustered data and provides methods for studying, and correcting for, the relation between probability of detection and cluster size. Point methods are particularly susceptible to bias arising from error, so it is very important to choose a good model for the data (see Section 10.6.4).

Whether using transects or points, it is important to standardise the method of data collection as much as possible. This includes removing possible sources of bias, for example by walking each transect at a standard speed and not surveying in difficult weather conditions.

Box 10.1   Methods of estimating distances by using the line transect method

Whenever estimating distances to objects on line transects, the critical distance is perpendicular to the line (see Figure B10.1a). A degree of error is possible in estimating perpendicular distances to objects that are a long way ahead of the observer and close to the line. These are often erroneously rounded to zero. Accurate angle measurement is important and, if distances are visually estimated, then thorough training and repeated self-checking against measured distances should be used. For band methods, the object only has to be recorded in the correct band, so the skill necessary in the field is less daunting.

If the location of the object is marked in relation to a tree, field edge or other feature, a tape measure can be used to check distances later. These days, it is much more usual to employ an optical range-finder. In projects in which objects are commonly recorded over 100 m, survey lasers are useful to determine distances accurately. Their cost is soon justified by the ability to precisely determine distances up to several hundred metres. Combined with a good-quality compass, distance from observer to object can be recorded along with angles and accurate perpendicular distances calculated by using trigonometry (see Figure B10.1b).

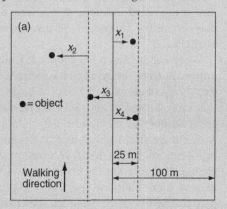
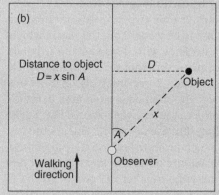

Figure B10.1

10.6.3   Field methods

Transects
Exact distances
The method involves walking along a transect and estimating the distance to objects either side of the line. The distance perpendicular to the line is measured, either directly or as a combination of distance and angle from the line (see Box 10.1).

Distance bands
Collecting exact distance data is the preferred method as it allows more sophisticated modelling of the detection function (Section 10.6.4), although similar levels of precision can often be obtained by using a fairly small number of distance bands. Another advantage is that distances can always be grouped into bands at the analytical stage if necessary, without being tied to a predefined grouping. For example, distances may be found to have been rounded in the field, and problems with heaping at, say, 10 m intervals can often be dealt with by forming appropriate distance bands.

A large number of intervals may improve the estimation of the detection function, but during fieldwork it will become more difficult to ascertain which distance band an object falls into the further away it is (unless laser range-finders are used).

Methods involve walking along a transect, estimating the distance to objects either side of the line and placing them in discrete distance bands, e.g. 0–10 m, 10–25 m, 25–50 m, 50–100 m and >100 m. The distance perpendicular to the line is measured.

There is no hard and fast rule to determine the width of the inner band. Ideally, there should be at least two bands within the distance for which detection is almost certain. If there is evidence that objects are moving away from the observer, however, it is important that the intervals are not so small that objects move between them before they are detected.

Conventionally, data from the outer unlimited distance band is omitted from analysis. This is because interpretation of data recorded to an infinite distance is complex and also because outlying observations can unduly affect the fit of the detection function. Although it is possible to calculate density estimates manually, use of the Distance software is recommended for simplicity (see Section 10.6.4). The detection function is usually assumed to be half-normal for two-band methods, but using more bands allows the choice of the optimal model using the Distance software (Section 10.6.4).

Point transects

The method involves counting objects for a fixed period of time at a point and either estimating the exact distance to them or placing them in discrete distance bands. The general field method principles are similar to those for transects.

In the case of birds, many of the contacts will be by sound only, and observers will need to be competent at estimating such distances accurately. Laser range-finders can be used to improve distance estimation to visible objects. Time spent at a point should be long enough to record everything in the vicinity but not so long that there is significant movement of objects into the area. Estimation of the optimum count time will require either existing knowledge of the behaviour of the species (e.g. song frequency in birds) or a pilot survey.

For mobile species, few will be recorded near to the point itself. This is both because it is where the observer stands and also because the area close to the observer is small. It is therefore useful to arrive at a point early, and spend a few minutes in silence so that your presence does not affect the behaviour of the target species. Movement of objects towards or away from the observer is another source of considerable bias in point transects.

10.6.4   Analysis

If distances are estimated, either exactly or in intervals, the decline of detectability with distance can be modelled and used to estimate the proportion of undetected individuals and hence to derive a density estimate.

Numbers of individuals detected at increasing distances from the observer can be plotted as a histogram, with distance from the line or point on the x axis and number of detections on the y axis. A curve fitted through the data describes the change in detectability with distance: this is termed the *detection function* (Figure 10.2). Detection functions will normally vary for different species in the same habitat and for the same species in different habitats. A separate detection function can be modelled for each species and habitat.

This function is best modelled by using the dedicated Distance software, which can be used to fit four basic mathematical models (known as key functions) to the data. Each model produces a differently shaped detection function based on a different assumption about the way in which detectability decreases with distance. These key functions have been chosen as they reliably reflect the nature of most biological distance data. For example, the detection function in Figure 10.2 is modelled with a half-normal curve.

If distance intervals are used, the number and spacing of intervals will depend on the level of accuracy required. Buckland *et al.* (2001) suggest that ideally there should be at least two distance bands on the 'shoulder' of the curve (i.e. before detectability begins to decline appreciably): see Figure 10.2. This will help to improve the model fit of the detection function. This modelling assumption is known as the 'shape criterion' and roughly means that detectability must remain certain, or near certain, for some distance from the line or point.

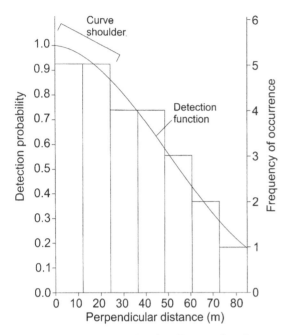

Figure 10.2. Histogram showing distance data for Lapwing *Vanellus vanellus* surveyed in grassland. A half-normal curve with one cosine adjustment term is shown as a model for the detection function.

Distance software provides ways of selecting the best model and testing the model fit. Careful selection of the best model is particularly important for point transect data.

It is often desirable to discard any outlying observations before fitting the detection function as these can have undue influence on the resulting model. If necessary, the function can be fine tuned to improve the fit by using a further set of 'adjustment terms' (for example, the detection function in Figure 10.2 has been adjusted with one term from a cosine series expansion). For details on the modelling procedure consult Buckland *et al.* (2001).

Clustered data, from herds or flocks for example, can also be handled by Distance. Each cluster (or group) is modelled as a separate record and the average group size used to provide estimates of density or population size. The possibility that small groups are less detectable away from the line can also be taken into account.

Once an acceptable detection function has been fitted, Distance will calculate estimates for population density and size with associated standard errors and confidence intervals.

One potential drawback of distance sampling is that sample sizes need to be quite large to model the detection function reliably. About 60 encounters are typically required to derive a reliable density estimate. Obviously for the scarcer species some intense surveying may be required. If the survey is repeated, then the model can be improved with additional data and old estimates re-analysed. Distance sampling methods are explained in relation to particular species in the relevant sections.

The computer program Distance is a fairly straightforward and versatile alternative to manual calculation. A Windows-based version is available to download from the internet via the Distance homepage at the University of St Andrews (www.ruwpa.st-and.ac.uk/distance). To keep up to date with information on Distance, it is recommended that you check the Distance homepage and subscribe to the e-mail discussion group. This is done by e-mailing jiscmail@jiscmail.ac.uk and typing: *join distance-sampling <your first name> <your surname>*.

Guidelines for modelling data by using Distance are described in the book *Introduction to Distance Sampling* (Buckland *et al.*, 2001). At the time of writing, an earlier version of this book could be downloaded from the above website.

10.7   LINE AND STRIP TRANSECTS

10.7.1   General principles

Transect methods involve moving along a line between two points and counting the number of objects observed on either side of the line. We consider the following methods:

- line transects (exact distances to each contact is estimated, or contacts are grouped at intervals into distance bands), already discussed in Section 10.6;
- line transects (infinite width);
- strip transects (species are recorded within a single defined perpendicular distance from the line); and

- line intercept or point intercept transects (counts are made of species that the line 'touches').

Of the above methods, only the first (in which distances are estimated exactly or measured in bands) will yield reliable density estimates if a substantial number of individuals remain undetected.

Infinite width transects can be useful to provide an index of abundance for a species for a long-term monitoring exercise. However, they cannot be used to compare the density of species in different habitats, because this would require some assumption about the shape of the detection function for each habitat. The lack of distance data would also preclude a reliable estimation of density within the sample area as there would be no way of knowing how many objects had been missed.

Strip transects require intensive surveying of the transect area in order to be sure that objects are not being overlooked. Line and point intercept transects require objects to remain stationary and are therefore applied only to sessile organisms such as plants.

10.7.2   Line transects: infinite width

Principles

Line transects of infinite width can be used to collect encounter rates, calculated as objects seen per unit time or per unit of transect length. Distances are not estimated, and therefore density estimation is not possible unless the species is very conspicuous and the habitat is open and detectability can therefore be assumed to be constant with increasing distance. This assumption is very unlikely to be met, so this method should only be used for deriving population indices.

Analysis

Counts made from transects with infinite width can be interpreted as indices of abundance, either between sites (if it can be proved that detectability remains constant) or over time in monitoring exercises. Counts can be compared over time by transforming the data (Part I, Section 2.6.4) and analysing with parametric statistics such as t-tests or analysis of variance or by using non-parametric

statistics such as the Mann–Whitney test or Kruskal–Wallis test.

10.7.3   Strip transects

Principles

A strip transect is essentially a long, narrow quadrat. It is assumed that all individuals within the strip are counted; individuals outside the strip are ignored. Strip transects can be used to sample immobile or sedentary species such as plants or snails, for which it is possible to be certain that individuals have not moved in or out of the strip while the search is being conducted. In this case, the strip will typically be very narrow (a few metres wide at most) in order to reduce the time taken to search the strip and increase the likelihood of counting all individuals.

Strip transects can also be used to sample mobile animals when it is not possible to search intensively before their positions change. This method is only likely to prove useful when detectability constraints are not a consideration, i.e. the terrain is uniform and species are conspicuous, for example rabbits or hares on short turf.

Analysis

Strip transects should be designed so that it can be reliably assumed that all individuals within them are certain to be detected. This is more likely to be the case for immobile species. Density may be calculated by simply dividing the number of objects by the area of the strip. A mean density and variance can be calculated from the sample of transects, and a total population estimate can be obtained by multiplying the mean density by the total area of similar habitat. Repeat counts from different years can be analysed by using methods such as t-tests and regression or their non-parametric equivalents.

For mobile species the optimum strip width is hard to determine. Observers may be surprised by how narrow such a strip needs to be, particularly in dense habitats such as scrub and woodland. If the aim of the project is to compare the abundance of a species at two sites or in two different environments this is especially important, as differences in detectability between sites could render the comparison of results invalid. It is therefore worth considering collecting distance data to enable adjustment for incomplete detection (Section 10.6).

10.7.4   Line intercept and point intercept transects

Principles

These are the most basic types of transect, in which the transect is a simple one-dimensional line. Only individuals that touch the line are recorded. Line intercept transects record touches continuously along the line. Point intercepts record touches at regular intervals along the line. This can be used to estimate relative abundance, cover and frequency. These transects cannot be used to survey mobile species, and are normally used for vegetation. See Part II, Section 6.4.6 for more details.

Analysis

The analysis of line intercept and point intercept transects is discussed in Part II, Section 6.4.6.

10.8   POINT COUNTS

10.8.1   General principles

Point counts involve counting and/or measuring distances to objects in all directions from a point. If distances are estimated to objects from the point, the method is also known as point transects (Buckland *et al.*, 2001) or variable circular plots (VCPs). A simpler method is to count the number of objects in a circle of known radius.

We consider the following methods:

- estimating exact distances to each individual or grouping into distance bands (already discussed in Section 10.6); and
- recording species within a single defined distance from the point or to infinity.

Fixed-radius circular plots can be used to provide density estimates providing that objects are only recorded to the distance within which they are certain to be detected. These counts are more likely to be suitable for sessile or slow-moving

species that will not flee from the observer. An infinite-radius plot may be used to provide an index of abundance for any one species. However, as with transects of infinite width, the lack of distance data would preclude any estimation of density within the sample area as there would be no way of knowing how many objects had been missed. It also means that the results cannot be compared between sites if the detectability of the species varies in different habitats.

10.8.2   Point counts in a circle of fixed radius or infinite distance

Principles

Point counts may be of infinite radius and used to collect encounter rates, calculated as objects seen per unit time. They may also be of fixed radius, with individuals recorded only if they are within a certain distance. The latter method may be used to derive density estimates providing it is certain that all objects were detected within the fixed distance. Detectability problems can have a profound effect on point count results and detection may only be certain to a short distance. Distance sampling methods may be more efficient as more data can be utilised from each point.

Field methods

The method involves carrying out a standardised, timed count from a point. If the species concerned is sedentary and a fixed-radius circle is used, then an intensive survey within the circle may reveal all the objects. If the objects are mobile, then the observer must ignore any observations made beyond the critical distance at which detectability declines significantly.

Analysis

Counts made to an infinite distance can only be interpreted as indices of abundance, either between sites (if it is proved that detectability remains constant) or over time in monitoring exercises. A fixed-radius point count designed to ensure that all objects within the area are certain to be detected may derive densities calculated by dividing the number of objects by the area surveyed. In habitats with dense vegetation such as woodland or scrub the radius may need to be particularly small. If the aim of the project is to compare the abundance of a species at two sites or in two different environments it is important to be especially careful, as differences in detectability between sites could render comparisons of the data invalid. It is therefore worth considering collecting distance data either in bands or as exact distances (Section 10.6).

The analysis of counts from point counts of infinite distance or fixed radius is identical to that described for line transects of infinite width (Section 10.7.2) or strip transects (Section 10.7.3).

10.9   TRAPPING WEBS

10.9.1   Principles

Trapping webs can be used for obtaining abundance estimates of animals that are not easily observed or efficiently surveyed by visual searching methods. They are most often used for small mammals and invertebrates. A trapping web is a

series of concentric circles of traps, each containing the same number of traps. The traps are usually arranged in lines like the spokes of a wheel, for convenience of relocation. The circles should be arranged so that they lie a constant distance apart, and so that the inner circle has a radius of half that constant distance (Figure 10.3).

Three basic assumptions are made:

1. that all the animals in the centre of the web are caught;
2. that population density is constant throughout the area of the trapping web; and
3. that probability of capture is homogeneous throughout all trapping occasions.

10.9.2   Methods and analysis

Animals are caught over several capture occasions until no more animals are caught in the central traps. It is likely that new animals will still be caught in the outer circles, for although the number of traps is constant they sit in a larger area, containing more animals, than do the inner traps. The number of animals caught in the outermost circles will be greater than the number caught in circles slightly further in, because the outermost traps will be catching animals from outside the web. If this immigration is obvious, the data from the outermost circles should be discarded.

It is best to mark and release captures rather than remove them unless one is sure that immigration will not occur. The removal of animals may simply create a vacant territory, which will be occupied by an individual from outside; this will bias results considerably, and cause the population to be overestimated.

Population estimation is a complex procedure, but is based on the fact that animals near the centre are more likely to be caught than those near the edge. It is then theoretically possible to work out differences in probability of capture, although this is complicated by the fact that the inner traps interfere with each other. See Greenwood (1996) and Anderson *et al.* (1983) for further details of analysis methods.

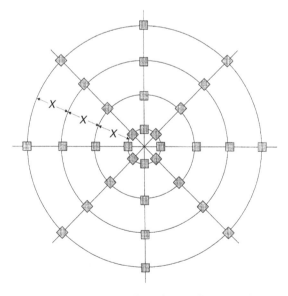

Figure 10.3. Illustration of trap layout for a trapping web. X is the constant separating rings of traps (see text).

10.10   REMOVAL METHOD

10.10.1   Principles and applications

The removal method is a way of estimating population size based on trapping, whereby trapped animals are removed from the population. In the extreme case, trapping continues until no more animals are being caught. The number of captures is then taken as the total population size. In practice, this usually requires too much effort. However, if the cumulative numbers caught in each trapping occasion are plotted against catch per unit effort (for example, mean number of catches per trap) a line can be fitted to the data with linear regression and extrapolated to obtain an estimate of the total population (see Figure 10.4). It is important that catch effort be evaluated correctly. For example, doubling the number of traps may not double the true catching effort if the traps interfere with each other. Alternatively, if there are not enough traps, the number of captures may be too small for reliable estimation.

The removal method is only appropriate for populations that are closed (i.e. no new individuals enter the population while trapping is taking place).

For monitoring purposes, this method is generally only applied to monitoring fish populations with electrofishing (Section 21.2.9): a section of water can be isolated with stop nets, and electrofishing is carried out until few fish are being caught. Catch per unit effort can be expressed as the number of fish caught in each sweep; the results are plotted as in Figure 10.4 and an estimate

of the total number of fish in that section of water can be obtained. Removal techniques are not usually applicable for monitoring terrestrial animals. Consult Seber (1982) and Greenwood (1996) for further information.

10.11   MARK–RECAPTURE TECHNIQUES

10.11.1   Principles

A sample of animals from a population is caught, marked and released back into the population. If the marked animals disperse throughout the total population, the ratio of marked to unmarked individuals in a second sample will be the same as the ratio in the whole population. The population size can thus be estimated from two trapping occasions.

This can be expressed algebraically as follows:

$$\frac{m_2}{n_2} = \frac{n_1}{N},$$

where m_2 = number of marked animals in second sample;

n_2 = total number of animals in second sample;

n_1 = total number of animals caught and marked in first sample;

N = total population size.

All mark–recapture techniques are based on this fundamental premise, although there are many refinements of the theory. Most methods that are commonly used require more than two trapping occasions.

There are some fundamental assumptions inherent in the use of mark–recapture models, which must be understood; if these assumptions do not hold for the population under study, the results may be invalid.

- Marked individuals must disperse throughout the entire population once released. If the marked animals stay in the group in which they were released, a second sample from the same area will contain a higher proportion of marked

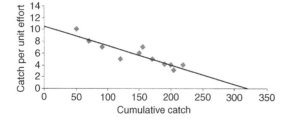

Figure 10.4. The removal method. The graph depicts a hypothetical removal experiment with the regression line added. The point at which the line cuts the x-axis is the estimated total population size.

individuals than exists in the whole population, and thus the population will be underestimated. Conversely, a sample from a different area will contain a lower proportion of marked individuals and the population will be overestimated.

- Every animal in the population must be equally at risk of capture on every trapping occasion. If animals become trap-happy (more likely to be recaptured) or trap-shy (less likely to be recaptured), the results will be biased. Refinements to some models have been made that allow for differences in trapping probability.
- Many models require the population to be closed. This means that no births, deaths, immigration or emigration should occur for the duration of the study. Some models have been developed that can cope with open populations. However, these tend to yield less precise population estimates.

A thorough knowledge of the ecology of the target species is therefore required if mark–recapture is to be used in order to select an appropriate model that does not contain assumptions that will be violated. For example, the assumption of a closed population can be made for adult newts in breeding ponds over a short time, but may not be justified over longer periods, especially if there are other ponds nearby.

It is important to realise that mark–recapture methods can produce disappointingly imprecise results given the amount of effort that is necessary. The higher the proportion of the population caught, the better the precision obtainable.

However, there are advantages with mark–recapture techniques: the standardisation of effort over time is not as essential as it is with other sampling methods. We are concerned with the ratio of new captures to recaptures, and therefore trapping occasions do not have to be standardised. For example, you can catch newts in pitfall traps, mark and release them, and catch them a second time in bottle traps. If marks are easily visible in the field (e.g. colour rings for birds), the ratio of marked to unmarked individuals can be estimated without any need for subsequent trapping. This also has the advantage of reducing the disturbance caused to the species and avoiding the problem of trap response.

10.11.2 Marking methods

A wide variety of methods can be employed to mark captured animals. The most preferable option is to use natural characteristics of the species for subsequent recognition so that the animals do not have to be marked at all. The belly patterns of Great Crested Newts, for example, are individually distinct. For animals that have to be marked, you should avoid intrusive marking methods (such as toe-clipping) wherever possible to avoid or minimise the risk of causing injury or distress, or altering the behaviour of the animals (for example, the pain of toe-clipping can deter animals from trap areas). It is also important that the mark does not make the individual more at risk of predation; if the marks affect mortality, population estimates will be biased. Methods for marking animals are discussed in the sections on species groups for which mark–recapture studies are appropriate survey and monitoring techniques. Note that in many cases a licence will also be required.

Animals can either be batch-marked, whereby every animal caught is given a mark that identifies the trapping occasion, or individually marked. Batch-marking is suitable for most mark–recapture models, but individual marking yields additional information and allows estimates to be made of variations in capture probability.

10.11.3 Mark–recapture models

A number of different models exist, which differ in the assumptions they make and statistical methods for analysis. The most widely used methods are briefly summarised in Table 10.1, but for further information, detailed equations and other methods based on trapping and marking refer to Bibby et al. (2000), Greenwood (1996), Pollock et al. (1990) and Seber (1982).

10.11.4 Mark–recapture analysis

It is beyond the scope of this *Handbook* to give detailed accounts of the analysis of mark–recapture data. For further information see Greenwood (1996), Pollock

Table 10.1. *A summary of some commonly used mark–recapture models*

Method	Summary
Petersen	The most basic method, involving two capture occasions. It requires closed populations with homogeneous capture probability. Also known as the Lincoln index. Mathematically simple.
Schnabel	Makes the same assumptions as the Petersen method, but can be applied to more than two capture occasions. Unmarked animals in each capture are marked. The method looks at the increase in the proportion of marked animals as the number of capture occasions increases, and extrapolates to the point at which the proportion is 1.0 and the number of marked animals equals the population size.
Burnham & Overton	Requires a closed population and several capture occasions but allows for heterogeneity of capture probability between individuals. Critical assumption is that capture probability does not change with time; trapping effort must be constant and trap response avoided.
Jolly–Seber	Can be used for open populations. Requires at least three trapping occasions and at least batch-specific marks. As well as allowing for gains and losses, the method estimates the number of animals entering the population and the survival rate.

et al. (1990), Seber (1982), Burnham & Overton (1978, 1979), Otis *et al.* (1978) and White *et al.* (1982).

Mark–recapture analysis can be very complex. Computer programs have been developed to carry out this analysis; software and instruction manuals can be downloaded free from the internet at www.mbr.nbs.gov/software.html. These programs include CAPTURE, a Windows-based program for analysing closed populations, which contains several different models to allow for variations in capture probability by time and individual. It also contains a model selection procedure, which chooses the most appropriate model for the data. Other useful programs are JOLLY, a DOS-based program for open populations, which estimates survival rates, and JOLLYAGE, a refinement of JOLLY, which allows age-class data to be included in the Jolly–Seber analysis. Methods from these programs are also available in the more user-friendly Windows-based package called MARK.

It is important that the theory behind the analysis is understood before using programs so that you can have confidence in the ecological explanation of model selection and population estimates.

11 • Fungi

The groups of fungi covered in this section are restricted to the macromycetes. This is not a precise taxonomic definition (it generally includes the basidiomycetes minus rusts, smuts and yeasts with some ascomycetes and myxomycetes), but it is convenient and commonly used (Watling, 1995). Although this grouping generally applies to the mushrooms and toadstools (correctly termed agarics), polypores and their relatives and jelly fungi, a few prominent ascomycetes such as the earth tongues, truffles and their allies are included. This grouping contains three different categories of fungi based on life strategy: biotrophs, which include basidiolichens and mycorrhizal species; saprotrophs, which include litter and wood rotters; and the necrotrophs or parasites. An informed biological approach should always be considered when dealing with members of each category. For example, a wood rotter may be restricted to a single tree trunk, whereas an ectomycorrhizal fungus may be associated with a widely spreading mycelial system that covers several square metres.

The survey and monitoring of fungi presents some difficulties that need to be taken into consideration when designing a monitoring strategy. Surveying for presence or absence of macromycetes depends upon the appearance of the fruiting body (sporome). The number of fruiting bodies is considered to reflect the health and spatial extent of a fungal colony, although there is little scientific evidence to support this. Sporome appearance is influenced by a number of environmental factors including temperature, amount and timing of rainfall, soil pH and nutrient status, and successional patterns of surrounding vegetation. It is thus very variable: in some years, a species might not fruit at all, whereas in 'good' years, fruiting may be extensive. It follows that an absence (or reduction in numbers) of the sporomes of a species in one year does not necessarily imply a reduction in range or numbers of that species; the species may very well still be present and will fruit again when conditions are favourable. Monitoring of fungi therefore must be undertaken with a view to making long-term studies. The minimum length of time over which actual changes in distribution or abundance can be realistically assessed is five years; Orton (1986) recommends 10 years as a reasonable minimum length. Studies of intervals of less than this period can do little more than confirm the presence of a species; for EIA studies, this may be all that can be realistically gained within the timescale of the overall project.

A further complication arises because of this need for longer-term monitoring. In addition to changes resulting from succession or alterations in site management practices, long-term trends caused by factors such as acid rain and climate change will also affect the data. Separating the effects of these factors, about the influence of which we know very little, is problematic.

The identification of some species of fungi may need to be carried out by specialists; although some species can be recognised in the field by generalist staff, there are many (particularly some of the rarer species) that will need experienced personnel to be certain of a correct identification. Although some of the rare fungi are difficult to identify, there are many that are not (for example the Pink Waxcap *Hygrocybe calyptriformis*; there is no other pastel pink *Hygrocybe* in Europe, nor is there another agaric like it in colour and size). The observer should, however, on first encountering a species have a specimen checked by an expert. It must be realised that even widespread species (e.g. *Laccaria* spp.) may require a microscope to identify them and therefore the help of a specialist should always be considered. Grouping into species complexes could be one way of dealing with such common and widespread fungi, and this would allow monitoring to proceed without any loss of accuracy.

With the peculiarities of fungal life strategies and the necessity of having at the present time to identify the taxa by reference to the fruiting body, these organisms are a special case; they are not the same as plants and must not be considered so. However, every effort must be made to tailor existing survey and monitoring activities to the fungal recording process, always bearing in mind the differences between the organisms. You should endeavour to marry monitoring of one group with that of another.

11.1   ATTRIBUTES FOR ASSESSING CONDITION

11.1.1   Habitat condition

Assessing the area of suitable habitat for fungi is a method of indirect monitoring that is particularly applicable to those species with specialised habitat requirements. For example, *Tulostoma niveum*, a UK BAP Priority Species, is restricted to dense patches of moss on limestone boulders and is found in only a very few localities in Scotland; the extent of habitat at this site can be accurately assessed and mapped. Quantifying the extent of potential habitat enables subsequent monitoring effort to be targeted efficiently.

For general methods for monitoring habitat extent, see Part II.

11.1.2   Population size

Counts of the number of fruiting bodies are the only way by which we can arrive at some idea of population size in the field, although there are problems with this approach (see above). With ectomycorrhizal fungi, a very small area on a tree root may produce many more fruiting bodies than a mycelium that is colonising many more roots and is therefore more widespread. Counting the fruiting bodies in as small an area as $2\,\mathrm{m} \times 2\,\mathrm{m}$ may in fact include the fruiting bodies of several distinct individual mycelia. The number of such individuals appears to decrease as the age of the vegetation in which they are found increases.

Counts can be made in a number of different ways (Section 11.2); monitoring for species of conservation interest will generally involve a combination of these methods.

11.2   GENERAL METHODS

Table 11.1 summarises the methods available for surveying and monitoring fungi.

11.2.1   Direct searches

Principles

If a species is restricted to a known area and has specific habitat requirements, a simple and reasonably efficient monitoring method is to conduct periodic searches of the area of suitable habitat and count the number of fruiting bodies. The entire area of fruiting will indicate the minimum extent of the vegetative colony. If the entire area can be searched at one time, the number of fruiting bodies can be taken as an estimate of the total population size or area covered by the mycelium or mycelia, which can then be compared with data from other years. If the site is too large to be completely covered by one survey, counts should be made for a set duration or along a set route or area (Sections 11.2.2 and 11.2.3).

The survey should be timed to coincide with the period of maximum sporome production. If this is not known, surveys may have to be carried out on a more regular basis (e.g. one per week) for one fruiting season to identify the period of maximum sporome abundance. However, this may itself vary from year to year depending upon weather conditions. A knowledge of the ecology of the target species is required if the fruiting period has to be predicted in advance when planning a survey or monitoring programme.

Field methods

The area of suitable habitat should be searched thoroughly for fruiting bodies of the target species.

Table 11.1. *Methods for surveying and monitoring fungi*

	Recommended species group	Population size data	Efficiency	Precision	Bias	Expertise required	Advantages	Disadvantages
Direct searches	Scarce species with discrete habitat areas	Estimate	Good when used for conspicuous species with restricted distribution	Good if whole area can be comprehensively searched	Low	Identification	Can be specifically targeted to individual species	New sites may be overlooked
Quadrats	Species found over narrow area	Estimate	Reasonable	Reasonable	Estimates can be affected by quadrat size	Identification	Enables density to be estimated	Affected by spatial as well as temporal variations in fruiting
Transects	Species found over wide area	Estimate	Good for conspicuous species	Reasonable	Cryptic species may be overlooked	Identification	Enables density to be estimated; covers larger areas with greater efficiency	Searching may be less thorough as longer distances must be covered
Fixed-point photography	Scarce species with discrete habitat areas	Presence–absence Estimate of population size	Reasonable	Good if photographs are of sufficient quality	Distortions can be caused if photographs of quadrats are not aligned properly	Identification; photography skills	Provides permanent photographic record; can be used to accurately reposition permanent quadrats	Requires initial outlay on equipment

It will often be worthwhile to record the condition of any sporomes found (i.e. fresh or moribund) (Fleming *et al.*, 1998), particularly if repeat surveys are to be made in the same season; this will allow estimates to be made of the lifespan of the sporomes.

Trampling has been shown to reduce fruiting, so searches should be undertaken with caution. If logs have to be moved for any reason they should be replaced in their original position.

For rarer species, the locations of sporomes can be mapped or marked so that follow-up surveys can be made of the same areas. This will allow assessments of range expansions and contractions to be made. Sporomes can be marked with Indian ink to ensure that the same sporome is not recorded more than once. Some fruiting bodies last for a comparatively long time, whereas others disappear after a few days. Recording the lifespan of sporomes allows the measurement of the longevity and biomass of a fungus (Richardson, 1970). Fixed-point photographs (Sections 11.2.4 and 6.1.4) can also be taken as an aid to future monitoring.

Although searches should concentrate on areas in which species of interest are known to exist, one should also spend some time searching outside the currently known population boundary so that broader-scale range expansions (or previously undiscovered colonies) can be identified.

The keeping of species lists should be encouraged, as information on fungal associations is limited; there may be cohorts of species that might be recognised and used as indicators of rare species that have yet to be recorded on a particular site. New species for a site can often be added, since many are very sporadic fruiters.

Surveying should be carried out over other periods of the year as well as the generally accepted survey time of autumn. Some ectomycorrhizal fungi will fruit from May until the first frosts. Good monitoring cannot be achieved by a casual visit to an area in autumn only. Essential field equipment is listed in Appendix 6.

Data analysis and interpretation
The extent of sporome production will vary greatly from one year to the next according to changes in environmental variables. Analysing data to identify actual changes in population size is thus not possible in the short term. Five- to 10-year means of annual count data should be calculated once regular monitoring has been established, and continued for several years. If methods are standardised, trends can be analysed statistically by using techniques such as regression. If resources are not available to undertake annual counts, the accurate identification of population trends becomes more difficult, because variations due to the environmental effects on fruiting are harder to adjust for.

11.2.2   Quadrats

Principles
Quadrats can be used to delineate known areas of suitable habitat for searching. The selection of quadrat locations is covered in Section 10.5 and in Part II, Sections 5.3.2 and 5.3.3. Searching a defined area enables more population parameters to be estimated, such as sporome density. For species of high conservation interest, permanent quadrat locations in areas where the species is known to occur should be used. However, some effort should be spent on searches outside these quadrats; because fruiting is very variable, the selection of permanent quadrat locations on the basis of short-term data may omit colonies that were not fruiting when the quadrats were initially chosen.

Quadrat size depends on the uniformity of vegetation and the species of fungus under consideration. Ectomycorrhizal fungi in normal arborescent communities can be monitored with $5\,m \times 5\,m$ plots, whereas $2\,m \times 2\,m$ plots are adequate in plantations (Richardson, 1970). On cliff tops and mountain tops with dwarf willows (*Salix* spp.), $2\,m \times 2\,m$ plots are also sufficient. In very variable arborescent communities, $50\,m \times 50\,m$ or even $100\,m \times 100\,m$ plots split into four equal units have been shown to be necessary. Even in seemingly uniform communities, the variation therein should be carefully scrutinised. Lange (1982, 1984, 1991) used $2\,m \times 2\,m$ plots in studies of fruiting periodicity. In woodland systems, $2000\,m \times 2000\,m$ plots have been used (Lange, 1993).

Quadrats can be used to study hypogeous (truffle-like) fungi, which may be first located by animal diggings (such fungi are dispersed by being eaten by rodents, pigs, etc.). If piles of dung are taken as the equivalent of quadrats then coprophilous fungi can be monitored, although the timescale of monitoring must be much reduced. At least one rare macromycete occurs on dung. Moss cushions and other small areas of habitat such as tree stumps or fallen trunks could also be treated as permanent quadrat units.

See Section 11.2.1 for the principles of fungal monitoring, which apply to all methods covered in this section.

Field methods

The marking of permanent quadrats is discussed in Appendix 5. Care should be taken not to disturb or damage the surrounding community when recording quadrats: this may have adverse effects on the species being monitored. Trampling has been shown to reduce fruiting, so setting up quadrats should be undertaken with caution. If logs have to be moved for any reason they should be replaced in their original position.

Quadrats should be set out in a line or along a transect, or randomly located in grassland or similar habitats if the species is distributed over a small area. The area of the quadrat should be carefully searched, and the numbers of sporomes and their condition recorded (see Section 11.2.1).

Quadrats can be photographed by using fixed-point photography (Section 11.2.4); this provides a useful permanent record of the condition of the surrounding habitat as well as the number of sporomes. Recommended field equipment is listed in Appendix 6.

Data analysis and interpretation

As discussed earlier (Section 11.2.1), natural fluctuations in the abundance of sporomes make the correct identification of trends in population size problematic. Five- or 10-year means of sporome counts or densities calculated from quadrat data should be used to identify trends. If appropriate sampling is used, data can be analysed statistically by using standard tests (Part I, Section 2.6.4 and Appendix 4).

11.2.3   Transects

Principles

Transects for monitoring fungi can be used to cover larger areas more efficiently than is possible with direct counts or quadrats. They are more suitable for species that occur over a wide area and thus are less efficiently monitored with direct searches or permanent quadrats.

Transect locations for monitoring fungi will generally be permanent. It is possible to use distance estimation methods (measuring or estimating the distance from the transect line to each sporome) and hence use computer software such as Distance for estimating density (Section 10.6). Alternatively, you can search for sporomes within a fixed distance of the transect line and calculate densities from this (Section 10.7).

See Section 11.2.1 for the principles of fungal monitoring, which apply to all methods covered in this section.

Field methods

Trampling has been shown to reduce fruiting, so setting up transects should be undertaken with caution. If logs have to be moved for any reason they should be replaced in their original position.

The transect should be walked along a standard route while surveying the immediate area for sporomes. The number and condition of sporomes should be recorded. The perpendicular distance from the transect line to each sporome can be measured, or a strip of fixed width can be searched (e.g. 2 m on each side of the transect line). Quadrats (Section 11.2.2) can also be set along the transect.

Transects should be timed to coincide with the maximum period of sporome abundance, unless there are sufficient resources available to survey on a regular basis throughout the year.

Transects designed for recording fungal fruiting bodies should be used for other or parallel monitoring activities, because the time of fungal fruiting will not be known exactly. Therefore, the longer the window of search time the better.

Fixed-point photography (Section 11.2.4) can also be used to make a permanent record, which can be useful for assessing successional changes that may influence the abundance of sporomes. The necessary field equipment is listed in Appendix 6.

Data analysis and interpretation

As discussed earlier (Section 11.2.1), natural fluctuations in the abundance of sporomes make the correct identification of trends in population size problematic. Five- or 10-year means of sporome densities calculated from transect data should be used to identify trends. If appropriate sampling is used, data can be analysed statistically by using standard tests (Part I, Section 2.6.4).

11.2.4   Fixed-point photography

Principles

Fixed-point photography is a useful technique for assessing successional changes, marking fruiting bodies to determine longevity and studying grazing factors. It is especially suited to species such as moss cushion inhabitants (e.g. *Galerina* spp. and *Tulostoma niveum*).

The photographs can be used to create overlays, which can be compared with those from other years to assess changes in sporome abundance and distribution. They can also be useful to assess successional changes in the surrounding vegetation, which may be influencing the distribution of sporomes.

If possible, all associated organisms should be recorded by the generalist; at present, there is a lack of information on fungal associates, which needs to be addressed. It was only because of careful monitoring and observation that the full association of certain species of disc fungi with species of moss and liverwort was discovered.

See Section 11.2.1 for the principles of fungal monitoring, which apply to all methods covered in this section.

Field methods

Fixed-point photography methodology is covered in detail in Part II, Section 6.1.4. Although more concerned with large-scale monitoring, the techniques of fixed-point photography described therein are straightforward to adapt to monitoring species such as fungi on a small scale.

Briefly, a camera tripod is set up at a fixed point, which is marked so that it can be precisely relocated on subsequent visits. Photographs are taken at a fixed angle and height, with the camera settings (aperture, film speed, etc.) kept constant from year to year.

The locations of individual sporomes can be traced from photographs on to acetate sheets to facilitate comparisons of photographs from different years. Field equipment requirements are listed in Appendix 6.

Data analysis and interpretation

As discussed earlier (Section 11.2.1), natural fluctuations in the abundance of sporomes make the correct identification of trends in population size problematic. Five- or 10-year means of sporome numbers per photograph or densities calculated by using the size of area enclosed by the photographs should be used to identify trends. If appropriate sampling is used, data can be analysed statistically by using standard tests (Part I, Section 2.6.4).

11.3   FUNGUS CONSERVATION EVALUATION CRITERIA

11.3.1   Key evaluation considerations

There are about twelve thousand fungus species (including the slime moulds) in the UK but the distribution of fungi is much less well known than that of other groups of vascular and non-vascular plants. As fungi are recognised by their fruiting bodies, which are present only at certain times of the year and are unpredictable in their occurrence, they are difficult to record effectively. Thus the distributional data are, on the whole, too scanty to produce lists of scarce or rare species to be assembled (Hodgetts, 1992). The current British checklist of basidiomycetes is due for completion and the checklist for ascomycetes is in need of revision. Work is under way to produce distribution data for certain fungus groups, which are being developed as a component of the National Biodiversity Network Species Dictionary Project (JNCC, 2004).

The British Mycological Society (BMS) (webpage: www.britmycolsoc.org.uk/) was founded in 1896. The Society is active in the promotion of conservation and field mycology, and established the BMS conservation group in 1996, part of the Fungus Conservation Forum. The conservation group's focus is to promote all issues related to fungus conservation, including involvement with the inclusion of fungi in the Bern Convention; the UK Biodiversity Action Plans for fungi; the UK 'Important Fungus Areas' report (see site designation criteria below); the British Basidiomycete Checklist and the revision of the UK Red Data List for fungi. Affiliated to the BMS as part of the BMS Recording Network there are Local Fungus Groups (LFG) that now exist in many parts of the country. These can be found on the webpage that has been set up for the LFG (www.britmycolsoc.org/LFG/index.html). The BMS has set up, in consultation with other organisations in the British Isles, a Fungal Records Database (BMSFRD), which currently contains over 600 000 records of fungi. There is a checklist of British fungi and also a list that contains links to over 2000 distribution maps of various species. The maps show 10 km squares for which there are records in the BMSFRD. The BMS is also developing a British Fungal Portal, which aims to create a pioneering integrated access system for information on British fungi, building on the voluntary activities of all sectors of the community. One of its functions is to improve implementation of current Biodiversity Action Plans for fungi, facilitate their development, and promote wide-scale conservation activities.

The Association of British Fungus Groups (ABFG) (webpage: www.abfg.org/) was founded in 1996. It acts as a national organisation for field enthusiasts who are interested in learning more about fungi, and recording fungi for local and national databases. The Association includes a nationwide network currently including 26 member groups and individual members (these can be found at www.abfg.org/groups.htm). It is closely involved in the conservation of fungi in the UK, working closely with Plantlife as a member of the Fungus Conservation Forum. The ABFG also work with other organisations surveying sites of potential mycological interest and advising on conservation measures.

The ABFG, working with Plantlife and English Nature, has been involved in funding current conservation programmes and the preparation of the Conservation of Wild Mushrooms Code of Practice. Several species of fungi are edible, and 'picking for the pot' is a common pastime. Overpicking of wild mushrooms and other fungi is becoming a problem, and a Code of Practice has been developed to help tackle the problem and give advice to mushroom pickers. The code can be found at www.bms.ac.uk/Code.html.

A number of surveys are currently being run. The Pink Waxcap Survey is a joint initiative of Plantlife, the British Mycological Society, the Association of British Fungus Groups and the RSPB. The Pink Waxcap *Hygrocybe calyptriformis* is listed under the UK Biodiversity Action Plan and is part of Plantlife's Back from the Brink programme, supported by English Nature, Scottish Natural Heritage and the Countryside Council for Wales. The survey also includes the Parrot Waxcap *Hygrocybe psittacina* and the Blackening Waxcap *Hygrocybe conica*. The Countryside Council for Wales is currently undertaking a survey of grassland fungi throughout Wales. The Environment & Heritage Service is organising a survey of Waxcap Grasslands in Northern Ireland and aims to survey all the 10 km squares in Northern Ireland looking for the best waxcap sites in each. SNH funded a survey of stipitate hydnoid ('tooth') fungi in Scottish pinewoods (Newton *et al.*, 2002) and a grassland fungus survey (Newton *et al.*, 2003).

11.3.2   Protection status in the UK and EU

No British fungi are listed in Annex I of the Bern Convention or in Annex II of the Habitats and Species Directive. The proposal to add 33 species of fungi (not all of which occur in Britain) onto Annex I of the Bern Convention has been withdrawn.

Four species of British fungus are listed in Schedule 8 (scheduled in 1998) of the Wildlife & Countryside Act 1981. The species are Sandy Stilt Puffball *Battarraea phalloides*, Royal Bolete *Boletus regius*, Oak Polypore *Buglossoporus pulvinum* and Bearded Tooth *Hericium erinaceum*. Twenty-six species are listed in Section 74 of the Countryside & Rights of Way Act 2000 as species of principal importance, though only the above four species have full protection. The species listed under Schedule 8 can be found on the JNCC web page www.jncc.gov.uk/page-2126 and those in Section 74 at www.defra.gov.uk/wildlife-countryside/cl/habitats/habitats-list.pdf.

The twenty-six species listed in Section 74, plus the Black Falsebolete *Boletopsis leucomelaena*, are current Priority BAP species. The species and their Biodiversity Action Plans can be found on the UK BAP web page www.ukbap.org.uk/fungus.htm.

11.3.3   Conservation status in the UK

The Red Data Book for UK macrofungi and some microfungi is due for completion in 2004. There is no equivalent for Ireland as yet but the development of a Red Data List for fungi in Ireland has been recognised as a Lower Priority or long-term additional work under Target 2 of the Plant Diversity Challenge (JNCC, 2004). Currently 38 fungi species are classified as extinct, ten as critically endangered, 63 as endangered, 95 as vulnerable on the IUCN list (designated 1998), and one as near threatened in the GB Red Data list.

11.3.4   Site designation criteria

Very few nature reserves have been set up to conserve fungi in Great Britain and Ireland. SSSI criteria for designating sites for fungal interest are described by Hodgetts (1992), which can be found on the JNCC web page www.jncc.gov.uk/publications/sssi/sssi_content.htm. In brief, the presence of colonies of Nationally Endangered, Vulnerable or Rare species as classified by the Red Data Book are eligible, although only strong colonies of Vulnerable and Rare species may be eligible.

The Common Standards Monitoring (CSM) Guidance has now been produced by JNCC. It provides guidance on the identification of interest features, attributes, targets and methods of assessment for species on designated sites. The Guidance for Lower Plants is still under development. Information on the Guidance can be found on the JNCC webpage www.jncc.gov.uk/csm/guidance.

The Important Fungus Areas (IFAs) report by Plantlife, the British Mycological Society and the Association of British Fungus Groups, helped with funding by English Nature, the Countryside Council for Wales and Environment & Heritage Service, has now produced an interim list of over 500 sites of great significance for fungi in England, Wales, Scotland and Northern Ireland. One major problem in the conservation of fungi has been the lack of criteria against which a site could be assessed as to its mycological importance. The object of this project was to build up a database of sites considered to be important for fungi by mycological recorders and to derive criteria against which sites could be assessed (Northern Ireland Fungus Group, undated). This interim list of IFAs will help target conservation efforts to ensure that key sites get proper protection. The criteria are as follows.

CRITERION A: The site holds significant populations of rare fungal species, which are of European, or UK conservation concern. A site should be considered if it includes at least five species from: the provisional UK Red Data List (1992), UK Biodiversity Action Plan and/or Schedule 8 or the European Red Data List (A & B) and/or Species of European Concern (Bern Convention proposals)

CRITERION B: The site has an exceptionally rich and well-recorded mycota in a UK context. A site should be considered if it has at least 500 recorded species

CRITERION C: A site that is an outstanding example of a habitat type of known mycological importance

CRITERION D: A nominated site that is considered to be important but for which further information is needed

The principles behind lichen survey and monitoring techniques are basically identical to those for other groups of lower plants. However, there are some considerations peculiar to lichen survey and monitoring, which must be considered when designing a suitable programme.

Many species of conservation importance are very scarce; some are known from only a single site. In the case of lichens, a single site can be something as small as a single tree, a rock or a tree stump. Many species are relict, and under prevailing conditions cannot colonise new habitats. The sites themselves may be small relics of larger areas of ancient habitat with long continuity and a history of minimal adverse disturbance. Thus the necessary conditions in which the species can persist may only occur in one location or in a series of distinct fragments. By definition, a relict species cannot colonise distant sites even if conditions are suitable. The destruction of ancient, unrecreatable habitat is an important cause of lichen rarity, but far from the only one.

Other lichens rely on extremely localised habitats. For example, *Gyalideopsis scotica* requires decaying bryophyte material on specific soils near the summits of a few Scottish mountains. *Cladonia botrytes* grows on dead pine (*Pinus* spp.) stumps at a particular stage of decay.

Lichens may therefore require ephemeral scarce habitats or ancient scarce habitats; in either case, their habitat requirements are often very specific and any alteration of the conditions under which lichen species will grow will frequently adversely affect the health of the colony. Most species are extremely intolerant of shade, pollution, changes in substrate pH and changes in management practices. Severe weather conditions (e.g. drought, cold) can also be detrimental to lichens. A scarce lichen on a particular tree is probably doomed if the tree dies or falls over.

This extreme sensitivity to environmental change, coupled with the scarcity of suitable habitat for many rare lichens, means that any survey and monitoring programme *must* consider the condition of the surrounding habitat as well as the health or size of the lichen colony itself. If monitoring does not include this component, then a species may well be lost before any remedial action can be taken. Transplanting lichens can be carried out if an isolated colony is in serious danger. For example, lichens growing on Beech *Fagus* spp. (which has a relatively short lifespan for a tree) may need to be moved to younger trees when their current host tree dies to prevent the species from dying out. Such transplants must only be carried out after expert consultation.

Another consideration that must be taken into account is that the identification of lichens, particularly in the field, requires much specialist knowledge. Although some species are conspicuous and reasonably distinctive, many others are extremely difficult to identify, and others can only be separated from related species in the laboratory. Monitoring such species will therefore require expert assistance. Unfortunately, it may not be possible for generalist field staff to undertake lichen surveys and monitoring themselves for those very species that most urgently need to be monitored. In this case, expert advice will have to be sought.

12.1   ATTRIBUTES FOR ASSESSING CONDITION

12.1.1   Habitat condition

Lichens often grow in very localised and specific habitats; it is therefore essential that the general habitat condition be assessed on every monitoring visit. If the habitat is deteriorating, recognising this will give advance warning of a subsequent deterioration of the health of the lichen colony and will provide more time for remedial action to be taken.

12.1.2   Colony numbers

Lichens generally grow in discrete colonies. A count of the number of colonies is therefore a simple indication of the status of a species. Monitoring the number of colonies can give an indication of population trends.

12.1.3   Colony size

Assessment and monitoring of the size of a lichen colony will give a straightforward indication of the health of that colony. Expansions or contractions of colonies can be monitored and related to changes in habitat condition, especially where a remedial conservation exercise has taken place.

12.2   GENERAL METHODS

Table 12.1 summarises the general methods for surveying and monitoring lichens.

12.2.1   Habitat condition

Principles

As mentioned previously, the habitat requirements of lichens, particularly those species that are scarce, are very specific. Any change in the surrounding environment of a lichen colony can therefore have detrimental effects. Useful information for lichen conservation can be gathered by monitoring their habitat. For those species that are restricted to very few locations, habitat monitoring is essential; species can quickly be lost if habitat conditions become unsuitable.

Habitat monitoring is not strictly within the scope of this chapter. However, because habitat condition is so crucial to the persistence of lichen colonies, a brief discussion of the factors that may need to be monitored is given. For further information, see Part II for general habitat monitoring methods.

Field methods

The field methods will vary depending on the habitat of the lichen species in question. Factors that may need to be considered and monitored will include the following.

- Pollution: local industrial pollution, brickwork and quarry dust, power station emissions, agricultural pollution, waste disposal.
- Habitat destruction by natural causes: windblow of trees on to colony, death of substrate tree, mollusc grazing.
- Increased shade: increased canopy, shrub layer (particularly Holly *Ilex* spp. and Rhododendron *Rhododendran ponticum*), Ivy *Hedera helix* invasion, basal shoot growth, Bracken *Pteridium aquilinum* and Bramble *Rubus fruticosus* agg. invasion, leaf litter.
- Changes in grazing regime and other management practices.
- Changes in substrate pH and other chemical properties (e.g. nutrient status).

Refer to Part II for details on the monitoring of these factors.

Data analysis and interpretation

Data analysis will depend upon the factors being monitored. For basic monitoring of habitat condition (e.g. health of tree), a subjective assessment of change will probably be sufficient provided the suitable habitat condition is properly understood. The use of an intelligent eye to assess all change is desirable. The change that could be most damaging to the colony might not be one that was thought of when the monitoring scheme was first put in place.

Table 12.1. *Methods for surveying and monitoring lichens*

	Recommended species group	Population size data	Efficiency	Precision	Bias	Expertise required	Advantages	Disadvantages
Habitat condition	All	Not applicable	Good	Not applicable	Not applicable	Ability to judge whether changes in habitat will be detrimental to lichens	Quick and easy method for monitoring the potential health of a colony	Does not in itself monitor the health of a colony directly
Quadrats	All	Presence–absence Frequency Cover Estimate of colony number	Good for species with few colonies	Good	Estimates of cover and frequency affected by quadrat size	Identification	Provides quantitative data with little expensive equipment	Colonies must grow on more or less two-dimensional surfaces. Species from ephemeral habitats may disappear from permanent quadrats, requiring repeat surveys to find new colonies.
Fixed-point photography	All, but particularly useful for scarce species with discrete habitats	Presence–absence Cover	Reasonable	Good	Distortions can be caused if photographs of quadrats are not aligned properly	Identification Photography	Provides permanent pictorial record; can be used to accurately reposition permanent quadrats	Can be time-consuming; requires intial outlay on equipment

For variables that require quantitative assessment such as pH, changes from the monitoring baseline of ideal condition can be analysed statistically by using standard tests, provided that appropriate sampling has been used.

The susceptibility of lichens to changes in habitat condition may not be fully understood. If this is the case it may be difficult to establish what level of change is acceptable (for example, how much does pH have to change before lichen health is affected?). Monitoring of habitat condition should therefore be closely correlated with monitoring of the health of the lichens themselves.

Changes in habitat condition that are thought likely to lead to detrimental effects on the lichens should be acted upon before the effects on the lichens become serious.

12.2.2   Quadrats

Principles
The principles of quadrat sampling are covered in Section 10.5. Most quadrat monitoring of lichen colonies will involve permanent quadrats; many rare species do not spread or colonise new areas. Some species that colonise ephemeral habitats may not be suitable for monitoring with permanent quadrats, but even if a particular site may not last for long it can be monitored with quadrats located in the same place for the duration of the colonies' persistence.

As well as the quadrat colony of the lichen under observation being recorded, a search should also be made for the presence of the lichen in other nearby areas. Habitat condition (Section 12.2.1) should also be recorded.

Field methods
Quadrat size
Quadrat size should be related to the size of the lichens that occur within the colony being surveyed. Some lichens are large, whereas others are less than half a millimetre in diameter. It is therefore important to select a practical quadrat size with a practical subsection size.

For monitoring large lichens (e.g. lichens of the genus *Cladonia*, section *Cladina*, which grow on dune systems) a quadrat of 1 m × 1 m divided into 16 sections will be an appropriate size. Presence or absence of species within each section can be recorded, or cover estimates made. For smaller species a 25 cm × 25 cm quadrat will be more appropriate.

Quadrat positioning and fixing
For lichens that grow on a horizontal surface, the position of the quadrat can be fixed with a peg, which is a known distance from a buried transponder. A tape run from the transponder to the peg will locate it and fix its alignment. Final adjustments to the position of the quadrat should be made by consulting previous fixed-point photographs (Section 12.2.3).

For lichens on a vertical surface, the quadrat can be suspended from a fixed peg. Certain adhesives (and the leachate from them) such as Araldite can be toxic to lower plants; the peg should therefore be fixed at some distance above the colony being monitored.

Where the quadrat is at an angle, a fixed point (e.g. an inert screw) can be placed within the study area so that exact positioning of the quadrat can be achieved.

The potential toxicity of materials used for markers should be considered. Brass markers should not be used; the leachate from brass is toxic to a range of saxicolous bryophytes, and there is a high probability that it will affect lichens as well. Totally inert materials must be used where any leachate might affect the lower plant communities beneath: stainless steel or a hard, inert plastic could be appropriate.

Great care must be taken not to disturb the colonies during the recording process. This applies particularly to species that grow on fragile substrates. Also, the quadrat itself should never be left *in situ*; this will frequently affect the growth of the lichens underneath it.

Data recording
Presence–absence of species in each quadrat division can be recorded. Alternatively, cover estimates

can be made, although this can be more accurately achieved with fixed-point photography (Section 12.2.3). In addition, notes should be taken of the number and size of colonies, their height from the ground and aspect, and their health. Lichen health can be recorded by noting necrotic patches and discoloration of the thallus. Any change in the number of fruits of fertile species should also be recorded. Sites such as trees with colonies can be discreetly tagged to aid relocation on subsequent visits.

Except for a few ephemeral species, there is no main season for recording lichens. However, lichens are more easily seen when damp, and woodland species are much more easily seen when there are no leaves in the canopy. Weather conditions permitting, with the exception of high-level Arctic–alpine species, the months from November to April are probably best.

For most species, monitoring should be carried out every three years, but a brief check every year to ensure that no catastrophic change is occurring is desirable, particularly for rare species with few sites and epiphytes. Essential field equipment is summarised in Appendix 6.

Data analysis and interpretation

Providing that appropriate sampling has been used, changes in frequency can be examined statistically by using standard tests (Part I, Section 2.6.4).

Decreases in cover or frequency will probably be correlated to a change in an underlying habitat variable (Section 12.2.1). Correlation or regression can be used to examine these relations, and the results can be used to suggest remedial action that may need to be taken to reverse any decline.

12.2.3   Fixed-point photography

Principles

Fixed-point photography is an invaluable method for monitoring lichen communities. Photographs provide a clear unequivocal record of the condition of a lichen colony and its surrounding environment, and useful data such as cover can be derived from photographs. They also provide a means of precisely relocating and realigning quadrats for

data recording (Section 12.2.2). In general, you should take three photographs per sample point; one of the quadrat itself in close-up, one of the quadrat and its immediate surroundings, and one of the area as a whole so that small- and large-scale changes in the habitat can be assessed.

Field methods

Methodology for fixed-point photography is covered in detail in Part II, Section 6.1.4. A heavy-duty tripod should be used, and as diffuse a light as possible should be obtained. Photography is best carried out when the sky is overcast; heavy or sharp shadows can often render photographs useless for comparing with previous photographs.

When photographing quadrats, it is important to have a second quadrat for the photograph, of identical size to that used for recording, which is undivided and therefore casts less of a shadow. The shadow from a divided quadrat will obscure the lichens and make analysis difficult at a later date. If the camera and tripod settings are noted and repeated exactly on each visit, a permanent 'quadrat' can be obtained without the need for a quadrat to be physically placed over the lichens. For details of such an approach carried out for corticolous and saxicolous lichens, see Perkins & Miller (1987a,b).

Photographs should be taken at similar times of year so that surrounding species are in a similar stage of development in each photograph.

As well as photographing the quadrat itself in close-up, it is also important to monitor the immediate area by recording the quadrat within its surroundings. This will greatly assist the identification of changes to the habitat that may have affected the lichens in the quadrat. A photograph of the habitat within a few metres as well as a broader-scale photograph taken with a wide-angle lens is ideal. A macro lens will normally be essential for close-up photographs of the quadrat. Slide films provide better definition than print films, although prints are more useful for annotating in the field; there is perhaps a case for using two cameras to record in both media if resources are available. The necessary field equipment is listed in Appendix 6.

Data analysis and interpretation

Diagrams showing the position and size of the colonies can be traced from the quadrat photographs and used as overlays. Areas of colonies can be calculated by using a grid overlay. Provided that appropriate sampling has been used, the change in areas between years can be analysed statistically by using standard tests (Part I, Section 2.6.4).

If slide film has been used, A3 prints can be made with colour copiers. Quality can vary; only the higher-quality photocopiers give results of sufficient detail at A3 from a 35 mm slide.

12.3   LICHEN CONSERVATION EVALUATION CRITERIA

12.3.1   Key evaluation considerations

Lichens occur in a wide variety of habitats. In woodland, they may be present on the bark, twigs, leaves and dead wood of the trees. They occur on both man-made and natural rock outcrops. Some species occur on compacted soil and others live on dead and decaying bryophytes. On coastal shingle, lichens colonise the pebbles and the sand between the pebbles as well as detritus which accumulates from dead vegetation. Some, such as *Xanthoparmelia mougeotii*, will grow quite happily on glass, and it is not unusual to find several species on older cars. Pieces of old leather on the beach are a habitat for several very rare species, and the lichens of mine spoil contaminated with heavy metals are a study in themselves. Churchyards are a rich source of lichens as they provide a wide variety of habitats. St Brelade's Church in Jersey holds the record number of lichen species for any individual churchyard: at the latest count, 206 species had been recorded.

Lichens are highly sensitive to the state of their habitat, and will disappear fast if conditions cease to be favourable. This fact was used to assess concentrations of sulphur dioxide in the atmosphere; the resulting maps gave an accurate indication of zones of pollution throughout the UK. Since the collapse of Britain's industrial base some twenty years ago, sulphur dioxide concentrations have declined dramatically. However, in recent years nitrogen-based alkaline pollutants have taken the place of industrial effluent gases in the atmosphere, and this is having a marked effect on lichens. Heathland species are suffering from invasive competition by aggressive higher plants of the habitat. The associations of species that grow on trees are also changing. The bark of mature trees in urban areas has been so impregnated by sulphur dioxide over the years that it remains acid. To assess the effects of alkaline pollution from car exhausts and intensive farming practice, the assemblage occurring on twigs and young branches is studied; this has shown considerable change in recent years.

There are few groups of organism that are as useful for studying the health and antiquity of habitats as lichens. Since the work of Dr Francis Rose on the link between the presence of a suite of lichen species and ecological continuity in woodland started in 1974, much work has been done in formulating lists of lichens that can be used for assessing ecological continuity. Rose published two lists of lichens for this purpose. The first was a list of 30 indicator species, which was used to establish the Revised Index of Ecological Continuity (RIEC) for a wood. This index was calculated as a percentage of the 30 species, based on a formula in which the number of species present was used to calculate a percentage of a wood with a hypothetical perfect ecological continuity. The presence of twenty species gives an RIEC of 100%. A theoretical wood with all thirty would have an RIEC of 150%. Some of our very best woods have been found to have an RIEC of more than 100%. This index is particularly useful in assessing the conservation value of a wood.

In 1992, the New Index of Ecological Continuity (NIEC) was published. This is a list of 70 species and is designed to assess ecological continuity. The NIEC is simply the number of species on the list that are present. The NIEC list of lichens contains species that are more difficult to identify, and therefore the index is designed for use by the more experienced lichenologist. Woods with a high degree of ecological continuity are likely to support rarer species, and this is taken into account in that bonus species may be added to the NIEC number to give a 'T' NIEC number. Sites with a 'T' NIEC number of more than 30 are considered to be of high conservation value for lichens. Those with fewer than 20 are likely to be of limited importance. However, in the southeast and eastern parts of England, woods with lower NIEC numbers may have greater conservation importance.

Recently, it was found that certain NIEC species held little significance as indicators of continuity in certain parts of the UK. Species such as *Lobaria pulmonaria*, whose presence is highly significant in Sussex, are virtually ubiquitous in Western Scottish woodlands. Coppins & Coppins (2002) have provided the most up-to-date list of lichen indices, building on the NIEC and RIEC developed by Rose. These indices include the following.

Western Scotland Index of Ecological Continuity (WSIEC)

This index is used in Western Scottish Highlands. It is a baseline list of fifty species to which notable bonus species may be added.

Eu-Oceanic calcifuge Woodland Index of Ecological Continuity (EuOIEC)

This index is used mostly for oak-dominated woodland in more upland and exposed situations in Western Britain. It has a base list of thirty species to which notable bonus species may be added.

Eastern Scotland Index of Ecological Continuity (ESIEC)

This index is used in eastern Scotland as well as in the England–Wales border country. It consists of 30 indicator species to which notable bonus species may be added. This index is used for assessing the native pine forests of Scotland.

Western Ireland Index of Ecological Continuity (WIIEC)

This index is used for assessing woodland in the extreme oceanic conditions of south-western Ireland. Lichen associations found here have a similarity with those of Macronesia. Fifty species are listed, and once again notable species may be used to establish a 'T' number.

The NIEC is now used for woodland in England, in Wales except for the area where the ESIEC is appropriate, and throughout most of Ulster and the Republic of Ireland. It may be used in conjunction with the EuOIEC in western, upland parts of these areas.

A similar list of indicator lichens has been suggested for the assessment of continuity by using saxicolous species growing on old buildings and in churchyards. This list was published in the Bulletin of the British Lichen Society provisionally by Rose, but is not yet widely used. Similar indices could be made for use in assessing ecological continuity in heathland, well-established bryophyte- and lichen-dominated calcareous grassland, stabilised dune systems and land contaminated by heavy metals.

As has been already stated, lichens associate closely with very specific ecological parameters. They can therefore be used to assess the nature of the substrate on which they are growing. Various geologies with a variety of climate, altitude and latitude all have their specific lichen floras. The lichens of the Arctic–alpine regions of Britain have been well studied by a small but dedicated group of energetic lichenologists. Lichens also grow in a wide range of coastal situations, and a few are even intertidal. There is also a lichen flora of unpolluted streams, rivers and lakes. Thus lichens may be used by competent lichenologists to establish the nature, continuity and health of a great variety of habitats, both natural and man-made.

Many lichens are known to be slow-growing and to live for extremely long periods of time. This has been used to age geological events such as rock falls and glaciation. There are also fast-growing species such as members of the genus *Peltigera* and *Lobaria* as well as ephemeral lichens. Some lichens are ephemeral in that their fruiting bodies are strictly seasonal. Many of the lichens associated with heavy metal contamination fall into this last category.

12.3.2   Protection status in the UK and EU

No British lichens are listed on Annex I of the Bern Convention or in Annex II of the Habitats Directive.

Thirty-two species of British lichen are listed on Schedule 8 of the Wildlife & Countryside Act 1981. Thirty-three species are listed on Section 74 of the Countryside & Rights of Way Act 2000 as species of principal importance, although only the thirty-two species listed in Schedule 8 have full protection. However, the species listings conflict; the most recent list of species listed under Schedule 8 can be found on the JNCC web page www.jncc.gov.uk/page-2124 and those in Section 74 at www.defra.gov.uk/wildlife-countryside/cl/habitats/habitats-list.pdf.

12.3.3   Conservation status in the UK

Many lichens are very rare and threatened. In 2003, the British Lichen Society published a new Red Data list of lichens. (Woods & Coppins, 2003). This supersedes all previously published lists including those prepared by JNCC.

The following Conservation Categories are used for the threatened species. The numbers given are taken from Woods & Coppins (2003).

Extinct	32 species
Critically Endangered	40 species
Endangered	30 species
Vulnerable	106 species
Data Deficient	226 species
Near Threatened	205 species
Least Concern	117 species
Not Evaluated	79 species
Total	1835 species

There are still a number of new species waiting to be described, and many of the parasymbionts and most lichen parasites are not included. However, non-lichenised fungi traditionally studied by lichenologists, such as *Stenocybe*, are included.

There are also lichens that are the subjects of Biodiversity Action Plans. These have been the subject of especially intensive searches by members of the British Lichen Society. In several cases, this has resulted in a considerable re-assessment of their rarity status. In at least one case, that of *Lecanactis hemisphaerica,* the species was found to be a churchyard variant of another species, *Lecanographa grumulosa.*

A new category of International Responsibility has also been designated. These are species that are rare internationally, and where Britain holds the majority or highly significant populations of the species. So far 180 species have been so designated.

Twenty-eight species are protected under Schedule 8 of the Wildlife & Countryside Act 1981. Originally, this consisted of 30 species, but two have been deleted following recommendations by the British Lichen Society. See the JNCC website for the most recent listings.

The above categories are for threat to, and conservation of, species. British Lichens are also listed by rarity; categories used are Nationally Rare and Nationally Scarce. Some 63% of the British lichen flora is either Nationally Rare or Nationally Scarce. A significant number of these are considered as being of least concern regarding their conservation status. Nationally Rare species are restricted to between 1 and 15 British ten kilometre squares. Nationally Scarce species are restricted to between 16 and 100 British ten kilometre squares. The British flora also contains endemic species. Figures for these categories are as follows.

Nationally Rare	646 species
Nationally Scarce	525 species
Endemic	32 species
Including possibly endemic	43 species

12.3.4   Site designation criteria

Many sites that are important for lichens will have been selected on the basis of habitat or vegetation types, although some sites, such as woodland with a distinctive *Lobarion pulmonariae* lichen association, may have non-vascular plants as the major interest but low vascular plant interest. However, since 1992 when the SSSI guidelines for non-vascular plants were published, it has been possible to designate SSSIs purely for their lichen interest. Several SSSIs now exist where the primary interest is the lichen flora (Church *et al.*, 1996).

SSSI criteria for designating sites for lichen interest are described by Hodgetts (1992), which can be found at the JNCC web page www.jncc.gov.uk/publications/sssi/sssicontent.htm.

All sites with viable populations of species listed on Schedule 8 of the Wildlife & Countryside Act 1981 can be selected for SSSI designation. All Red Data Book species' localities can be considered as candidate sites. In addition, a scoring system for Nationally Rare and Scarce species and species characteristic of certain climatic conditions can be employed, with a threshold score for a nationally important assemblage of 200 for most parts of Britain and 300 in parts of the south-west, Wales, the Lake District and most of Scotland. Schedule 8 species score 200, Nationally Rare 100, and Nationally Scarce 50. The Indices of Ecological Continuity (see above) can also be used to select ancient woodland and parkland sites for SSSI designation.

13 • Bryophytes

Surveying and monitoring bryophytes poses considerable problems. Most are so small and difficult to identify that anything other than qualitative or at best semi-quantitative data is time-consuming and expensive to acquire. Some species are difficult to identify even for specialists, and some always require confirmation with a microscope. Working with bryophytes takes longer than working with most vascular plants. Many species grow in association with other species, and trying to quantify the amount of a target species can easily cause considerable damage to the habitat.

There are very few published studies on surveying and monitoring bryophytes in Britain. Most monitoring has consisted of merely checking that species are still present, with only limited attempts at recording population size.

A feature of some bryophytes is that they may be strongly associated with other plant species. This is obviously true with epiphytic species (e.g. *Orthotrichum obtusifolium,* which only occurs on trees with nutrient-rich bark) or *Jamiesonella undulifolia,* which is restricted to *Sphagnum* hummocks.

13.1 ATTRIBUTES FOR ASSESSING CONDITION

13.1.1 Presence–absence

Monitoring of bryophytes has in the past concentrated upon establishing that a species of interest is still in existence on sites where it has been previously recorded. Presence–absence in a series of samples (e.g. quadrats or transects or individual host plants for epiphytic species) can be used to establish frequency and to generate broad distribution maps for target species.

13.1.2 Population size

Semi-quantitative or quantitative methods will involve some measurement of extent. For most bryophytes it is not feasible to count individuals, because it is never known whether a clump represents one individual or many. Species that form discrete cushions, mats or turfs can be counted in these units. Otherwise, area can be estimated and treated as an index of population size (the greater the extent, the healthier the population is assumed to be, even if the number of individuals comprising that extent is unknown).

Cushion-formers tend to occur in monospecific cushions and are thus suitable for direct counting of cushions and area measurement. Some turf-formers can also be monitored in this way, but others occur in association with other species, giving rise to the added complication of estimating the proportion of the turf occupied by the target species. Similar problems occur with mat-formers; few species form discrete monospecific stands.

Techniques suitable for long-lived perennial bryophytes will rarely be useful for annual or 'short-term shuttle' (see During, 1992) species. Fixed-point photography and permanent quadrats are not suitable for monitoring short-term species over time; for these species, presence–absence in defined areas could be used. Populations of ephemeral species are often subject to wide fluctuations, so the identification of trends may require the calculation of at least 5-year means of data.

Within the ephemeral group there are species for which the time of year of monitoring may be critical; for example, those that can only be identified from mature sporophytes or those that may be inaccessible in winter.

13.2   GENERAL METHODS

The general methods for monitoring bryophytes are summarised in Table 13.1.

13.2.1   Total counts

Principles

Counting individuals is rarely an option with bryophytes, because most species form turfs, cushions or mats comprising aggregates of stems, which may or may not be a single individual. Not all of these life forms are discrete, so if some form of quantitative technique is required it is vital from the outset of monitoring to establish what is to be counted.

Counting cushions is an effective way of quantifying the amount of cushion-forming species, but you cannot be sure that each cushion is an individual. By considering each cushion as a circle, measuring the diameter gives a means of estimating total area, but where large numbers of cushions occur this can be time-consuming and cause considerable disturbance.

Field methods

If the target species is confined to a reasonably small location, total counts can be made of all the individual units in that area. In larger areas, a more efficient means of estimating numbers can be achieved by using timed counts, transects (Section 13.2.3) or quadrats (Section 13.2.4).

The area to be searched should be examined carefully for the target species. Non-ephemerals can be marked with a discrete tag or stake to ensure that clumps are not counted twice; this will also enable data to be collected on the longevity of individual units. The best method is to mark all individuals, cushions or patches and then count the markers. Data on extent of cushions or patches can be added if required.

Samples of some species may need to be taken for later identification by a specialist. This is obviously undesirable for rare species, but is unavoidable for those species that require microscopic analysis to confirm identification. Recommended field equipment is listed in Appendix 6.

Data analysis and interpretation

Providing methods are suitably standardised, counts from different years can be compared statistically using techniques such as regression (Part I, Section 2.6.4). If individual cushions have been marked and re-found at a later date, estimates can be made of the mean lifespan of a clump.

13.2.2   Visual estimates

Principles

Where bryophytes are conspicuous because of their size, colour or other characteristics, and where the population is relatively large and confined to a well-defined site or habitat, visual estimates can be a rapid means of recording frequency or abundance. Within stands that contain the target species, it is rare that the species will be sufficiently abundant to allow commonly used scales, such as the Domin scale, to be used. It may therefore be necessary to define a scale that is sensitive enough to reflect the abundance of the target species in all stands.

Most visual estimate scales such as the DAFOR scale are semi-quantitative and involve a certain amount of subjectivity. It is therefore essential that the scale to be used is clearly defined before monitoring starts, or at least established with a pilot study when baseline data are being gathered. It will usually be appropriate to make visual estimates within quadrats (Section 6.4.2) in order to standardise recording techniques.

Field methods

Making visual estimates of bryophytes is carried out in a similar manner to that used for vascular plants, with adaptations of the scales used if required. This is covered in more detail in Part II, Section 6.4.2. The essential field equipment is listed in Appendix 6.

Table 13.1. *Methods for surveying and monitoring bryophytes*

	Recommended species group	Population size data	Efficiency	Precision	Bias	Expertise required	Advantages	Disadvantages
Total counts	Large, conspicuous species forming discrete patches	Presence–absence Index of population extent	Good if species confined to small area	Good if species readily distinguishable	Low	Identification	Produces quantitative data	Can cause considerable disturbance
Visual estimates	Conspicuous species with large, well-defined habitats	Semi-quantitative index	Reasonable	Low if subjective cover scale is used	Subjectivity will introduce errors based on surveyors' interpretations	Identification	Quick and simple method of assessing abundance	Species usually too scarce to use Domin or DAFOR scales; scale may need to be devised especially for rarer species
Transects	Frequent and reasonably sized species	Estimate of number of units or cover	Good for single line transects; band transects take longer	Reasonable	Low	Identification	Covers larger areas quicker than other methods and allows extent to be extrapolated	May not be sensitive enough to detect change adequately
Quadrats	Permanent quadrats for long-lived and perennial species Temporary quadrats for short-term species and annuals	Presence–absence Estimate of cover, frequency and number of units	Better for temporary quadrats; permanent ones take time to relocate	Good for permanent quadrats	Size of quadrat affects measures of cover and frequency	Identification Marking of permanent quadrat locations	Good for monitoring of small areas of perennial species accurately	Permanent quadrats unsuitable for short-term species
Photography	Long-term and perennial species and broader scale habitat quality	Estimate of extent and/or number of clumps	Reasonable	Good if photographs are of sufficient quality	Distortions can be caused if fixed-point photographs of quadrats are not aligned properly	Identification Photography	Provides permanent pictorial record; can be used to pinpoint stands and accurately reposition permanent quadrats	Requires initial outlay on equipment

Data analysis and interpretation

Refer to Part II, Section 6.4.2 for details of how to analyse visual estimate data. Data obtained by using subjective scales similar to the DAFOR scale are imprecise and can only indicate broadscale changes in abundance. More quantitative scales such as the Domin and Braun–Blanquet scales are more sensitive to change. The appropriate scale for bryophyte monitoring will need to be sensitive enough to detect the level of acceptable change of the abundance of the target species.

13.2.3   Transects

Principles

Monitoring bryophytes with transects is an appropriate method when the target species is known to be frequent within a defined area and forms cushions or turfs of a reasonable size so that a sample will give a reasonable reflection of the population as a whole.

Field methods

Field methods for transects will generally follow those for vascular plants (Sections 10.5 and 10.7 and Part II, Section 6.4.6). Refer to Appendix 6 for the necessary field equipment. The simplest transect form of counting species along a line (Section 10.7.4) can be used, but even with species that are frequent within the habitat this method may not be sufficiently sensitive to monitor populations accurately, and single strip transects (Section 10.7.3), whereby all stands within a set distance from the transect line are counted, can be used instead. It may be necessary to adjust the transect line to accommodate non-linearity of bryophyte habitat.

Data analysis and interpretation

See Sections 10.5 and 10.7 and Part II, Section 6.4.6, for details of how to analyse transect data.

13.2.4   Quadrats

Principles

Making counts (Section 13.2.1) and visual cover estimates (Section 13.2.2) may require randomly selected temporary quadrats to allow comparable

and representative data to be gathered for species that are spread over a large area or those that are not conspicuous.

If the performance of individual stands of a target species is to be assessed over a period of time (i.e. for rare species restricted to a very few sites), permanent quadrats can be used.

The scale of the bryophyte species being monitored and the problems of identification need to be established at the outset of monitoring. For many species of conservation importance, including most UK BAP Priority Species, quadrat sizes need to be small (50 cm × 50 cm maximum size). The method is best suited to those that form cushions and well-defined turfs or mats.

The procedure for randomly selecting quadrats and a discussion of the pros and cons of temporary and permanent quadrats is given in Part I, Sections 2.3.4 and 2.3.3, respectively.

Field methods

Location of random quadrats is covered in Part I, Section 2.3.4. Marking locations of permanent quadrats is of great importance if the quadrats are to be accurately relocated. Quadrats can be marked with transponders as for permanent lichen quadrats (Section 12.2.2), and many of the same considerations apply. Quadrats themselves should not be left permanently *in situ*, and care must be taken not to damage the species or habitat. The problem of damage to the habitat caused by large numbers of quadrats should be taken into account when deciding how many quadrats to use. A summary of the recommended field equipment is given in Appendix 6.

Data analysis and interpretation

Provided that sampling is representative, data can be analysed statistically by using standard tests (Part I, Section 2.6.4). See also Section 10.5 and Part II, Section 6.4, for details of how to analyse quadrat data.

13.2.5   Photography

Principles

Photographs of broad-scale bryophyte habitat can serve as a useful alternative to sketch maps for recording areas where target species occur and can be used to examine successional trends, which could be used as an indicator of the development of unsuitable conditions. In practice, the presence–absence of the target species in stands on marked photographs is likely to be the most popular form of monitoring, as it is relatively quick and cheap, but it is not suitable on a smaller scale.

Fixed-point photography can be used for long-lived species. The technique is similar to that used for lichens (Section 12.2.3) and vascular plants (Section 15.2.5).

Field methods

For broader-scale habitat photographs, individual stands can be marked with easily visible markers and the area in which the species occurs can be marked on the photograph after developing. The photographs should be clearly aligned to illustrate the site and to include easily recognisable features to aid relocation on subsequent visits.

For fixed-point photographs the scale must be sufficient to allow recognition of the species from the photograph, and so this technique is only feasible for those species that form readily identifiable cushions, turfs or mats. Refer to Section 12.2.3 for details on fixed-point photography methods and Appendix 6 for a summary of the field equipment required.

Data analysis and interpretation

Diagrams showing the position and size of the cushions, mats or turfs can be traced from the quadrat photographs and used as overlays. Areas can be calculated by using a grid overlay. Provided that appropriate sampling has been used, the change in area between years can be analysed statistically by using standard tests (Part I, Section 2.6.4, and Appendix 2).

If slide film has been used, A3 prints can be made with colour copiers. Quality can vary; only the higher-quality photocopiers give results with sufficient detail at A3 from a 35 mm slide. More versatility is available with digital format.

13.3   BRYOPHYTE CONSERVATION EVALUATION CRITERIA

13.3.1   Key evaluation considerations

The UK contains about a thousand bryophyte species. About sixty-five percent of the known European bryophyte flora occurs in the UK, which has a unique blend of northern Atlantic, Mediterranean and Lusitanian elements (JNCC, 2004). The extremely rich bryophyte flora of Britain is widely recognised as a biological attribute of major international importance (Church *et al.*, 2001). Knowledge of the taxonomy and distribution of bryophytes has always lagged behind that of vascular plants, for the simple reason that they are so much smaller and less conspicuous (Hill *et al.*, 1991).

The British Bryological Society (BBS) (www.britishbryologicalsociety.org.uk) has co-ordinated the collection of data on the distribution of species in both Britain and Ireland since its foundation (as the Moss Exchange Club) in 1896. The BBS Mapping Scheme was set up in 1960 to map the 10 km square distribution of the bryophyte flora of the British Isles. The data collected were used to create a database on the geographical distribution of British bryophytes and to produce maps of the British bryophytes at the 10 km square scale, distinguishing recent from older records (Hill *et al.*, 1991). In 1991 the first (covering liverworts) of the three volumes of the *Atlas of the Bryophytes of Britain and Ireland* by Hill *et al.* (1991 *et seq.*) was published, with the two subsequent volumes published in 1992 and 1994. It is clear from the maps that there are several areas in Great Britain that are seriously under-recorded and that there remains a great deal of scope for fieldwork in Ireland. The BBS plans to continue to record bryophytes at a 10 km square scale, in order to build on the foundation laid by the *Atlas*. Experience with other taxonomic groups shows that the publication of an *Atlas* for any taxonomic group is the most effective way of identifying recording errors and drawing attention to under-recorded areas (Hill *et al.*, 1991). The BBS have a network of Regional Recorders who co-ordinate bryophyte recording in individual vice-counties. New or updated records from vice-counties are published each year in the

Bulletin of the British Bryological Society. Periodically, these are compiled in a vice-comital *Census Catalogue* (e.g. Blockeel & Long, 1998).

Bryophytes are a characteristic component of cultivated land in Britain, but knowledge of their status, distribution and ecology lags well behind that of arable vascular plants (Porley, 2000). Bryophytes are included in several current conservation programmes. Under the Scottish Cryptogamic Conservation Project, known sites of selected threatened species have been surveyed and conservation recommendations drawn up. English Nature's Species Recovery Programme, a programme of action for bringing threatened species back from the brink of extinction, includes several bryophyte species (Church *et al.*, 2001). CCW continue to survey and monitor key sites for rare bryophytes, with attention focusing primarily on BAP species. However, most targeted action for species conservation now takes place under the UK Biodiversity Action Plan.

The key considerations with regards to evaluating species at a site are listed below.

1. Check lists of species of conservation importance and protection status (see below for information on which lists to check and where to obtain the relevant information).
2. Carry out a preliminary (scoping) survey to identify whether there is a need for a detailed survey. This kind of assessment should involve looking for BAP and nationally notable (NS, S8, RDB, NT, etc.) species on the list and then assessing the assemblages of woodland taxa if in lowland Britain or the Atlantic Assemblage (oceanic species that occur along the Atlantic seaboard – Atlantic fringe of Europe where there is higher rainfall and atmospheric humidity) if in the west (see Hodgetts, 1992). What part of the country the site is in should be taken into account, as there is a gradient of decreasing diversity roughly from the north-west to the south-east. If a reason has been identified for carrying out a detailed survey then one should be carried out by an expert bryologist.
3. A local county bryological recorder could be contacted. The list for these can be found on the British Bryological Society web page (see above). They may have information on whether the site contains suitable habitat for bryophytes. If they have already been to the site they may have a species list or records for rare or scarce species that occur there. If notable species have been found then records should be sent to the local county recorder along with specimen samples of these species.

13.3.2   Protection status in the UK and EU

Four British bryophytes are listed in Annex I of the Bern Convention: *Marsupella profunda* (Western Rustwort), *Petalophyllum ralfsii* (Petalwort), *Buxbaumia viridis* (Green Shield-moss) and *Hamatocaulis vernicosus* (Slender Green Feather-moss). There are no bryophytes listed under the protection for species themselves in the Habitats Directive, but the above four species require Special Areas of Conservation (SACs) to be designated for their protection (Annex IIb). *Sphagnum*, as a generic inclusion, and *Leucobryum glaucum* are afforded protection by inclusion in Annex Vb of the Habitats Directive to avoid excessive damage by commercial moss collectors.

Thirty-seven species of British bryophyte (nine liverworts and twenty-eight mosses) are listed in Schedule 8 of the Wildlife & Countryside Act 1981. The species listed under Schedule 8 can be found on the JNCC web page www.jncc.gov.uk/species/plants/p5.htm. Forty-six bryophyte species (eleven liverworts and thirty-five mosses) are listed in Section 74 of the Countryside & Rights of Way Act 2000 as species of principal importance. The list can be found at www.defra.gov.uk/wildlife-countryside/cl/habitats/habitats-list.pdf.

Sixty-four species (thirteen liverworts and fifty-one mosses) are currently priority BAP species. The species and their Biodiversity Action Plans can be found on the UK BAP web page www.ukbap.org.uk/lichens.htm. Bryophytes have also been taken into account in several of the Habitat Action Plans, for example in the Action Plan for upland oakwoods (Church *et al.*, 2001).

13.3.3   Conservation status in the UK

The Red Data Book for bryophytes has been completed for Britain but there is no equivalent for Ireland as yet. The development of a Red Data List for bryophytes in Ireland has been recognised as a Medium Priority additional work under Target 2 of the Plant Diversity Challenge (JNCC, 2004). Eighteen bryophyte species (one liverwort and seventeen mosses) are classified as extinct, twenty-four as critically endangered (two liverworts and twenty-two mosses), forty-two as endangered (four liverworts, one hornwort and thirty-seven mosses), sixty-six as vulnerable (twenty-five liverworts and forty-one mosses), seventy-six as near threatened (twenty-four liverworts and fifty-two mosses) and twenty-four as data deficient (six liverworts and eighteen mosses) in the GB Red Data list. Of the species that are without IUCN classification, a group of fourteen species are classed as nationally rare (four liverworts and ten mosses) and two hundred and fifty-four as nationally scarce (eighty liverworts, two hornworts and one hundred and seventy-two mosses). In time, these species will also be assessed against IUCN criteria. A full list can be found on the JNCC web page www.jncc.gov.uk/species/Plants/threatened/default.htm. However, as this list relies entirely on records from the BBS *Atlas*, some species that it includes are merely under-recorded.

The World Red List of Bryophytes currently includes 92 species. This list is only a small subset of globally threatened species. The list can be found on the IUCN Species Survival Commission Bryophyte Specialist Group web page via the BBS web page mentioned above.

13.3.4   Site designation criteria

Many sites that are important for bryophytes will have been selected on the basis of habitat or vegetation types: bogs are a prime example. Similarly, bryophyte-rich Atlantic woodlands sometimes do not form particularly good examples of woodland community types, and as a consequence a few woods of great importance for bryophytes had escaped notice before 1992 (Hodgetts, 1992). However since 1992 when the SSSI guidelines for non-vascular plants were published, it has been possible to designate SSSIs purely for their bryophyte interest. Several SSSIs now exist where the primary interest is the bryophyte flora (Church *et al.*, 2001).

SSSI criteria for designating a site for bryophyte interest are described by Hodgetts (1992), which can be found at the JNCC web page www.jncc.gov.uk/publications/sssi/sssi_content.htm. In brief, the main requirements for site selection are the presence of the largest population of a Schedule 8 or Red Data Book species within an Area of Search or the presence of an assemblage of notable species that scores above a certain threshold . The latter uses a scoring system that includes rare and scarce species, Atlantic, sub-Atlantic and western British bryophytes, 'woodland indicator' bryophytes (for use in eastern, south-eastern and midland lowland woods), endemic species, non-endemic species threatened in Europe, declining species, and species at the edge of their range (Hodgetts, 1992). A refined version, assessing individual elements separately, may be developed in time. For full details see the Guidelines.

The Common Standards Monitoring (CSM) Guidance has now been produced by JNCC. It provides guidance on the identification of interest features, attributes, targets and methods of assessment for species on designated sites. The Guidance for Lower Plants is still under development. Information on the Guidance can be found on the JNCC web page www.jncc.gov.uk/csm/guidance.

Aquatic macrophytes and algae can be divided into two relatively distinct groupings: (a) the micro-algae, such as diatoms and most green and blue-green algae, which can only be seen, identified and counted with the aid of a microscope; and (b) those vascular plants and macroalgae that can be seen and assessed by the naked eye. Macroalgae include, in marine systems, the seaweeds and certain filamentous algae, and in freshwater systems the stoneworts (e.g. *Chara* and *Nitella* species) and filamentous algae (often lumped under headings such as 'blanket weed').

The methodology for surveying and sampling microalgae in their various forms, e.g. single-celled phytoplankton, diatoms growing on substrates and benthic mats, and in various habitats, e.g. freshwater, estuarine and marine systems, has been developed over the years and such methods are generally well described. This section provides an overview of some of the main aspects of the different techniques for surveying and monitoring aquatic microalgae; the reader needs to consult some of the recommended sources at the end of the book for further details or seek advice from an appropriate specialist. Different techniques are required for aquatic macrophytes; perhaps surprisingly, methods are still being developed to ensure that reliable surveying and sampling can be undertaken in a systematic and repeatable form.

Monitoring macrophytes in the aquatic environment presents some problems that have necessitated the development of techniques that are distinct from those used for monitoring terrestrial plants. In shallow, clear waters, adaptations of terrestrial techniques can often be used, but in deeper or turbid waters the following problems must be addressed.

- Access to the plant being monitored: plants in deep water will require boats and possibly divers (either snorkel divers or those with subaqua equipment).
- Visibility: turbid conditions will hinder visibility and make observations difficult. A bathyscope (glass-bottomed bucket) can be used, but problems may still occur.
- Substrate: if the sediment is soft, wading may be impracticable even in shallow waters; risks must be fully assessed. Sediment can also be disturbed by divers or by quadrats, leading to impaired visibility.
- Annual and seasonal fluctuations: the extent of fluctuations in growth in some aquatic plants is considerable. This means that survey timing is of critical importance when you are examining long-term population changes.
- Relocation of sample points: accurately fixing your position on large water bodies can be difficult. Various methods can be employed; these are detailed in the following sections.

Because of these difficulties, most methods for monitoring deeper-water species do not provide fully quantitative estimates. Using divers can yield quantitative data but is time-consuming and requires training and specialist equipment, although sub-aqua equipment is not always necessary. Such methods are similar to those used for aquatic habitat monitoring; see Part II, Section 6.3 for more information.

There are also particular safety aspects to consider when working in or near water. In particular, personnel should be trained in the relevant aspects of aquatic safety and the use of appropriate safety equipment. Surveyors should work in pairs and carry mobile phones or radios if working in remote areas. These should be used to contact colleagues at agreed times to confirm that sampling is proceeding safely and according to schedule. Boots or waders are a necessity but chest waders should be avoided, as they can seriously hinder mobility if they fill with water. Sampling should not be carried out when a river is in spate or when weather conditions are particularly bad. Before attempting to gain access to a water body, water depth and substrate stability should be checked (with a net pole or similar) to make sure that it is safe to sample.

Other safety aspects listed in Part I, Box 2.11, should be followed as appropriate.

14.1   ATTRIBUTES FOR ASSESSING CONDITION

14.1.1   Presence–absence

Monitoring of aquatic macrophyte and particularly algal communities is often undertaken as part of water quality monitoring. These methods can be used for species monitoring; presence–absence in vegetation samples can be used to map the distribution of individual species, and semi-quantitative frequency data can be derived.

Some aquatic plants are annuals, with considerable year-to-year fluctuations in range and number. Others can vary considerably in seasonal abundance depending on conditions such as climate, nutrient load and competition from other plants (including algal blooms). Presence–absence in areas of suitable habitat may be the most efficient way of monitoring these species. Monitoring areas of suitable habitat is not covered in this part; refer to Part II (Sections 5.9, 5.10 and 6.3.1) for further details.

Presence–absence of algae can also be used as a monitoring tool. For large benthic algae, samples can be taken from marked areas. For smaller algae and phytoplanktonic algae, more specialist extraction and analytical techniques are required.

14.1.2   Population size

More detailed monitoring of macrophytes will require estimates of population size such as cover and density. These can be estimated by using adaptations of methods for terrestrial vegetation such as quadrats and transects. Each of these approaches will require different methods, which need to be considered when any work is being planned.

Estimates of planktonic algal density can be made in the laboratory from water samples collected in the field. These will require specialist techniques and identification skills, which will not necessarily be covered by field staff. There are many different types of algae: filamentous, unicellular or multicellular, epilithic or epiphytic. It is beyond the scope of this *Handbook* to cover all these types in detail. Refer to the recommended sources at the end of the *Handbook* or an appropriate specialist for further guidance if required.

14.1.3   Community composition

This may be an appropriate attribute to monitor for aquatic macrophytes and microalgae; species lists compiled from samples can be used to identify associations of species, which can be monitored for changes in composition, or species richness can be compared from different surveys.

14.2   GENERAL METHODS

Table 14.1 gives a summary of the general methods suitable for monitoring aquatic macrophytes and algae.

14.2.1   Quadrats and transects

Principles

In water bodies shallow enough to be waded, techniques used for terrestrial vegetation such as quadrats and transects can be used (with suitable methodological adaptations). If the water is clear, visual methods can be used in deeper water for presence–absence surveys from a boat. It is also possible to carry out sampling in deeper water with snorkelling or diving equipment. Fully quantitative data can be collected (e.g. density and cover), which cannot be obtained with grapnel surveys (Part II, Section 6.3.2).

Table 14.1. *Methods for surveying and monitoring aquatic algae and macrophytes*

	Recommended species group	Population size data	Efficiency	Precision	Bias	Expertise required	Advantages	Disadvantages
Grapnel surveys[a]	Macrophytes Charophytes Large benthic algae	Presence–absence Semi-quantitative frequency	Reasonable	Fairly good for presence–absence Moderate for frequency	Small rosette and fine-leaved plants are under-recorded	Boat handling Identification from fragments	Cheapest way of semi-quantitative sampling of deep-water communities	Underestimates some species Only suitable on still or slow-moving waters Destructive
Quadrats and transects	Macrophytes Charophytes Large benthic algae	Presence–absence Frequency, cover and density	Good in shallow water; expensive if diving is required	Potentially good, but will depend on exact method	Potentially good, but will depend on exact method	Identification Boat handling Diving (deeper per water/ poor visibility)	Provides full quantitative data	Expensive in deep waters Turbid water makes recording difficult
Water/ substrate sampling	Microalgae	Presence–absence Density Community composition	Low: laboratory equipment and time required	Reasonable if methods are sufficiently standardised	Smaller species will slip through net Some species hard to dislodge from substrate	Boat handling Identification	Only way to sample algal community with any degree of precision	Identification is expensive and time-consuming

[a] see Part II, Section 6.3.2. for details.

The principles of quadrats and transects are covered in Sections 10.5 and 10.7, and further information on their applications for vegetation monitoring is given in Part II, Sections 6.4.2 and 6.4.3 (quadrats) and 6.4.6 (transects). Guidance on the selection of appropriate quadrat size is given in Appendix 4.

Field methods

Quadrat or transect locations can be either permanent or temporary. For scarce species of conservation interest with a restricted distribution, permanent sample locations can be used. However, for those species that are widely distributed, or that fluctuate considerably in distribution (for example, those that occur in ephemeral habitats), temporary quadrats will be more suitable.

Marking the locations of permanent sample points can be difficult; markers will need to be more robust than those used for terrestrial locations, particularly in fast-flowing waters. Coloured plastic stakes driven into the substrate can be used, although if the substrate is soft and deep markers can still be lost or buried.

The use of global positioning systems (GPS) to relocate sample points can be considered if the system is sufficiently accurate. Triangulation can achieve a high level of precision. Alternatively, compass bearings on two features on land at 90° from each other can be used. Good accuracy can also be achieved by lining up two features on land in one direction and two in another. This could involve lining up a feature on the shore with one on the horizon, but the features must be permanent. Alternatively, stakes can be put on the shoreline. It is easier for a boat operator to steer a transect by keeping two markers in line than to hold to a compass bearing. Divers can swim out to where the lines cross and will know when to dive down to search for submerged permanent markers. An even more accurate method for work near the shore is to put posts in at regular intervals and measure the distance from the nearest two posts to the sample point.

Data recording can be inhibited by turbid water or by reflected sunlight. Polaroid sunglasses and/or a glass-bottomed box can be used to gain a clearer view of the vegetation, although if there are several layers of vegetation it can be difficult to part the upper layers to see what is beneath. If samples are being recorded by using divers, this problem will be less acute, but difficulties may still occur in very cloudy water. Soft substrates can be stirred up by the movement of divers' fins, which will hinder accurate identification and recording, and quadrats may sink below the sediment surface. Problems may also occur in eutrophic lakes later in the summer if algal blooms occur. A stick with a hook on the end can be useful for collecting particular plants for closer examination. The equipment required for field recording is summarised in Appendix 6.

Surveys should be carried out during the period from June to September, but the precise timing will depend on the species. Some species (e.g. those from ephemeral pools in dune slacks) may require earlier surveys. Repeat surveys should be at similar times of the year, unless seasonal variation is being investigated, and repeated at least every three years for larger and typically more stable habitats, e.g. large lakes, and annually for smaller habitats such as drainage ditches, channels and ponds in which change is more rapid. Some rarer species may require monitoring more frequently. Initial surveys may have to be more frequent to establish how much variation occurs, both seasonally and annually, and to determine the optimum monitoring time.

Some species cannot easily be identified under water; it can be difficult to see important characteristics, and using a hand lens is not feasible. Samples will therefore have to be taken of these species for identification either on the surface or later in the laboratory.

Suitable safety clothing should be worn. Workers should also be aware of the risk of catching Weil's disease; toxic blue-green algae are also a hazard at certain times of year.

Certain established survey and assessment methodologies have included aquatic macrophytes as part of the data collected. These include River Corridor Surveys (National Rivers Authority) and River Habitat Assessment (Environment Agency).

Data analysis and interpretation

Analysis will depend on the information gathered (e.g. cover, density and frequency). See Part II, Sections 6.4.2, 6.4.3 and 6.4.6 for details on the analysis of vegetation data from quadrats and transects.

14.2.2   Water and substrate sampling

Principles

Monitoring of microalgal species may be undertaken for a variety of reasons: to assess overall importance of phytoplankton or benthic algae, to indicate the trophic status of a water body, to assess the population of a rare species, or to record a toxic species (e.g. blue-green algae), a species particularly used as a food plant by a larger organism of conservation interest, or an indicator species known to be associated with a rich community or healthy conditions. Many methods exist for taking and analysing freshwater algae. Some methods involve specialised electronic equipment for *in situ* counting, but if you are interested in particular species, samples must be taken to the laboratory for analysis. This section covers only the basics of algal sampling. For more technical details and methods consult Bailey-Watts & Kirika (1981) and HMSO (1984).

Field methods
Phytoplankton

The aim of surveying a water body for phytoplankton could be to determine presence–absence of species but is more usually to achieve a measure of the number of cells and/or filaments of species per unit volume of water. A water body can be sampled with a sample bottle or other container (particularly suitable for eutrophic water bodies) or with a plankton net (a fine-mesh net with a bottle at the end). Both can be used for taking standardised samples of known volumes of water. The area of the net frame can be simply calculated. The volume of water sampled can be calculated from the area of the net frame, the speed of water flow, the speed of dragging the net and the time taken per sample. The volume should be standardised for all samples. Phytoplankton communities change with depth; you should therefore either sample at a constant depth or sweep the net through the entire water column. Sampling at a set depth requires nets that can be opened and closed remotely. The net can be fixed to a pole or towed behind a boat.

Samples should be taken from strategic locations, e.g. along a transect for larger water bodies, or at regular distances along a river. For larger water bodies a GPS may be required to locate sample points accurately (see Section 14.2.1 or the site can be marked by a buoy.

Algal cells will decay rapidly after collection and should be placed in a suitable preservative as soon as possible. Lugol's iodine solution is the commonest preservative used (see Bullock (1996) for further details). Samples should be kept in lightproof containers.

Densities of species can be determined by counting subsamples of each sample with a microscope (some microscopes are specifically designed to facilitate counting algal cells, e.g. inverted microscope). The identification of phytoplankton is time-consuming and will probably require expert assistance. Several pieces of equipment are available to facilitate counting. The most commonly available is a counting chamber modelled on the haemocytometer (developed to count red blood cells). This holds a precise volume of water in which you can count the numbers of each species. Several subsamples should be counted from each sample.

Phytoplankton populations can fluctuate dramatically within a few weeks and the timing of peaks will vary from year to year depending on weather conditions. Samples will therefore need to be taken at regular intervals throughout the year.

Benthic or epiphytic algae

Microalgae can grow on a wide range of substrates, e.g. stones, leaves, sediment and concrete, in most if not all aquatic and semi-aquatic habitats. The range of techniques for assessing the presence–absence and abundance of algal species is, not surprisingly, equally varied. The methods can be broadly divided into the following approaches.

- Direct observation of the colonised surface, e.g. viewing a leaf surface under a microscope and identifying and counting cells per unit area
- Removing the algal cells from an area of the substrate, for quantitative estimates, from a known area of leaf, rock or other surface. This can be achieved by removing, e.g. scraping the cells off *in situ*, or removing the cells in the laboratory, e.g. by washing or scraping. The cells are then suspended in a known volume of water and can be counted using similar techniques as described for phytoplankton
- Provision of artificial substrate in the water body for cells to colonise. These can be of such material as stones (cleaned of any algae), plastic plates or glass. The artificial surfaces are typically returned to the laboratory and sampled as described in the section immediately above
- Sampling of soft sediment, e.g. by using a quadrat and taking a sample with a large syringe or other suction device

For large mats of algae, cover estimates can be made by using quadrats (Section 14.2.1).

Laboratory analysis is carried out in the same way as for phytoplankton samples. Counting of algae from sediment samples is problematic; small species will be obscured by sediment particles. Such techniques are described in texts such as Flower (1985) and Bullock (1996).

Data analysis and interpretation

Presence–absence data from samples can be used to generate species lists for water bodies, which can be compared with those of other water bodies in order to determine, for example, level of eutrophication or salinity. Such a process can be developed by using quantitative data; sample data can be analysed with multivariate statistical programs such as DECORANA (see Section 20.2.1) to examine differences in algal community structure between water bodies or at different times of year. Data can be compared with data collected from other years, e.g. density measures, by using standard tests (Part I, Section 2.6.4).

14.3   REQUIREMENTS FOR SPECIES OF PARTICULAR CONSERVATION IMPORTANCE

14.3.1   Introduction

Aquatic macrophytes and microalgae present a diversity of form and taxa that will dictate the survey techniques necessary to assess status. Those species of aquatic vascular plant that grow only as emergent species can in large measure be treated as terrestrial plants. The majority of species pose particular problems and can be usefully divided into the following categories, some species falling into more than one category.

- Species with different growth forms, for example exhibiting floating leaves in some conditions but in others only submerged leaves (e.g. Floating-leaved Plantain *Luronium natans*). Some species can have emergent, floating and/or submerged leaves, e.g. Arrowhead *Sagittaria* species.
- Species present as submerged plants only, which can either only be seen from a boat or by a snorkel or subaqua diver, or in turbid conditions only seen by divers or by using a remote sampling method, e.g. grapnel or grab.
- Species present only in a dormant form, which can be short-term, i.e. a winter bud, or long-term, e.g. certain types of turion. It is important to remember that a number of species of aquatic plant of conservation significance can be dependent upon such propagules and that their apparent absence from a water body can be transitory, e.g. the stoneworts (*Chara* and *Nitella* species) and pondweeds (*Potamogeton* species).
- Some scarce species of microalga can occur at low density, e.g. mesotrophic and oligotrophic species in regions where most of the water bodies have become eutrophic. Sampling strategies must reflect this situation.

An example is provided to give an insight into a particular species, Slender Naiad *Najas flexilis*.

14.3.2   Slender Naiad *Najas flexilis*

The Slender Naiad is a protected species under Schedule 8 of the 1981 Wildlife & Countryside Act and Annexes IIb and IVb of the EU Habitats and Species Directive, and is listed on Appendix I of the Bern Convention. It is also the subject of a UK Species Action Plan.

Slender Naiad is a submerged macrophyte, occurring only in a submerged form. It is rare throughout its European range and is found in clear lowland lakes with low (oligotrophic) or medium (mesotrophic) plant nutrient concentrations. Underlying shell sand or limestone outcrops are often present, making the water lime-rich.

A monitoring protocol for the Slender Naiad recommended that the plant should initially be monitored on an annual basis for 3 years to establish a baseline, and then surveys should be repeated at 3 year intervals.

Surveying for this species has been undertaken by using various techniques including grapnelling, snorkelling and diving, although monitoring requirements vary depending on the abundance and distribution of the species.

Slender Naiad grows in beds at a depth of usually between 1.0 and 2.2 m. Diving surveys are therefore required to monitor this species. The first requirement is to map the location of the beds accurately. This may require the use of a GPS. Once the beds have been located and mapped, they should be marked and subdivided with permanent markers so that transects or quadrats can be relocated with accuracy.

The optimal monitoring time for the species is late July to early August when the plants are approximately 15 cm in height and have shining white nodes, which makes them stand out from other species.

The species grows on fine silty mud and this can be a problem when placing quadrats as the mud becomes disturbed. Permanent transects, marked with coloured plastic shafts driven into the substrate and weighted lines, are recommended in areas where the mud is deep, and can be used for all Slender Naiad sites. The recording method should be a belt transect 1 m wide with counts of shoots every square metre or every other square metre.

14.4   AQUATIC MACROPHYTE CONSERVATION EVALUATION CRITERIA

14.4.1   Key evaluation considerations

Owing to their special nature, aquatic macrophytes and microalgae have often been considered separately in terms of their evaluation and site evaluations from other elements of the flora. Aquatic macrophytes in fresh waters pose particular problems in terms of even determining presence and absence; separate programmes of survey, evaluation and monitoring are typically undertaken, especially with regard to the truly aquatic component, submerged species in particular, of lakes, reservoirs, rivers and canals.

However, the same range of legislation and designation as all other vascular plant taxa governs vascular aquatic macrophyte species. They are included in reviews of scarce and rare species, e.g. those by Stewart *et al.* (1994) and Wigginton (1999), and are a recognised component of site designation such as SSSIs (e.g. pondweed *Potamogeton* species).

Although there are no alien freshwater macrophytes to which legislation might apply, there is an increasing imperative to include alien invasive or potentially invasive aquatic species within the survey, evaluation and monitoring of aquatic habitats. In the case of freshwater macroalgae, on the one hand, the stoneworts (e.g. *Chara* and *Nitella* species) are dealt with similarly to vascular plants; for example, rare species are recognised under the Wildlife & Countryside Act and are considered in designation of sites such as SSSIs. They have their own Red Data Book (Stewart & Church, 1992). Filamentous algae, however, e.g. species of *Cladophora*, *Vaucheria* and *Spirogyra*, are generally regarded as nuisance species; no rare or scarce species has been identified and dealt with in the same way as aquatic vascular plants and stoneworts. They are considered with the microalgae.

Microalgae (including the macrofilamentous algae) have not attracted the same attention as the vascular plants and stoneworts and there is no requirement that either the species themselves or their indicator value in terms of assessing status of a freshwater habitat be taken into consideration. Unusually, an algologist has provided data for a given site that identifies its value for particular species and which, alongside other characteristics, have led to designation or site safeguard, e.g. unusual or rare desmid species in a series of ponds or an algal species indicating mesotrophic conditions.

14.4.2   Protection status in the UK and EU

The chapter dealing with vascular plants in general (Chapter 15) applies to aquatic vascular plants and in large measure to the stoneworts.

Although able to invade a range of habitats, Japanese Knotweed *Fallopia japonica* and Giant Hogweed *Heracleum mantegazzianum* are often considered as 'aquatic' species owing to their favouring the banks of rivers, streams, canals and lakes. These alien invasive species are legislated under the Wildlife & Countryside Act such that it is an offence to spread them into the 'wild'. The presence of one or both species in a site is considered to degrade its nature conservation value.

14.4.3   Conservation status in the UK

The Red Data Books for vascular plants in the UK and Ireland apply to aquatic vascular plants. The stoneworts of the British Isles have their own Red Data Book (Stewart & Church, 1992).

Relative to non-aquatic vascular plants, knowledge on the distribution and health of populations of aquatic vascular plants and stoneworts is relatively poor owing to such problems as the inaccessibility of habitats, the underwater growth particularly of submerged species and the relative difficulty in identification, e.g. the stonewort species and pondweeds (*Potamogeton* species). Both these groups contain a number of scarce and rare species and both groups are valuable indicators of the conservation of wetlands and waterbodies.

14.4.4   Site designation criteria

Aquatic macrophytes are an important component in the designation of sites of nature conservation value. They are taken into consideration in the same way as other vascular plants and stoneworts. There are no special SSSI criteria for designating a site for these plants as there are, say, for bryophytes (Hodgetts, 1992).

Aquatic macrophytes are an important source of food, either directly or indirectly, for wildfowl; the extent and health of aquatic macrophyte populations are increasingly being taken into consideration in those water bodies that do or that might support nationally or internationally significant populations of waterfowl species.

As described above, the presence of Japanese Knotweed and Giant Hogweed, species erroneously described as 'aquatic', along with other aquatic alien invasive species, e.g. Australian Swampstonecrop *Crassula aquatica*, is a negative aspect of the flora of freshwater bodies.

There are a series of general problems that can be encountered when monitoring vascular plants, not all of which will apply in every case. The type of plant being surveyed, the methods used and the recorders can all affect the results (Rich & Woodruff, 1990).

Defining an individual
Defining an individual plant can be a problem; opinions differ between botanists. With annuals or biennials there are rarely difficulties as their growth forms are generally simple. Perennials have more varied growth forms. If the species grows in dense clumps, the clumps might be composed of one or more individuals, and species spreading by stolons or rhizomes may form single or mixed patches of clones. Clonal perennials may also fragment, resulting in two or more parts of the original plant. Trees tend to be counted as individual trunks, although some trees such as Aspen *Populus tremula* spread by suckers.

Alternatively, proxy measures of abundance can be used such as the number of ramets or shoots, or percentage cover, rather than the number of individuals.

The method by which an individual is defined should be clearly stated at the outset of survey and monitoring, so that this can be followed subsequently.

Defining populations
The definition of the extent of a population varies between botanists. It is possible to delimit populations by compartment, habitat, site, ownership or other boundaries, distance to nearest neighbouring populations, or by 1 km square, etc. Populations that fluctuate from year to year may form discrete patches in some years when numbers are low, but merge when they are high. Again, it is best to state how populations are defined. A long-term view of the functioning of metapopulations may be very difficult to obtain.

Method selection according to growth patterns
The monitoring methods must also allow for patterns of growth. For instance, Carnation Sedge *Carex panicea* is a clonal species, which grows radially outwards from the initial plant; the centre of the patch then dies off. A permanent quadrat centred on a young plant will thus show an initial increase and then a longer-term decrease as the plant grows outwards. Most species show clustered microdistribution patterns.

Vegetative and flowering plants
Most populations consist of both flowering and vegetative individuals. Consequently, counting only flowering individuals will underestimate total population size. Surveyors should therefore be able to identify species from vegetative growth, and it may be worthwhile distinguishing the proportions of flowering and vegetative plants. There are relatively few vegetative identification keys available (see Rose, 1981; Rich & Jermy, 1998).

Plants in flower may be easier to see than vegetative ones; simple presence–absence can be rapidly assessed on this basis. The number of flowering plants can be used as a proxy measure of the abundance of a colony for example, as used for monitoring Alpine Milk-vetch *Astragalus alpinus*.

Variation due to timing of survey

Individuals may have a period of dormancy below ground when they do not appear for a year or more. For instance, individual plants of Early Spider Orchid *Ophrys sphegodes* may be dormant for one or two years (see Hutchings (1987a,b), but see also Sanger & Waite (1998)). Some plants show seasonal variation in appearance, and are only visible or identifiable at particular times of year. For instance, leaves of Lesser Celandine *Ranunculus ficaria* appear in the winter and plants flower in the spring; there are no visible signs of the plants from about July to November. Other species such as Small Cow-wheat *Melampyrum sylvaticum* or Mountain Scurvy-grass *Cochlearia micacea* are only readily identifiable when flowering and/or fruiting. The timing of surveys should therefore be specified and standardised.

Population sizes may vary depending on when the surveys are carried out for other reasons. Populations of annuals may increase through the summer owing to continued recruitment from seed. In this case, seedlings can be recorded separately from established plants, but the problem then becomes one of deciding when a seedling becomes an established plant. For example, Kidney Vetch *Anthyllis vulneraria* seedlings are often abundant in May, but few survive to flowering; counts including seedlings will be much higher than counts of established plants only. There are often large fluctuations from year to year due to climate, especially in annuals, and biennials (e.g. gentians, *Gentianella* spp.) may be abundant in alternate years. It may be best to survey some species only in good years, or to survey in greater detail in good years.

Dates of surveys must be recorded to aid the determination of future survey dates, and to aid data interpretation if counts are unexpectedly high or low (e.g. past the main flowering time for counts of flowering shoots). Poor weather should ideally be avoided, but if this is impossible, the weather conditions should be recorded. If the objective of monitoring is to gain accurate information on population sizes, the survey date should be adjusted to take into account yearly variations in growing and/or flowering times caused by weather conditions (e.g. an early or late spring). If flowering times are delayed, this should be noted and the survey postponed.

Observer bias

The recorders themselves are a major source of variation (Rich & Woodruff, 1990), (Bibby *et al.* (2000) give comparable assessments for bird surveys); recorders are better at repeating their own work than other people's. Experienced botanists almost always provide better information than inexperienced surveyors, whereas experts may be needed for particularly critical species (e.g. *Taraxacum clovense*). However, even experts make mistakes. Factors such as weather, season, the level of fatigue of the recorders, and even biting insects in some locations, result in subjective variation from day to day.

Large, broad-leaved or clumped taxa are better recorded than small, well-dispersed or fine-leaved taxa. Species at ground level in tall or dense vegetation (e.g. Adder's Tongue *Ophioglossum vulgatum*) can be easily overlooked.

Surveys of small, intensively searched areas are more repeatable than surveys of larger, less intensively searched areas. Semi-quantitative surveys based on objective measurements (e.g. presence–absence) are more repeatable than are quantitative surveys based on more subjective measurements (visual cover estimates in particular are often inconsistent).

Accessibility

Some types of habitat, such as cliffs and wetlands, can be difficult to survey thoroughly. Health and safety considerations may require pairs of surveyors, with consequent increases in costs.

Frequency of monitoring

Guidance on establishing the required frequency of monitoring is given in Part I, Section 2.1.5. However, of prime importance is the need to ensure that changes are detected before they become irreversible. The optimum frequency of monitoring therefore needs to be based on potential intrinsic rates of change and the likelihood of extrinsic factors influencing a feature. Plants with the highest potential rates of change and those that may require the most frequent surveying and monitoring are:

- annuals or short-lived perennials;
- species with a small population (i.e. only a few individuals or a few small colonies);
- species with a very restricted, local distribution (rather than a widely scattered distribution);
- species with low reproductive output;
- species in vulnerable or dynamic habitats; and
- species in habitats subject to sudden changes in management.

From the above, a priority list can be devised for the survey and monitoring programme. However, priorities may change with time; for example, if the status of a species shows some stability over a long period of time then the frequency of monitoring can be reduced.

Key points for survey

- If the species is easily detected, populations can be counted directly or estimated from samples; if the population is localised or relatively small, then whole-population methods can be employed; otherwise, samples should be taken. Demographic techniques are required to detect changes in population structure (Section 15.2.4). Photography (Section 15.2.5) can provide general information about the habitat as well as about the plants themselves.
- If some colonies of a specific species are inaccessible (such as cliff-face species), only a sample of the total population may be available for survey; the proportion surveyed will be an unknown percentage of the total population.
- For statutorily protected species, such as those listed on Schedule 8 of the 1981 Wildlife & Countryside Act, total counts should be conducted at least every 5 years as part of their quinquennial review.
- Populations often contain a significant proportion of non-flowering individuals. Population size therefore cannot be assessed from number of

flowering plants alone. Vegetative identification skills may be required.

15.1   ATTRIBUTES FOR ASSESSING CONDITION

15.1.1   Presence–absence

For some plants, basic monitoring may simply involve establishing whether or not they are still present at a site. This will also apply to baseline surveys of new sites, during which a species list can be drawn up to identify priority species for monitoring. More detailed monitoring based on presence–absence in grid cells (e.g. 1 km × 1 km or 50 m × 50 m squares) can be used to map the range of a species. Repeat surveys can then be used to assess whether the species' range is expanding or contracting.

15.1.2   Population size

Determining the size of a species' population is key to assessing its status. However, as discussed above, there may be difficulties in distinguishing individual plants to ascertain the actual population size. Counts of shoots, number of flowers, number of flowering stems, cover or percentage frequency, etc., can be used as proxy measures of population size.

Further discussion of measures of plant species abundance is provided in Part I, Section 2.1.2.

15.1.3   Plant growth and reproduction

The relative size of plants or parts of plants (e.g. height, clump diameter) can give an indication of how well the plants are growing in a certain habitat. The basic assumption is that the larger the plants, the better they are growing. Additionally, if plant size is measured between two points in time and growth rate is calculated, a high growth rate relative to that plant's growth capability will indicate good conditions. Surveys of plant size can also give information on population structure and life history for some species. Similarly, the number of flowers, flowering heads, flowering stems, flowering plants or fruits indicates the reproductive health of the population; the assumption again is that the more flowers, fruit, etc., the better the plants are growing. Both measures are sensitive to environmental factors such as grazing and weather.

When assessing the numbers of flowering shoots it must be remembered that aerial shoots can be grazed, thus reducing apparent numbers, and that not all individuals will flower every year. Also, as a result of the variability of growth and flowering between years and the short flowering period of some species, assessments should be conducted annually at the same time of season (although actual calendar dates may vary if a season is delayed or advanced compared with the average). To obtain accurate results, if the attribute is dependent on a period of a certain type of weather (such as wet weather for frond production or sunny weather for flower emergence), the timing of the survey should be such that the survey is only conducted after this critical weather has occurred. For example, surveys of shoots of Oblong Woodsia *Woodsia ilvensis* are only conducted after a period of wet weather and between two specific calendar dates (Geddes, 1996).

Any monitoring of plant size is likely to be long-term and will probably involve tracking the progress of individual plants. Such methods are probably best used to gain broad indications of the health of the population and are useful in that they are relatively rapid to conduct. Results should then be used as a trigger for more intensive studies should plants appear to have a reduced growth rate compared with what is expected or has previously been observed.

The size of clonal plants can be estimated by the total area covered by the plant or the sum of the dense patches of shoots within a total area.

Measures of plant size over an extended period, coupled with observations such as the size at which sexual maturity is reached or the plant ceases to flower, can give useful information on the life history of a species and are a step towards detailed demographic studies.

The variables that can be measured include height, diameter of clump, rosette or trunk,

number of leaves or fronds, and number of shoots. The length of shoots produced in the current field season can be measured, but the timing of this should be restricted until after the growing season. This can be difficult if there is a mild winter and the plants keep growing.

The frequency of survey should be tailored to the growth rate and longevity of the species. Annuals or biennials may require several surveys in the same growing season whereas herbaceous perennials, shrubs and young trees may only require measurement once a year. Similarly, older trees may only require surveying once every 4–5 years.

Analysis of trends in plant size are likely to be more meaningful if there is an indication of why plant size is being affected and what environmental factors may be acting on the plants. Techniques such as regression analysis may be appropriate to examine the effect of environmental factors on the health of a population.

Plant size distribution within a population can give some information about population structure. The simplest measures used to characterise the distributions are:

- mean plant size;
- variability in plant size; and
- skew, i.e. whether the size distribution has long tails to one side or another, implying that there are some individuals that can be very different in size from the majority.

Analysis of these parameters may be used for limited predictive purposes. If the distribution is seen to be changing so that the numbers of small plants (new recruits) are decreasing, it may imply that the population has low numbers of young plants and could be on the verge of a population crash.

For detailed accounts of the methods for surveying and monitoring the size and flowering of plants, see Section 15.2.4.

15.1.4   Population dynamics and structure

The long-term status of a species is generally dependent on many more factors than distribution and population size. A population's viability will also depend on its structure and dynamics, including longevity, recruitment, mortality and other aspects of life history. Such attributes may, therefore, require monitoring (see Part I, Section 2.1.2). This information may help to identify the stages of a species' life cycle at which it is more vulnerable, which will in turn aid the targeting of management actions and resources. Monitoring such attributes will be particularly important for rare species, which are confined to only a few sites or populations.

Details of the population structure and dynamics of a species can be gained from two types of survey.

1. Surveys measuring performance indicators such as cover, numbers of flowers, etc. and size of plants (e.g. where it is hard to identify an individual plant).
2. Surveys that use demographic techniques to gain detailed information on the life cycle of a species and to identify vulnerable stages at which population numbers decrease compared with the previous stage (Section 15.2.4).

15.2   GENERAL METHODS

Table 15.1 outlines the general techniques for surveying and monitoring higher plants.

15.2.1   Look–see method

Principles
This method is appropriate where it is only necessary to establish the presence of a species or to gain a rough estimate of a population size. Population sizes can either be obtained by total counts or estimated from crude samples obtained by timed counts or standard walks.

The look–see method is widely used and probably applicable to the widest variety of situations but is somewhat subjective and provides relatively crude data. It is often used as a preliminary method to obtain a general impression of the status of a plant (e.g. Mountain Scurvy-grass (Dalby & Rich, 1994)).

This method has the advantage that it is quick to carry out; large areas can therefore be assessed within an acceptable timescale. Site maps showing locations of plant populations can be annotated with additional information such as the presence of nearby colonies or soil types.

Field methods
In its simplest form, you walk through the site, visiting the appropriate habitat(s), and estimating each population size by eye or by counts if possible. Population estimates can either be exact figures, where sufficient time is available, or based on the logarithmic scale (1–10, 10–100, 100–1000 plants, etc.) to give an order of magnitude. Alternatively, a crude indication of the population size can be given by using the DAFOR scale (Part II, Section 6.4.2).

These methods are somewhat subjective and estimates vary between observers. Estimates of population size may vary depending on the effort taken or the time spent recording. If a variety of sites are to be surveyed and compared, a standard amount of time per unit area or a standard route should be allocated for recording to make the data more comparable.

Methods based on timed searches or standard walks are recommended for assessing large areas of vegetation and where the use of systematic total counts (Section 15.2.2) or sample-based estimates is not possible or too time-consuming. Standard walks follow a fixed pattern, such as a 'W', and start at the same place in each survey. To increase consistency further, it is also useful to fix the time spent searching along the route. Timed searches may also use haphazard searches of suitable habitat or random rather than standard walks. Random walks are conducted by calculating a random compass bearing, walking on that bearing for a certain distance, then walking on another random bearing for the same distance and so on. Every plant of the target species within a defined band (e.g. 1 m) adjacent to the standard or random walk is then counted, forming an incomplete total count.

The value of these methods is considerably enhanced if the areas searched and the locations of any populations detected are marked on a map.

Data analysis and interpretation
At its simplest, the results of this method are used to establish whether a species is present or its

Table 15.1. *Methods for surveying and monitoring higher plants*

	Recommended species groups	Population size data	Other attributes	Efficiency	Precision	Bias	Expertise required	Advantages	Disadvantages
Look-see	All	Presence–absence Minimum estimates		High, for intended purpose	Low	Observer bias, tends to underestimate population size where estimates made	Identification skills	Rapid	Accuracy dependent on time spent surveying; does not show flux in population structure
Systematic total counts	All; limited to small, localised populations	Presence–absence Exact totals of population		High, labour-intensive	Very high	If grids are used, they may follow a pattern in the vegetation such as ridge and furrow	Identification skills	Very precise and normally accurate	Only appropriate for small, localised populations
Frame quadrats for cover/density[a]	All ground flora and shrubs	Presence–absence Cover Density	Height Flowering	Relatively time-consuming, especially if very accurate cover values required	Cover values can be very imprecise	Conspicuous species often overestimated by cover estimates	Identification skills and experience of cover value estimation	Cover values provide good description of the contribution of a species to a vegetation community	Cover estimates can be imprecise Cover scales such as Domin are non-linear and thus statistical analysis is limited

Method	Habitat	Data recorded	Other attributes	Accuracy	Precision	Bias	Skills required	Advantages	Disadvantages
Frame quadrats for frequency[b]	Ground flora	Presence–absence Frequency	Height Flowering	Good	Low	Biased against species with clumped distributions; shoot frequency is biased against smaller plants	Identification skills	Data are quick to collect Method is easily repeatable by different surveyors	Requires large number of quadrats Tall and coarse vegetation causes difficulties with small quadrats
Point quadrat[c]	Short ground flora	Presence–absence Cover	Vertical canopy structure	Low	High	Low, but over-estimates cover of spreading species	Identification skills and experience with method	Most objective, precise and accurate way of measuring cover	Very time-consuming and requires large number of samples to detect rarest species
Line and point intercept transect[d]	All, but especially useful in tall or sparse vegetation	Cover Frequency		High	High	Over-estimates spreading species	Identification skills	Quicker to record than quadrats	Not suitable for individual species in dense habitats
Belt transect[d]	All, but especially useful in tall or sparse vegetation	Frequency Cover Density	Height Flowering Size	Relatively time-consuming, especially if very accurate cover values required	Cover values can be very imprecise	Conspicuous species often give over-estimated cover estimates	Identification skills and experience of cover value estimation	Cover values provide good description of the contribution of a species to a vegetation community	Cover estimates can be imprecise Cover scales such as Domin are non-linear and thus statistical

Table 15.1. (cont.)

	Recommended species groups	Population size data	Other attributes	Efficiency	Precision	Bias	Expertise required	Advantages	Disadvantages
									analysis is limited
Permanent plots[e]	Trees and shrubs	Frequency Cover Density	Population structure and dynamics	Low if data on performance of individuals are collected	High, but cover values can be imprecise	Plots may not remain representative of wider habitat	Identification skills	Very detailed data can be collected Observed change can be related to performance of individuals	Time-consuming Plots may become lost or unrepresentative over long time periods
Temporary plots[f]	Trees and shrubs	Frequency Cover Density	Height Size	Quicker to record than permanent plots	High, but cover values can be imprecise	Generally low	Identification skills	Quicker than permanent plots Randomisation ensures sample remains representative	Data collected are less detailed than for permanent plots
Plotless sampling[g]	Trees and shrubs	Density	Height, etc., if required	High	Varies with type of sampling method	Serious bias occurs if species distributions are not random	Identification skills	Quick method, which requires little equipment	Biased if trees are non-randomly distributed Does not select a random sample of trees
Selected colonies	Species that form discrete colonies	Presence–absence	Can be used to study population structure	High	High	Colonies may not be representative of the entire population if not randomly selected	Identification skills	More efficient use of available time with large populations	Extrapolation to whole population difficult if few colonies monitored or

Technique	Taxa	Data type	Cost/effort			Skills needed	Advantages	Disadvantages
Demographic techniques	All	Presence–absence Absolute counts Life history data, vegetative and sexual recruitment	Low, very labour-intensive	High	None	Identification skills and experience with mapping methods	Yields detailed data with high degree of confidence	Survey must run for a considerable length of time and frequent surveys needed non-randomly selected
Photography	All	Presence–absence Extent Cover General habitat information	High	Not applicable	Under- or over-estimation due to difficulty of interpretation	Identification skills Photography skills	Enables rapid assessment of the environment and provides permanent pictorial record	Difficult to analyse objectively or with any accuracy

[a] See Section 6.4.2.
[b] See Section 6.4.3.
[c] See Section 6.4.5.
[d] See Section 6.4.6.
[e] See Section 6.5.2.
[f] See Section 6.5.3.
[g] See Section 6.5.4.

population is above a threshold level (i.e. a change limit, which may be the minimum requirement for monitoring). Thus, there is no doubt over a positive result, but if the species is not found in sufficient numbers care must be taken in interpreting such negative results. This is particularly important for EIA studies. In particular, there are inherent problems with observer bias. Some surveyors will tend to overestimate population sizes by this method, whereas some will underestimate. Some surveyors will be consistent in population estimation and some will not. The look–see approach tends to underestimate population size compared with more systematic approaches.

The inconsistencies of approach with this method will make comparison of repeat surveys from different years difficult. If count time, count area or both are standardised, comparisons are more valid, but differences due to observer bias and the relatively crude data that are obtained will mean that the reliable identification of changes will be unlikely unless they are large. As annual counts are not based on samples, no measure of variation is obtained and consequently differences between two years cannot be compared statistically. Similarly, trends over a number of years might be examined informally, but results should be treated with caution. To maximise the sensitivity of the technique to detecting trends, assessments should be made as often as possible, ideally on an annual basis.

15.2.2   Systematic total counts

Principles
Systematic total counting is a method that can be used to ensure that all areas are covered and all plants counted. This method increases consistency and therefore produces more accurate results, but it is more time-consuming and costly than the look–see method (Section 15.2.1). Systematic total counts can only realistically be carried out on small populations.

Field methods
The aim is to count all individuals in the population. Techniques to improve accuracy include marking individual plants and the use of grids and transects to delineate search areas.

To ensure consistency between searches, it is important to ensure that a record is kept of the area searched (preferably on a map), the methods used and the total search time.

Maps and diagrams
The location of individual plants or colonies should be marked on a small-scale site map (1:5000 or larger). If a map of the site with a superimposed grid (see below) is used, the cells of the grid can be marked as they are surveyed, to ensure that no cells remain unsurveyed. Using a grid also makes mapping more accurate because the lines of the grid can be numbered, giving each cell unique co-ordinates which can assist the relocation of plants on future surveys. Maps, sketches and photographs can also assist the relocation of plants on subsequent surveys. Maps can be annotated with other information such as the presence of nearby colonies, features to aid relocation and general habitat information (e.g. vegetation height and presence of other species).

Plant or population location markers
Individual plants can be marked by using flags, canes, tags, hat pins, etc. to ensure that all are counted. Marking plants also helps to avoid trampling, as well as delineating the extent of the colony and making the plants more visible in photographs (Section 15.2.5). Permanent markers can be valuable for relocating populations but should be discreetly positioned to avoid attracting interest from members of the public or livestock. A map will probably be necessary showing the relation of the marker to the plants.

Tape measures
For perennial species, a pair of tape measures with fixed permanent starting points can be used to record the 'co-ordinates' of plant locations. They can also be used as transect lines or to set up grids to aid systematic coverage.

Grids
A grid can be superimposed on a site. This can assist a surveyor in locating positions within the site,

determining the location of a plant or simply checking that every part of the site has been surveyed. The numbers of plants in each cell can then be counted. Sufficient details should be given to ensure relocation of the grid in subsequent surveys.

The grid is merely an aid for the surveyors and thus the size of the component cells can be tailored to the individual site and particularly to the size of the plants under survey. The orientation of the grid should be such that it is easy to use; if the habitat is an obvious rectangular shape, then one of the boundaries of the habitat can be used as the edge of a row of cells. More usually, the habitat is an irregular shape and in these cases it is easier for the surveyor if the orientation of the grid is aligned to a straight feature such as a path or fence line. In the absence of any helpful features the grid can be oriented on simple compass bearings (e.g. north–south). If other features are used, the bearing of these features should be taken and used for defining the grid.

It should not be forgotten that there is a difference between magnetic and true north. Thus the compass will read the magnetic north, but bearings worked out from a map will be based on true north and will need to be converted to magnetic north before use. (Useful acronyms to remember are: MUGA, Map Unto Ground Add (6 degrees); and GUMS, Ground Unto Map Subtract (6 degrees).)

The cells of the grid should always be located by using compass bearings to maintain accuracy. Ordinary compasses have been found to be very inaccurate for this type of work; a sighting compass is essential. When setting out the grid it is helpful to have two people, one to walk ahead to the next grid intersection point (pulling out a tape measure while walking for the length of the cell). The other remains at the last intersection point, 'sights' the first person (i.e. checks that they remain on the correct bearing) and winds in the tape measure. This speeds the procedure up, especially if, once the second intersection has been identified, the original sighter walks up to the person ahead and keeps on walking to the third point, this time being sighted themselves. If the ground is uneven, the person ahead may be lost from view by the sighter

if the full distance to the next point is walked. In such situations, carry out the process in stages. If the ground is very uneven, decrease the cell size to save time.

The grid, or key parts of it (e.g. corners), can be permanently marked (which considerably enhances the accuracy of relocation), but relocation should also be possible by using grid bearings in case these markers are lost. In addition, a location map of the origin of the grid should be drawn up (see Appendix 5 for further information on permanent markers). A small grid can be marked with string but larger ones are better marked at the intersection points with canes or string around trees, etc. These markers should be highly visible; attempting to distinguish a bamboo cane at 100 m against a woodland with bracken understorey is impossible. Attaching highly visible tape to the canes assists visibility. Cell corner markers should only be removed once the cell and adjacent cells have been surveyed.

Cell size is usually determined by the detectability of the plant being searched for. There is little point in having to subdivide the cell in order to search it, so keep the cells small. Suggested sizes are 50 m × 50 m when surveying an open woodland or other open habitats, and 30 m × 30 m in dense woods or other closed habitats.

Also note that there will usually be a large number of partial cells around the perimeter of the grid that have some of the habitat to be surveyed and some of the adjacent habitat. It is useful to be familiar with the area of each cell so that you can visually estimate or measure the area of habitat within these partial cells and adjust the counts accordingly, especially if estimating density. Alternatively, only survey full grid cells, although this will remove any edge effects from the results.

The location and relocation of grid cells can be a time-consuming process; it may be more feasible to sample a random selection of grid cells rather than attempting to count in every cell. In this case the survey is no longer a total count, but estimates of density, etc., from the sample of cells can be extrapolated across the entire site.

The equipment required for field surveying and monitoring is summarised in Appendix 6.

Data analysis and interpretation

In theory, changes in abundance are simply measured by calculating the difference in the total counts between one survey and the next. Increases or decreases can be expressed as percentages of the initial population. In practice, however, some individuals will probably be missed, so populations will be underestimated. This underestimation is unimportant if an index of population size can be used for detecting change, provided that the bias caused by failing to detect all individuals remains constant from year to year.

However, it may be difficult to separate significant trends from natural fluctuations in population size; 5–10 year means of counts can be used to eliminate some of this variability. Regression analysis or other techniques can be used to statistically assess the significance of trends in population size. Time-series analysis can also be used for long series of data to separate cyclic fluctuations from underlying trends in population size.

15.2.3   Selected colonies

Principles

This method involves estimation of the population size of one or more selected colonies of the target species. These colonies are used as sample indicators of the health of a population as a whole. The method is applicable to species that have some colonies in areas where access is problematic; in this case, you can monitor easily accessible colonies and make the assumption that the health of these colonies is indicative of the health of others. A decrease in colony size should trigger surveys of other populations. This method is also appropriate for a population consisting of numerous scattered small colonies. In such cases it may be very costly to attempt to survey the entire population comprehensively to an adequate level of detail.

Because the survey area is not an arbitrarily defined area such as a quadrat, but an existing colony, a better picture emerges of how each colony size is changing and/or whether each colony is moving but not increasing in size. This might be the case with species that possess underground rhizomes and grow outwards from the colony origin (e.g. Carnation Sedge *Carex panicea* or Sand Sedge *C. arenaria*). If a permanent quadrat is used for such species, and a colony grows beyond the boundaries of the quadrat, counts of shoots within the quadrat will eventually decrease in number; such a decrease could be misinterpreted as a decrease in the size of the colony. A survey of the colony with the boundaries of the survey area defined as the boundaries of the colony would not encounter this problem.

Selecting discrete colonies provides an ideal opportunity to investigate a species in detail, either by using demographic studies or by collecting data on performance indicators, which can be used to calibrate data from other colonies.

If a particularly good flowering year is noted from flowering stem counts, it may be worth while conducting a census of the whole population at the site; new colonies may be found in this way. In addition, this type of count repeated in 'good years' may serve on its own as a method of assessing trends in population size.

Wherever possible, colonies should be selected on a random or stratified random basis (see Part I, Section 2.3.4) and statistical methods should be used to determine the number of colonies required to yield results with adequate precision and accuracy (see Section 2.3.5).

If monitoring resources are limited, it may only be possible to monitor one 'representative' colony. In this case, no information will be obtained on the variability of the condition of colonies. The worst case scenario would be that the selected colony thrives while the others, which are not being monitored, decline. Caution should therefore be exercised when monitoring a larger population from one or a small subset of colonies; other sites should at least be checked occasionally on a presence–absence level. Any decisions on a change in management as a result of a single-colony survey should be made only after further surveying of other colonies.

Field methods

Colonies should ideally be randomly selected for survey and monitoring. However, colonies that are especially remote and thus costly to survey, or located in inaccessible areas, may have to be removed from the pool of possible colonies to survey. If less than 10% of the colonies are excluded on these grounds, departures from strict random sampling are unlikely to be significant. However, if more colonies are excluded, the results will not be representative of the entire site. Nevertheless, the results will provide an indication of the status of the colonies over the site and the whole population.

However, if all the colonies from one habitat type cannot be surveyed, any results from other colonies cannot be extrapolated to the unsurveyed habitat without further sampling. For example, if you are monitoring a species that occurs on acid grassland habitats in open ground and acid grassland on ledges surrounded by cliffs and all the cliff sites are inaccessible, then the results of the survey are only strictly applicable to the grassland, not to the entire species population. If this problem is unavoidable, supplementary data should be collected on other sites.

If the colonies to be surveyed must be selected by judgement, then care must be taken to include sites that are representative of the entire distribution of that species, thus including the whole range of habitat types and environmental factors that may affect that species. Again using cliff sites as an example, it may be possible to conduct a less intensive survey on that habitat, such as a ground-based surveillance with binoculars, which at least yields some data from that habitat type. Any information regarding environmental influences can be used to supplement the floristic survey, particularly when comparing inaccessible sites with surveyable sites. These factors can then be used to help explain any differences in population size between samples, and may highlight the need for more detailed surveys.

If the habitat type (e.g. blanket bog) is particularly fragile, there is good reason to locate the sampling site at the edges of the habitat (although far enough into the habitat to avoid sampling transitional vegetation or areas subject to edge effects) to avoid damaging the vegetation by trampling.

Colony population size can be estimated by using the look–see method (Section 15.2.1), systematic total counts (Section 15.2.2) or quadrats (Part II, Section 6.4.2). Refer to these sections for details of field methods. Selected colonies are good candidates for conducting demographic studies to measure the longevity and turnover of individuals (Section 15.2.4).

It is also recommended that a wide range of colonies (or even the entire population) be surveyed briefly on a regular basis (e.g. with the look–see method every 3 years). First, this serves as a quality control exercise to check that the selected colonies remain representative of the entire population and that any trends affecting these colonies are not unique but apply to the population in general. Second, results from detailed surveys of selected colonies should be used as a trigger for a wider survey if a decline in numbers is observed. If baseline surveys have not been conducted on the remaining colonies, you cannot be sure that a decline in the selected colonies is indicative of a decline in the population as a whole; more surveys would be needed to determine this, which would result in a delay before remedial action could be taken.

Data analysis and interpretation

If several colony locations have been selected by using random or stratified random sampling then conventional statistical analysis can be carried out with standard tests (Part I, Section 2.6.4). Given that it is unlikely that colonies will be the same size, results must be expressed in a standardised way (e.g. shoots per square metre, flowers per stem, etc.) to enable comparisons to be made.

If only a single colony is surveyed and monitored, results indicating a decline in the health of the colony should be used to trigger immediate monitoring of other colonies.

15.2.4   Demographic techniques

Principles

Demographic surveys of plant populations involve following individuals throughout their entire life history. The aim is to understand the life history and longevity of the species and the factors that affect various stages of the life cycle. The type of information that can be obtained includes:

- longevity of individuals;
- growth patterns of rhizomes;
- percentage recruitment from seedlings;
- percentage recruitment by vegetative reproduction;
- length of time an individual remains fertile; and
- mortality rates at different growth stages.

Demographic data can be correlated against environmental factors (e.g. grazing, rainfall, temperature) to determine which factors significantly affect the population. They can give powerful insights into population structure, which can be of key importance for understanding the conservation requirements of species and the effectiveness of management regimes. Management can then be tailored to protect the vulnerable stages in the life cycle.

Demographic studies are time-consuming and expensive; there are relatively few examples of such studies in the literature. One example is the long-running research by Hutchings (1987a,b) on the Early Spider Orchid; the method used for this study can be applied to all species.

Owing to the high costs of the method, demographic studies are only likely to be used for monitoring the highest-priority species. It is only feasible to monitor a subset of the population by using this technique (unless the population is very small), so resources should also be allocated to less intensive monitoring of the rest of the population.

Field methods

Surveys are usually conducted annually, or more regularly if dormancy occurs (Sanger & Waite, 1998), at flowering or fruiting time to collect the maximum amount of data.

A permanent plot is established (see Appendix 5) and the location of every plant within the plot is mapped. The appropriate mapping method depends on the scale of the study and the density of the target species. Plants can be mapped within permanent quadrats by fixing a scale on to the frame or dividing the quadrat into a grid and determining co-ordinates in relation to the frame by using rulers or measuring tape. If the quadrat is small enough (e.g. 1 m^2) and the vegetation is sufficiently short, the location and outline of the plants can be traced with a pantograph or by using the grid as a guide to sketch by eye while standing over the quadrat. Alternatively, a 'mapping table' can be used. This is a sheet of Perspex, mounted on legs, which is placed directly over the quadrat. The positions of plants are marked on the perspex with a felt-tip pen while looking vertically down on to the quadrat. Once all plants have been marked, the pattern of plant locations can be traced from the perspex on to paper for permanent recording. Accuracy is important when using methods such as this to map individuals, particularly if the density of individuals is high; it will be necessary to relocate each individual on later surveys.

Individuals can be marked by a variety of methods (e.g. numbered posts, canes or plant labels). If the plants can be individually identified, the performance of each plant (e.g. survival, growth rate etc.) can be measured. Mapping the outlines of the individuals will allow the calculation of their basal areas. If all individuals in the sample area are being mapped and marked for compiling a total count, new individuals will be detected during each repeat survey, which can then be added to the map (Bullock, 1996). However, it can be difficult to tell whether plants have died and been replaced by new individuals unless the site is visited regularly.

Aerial photographs form a useful supplement to ground surveys when initially locating individual large trees.

The actual data recorded will depend upon the objectives of the survey. In many cases, presence–absence data of individual plants may be sufficient. In addition, data on the plant characteristics such as size can be recorded, including height (non-flowering and flowering shoots), cover, number of leaves in basal rosettes, length of stolons between rosettes, number of flowers, etc. For details of methods for recording tree condition see Part II, Section 6.5.2.

These measurements are repeated on a regular basis, typically annually or more frequently (e.g. on a monthly basis) to monitor the fate of individual plants through a season. Counts of individuals at every stage of the life cycle such as seedling, vegetative, flowering and senescent should also be made. Alternatively, proxy measures of age such as size can be recorded. Environmental variables such as rainfall and temperature can also be directly measured. The equipment recommended for field surveying and monitoring is summarised in Appendix 6.

Data analysis and interpretation

Spatial distribution maps or tables should be produced on an annual basis (or perhaps more frequently for species that exhibit dormancy), to enable the life history of every individual to be recorded and analysed. These are compiled from the co-ordinates of individuals and will give information on the longevity of individuals and the growth patterns of rhizomes. In addition, elasticity matrices can be used to assess mortality rates at different stages in the life cycle, to identify key stages that determine the structure of the population. The analysis of demographic studies and in particular the use of elasticity matrices is highly complex and for this reason is not described in this *Handbook*. Further information can be obtained from Hutchings (1987a,b), Wells & Willems (1991), Watkinson (1986) and Sanger & Waite (1998). Information on the management of species exhibiting dormancy can be found in Farrell (1991).

15.2.5   Photography

Principles

Photographs can enhance the accuracy of a survey by reducing the error involved in the relocation of permanent sample points. They can also provide helpful information such as an impression of the density of the plants, or the height or structure of the vegetation. Photography can be a quick way to record the presence and extent of an entire population, although it cannot provide a substitute for conducting on-site counts and the information provided is largely qualitative rather than quantitative.

Photographs can also record seasonal advancement to aid comparisons of data with other years, the degree of events such as poaching and grazing, and other variables such as the amount of bare ground and vegetation height.

Fixed-point photography in particular (see Part II, Section 6.1.4) is useful for providing a permanent pictorial record of successional habitat changes on a site over time, and can also be applied to monitoring colonies of small plants if individual quadrats are photographed. For example, lichens (Chapter 12) are commonly monitored with fixed-point photography.

Field methods

A detailed discussion of the methodology for fixed-point photography is provided in Part II, Section 6.1.4.

It is important that the following are noted:

- date and time of day that the photograph is taken;
- stance, location and direction faced;
- film speed used (SLR camera); and
- an idea of scale, such as a tape stretched out along the horizontal axis.

Photographs should be taken with a record of the quadrat number and location positioned in one corner. Dry-wipe boards are very useful for this purpose, as it is easy to change the information for each quadrat.

Individual plants can be marked in the field to assist the interpretation of the photograph (see Section 15.2.2). The extent of a colony can be highlighted by running a tape around the edge. Alternatively, it may be useful to use Polaroid prints as these can be annotated in the field with felt-tip pens. However, they tend to be of poorer quality and can also fade with time unless kept in light-proof storage.

Tripods are a valuable aid in poor light and for close-ups and are essential for fixed-point photography. Prints can be laminated for field use and can considerably aid the relocation of sampling points. Appendix 6 lists the essential field equipment.

Data analysis and interpretation

Total counts should not be made from photographs unless the detail is sufficient to distinguish individual plants.

Diagrams showing the position and size of the colonies can be traced from fixed-point photographs and used as overlays. Provided that appropriate sampling has been used, estimated colony areas from different photographs can be analysed statistically by using standard tests (Part I, Section 2.6.4).

15.3   VASCULAR PLANT CONSERVATION EVALUATION CRITERIA

Key evaluation considerations

The status of the British flora has recently been reviewed by Rich (2001). In the British Isles, there are currently about 1390 native seed plants and ferns (*c.* 2200 including named critical species in *Hieracium*, etc.), and over 1100 reasonably well-established aliens. There are *c.* 450 endemic species in the British Isles (*c.* 20% of the flora) mostly contained in the critical genera such as *Sorbus* and *Taraxacum*, and 10 non-critical species and 29 endemic subspecies (Rich *et al.*, 1999).

The UK also holds internationally important plant assemblages such as oceanic western and Atlantic–alpine communities. The UK has a responsibility for species for which the country has a large proportion of the world's population. For example, between 25% and 49% of the world's Bluebell *Hyacinthoides non-scripta* population is found in the UK. Furthermore, a number of the UK's flowering plants are growing at the edge of their range, some recognised as endemic subspecies.

The Botanical Society of the British Isles (BSBI) is the largest organisation devoted to the study of botany in the British Isles. It produces national atlases and county floras of the distribution of plants, most notably the recent *New Atlas of the British and Irish Flora* (Preston *et al.*, 2002a), the first comprehensive update of the distribution of vascular plants in Britain since 1962. The 2002 atlas provides colour maps for over 4000 taxa, showing native and alien distributions, in three date classes, for every 10 km square in Great Britain, the Isle of Man, Ireland and the Channel Islands.

The BSBI has joined forces with Plantlife, dedicated to conserving all forms of plant life in its natural habitat, to deliver the exciting and innovative programme *Making it Count for People and Plants*, which is supported by the Heritage Lottery Fund.

The purpose of the programme is to build a clear picture of the state of the UK flora by carrying out a range of surveys to identify changes and trends in the UK's wild plant species. This information will then be used in the development of appropriate conservation management plans, which will respond to the changes and promote a healthy environment for wild plants. Four surveys are being run, which have been designed to cater for people's differing botanical skills. These are:

- Annual single-species survey;
- Common Plants Survey;
- BSBI Local Change survey;
- Rare Plant Recording.

Further details on the results of the surveys and how to participate in forthcoming surveys can be found on Plantlife's website at www.plantlife. org.uk/html/about_plantlife/about_index.htm.

Individual species of vascular plant are included in several current conservation programmes. In 1993, Plantlife International launched *Back from the Brink*, a programme designed to halt species loss and decline in Britain. Twenty-one flowering plants in Great Britain and eleven in Ireland (excluding critical species) have been lost since detailed records began, although this is only a fraction of the number that have suffered population crashes and are still declining owing to the pressures of agricultural intensification, habitat neglect or destruction. In 1995, the UK BAP identified a further 168 plant species threatened with extinction or severe decline. A total of 101 species are in the *Back from the Brink* programme, with more than 40 species projects operating in England, Wales and Scotland. The programme combines laboratory and field research with hands-on management to produce effective, practical action for rare plants. More information on the programme and the list of *Back from the Brink* species can be found on Plantlife's website: www.plantlife.org.uk/.

English Nature's *Species Recovery Programme*, a programme of action for bringing threatened species back from the brink of extinction, includes species listed in Annex II/IV of the Habitats Directive, as well as UK BAP species, the IUCN Red

List for Britain and nationally scarce species for which it has been proven that they would be threatened by a drastic decline in range or numbers. Species and sub-species endemic to Britain are also included, as well as ones found in only one or two other countries. The programme uses similar techniques to the Plantlife *Back from the Brink* programme (which it sometimes funds in part) to further the conservation of these species. Further information and a list of species included in the programme can be found on English Nature's website at www.english-nature.org.uk/science/srp/default.asp.

At The Hague in April 2002, the 'Global Strategy for Plant Conservation' was endorsed by the parties to the Convention on Biological Diversity, the long-term objective being to halt the continuing loss of plant diversity. Sixteen outcome-orientated, global targets for plant conservation were set, to be completed by the global community by 2010. The UK is committed to implementing the strategy and the *Plant Diversity Challenge* (JNCC, 2004) report is its response. The sixteen targets are grouped under five objectives:

1. Understanding and documenting plant diversity;
2. Conserving plant diversity;
3. Using plant diversity sustainably;
4. Promoting education and awareness about plant diversity;
5. Building capacity for the conservation of plant diversity.

Each of the major partner organisations (JNCC, Plantlife International and the Royal Botanic Gardens, Kew) has a remit to look after a particular group of targets. Further information on the strategy can be found on the JNCC website at www.jncc.gov.uk/species/Plants/default.htm. The report can also be viewed or downloaded from this site.

The key considerations with regards to evaluating vascular plants at a site are listed below.

1. Check lists of species of conservation importance and their protection status (see below for information on which lists to check and where to obtain the relevant information).

2. Check existing designation status of the site. For EIAs, the search area should extend to 2 km from the boundary of the site. This will inform the results of the preliminary scoping survey and highlight any areas of land that hold species of conservation importance.

3. Carry out a preliminary (scoping) survey to identify the potential for species of conservation importance. A Phase I habitat survey (see Section 6.1.4 for methodology), augmented by land management information, should identify habitat types that may potentially hold such species. For example, arable land on an organic farm with wide cereal margins may hold one or more rare UK BAP arable weeds.

These three steps should enable the determination of Valuable Ecosystem Components (VECs) (in terms of vascular plant species) that may *potentially* be present. To establish the *actual* presence or absence of a VEC, further survey may be necessary at an appropriate time of year.

A further key consideration is the viability of the population of any species of conservation importance. A small population of a nationally important species may rank lower than a large, ecologically viable population of a regionally important species. However, the nationally important species may be so rare in the UK that all occurrences of the species are to be conserved.

Currently there is surprisingly little conservation emphasis on either endemics or rare critical species in large genera such as *Hieracium* and *Taraxacum* in Britain, despite the SSSI selection guidelines (see below). Advice should be sought about the likely occurrence of such taxa in any area of search.

Protection status in the EU and UK

Appendix 1 of the Bern Convention lists nine vascular plants native to Britain and threatened in Europe as a whole, for which special protection is required. They are all included on Schedule 8 of the Wildlife & Countryside Act. Annex IIb of the EU Habitats Directive contains the same nine vascular plants as in Appendix 1 of the Bern Convention.

For these species, the Directive specifies that Special Areas of Conservation (SACs) will be designated. The same species are also listed in Annex IVb of the Directive, requiring their strict protection. As such, the species are protected in Britain under both the Wildlife & Countryside Act (1981, as amended) and the Conservation (Natural Habitats, & c.) Regulations. A list of the vascular (and non-vascular) plants listed under international agreements can be found on the JNCC website at www.jncc.gov.uk/species/Plants/p6_3.htm.

In Britain, all wild plants are protected against unauthorised uprooting under Section 13 of the Wildlife & Countryside Act (1981, as amended). Plants listed on Schedule 8 of the Act enjoy special protection against picking, uprooting, destruction and sale. The Schedule is reviewed every five years, but currently it contains 107 vascular plants, 33 bryophytes, 26 lichens and 2 charophytes (stoneworts) (JNCC, 2004). The list of vascular (and non-vascular) plants currently on Schedule 8 of the Wildlife & Countryside Act can be viewed on the JNCC website at www.jncc.gov.uk/species/Plants/p5.htm.

Section 74 of the CRoW Act requires the Secretary of State for England and the National Assembly for Wales each to publish a list of species and habitat types that are of principal importance for the conservation of biological diversity in England and Wales, respectively. The Section 74 list for England can be viewed on the DEFRA web page www.defra.gov.uk/wildlife-countryside/cl/habitats/habitats-list.pdf. The equivalent list for Wales can be viewed on the National Assembly for Wales web page www.wales.gov.uk/subienvironment/content/guidance/species-statement-e.htm. These two lists are based on UK Bio-diversity Action Plan (UK BAP) Priority Species and Habitats lists. Further information on the UK BAP process and the current list of UK BAP species and habitats can be found on the UK BAP website at www.ukbap.org.uk/.

Conservation status in the UK

The assessment of conservation status for species, including the IUCN criteria for assessing threat status, has led to the publication of Red Data Books for a range of taxa in a number of countries.

In addition to IUCN criteria, there are also criteria to define nationally rare and nationally scarce. Currently these are defined to be: Nationally Rare (NR), occurring in 15 or fewer hectads (a hectad is a 10 km × 10 km square of the National Grid) in Great Britain; Nationally Scarce (NS), occurring in 16–100 hectads in Great Britain.

The vascular plants include the flowering plants as well as conifers, ferns and allied species. Vascular plants have been assessed against 1994 IUCN criteria by Wigginton (1999) but require revision against the 2001 criteria. More recently, the distribution of all vascular plants has been mapped by Preston *et al.* (2002a). This has also critically reviewed the native status of species; only those species that are considered as native or archaeophytes are given a conservation status. The publication of the *New Atlas* has substantially updated knowledge of species distribution and declines and has resulted in a considerable number of species being listed as rare or scarce for the first time. Some of these species may warrant an IUCN designation, but as yet they have not been assessed against IUCN criteria. The most recent date class (1987–99) has been used to assess rarity status, except when taxa are known to have been under-recorded. Vascular (and non-vascular) plants listed under the various IUCN threat categories and Nationally Rare or Scarce can be viewed on the JNCC website at www.jncc.gov.uk/species/Plants/threatened/default.htm.

Following the publication of the Red Data Book for vascular plants in Britain, the *Threatened Plants Database* was initiated to create a 'live' database of records of threatened plants. A joint venture between the statutory nature conservation agencies, BSBI and Plantlife, the database is intended to contain information on the state of populations of threatened species and hence to inform conservation initiatives such as the UK BAP programme. More information on the database and a list of the 400 or so plants included in the project can be found on the BSBI website at www.bsbi.org.uk/html/tpdb.html.

Site designation criteria

SSSI criteria for designating a site for its vascular plant interest are described by NCC (1989 and subsequent amendments), which can be found on the JNCC website at www.jncc.gov.uk/Publications/sssi/default.htm. Briefly, sites are considered for selection on the basis of their vascular plants on the following criteria.

1. All sites with viable populations of a Wildlife & Countryside Act Schedule 8 species should be selected.
2. The localities of all Red Data Book species are to be considered as candidate sites. Various criteria determine whether a site qualifies for selection based on the presence of one RDB species.
3. A simple scoring procedure is used to assess combinations of species within the two classes Nationally Rare and Nationally Scarce (i.e. occurring in 1–100 10 km squares). With this scoring system, the presence of two RDB species, for example, qualifies a site for selection.
4. The largest population of endemic species in each area of search (AOS) should be selected.
5. In each AOS, the best population of each of the six non-endemic species threatened in Europe, which are neither listed on Schedule 8 of the Wildlife & Countryside Act nor RDB species, should be selected.
6. If an AOS contains species that are known to have declined markedly within Britain but are not yet in the Nationally Rare or Scarce categories, particularly large populations may be selected.
7. Floristic assemblage: sites with more than 75% of the total vascular plant species list for a community type of the NVC should qualify for selection.
8. All microspecies and recognised, regularly occurring hybrids should be represented on at least one SSSI somewhere in Britain.

Further information on each of the above criteria can be found in NCC (1989).

Evaluation of vascular plants

The evaluation of Valued Ecosystem Components (VECs) (both species and habitats) for EIAs should ideally follow the guidelines presented in Part I of this *Handbook*. These recommend grading the importance of sites or components thereof against the following levels of value:

1. International;
2. National;
3. Regional;
4. County/Metropolitan;
5. District/Borough;
6. Parish/Neighbourhood.

The guidelines take into account the size (and therefore viability) of populations of species when attempting to rank these against each other. Part I of this *Handbook* also provides information on other methods for ranking the importance of species and habitats.

Vascular plants found on a site should be evaluated in relation to the species listed on Annexes II and IV of the EU Habitats Directive, which are of international importance. In terms of national importance, the UK BAP (Section 74) Priority Species list should be consulted, as well as the national Red Book for vascular plants (Wigginton, 1999) and *Scarce Plants in Britain* (Stewart *et al.*, 1994). Reference should also be made to the JNCC list of threatened plants (www.jncc.gov.uk/species/ Plants/threatened/default.htm) and the SSSI selection guidelines (NCC, 1989).

Below the national level of importance, the species list for a site should be checked against County Red Data Books, where they exist. Local biodiversity partnerships may also have published, through the production of local BAPs, lists of species of local conservation importance that, if available, should also be used for evaluation purposes. Guidelines for the selection of sites of conservation importance at a County level, available from the Local Authority or local Wildlife Trust, may include criteria based upon particular vascular plant species.

16 • Dragonflies and damselflies

Dragonflies and damselflies (Odonata) have an aquatic larval stage, which can last for a few years, followed by emergence, mating and dying all in the same season. As larvae can live for long periods before pupating, an absence (or decrease) of adults in one year does not necessarily imply that the population is in decline. Several years of negative results are required to confirm an absence.

Surveys of Odonata can provide a useful indicator of water and habitat quality where regional differences in diversity are taken into account. This is one reason why they are a useful group to survey as part of EIA studies.

Monitoring areas of suitable habitat may be appropriate, particularly if resources are not available for more detailed survey methods. Monitoring of micro-habitats is not specifically covered in this *Handbook*. However, some of the techniques in Part II may be adapted for this purpose.

16.1 ATTRIBUTES FOR ASSESSING CONDITION

16.1.1 Population range

Area of occupancy is an important attribute to monitor and can be best assessed by mapping presence – absence in suitable micro-habitats. Note that presence in the only pond in a 100 ha site gives 100% occupancy, even though most of the site lacks the species. At the same time, a presence in 50 ponds in the same area is only 50% occupancy if there are 100 ponds. Area of occupancy must therefore be defined in terms of the area of suitable micro-habitat occupied. Repeat surveys will illustrate expansions or contractions of range.

16.1.2 Population size (larval and adult)

The dragonfly and damselfly life cycle has three stages (the egg, an aquatic larval stage and a terrestrial adult stage) but only two of these, the larval and adult stages, are of value in monitoring. Monitoring populations of Odonata can therefore entail the monitoring of either or both of these. In general, populations of adult Odonata are estimated either from the number of exuviae (discarded exoskeletons of the larvae) found on emergent vegetation or by counting adult males as they display over water. Larval populations can be sampled as part of general aquatic invertebrate monitoring (see Chapter 20).

16.1.3 Population structure

For a population to be deemed viable there must be sufficient recruitment from the larval to the adult stage and sufficient successful breeding to establish a new generation of larvae.

The successful recruitment of adults from the larval stage may need to be monitored for rarer species. This can be estimated from a comparison of larval counts with counts of exuviae. Mortality of adults will reduce the number of newly emergent adults that return to breed in the following year. Comparison of year-to-year counts will reveal trends in larval and adult mortality.

16.2 GENERAL METHODS

General site survey methods for invertebrates are provided in Chapter 10.

The general methods for surveying and monitoring Odonata are outlined in Table 16.1.

Table 16.1. *Methods for surveying and monitoring dragonflies and damselflies*

	Recommended species group	Population size data	Efficiency	Precision	Bias	Expertise required	Advantages	Disadvantages
Sampling larvae (see Chapter 20)	Odonata	Presence–absence Index Estimate	Depends on method chosen	Depends on method chosen	Depends on method chosen	Identification Some ecological knowledge required for species-specific work	Depends on method chosen but invariably will be weather independent	Depends on method chosen; possible health and safety implications for some water bodies
Exuviae counts	Odonata	Presence–absence Estimate	May be time-consuming if dense vegetation must be searched	Good in theory	Number of exuviae counted will depend on density of vegetation and ease of access to waterside	Identification	Can be undertaken in most weather conditions except very windy or wet weather	Number of exuviae not necessarily a good estimate of adult population returning to breed, though it allows a good year-on-year comparison
Transects	Odonata	Index	Good if terrain is easily traversed	If conditions are ideal, results should be reasonably precise	Gives reliable counts of only adult males and tenerals	Identification	Enables comparable results to be taken from different observers Good for EIA	Can only be carried out during certain weather conditions
Timed counts	Odonata	Index or estimate	Best for small areas or difficult terrain	If conditions are ideal, results should be reasonably precise	Gives reliable counts of only adult males and tenerals	Identification	Gives total counts for small ponds Good for EIA	Can only be carried out during certain weather conditions

16.2.1   Sampling larvae

Odonata larvae should be sampled by using the techniques described for aquatic invertebrates (Chapter 20). The appropriate method will depend on the time and resources available and the level of detail required. In general, it will probably be sufficient to sample by using netting (Section 20.2.2) or kick sampling (Section 20.2.3), although dredging bottom mud and taking weed samples in addition will often yield a higher count. Only final-instar nymphs – those in which the wings reach to or beyond the rear margin of the third abdominal segment – can be identified reliably and even with these it is not possible for all examples to be identified to species level. Identification from exuviae is possible with similar limitations. The keys in Askew (1988) should be used, as some other British keys are unreliable.

16.2.2   Exuviae counts

Principles

Odonata emerge from the larval stage on plants or objects standing in the water body or around its edges. The larval skin splits open and the adult emerges; the empty larval skins (exuviae) remain on the plants or objects and can be counted.

According to Askew (1988), libellulids, corduliids and some gomphids use horizontal supports with the head only slightly raised; aeshnids hang between 90° and 180° to the vertical so that they are belly-up (i.e. on the underside of sloping surfaces) and all European Zygoptera hang head upwards from a near-vertical surface.

If all the exuviae at a particular water body could be collected and identified in a year, the total would represent the size of the emergent population from that water body in that year. However, it is likely to be impracticable, if not impossible, to count all the exuviae because, although they can remain on vegetation for some weeks if undisturbed, they can be dislodged and lost during rainy or windy conditions. In addition, surveyors can easily miss exuviae, particularly those of damselflies. The nature of the habitat and the accessibility of the water margin to

the surveyor will therefore affect the accuracy of counts. As a compromise measure, counts of exuviae should be made each day, removing each one as it is encountered so that subsequent counts do not duplicate numbers.

However, exuviae counts will at best provide only an index of the emergent adult population in one year.

Field methods

Surveyors should walk around the water body, closely examining emergent vegetation for exuviae. Those that are found should be collected for later identification to species level where technically possible. If it is not practicable to survey the entire water body margin in the time available for the survey, either survey a fixed length of bank or search for a fixed length of time on each visit. This will standardise observations and enable valid comparisons to be made.

Surveyors should be experienced in the recognition of exuviae and be aware of the likely places where they can be found. To increase the likelihood of finding exuviae it may be desirable to place sticks or other artificial supports around the water-body edge at regular intervals to encourage emergence in accessible areas; these sticks can be more easily searched but care must be taken to place them at the appropriate angle (see above for details on adult emergence positions). However, even if sticks are used, the vegetation should still be thoroughly examined.

Timing and frequency of counts will depend upon availability of resources and the species being monitored. Moore & Corbet (1990) recommend that counts should be made weekly. However, this is not likely to be feasible unless visits can be integrated with other monitoring work. Visits can be timed to coincide with the emergence of a particular species of interest; otherwise you should aim to visit at similar times each year, or every 3 years, depending on the degree of accuracy required from the study. Frequency and timing of visits should be standardised once a survey and monitoring regime has been decided upon. If weekly counts cannot be made, a problem may arise when attempting to standardise survey timing: the date of the peak population will vary from year to year depending on weather conditions. Therefore, a count made on the same date each year may produce very different estimates of similar population sizes. Surveying only during periods of suitable weather conditions (see below) and attempting to survey at a similar *seasonal* time each year will help to mitigate this bias. However, weekly counts are preferable, because this enables the peak count to be identified. The equipment required for surveying and monitoring in the field is listed in Appendix 6.

Data analysis and interpretation

If several counts of adults are made in one year, the data can be summed to provide an estimate of the total number of adults emerging. In practice, this should be treated as an index, rather than an actual estimate of population size. Time constraints will generally mean that only a proportion of each year's exuviae will be collected.

Provided that sampling is representative, data can be analysed statistically by using standard tests (Part I, Section 2.6.4). Other kinds of statistical analysis may also be appropriate (see Section 2.6.4).

It is important to consider that exuviae counts only provide a partial picture of the size and health of a population. If counts are falling, the decrease could be due to mortality of adults (not surviving to breed) or of larvae (not surviving to emergence).

Adult Odonata do not survive over winter; they breed in the same season of emergence. Therefore, the exuviae count for one year gives the potential number of breeding adults in that year. Most dragonfly larvae take more than one year from hatching to emergence, so adults laying eggs in one year will not produce the next year's final-instar larvae. Therefore the count of exuviae from one year is not related to the previous year's count. Knowledge of the ecology of individual species is required to identify which year of adult counts relate to which year of larvae. The situation is further complicated by the fact that larvae can 'lie over' (i.e. not emerge) in unfavourable seasons; the life cycle is not necessarily completed in the same length of time.

In order to examine further any trends identified with exuviae counts, surveys of adults and larvae will be required. However, exuviae counts

in isolation are still a useful and relatively simple index of population size.

16.2.3   Transects

Principles

Adult Odonata are highly visible and relatively easy to identify in the field. A standard technique involving transect walks along water body edges has been developed (RSPB/EN/ITE, 1997). This method is particularly suited to damselflies and libellulid dragonflies (Brooks, 1993) and allows different observers following a set route to produce comparable results.

In general, it is only adult males that display over water, and then only at times when air temperature is high. Adult males at other times, females for most of the time and immature adults of both sexes are generally found away from water. The only meaningful counts of mature adults are of adult males by water during good conditions (Moore & Corbet, 1990). Teneral adults (adults that are less than a day old with wings and body still soft) can also be counted; these tend to fly away from water after emergence but do not travel far on their first flight. Teneral adults near a water body are therefore very likely to have emerged from that water body and can be counted separately from adults to estimate numbers of newly emergent Odonata.

Field methods

Set routes for transect locations should be identified, mapped and divided into sections before surveying commences. Counts should be made at regular intervals, and at the same time each day during optimal conditions for recording Odonata. Maximal numbers of Odonata are found over water within an hour or two of midday on warm days with little or no wind (Moore & Corbet, 1990), although these data probably apply to southern Britain. Surveys should take place between 10.00 and 14.00 hours on days when air temperature in the shade is above 17 °C, there is at least 50% sunshine and wind conditions are light (if trees are bending, the wind is too strong). It is permissible to vary these parameters to accommodate local climatic conditions provided that repeat surveying in subsequent years is carried out under the same conditions. All these conditions should also be recorded alongside the insect counts.

Surveys can also be directed at particular species; in this case, surveys can be timed to coincide with the flying period of that species (see Merritt *et al.*, 1996).

The transect should always be walked by the same route, at a continuous slow speed, keeping to the edge of the water body. In each section of the transect, every identifiable specimen is recorded (flying or perched) in front of and to the side of (but not behind) the surveyor. It is recommended that transects should be walked every week during the summer period: 1 May to 30 September (Moore & Corbet, 1990; RSPB/EN/ITE, 1997). If time constraints do not allow this, visits from different years to the same site should be made at similar times to enable comparable data to be collected. Appendix 6 lists the necessary field equipment.

Data analysis and interpretation

If transects have been regularly surveyed during one field season, the maximum count of adult males can be taken as an estimate of the breeding male population. If site visits have been less frequent, data can only reasonably be interpreted as an index of population size. Data can be expressed as the number of individuals per metre or per transect and multiplied by the total length of water body margin to obtain an estimate of the total population at that site.

Provided that sampling is representative, data can be analysed statistically by using standard tests (Part I, Section 2.6.4). Comparisons within one year of exuviae counts (Section 16.2.2), teneral adult counts and adult counts can give an indication of adult mortality if it is possible to sex exuviae and tenerals. Exuviae are sexable if the gonapophyses are undamaged; this is usually the case, but the careful detachment of exuviae from surfaces is required. Teneral adults are sexable but must be captured: this may prove impracticable in reality.

16.2.4   Timed counts

Principles

Timed counts are an alternative to transect counts (Section 16.2.3) and can be useful if the habitat is

not easily walked because of uneven terrain or dense vegetation, or if it is too small (i.e. small ponds) to require transects. The principles of survey timing and applicability are identical to those for transects, except that surveys are carried out for a set period of time while remaining in the same place.

Field methods

Some ponds may be small enough to be surveyed in their entirety from one location. Larger areas may require sample points at regular intervals. In this case, points should be far enough apart to avoid counting individuals twice. If you walk all the way around a lake, you may encounter individuals that were counted earlier on the far side and so be counting the same one twice. A section or sections of bank should be selected very carefully: some dragonflies can move a long way and often feed over the entire surface area of a lake. Length of counts at each point should be standardised; given that Odonata are highly mobile, a short count duration is preferable, since it is less likely that individuals will be counted more than once.

The timing and suitable conditions for timed counts are the same as for transects (Section 16.2.3). The surveyor should stand in the same spot, regularly scanning through 360° and recording all individuals seen (flying or perching). You should try not to count the same individual twice, but this may be unavoidable if counts are undertaken over longer periods. For flowing waters, such as rivers, directional counts are useful. The numbers seen flying downstream plus numbers flying upstream gives the maximum possible count. Numbers flying upstream minus those flying downstream (or vice versa to obtain a positive number) gives the minimum. The recommended field equipment is listed in Appendix 6.

Data analysis and interpretation

Data analysis is carried out in a similar manner to that for transects (Section 16.2.3). However, if a site is small enough to be surveyed from one point, numbers from that count can be taken as an estimate of the male breeding population rather than as an index.

16.3   ODONATA CONSERVATION EVALUATION CRITERIA

16.3.1   Key evaluation considerations

Around 38 species of dragonfly (including damselflies) breed in Britain. Some are supplemented by migrants from the continent, which can bring large fluctuations in abundance of a species between years. In addition, there are species that are colonising Britain (or possibly recolonising after a long period of absence), such as the Small Red-eyed Damselfly *Erythromma viridulum*.

The last BRC atlas covering the dragonflies of Great Britain and Ireland was produced in 1996. Since then, the Small Red-eyed Damselfly has started breeding and spreading in England, and other species that were previously occasional migrants have also started to breed here in recent years. The British Dragonfly Society has accumulated survey data since the atlas was published. It is therefore important to consult local record centres and naturalist societies for up-to-date information on recorded dragonfly distribution for a particular area.

16.3.2   Protection status in the UK and EU

No dragonfly species are listed in Appendix III of the Bern Convention.

Two species are strictly protected under Schedule 5 of the Wildlife & Countryside Act 1981 as amended by the Countryside & Rights of Way Act 2000: the Norfolk Hawker *Aeshna isosceles* and Southern Damselfly *Coenagrion mercuriale*.

The Southern Damselfly is the only species still occurring in the UK that is listed in Annex II of the EU Habitats Directive of species of community interest whose conservation requires the designation of Special Areas of Conservation (SACs). The Orange-spotted Emerald dragonfly *Oxygastra curtisii* is also listed, but is considered extinct in Britain.

The Southern Damselfly is currently the only priority BAP species.

16.3.3   Conservation status in the UK

Four species are classified as endangered in the British Red Data Book (Shirt, 1987), but are all considered extinct apart from the Norfolk Hawker. Two species are classified as Vulnerable and three as Rare in the British Red Data Book.

16.3.4   Site designation criteria

SSSI criteria for designating sites for dragonfly interest are described by the NCC (1989). In brief, all sites supporting populations of endangered species qualify for selection. Sites containing a single Nationally Rare or Scarce species can qualify if the site supports:

- the largest population of the species in the area of search;
- a strong population of the species on a site supporting a good example of a habitat type;
- a strong population of the species within an area of search that encompasses a substantial proportion of the localities for the species; or
- a strong population at the edge of the species geographical range.

In addition, where a site has a number of species that meets or exceeds a number considered to form an outstanding assemblage, the site should be considered for selection. This number varies across Britain: 17 – 15 species for southern England and Wales, 9 in Scotland, and fewer in the surrounding islands. The site to be selected should include semi-natural habitats used for resting and feeding in addition to the water body that provides the breeding site, and some of the associated catchment if that is necessary to protect the supply and quality of the water (NCC, 1989).

17 • Butterflies

Butterflies are mobile and often highly visible species. Some species exhibit a metapopulation structure, with colonies in discrete areas of suitable habitat. Colonies may become extinct, and the areas are then recolonised. Failing to find a species on a site in one or more years can therefore not be taken as proof of absence; negative results from several years would be needed to confirm this.

Presence–absence of adults is the simplest method for monitoring butterfly populations and will usually be used to establish baseline data at sites that have not previously been surveyed. More detailed survey and monitoring of larval or egg numbers can be made by using timed counts or quadrats and transects once presence has been established. For species of conservation importance, some sites will have already been identified and monitoring schemes will normally already be in place. However, surveys of other sites are obviously required, since it is unlikely that all breeding areas have been identified, and you will need to look for range expansions out of known sites.

17.1   ATTRIBUTES FOR ASSESSING CONDITION

17.1.1   Population range

Area of occupancy is an important attribute to survey and monitor and can be best assessed by mapping presence–absence in areas of suitable habitat. Repeat surveys will illustrate expansions or contractions of range. Monitoring habitat extent with occasional confirmation of presence may be the most practical approach in some cases.

17.1.2   Colony numbers

Butterflies often live in breeding areas defined by areas of suitable habitat. Separate breeding areas may also exist within areas of suitable habitat. The number of breeding areas on a site is a straightforward indication of the health of a population. The number of breeding areas may also vary with species: some species will occupy a single large breeding area and others will form smaller, more discrete population units. A small number of breeding areas on one particular site does not necessarily imply that a species is not at its optimal level, especially if the site is a part of the edge of the main area for the species.

Numbers within a breeding area are relatively simple to establish: presence of individuals can be used to imply the presence of a breeding area. However, failure to find evidence of a species in one year alone cannot be taken as evidence of absence; several surveys with a negative result will be needed to confirm an absence, particularly on sites where a species has previously been recorded.

17.1.3   Population size

A more detailed assessment of butterfly populations will entail estimates of population size. Estimates can be made by counting adults or larvae along transects set up through areas of suitable habitat. Transect methods may need to be tailored to suit particular species.

17.1.4   Population structure

For a population to be deemed viable there must be sufficient recruitment from the larval to the adult stage and sufficient successful breeding to establish a new generation of larvae. Butterflies can be surveyed at the larval stage by counts on food plants. Such counts can be compared with adult counts to examine changes in population structure from year to year.

17.2   GENERAL METHODS

General site survey methods for invertebrates are provided in Chapter 10.

Table 17.1 outlines the general methods for surveying and monitoring butterflies.

17.2.1   Larval or egg counts: timed searches

Principles

Counts of larvae and eggs are a reliable method for establishing the presence of butterfly species. Although adult butterflies are often conspicuous, they tend to fly only during periods of fine weather. Searches for eggs and larvae are less dependent upon sunshine than searches for adults and are by definition carried out at a different time of the year. It is thus possible to monitor one species by two methods at two different times in the same year.

Field methods
Establishing presence–absence

This is a variant of a timed count in that you must establish an arbitrary time beyond which it is decided that the species can be considered absent. Generally, the surveyor will walk around the site in a random manner, searching for larvae or eggs; this may require more than one surveyor, because not every fieldworker will have sufficient knowledge of all butterfly species.

If one particular species is being looked for, then it may be possible to narrow down the search area considerably if the larval food plant(s) of the species is known. The complete range of food plants for several species, especially the grass-feeders, is not known; looking for a species solely on a food plant known from one site may result in missing the species if it has adapted to different conditions on another site. For example, Emmet & Heath (1989) reported that Wall Brown *Lasiommata megera* larvae in Cheshire feed on Cocksfoot *Dactylis glomerata*, Wavy Hair-grass *Deschampsia flexuosa*, Yorkshire Fog *Holcus lanatus* and bent grasses *Agrostis* spp. but not on all of those at any one site, and that differences occur between sites.

If eggs, larvae or signs of larvae are found then a presence is confirmed and a more rigorous monitoring scheme must be devised if abundance data are required. If nothing is found after a set time period has elapsed then the species can be classified as absent from that site on that occasion. However, failure to find a species on only one occasion does not imply that it is definitely absent. Butterflies have natural cyclical population patterns, and in some years they may be numerically common whereas in other years they may be scarce. During these naturally occurring years of scarcity, the few that are around may be absent from one survey plot, but may return the next year as their numbers build up again. The effect of weather is also important: a thorough knowledge of the ecology of each species is needed as some species can react to adverse weather by not emerging from the pupa (this happened with a lot of moths in 1998) but these will certainly emerge in the following year. Other species may react in different ways. A single year of absence is not enough to confirm absence. The number of years required will vary between species and according to the reasons for the temporary absence of the life cycle stage being searched for, but it will always require at least two successive years as an absolute minimum.

The surveyor must be familiar with the habitat requirements of the target species and be able to identify the larval food plant(s) and larvae with confidence.

Timed counts

Timed counts can be used to produce an index of larval population size in the form of numbers found per unit time (or per search if search times are kept constant). To make the most efficient use of time, searches should be concentrated on areas of suitable habitat. This non-randomness means that data are not comparable between sites, but

Table 17.1. *Methods for surveying and monitoring butterflies*

	Recommended species group	Population size data	Efficiency	Precision	Bias	Expertise required	Advantages	Disadvantages
Larval or egg counts: timed searches	Larvae (Northern Brown Argus; Small Blue, eggs; Marsh Fritillary, larval webs)[a]	Presence–absence Index Estimate	Reasonable	Good	Inconspicuous larvae or eggs may be missed	Identification	Can be carried out in most weather conditions	Does not estimate number of adults Not appropriate for all species
Larval or egg counts: quadrats or transects	Larvae (Northern Brown Argus; Small Blue, eggs; Marsh Fritillary, larval webs)	Index Estimate	Good	Reasonable	Inconspicuous larvae or eggs may be missed	Identification	Entire colony areas can be searched	Standardising search methods may be difficult Not appropriate for all species
Transects	Adults (all species)	Index	Good if transect access straightforward	Will vary according to weather conditions at time of survey	Some species may be relatively under-recorded	Identification	Usually reliable method, which produces comparable results	Survey times restricted by appropriate weather conditions

[a] Latin names: Northern Brown Argus *Aricia artaxerxes*; Small Blue *Cupido minimus*; Marsh Fritillary *Eurodryas aurinia*.

provided survey times are kept constant and provided that identical techniques are used in the same area of land each year, data can be compared between years from the same site.

Knowledge of the timing of larval emergence and their habitat and food preferences is essential to make good use of survey time. Surveys will in all cases need to be tailored to suit the life cycle of the target species, and the counting methodology may also depend upon the ecology of the species concerned. For example, when counting Marsh Fritillaries *Euphydryas aurinia* you should count larval webs rather than eggs (Section 17.3.1), whereas for the Chequered Skipper *Carterocephalus palaemon* you should select a transect including at least 50 Purple Moor-grass *Molinia caerulea* tussocks close to the transect used for monitoring adults (Section 17.2.2).

The habitat should be searched thoroughly during the survey, and signs of egg and larval presence should be noted and counted. It should not be necessary to take samples from the field; with rare species this is obviously undesirable. Often it will also be desirable to estimate the area covered by the food plant.

Surveys for monitoring purposes should ideally be carried out every year. For EIA studies one needs to be aware of the intra- and inter-annual variations in abundance. Hence, a survey undertaken in one year only may not be representative of the Lepidoptera population of a site. For less threatened species a count every 3 years may be sufficient. In all cases, however, if an apparent absence is detected in one year, annual surveys should be carried out for at least two further seasons before the conclusion can be drawn in the third that the species is probably absent. The necessary field equipment is summarised in Appendix 6.

Data analysis and interpretation

As long as methods are standardised between years, trends in count data can be analysed by using techniques such as regression (Part I, Section 2.6.4). Other kinds of statistical analysis may also be appropriate, provided that sampling is representative (see Section 2.6.4). If data are collected on the abundance of the food plant

and larval or egg density then an estimate can be made of the total number of larvae or eggs. For example, if an average of two Chequered Skipper larvae are found on each *Molinia* tussock, the tussocks are on average distributed at two per square metre and cover an area of $100\,m^2$ then the total number of larvae can be estimated as $2 \times 2 \times 100 = 400$. Confidence intervals can also be estimated under appropriate sampling conditions.

17.2.2   Larval or egg counts: quadrats and transects

Principles

Transects or quadrats can be used for monitoring larval or egg numbers. Transects can be laid out across areas of representative habitat, or quadrats can be selected and sampled. Unless a large quadrat size is used, most quadrats will only contain part of one or two clutches of eggs. These data will be of limited use for estimating population size, but will provide supplementary information for estimating clutch size, which will be of use if population structure is being monitored. If transects or quadrats are chosen on the basis of habitat suitability then data can be used as an index of abundance. If transects or quadrats are randomly selected over the whole site then an estimate can be made of numbers at that site. For rare species, which are found only in restricted areas, quadrats or transects will usually be placed in areas where the species are known to occur; this will make the most efficient use of survey time.

As with timed searches (Section 17.2.1), the surveyors will need to be experienced in the recognition of larvae, eggs and food plants. Knowledge of the timing of larval emergence will also be necessary.

Field methods

The principles of quadrat and transect selection are covered in Part I, Section 2.3.3. When monitoring rare species, sample points will generally be selected by judgement to include areas of suitable habitat for the species in question. Transect length and quadrat size will depend on the habitat being surveyed and the colony size of the species being monitored.

The precise methodology will vary according to which species is being surveyed and monitored. In general, however, you will walk transects or search quadrats systematically looking for larvae, eggs or pupae. Timing of surveys will depend upon the ecology of the species concerned; see Emmet & Heath (1989) for more information.

Methodology and transect length or quadrat size should be standardised for each site and species so that different surveyors can produce comparable data. Surveys should ideally be carried out every year. For less threatened species a count every 3 years may be sufficient. The field equipment requirements are listed in Appendix 6.

Data analysis and interpretation

Provided that sampling is representative, data can be analysed statistically by using standard tests (Part I, Section 2.6.4). Other kinds of statistical analysis may also be appropriate (see Section 2.6.4). Data from samples selected by judgement can only be treated as an index of abundance unless the area of suitable habitat is known and is reasonably homogeneous. Larval population estimates can be made if such data are gathered (see Section 17.2.1).

Interpretation of larval population estimates should be made with reference to counts of adults (Section 17.2.3); many larvae will not survive to reach adulthood, and the number of larvae will be greater than the number of adults that produced those larvae, as each female lays more than one egg. Larval numbers, therefore, are an index of the adult population that produced that generation, and of the next generation of adults, but the numerical relation between these will vary depending upon the species in question and environmental effects.

17.2.3   Adult counts: transects

Principles

A national scheme for recording butterfly numbers by using standardised methods has been in operation since 1976. The Butterfly Monitoring Scheme (BMS) methodology is described in Pollard (1977), and reviews can be found in Pollard et al. (1986) and Pollard & Yates (1993). The methods developed are both species- and site-specific.

The advantage of using standard methods across all sites is obvious: you can compare data not only between years for the same site but between sites, and monitoring is made much simpler if everyone uses similar methods.

Field methods
BMS methodology

A series of counts are made along a fixed route at each site; recording should ideally be carried out weekly from 1 April to 29 September. For each count the surveyor walks at a uniform pace along the transect and records all butterflies seen within 5 m on either side of the transect.

To ensure comparability of counts, certain weather criteria must be met. Counts are not made when the temperature is below 13 °C; from 13 °C to 17 °C counts are made only when there is 60% sunshine, and above 17 °C counts can be made even in cloudy conditions. In northern and western upland sites, the minimum recording temperature in 60% sunshine may be reduced to 11 °C. Counts are carried out between 10.15 and 15.45 hours BST.

Each transect is divided into sections that broadly coincide with distinct habitat types within the broader site. The equipment necessary for field monitoring is listed in Appendix 6.

Data analysis and interpretation

Data from butterfly transects will generally be treated as an index of population size. Provided that sampling is representative, data can be analysed statistically by using standard tests (Part I, Section 2.6.4). Other kinds of statistical analysis may also be appropriate (see Section 2.6.4). However, although year-to-year changes on a site may be due to the effects of site management (Pollard, 1982) they may also be related to national trends, which may be caused by weather patterns (Pollard & Lakhani, 1985; Pollard, 1988) or other factors. Caution is therefore required in the interpretation of data; comparisons with other sites are invaluable.

17.3 BUTTERFLY CONSERVATION EVALUATION CRITERIA

17.3.1 Key evaluation considerations

Compared with other invertebrate groups in the UK, butterflies receive considerable attention from the public and policy makers. The Butterflies for the New Millennium project, organized by Butterfly Conservation and the BRC, has brought together data from a variety of sources to produce the *Millennium Atlas of Butterflies in Britain and Ireland* (Butterfly Conservation, 2001). This atlas provides an assessment of the habitats and threats facing butterflies, as well as changes in distribution since the previous atlas (Heath *et al.*, 1984).

Further sources of data that have been used in the production of atlases include the Butterfly Monitoring Scheme run by the Centre for Ecology and Hydrology at Monks Wood. This scheme monitors changes in butterfly numbers based on transects carried out throughout the summer at a series of set monitoring sites throughout the UK. However, most rare species are not included in this. A less formal scheme is the Garden Butterflies Count organised by Butterfly Conservation on an annual basis. This provides much wider coverage than the Butterfly Monitoring Scheme, but is less reliably standardised.

17.3.2 Protection status in the UK and EU

Appendix II of the Bern Convention lists three species of butterfly that occur or occurred in Britain and have consequently been included in the Wildlife & Countryside Act 1981: Large Blue *Maculinea arion*, Large Copper *Lycaena dispar* and Marsh Fritillary.

Twenty-five of the 59 species of British butterfly are listed in Schedule 5 of the Wildlife & Countryside Act 1981, although only six receive full protection as amended by the Countryside & Rights of Way Act 2000. The other 19 are protected from sale only.

The Large Blue is the only butterfly listed in Annex IV(a) to the EU Habitats Directive, for species in need of strict protection, whose range includes any part of Great Britain. This is implemented in UK legislation by being listed in Schedule 2 of the Conservation (Natural Habitats & c.) Regulations 1994.

The Marsh Fritillary is the only butterfly listed in Annex II to the EU Habitats Directive of species of community interest whose conservation requires the designation of Special Areas of Conservation (SACs). The Large Copper, also listed in Annex II and IV of the Habitats Directive, is considered extinct in the UK.

Eleven species are currently priority BAP species, and a further 14 are BAP species of conservation concern.

17.3.3 Conservation status in the UK

Two resident butterfly species are classified as Endangered, three as Vulnerable and two as Rare in the British Red Data Book 2: Insects. However, the Red Data Book was published in 1987 and butterfly populations and distributions have changed since. For example, one of the endangered species, the Large Tortoiseshell, is now considered to be extinct.

Five of the resident species of butterfly have become extinct in the UK since the nineteenth century, and over half have declined substantially in distribution. Habitat specialist species, i.e. those that use more localized habitats such as chalk grassland or ancient woodland, have tended to decline, whereas most wider countryside species have not suffered as much. However, some wider countryside species such as the Small Copper *Lycaena phlaeas* and the Wall Brown have declined severely, and there is evidence to suggest that although they are still widespread at the 10 km grid square level they have declined in abundance and distribution within those squares (Butterfly Conservation, 2001).

Of the 11 priority BAP species, over the past two decades seven have continued long-term declines (typically in excess of 30%), two have recovered slightly, and one, the Large Blue, has been reintroduced. Most of the species of conservation concern have also undergone substantial declines, with the Wood White *Leptidea sinapis* in particular, by the time of publication of the *Millennium Atlas of Butterflies in Britain and Ireland*, having disappeared from 62% of the 10 km grid squares in which it was recorded in 1970–82 (Butterfly Conservation, 2001).

17.3.4   Site designation criteria

SSSI criteria for designating sites for butterfly interest are described in NCC (1989). In brief, the presence of colonies of Nationally Endangered, Vulnerable or Rare species as classified by the Red Data Book are eligible, although only strong colonies of Vulnerable and Rare species may be eligible. All sites with endemic races of the Grayling *Hipparchia semele* and Silver-studded Blue *Plebeius argus* qualify.

For nationally scarce species, the three strongest colonies within an AOS qualify, or five strongest colonies in an area that contains a substantial proportion of the British colonies. Within an AOS, sites with the two strongest colonies of a further 15 species that have experienced substantial local declines can also qualify, although they should ideally also support colonies of some nationally rare or scarce species. An Area of Search is based largely on counties in England, and largely on districts in Scotland and Wales.

18 • Moths

This chapter refers largely to the macromoths, although many of the techniques are also applicable to micromoths. Most macromoths are nocturnal, and this poses some problems for survey and monitoring. For many species, light traps are the only reliable way of confirming the presence of adults.

Adult moths are mostly highly mobile and rarely site-specific, but larvae often live in discrete areas of suitable habitat. Such habitats may be large in the case of grass-feeding species or very small and discrete in the case of leaf miners. Separate populations may also exist within areas of suitable habitat.

Monitoring areas of suitable habitat may be appropriate, particularly if resources are not available for more detailed survey methods. Monitoring of micro-habitats is not specifically covered in this *Handbook*. However, some of the techniques in Part II may be adapted for this purpose.

18.1 ATTRIBUTES FOR ASSESSING CONDITION

18.1.1 Population range

Area of occupancy is an important attribute to monitor and can be best assessed by mapping presence–absence. Repeat surveys will illustrate expansions or contractions of range.

18.1.2 Colony number

As mentioned above, adult moths are highly mobile whereas larvae often live in discrete areas. The number of colonies may therefore apply more to larval populations than to adults.

The number of populations occurring in a site is a straightforward indication of the overall health of

the species in the defined area. A small number of colonies on one particular site does not necessarily imply that a species is not at its optimal level, especially if the site is a part of the edge of the main area for the species.

Colony numbers are relatively simple to establish: presence of individuals can be used to imply the presence of a colony. However, failure to find evidence of a species in one year alone cannot be taken as evidence of absence; several surveys with a negative result will be needed to confirm an absence, particularly on sites where a species has previously been recorded.

18.1.3 Population size

A more detailed assessment of moth populations will entail estimates of population size. This can be achieved by counting adults (diurnal moths only), larvae or eggs along transects set up through areas of suitable habitat. For species with discrete colonies, counting larvae on all the food plants in the area as part of a timed count may be better than transect counts. Transect recording methods may need to be tailored to suit particular species. Some species of nocturnal and diurnal adult male moths can be monitored by using pheromone traps or attracted to purposely bred virgin females. Over a period of years, annual numeric totals from light traps will reveal population trends.

18.1.4 Population structure

Some moths can be surveyed and monitored at the larval stage by counts on food plants. If the life history is known then counts of larval workings can be made instead (especially for internal leaf feeders). Changes in the ratio of larval counts to adult counts can be used as an indication of changes in population structure, which may be caused by a number of factors such as increased larval or adult mortality.

18.2   GENERAL METHODS

General site survey methods for invertebrates are provided in Chapter 10.

The general methods for surveying and monitoring moths are outlined in Table 18.1.

18.2.1   Light traps

Principles

Most species of night-flying moth are attracted towards light, particularly towards the ultraviolet (UV) end of the spectrum. They can then be caught in a trap for identification. Light traps can, in ideal weather conditions, catch very large numbers of moths. However, the numbers of moths caught is strongly dependent upon the prevailing weather conditions, and therefore traps cannot realistically be used for monitoring moth populations unless they are used almost every night over a period of some years (Ausden, 1996). Light traps are therefore best used for obtaining presence–absence data.

Field methods

The simplest light trap consists of a light (high-pressure MB mercury vapour bulbs are best, as they emit both UV-a and visible radiation between 350 and 650 nm) (Fry & Waring, 1996) on a cable hanging outside a building; moths can be caught with nets as they circle the light.

Catches can be increased by using moth traps (Figure 18.1), which also have the advantage that they can be left overnight without an operator being present (although many species of Geometridae and many families of micromoths will settle on the outside of the trap and subsequently take to flight again at first light).

Traps should be situated so that the light source is not heavily shaded by surrounding foliage, because this reduces the area over which the light will be visible. The effective radius of a 125 W white MB high-pressure bulb is 60 m. Light traps catch the greatest number of moths on warm, still and overcast nights. If possible, you should try to use the traps during similar conditions on different nights. Never use traps during heavy rain unless a rain shield is fixed to the trap, or the bulb may crack if water falls on it. However, trapping during light rain on a muggy summer evening can be extremely productive.

If the trapping location is not near a mains electricity supply, batteries will be needed. Light traps come in various designs and can be obtained from entomological supply merchants. It is also possible to construct them from scratch. In order to achieve some degree of standardisation, operate the trap for the same length of time on each occasion. The field equipment requirements for monitoring moths are listed in Appendix 6.

There are a large number of macromoth species; some exhibit considerable phenotypic variation. Surveyors should therefore be experienced at identification. Skinner (1998) is the standard work on moth identification. For many rare species listed in site citations, light trapping is the best – perhaps the only – option for recording a presence–absence.

Data analysis and interpretation

The variability of light trap data, depending on the weather, makes quantitative or semi-quantitative analysis impracticable for monitoring purposes. For example, an increase in wind speed will reduce the numbers caught by a considerable amount. Light trap data can, however, be used to establish the presence of species, which is most useful in EIA studies. Moth monitoring has been patchy in the past; in many areas there will be little information on the species present so it will be difficult to make regional evaluations for a particular site. Light trap data can therefore be useful when surveying sites that have not been previously surveyed for moths, and can also be used as an effective means of detecting the presence of species of conservation interest.

18.2.2   Pheromone traps

Principles

Pheromone traps use pheromones that have been isolated from female moths, or synthesised in

Table 18.1. *Methods for surveying and monitoring moths*

	Recommended species group	Population size data	Efficiency	Precision	Bias	Expertise required	Advantages	Disadvantages
Light traps	Night-flying moths	Presence–absence	Low if traps and batteries must be transported long distances. Depends to some extent on species	Reasonable	Biased towards species attracted to light. Location of trap influences species caught	Identification. Trap operation	Can attract large numbers of moths	Only qualitative data obtained: results greatly affected by weather
Pheromone traps	Moths with available pheromones	Presence–absence. Index	Depends on costs of pheromones and species being trapped	Low	Will only attract certain species; not all moth pheromones are available	Identification. Trap operation	Will attract all adult males if left long enough	Pheromones are very expensive. Cannot be used for some species. Does not attract females
Larval or egg counts	Most moths	Index. Estimate	Good	Reasonable	Inconspicuous larvae or eggs may be missed	Identification	Entire colony areas can be searched	Standardising search methods may be difficult
Transects: adults	Diurnal moths	Index	Good if transect access straightforward	Will vary according to weather conditions at time of survey	Small, cryptic species may be under-recorded	Identification	Usually reliable method, which produces comparable results	Survey times restricted by appropriate weather conditions. Only applicable to diurnal species

laboratories, and used to 'bait' traps, which will attract and catch adult males. They have some advantages over light traps in that they are more attractive over a greater distance and will therefore catch more male moths, but only from downwind and often from considerable distances. Attracted males may not therefore truly relate to the survey site, whereas light traps only attract individuals that are close by. Data will still vary according to weather conditions, but if the trap is left out for a sufficiently long period of time, which encompasses a range of conditions, some amount of standardisation can be achieved.

There are a number of commercially available pheromones but they are not available for all species. Some are not species-specific and so can be used to attract a range of species. A fuller description of the use of pheromone traps to attract clearwing moths (Sesiidae) can be found in de Freina & Witt (1997). A cheaper and equally effective method of attracting males is the use of purpose-bred virgin female moths, which are placed in the traps instead of pheromones. These will select only the males of the particular species chosen. See Ekkehard (1986) for details about breeding moths in captivity.

Field methods

A pheromone trap operates in a similar manner to a light trap (Figure 18.1); moths are attracted into a chamber, which contains cover for them to hide underneath and from which they cannot easily fly out. The pheromones come in liquid form and can be poured onto cotton wool or other absorbent material.

In order to counter the effects of weather on the numbers of trapped moths, the traps should be left open for at least a week during the peak flight season of the target species. Over this period of time, it should be possible to trap all the males in the surrounding downwind area. The range over which pheromone traps are effective depends on the species concerned. For example, Emperor Moth *Saturnia pavonia* males can be attracted over a distance of 8 km, whereas Vapourer Moths *Orgyia antiqua* are apparently attracted over much shorter distances.

Pheromone traps retain male moths, which are thus removed from the population. Prolonged use of pheromone traps can seriously deplete the

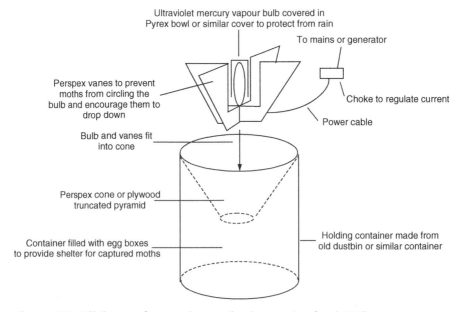

Figure 18.1. A light trap for trapping moths. Source: Ausden (1996).

males in a given population (indeed, they are used as a pest removal tool in Kentish orchards, for example). Appendix 6 outlines the field equipment necessary for trapping moths.

Data analysis and interpretation
Counts obtained by using pheromone traps will be an estimate of the total number of adult males. The sex ratio of moths is extremely variable between species; counts of males should therefore be used as an index of total population size.

Provided that sampling is representative, data can be analysed statistically by using standard tests (Part I, Section 2.6.4). Other kinds of statistical analysis may also be appropriate (see Section 2.6.4). Comparisons will only be valid if fluctuations due to weather have been accounted for by using traps for a sufficient length of time. Otherwise, the data will reflect differences in trapping caused by factors such as wind speed and temperature more than any real changes in the abundance of target species.

18.2.3   Larval or egg counts

Principles
Some moth eggs and larvae can be monitored by using the methods described for butterfly eggs and larvae: timed counts (Section 17.2.1) and quadrats or transects (Section 17.2.2). The surveyor will need to be experienced in the identification of moth larvae, eggs and food plants; consult Young (1979), Bradley *et al.* (1973; 1979) or Emmet & Heath (1989) for further details on the ecology of moths. Surveys should be timed to coincide with peak numbers of larvae or eggs.

Such surveys are highly specific and results may not be as simple to interpret as light trap data. However, they can be very effective for some species, such as the Welsh Clearwing *Aegeria scoliaeformis*, which can be surveyed by counting pupal cases protruding from birch (*Betula* spp.) trees.

Field methods
See Sections 17.2.1 and 17.2.2.

Data analysis and interpretation
See Sections 17.2.1 and 17.2.2.

18.2.4   Transects

Principles
Adult diurnal moths can be monitored by using the methods of the BMS or, for regional variation. These are described in Section 17.2.3 and in Pearce *et al.* (1996).

Field methods
See Section 17.2.3.

Data analysis and interpretation
See Section 17.2.3.

18.3   MACROMOTH CONSERVATION EVALUATION CRITERIA

18.3.1   Key evaluation considerations

There is currently no comprehensive national dataset that can be used to assess the distribution and conservation status of the 900 or so UK resident macromoths, although Butterfly Conservation is planning a National Macromoth Recording Scheme.

Atropos and Butterfly Conservation currently organise an annual Moth Night that includes preselected 'target species': scarce species that may occur more widely. This has generated useful information, including new county records and new sites for scarce species.

There is a network of county recorders for moths, with county distributions of moth species also available on some web pages, e.g. on those of the Suffolk Moth Group (www.suffolkmothgroup.org.uk).

18.3.2   Protection status in the UK and EU

There are no resident moth species listed in Appendixes II or III of the Bern Convention, although some, such as the Willow Herb Hawkmoth *Proserpinus proserpina*, are found as occasional migrants in the UK.

Eight species of British moth are listed in Schedule 5 of the Wildlife & Countryside Act 1981 and are strictly protected as amended by the Countryside & Rights of Way Act 2000.

No UK resident moths are listed in Annex IV(a) of the EU Habitats Directive, for species in need of strict protection, and hence no moth species are listed in Schedule 2 of the Conservation (Natural Habitats & c.) Regulations 1994.

The Jersey Tiger *Euplagia quadripunctaria* is the only moth species occurring in the UK that is listed in Annex II of the EU Habitats Directive of species of community interest whose conservation requires the designation of Special Areas of Conservation (SACs). However, this species is considered to be outside its native range in the UK, so does not require site protection.

Fifty-three moth species are currently priority BAP species, and many more are species of conservation concern.

18.3.3   Conservation status in the UK

Twenty-one resident macromoth species and subspecies are classified as endangered, twelve as vulnerable and fifty-three as rare in the British Red Data Book 2: Insects. A further four micromoths are classified as endangered and seven as vulnerable. However, moth populations are likely to have changed since the Red Data Book was published, and without a national dataset, establishing the current national status of these and other species is difficult.

18.3.4   Site designation criteria

SSSI criteria for designating sites for butterfly interest are described in Guidelines for Selection of Biological SSSIs (NCC, 1989). Moths are treated in general terms, i.e. as for other invertebrate groups except butterflies and dragonflies, which are sufficiently well known to have separate treatment within the guidelines. The site designation criteria for moths are therefore included in Section 19.3 (Other terrestrial invertebrates).

Insects and other arthropods account for 26 000 of the 88 000 species of all groups recorded in Britain. This figure excludes the terrestrial component of the non-arthropod invertebrates such as molluscs (Anon., 1995). These species take a huge variety of forms, occupying many trophic levels and having a variety of either broad or narrow habitat requirements (Strong *et al.*, 1984). Species occupy tree and shrub canopies, grass and herbaceous vegetation, and roam the surface and subterranean components of soil. Species that undergo metamorphosis often have life stages adapted to contrasting habitats or resources within a habitat. Different species can reproduce at different times of the year and in one or more generations a year. There are also temporal considerations important in the design of sampling protocols. The varied life histories of different species translates to varied activity through the season. Different species can also be active during the day, others are active nocturnally, and some are crepuscular. The number of different groups and species in this category is immense. It is therefore not feasible to give specific methods for all groups.

This chapter presents general methods for invertebrate monitoring, which can be adapted to suit the requirements of most groups. However, given the above constraints, as well as the difficulty in identifying many species, there will be many situations in which the only practical course of action will be to engage an appropriate specialist (who may sometimes be a local amateur entomologist) either to design the procedure or to carry out the monitoring work in person. For more information regarding the monitoring of specific groups see New (1998), Southwood (2000), Greenslade (1964), Morris (1991), Okland (1996), Roberts (1996),

Prys-Jones & Corbet (1991), Oggier *et al.* (1998), Yarrow (1995), Stubbs (1972), Blackshaw (1994) and Usher (1990).

Clearly, given the number of species and variety of life histories, invertebrate monitoring is a complex and time-consuming process. For general invertebrate monitoring, resource constraints may not permit the use of some of the more detailed methods described here. It may be necessary simply to monitor invertebrates indirectly by assessing the extent of suitable habitat and confirming presence–absence of particular (selected) species on an occasional basis. See Part II for details on habitat monitoring methods. For species of conservation importance, however, more detailed monitoring may be necessary.

Monitoring is often carried out on a site-specific basis; methods for the same group may vary according to the class and complexity of the habitat and conditions pertaining at different sites. Again, it is not feasible to cover this aspect in detail. However, a combination of one or more of the methods described could be adapted to establish site-based monitoring for species of interest in particular situations. For further information consult New (1998).

The monitoring of many invertebrate groups requires specialist knowledge about their seasonal and daily activity, broad efficiency in the habitat (e.g. the host plant species of herbivores) and identification. Identification of invertebrates will also often require specialist taxonomic knowledge, particularly because there is a lack of published identification keys for a significant proportion of invertebrate taxa. Despite some species being distinct and recognisable in the field by generalist ecologists, species of taxa for which published keys are available will require identification by using microscopy in the laboratory. This can be a lengthy process; voucher specimens of species identified in this way and unidentified specimens of taxa with no available published keys will need to be sent away for verification and identification by the recognised expert or recorder for that group.

Specific methods that have been developed for particular species of conservation interest are not covered in detail; references for BAP Priority Species, where available, are given in Appendix 1.

19.1   ATTRIBUTES FOR ASSESSING CONDITION

19.1.1   Population range

Surveying and monitoring for the majority of invertebrates will generally consist of establishing presence or absence at a particular site or part of a site and setting this in context. Care should be taken when a species is not found on one survey at a site where it has previously been recorded; natural population fluctuations may be responsible. It is not at all possible to regard a species as definitely absent until many years of appropriate survey yielding a negative result have elapsed; this is particularly the case with some saproxylic beetles, which may spend ten or more years as larvae feeding inside timber. On the other hand, when an entire assemblage of species associated with a single microhabitat declines or disappears, there may be cause for more immediate concern. Knowledge is always required of the season of activity of the different stages in the life cycle of the target species. Repeat visits or continuous sampling methods will certainly be required if several species of different taxa are to be monitored.

Although the fact that a species is not recorded on one survey does not *prove* absence, it only takes one record to prove presence. However, captures of single specimens of a species must be carefully considered in relation to the sampling method employed. Occasional captures of species from remote habitats are expected in samples from pitfall and window traps. Confidence in sampling small numbers of specimens will require discrimination of rare species

from occasional visitors. This is best achieved when the target species are known to be either sedentary or weakly dispersing species, and will invariably imply a need for discussion with an appropriate expert.

19.1.2   Population size

For species of conservation interest that require more detailed monitoring, estimates of population size may be required. This will entail more detailed sampling of the population, in terms of number of samples and the time over which they are collected. The methods detailed below will provide an index of population size rather than absolute estimates. Several of the general sampling methods are capable of providing measures of relative trap abundance. However, interpretation of trap to actual abundance is a species-specific problem, depending on the sampling efficiency of the method, usually related to the size, mobility and form of attachment of the species and the complexity of the sampled substrate. Invertebrates are small and often numerous and widely dispersed; it is therefore unlikely that monitoring will be able to achieve the level of precision necessary to make estimates of the total population for more than just a few selected species.

19.2   GENERAL METHODS

19.2.1   Purpose

An initial assessment to judge whether a site is likely to require a more in depth evaluation for invertebrates may be required, if there is insufficient information on the invertebrate interest of the site (see Section 10 on general site survey). Such an assessment should be brief, but sufficient to assess the likely presence of important terrestrial invertebrate species.

19.2.2   Method

A site appraisal should be carried out by walking over it. Habitat features of invertebrate interest should be largely visible at any time of year, but important invertebrates themselves are more likely to be visible from May until September. Within this time span, it should be noted that certain species will often only occur in a more readily observable form over a much shorter time period, which can be under a month.

The initial survey should ideally be carried out in warm, sunny weather so that as many invertebrate species will be readily observable as possible. Guidelines for the Butterfly Monitoring Scheme (see Section 17.2.3) suggest weather conditions that will also be suitable for a wide range of invertebrates other than butterflies. In brief, assessment should not be made when the temperature is below 13 °C (11 °C for northern and western upland sites); from 13 to 17 °C there must be a minimum of 60% sunshine; above 17 °C, the weather can be cloudy so long as it is not raining. The windspeed should not be above 5 on the Beaufort Scale.

While the surveyor is walking over the site, habitat features of invertebrate interest should be noted. These will include such features as dead wood, bare ground, soil types, variety of vegetation heights, habitat mosaics, and presence of flowering plant species (particularly Umbelliferae and Asteraceae). In addition, direct evidence of invertebrate species should be noted, particularly for many species of groups such as Orthoptera (presence will frequently be determined by sound rather than sight), Hymenoptera, and especially day-flying Lepidoptera. Many species of Diptera, although typically active and potentially visible during the day, are likely to be missed because of their rapid response to disturbance. Attention should be paid to the invertebrates present on flowers, dung and carrion and under loose objects, which can reveal important species of Coleoptera and other less obvious invertebrates. Careful searches of vegetation, along the lines of the methods described below in Section 19.2.6, can particularly reveal further species of Coleoptera, especially leaf beetles (Chrysomelidae), in addition to Hemiptera and molluscs. Ideally, this latter method can be used in conjunction with some sweep-netting: the sweep-netting will reveal insects missed in the search, and the search will reveal invertebrates that are easily missed by sweep-netting because of their rapid response to disturbance.

Checking of roads on or in the vicinity of the site can give information on larger invertebrates killed by cars, especially the larger beetles such as Stag Beetles *Lucanus cervus* (Hawes, 2003) and chafers.

Those species that are not readily identified on site, either because of the requirement for a microscope or because of the need to refer to keys, can be caught by using a butterfly net or pooter as appropriate.

19.2.3   Interpretation of results

If protected species have been recorded in the area, then a more detailed survey of the site for those species would be required regardless of the findings of an initial survey. The presence of habitat features suitable for a protected species identified in the initial survey should necessitate a further survey for the protected species if the protected species is known to occur locally, even if the species has never been recorded from the site before (because the species may have recolonised the site since previous surveys, especially if it exists as a metapopulation), or if the site and the local area are not known to have been surveyed for the species before. If the usual range of the species were known, then in theory it should be possible to determine how close a site for evaluation should be to a known protected species site in order to require checking for the protected species. However, in most cases the likely range is not known, and furthermore, information on the presence of small patches of suitable habitat between the site with the protected species and the site for evaluation that could act as 'stepping stones' is unlikely to be available.

In cases where other species of conservation interest are concerned, observation of one or more of these species on the initial survey should require further, more detailed surveys to be carried out (a species of conservation interest being species considered of interest to the site, whether they are priority BAP species or Species of Conservation Concern). Because only a small proportion of the invertebrate fauna of a site would be directly observed on an initial survey, the presence of even a single species of conservation interest during the initial survey suggests that other species of conservation interest are likely to be present.

If the initial survey reveals a wealth of habitat features of invertebrate interest, and additionally a rich diversity of invertebrate species are observed, even if no species of conservation interest were seen then the site merits further surveys. A site rich in suitable features and with a diversity of even common invertebrate species is likely to possess features and characteristics suitable for species of conservation interest to be present.

The general methods for surveying and monitoring invertebrates are outlined in Table 19.1.

19.2.4   Searches of adult and larval feeding or resting sites

Principles

Surveying and monitoring of invertebrates is often carried out in an informal or targeted way; the diversity of invertebrates is considerable and the degree of niche specialisation means that a species of interest may occur only on a very localised scale, or will occupy a very specialised micro-habitat. For sites notified for their invertebrate conservation interest, the habitat requirements of these species, and the area in which they are found, will sometimes be known, and possibly marked. In this case, a straightforward and cheap survey method is simply to search areas of suitable habitat for the target species, and draw up a basic distribution map based on presence–absence of the species in areas that could potentially support it. There is a presumption in this situation that the species can be easily found and identified in the field.

This *ad hoc* method has the advantage of being relatively quick and simple to carry out and being directly targeted at species of conservation interest. If monitoring resources are limited, this method, although incapable of providing comparable quantitative data, provides one of the most efficient methods for monitoring species with specialised niche requirements.

A disadvantage of the method is that it cannot provide estimates of the population size of target

species, because *ad hoc* search data cannot be compared with other data. This means that, although an idea of the extent of the species can be obtained from presence–absence in suitable areas, you cannot ascertain with any degree of precision whether the population is increasing, stable or decreasing. If a more detailed survey of species of interest is required, one of the other methods outlined in Sections 19.2.2–19.2.7 should be considered.

The efficiency of this method will depend on the surveyor's knowledge of the site and of the species; if you have to spend time searching first of all for areas of habitat, efficiency will be reduced. It is thus preferable that *ad hoc* searches be carried out by staff with experience of the site and of the habitat requirements of the species being monitored.

Invertebrates can also be indirectly monitored by measuring the area of suitable habitat (and perhaps establishing presence–absence in a sample of that area). Clearly, it is a major assumption that the invertebrate species would be present, simply as a product of the habitat condition. There are commonly empty niches in nature in which the prevailing environmental conditions exclude species from apparently favourable habitat (Strong *et al.*, 1984; Sparks *et al.*, 1994; Dennis *et al.*, 1995). Methods for surveying and monitoring habitat extent are covered in Part II of this *Handbook*.

Field methods

The surveyor should carefully search the micro-habitat of the target species. The method of searching will depend upon the species and habitat in question; there is not much in the way of specific guidance that can be given in a general methods book, and appropriate expert advice should always be sought before inexperienced staff begin work. Consult some of the recommended sources at the end of this *Handbook* for further information on the ecology of invertebrate groups and species. Time of season, time of day and prevailing weather conditions will be among the many critical factors for a successful survey. The timing of surveys should coincide with the time of maximum abundance of the target species(e.g. mating flights or larval emergence).

If you are aiming to draw up a distribution map of the target species, it may be desirable to divide

Table 19.1. *Methods for surveying and monitoring other terrestrial invertebrates*

	Recommended species group	Population size data	Efficiency	Precision	Bias	Expertise required	Advantages	Disadvantages
Searches of adult or larval feeding or resting sites	All	Presence–absence	Good if area to be searched is small	Low if not all of area is searched or timing is not synchronised with period of activity of target life stage	Cryptic species often over-looked; Mobile species may escape; Effects of timing will bias results	Identification; Knowledge of habitat requirements of species	Straightforward method of establishing presence. Most usual method in EIA	Data not comparable
Timed searches	All	Presence–absence; Index	Reasonable	Reasonable: as above	Cryptic species often over-looked; Mobile species may escape	Identification; Knowledge of habitat requirements of species	Enables comparable data to be collected; Results can be extrapolated over wider area	Variations in surveyor effort difficult to standardise
Quadrat searches	Ground-dwelling species	Presence–absence; Index; Estimate	Reasonable	Good for distinctive species: as above	Mobile species may escape	Identification; Knowledge of habitat requirements of species	Narrows down search area; Results can be extrapolated over wider area	Data variability high in heterogeneous habitats
Pitfall traps	Ground beetles and other	Presence–absence; Index	Good	Difficult to measure	Species not equally likely to	Identification; Knowledge	Collects large number of invertebrates	Results reflect activity as well as numbers

Table 19.1. (cont.)

	Recom-mended species group	Population size data	Efficiency	Precision	Bias	Expertise required	Advantages	Disadvant-ages
	epigeal or surface-active invertebrates				be caught Weather and habitat complexity affects activity and hence numbers trapped	of habitat requirements of species	with min-imum effort	
Suction samplers	Invertebrates in low vegetation	Presence–absence Index Estimate	Low to reasonable dependent on device	Good	Mobile species and species firmly attached to vegetation are undersampled; other species may be over-sampled by suction at edge of nozzle	Identifi-cation Knowledge of habitat requirements of species Operation of sampler	Reasonably accurate and easily standardised methodology	Cumbersome and expensive Requires transport of equipment and fuel, which is problematic in remote areas D-vac requires regular servicing
Window traps	Flying insects	Presence–absence Index	Reasonable	Reasonable	Nature and height of trap affects types of species caught	Identifi-cation Knowledge of habitat requirements	Simplest way of sampling flying insects	Traps must be regularly checked Data analysis problematic

Malaise traps	Flying insects, particularly Diptera	Presence–absence Index	Reasonable	Reasonable	Trap aspect	of species Trap construction Identification Knowledge of habitat requirements of species	Simple method for sampling flying insects	Traps must be regularly checked Data analysis problematic
Artificial refugia	Molluscs	Presence–absence Index	Good	Reasonable	Weather-dependent: dry conditions lead to undersampling, wet card can compensate for this	Identification Knowledge of habitat requirements of species	Straight-forward method of assessing abundance	Requires transport of slates, which is problematic in remote areas

the habitat area up into a grid and search for presence in each cell. The size of the grid cells will depend upon the level of detail required (for example, you may be interested in presence–absence in 1 km squares or in 10 m squares). Steel pegs can be used to mark the location of the grids permanently for annual or longer re-survey. These can be relocated with a metal detector. Setting up a grid is covered in more detail in Section 15.2.2.

If the species is readily identifiable in the field, you can simply record the number of sightings. If this is not the case, specimens will have to be collected for later identification. Collecting equipment, such as pooters or aspirators and specimen tubes, will be required, with a suitable killing agent and, if appropriate, a suitable preservative.

If it is necessary to collect invertebrates as part of the study, careful thought should be given to the number of individuals that are taken, particularly for species restricted to a small number of micro-habitats or a limited area of the site, or where the site contains a large part of the local, regional or national population; in such situations, this methodology may perhaps be judged inappropriate. If you are simply concerned with presence–absence, the removal of several specimens is not necessary.

It may be necessary to take samples (e.g. litter or soil) and search these in the laboratory. This will apply in the case of species that cannot easily be seen in the field. You should therefore consider the destructiveness of the search method. If it requires considerable disturbance to the micro-habitat (for example, searching for dead-wood invertebrates), and that micro-habitat is not widespread or will take time to recover, you should consider only searching a portion of the habitat, perhaps by using timed or quadrat searches (Sections 19.2.2 and 19.2.3) to minimise damage. The recommended field equipment is listed in Appendix 6.

Data analysis and interpretation

Data from *ad hoc* searches can only be used to establish presence–absence. If the habitat of the target species is mapped, a grid can be overlaid and a distribution map drawn up based on presence–absence in each square. Repeat surveys within permanently marked grids can be compared to examine range expansions or contractions.

19.2.5   Timed searches

Principles

In the previous section, *ad hoc* searching was considered as a cheap and relatively efficient way of determining the presence or absence of species. The method has its limitations, some of which can be addressed by using timed counts. Timed counts bring an element of standardisation, enabling semi-quantitative data to be collected, which can be compared across years or sites. They also enable larger sites to be surveyed on a more rigorous basis.

Timed counts can also be useful when monitoring species that require destructive sampling (e.g. dead-wood invertebrates). A timed search method for dead-wood species could involve a 30 minute search of randomly selected 50 m × 50 m plots in a woodland; this would avoid the destruction of all the dead wood in one area.

In a timed count, an area is searched for a fixed time and all individuals of the target species are counted or collected. Counts can therefore be expressed as numbers found per unit time and, if search methods are reasonably standard between surveyors, data can be compared. This method can produce indices of abundance and relative abundance. It cannot produce estimates of population size: you can never be sure that all individuals in a given area will be found during the search (this is extremely unlikely).

Timed searches can be based on simply searching a set area for a standard period of time, or they can be combined with further subsampling of the area by plots, quadrats or transects (e.g. divide the area up into squares, select a sample of these and search for a set time in each selected square).

Field methods

Selection of the appropriate field method will involve the same considerations as in Section 19.2.1 and will depend upon the ecology of the target species. It is beyond the scope of this *Handbook* to consider detailed methods for every group of invertebrates. The reader should consult some of the recommended sources at the end of the *Handbook* for further information.

Searches should be informed (i.e. only search in areas likely to harbour the target species) and if possible conducted with a standardised methodology so that other surveyors can repeat the survey and obtain comparable results. The length of search will depend upon the time available and the area that must be covered, but as a general rule, counts should be 30–120 minutes long.

Frequency of repeat surveying will depend upon available resources and on the length of the various stages of the life cycle of the target species. The necessary field equipment for timed searches is outlined in Appendix 6.

Data analysis and interpretation

Data from timed counts can be expressed as numbers found per unit time assuming the search focuses on identifiable features on each occasion. If the site has been subdivided into equally sized sample units, data can be expressed as numbers found per unit time per size of area searched (assuming the habitat structure within each subunit is of equivalent complexity). Regardless of the units chosen to express the data, counts can be analysed statistically provided that methods are standardised from year to year and appropriate sampling has been used (see Part I, Section 2.6.4).

19.2.6   Quadrat searches

Principles

Quadrat searches are used to delineate small areas of ground vegetation for intensive searching. They can be particularly useful for species that have specialised habitat requirements and therefore are only found in a few small areas; in this case, the area of search is already narrowed down quite considerably. The use of quadrats to define smaller plots for searching within these areas can improve efficiency and will produce comparable, quantitative data. To further standardise methods, each quadrat should be searched for a set length of time, or vegetation within each quadrat can be

clipped and sieved or searched in a standard way (Williamson *et al.*, 1977; Southwood, 2000).

Quadrat searches are best suited to less mobile species such as snails. Fast-moving invertebrates may be under-recorded if they leave the quadrat area before the search is complete. If the search is sufficiently thorough, you may be able to detect all individuals in a quadrat and thus derive population estimates. For species that are highly mobile or cryptic, counts should be treated as population indices.

Field methods

A standard frame quadrat of size $0.25 \, \text{m}^2$ is generally used for sampling invertebrates. The selection of quadrat locations is covered in Part I, Section 2.3.3. If you are targeting a particular species, you should restrict quadrat locations to areas of habitat suitable for that species, to maximise search efficiency.

The quadrat should be laid on the ground and the vegetation or leaf litter within carefully searched for a set time (ideally 2–5 minutes depending on the proportions of bare soil and plant cover and the complexity of the vegetation). A longer search time should be allowed for cryptic species.

It may be necessary to search two or three trial quadrats not used in the analysis before starting on the specified sample, as it is an inevitable fact that finding efficiency increases with time as observers 'get their eye in'.

A minimum of five quadrats should be taken from each sample area. A pooter or aspirator and collecting bottle with a suitable killing agent will be needed to collect invertebrates for later identification if the species cannot be identified in the field. Species that can be readily identified on site should be placed in a container until the search is completed and then released back to the searched area.

Timing of counts will depend on the ecology of the target species. However, you should always aim to make counts during similar weather conditions: invertebrate activity is strongly weather-dependent. The field equipment required for quadrat searches is listed in Appendix 6.

Data analysis and interpretation

Data can either be expressed as numbers found per quadrat (and hence per square metre) or, if several quadrats have been taken, presence–absence in each can be used to calculate frequency. If the latter measurement is used, you should remember that quadrat size could affect estimates of frequency (Appendix 5). In general, estimates of density should only be made if you can be reasonably certain that all individuals in the quadrats were found. This will not be the case with more mobile, cryptic or subterranean species; counts for such species should be treated as population indices.

Data from different years can, potentially, be analysed statistically by using standard tests (Part I, Section 2.6.4). Comparisons of counts for monitoring should only be made between areas of similar habitat; habitat variables will affect counts and may obscure any underlying trends in abundance. As with all experimental work, a control should be established where possible. This may take the form of parallel monitoring of another common species that can generally be guaranteed to be present so that fluctuations in its population can be compared statistically with fluctuations in the population of the target species.

19.2.7   Pitfall traps

Principles

A pitfall trap is a vertical-sided container that is dug into the ground so that the top is level with or below the ground surface; invertebrates walking along the ground inadvertently fall into the trap. Pitfall trapping is probably the most widely used method for sampling invertebrates, and is a cheap and straightforward way of catching a large number of invertebrates with the minimum amount of effort.

As a monitoring method for comparing numbers caught over time, pitfall trapping has the disadvantage that invertebrate activity is greatly affected by the surrounding vegetation and by weather (Greenslade, 1964; Baars, 1979). When comparing counts from different years, you must attempt to standardise the micro-habitat in which the traps are placed and the weather conditions at

the time when trapping occurs (Honek, 1988). Otherwise, variations in trapping data could reflect changes in environmental conditions rather than in the abundance of species. If monitoring is targeted towards a species with particular habitat requirements, the traps will necessarily be placed in areas of similar habitat from year to year, so the first consideration will be met in most cases. Trapping in standard weather conditions is more difficult. One solution is to leave traps open for a reasonably long period of time (e.g. 1 month); unless the weather varies greatly from year to year, the average conditions over a 1 month period should be similar enough to allow valid comparisons to be made.

There are also variations in the capture rates of different species of ground beetle (Carabidae) depending on their mobility, visual acuity and climbing ability, such that the relative abundance of species in pitfall traps does not reflect the true relative abundance of the species (Halsall & Wratten, 1988). In addition, some species of ground beetle emit pheromones that attract other individuals to the trap (Luff, 1986). Pitfall traps tend to catch more invertebrates greater than 3 mm long (Ausden, 1996), but this may be due more to the mesh size used to sieve samples after collection; a smaller mesh size will probably increase the number of smaller invertebrates detected. You should therefore be wary of extrapolating relative abundance from pitfall trap data to relative abundance of overall populations. Pitfall traps should mainly be used for monitoring indices of population size. It is possible to sample for long periods (continuous trapping through a season) to overcome these inter-species differences in ease of capture and variations in season of activity, which affect the proportions in traps during short trapping periods (Baars, 1979).

Field methods

Any straight-sided container can be used as a pitfall trap (Figure 19.1). For example, large yogurt pots with snap-top lids are suitable and cheap. Monopots with snap lids are cheap but can be used only once and often leak fluid; screw-top honey pots are more durable but the Environmental Change

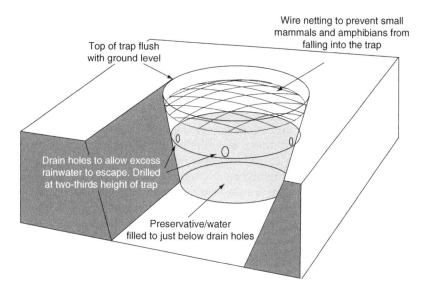

Figure 19.1. An invertebrate pitfall trap. See text for details.

Network (ECN), a UK-wide monitoring scheme, uses standard pots 7.5 cm in diameter and 10 cm deep from A. W. Gregory Ltd (Eyre *et al.*, 1989).

The traps are dug into the ground so that the rim of the trap is flush with the ground surface. A circular piece of wire mesh or chicken wire should be wedged into the top of the trap to reduce the chances of amphibians and small mammals from falling into the trap. The mesh size should be large enough to allow invertebrates to enter the trap but small enough to discourage larger species such as shrews. Alternatively, the ECN protocol uses a small rectangular sheet of chicken wire laid over the trap and surrounding ground, pinned down with metal staples.

If traps are to be left open for any great length of time during wet conditions, a raised lid on legs can be placed over the trap to prevent it from filling up with rainwater, although not where grazing animals have access. However, it should be noted that lids over pitfall traps may reduce the number of spiders entering the traps, although it may increase the catch of ground beetles. Holes should be drilled in the trap approximately two-thirds of the way up from the base to allow excess rainwater to drain out and prevent the trap from flooding.

To prevent captured invertebrates from eating each other in the trap, the bottom should be filled to just below the level of the drain holes with a preservative. A standard preservative is 40% ethylene glycol (commercial antifreeze), 5% formaldehyde and 2% sodium chloride in water, with a detergent additive to reduce surface tension (a small squirt of washing-up liquid). The use of formaldehyde is governed by the COSHH (Control of Substances Hazardous to Health) regulations; it is not absolutely essential to the mixture although it acts to prevent decomposition and thus reduces the attractiveness of the traps to carrion-feeding species of invertebrate and to foxes, which may otherwise dig the traps out. Salt helps to coagulate slug mucus.

If the trap is to be emptied *in situ* more than once, it can be helpful to place the trap in a tight-fitting plastic collar (e.g. a length of drainpipe) before digging it in. The trap can be removed from the collar without causing the sides of the hole to fall in. An alternative is to use two plastic vending machine cups, one inside the other. This also makes digging in the trap easier: the inner cup can be removed and soil that fell in during setting shaken out so that a clean trap is presented. If this design is used, it is important to drill drain holes in both cups, because there is no soakaway for overflowing rainwater.

The selection of locations for pitfall traps will depend on the size and nature of the area to be sampled and upon the ecology of the target species. Traps are unsuitable in very stony, shallow or waterlogged soils. If a large area is to be surveyed, it will be best to subdivide the area into equally sized squares and select a sample of these in which to put traps.

A total of ten (five at a squeeze) traps should be placed in a straight line, 2 m apart in each sample area. This makes the traps easier to find on subsequent visits; they may often become hidden by fallen leaves. You should always make notes of trap locations; it is frustrating and time-consuming to have to search for traps on each subsequent visit. Vegetation growth over the traps can obscure the trap from view even when the location is found. Sometimes a garden fork can be gently pressed into the vegetation systematically through the approximate location; the chicken-wire cover is often detected in this way, even below a layer of annual vegetation growth.

When traps are emptied, the liquid from the traps (if it contains anything other than water) should not be allowed to run out on to, and hence pollute, the site; strain the liquid from the traps into an empty container and remove from the site. The liquid should be strained, because the movement resulting from transporting specimens in a fluid (especially if mixed with small stones) will cause damage. The trap contents should be poured on to a muslin cloth, nappy liner or similarly fine and soft filter. The mesh sizes of any series of filters used must be sufficiently small to retain invertebrates as small as 1 mm in length. The pot should then be rinsed and again emptied into the filter to avoid the loss of very small specimens. Larger stones and other debris may then be picked out for disposal after first being washed by hand in a jam-jar of water to ensure that no invertebrates are attached. The wash water is then also passed through the filter. The filter is then folded, specimens inwards, and placed in a plastic bag for transport to base. On returning to base it can be placed directly in a preservative for later examination.

Note that slugs and earthworms should be collected in a separate container because the mucus associated with these species can foul up traps so that other material cannot easily be separated. If the traps are to be emptied more than once, the liquid can be reused, although it may require topping up. The ECN protocol suggests replacement with a new cup already containing preservative; the lid of the cup can simply be transferred from the new to the old pitfall cup.

Filters are best floated invertebrate-side downwards on a bowl of water and any invertebrates that remain attached removed with a wash bottle (squeezy bottle filled with water) and an artist's paint brush. Stones, leaves and other debris may now be removed and the water in the bowl is then passed through a muslin or nappy liner filter held in a funnel. The pellet of invertebrates is stored in an appropriate preservative for examination.

Appendix 6 summarises the field equipment that will be needed for pitfall trapping.

Data analysis and interpretation

Pitfall trap data can be expressed as number of individuals found per trap: an average number from all traps put down (Southwood, 2000). If the site was subdivided or stratified, data can be expressed as number per sample unit (total number from all traps in one unit) and numbers from sample units from areas with different habitats can be compared (Luff & Rushton, 1989).

It is difficult to relate trap data to density unless you have an idea of the range over which individuals of the target species forage. It is thus not practicable to estimate absolute abundance from pitfall trap data unless trapping periods are long and samples are accumulated for the whole period (Baars, 1979). Data from several years can, potentially, be analysed statistically by using standard tests (Part I, Section 2.6.4).

If using such data to identify trends, you must be careful: numbers trapped can vary according to the weather or surrounding vegetation. A change in numbers over time could be due to changes in activity influenced by successional changes in the vegetation rather than an actual change in the number of individuals. Successional changes may in themselves be affecting numbers in one particular area, but the overall number may remain stable unless the area of suitable habitat is itself decreasing. Most confidence in invertebrate data from varied habitat complexity in space or time is achieved when catches are higher in the more complex vegetation, because you would expect reduced mobility of invertebrates (Greenslade, 1964).

19.2.8   Suction sampling

Principles
Suction sampling is used to sample invertebrates from vegetation, leaf litter and the soil surface. It collects far more species from more invertebrate taxa than does sweep netting (Southwood, 2000). Sweep netting collects from the vegetation and is dependent on the standing biomass of vegetation; it is therefore too variable to be used as a monitoring tool, whereas suction sampling methods can be sufficiently standardised to produce comparable data. Invertebrates from a set area of vegetation are sucked into a net by using a mechanical suction device (Dietrick, 1961; Macleod et al., 1994; Stewart & Wright, 1995; Samu et al., 1997). Comparisons can be made between suction samples from different years provided the same size area is sampled.

Suction sampling by D-vac (see below) is only really effective in vegetation that is less than 15 cm high and not flattened by wind, rain or trampling (Duffey, 1980; Ausden, 1996). The use of modified leaf blowers with a steel ring enclosure increases efficiency significantly (Stewart & Wright, 1995; Samu et al., 1997). Samplers also cannot be used in damp conditions. Large invertebrates that are quick to take shelter, or are firmly attached to the vegetation, will be undersampled. Some invertebrates may also be disturbed by the noise of the engine.

For those invertebrates that are easily dislodged and sucked up (e.g. Hemiptera and linyphiid spiders), you can assume that practically all the individuals in the sample area have been caught. In this case, you can derive total population estimates from suction sample data. For other invertebrates (e.g. Lycosidae, which are large hunting spiders), data should be treated as a population index rather than as a total population estimate.

Field methods
The most commonly used purpose-built sampler is the Dietrick sampler, or D-vac (Dietrick et al., 1959). This is a large and expensive piece of equipment, which is carried on the surveyor's back. Smaller and more lightweight samplers have been developed from suction machines originally designed for the removal of leaves and other garden litter. These generally have greater suction power than D-vacs, owing to the smaller nozzle size, and are about a third of the purchase price. In addition, the leaf blowers require less servicing than the D-vac (Macleod et al., 1994; Stewart & Wright, 1995) and are therefore more efficient and produce more accurate results when used in conjunction with a metal ring quadrat, e.g. $0.25\ \mathrm{m}^2$ size (Macleod et al., 1994; Samu et al., 1997).

There are two basic field methods for sampling a patch of vegetation. If the collecting nozzle is large, it is pushed vertically into the vegetation and held for a set length of time (30–60 seconds) to collect invertebrates from an area the size of the nozzle. This should be repeated five times for each sample (Dennis et al., 1998). Alternatively, a plot of a given size can be sampled for a set length of time.

After sampling, the net containing the invertebrates should be checked to remove newts, mice and other things sometimes inadvertently collected, then emptied into a plastic bag. A cotton-wool ball soaked in ethyl acetate should be introduced to the bag before closing it. Note that ethyl acetate is a solvent and will dissolve polythene; it is worth while experimenting with the container before collecting to ensure that it will not be dissolved. The bags should be stored in a freezer until they are taken to the laboratory for sorting and identification. It will be necessary to separate plant debris from the sample; this is usually done by dry sieving (Dennis et al., 1998). The field equipment necessary for suction sampling is listed in Appendix 6.

Data analysis and interpretation
Analysis will depend to some extent on the sample method; if a sampler with a large nozzle of standard area was used, you can assume that all invertebrates immediately under the nozzle were

sampled (some can be oversampled; see Samu *et al.*, 1997) and you can therefore estimate invertebrate density. By extrapolation, you can derive population estimates if the area of similar habitat to that sampled is known.

If a defined plot was sampled for a given length of time, data can be expressed as numbers found per unit time or per plot area, but these can only be used as population indices, because you cannot be sure that all invertebrates were collected.

Data from different years can, potentially, be analysed statistically by using standard tests (Part I, Section 2.6.4).

19.2.9   Window traps

Principles

Flying insects can be difficult to sample by using timed searches or other methods detailed in this section; they can be hard to catch and are rarely easy to identify in flight. Window trapping is a way round this problem. Many species of flying insect are attracted to particular colours. A window trap combined with a perpendicular clear, perspex sheet both attracts and intercepts flying insects, capturing them in a water-filled coloured tray. These traps can be used to sample flying insects in most habitats.

The colour of the trap and the height of the trap above the surrounding vegetation will affect the types of insect that are caught by attraction. Yellow traps are best for catching Diptera and Hymenoptera, whereas white ones attract Diptera but are less efficient for some species of Hymenoptera. Neutral colours such as blue or grey can be used; these have the least attractant or repellent effect and thus reduce the sample selectivity (Usher, 1990; Disney, 1986, 1987; Okland, 1996).

The height at which traps are set will depend upon the aim of the survey. If you are establishing a baseline species list as a basis for future monitoring, a variety of different coloured traps should be set at a variety of heights. If traps are used for surveying and monitoring a particular species over time, identically coloured traps should be used at a constant height. Trap catches are highest

when the trap is set just above the level of the surrounding vegetation (Usher, 1990).

It is also possible to bait traps (for example, with a sugar solution) to increase their attractiveness. Whether or not the trap is baited, you cannot be sure of the size of area from which insects are attracted, and therefore population estimates for a site cannot be made.

The numbers of insects caught in traps will also vary according to their activity, which is affected by weather and the surrounding vegetation, as well as reflecting variations in actual abundance. It is therefore hard to standardise methods sufficiently to enable quantitative data to be collected; a semi-quantitative index of population size is the best estimate obtainable from window traps for monitoring purposes.

Field methods

Details of window trap construction are shown in Figure 19.2. Traps consist of a platform mounted on a wooden stake, which is driven into the ground. The tray filled with water is placed on the platform and secured with string or elastic.

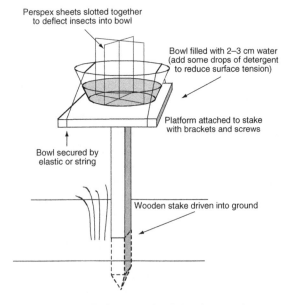

Figure 19.2. A window trap for flying insects. See text for details.

Traps will need to be checked regularly, because the water will eventually evaporate and trapped insects will decay or be eaten. Alternatively, the trap may fill up with rain and overflow if it is not regularly emptied. If rain is expected, drain holes should be drilled just below the top of the trap sides. The trap can be filled with a non-evaporating preservative, such as 40% ethylene glycol, 5% formaldehyde and 2% sodium chloride in water, with a detergent additive to reduce surface tension, but this will affect the attractiveness of the trap. Better results are obtained with plain water and a squirt of washing-up liquid to reduce surface tension, so avoiding a lingering death for the insects (tip: add the detergent to the filled trap; if you make up the mixture before leaving base you will have nothing but bubbles to pour into the trap), but this requires the trap to be emptied at least every other day to avoid decomposition. Methods must be standardised if results are to be used for monitoring.

The decision as to where to place traps and at what height will depend upon the species being surveyed (Okland, 1996; McWilliam & Death, 1998). Where grazing stock, Rabbits or deer are present, ground-level traps are not advised. The timing of trapping should coincide with the maximal abundance of the species in their flighted phase. If this is not known in advance, trapping should be continuous, with frequent changeover of preservative, to establish when peak numbers occur. However, numbers will be influenced by other factors such as weather, so identifying peaks of abundance will not be straightforward (the convention is to sample continuously throughout the season (spring and summer) for general invertebrate surveys).

When traps are emptied, strain the liquid through a muslin cloth, nappy liner or other soft and fine filter (see Section 19.2.7 on pitfall traps) and place the insects into a bottle or jar filled with a preservative such as a 70% alcohol and 1% glycerol solution. The contents should be sorted and identified in the laboratory. The equipment required for window trapping in the field is summarised in Appendix 6.

Data analysis and interpretation

Analysing window trap data can be problematic: you will not necessarily be certain of the range of the species under consideration. In a small site, presence in a trap does not prove presence on the site; individuals may have been attracted to the trap from outside. For larger sites, presence in a trap will confirm presence, but absence cannot be taken for granted until several years of data have been collected. If monitoring times are infrequent (i.e. every few years) it will be difficult to establish trends reliably.

Counts of insects from window traps can be treated as indices of abundance and can, potentially, be analysed statistically by using standard tests (Part I, Section 2.6.4) or non-parametric equivalents. Interpreting such data is again complicated by the fact that the area of influence of the trap is not certain, and in any case it will vary depending upon the weather conditions at the time of sampling.

Despite these drawbacks, window traps are a good method for monitoring flying insects that cannot always easily be sampled by using the more quantitative methods in this section.

19.2.10   Malaise traps

Principles

A Malaise trap is a tent-like net, erected in the habitat to be sampled. Insects collide with the central net wall and are funnelled upwards to a catching chamber. This method almost always generates huge volumes of material; several days are normally required to sort and identify specimens from a single trap session. They can be run all year without a break, though samples should be collected at least monthly. Malaise traps are an incredibly effective method for sampling all flying insects and often record insects that have not been found by any other method. An average Malaise trap sample for the month of July in a varied habitat in southern Britain could contain a hundred thousand insects or more.

Field methods

Caution should be taken in the use and positioning of such traps, as the size and shape of Malaise traps will tend at best to arouse curiosity from the general public, and at worst they may be vandalised.

The choice of habitat and aspect for setting up of a Malaise trap will affect the species caught; simply to survey for the maximum number of species on a site, positioning the trap on the boundary between habitat types or features of invertebrate interest is likely to produce the best results.

Traps are usually left all year and the catching chamber is charged with alcohol or another preservative so that it may be emptied infrequently: fortnightly in the summer or monthly when the volume of insects caught is less.

Data analysis and interpretation

Caution must be exercised in interpreting results from Malaise traps. By definition, the traps work best when placed across flight-lines and as a consequence are very likely to catch insects that are merely passing through the site rather than resident thereon. Large numbers over a lengthy period do not necessarily indicate residence as there may have been a single large movement of individuals. A greater degree of reliability can be obtained from shorter time period samples if unexpected species are either not repeated on subsequent dates (indicating a passing species) or if they occur in all samples (suggesting residency on site). Traps placed in dense cover in central areas of sites are far more likely to record site-related species than traps situated in rides or across hedge lines.

Counts of insects from Malaise traps can be treated as indices of abundance and can, potentially, be analysed statistically by using standard tests (Part I, Section 2.6.4) or non-parametric equivalents. Other kinds of statistical analysis may also be appropriate (see Part I, Section 2.6.4). Interpreting such data is again complicated by the fact that the area of influence of the trap is not certain, and in any case it will vary depending upon the weather conditions at the time of sampling.

In spite of these drawbacks, Malaise trapping is the single most effective method of sampling overall insect species diversity at any site. There is inevitably an implication for an inordinate amount of time (and hence cost) in identifying the large samples. In smaller studies, target taxa can be sorted from the bulk samples to provide a realistic snapshot of the invertebrate assemblage; in larger

or long-term studies Malaise trapping is, however, the methodology most likely to reveal the true extent of the on-site invertebrate biodiversity.

19.2.11   Artificial refugia

Principles

Cardboard, slate, ceramic or wooden tiles can be used for monitoring slugs and snails. These species will generally conceal themselves under objects on the ground during the day. If you lay down tiles to encourage slugs and snails to use them, they can be surveyed by simply turning the tiles over during the day and counting any species that are found.

Density estimates can be made from such data if the slates are randomly distributed in similar habitat (Williamson et al., 1977; Oggier et al., 1998).

Field methods

The tiles (10 cm × 10 cm in size) should be placed out in a random pattern at an average density of four per square metre in areas of habitat suitable for the species of interest. Once a suitable period of time has passed to allow for acclimatisation, the tiles should be turned over and any individuals found under the slate can be identified and counted. It may be necessary to collect specimens for identification in the laboratory; in this case, collecting jars will be needed with a suitable killing agent and preservative.

The best time for surveying and monitoring slugs and snails is overnight after a rainy day, hence tiles should be placed out on a wet evening and reviewed the following morning. Tiles should be used to survey the habitat on at least three occasions each season to obtain an average (Oggier et al., 1998). The activity of slugs and snails is strongly influenced by the wetness of the weather; you should therefore aim to collect data only during periods of warm, wet weather. The gastropod species per site are effectively sampled when more than 150 tiles are used in the sampling procedure. A soil core method requires only 10 samples of dimensions 25 cm × 25 cm × 10 cm to achieve the same degree of accuracy, but demands a time-consuming extraction procedure in the laboratory (Oggier et al., 1998). Appendix 6 outlines the essential field equipment required for monitoring by using artificial refugia.

Data analysis and interpretation

Counts can be used to estimate density over the area sampled with tiles. If the area of similar habitat is known, this density can be extrapolated to gain an estimate of the population in that area. However, this is likely to be an underestimate, because it is doubtful that all individuals will be found under tiles; results should therefore be treated as an index of population size rather than as an estimate of the total population.

Results from different years can, potentially, be analysed statistically by using standard tests (Part I, Section 2.6.4), particularly where the population is sampled appropriately.

19.3   TERRESTRIAL INVERTEBRATE CONSERVATION EVALUATION CRITERIA

19.3.1   Key evaluation considerations

'Terrestrial invertebrates' covers a very wide range of species, but the largest groups of concern are beetles, bees and wasps, probably because in this country they are among the better studied of the terrestrial invertebrates outside of the Lepidoptera.

In terms of information available to assess a site for its invertebrate value, the Invertebrate Sites Register was set up in the late 1970s to bring together occurrence data on rare and scarce species. The paper records of the Invertebrate Sites Register has been archived at Monks Wood BRC since 1996, and its role is due to be taken over by the National Biodiversity Network, which aims to link information held by local record centres and national recording schemes (Key *et al.*, 2000).

Invertebrate distribution atlases produced by the BRC since 1997 have included land and freshwater molluscs (Kerney, 1999), aculeate Hymenoptera (Edwards, 1997, 1998; Edwards & Telfer, 2001, 2002), spiders (Harvey *et al.*, 2002), Orthoptera (Haes & Harding, 1997) and hoverflies (Ball & Morris, 2000). Provisional atlases have included Cantharoidea and Buprestoidea (Alexander, 2003), ground beetles

(Luff, 1998) and longhorn beetles (Twinn & Harding, 1998). For a full list of available atlases, refer to the BRC website (www.brc.ac.uk).

Invertebrate distributions can alter significantly over a period of a few years, and caution should be taken with the interpretation of distribution and rarity data, particularly if it is more than five years old, as is frequently the case with published atlases.

19.3.2   Protection status in the UK and EU

Two species are listed in Appendix III of the Bern Convention: the Stag Beetle *Lucanus cervus* and Roman Snail *Helix pomatia*. The Roman Snail is an ancient introduction to this country, and as such has not received protection in UK legislation. However, recent concerns about collection of this species for food have led to the proposal in the fourth quinquennial review of Schedules 5 and 8 of the Wildlife & Countryside Act 1981 that this species receive partial protection through legislation.

Three terrestrial beetles, one hemipteran bug, three orthopterans, two spiders and one terrestrial mollusc species are listed in Schedule 5 of the Wildlife & Countryside Act 1981 and are strictly protected as amended by the Countryside & Rights of Way Act 2000. In addition, the Mire Pill Beetle *Curimopsis nigrita* receives only protection against damage to its place of shelter, and the Stag Beetle is only protected against sale.

Two species of beetles, the Stag Beetle and Violet Click-beetle *Limoniscus violaceus*, in addition to four whorl snails that occur in the UK, are listed in Annex II of the EU Habitats Directive of species of community interest whose conservation requires the designation of Special Areas of Conservation (SACs).

Of the terrestrial invertebrates, there are currently 73 beetles, 33 hymenopterans, 4 orthopterans, 22 flies, 5 molluscs, 6 spiders and 3 hemipterans that are priority BAP species. Around 40% of the species in the well-known invertebrate groups are Species of Conservation Concern (Buglife, 2003).

19.3.3   Conservation status in the UK

Around 500 invertebrate species are classified as endangered, and over 1000 further species are classified as vulnerable and as rare in the British Red Data Books.

Since the British Red Data Books for insects and other invertebrate groups were published, some of the species in them have become extinct. Others have become much more widespread, e.g. the Bee Wolf *Philanthus triangulum* (Key *et al.*, 2000) and for other species there are probably insufficient data to assess their changing status.

19.3.4   Site designation criteria

SSSI criteria for designating sites for invertebrate interest are described in NCC (1989).

The criteria laid out for designating SSSIs are currently rather sketchy. The most definite of the criteria is that all sites with populations of species on Schedule 5 of the Wildlife & Countryside Act 1981 qualify for consideration. Other criteria are that any site supporting the strongest population in the UK of a Red Data Book species should be considered, as should sites within an Area of Search supporting strong populations of Red Data Book species in the better recorded groups. Nationally Scarce species should be included in the SSSIs within each Area of Search where they occur, and all regionally scarce species within Areas of Search where they have this status.

The criteria give room for the consideration of species assemblages where it is possible to assess the quality of that assemblage. Methods for assessing sites according to the assemblages present have been developed for saproxylic beetles (the Saproxylic Quality Index) and are under development for the beetle fauna of exposed riverine sediments.

Criteria for designation of Ramsar sites also cover invertebrates. The most relevant criteria are criteria 2 and 3. Criterion 2 guidelines urge contracting parties to include in the Ramsar list wetlands that include threatened communities, or wetlands that are critical to the survival of species identified as vulnerable, endangered or critically endangered within national endangered species programmes or international endangered species frameworks, such as the IUCN Red Lists. Criterion 3 guidelines cover species considered internationally important for maintaining the biological diversity of a particular biogeographic region. Characteristics sought under this criterion are 'hotspots' of biological diversity, centres of endemism, the range of biological diversity occurring in a region, a significant proportion of species adapted to special environmental conditions, and wetlands that support rare or characteristic elements of biological diversity of the biogeographic region.

A considerable range of techniques are available for sampling aquatic invertebrates, a comprehensive description of which is beyond the scope of this *Handbook*. Section 20.2 summarises the most widely used methods, but variants have evolved for most of the techniques and equipment described. A detailed account of sampling methods is given in Hellawell (1978, 1986) and Southwood (2000). A summary can also be found in Ausden (1996) and RSPB/NRA/RSNC (1994).

The timing of any survey of aquatic invertebrates is very important. Some species may not be detectable at certain times of the year (e.g. when they have emerged as flighted adults, are present as eggs attached to vegetation, or as very small instar stages). For this reason, fluctuations in community structure occur throughout the year and for comprehensive surveys it is therefore necessary to sample in various seasons to maximise the number of species captured. The protocol developed and effort expended will vary according to the objectives.

There are also particular safety aspects to consider when working in or near water. In particular, personnel should be trained in the relevant aspects of aquatic safety and use appropriate safety equipment. Surveyors should be aware of the risk of catching Weil's disease from water contaminated with rat urine. Surveyors should work in pairs and carry mobile phones or radios if working in remote areas. These should be used to contact colleagues at agreed times to confirm that sampling is proceeding safely and according to schedule. Boots or waders are a necessity but chest waders should be avoided, as they can seriously hinder mobility if they fill with water. Sampling should not be carried out when a river is in spate or when weather conditions are particularly bad. Before attempting to gain access to a water body, water depth and substrate stability should be checked (with a net pole or similar) to make sure that it is safe to sample. Other safety aspects listed in Part I, Box 2.11, should be followed as appropriate.

Surveying areas of suitable habitat may be appropriate, particularly if resources are not available for more detailed survey methods. Surveying of micro-habitats is not specifically covered in this *Handbook*. However, some of the techniques in Part II may be adapted for this purpose.

20.1 ATTRIBUTES FOR ASSESSING CONDITION

20.1.1 Community composition

The aquatic invertebrate community is composed of numerous organisms with a range of attributes and habitat requirements. Therefore, when surveying the aquatic invertebrate community in general (rather than when concentrating upon a particular species of interest) it is often common practice to condense complex community inter-relationships into a single index of species diversity. A good review can be found in Metcalfe-Smith (1994). The diversity index accommodates species data; however, within the water industry, macroinvertebrates have been traditionally sampled for water quality assessment, for which it was considered adequate to identify to family level only. Thus, biotic scores are often based on family-level identification (rather than on species-level), which is obviously easier and cheaper to do. However, fuller surveys with identification to species will be required to survey or monitor populations of species of conservation interest and to search for species new to the site that may require more detailed monitoring. Invertebrate sampling methods are fairly indiscriminate, in that they will capture members of more than one invertebrate group (although different methods will yield different results). Therefore, unless you are concerned only with a particular species, community composition can be examined. A reduction in the diversity scores recorded at a particular site can be used as a trigger to start more detailed monitoring programmes and also to provide an index of habitat quality.

20.1.2   Presence–absence

Species of particular interest will need to be surveyed in more detail than can be obtained from a community diversity index. It may be sufficient merely to establish whether or not a species is present at a site or subdivision of a site, and thus map the distribution of the species. In this case, surveys will be targeted towards one particular species, but general sampling methods will often be similar to those used for community sampling.

Monitoring for presence–absence can therefore be directed towards range expansion or contraction of species of interest. In most EIA studies, for example, presence–absence is all that can be collected within a given time-frame and these data are then used to assess the number of species of particular conservation importance; less emphasis is placed on determining abundance.

20.1.3   Population size

For particularly rare or otherwise important species, it may be desirable to obtain an estimate of population size so that population fluctuations can be monitored and downward trends identified before falling numbers lead to local extinctions.

Populations of aquatic invertebrates are generally expressed in terms of density (individuals per square metre or individuals per sample unit).

20.2   GENERAL METHODS

Table 20.1 outlines the general methods used for surveying and monitoring aquatic invertebrates.

20.2.1   Vegetation sampling

Principles

Many species of aquatic invertebrate can be found on or among submerged aquatic vegetation. If you sample this vegetation for invertebrates an idea can be obtained of the species present, their abundance per unit of habitat or sampling time, and their overall relative abundance.

In general, this method is best used for determining presence–absence of species. Population density estimates are problematic: since determining the density of aquatic plants being sampled is not always straightforward. Comparisons between sites are influenced by factors such as vegetation type and density, which would have to be standardised before meaningful quantitative comparisons could be made.

An alternative method is to search the vegetation *in situ* for a fixed period. This enables comparisons between samples to be made on the basis of numbers per unit effort and has the advantage of being less destructive.

Field methods

A sample of aquatic vegetation is collected in a net or other receptacle and taken back to the laboratory, where it is searched for invertebrates.

If sampling in flowing water, position the net downstream of the patch of vegetation to be sampled and cut or pull out the vegetation so that it is carried into the net. This will help to ensure that invertebrates that are disturbed by the cutting of the vegetation are also directed into the net by the current flow. When sampling in still water it is probably best to cut and enclose the vegetation as quickly as possible to minimise the number of fast-moving invertebrates that escape.

This method is best suited to vegetation in shallow waters and near banks; deeper waters will cause problems with sampling because it will take time to pull the vegetation to the surface, which will allow more invertebrates to escape or become dislodged.

When searching vegetation in the laboratory, the best results are obtained by placing the plants in a shallow white tray and removing invertebrates

Table 20.1. *Methods for surveying and monitoring aquatic invertebrates*

	Recommended species group	Population size data	Other attributes	Efficiency	Precision	Bias	Expertise required	Advantages	Disadvantages
Vegetation sampling	Species on submerged vegetation	Presence–absence Index	Vegetation community composition Biotic scores[a]	Requires time to search through vegetation in laboratory	Varies with density of vegetation	Biased in favour of sedentary spp.	Identification	Samples can be searched thoroughly in laboratory	Destructive Comparisons difficult between different vegetation types
Sweep netting	Species in the water column and on submerged vegetation	Presence–absence Index	Water column and vegetation community composition Biotic scores[a]	Reasonable	Varies with density of vegetation	Highly mobile organisms may be under-recorded	Identification	Quick and simple field methods	Difficult to standardise effort between surveyors
Kick sampling	Species amongst sand, gravels and pebbles in flowing water	Presence–absence Index	Benthic community composition Biotic scores[a]	Reasonable	Reasonable	Biased against firmly attached and heavy spp.[a]	Identification	Quick and simple field methods	Difficult to standardise effort between surveyors
Cylinder sampling	Species among sand and gravel in flowing water	Abundance	Benthic community composition Biotic scores[a]	Requires time to set up equipment May be costly	Good	Low	Identification Equipment set-up and operation	Enables density estimates to be made	Requires expensive equipment
Artificial substrates	Bottom-dwelling species	Abundance	Benthic community composition Biotic scores[a]	Time needed between putting down substrate and colonisation	Good	May not sample slow colonisers	Identification	Removes substrate variability	Takes time before samples are ready

[a] When combined with samples of other community components.

361

as they are found. The greatest variety of invertebrates will be found if the plant material is left overnight in a water-filled, covered bucket. The oxygen depletion and reduction of water quality will encourage invertebrates to come to the surface, where they can be more easily seen. The equipment required for vegetation sampling is summarised in Appendix 6.

Data analysis and interpretation
In general, invertebrate samples can be processed similarly, irrespective of the method used to collect them. This section therefore can be used when considering qualitative and semi-quantitative analysis for all the sampling methods described in this chapter. Quantitative population estimates are generally derived from data collected from solid substrata: see Section 20.2.4. For further information consult the references listed at the end of the book.

Invertebrates should be sorted, identified to the required level and counted. If the data are to be used for biotic scores, identification is usually only necessary to family level. More detailed studies will require identification to species level, which requires a greater level of expertise.

A key use of invertebrate community data is to calculate biotic scores as an indicator of water quality. A recent development of the method by the Environment Agency has been to compare actual invertebrate biotic indices with those predicted by RIVPACS (River Invertebrate Prediction and Classification System) to produce a biological General Quality Assessment (GQA). RIVPACS uses the environmental characteristics of a site to predict the invertebrate community to be expected in the absence of environmental stress. The standard nationally used biotic index is the Biological Monitoring Working Party (BMWP) score system (National Water Council, 1981). Scores are based on the total number of families present, each weighted according to its sensitivity to water quality. Comparison between different years can be made, although it should be remembered that biotic scores are effort-dependent (i.e. the longer the search, the higher the score); the survey effort should therefore be standardised as much as

possible. For further information on the subject see RSPB/NRA/RSNC (1994) for a useful summary; Metcalfe-Smith (1994), Hellawell (1986, 1997) and Wright *et al.* (1994) for reviews; and Hellawell (1978) and HMSO (1978, 1980, 1983) for methodological techniques. An account of the RIVPACS approach, including some examples of RIVPACS II predictions, is provided by Wright *et al.* (1997).

Analysis of data for species monitoring is generally more complex. Relative abundance can be compared over time to examine changes in community structure, but effective comparisons can only be made if sampling effort is kept constant.

Comparisons of presence–absence data allow expansions or constrictions in the ranges of target species to be evaluated. This is best achieved by looking at the frequency with which a species occurs within a series of samples collected at a range of points over a fixed period (i.e. presence–absence in each sample converted to percentage frequency: a species present in 2 out of 10 samples has a percentage frequency of 20%). Changes in frequency over time can be analysed with a χ^2 test.

There is also a range of more complex multivariate analyses, which can be used to look at changes in community structure. Computer programs are available, such as TWINSPAN, which uses classification techniques, and DECORANA, which uses DEtrended CORrespondence ANAlysis (DCA) to condense variance within data into component axes, which can be plotted, allowing you to identify groups of roughly similar communities. Comparisons of plots from different years will enable you to identify shifts in community composition. Alternatively, several years' data can be plotted together; if the different years are separated, this can be taken as evidence that the community is changing. Multivariate analyses such as DCA should be used to identify possible changes, which should then be examined by using more rigorous analysis. The use of multivariate analysis is commonly applied to vegetation data but can be equally well applied to other organisms. For more information on these and other multivariate techniques see Kent & Coker (1992), Manly (1986), Cushing *et al.* (1980) and Omerod & Edwards (1987).

20.2.2   Sweep netting

Principles

Sweep netting can be used to sample invertebrates that colonise submerged aquatic vascular plants, algae and the submerged surfaces of emergent vegetation. The principles are similar to those applying to sweep netting for terrestrial invertebrates: the net is passed for a set distance through the vegetation for a set number of times. Comparisons between surveys can be made as long as sampling effort is kept constant.

The method is best suited to still or slow-flowing waters; there is a risk that invertebrates will not be caught in the net in fast-flowing waters.

Field methods

This method is applicable to vegetation in waters that are shallow enough to be waded or vegetation accessible from banks. The net should be swept with alternate forehand and backhand strokes. Try to sweep the same distance from side to side and to sweep for the same number of strokes for each different sample. The greater the number of sweeps, the greater the number of species that will be caught; standardisation is therefore essential if comparisons are to be made.

If you are searching for a particular species rather than carrying out a general survey it may be possible, if the species is conspicuous, to pick out individuals from the net immediately. If the water is cloudy or full of debris, it will be preferable to sort through the samples in the laboratory. In this case, transfer the contents of the net into a collecting bottle.

Refer to Section 20.2.1 for further information on the sorting of samples in the laboratory. Appendix 6 summarises the field equipment requirements for sweep netting.

Data analysis and interpretation

In general, sweep netting will yield qualitative or semi-quantitative data. For details on the analysis of this type of data, see Section 20.2.1.

20.2.3   Kick sampling

Principles

Kick sampling is the most commonly used method for obtaining qualitative data in flowing waters of wadeable depth (Furse et al., 1981). If kicking effort is kept constant, it is possible to obtain comparable samples from which estimates of relative abundance can be derived. It has also been shown that when a known area is systematically sampled, it is possible to derive approximate population density estimates (e.g. animals per unit area) (Armitage et al., 1974). In general, however, kick sampling is used for generating qualitative and semi-quantitative data.

Field methods

The majority of invertebrates in flowing water are found among stones, gravel and silt on the stream or river bed. Kick sampling disturbs the substrate and catches the dislodged invertebrates in a net placed immediately downstream.

Kick nets are flat bottomed so they can rest firmly on the substrate with no gaps under which invertebrates could escape. The net is placed on the substrate, and the sediment in front and upstream of the net entrance is kicked a set number of times. The current carries the invertebrates into the net. The sample is then transferred to a collecting bottle for sorting and identification in the laboratory (Section 20.2.1).

A further adaptation of the kick-sampling method is the Surber-type sampler, which delineates (by means of a square frame that rests flat on the stream or river bed) an area of substrate to be disturbed. This gives a more quantitative sample area measurement, although numbers may be influenced by the vigour with which the enclosed area is disturbed. In consequence, the Surber-type sampler may indicate numbers of organisms in a sample rather than the number per unit area of substratum. However, provided the substratum is disturbed systematically and thoroughly it is possible to derive quantitative data. Surber-type samplers are best suited to slow-flowing water; there is a problem with specimen loss around the sides in fast-flowing water.

The recommended field equipment for kick sampling is listed in Appendix 6.

Data analysis and interpretation

For information on analysing qualitative and semi-quantitative aquatic invertebrate data, see Section 20.2.1.

20.2.4   Cylinder sampling

Principles

Cylinder sampling provides a method for obtaining quantitative data on aquatic invertebrate populations. The method was designed to overcome the problem of sample loss around the edges of kick samplers or Surber-type samplers in deep or fast-flowing water. Cylinder samplers are particularly suitable for sandy substrata and enable animals that may burrow at depths of up to 30 cm to be captured.

An area of substrate of known size is sampled by pushing the cylinder a small distance into the substrate; in principle, this will collect all the invertebrates present, thus enabling population densities to be calculated. Cylinder samplers are available in a wide variety of designs, some of which are described in Southwood (2000).

Field methods

The exact method for sampling with cylinders will depend to some extent on the type of cylinder being used. The simplest and cheapest cylinder samplers are merely open-ended metal cylinders (usually stainless steel), often with teeth on the bottom edge to ease their insertion into the substrate. There is a hole near the base of the cylinder to which a bag-like net is attached, opposite which is an oval aperture covered by a metal grille. The sampler is pushed into the substrate with the net downstream of the grille so that water flows through the grille into the cylinder and out through the net. In this way, a known area of substrate is completely enclosed and can be disturbed to dislodge invertebrates, which then collect in the net.

A more sophisticated design, the airlift sampler, comprises a vertical tube, which is submerged in the water with its base pushed into the substrate. Compressed air from portable tanks is pumped into the lower end of the tube, causing it to vibrate and dislodge gravel and other benthic material. The mixture of air, water and sediment is pushed up the pipe and into a bag net at the surface. This sampler is not recommended for use on mud. For further information on airlift sampling techniques see Drake & Elliot (1983). The field equipment required for cylinder sampling is listed in Appendix 6.

Data analysis and interpretation

Qualitative and quantitative data can be obtained with cylinder samplers as outlined in Section 20.2.1. Population density estimates (and therefore population size estimates) can be made with samplers that quantify the area or volume being sampled. Population density (numbers per unit area) can be multiplied by total area of substrate to give an absolute population estimate. These values can be compared over time by using multivariate analysis for community data (see Section 20.2.1) or by using standard tests (Part I, Section 2.6.4).

20.2.5   Artificial substrates

Principles

One of the most precise methods of sampling benthic invertebrates is to place a bag, tray or box on the bed of the river or lake and either replace the substrate or allow sediment to accumulate naturally and invertebrates to colonise Southwood, (2000). The box is then removed and the sediment searched for invertebrates in the laboratory. One problem with this method is that the population of invertebrates found on artificial substrates may be different from that found on natural ones; however, placing the same artificial substrate in different areas gives a degree of standardisation and hence enables data from different sites to be compared.

Because the area of artificial substrate is known, quantitative density estimates can be made. If the sample unit can be taken to the surface without any sediment being lost, the estimates will be reliable.

Field methods
The type of artificial substrate to be used must first be determined. These can range from simple trays or baskets to the more complicated Ford box (Ford, 1962), which has two fixed sides and a bottom and is placed in a hole on the water-body bed (with the sides parallel to the direction of stream flow if used in flowing water). After a given time (Ford left his boxes for 6 weeks), the other two sides are slid into position, and the box is lifted out with the sample undisturbed.

The number of boxes used and the length of time they are left will depend upon the time and resources available for the study and should also reflect the aim of the study; the number and distribution of samples should be calculated to enable statistically robust conclusions to be made (Part I, Section 2.6). It is important that time is kept constant to enable comparisons to be made.

For rocky areas of substrate, blocks or plates of regular size can be left and then turned over and searched at a later date. Again, time and search effort must be kept constant.

Once the sample has been collected the invertebrates must be separated from other benthic material and counted. If the sample is large or contains a large number of animals, which are evenly distributed throughout the sample, subsamples can be taken. Hand sorting is the most widely used method for examining samples; see Section 20.2.1 for further details. The equipment needed for monitoring aquatic invertebrates by using artificial substrates is summarised in Appendix 6.

Data analysis and interpretation
Data obtained by using artificial substrates can be analysed with qualitative or semi-quantitative methods (Section 20.2.1). If sample area and time

are constant, quantitative estimates of abundance can be made (Section 20.2.4).

20.3   REQUIREMENTS FOR SPECIES OF PARTICULAR CONSERVATION IMPORTANCE

20.3.1   Freshwater Pearl Mussel *Margaritifera margaritifera*

The Freshwater Pearl Mussel is protected under Schedule 5 of the Wildlife & Countryside Act 1981 and Annex IIa of the EU Habitats Directive. The UK is one of the last remaining strongholds for this species in Western Europe.

A monitoring strategy has been developed by Young (1995). It should be noted that this survey procedure requires the surveyor to be licensed, because it involves the disturbing of mussels. Surveyors will also need to be familiar with preferred substrate types (coarse sand set among cobbles or boulders but sometimes solely coarse sand). Surveys should be concentrated in the most favourable substrate types in order to maximise search efficiency.

Searches should be made with a glass-bottomed viewing bucket during favourable conditions in shallow water. If no mussels are found after 2 hours a negative result can be reported. If mussels are found, then a more systematic search is made, along a 50 m × 1 m transect from the point where the first mussel is found. All mussels are then counted within this transect. Two 1 m² quadrats should also be selected and carefully searched for juvenile mussels.

20.4   AQUATIC INVERTEBRATE CONSERVATION EVALUATION CRITERIA

There are specific characteristics of aquatic invertebrates that must be taken into consideration when evaluating the importance of aquatic habitats for conservation.

First, the collection of aquatic invertebrates requires specialised techniques and, as many species are cryptic, once they are captured their identification requires significant experience or specialist keys. Consequently, information about the abundance and distribution of aquatic invertebrates is less complete than for other taxa in the UK.

Second, very few aquatic invertebrates are either listed on international conservation treaties (e.g. the Bern Convention) or protected under EU and UK legislation, and so these instruments provide a limited basis for determining the conservation status of most species. Assessments of species rarity are, therefore, reliant on other sources such as Red Data Books.

Third, the composition of macro-invertebrate communities is closely linked to the physical and chemical status of aquatic habitats. This is because taxa respond differently to environmental stressors such as pollution, reduced flow and introduced species. Heavily modified, more uniform habitats tend to support fewer species than do naturally diverse ponds, rivers and streams. Aquatic invertebrate conservation has, therefore, tended to emphasise the importance of species assemblages as much as the occurrence of specific species.

Bern Convention

Signatories to the Bern Convention have agreed to protect invertebrate species listed in Appendix II and III. Four of these are extant, native species that, for at least part of their lifecycle, depend on aquatic habitats within the UK: White-clawed Crayfish *Austropotamobius pallipes*, Southern Damselfly *Coenagrion mercuriale*, Medicinal Leech *Hirudo medicinalis* and Pearl Mussel *Margaritifera margaritifera*.

Habitats Directive

Annex II of the EU Habitats Directive (92/43/EEC) includes the same species listed on Appendix II and III of the Bern Convention but obliges member states to take steps to conserve the habitats that support important populations of these species.

Ramsar Convention (The Wetlands Convention)

The Ramsar Convention establishes criteria by which signatory countries may identify internationally important wetlands. Three of these criteria are potentially applicable to the habitats of aquatic macro-invertebrates.

Criterion 2: A wetland should be considered internationally important if it supports vulnerable, endangered, or critically endangered species or threatened ecological communities.

Criterion 3: A wetland should be considered internationally important if it supports populations of plant and/or animal species important for maintaining the biological diversity of a particular biogeographic region.

Criterion 4: A wetland should be considered internationally important if it supports plant and/or animal species at a critical stage in their life cycles, or provides refuge during adverse conditions.

Wildlife & Countryside Act

Section 9 of the Wildlife & Countryside Act 1981 (as amended) provides protection for those aquatic invertebrates listed on Schedule 5. Some, such as Lesser Silver Water Beetle *Hydrochara caraboides*, receive full protection, others are protected to a lesser degree. White-clawed Crayfish, for example, is protected only from taking (capture) and sale.

For those species at most threat the British Red Data Books (RDB) provide the most widely accepted categorisation of rarity (see, for example, Shirt, 1987; Bratton, 1991). There are three relevant RDB categories that can be used for this purpose.

- *Endangered* (RDB Category 1): species in danger of extinction because numbers have declined to critical levels or habitats have been dramatically reduced.
- *Vulnerable* (RDB Category 2): species likely to become *Endangered* unless measures are taken to reduce threats.
- *Rare* (RDB Category 3): species with small populations that are in neither of the above two categories but which are still at risk.

It should be noted, however, that invertebrate populations can change rapidly, often as a result of extraneous factors, and that RDB listings may not necessarily reflect current conservation status.

Beyond these species, conservation status is further defined on the basis of geographical restrictedness. JNCC identify species that occur in fewer than a hundred 10 km squares within Great

Britain as 'notable', analogous to the Pond Action category of 'nationally scarce'. Regionally Notable species are those species that occur in more than a hundred squares but which are uncommon in some regions. Species of Local Conservation Importance are those species that are confined to limited geographical areas or specialised habitats, that are widespread but nowhere common, or that are suspected of being under-recorded.

The evaluation of the conservation value of a site, however, involves an assessment of the rarity of the species present as well as of the richness of the macro-invertebrate community it supports.

Aquatic invertebrates have been widely seen as a useful indicator of the status of aquatic habitats. 'Healthy', natural habitats with high physical diversity and good water quality will tend to support more species, particularly species that are intolerant of pollution, than heavily modified habitats.

Various indices have been developed to facilitate the evaluation and monitoring of aquatic habitats. A variety of indices have also been developed to express these combined assessments and to allow comparisons of the status of different sites or the same site over time. Some of these (e.g. RIVPACS, SERCON) compare the observed community with that expected for the habitat present in an undisturbed state. In this way the index is used as an indicator of the general ecological condition of a site and measures the extent to which it diverges from the ideal, owing to, for example, degraded water quality.

Other indices provide a more direct indication of the conservation status of a site. The Species Rarity Index (SRI) (Pond Action, 1999), for example, scores pond species on the basis of their national rarity. These scores are summed for the species recorded at a site and the total divided by the number of species present to generate an average rarity score.

The Community Conservation Index (CCI) (Chadd & Exstence, in press) is an index applicable to lotic and lentic aquatic systems in Great Britain. It is a useful tool for the evaluation of the conservation status of sites that integrates information about the rarity and richness of the species recorded at a site. More importantly, it is sufficiently flexible that it can be adapted to national and regional contexts.

Both SRI and CCI require species-level information. Their data requirements are, therefore, significantly greater than those of indices such as the BMWP, which focuses on 76 families.

21 • Fish

The UK has some important natural fish communities, which require active conservation via habitat protection and ensuring that other fish species that may upset the existing ecological balance are not introduced to these key sites.

Where sites contain Lampreys, Vendace, Shad, whitefish, Smelt, Charr *Salvelinus alpinus*, Bullhead or other fish species of conservation concern, information on the status of stocks is particularly important.

Whether a fish stock is self-sustaining in the long term is an important attribute: some exploited freshwater fish (e.g. Brown Trout *Salmo trutta*) are now routinely stocked with hatchery-reared individuals. Stocking can have impacts on locally adapted fish populations, and stocked fish can give the impression that a population is abundant when, in fact, it is not self-sustaining. The distribution of successfully reproducing fish is a valuable measure of the ecological condition of a given river system. Tributaries or main river stretches in which fish are unable to spawn successfully may indicate, for instance, habitat degradation of various forms or barriers to migration. Fisheries surveys can therefore produce important insights into the health of the overall aquatic environment.

All natural fish stocks fluctuate in abundance in response to changing environmental conditions and degrees of exploitation. Any single measure of abundance is therefore of limited value unless it is viewed in the context of historical change. Long-term catch records, for instance for Atlantic salmon *Salmo salar*, can be particularly valuable in helping to determine likely trends in population abundance. Note, however, that indirect measures such as catch need careful interpretation before assumptions are made concerning real changes in fish abundance.

It can be valuable to examine and monitor the species composition of fish assemblages; not only can fish communities be important features in themselves but observed changes in species composition may be used as an indicator of fluctuating environmental quality. Some methods such as gill netting may provide information on a range of species, but in some circumstances a range of methods may be required to assess community structure properly.

The survey methods described in Section 21.2 are divided into those suitable for running and still waters, running waters only, and slow-flowing or still waters only (Table 21.1).

The type of information obtainable with a method (presence–absence, population index, population estimate, etc.) will depend on how it is applied, or whether it is used in conjunction with another method such as mark–recapture (Section 21.2.3). The information obtainable with each method is described in Table 21.2.

21.1 ATTRIBUTES FOR ASSESSING CONDITION

21.1.1 Population size

Population size is the key criterion for determining the condition of fish stocks. Sometimes these are expressed as numbers per unit area where they are based on fisheries survey (e.g. electrofishing) data. Care needs to taken when comparing survey data, as juvenile fish densities change rapidly with age: surveys conducted at the same time of year and in

Table 21.1. *Methods for surveying and monitoring fish according to type of water body*

Methods suitable for running and still waters	Methods suitable for slow-flowing or still waters	Methods suitable for running waters
Visual surveys: small pools and clear streams (21.2.1)	Hydroacoustic sonar counters (21.2.1)	Electronic counters (21.2.1)
Catch returns (21.2.2)	Gill netting (21.2.4)	
Traps (21.2.3)	Seine netting (21.2.5)	
Lift, throw and push netting(21.2.7)	Trawl netting (21.2.6)	
Electrofishing (21.2.8)		

the same areas are required for valid comparisons. For commoner fish species, making estimates of population size has been an integral part of commercial fisheries monitoring and research for many years.

Consequently, a large number of techniques have been tried and tested over a long time period. Because many species of fish are very mobile and migratory, population estimates will usually be made of a species at a certain stage of its life cycle. Censuses can be made of adult migratory fish returning to streams (e.g. Salmon *Salmo salar*, Sea Trout), or to the sea (Eels *Anguilla anguilla*) to breed or while they are breeding (e.g. salmonid redd numbers and distribution). Censuses can be made of juvenile fish as they swim downstream as smolts and out to sea (salmonids, Shad).

Fish that spend their whole life cycle in fresh water are normally sampled as adults or juveniles within specific areas of habitat, for instance within juvenile nursery habitats.

Artificial structures such as fish passes, which concentrate all fish through a narrow channel, are particularly useful for setting up monitoring schemes for migratory fish, such as Salmon and Sea Trout; where efficient traps are operated, exact population counts can be obtained. This is generally only possible on small-scale systems. Indirect assessments of breeding adult population size can be made by counting the number of spawning sites (e.g. Salmon redds).

21.1.2   Breeding success and population structure

The successful recruitment of juveniles and survival of adequate numbers of fish to the mature adult stage are of fundamental importance when defining the condition of a fish stock (population). The numbers of young fish surviving each year ('year class strength') is naturally variable and the scale of these fluctuations in self-sustaining stocks needs to be appreciated before decisions on significant departures in stock abundance can be reached. In addition, the physical size and condition of maturing fish has a major effect on reproductive output. Some Salmon stocks, for instance, are dominated by small summer-running grilse (fish that have spent only one winter at sea before returning to fresh water to breed). Such fish are much less fecund (produce fewer eggs) than 'multi-sea-winter' (MSW) Salmon, which have spent 2 or more years at sea before returning to spawn at much larger sizes. Complex fish populations, which contain these sub-stock components, must therefore be sampled for size and/or scales to determine size and age distributions. Within species such as Sea Trout, scale reading can also often reveal the presence within the population of large individuals, which have spawned on several previous occasions; such information is invaluable in understanding the population dynamics and resilience to exploitation of a given stock. Repeat spawning

Table 21.2. *Methods for surveying and monitoring fish*

Method	Recommended species group	Population size data	Other attributes	Efficiency	Precision	Bias	Expertise required	Advantages	Disadvantages
Direct counts: visual surveys	Visual surveys are of very limited application (small pools and small clear streams) Only suitable in clear waters for non-cryptic open-water-dwelling species	Simple presence/absence or, at best, rough index (bankside counts)	Can produce rapid and valuable assessment of breeding distributions (redd counts) and location of spawning shoals Diving studies good for habitat use by individual fish	Bankside counts provide basic information only	Low	Biased towards more visible species Likely to yield severe under-estimates	Identification Diving skills Field craft for bankside counts	Bankside counts require no specialist equipment	Limited applicability and do not produce population size estimates
Direct counts: electronic counters/echo-sounding (sonar)	Hydroacoustic counts estimate good for pelagic lake species and migratory riverine fishes	Estimate	Hydroacoustics good for pelagic shoals	Methods require expensive equipment but generate a large amount of data	Good for electric counters under usual stream flow conditions	Counters can be very unreliable high flows and species may be difficult or impossible to distinguish	Operation of electronic systems Interpretation of sonar signals	Provides direct estimate of population size	Electronic systems can be expensive to construct and maintain Counts need validation

				Counters can be validated via video taping. Large lake sonar studies require large data sets to cover water	Sonar methods can be difficult to interpret if similar species present			
Catch returns: catch per unit effort (CPUE)	Of very wide application, from marine or river commercial netting operations to anglers' catch record books or research trap data	Index that may not be related directly to varying stock abundance	Can yield population structure data if requests made to anglers/netsmen	Good if catch returns and effort data adequately reported	CPUE data must be treated with care: poor catches may not reflect low stocks and vice versa — True catches are often under-reported. Effort data are rarely available	Analysis and interpretation of CPUE data and local knowledge of fishery	Does not require equipment or fieldwork except where subsampling catches for age/length/body mass data	Method dependent upon honest catch-return data being gathered from anglers and/or netsmen. There is potential for either over- or underdeclaration of catches, depending upon circumstances

Table 21.2. (cont.)

Method	Recommended species group	Population size data	Other attributes	Efficiency	Precision	Bias	Expertise required	Advantages	Disadvantages
Traps	Adult migratory fish and smolts Resident adult and juvenile fish of any species	Can be absolute estimate or index depending upon local circumstance	Population structure	Variable, can be very good but spates often ruin sampling efficiency	Low for passive traps Good for intercept traps	Results depend on reaction of fish to traps; trappability can vary greatly with season (e.g. Perch seek out traps when spawning)	Identification Trap deployment	Large amounts of fish can be caught with minimal effort Estimates of population structure can be made Intercept traps make good assessment of populations	Passive traps do not generate quantitative population estimates unless combined with a mark–recapture sampling programme
Seine netting	Any sized fish in slow-flowing river sections and on lakes	Index Estimate via reduced catches over series of sweeps	Population structure	Good for small areas	Good if net is of correct design for site and if deployed correctly	Bottom dwellers and active open-water fish may be missed Mesh size of net dictates whether smallest year classes sampled	Identification Net selection and deployment	Can catch large numbers of fish in one sample period (this may necessitate stratified subsampling to maximise value of	Can only be used in waters free of obstructions unless divers are available to de-snag net Requires smooth substrate for efficient capture of benthic

								operation and minimise fish casualties)	species. Even here, fish often burrow into silt to evade net
Gill netting	Usually used on still waters but can be used on rivers where there is little floating debris Most effective with open-water species Note that this method is destructive: few fish survive release from gill nets	Index	Population structure	Variable: can be high for migrating fish in rivers (often used by poachers) but low for shoaling fish in lakes	Can be high or low depending upon local circumstances	Open-water dwellers more catchable Size classes of fish caught depend entirely on size of mesh used For population surveys, gangs of varying mesh-size nets should be used in various locations	Identification Net deployment	Can enable low-cost quick surveys to establish presence–absence in difficult habitats (e.g. Charr or whitefish in deep lakes) Can yield good population data if programme well designed	Can be destructive of large numbers of fish relative to population if used indiscriminately Largely unselective for target species Care needed for rare species
Trawl netting	Bottom-dwelling or pelagic fish Usually used in inshore waters or estuaries, but also in slow-flowing rivers and lakes	Estimate	Population structure	Low	Low	Fast-moving species may escape	Identification Net deployment Boat handling	Good for large water bodies where seine netting is impracticable	Damages substrate Expensive Requires water to be free of obstructions

Table 21.2. (cont.)

Method	Recommended species group	Population size data	Other attributes	Efficiency	Precision	Bias	Expertise required	Advantages	Disadvantages
Lift, throw and push netting	Can be adapted for use in all habitats for various species and size classes	Index Estimate	Population structure	Good for lower sample numbers	Reasonable	Fast-moving species may escape	Identification Net deployment	Cheap and reasonably efficient for small samples	Use restricted to shallow waters
Electro-fishing	All Most efficient in shallow streams, less so in larger rivers Still waters need netting off into sections	Estimates via depletion techniques	Population structure	May be time-consuming for fully quantitative work but quick for base surveys	Good	Size-selective, depending on pulse frequency, and species-selective, depending on behaviour	Identification Equipment operation Boat handling	Good method for catching most species	Potentially dangerous Requires training Expensive equipment

is much less frequent in most salmon stocks than with Sea Trout but common, for instance, amongst cyprinid (carp family) fish species such as Chub *Leuciscus cephalus*, Roach *Rutilus rutilus* and Dace *L. leuciscus*. Some species such as Lampreys and Eels are thought invariably to die after a single spawning.

For successful stock management and conservation, therefore, estimates will often need to be made of the numbers of adult spawning fish (spawning escapement), their size and age distributions, and densities of surviving juveniles in nursery habitat areas. As mentioned above, the geographical distribution of successful spawning within a catchment is also an important criterion.

Different methods are usually required to monitor the different life stages of fish populations. For many methods that involve capturing fish, mark–recapture techniques can be applied to generate more precise estimates of population size. Mark–recapture theory is summarised in Section 10.11; the applications of the method to fish monitoring are briefly considered in Section 21.2.3.

21.2   GENERAL METHODS

21.2.1   Direct counts

Principles

Many methods for surveying and monitoring fish involve capture. However, in some cases this can be avoided. A variety of counting methods can be used to make direct counts, ranging from simple bankside observations, through scuba-diving surveys to the installation of sophisticated electronic or acoustic counters.

Counts made by trained observers have the advantage that species can be distinguished and estimates can also be made of spawning sites and other attributes of fish populations. Data are, however, usually limited to presence of a given species (absence always being difficult to determine definitively). Note, also, that it is not usually possible to determine the sex of fish from bankside observation. Bankside visual counts are cheap, quick and cause minimal disturbance to fish but are generally very inefficient, as many fish use available cover during daylight hours. They are, however, sometimes appropriate for waters that are too shallow to be sampled easily with other techniques and for particular age-classes of fish that inhabit shallow-water areas. For Bullheads, visual stone-turning searches are valuable for presence–absence or rough population index measures.

Counts can also be made underwater with the aid of snorkel or scuba-diving equipment; micro-habitat selection by stream-dwelling trout, for instance, has been studied by using this method, which is generally best suited to clear or calm waters.

Automatic counters are often used for counting migrating salmonids; they do not always distinguish between sizes or species of fish (photographic equipment can be helpful) but they do provide continuous data coverage, given suitable water conditions, and technological developments are increasing their accuracy. Sometimes a size limit (e.g. of 50 cm) is used to split Salmon and Sea Trout: this is not totally accurate (often lumping large sea trout with salmon), but is a useful method to obtain broad estimates of numbers of upstream migrating fish. Counters themselves are not overly expensive, but on larger rivers the structures in which they must be sited can be costly.

Hydroacoustic systems can also be used to count fish. They can be oriented to sample the water column vertically or horizontally and can be fixed or mounted on boats. They are generally unsuited to shallow weedy waters and have been used mostly to determine the distribution and abundance of shoaling species in large open reservoirs and natural lakes.

Safety is a key consideration when carrying out fieldwork in aquatic habitats. Some key points are described in the previous section, but all safety recommendations listed in Part I, Box 2.11 should be followed where appropriate.

Field methods
Bankside counts

This technique is of limited application. The water should be surveyed cautiously, wearing unobtrusive clothing, polarised glasses and a hat with a brim to shield the eyes.

Counts should be of sufficient duration to record all the fish in view but not too long; if fish move into the count area from outside during the count, the results will be biased upwards. Remember that it will usually be the case that many fish of all species will be remaining under or within physical cover (e.g. weed beds), making them difficult to see. The area of water visible from each location should be estimated, preferably in advance of the survey.

Underwater counts

Underwater counts can be either transects or point counts (Sections 10.5 and 10.6). They can be made by using snorkelling or scuba-diving equipment. The choice will depend on the depth and clarity of the water; in general, observations deeper than 1.0–1.5 m in turbid freshwater lakes will require scuba-diving equipment (Perrow *et al.*, 1996).

For transects, the surveyor swims along a fixed cord marked at regular intervals. The number and size of fish within a given distance of the transect line are recorded. This distance will depend on the range of visibility. If the limit of visibility is measured, the transect area can be calculated. It is best to record fish at a small distance ahead, because they may well move out of the transect area at the approach of the observer. Swimming speed should be kept constant and slow; faster speeds will introduce greater inaccuracies.

Point counts are generally carried out with scuba-diving equipment from a set location for a set amount of time. Surveyors should remain still on the bottom for a while before starting the count to let the fish become accustomed to their presence. The radius of visibility should be estimated after the count in order to calculate the area surveyed.

A GPS can be used to relocate sample points with a greater degree of accuracy than is obtainable with compass bearings on large water bodies.

Electronic counters and hydroacoustic systems

Automatic electronic counters record the upstream or downstream movement of fish. Resistivity counters detect fish passing over electrodes beneath the counting chamber; hydroacoustic counters use echoes bouncing off fish to form the basis of the counts. Resistivity counters can detect fish of various size ranges and whether they are passing up- or downstream. Counters generally need to be located at permanent sites such as weirs or fish passes, although semi-permanent units can be utilised on small streams for investigatory work. In clear waters, the videotaping of fish in a counting chamber can be used to verify counts and identification of different species. In principle, absolute population estimates can be achieved, but in practice counts tend to be incomplete and can therefore miss an unknown component of a migratory run of fish. This usually happens under spate conditions.

Hydroacoustic systems offer the advantage on some rivers of fulfilling a similar function to electronic resistivity counters, but they are inefficient under turbulent conditions and thus require careful siting. Sonar set-ups can, however, be used to survey in areas in which other techniques are not practical, for instance, in the depths of deep lakes and lochs. Shoals of fish show up as clouds of echoes on the screen, with air-filled swim bladders giving distinctive traces. Differing species and sizes of fish can be discerned by experienced operators.

It is beyond the scope of this *Handbook* to cover the design and installation of fish counters or sonar equipment; for further information, see Cowx (1996) and Templeton (1995). At the time of writing the Environment Agency is undertaking a fundamental fisheries monitoring review, including the efficiency and applicability of fish-counter facilities. Appendix 6 lists the field equipment required for surveying and monitoring fish by direct counts.

Data analysis and interpretation
Bankside counts

Observation data will often be limited to presence of a given species. Data from each sample location can be used to estimate minimal density if the area visible from the sample points has been estimated. If the whole river has been surveyed, an index can be derived of the total number of fish. This method will normally underestimate fish populations, because many fish will be hidden during the count period. However, during the breeding season, when some species of fish hold territories or are concentrated into small areas for spawning, this error may not be too great. Counts can otherwise be used as an index of population size.

Statistical analysis of bankside count data should only be made if the data are reliable (i.e. the bias is consistent and understood). Statistical comparisons of counts from different years can be made by using standard tests (Part I, Section 2.6.4).

Underwater counts and transects

Analysis of underwater point count or transect data should follow the principles detailed in Sections 10.7 and 10.8. If the area of visibility is known, a simple density estimate can be made from this and the total count, but some effort should be made to account for the decrease in detectability as distance increases (Section 10.6) unless fish were only counted in an area of 100% visibility. Counts or density estimates can, potentially, be analysed by using standard tests (Part I, Section 2.6.4). Other population parameters such as age-class ratio (based on size) can also be estimated and tested if recorded.

Electronic counters and hydroacoustic systems

Analysis of electric counter data can be made by calculating the total number of fish passing the counter over a set period and comparing counts between years. Trends may be established by using techniques such as regression analysis.

Analysis of hydroacoustic data is a specialised field, and cannot be covered in detail here. Refer to Templeton (1995) for further details.

21.2.2   Catch returns

Principles

The collection and analysis of catch information from fishermen (anglers and netsmen) potentially gives access to a large amount of data. Catch returns can be used to calculate CPUE (catch per unit effort) data (e.g. fish angled per hour or Salmon caught per haul of a seine net) if the amount of time spent by the angler in catching fish or the number of net or trap days is known. The more fish caught per unit effort, generally speaking, the higher the number of fish present.

CPUE data can therefore provide an index of actual fish population size as long as the results are treated with caution. Recent research on long-term fluctuations in Sea Trout catches from a variety of English and Welsh rivers indicates that catch data probably do represent a useful index of fish population size.

Note, however, that spring Salmon can be very susceptible to capture by angling soon after entering a river but less susceptible after being in fresh water for some time. Under suitable conditions, low fish stocks can give rise to good catches whereas under adverse conditions high stocks may be virtually uncatchable. The likelihood of capture of fish can change with length of time in fresh water, recent movement history, sexual maturation, weather, angler skill, type of netting gear or angling technique and skill of deployment, etc. A detailed knowledge of the fisheries concerned is a prerequisite for sound analysis and judgement of likely trends in abundance.

Always compare 'like with like' CPUE data when assessing whether fish stock abundance may be changing year on year. Be particularly careful to allow for season and method restriction changes as these may not be quoted in any overall catch return figures. Further problems with CPUE analyses can involve the difficulty of obtaining accurate net and rod catch returns from anglers, and the problem of establishing actual effort expended. Differences in the technological sophistication of angling or commercial fishing equipment (e.g. a change from traditional multifibre to nylon monofilament nets) result in differently sized catches for the same time spent fishing. More information must therefore be collected to enable actual effort deployed to be estimated.

Field methods

A variety of methods can be used to collect angler and commercial fishery catch data. Most methods involve the use of third-party recording, including the use of log books and postal questionnaires or sub-sampling commercial catches and the collection of statutory catch returns. Allowances have to be made for under-reporting of commercial catches and potential over-reporting from angling fisheries (which could raise the capital value) if any true relationship with actual fish stock abundance is to be reliably established. For a more detailed treatment of this subject see Cowx (1996) and King (1995). Data can also be obtained from fish caught in intakes and screens.

Data analysis and interpretation

Problems associated with the use of CPUE data include the ability and willingness of anglers and netsmen to make accurate returns, species bias, and the quantification of effort. This last point, in particular, makes analysis and interpretation of results difficult. Where long-term datasets are available they can, however, be very useful. Examples on major rivers have shown previous declines in the abundance of multi-sea-winter (MSW) fish and corresponding increases in grilse abundance. Such results show, for instance, that current Salmon declines could be a periodic, rather than a one-off phenomenon.

In principle, the numbers of fish caught by anglers of a certain species in a particular river or water body over a certain period can be treated as an approximate index of population size. Data for differing species will produce varying relationships between CPUE and actual stock abundance.

Data from intakes or screens can be used for presence–absence of species and indices of abundance of a given species from year to year. In principle, many other types of data can be collected from dead fish obtained from intakes, screens etc., such as growth rates, age, DNA and morphometrics. However, this is likely to be far beyond the scope of most survey and monitoring programmes.

Provided the problem with catch return data can be addressed, trends in catch returns from different years may be analysed with techniques such as regression. Other kinds of statistical analysis may also be appropriate (see Part I, Section 2.6.4).

21.2.3   Traps

Principles

Trapping fish allows the possibility of establishing direct population counts, inferred estimates by depletion or mark–recapture experiments, or population indices by fixed-effort sampling programmes.

Fish traps fall into two broad categories: those such as baskets, pots and fyke nets, which are portable and used for both non-migratory and migratory fish species, and those that intercept up- or downstream migrants based on trapping barriers or weirs.

Non-interceptory traps come in a variety of designs, but most rely on the funnel principle whereby fish pass easily through an entrance hole but are unable to find their way out again. Returns from these traps are dependent upon the behaviour of the fish in relation to the type of trap used. They are thus considered generally unsuitable for the quantitative assessment of non-migratory fish populations. However, they can be useful for determining other population parameters of target species (e.g. estimating age structure, growth or condition (Cowx, 1996)).

Traps for migratory fish are usually permanently installed on structures such as weirs or salmon ladders, and are a convenient method of catching returning adults, downstream-migrating juveniles or Eels. Population estimates can be made from larger rivers by using mark–recapture techniques between traps, and direct total population counts can be made on small, intensively trapped channels. Partial estimates (in which an unknown proportion of the run is caught at a given point) can be combined with mark–recapture studies to obtain total migrating population estimates for a given river system.

Field methods
Baskets, pots and fyke nets

These traps (Figure 21.1) are portable. They can be set in a pattern along the shoreline or partially across a river and used to catch Eels, salmonids and other species. Pot and basket traps can be thrown from boats or from the bank or placed by wading in shallow water. The position of each trap should be marked with a float; traps in deeper water should be on ropes so that they can be easily retrieved. Fyke nets need to be more carefully set and fitted with Otter guards to prevent drowning of these animals. When set from a boat the net should

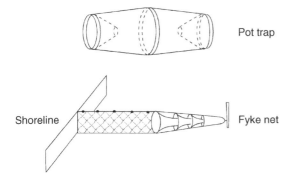

Figure 21.1. Pot traps and fyke nets. Source: Perrow *et al.* (1996)

be placed on the bow with the leader on top. The end of the leader is anchored, and is let out as the boat moves backwards. The hoop net is put overboard, stretched out and the end is anchored. One leader should extend perpendicular to and near the shore to prevent fish from swimming around the trap.

Permanent traps

These traps can be designed around previously constructed structures such as weirs or fish ladders or sited in purpose-built facilities. These will require engineering design and will therefore tend to be expensive, especially on larger rivers. The design and construction of these will depend upon the location for which they are intended. For further details see Templeton (1995) and Cowx (1996).

Whichever method of trapping is used, traps should be checked at least once a day, and the trapped fish should be identified, aged and released. Trapped fish can be tagged or marked in a number of ways for a mark–recapture study.

Marking fish

The most commonly used and successful method is to mark the fish with Alcian blue dye, using either a syringe or a 'Panjet' (compressed air tattoo gun) inoculator. Recently, fluorescent biocompatible silicone-based elastomers have been produced. These can be injected under the skin or between fin rays to allow batch marking of differing classes of fish. Retention should be checked by a double-marking procedure (e.g. elastomer and a

fin clip) before reliance is placed on quantitative results. Fish can also be fin-clipped to allow identification. This can be combined with microtagging in the nose cartilage with tiny coded wire tags, which are electronically read on recapture of the fish. This system is widely used for batch or individual tagging of Salmon parr and smolts to determine, for instance, the survival at sea of wild smolts or the survival of hatchery-produced stocked juvenile Salmon. Other forms of external tag (e.g. numbered Floy tags) can also be used on fish. For further details on the marking of fish see Templeton (1995). For further information on mark–recapture theory see Section 10.11. Refer to Appendix 6 for a list of the equipment required for monitoring fish by trapping.

Trapping should usually be carried out continuously for the period of fish movement under observation. Many fish move under cover of darkness or during spates, and trap emptying should take account of this behaviour. If migratory fish are being monitored, trapping should be timed to coincide with the peak of adult or juvenile migration.

Data analysis and interpretation

The analysis of passive trap data is complicated by the fact that captures will depend upon the behaviour of the fish and the size of the trap. It is unlikely that a previously captured fish would exhibit the same likelihood of being caught again and this change in awareness (i.e. trap shyness) biases recapture frequencies. In addition, some fish (e.g. Perch *Perca fluviatilis*) differ greatly in trap susceptibility through the year. Population estimates cannot therefore be made with any degree of reliability with these types of trap. However, a population index, such as the mean number of fish per trap or fish caught per day, can be used. Results can potentially be compared statistically by using standard tests (Part I, Section 2.6.4).

Intercept trap data can be used to derive total population counts. For example, if a trap is set in a fish pass you can be reasonably certain that all the fish that pass through have been caught. In intensively trapped narrow channels, this can be treated as an estimate of total population size. In wider channels, only a proportion of the population will be caught. That proportion can be estimated by marking all the fish caught in one trap and looking at the proportion of marked fish caught in another trap further along the migratory route. The analysis of mark–recapture data is covered in more detail in Section 10.11.

21.2.4   Gill netting

Principles
Synthetic twine or nylon monofilament gill nets are supplied in a wide variety of mesh sizes, measured either along one side of the square ('bar length') or as a 'stretched mesh' (pulled tight corner to corner). The nets are readily available and inexpensive. The top line is buoyed up by a row of cork or polystyrene floats and the bottom lightly weighted. Gill nets catch fish by enmeshing them, usually behind the gill covers. Spiny-finned species such as Perch can take some disentangling, and waters in which there is a great deal of floating debris cause gill nets to become clogged, necessitating long tedious cleaning sessions. In relatively clear open water, however, gangs of gill nets can be set anywhere from the surface down to the bottom and, in skilled hands, can represent a cost-effective form of fisheries survey. Care must be taken not to set too many nets in a given water body as, on occasions, shoaling species can be caught in large numbers and this could adversely affect the conservation status of rare fish and create logistical problems of handling time. Lost nets may carry on fishing for long periods in the depths of a lake and so it is important to tether and recover them securely. In addition, it is unusual for fish to survive gill netting: the skin and/or fins are often badly damaged, either through abrasion while in the net or during the process of removing the fish from the net. Gill-netted fish are therefore often killed and used for complete analyses of length, mass, sex, growth, dietary and, perhaps, DNA, or other, studies.

21.2.5   Field methods

Gill nets set on a lake bed are usually set from a flat board on the back of a rowing boat. The boat is rowed slowly along as the net is paid out. Skill is needed for gill nets to be routinely untangled and set so as to fish efficiently. Each end of the net has a long cord with a buoy attached for judging the position of the set net and to aid relocation. For a general survey of an unknown 5 ha still water, where the investigator wishes to assess the fish community structure, it might be sufficient to set a total of six different 30 m lengths of nylon gill net with mesh sizes from 1 cm up to 5 cm bar length. The nets should be set from the shallow littoral down into the depths to fish for a single night and recovered early the next morning. Care is needed where rare fish-eating birds occur, as it is not unusual to drown birds in nets as they seek to plunder the enmeshed fish. Gill-netted fish are usually killed immediately by concussion and then stored in a coolbox for subsequent laboratory analysis. Where fish are intended for release they should be handled very carefully. Greater survival is likely from relatively thick and soft-meshed nets, which have been fished for short periods (an hour or two) only. As a last resort with important specimens, nets can be cut to release fish quickly and with minimal damage. On some waters enmeshed fish are often attacked and partly (or completely) devoured by Eels; the likelihood of this can be lessened by daytime fishing with gill nets although this, in turn, will bias the sizes and species of fish likely to be caught.

Data analysis and interpretation
Interpretation of gill-net catch data is not easy as catches tend to be very variable. This is particularly the case in large lakes and with shoaling species such as white fishes. Experience of netting a given site brings with it a degree of predictability of catches. Presence (but not absence) data and CPUE (Section 21.2.2) are the most reasonable analytical approaches. Note that gill-net catch data are, by the very nature of the equipment used, very size-biased. Scale readings can be used with many species to check that all year classes are represented in catches.

21.2.6   Seine netting

Principles
A seine net is a wall of netting with floats at the top and weights at the bottom. Seine nets are often the

only practical way of catching smaller fish in still waters. They can be adapted to suit many situations and are efficient in terms of costs and labour provided the net is not too large. Nets are designed for specific water bodies; a truly general-purpose net is not available. Water depth, substrate type, fish species, and specified mesh size and length of net will all affect the specific design of net required.

Seine nets are limited principally by the requirement of a good bed profile over which to set and haul in the net. They are used most easily in relatively shallow waters, free of obstructions (natural or artificial); if a scuba-diver is unavailable, snagging the net may tear it and incur considerable expense as well as wasting time while the net is freed.

The method is relatively unselective, although fish in the littoral margins are undersampled and fast-moving species or those able to burrow into a soft substrate may escape.

Field methods

The length and width of the net will depend on the size of the water body. In shallow water the depth should be 1.5 times the depth of the water (Buckley, 1987). A reasonable number of hauls should be made to obtain a good sample of the population. This needs to be judged on the site according to the success of the operation. It is usual to subsample size classes of fish at random when collecting scales, length or body-mass data for subsequent analysis.

A known area of water is encircled with the net. The net is fixed at one end (to the shore, a boat or a buoy), and the rest of the net is laid out (from a boat, or by wading in shallow water) in an arc or semicircle and then returned to the fixed point. Potentially, the fish may be frightened away while the net is being set. To minimise this problem, set the first part of the net quietly and close the gap to the fixed station as quickly as possible.

Hauling the net in is usually done by at least two people, one on the rope at each end of the net. If the net is in shallow water and covers the entire water column, the float line is pulled first, and slowly to ensure that the bottom of the net does not rise up. When the haul is almost complete, the weight line is pulled up and out from underneath the net, trapping the fish. In deeper water, when the net is not in contact with the substrate, both lines are pulled quickly at once; this is a very hit-and-miss approach and is unlikely to produce unbiased results in terms of fish community structure.

Removing the trapped fish from the net is done in small stages by pulling the net in by a small distance each time and removing fish with a dip net or by hand. The fish should be identified and other attributes measured if required. Fish can also be marked for mark–recapture studies (see Sections 21.2.3 and 10.11). The field equipment required for monitoring fish by seine netting is listed in Appendix 6.

Data analysis and interpretation

Density of fish can be estimated from the number of fish caught in a seine net spread over a given area, and depletion techniques can be applied to data from successive nettings. This estimate will probably be lower than the actual amount, because some fish will not be captured. Estimates obtained with seine nets are indices of population size, unless the entire water body is netted, which is only possible for small ponds. Even then it is usual for many fish to remain in the mud at the bottom, evading capture. Counts or densities from different years can potentially be compared statistically by using standard tests (Part I, Section 2.6.4). For details of the analysis of mark–recapture data see Section 10.11.

21.2.7   Trawl netting

Principles

Trawl netting is used for catching fish that live on or near the bottom of large rivers and lakes. The applicability of this method is limited by the need for a boat capable of handling trawl nets and the size of water body on which boats of a suitable size can be used.

A cone-shaped net is towed along the bottom, or through the water column at a set depth. There are several types of trawl net; the most commonly used ones are:

- mid-water or surface trawls, in which the mouth of the net is fitted with floats at the top and weights at the bottom to keep it open;

- beam trawls, which have a horizontal bar on the headrope and a rectangular frame and rows of chains set in front of the groundrope to disturb fish in the bottom sediment; and
- otter trawls, another type of bottom trawl in which the net is kept open by water pressure on boards attached at an angle to the towing line.

The different types of net are shown in Figure 21.2. Beam trawls can cause significant damage to the substrate, and all trawls can injure fish when they are packed together in the net.

Trawling is useful for slow-flowing water bodies in which the flow would make seine netting impracticable, and for water bodies such as tidal rivers, which are too saline for electrofishing. However, it is limited to waters that are relatively free of obstructions and is a time-consuming and expensive method of monitoring fish. An alternative approach in large slow-flowing rivers is to use an electrofishing boom boat, which has built-in cathodes and hand-held anodes. Fish are attracted to the anodes, stunned and netted out.

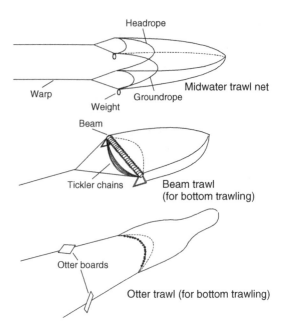

Figure 21.2. Types of trawl net. Source: Perrow *et al.* (1996).

Field methods

For both bottom and mid-water trawls, the net is towed from the stern of a boat. The net is fed into the water by hand (requiring at least two people). When the net has been let out, the otter boards (if an otter trawl is used) are lowered into the water and positioned by keeping the lines tense. The lines are fed out evenly and kept under tension by two people. Marks along the lines are used to feed out the required amount of line for the desired trawl depth. The lines are fastened to the stern of the boat.

The net must be towed at a speed faster than that which the fish can sustain, tiring individuals gradually dropping back into the bag of the net and being captured. The most effective trawling speed varies from 1.5 knots for slow-moving bottom-dwelling fish to 5 knots or over for faster species (Perrow *et al.*, 1996). Line length for bottom trawls should be roughly three times the depth of the water. Towing a mid-water trawl at the correct depth can be achieved by measuring the angle of the lines relative to the vertical.

Trawl depth equals line length multiplied by sin (90° − angle).

When the trawl is complete, the lines are pulled in. Care should be taken to ensure that the net does not catch the propeller or engine of the boat. To standardise surveys and estimate the volume of water or area of substrate sampled, the distance covered by the net must be known. This can be achieved either by trawling between two markers set on the banks or by towing at a set speed for a set time period. The latter method is more appropriate on larger water bodies. Appendix 6 summarises the equipment that will be needed for surveying fish by trawl netting.

Data analysis and interpretation

Trawling produces a semi-quantitative index of population size. Catch per unit effort statistics can also be calculated from trawl data. The numbers of fish caught over a certain length of trawl can be used to monitor populations, and comparisons can potentially be made statistically by using standard tests (Part 1, Section 2.6.4).

21.2.8   Push, throw and lift netting

Principles

These methods involve small hand-operated traps, which are typically used to capture small fish in shallow waters, which are still or slowly flowing. Salmon fry can also be captured on fast-flowing sections by the use of a 'banner net': a simple bag of mesh spread between two rods and held downstream of an electrofishing anode. Hand-held nets can be used to make absolute estimates of local population density, which can be expanded to an overall population estimate if the traps are deployed in a sufficient number of representative discrete sampling points. As they are not passive traps, they are less dependent on the behaviour of the fish in relation to the trap and so produce results that are fully quantitative.

Field methods
Push nets

Push nets are similar in design to trawl nets in that they have a net attached to a frame, which keeps the net open. The frame has handles, which are used to push the net through shallow water by wading. The number of steps taken should be standardised on each occasion.

Throw nets

Throw nets are circular with weights around the edge. They have a central line, which is used to pull the net in after casting. It requires practice to throw the net correctly so that it opens to its full extent before hitting the water. This is important in order to ensure that methods are standardised. Fish are trapped in the net as it folds up when pulled in. One design has a purse line, which closes the bottom of the net to prevent fish from escaping as the net is pulled in.

Lift nets

Lift nets come in two basic types. Hand-held scoop nets are simply pushed below the surface and brought up rapidly. Buoyant nets lie on the bottom attached to a weighted frame with dissolving tape, glue, or (originally) a Polo mint. When the attachment dissolves, the net rapidly rises to the surface, catching the fish above it as it does so. Buoyant nets are particularly good for capturing fish larvae and small fry in still waters.

All these methods are simple to perform and easily standardised after some practice. They are cheap, but can be labour-intensive if a large number of samples are required.

Redd nets

Mesh netting, which catches emerging fry, can be pinned down around a salmonid redd to obtain estimates of the numbers of young fish emerging in the spring after winter incubation. This technique can be used on silt-laden rivers to help establish whether ovum incubation success is high or low.

The equipment necessary for surveying and monitoring fish by push, throw and lift netting is listed in Appendix 6.

Data analysis and interpretation

Data from push, throw and lift nets can be used to generate absolute population estimates if sample points are representative of the water body as a whole. The number of fish caught in a given area can be extrapolated over the whole site area to give a total estimate. Care must be exercised with data analysis as fish often shoal, leading to non-uniform distributions within water bodies.

Data from different years can potentially be analysed statistically by using standard tests (Part I, Section 2.6.4).

21.2.9   Electrofishing

Principles

Electrofishing is one of the most commonly used methods of catching fish for surveying and monitoring purposes. It can be applied to most species and locations, but it is particularly useful for monitoring juvenile fish populations in rivers and streams.

An electric current is passed through the water through electrodes; the current draws fish towards the anode ('galvanotaxis'), stunning them and making them easy to capture and record. Electrofishing units may be AC or DC; pulsed DC is most commonly used because it causes less damage to the fish. Amperages of currents used must be carefully regulated so that the fish are stunned effectively without the current being so high that their muscles are thrown into severe contractions, damaging their vertebrae and spinal nerves. The strength of current passing between the electrodes is affected by water chemistry (conductivity) and physical factors such as the amount of weed growth. The frequency with which the DC is pulsed through the water affects the length of fish most efficiently stunned. For this reason it is important that any comparisons of electrofishing data should ideally be made by using similarly set machines operated by the same team of people. This will ensure that minimal variability is introduced into the dataset and that comparisons are valid. It is also worth noting that the efficiency of electrofishing is affected by turbidity, current velocity, water depth and the alertness of the netting personnel.

Electrofishing can be used to make total population estimates for a given stretch of river by using multiple catch techniques (fishing upstream two or three times between stop nets) or indices of population size (semi-quantitative sampling) by using single fishing surveys (often downstream, down the centre of the river). It is possible to establish regression relations between multiple-catch estimates and single-sweep estimates for a given type of river such that single-sweep estimates can subsequently be corrected reasonably accurately to provide reasonable quantitative population estimates (see Section 21.2.3, Salmon juveniles).

Field methods
A detailed methodology for electrofishing is not included here. Electrofishing can be a highly dangerous operation and users should be adequately trained and experienced in the method. It is therefore recommended that anyone wishing to undertake electrofishing surveys should attend a training course and consult more specific methodological references before attempting to carry out any survey work. Refer to Cowx & Lamarque (1990) and Cowx (1990) for further information on the operation of electrofishing equipment.

Puhr (1998) has produced an electrofishing protocol, which sets out a standard survey methodology with the aim of producing data that are comparable between sites. This should be followed where appropriate.

Electrofishing is generally carried out by chest wading or from boats, although smaller streams and ponds can be fished on foot with thigh waders. Sections of a set length are fished, and stunned fish are recorded (e.g. length, mass, etc.). Sections can be marked out with stop nets; in this case, the contained area can be fished repeatedly until most of the fish have been caught; total numbers can then be estimated by using the removal method (Section 10.8). This produces numbers per unit area of habitat with associated confidence intervals around the population density estimates for each species.

Data for individual species can be broken down into size classes and presented as separate analyses. Mills (1989) provides a useful description with respect to Atlantic Salmon ecology. It is worth noting that, of all the methods described in this section, electrofishing is by far the most widely used for juvenile salmonid population assessment. The field equipment requirements for surveying and monitoring fish by using electrofishing are listed in Appendix 6.

Data analysis and interpretation
Estimates of total population density can be made by using the removal method (Section 10.10) if a set area is marked out and fished intensively. Alternatively, numbers caught along a transect can be treated as population indices. It has now been established that single-run electrofishing surveys ('semi-quantitative surveys') bear a fairly good relation to fully quantitative approaches, thus saving much sampling effort and expense while sacrificing little precision.

Indices or estimates can potentially be analysed by using standard tests (Part I, Section 2.6.4).

21.3   FRESHWATER FISH CONSERVATION EVALUATION CRITERIA

Key evaluation considerations

Catch data can provide a large amount of information from which the status of fish populations may be determined. However, these data are subject to certain sampling errors, particularly the variability in fishing effort, which may change with environmental variables, such as weather, as well as human factors such as angling skill and accuracy of reporting.

Fish records from the Environment Agency and others have been brought together in the DAFF (Database and Atlases of Freshwater Fishes) project, from which an atlas has recently been produced. (Davies *et al.*, 2003). Previously, the most recent distribution data were published in 1972 in the *Key to Freshwater Fishes* by Peter Maitland.

Protection status in the UK and EU

Bern Convention

Signatories to the Bern Convention have agreed to protect fish species listed in Appendix III. Freshwater fish species occurring in the UK that are listed in the Bern convention include the River Lamprey *Lampetra fluviatilis*, Brook Lamprey *Lampetra planeri,* Sea Lamprey *Petromyzon marinus*, Allis Shad *Alosa alosa*, Twaite Shad *Alosa fallax,* Vendace *Coregonus albula*, Whitefish *Coregonus* spp., Grayling *Thymallus thymallus*, Atlantic Salmon *Salmo salar*, Spined Loach *Cobitis taenia*, Wels *Siluris glanis* (introduced to Britain) and Common Goby *Pomatoschistus microps*, an estuarine species.

Additional details on the Bern Convention can be found online at www.nature.coe.int/English/cadres/bern.htm.

Habitats Directive

Annex II of the EU Habitats Directive (92/43/EEC) includes the following species as requiring the designation of Special Areas of Conservation (SACs): Sea Lamprey, Brook Lamprey, River Lamprey, Sturgeon *Acipenser sturio*, Allis Shad, Twaite Shad, Atlantic Salmon, Spined Loach and Bullhead *Cottus gobio*.

Although the Sturgeon, a priority Annex II species, has occasionally been found in UK rivers, it is very infrequent and may be extinct in the UK at present, and as such no SACs have been put forward for this species in the UK. Similarly, Houting *Coregonus oxyrhynchus* is also listed in Annex II but has no UK designated sites as it is now considered extinct in the UK.

Sturgeon and Houting are the only UK or formerly UK species that are listed in Annex IV of the Habitats Directive as species of community interest in need of strict protection.

Annex V of the EU Habitats Directive includes the following UK species whose taking in the wild and exploitation may be subject to management measures: Sturgeon, River Lamprey, Grayling, Vendace, Whitefish species, Atlantic Salmon, Barbel *Barbus barbus*, Allis Shad and Twaite Shad.

Ramsar Convention (The Wetlands Convention)

General criteria for the designation of wetlands of international importance that cover fish are criteria 2, 3 and 4.

Criterion 2 guidelines urge contracting parties to include in the Ramsar list wetlands that included threatened communities, or wetlands that are critical to the survival of species identified as vulnerable, endangered or critically endangered within national endangered species programmes or international endangered species frameworks, such as the IUCN Red Lists.

Criterion 3 guidelines cover species considered internationally important for maintaining the biological diversity of a particular biogeographic region. Characteristics sought under this criterion are 'hotspots' of biological diversity, centres of endemism, the range of biological diversity occurring in a region, a significant proportion of species adapted to special environmental conditions, and wetlands that support rare or characteristic elements of biological diversity of the biogeographic region.

Criterion 4 guidelines seek to include wetlands that provide habitat to support species at a critical stage of the life cycle or provides refuge during adverse conditions. This could cover areas that provide habitat for breeding fish.

Fish-specific criteria for the designation of wetlands of international importance are criteria 7 and 8.

Criterion 7 indicates that a wetland can be designated as of international importance if it supports a high diversity of fishes and shellfishes. Diversity in this context includes not only species richness, but also interactions and life history stages.

Under criterion 8, a wetland should be considered as of international importance if it represents an important resource for fish stocks in terms of food, spawning ground, nursery, or migratory pathway.

Wildlife & Countryside Act

In the UK fish that are protected under Schedule 5 of the Wildlife & Countryside Act 1981 (amended 1985) include the Sturgeon, Allis Shad, Twaite Shad, Vendace, Whitefish *Coregonus lavaretus* (Gwyniad, Skelly or Powan), and Burbot *Lota lota* (which is probably extinct in Great Britain). These species receive strict protection, apart from Allis Shad, which is protected against killing, injuring and taking, and Twaite Shad, which is only protected against damage to its place of shelter or protection.

Conservation status in the UK

Of the 38 species of freshwater fish native to Britain, two are rare, three vulnerable, and three endangered. Some other species, such as Eel and Sea Trout, have also declined in numbers in recent decades (Environment Agency, 2004).

Pressures on UK freshwater fish are mainly from obstructions to migration, pollution and habitat alterations. Many fish species require clean, well-oxygenated water for their eggs to develop. Species such as the salmonids, which lay their eggs in gravel, require a substrate that is free of fine sediments that would hinder the flow of water (and therefore dissolved oxygen) around the eggs. Dredging, changes in the flow rate of rivers, bank erosion and possibly soil and organic matter washed off arable fields in winter may all contribute to the silting up of previously suitable breeding sites.

Decline of some fish populations can be attributed to the introduction of non-native fish species such as the Zander *Stizostedion lucioperca*, which eats native fish species. Introduced fish may also bring new diseases to river systems.

UK BAP

Fish species in the UK BAP include the Allis Shad, Twaite Shad, Vendace, Pollan *Coregonus autumnalis*, Houting and Burbot. The BAP for the UK-extinct Burbot seeks to find out the causes of the extinction and consider the feasibility of reintroduction. The BAP for the UK-extinct Houting seeks to continue monitoring for the presence of the species and protect the species in UK waters if re-discovered. Further information is available at www.uk-bap.org.uk/library.

Sites of Special Scientific Interest

SSSI criteria for designating sites for freshwater and estuarine fish interest are described in the *Guidelines for Selection of Biological SSSIs* (NCC, 1989).

One aspect of the criteria is that diversity will not usually be a valid criterion for selecting SSSIs, because of the distortion of fish populations by introductions. Therefore, criteria are based upon ecotypically or genetically distinctive fish populations, for which the site with the largest population of any fish in an Area of Search may be selected, and nationally rare species, for which all breeding sites qualify. The nationally rare species are defined in the guidelines as:

- Vendace
- Whitefish
- Allis Shad
- Twaite Shad
- Burbot (probably extinct).

Some breeding sites of the nationally uncommon species Smelt *Osmerus eperlanus* also qualify.

Amphibians have a terrestrial and an aquatic phase to their life cycle, with the larvae being exclusively aquatic until they metamorphose. Adults return to water every year to breed but spend a proportion of each year on land. Amphibians also hibernate over winter. Most surveying and population monitoring of amphibians focuses on population studies of adults at breeding sites. It is important to remember that the numbers of amphibians counted by using most methods are influenced by air and soil temperature: a cold spell may reduce activity considerably. This must be taken into account when comparing studies between years or between sites or when assessing a site as part of an EIA study.

22.1 ATTRIBUTES FOR ASSESSING CONDITION

22.1.1 Population size

Estimates of population size for amphibians are generally best made during the mating season, when most adults will be gathered at their breeding sites. Breeding population size can therefore be estimated for each pond, with a total estimate for an area obtained by totalling numbers from each pond. This will probably be an overestimate of population size, because movement between ponds is likely.

22.1.2 Breeding success

Whether or not amphibians are breeding successfully can generally be examined in two ways. First, egg searches will establish if mating has taken place and eggs have been laid. With some species, population estimates can also be made from the number of egg clusters. Second, trapping larvae at various stages of development will establish whether eggs are hatching and larvae are surviving.

Breeding success may be estimated by observing the number of metamorphs (the term for the stage immediately after metamorphosis, when the animals emerge from their natal pond) leaving the pond during summer, and making a comparison with adult population estimates. This provides an indication of the productivity of the pond. Evaluating metamorph output requires careful monitoring of larval development in order to ascertain when emergence is imminent. For anurans (frogs and toads), absorbance of the tail provides an indication of immediate emergence, although the tail is not entirely absorbed prior to emergence. For common toads, metamorph emergence normally occurs in late summer, and toadlets will leave the pond *en masse*. Emergence of Natterjack *Bufo calamita* toadlets may be staggered. Metamorph output is variable (Oldham, 1994; Cooke 1995) and therefore evaluation of sites should not be based on data from a single year.

Young amphibians do not migrate *en masse* to the breeding site, so the number of juveniles caught entering the pond at the start of the breeding season will not be a representative sample of the total juvenile population. Little is known about the life history of juvenile amphibians; estimates suggest that the adult population represents only about 20% of the total population for Great Crested Newts *Triturus cristatus* (Oldham, 1994) and 10% for Common Toads *Bufo bufo* (Latham, 1997).

22.1.3   Survival and mortality

Estimates of survival and mortality can only be made reliably by mark–recapture studies; survival is calculated through analysis of marked individuals recaptured on subsequent occasions. Unless dead animals are found, it is not usually possible to distinguish between mortality and emigration. Similarly, immigration and births can be easily confused, unless you are certain that the population is isolated.

For toads and Great Crested Newts it is believed that dispersal occurs during the juvenile stage. Given that most population marking is centred on the adult population, emigration and immigration may be considered to be unimportant. Survival of juvenile cohorts can be estimated by comparing estimates of metamorph output with numbers of adults.

22.2   GENERAL METHODS

A general survey for amphibians would start with an assessment of the suitability of the habitat. A key requirement is a water body, but even if this is absent, amphibians may be present in the terrestrial phase of their lifecycle. Once the habitat has been assessed, the survey can start. Table 22.1 outlines the general methods available for surveying and monitoring amphibians, but the survey techniques used will vary according to the aims of the survey, the time of year, and the target species. Further guidance can be found in Buckley & Inns (1998).

For designated sites (i.e. ASSIs, SSSIs, SACs) the JNCC have outlined common standards of monitoring, to ensure that monitoring methods, timing and duration are comparable across all areas designated for their amphibian fauna. These can be found at http://www.jncc.gov.uk/csm/guidance/.

It should be noted that both Natterjack Toads and Great Crested Newts are highly protected species in Great Britain (see Section 22.3 below) and a licence is required from the relevant government agency to survey for them. In Northern Ireland, a licence may be required to survey for Smooth Newt *Triturus vulgaris*.

22.2.1   Newts

The English Nature guidelines for Great Crested Newt mitigation (English Nature, 2001) provide a suitable survey standard to establish presence-absence, and a population size class estimate. These can be applied to all newt species in the UK and provide guidance on the survey intensity and timing required. The guidelines are summarised in Table 22.2.

22.2.2   Natterjack Toad

Qualitative surveys for the Natterjack Toad can be carried out by listening for calling males, or by searching for animals in refugia, for spawn strings, or for animals at night. To assess the population size, estimates can be made by counting spawn strings. Searching for adults should be carried out between spring and autumn, on humid warm nights. Spawn strings will be present in ponds from early April to June. It is recommended that the ponds be surveyed weekly during this period to establish population size (Beebee & Denton, 1996).

22.2.3   Torch counts

Principles

Torch counts are most appropriate during the breeding season for species that exhibit aggregating behaviour. For example, newts can be surveyed by conducting torch counts around ponds in which they are breeding. After nightfall, male newts hold territories and display around the pond edges to attract females; provided that the water is clear and not covered with floating vegetation, a walk around the pond counting all newts seen will provide an estimate of abundance. It is also possible to count different species and sexes, although you cannot distinguish between Smooth and Palmate Newt *Triturus helveticus* females without catching them.

Torch counts are useful for estimating breeding populations, but it should be borne in mind that, for territory-holding species, if numbers are high, some animals may not be holding territories and so

Table 22.1. *Methods for surveying and monitoring amphibians*

	Recommended species group	Population size data	Other attributes	Efficiency	Precision	Bias	Expertise required	Advantages	Disadvantages
Torch counts	All	Presence Index Estimate	Sex ratio (night counts)	Good if water is clear	Low	Under-estimate	Identification	Quick method for assessing presence	Will not detect all individuals
Bottle traps	Newts	Presence Index Estimate[a]	Sex ratio	Requires several visits	Low	Under-estimate[b]	Identification Handling	Many animals can be caught with minimum effort	Will not detect all individuals Tends not to catch juveniles
Netting	Newts Anuran tadpoles	Presence Index Estimate[a]	Sex ratio	Good for presence in small ponds Poor for estimation	Low	Under-estimate	Identification Handling	Quick and simple capture method	Will not detect all individuals Causes disturbance to pond
Pitfall traps	All	Presence Index Estimate	Sex ratio Population structure Age ratio	Labour-intensive: traps must be checked at least every morning	Good (if traps are in place long enough)	None in theory	Identification Handling Construction	Possible to catch most animals returning to pond	Requires long intensive sampling period and construction of fence Expensive
Terrestrial transect searches	Frogs Toads	Presence Index	Sex ratio	Can be time-consuming if large areas are searched	Generally low	Under-estimate	Identification	Estimates numbers outside ponds	Counting dispersed animals requires a wide search area; method is less efficient

Table 22.1. (cont.)

	Recommended species group	Population size data	Other attributes	Efficiency	Precision	Bias	Expertise required	Advantages	Disadvantages
Egg searches	All	Presence Estimate (frogs and Natterjacks)	Occurrence of breeding	Good for small ponds	Reasonable if spawn clumps or strings can be distinguished	Count varies by time of survey	Identification	Simple methodology	Does not estimate numbers (except for frogs and Natterjacks)
Mark-recapture	All	Estimate	Survival Emigration Immigration Recruitment Population structure	Requires several trapping occasions and data analysis can be time-consuming	Good if assumptions are met and trapping effort is sufficient	Low if correct model is applied	Identification Photography (or other method) Data analysis	Can provide most accurate, unbiased results	Requires several trapping occasions Analysis can be complex

[a] If combined with a mark-recapture study.
[b] Unless combined with a mark-recapture study.

390

Table 22.2. *English Nature requirements for Great Crested Newt surveys*

Great Crested Newt Survey aim	Methods	Number of visits per method	Timing
Presence–absence (Pond)	Three of these four methods: • bottle trapping; • torch survey; • egg searching; • netting.	4	Mid-March to mid-June, with at least 2 visits mid-April to mid-May
Presence–absence (Terrestrial)	Transects, search by hand (preferably include pitfall trapping and drift netting)	60	March–October
Population size class assessment	Bottle trapping or torch survey.	6	Mid-March to mid-June, with at least 3 visits mid-April to mid-May

may not be counted. For Natterjack Toads, counting the number of croaking males can be used to estimate numbers, but it is possible that the presence of the surveyor will cause the males to stop calling, and in any case they can be difficult to pinpoint, making counts potentially inaccurate.

The torch count method will generally underestimate total population size but will give a useful index of breeding population size, and is one of the quickest and easiest methods for establishing presence or absence of a species in a particular pond. Several counts will need to be made, possibly combined with other survey methods such as bottle traps (Section 22.2.2), before an absence can be taken as confirmed; on the other hand, it only takes one sighting to confirm presence.

Torch count surveys can provide census data for annual monitoring. However, they need to be used with caution. For the data to be truly effective, a site should be visited several times during the breeding season to ensure that the count represents the peak number of animals. When comparing counts from different populations the ease of making the count must be taken into account. Highly turbid water, inaccessible areas of bank, and weather conditions will influence the count and make comparisons difficult. Latham (1997)

found that night counts of toads in different ponds found between 5% and 50% of the total population, as estimated by mark–recapture studies. Differences in the percentage of the total population confirmed by torch counts will be site-specific. Therefore, although torch counts are valuable for determining presence and suggesting abundance, comparison of counts from pond to pond requires an assessment of sampling efficiency.

Field methods

When surveying ponds, the simplest method is to start at one point and walk slowly around the pond, scanning the water with a torch. If the water is fairly opaque, or if aquatic plants are common, it may be necessary to stop and scan the pond carefully at regular intervals. A count is made of each species. For newts, distinguishing the sexes is reasonably straightforward; numbers of males and females can be counted to obtain an estimate of the sex ratio. This is not straightforward for toads and frogs; single males and pairs should be counted (single females are very rare).

The site should be surveyed at similar times on more than one date. It should be noted that the behaviour of amphibians is strongly influenced by weather: they are more active during wet and warm conditions. Survey times should take account of this, and surveys should be carried out during a range of different conditions.

If counts from different surveys are to be averaged or otherwise compared, care should be taken to standardise the survey methods; each visit to one pond should be the same length of time. Obviously, larger ponds will take longer to survey, but as long as all visits to one pond are of the same duration, data for that pond over time can reasonably be compared. Another method of standardisation to allow comparisons between different populations is to divide the bank into 2 m segments and express counts as number of animals per 2 m length of bank.

When surveying frogs and toads with this method, it should be remembered that these two groups are explosive breeders; numbers in a pond will rapidly reach a peak and will tail off soon after mating has occurred. This happens over a 2–3 week period. In order to obtain a maximum count, at least five counts will be needed to ensure that the peak is captured. This requires some prediction of when the population will move to the pond. By watching roads and paths close to the pond, it should be possible to notice when large numbers of frogs or toads are active, and you can start counts after this has been observed. A night temperature of over 6 °C combined with damp conditions will produce a rapid movement. As a rule, it takes five days from the time of the first animals reaching the pond until the peak of toad numbers is reached. Frogs are often quicker breeders, and can be in and out of ponds in a matter of days. They are also more elusive, so torch counts are less reliable for frogs than for toads and newts.

When surveying at night, safety precautions must be taken. Surveyors should work in pairs and carry mobile phones or two-way radios. Working on slippery pond edges in darkness is particularly hazardous. Monitoring amphibians by torch counts has very simple equipment requirements (Appendix 6).

Data analysis and interpretation

Data analysis will depend on the type of survey being carried out. If ponds are merely being surveyed for presence–absence, analysis is restricted.

When several ponds in a site are being surveyed, a percentage of occupied ponds can be calculated.

If numbers are being counted, a graph can be plotted of numbers against date to obtain an idea of the change in numbers over the course of a breeding season.

Care should be taken when looking at changes in count data over the course of one year. Newt numbers will drop off during the spring–summer period as individuals breed, lay eggs and leave the pond. For Great Crested Newts, which tend to breed in ephemeral ponds, numbers will also go down as the ponds dry out. It is therefore best to restrict sampling to early in the breeding season, when the greatest number of animals will be present in the pond. A classic flaw of many EIA surveys of amphibians is that they are often carried out at the wrong time of year and provide little useful information.

Torch count data for frogs and toads will generally be from a much shorter time period than for newts, because their mating and egg-laying period is shorter. However, it is feasible to treat torch count data as an estimate of total breeding population rather than an index if the count period includes the peak of animals in the pond. The peak count of males can be converted into an estimate of total adult male population (Halley *et al.*, 1996) by multiplying by 2.5. This multiplier is based on detailed mark–recapture studies. The sex ratio can also be estimated from the proportions of the two sexes caught in pitfall traps (Section 22.2.4).

For longer-term monitoring, peak torch counts in each year can be compared to ascertain population trends. Potentially, these can be analysed by using methods such as regression. If a sample of ponds has been studied, statistical tests may be useful to compare ponds and made even more useful if habitat and physical characteristics data are collected (Part I, Section 2.6.4). Application of these methods will depend on effective standardisation of fieldwork.

22.2.4   Bottle traps

Principles

Bottle trapping is a useful method of trapping newts in ponds for simple counts or for

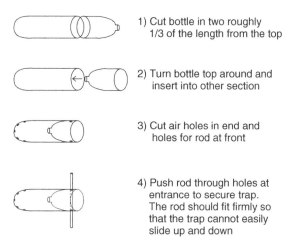

1) Cut bottle in two roughly
1/3 of the length from the top

2) Turn bottle top around and
insert into other section

3) Cut air holes in end and
holes for rod at front

4) Push rod through holes at
entrance to secure trap.
The rod should fit firmly so
that the trap cannot easily
slide up and down

Figure 22.1. Construction of bottle traps. Note that the rod should be longer than shown here. Traps without air holes may also be required if the traps must be completely submerged.

mark–recapture studies. Bottle traps are designed to ensure that newts can easily enter them but cannot easily leave. They are best used during the breeding season when newts are engaging in breeding behaviour, but can also be used for trapping larvae (of newts and other species) later in the year. Peak bottle catches of adult newts are obtained in March–April when activity is greatest at the start of courtship (Oldham, 1994). Metamorphs emerge in late summer and early autumn, so trapping at the start of this period will yield the greatest number of metamorphs.

Bottle trapping is the best method for ponds that are heavily vegetated, making netting and torching difficult.

Field methods
Trap construction
Bottle traps can be cheaply constructed from 2l plastic drink bottles and thin garden bamboo canes or dowel rods (see Figure 22.1). It is recommended that the rods be painted white to enable them to be found again more easily.

Trap placement
Bottle traps can be placed either around the pond edges or deeper in the centre of the pond. In the latter case, the oxygen supply for trapped animals is limited; traps must therefore not be left unchecked for more than a few hours, especially in warmer weather. Submerged traps, which do not allow breathing, must not be left unchecked longer than 12 hours in March and April, 10 hours in May, 8 hours in June, 7 hours in July and August, and 8 hours in September (see, for example, SNH Great Crested Newt survey licence guidelines). They must be held firmly in place to prevent tilting and loss of the air bubble. Traps that allow air breathing must not be left unchecked longer than 17 hours overnight and should be checked between 06.00 and 11.00 hours. It is generally recommended that traps with air holes are placed around the edges of the pond with the trap entrances facing towards deeper water and the bottom of the trap resting on the pond substrate (Figure 22.2).

It should be remembered that water levels can fluctuate considerably in ponds, particularly if it is raining. It is therefore important to have a long length of rod sticking out of the water so that the traps can still be pinpointed if the water level rises. This is especially useful if the pond water is cloudy.

There is a risk that newts will drown if water levels rise to the extent at which traps with air holes are completely under water. If it is known that water levels are likely to rise during a trapping occasion, the traps can be attached to bricks with

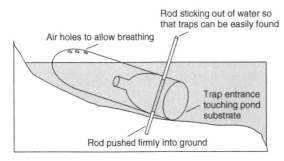

Figure 22.2. Placing bottle traps

string and floated on the water surface; the slack in the string will prevent the trap from being totally submerged.

The traps are placed at regular intervals around the pond, usually at intervals of 1–2 m. Place the traps just before dusk, and return to check them early in the morning. If trapping during warm weather, do not place so many traps that some will not be checked until late morning; there is a risk of mortality if trapped newts are exposed to heat.

Bottle catches are affected by several variables, including weather, trap spacing and the stage of the breeding season. The peak in breeding activity will be influenced by the geography of the site, so it is recommended that trapping be done in March, April and May (March may be too early in some years, depending on temperature). Trapping duration should be three blocks of a minimum of three consecutive days.

Appendix 6 outlines the field equipment necessary for surveying and monitoring with bottle traps.

Data analysis and interpretation
If newts are being captured for a mark–recapture study, refer to Section 22.2.7 for details of methods for marking or otherwise recording individual animals and subsequent data analysis.

If trapping data are not to be used for mark–recapture studies, then a simple calculation of mean number of animals caught per trapping occasion can be calculated for each breeding season. However, as it is unlikely that all newts will be caught, data are best treated as a population index. In addition, although there is no evidence that Smooth or Palmate Newts show a trap response, a bias towards males is normally observed, but not for Great Crested Newts (Griffiths & Inns, 1998). An index can be derived from numbers trapped per unit effort (number of days and number of traps). The number of newts caught will be roughly proportional to the number of traps used; if trapping is standardised to one trap per 2 m length of shoreline, the total catch will be between 2% and 28% of the population on any one night at the peak of the mating season (Griffiths & Raper, 1994). Statistical tests to compare years or to look for trends may be applicable (Part I, Section 2.6.4).

It is recommended that, in order to obtain the best estimates of population size, bottle trapping be used as the basis for mark–recapture studies; the extra time involved in marking and identifying individuals will provide a much clearer and more accurate estimate of population size, as well as enabling other population parameters to be estimated. See Section 22.2.7 for further details.

22.2.5   Netting

Principles
Netting animals in ponds is a relatively quick and simple method of catching amphibians, provided the pond is small enough; larger, deeper ponds may require waders and other safety equipment. This method should, however, be carried out sparingly, especially in small ponds, because considerable disturbance is caused to both the pond and its wildlife.

Netting is probably most useful for checking the development of amphibian larvae and thus gaining an idea of breeding success. Estimates of adult population size cannot realistically be achieved with this method; the disturbance caused by netting will frighten animals away and make them harder to catch. Netting will therefore only catch a small percentage of animals in a pond unless carried out intensively, but this is not recommended.

Field methods

A sweep net should have a solid frame, as weaker heads cannot usually cope with the vegetation and debris encountered. The net is raked through the water along the bottom of the pond. When the net is removed from the pond, the debris caught in the net is sifted for amphibians. Be sure to return any other species caught to the pond as soon as possible, and place any amphibians in a holding tank for identification and counting. The field equipment required for monitoring by sweep netting is summarised in Appendix 6.

Try not to leave amphibian larvae in tanks for too long before release; most species are carnivorous at this stage, and may predate each other.

If you are attempting to do more than just confirm presence or successful recruitment of juveniles, the netting methodology must be standardised to ensure that data are comparable between sites and visits. As an example, one sweep at each 5 m interval around the pond edge, or five sweeps at three set points per visit, could be used as a standard.

Data analysis and interpretation

Netting data are usually used to confirm presence of animals in a pond, particularly of larvae. If the netting method has been standardised, numbers caught at different times (within or between years) can be treated as an index of population and compared over time, although relating this index to actual population size is not practicable. Data can potentially be analysed statistically by using standard tests (Part I, Section 2.6.4).

22.2.6   Pitfall traps

Principles

Pitfall traps are constructed around breeding ponds or hibernacula or across routes that amphibians are likely to traverse, in conjunction with drift fencing. An amphibian encountering fencing will travel along the fence trying to find a way around (the usual movement is a zigzag pattern along the fence). It then has a chance of falling into one of the pitfall traps, which are situated immediately adjacent to the fence line. Most species of amphibian can be caught by using this method, although frogs can often jump out of the traps if they are too shallow.

If a pond is surrounded by fencing and traps before the animals emerge from hibernation, it is possible to catch most animals as they return to the pond (assuming that the fence is secure) and thus make a reasonably accurate and unbiased assessment of the population entering that particular pond, provided that the traps are left in place for a sufficient length of time. In practice there may well be some animals that overwinter in the pond itself, or a part of the fence that some animals may penetrate, but pitfall trapping does provide a good estimate of the population of a pond when applied in this manner.

Fences are at best 80% effective unless constructed as permanent structures. If traps are installed on both sides of the fence, estimates can also be made of the number of adults and metamorphs leaving the pond, and thus breeding success and recruitment can also be measured. Trap design will need to take account of species and life history; traps for adults are not necessarily suitable for metamorphs because of the size difference.

Traps and fencing can also be constructed in terrestrial amphibian habitats. In this case, the fence is built in a straight line, and serves to direct any animals encountering the fence into the traps. This will trap a greater number of animals than would be caught by using traps alone.

A further use of traps is to construct a trapping web (Section 10.9), which can be used to estimate density. However, the most common use of pitfall traps when monitoring amphibian populations is to install them around ponds to obtain estimates of the breeding population or a population index.

Field methods

Drift fencing must be constructed to prevent animals from climbing over, through or under it. The fence consists of black polythene sheeting (1000 gauge is recommended) of 750 mm width, stapled to wooden stakes 38 mm × 38 mm × 850 mm (other types of polythene can be used; lighter sheeting is cheaper but is more likely to tear).

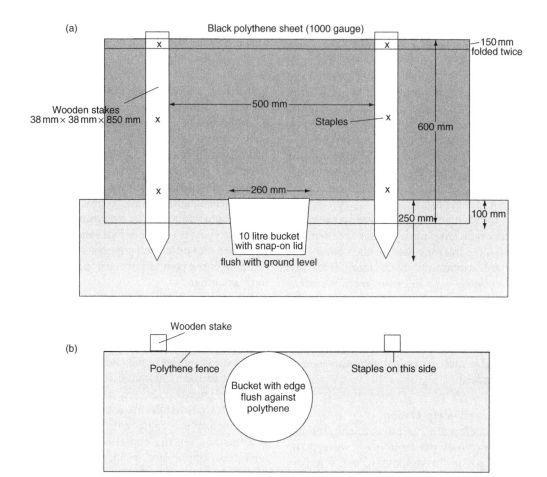

Figure 22.3. Construction of pitfall traps and fencing. (a) Front elevation; (b) plan view.

The sheeting is buried to a depth of 100 mm and should be 600 mm tall, with the last 150 mm folded over at the top. The traps are usually 10-litre buckets, with snap-on lids. These are buried flush with the ground and with the fence line. The stakes should be 0.5–1.0 m apart. Distance between traps must be kept standard so that sampling effort is kept consistent; one trap every 10 m should be sufficient. For smaller ponds, traps can be placed closer together. Details of fence construction and trap placement are shown in Figure 22.2. The buried lip prevents animals from burrowing under the fence, and the rolled-over lip at the top prevents animals from climbing over.

The stakes should be on the side away from the traps, unless traps are to be placed on both sides of the fence.

When digging out the fence line it is usually easiest to dig a fairly wide, deep trench; this makes placing the stakes and sheeting more straightforward and allows you to curl the bottom of the sheeting away from the stakes, providing a greater barrier to any animals that may attempt to burrow under. The trench must be backfilled and compacted, so that there are no cracks or gaps that might enable animals to burrow down alongside the fence.

The sheeting can be attached to the posts with two 14 mm staples placed through a 25 mm × 25 mm plastic or plastic-coated washer at the top, middle and bottom of the fence. A quicker method is simply to use one staple at each point, put in with a staple gun. The sheeting should be taut and should not have any creases; amphibians, particularly newts, are capable climbers and could potentially scale the fence by means of diagonal or vertical creases in the sheeting.

The traps should be flush with the ground and the fence; if the traps are raised above the ground, animals turn back at the lip, whereas if the traps are not tight against the fence animals might be able to walk between the lip of the trap and the fence without falling in.

Put some leaves or grass into the traps as cover for any animals that are caught, otherwise there is a risk of predation from birds or other animals. Also make sure that the plant material is kept damp. Some small holes should be pierced at the bottom of the traps to allow water to drain away if it rains during the trapping period, unless the ground is permanently boggy or waterlogged. If the traps are prone to flooding, bark or wood 'islands' should be placed in the trap to reduce the risk of animals drowning.

If it is likely that small mammals may be captured, especially shrews, 'mammal ladders' must be provided in the traps (Griffiths & Inns, 1998) or a separate trapping licence must be obtained. Mammal ladders are commonly narrow strips of wood or thick rough stems that reach from the middle of the trap bottom to the top. It should be remembered that these will also allow the escape of some of the target species, which will bias results downwards.

The traps should be checked daily while in place, and should be visited as early as possible in the morning. Search the litter in the trap very carefully; newts will play dead when disturbed, and it is easy to overlook individuals, particularly small juveniles. If trapping around a pond, place trapped animals into the pond once they have been counted, photographed, marked or otherwise recorded. If the traps are not to be checked daily, the lids must be fitted between trapping periods to avoid the risk of trapped animals being eaten or starving.

If trapping is being carried out with the intention of trapping all animals returning to a pond, the fence and traps must be left up until trapping effort outstrips the number of animals captured. If you are trapping for a mark–recapture study, the traps can be removed once it is considered that a reasonable proportion of the estimated population has been caught.

When pitfall trapping frogs or toads, you should be prepared to catch a large number of animals; it is not unusual to catch as many as 80 toads in a single trap, and populations can be in the thousands in good ponds. Frog populations are generally smaller but may be caught in a short space of time. Traps for frogs need to be adapted; they can jump out from 10-litre buckets. They are less likely to escape from wet traps (i.e. traps with water at the bottom), but to make a trap fully escape-proof a cage needs to be constructed over the trap. The field equipment requirements for surveying and monitoring by pitfall trapping are listed in Appendix 6.

Data analysis and interpretation

When trapping around a pond, if you are certain that the traps were set up before any individuals reached the pond and were not taken down until no more animals remained to be caught, the total number of animals trapped can in theory be taken as the exact number of animals breeding in the pond. In practice, there will be some inaccuracy as animals may overwinter in ponds, breach the fence, or arrive late to the pond, but this nevertheless remains a good and accurate (although expensive and time-consuming) method of assessing population size.

Trapping for a set number of days each year will yield a population index, which over time can be examined for trends by using methods such as regression (Part I, Section 2.6.4).

Another use of pitfall trap data is in conjunction with a mark–recapture study (Section 22.2.7). This combination has the advantage that trapping duration need not be constant from one year to the next, as long as a reasonable proportion of the population is caught each time. For further details of mark–recapture analysis and methods see Sections 22.2.7 and 10.11.

Trapping metamorphs leaving the pond is a good way of estimating the breeding success and annual recruitment of a population. Oldham (1994) describes a study that used pitfall traps on both sides of a fence around a Great Crested Newt pond for an entire year. This kind of intensive monitoring enables detailed and accurate assessments to be made of population size and breeding success, as well as providing information on the timing of movements of animals at different stages of the year. It is unlikely that a monitoring programme would be this intensive, but the data gathered from such experiments is useful when designing monitoring schemes.

22.2.7   Terrestrial transect searches

Principles
Terrestrial transect searches are used to estimate amphibian numbers on land, as opposed to most other methods, which are based around pond searches. Transects of a standard length are selected and are searched with consistent effort. This is not a suitable method for accurately estimating population size unless combined with a mark–recapture study (Section 22.2.7). However, the number of animals detected per unit of person-hours provides an index of population size.

Field methods
Transects are searched by the surveyor carefully (i.e. on hands and knees) and cover objects within a specified distance of the line are searched for amphibians, as are any traps that may have been placed along the transect. For example, rocks and logs should be turned over, because amphibians often hide underneath them. If surveying at night with a torch, particularly in damp conditions, the animals may be more mobile and can be seen more in the open. In upland grassland or moorland habitats, frogs can be more visible in daylight and it may be possible, in some cases, to index the population while walking a transect during daylight hours.

For anurans (frogs and toads), terrestrial searches should be conducted with torches during the evening, after the breeding emigration from the pond. Although the habitat will affect the ease of the search, search times should be standardised for each habitat and for each visit.

For newts, terrestrial searches are best conducted during the day, and any suitable refugia should be investigated. Appendix 6 summarises the equipment required for surveying and monitoring by using terrestrial transect searches.

Data analysis and interpretation
For details of how to analyse transect data, see Sections 10.6 and 10.7. It should be remembered when interpreting transect data that amphibian densities in terrestrial habitats will be lower than when they are concentrated together in ponds. They are also much harder to find on land, which will tend to bias results downwards. Standardising search effort between observers can also be problematic.

Estimating abundance with transects is more problematic than estimating abundance at breeding sites.

22.2.8   Egg searches

Principles
Egg searches are generally used to obtain evidence of amphibian breeding. Amphibian eggs are usually easily recognisable, and can be attributed at least to frogs, toads or newts.

Frog populations can be estimated from the number of spawn clumps; it is assumed that each female lays one clump, and that the sex ratio is 1 : 1. Egg searching is an effective means of establishing newt presence. However, egg laying is not uniform throughout the season, and it is therefore difficult to estimate newt population size from egg counts. It is not possible to distinguish between Smooth Newt and Palmate Newt eggs.

Natterjack Toad spawn strings are relatively easy to identify given the shallow and ephemeral nature of the ponds used for breeding by this species. This is a standard method for assessing the number of breeding females. Common Toad spawn strings are often harder to count as they are often wrapped around aquatic vegetation and may be in fairly deep water.

Field methods
Newts

Newt eggs are laid singly in folds on aquatic vegetation; the egg is laid on the underside of the leaf, which is then folded over to protect the egg. With practice, the folded leaves can be seen from the bank. Great Crested Newt eggs can be distinguished from those of the two smaller native newt species by their larger size and their colour: they are about 2 mm in diameter, surrounded by a clear jelly capsule about 4.5 mm long, whereas smooth and palmate newt eggs are about 1.5 mm diameter in a 3 mm capsule (Buckley & Inns, 1998).

Egg sticks, which are strips of black polythene stapled to bamboo canes, can be placed in the pond to provide extra laying sites. These can be more easily searched, and can be used to standardise effort for each pond and each visit: a set number can be placed in each pond, and these can be searched each time a visit is made.

Egg counts will reach a peak around May and cannot easily be used for population size comparisons unless the counts are made in each pond at the same phase of the egg laying season (Oldham, 1994). Alternatively, if several counts are made at each pond over a period that includes the peak count, peak numbers can be compared between ponds.

Frogs and toads

Frog spawn is laid in large globular clumps, and one clump is laid by each female. These clumps float when freshly laid but sink to the bottom after a few days. Consequently, if frog populations are being estimated by counting clumps, several visits will need to be made to obtain a peak number of spawn clumps.

In good ponds, so much spawn can be laid that it forms a mat and it becomes hard to separate clumps. In this case, you can either sort through the spawn by hand to separate and count the clumps (possible in smaller ponds), or make an estimate of the surface area of the pond covered by one clump and extrapolate this across the area covered in spawn. This method has been detailed by Griffiths *et al.* (1996) and is summarised by

Griffiths & Inns (1998). It has been found that there is a good positive correlation between number of spawn clumps and mat area, and a graph has been produced that can be used to estimate the number of spawn clumps from spawn mat area (roughly 80 clumps per square metre of spawn mat). Untrained surveyors were considerably less consistent in their estimates of spawn clumps, so some degree of experience is necessary if precise estimates of frog numbers are to be obtained.

Toad eggs are laid in long strings, and it is not always easy to separate them into single strands. Common Toads usually lay two parallel spawn strings; Natterjacks usually lay one string, but may spawn twice in one year.

Egg searches for Common Toads are therefore mainly used for determining presence and breeding, although the number of breeding female Natterjack Toads can be assessed by counting spawn strings, because they can usually be distinguished in the shallow ponds favoured by this species.

Appendix 6 outlines the field equipment required for surveying and monitoring amphibians by using egg searches.

Data analysis and interpretation

Egg searches are generally used to establish the presence of amphibians. However, it is not possible to separate the smaller newt species by using this method. The use of egg counts to estimate numbers is possible with frogs and natterjack toads as long as you are careful to count different ponds at the same time of the egg-laying season, and provided the peak count is captured during the surveying period.

With standardisation of fieldwork, counts can be compared over time or between ponds and statistical tests may be applicable (Part I, Section 2.6.4).

22.2.9   Mark–recapture studies

Principles

The principles of mark–recapture theory are discussed in Section 10.11. Essentially, animals are trapped by using one of the trapping methods described above, then marked in some way so that recaptures can be identified, and finally released. Subsequent trapping will reveal the ratio of recaptures to new captures, which is used to estimate total population size.

Mark–recapture studies provide a population estimate together with a confidence interval and are therefore the most effective method for population studies. They also allow the estimation of other population parameters such as births, deaths, immigration and emigration, provided a suitable model is used.

The type of mark chosen will depend upon the type of mark–recapture analysis that is to be used. Some methods require individual recognition, whereas others only need batch marking (i.e. all animals caught on one occasion are given the same mark). Again, see Section 10.11 for details, and also Baker & Gent (1998).

Invasive marking methods should only be carried out by trained personnel; a Home Office licence under the Animals (Scientific Procedure) Act 1986 is usually required. A licence is also required, for example, from SNH to take and disturb protected species (e.g. Great Crested Newt), so two licences may be required, depending on the method used.

Field methods

Marking amphibians for later identification can be done in several ways. The techniques most commonly used are outlined below. It should be borne in mind that invasive marking methods such as skin staining and PIT (passive integrated transponder) tags require trained and licensed personnel. For more details concerning licensing see Part I, Section 2.4.3.

Photography of belly patterns: Great Crested Newts

Adult and sub-adult Great Crested Newts do not require marking, as they can be individually distinguished by the orange and black belly patterns. Newts are photographed with a camera fitted with a macro lens, and photographs from different trapping occasions compared to identify recaptures.

To hold newts still while photographing them, use a transparent box such as a small computer disk case and a piece of ordinary household sponge with a newt-sized hole cut out. The newt is inserted gently into the hole, with its belly against the transparent box. Apply slight pressure to the back of the sponge to hold the newt in place, and hold the box up to take the photograph. With practice, each newt can be photographed in a very short space of time and returned to the pond quickly, thus minimising disturbance. A purpose-built camera rig for photographing newt bellies is described in Baker & Gent (1998).

Remember to label each photograph individually as it is taken with details of date, capture point, sex of newt, etc. This is most easily done by writing on sticky labels and fixing them to the outside of the photography box.

Skin staining: toads

Toads can be individually marked or batch marked by using a dental 'Panjet' tattoo gun, which fires ink at high speed. This can be used on the bellies of toads (the bladder area should be avoided to prevent internal damage) and produces a mark that will last for 18 months and can therefore be used for two breeding seasons. Frogs' skin is thinner, and this method is therefore not suitable for frogs. This is an inexpensive method, and if used with care will not cause any injuries. If the mark–recapture study is to last longer than 18 months, a more permanent method of marking will be required. See Wisniewski et al. (1980, 1981) for a fuller discussion of Panjet marking.

PIT tags: all amphibians

PIT (passive integrated transponder) tags are small electronic tags, which generate a response to a signal produced by a scanner. The tags are inserted under the skin, and recaptures are 'read' with a portable scanner, which identifies each tag (Fasola et al., 1993) and allows individual recognition of a potentially large number of animals. This is a much more invasive method of marking than Panjets, and requires a Home Office licence.

PIT tags and scanners are expensive but are often cost-effective because of the amount of information they can provide an individual. They can be obtained from Trovan, UK ID Systems Ltd, Riverside Industrial Park, Preston, Lancashire PR3 0HP; Fish Eagle Co., Lechlade, Gloucestershire GL7

3QQ; and Labtrac Ltd, Holroyd Suite, Oak Hall, Sheffield Park, Uckfield, East Sussex TN22 3QY. Different systems are not compatible. Another disadvantage of this method is that infections can occur; this may increase the mortality of marked individuals and therefore bias the results.

Appendix 6 outlines the field equipment required for marking amphibians.

Data analysis and interpretation

There is a considerable amount of literature devoted to the analysis of mark–recapture data; references are given in Section 10.11.

It is important that the assumptions behind whichever model is chosen to estimate populations are fully understood and are met by the study. For example, the computer program CAPTURE assumes that no animals enter or leave the population during the time of the study (i.e. a closed population). This assumption can be made if the study takes place over a relatively short space of time, particularly early on in the breeding season.

One of the advantages of compiling a capture history of individual animals is that data from one trapping occasion can be used in several different analyses. For example, trapping data from one breeding season can be used to derive an estimate of population size for that year. The same data can also be used in a longer-term analysis in conjunction with data from other years to obtain not only population size estimates but also estimates of parameters such as recruitment and survival.

Mark–recapture studies over one field season can only be used for males of frog and toad species, as the females will leave the pond after spawning and thus their residency in the pond is shorter. Female population size can be derived from the sex ratio observed from pitfall trapping or breeding counts.

22.3   AMPHIBIAN CONSERVATION EVALUATION CRITERIA

22.3.1   Key evaluation considerations

As previously stated, when considering the conservation value of a site or population it is necessary to consider the status of the species at the local and national scale. There are ongoing survey and monitoring programs for certain amphibian species. English Nature holds a Natterjack Toad Site Register, which is updated annually, and monitors the status of the Natterjack Toad. For understandable reasons this is a confidential database, but further information can be obtained from English Nature, Peterborough. Information about the local status of a species can sometimes be obtained from the County Recorder or Biological Information Centre (or BRC) or the local amphibian and reptile group. Other sources of data are local Red Data books, local amphibian atlases, and Local Biodiversity Action Plans.

Protection status in the UK and EU

Of the six amphibian species resident in the UK, two (Great Crested Newt and Natterjack Toad) are fully protected on Schedule 5 of the Wildlife & Countryside Act 1981 (as amended), which affords them protection under Section 9. This makes it an offence to:

- intentionally (or recklessly, in Scotland) kill, injure, take or possess these animals;
- intentionally or recklessly damage, destroy, obstruct access to any structure or place used by a scheduled animal for shelter or protection, or disturb any animal occupying such a structure or place;
- sell, offer for sale, possess or transport for the purpose of sale (live or dead animal, part or derivative) or advertise for buying or selling these animals.

Smooth or Common Newts are protected under Schedules 5 and 7 of the Wildlife (Northern Ireland) Order 1985. In Northern Ireland, the word 'recklessly' is not included in the legislation.

In addition, Great Crested Newt and Natterjack Toad are Schedule 2 species protected under Regulation 39 of the Conservation (Natural Habitats & c.) Regulations 1994 (as amended). As such, in addition to the above offences, the Conservation Regulations make it an offence to

Table 22.3. *NCC population size class assessment for different amphibian species*

Species	Method of search	Count for low population	Count for good population	Count for exceptional population
Great Crested Newt	Netted or seen (daytime)	< 5	5–50	> 50
	Night count	< 10	10–100	> 100
Smooth Newt	Netted or seen (daytime)	< 10	10–100	> 100
	Night count	< 10	10–100	> 100
Palmate Newt	Netted or seen (daytime)	< 10	10–100	> 100
	Night count	< 10	10–100	> 100
Common Toad	Estimated	< 500	500–5000	> 5000
	Counted	< 100	100–1000	> 1000
Common Frog	Spawn clumps counted	< 50	50–500	> 500

Source: NCC (1989).

damage or destroy a breeding site or resting place of these species (not just intentionally, deliberately or recklessly). Great Crested Newts are also listed on Annex II and Annex IV of the EU Habitats Directive; Natterjack Toads are listed on Annex IV. They are both UK Biodiversity Action Plan Species. In Northern Ireland, the Wildlife (Northern Ireland) Order 1985, the Nature Conservation and Amenity Lands (Northern Ireland) Order 1985 and the Conservation (Natural Habitats, etc.) Regulations 1995 replace the Wildlife & Countryside Act.

Common Toads, Common Frogs, Palmate Newts and Smooth Newts are all afforded protection against sale only under Schedule 5 of the Wildlife & Countryside Act 1981.

The status of the Pool Frog *Rana lessonae* in the UK is uncertain; it may be a native species. There is a UK Biodiversity Action Plan for the species, which aims to establish its status. Should it be deemed to be native, it will likely become fully protected on Schedule 5 of the Wildlife & Countryside Act. It is listed on Annex IV of the EU Habitats Directive.

All species may be Local BAP species depending on their local distribution.

Conservation status in the UK

The assessment of population status in the UK for each amphibian species is based on tables available on the DEFRA website (http://www.defra.gov.uk/environment/statistics/wildlife/index.htm, assessed in 2004).

The Great Crested Newt is an IUCN Lower Risk/Conservation dependent species (i.e. should conservation efforts cease, it would qualify for one of the higher-risk categories within 5 years) (IUCN, 2003). It is distributed across lowland Britain, being absent from parts of Wales and Scotland and parts of southwest England (Beebee & Griffiths 2000), and is one of the more endangered species in the UK. It is not found in Northern Ireland.

The smooth newt is a common and ubiquitous species in the UK, although it is rare in the Highlands, the far South West of England, and parts of Wales (Beebee & Griffiths, 2000). Palmate Newts are more patchily distributed across Britain, being rare across the Midlands, East Anglia and the Highlands, and are regarded as common. They are not found in Northern Ireland (Beebee & Griffiths, 2000).

The Natterjack Toad is mostly restricted to coastal sites in Britain, although there are a few remnant populations on heathlands (Beebee & Griffiths, 2000). It is rare in the UK and is the subject of an English Nature Species Recovery Programme (Beebee & Denton 1996). Both Common Toad and Common Frog are widespread and abundant in Britain (Beebee & Griffiths, 2000) and are considered common.

Table 22.4. *NCC scoring system for the selection of potential SSSI sites*

Item	Score
Low population (per species)	1
Good population (per species)	2
Exceptional population (per species)	3
Four species present	1
Five species present	2
Natterjack Toads present	2

Source: NCC (1989).

As previously stated, the status of the Pool Frog is uncertain in the UK; native or not, it has a very restricted range, with possible remnant populations in Norfolk, Northamptonshire and Cambridgeshire. It may even be extinct and is part of an English Nature Species Recovery programme.

Natterjack Toad, Common Frog and all newt species are thought to be in decline in Britain (Beebee & Griffiths, 2000); amphibian populations are thought to be in decline globally (Gardner, 2001).

Site designation criteria

Sites of international importance for their amphibian fauna (i.e. candidate SACs) can be assessed by using the approach outlined in Chapter 3 of this *Handbook* (based on IEEM guidelines 2002); it would be difficult to give more precise selection criteria.

The SSSI designation criteria, outlined in NCC (1989), can be used as a standard to assess whether sites are of national importance. All important and established (i.e. viable population at the site for the last five years) colonies of Natterjack Toad should be considered of national importance. Important colonies are sites with more than 100 individuals or 25 spawn strings counted on site for two out of the preceeding five years, sites on heathland, or the best sites in that vice-county.

For Great Crested Newts, any site that has contained an 'exceptional' population for the previous three years is eligible for designation as a SSSI (Table 22.3). In addition, there is a scoring system (NCC, 1989) to identify 'outstanding assemblages', as shown in Table 22.4. Sites qualify if they score a minimum of ten points, with a species assemblage of at least four species.

A site is considered to be of County importance if it contains a regularly occurring locally significant population of a Local Biodiversity Action Plan species or species listed in the County Red Data Book.

For levels of importance below this, please refer to Part I as more specific guidance cannot be given here.

23 • Reptiles

Reptile surveying and monitoring can be problematic; reptiles are active, shy creatures, which do not aggregate for breeding as do amphibians. Their behaviour is also heavily influenced by the weather. Most methods for surveying and monitoring reptiles do not generally produce sufficient data to enable population size to be estimated, unless mark–recapture techniques are used.

23.1 ATTRIBUTES FOR ASSESSING CONDITION

23.1.1 Population size

Estimates of population size for reptiles are made during April–October. Most methods for estimating total population size employ mark–recapture studies. Population indices can be obtained without mark–recapture work, but results are less accurate.

23.1.2 Breeding success

Whether or not reptiles are breeding successfully can generally only be ascertained by counting the number of young animals entering the breeding population each year.

23.1.3 Survival and mortality

Estimates of survival and mortality can only reliably be made by mark–recapture studies; the survival of individually marked animals from one trapping occasion to the next can be estimated. Unless dead animals are found, it is not usually possible to distinguish between mortality and emigration. Similarly, immigration and births can be easily confused, unless you are certain that the population is isolated.

23.2 GENERAL METHODS

A survey for reptiles should start with an assessment of the habitat suitability for different species, to establish which, if any, reptiles are likely to occur in the area. For example, Grass Snakes *Natrix natrix* are more likely to occur in areas with freshwater bodies; a summary of the habitat requirements of the different species can be found in Gent & Gibson (1998). For establishing the presence–absence and approximate abundance of reptiles on a site, the most commonly used methods are a combination of walked transects and placing of artificial refugia, as outlined below. A standard number of 7 survey visits is recommended to establish presence–absence, 15–20 to estimate population size, ensuring that visits occur at the appropriate time of year, in suitable weather. The general methods available for surveying and monitoring reptiles are summarised in Table 23.1.

For designated sites (i.e. ASSIs, SSSIs, SACs) the JNCC have outlined common standards monitoring, to ensure that monitoring methods, timing and duration are comparable across all areas designated for their reptile fauna. These can be found at http://www.jncc.gov.uk/csm/guidance/.

It should be noted that a licence from the appropriate statutory body is required to survey for Sand Lizards *Lacerta agilis* and Smooth Snakes *Coronella austriaca*, and should be obtained when surveying in areas where these are likely to occur. Adders *Vipera berus* are the only venomous snake in the UK; although bites are rare, care should be taken in areas where they are likely to occur.

Table 23.1. *Methods for surveying and monitoring reptiles*

	Recommended species group	Population size data	Other attributes	Efficiency	Precision	Bias	Expertise required	Advantages	Disadvantages
Artificial refugia	All	Presence Estimate	Density Survival rates[a]	Reasonable		Affected by weather	Handling Identification	Most species can be found either under, or basking on, sheets; Can be easily standardised between sites	Expensive outlay to purchase sheets at start of study; Requires time and effort to lay out sheets
Standard walk transects	All except Slow-worms	Presence Index	None	Low	Generally low	Affected by weather	Identification	No expensive equipment required	Number of animals seen is generally small
Trapping	All	Presence Estimate	Survival[b]	Reasonable			Handling Identification Trap construction	Good way of trapping animals for mark–recapture studies	Traps must be regularly checked and maintained
Mark-recapture	All	Estimate	Survival rates	Depends on method of capture	Good if large numbers caught	None in theory; small, fast-moving animals may not be caught	Handling Identification Marking (licence may be required)	Obtains best estimate of population size	Time-consuming

[a] If combined with a mark–recapture study.
[b] Unless combined with a mark–recapture study.

23.2.1   Artificial refugia

Principles

Reptiles are often found underneath refuges such as logs. Slow-worms *Anguis fragilis* in particular are commonly found in this manner, but the other lizard and snake species will also readily use such cover. Putting down artificial refugia, such as sheets of metal or roofing felt, will encourage reptiles to shelter underneath them. The sheets are periodically turned over, and any reptiles underneath them are identified and counted. If the sheets are laid out in a grid, estimates of density as well as presence can be made. The sheets will often also be used by both Sand and Common Lizards *Lacerta vivipara* as basking sites.

The advantage of this method is that refuges can be spaced out systematically and added to areas where searching natural cover for reptiles would be time-consuming. The distance walked between refuges can also be treated as a transect (Section 23.2.2) for recording purposes. Refuges should be hidden from plain view, as reptiles under them are vulnerable to disturbance and collection by unauthorised people.

The numbers of reptiles found will vary depending on the prevailing weather conditions, and this should be taken into account when comparing results.

Field methods

Reading (1996) proposes a standard survey methodology for reptile surveys. Refuges should be made from 76 cm × 65 cm rectangles of galvanised, corrugated sheet steel, painted black (e.g. with Hammerite paint) on the upper surface to increase heat absorption on cool days. The standard survey involves a basic hexagonal array of 37 sheets spaced 10 m apart in a grid pattern of 4, 5, 6, 7, 6, 5, 4 on the survey area. This covers 0.29 ha and fits into an area 60 m × 60 m with the middle refuge at the centre of a circle with radius 30 m (Figure 23.1). Alternatively, a rough rule of thumb is 5–10 refuges per hectare (Froglife, 1999). Refuges should be placed horizontally and as close to the ground as possible, although not on bare ground. Larger areas

37 sheets in total
Each sheet is 10 m from its neighbours
Covers 0.29 ha and fits into 60 × 60 m area.

Figure 23.1. Grid pattern for artificial refugia. See text for details.

can be surveyed by using multiples of the basic 37-refuge array.

To check the refuge (reptiles can bask either on or under refuges), gently lift one edge of the tin or felt and watch for any reptiles; if they are present, allow them to move off before replacing the refuge (Froglife, 1999). In areas where adders may be present, use thick gloves when lifting refuges, and wear high boots or gaiters.

The best time of year to set up the refuges is during the winter, so that they are in place before the reptiles emerge from hibernation in the spring. Placing refuges after reptiles have emerged may result in a period in which they will be undiscovered, and thus bias the results downwards. In many EIA studies, however, the refugia may have to be placed out only a short time before the survey period begins.

In order to encounter at least 90% of the reptiles present, and determine the approximate population size, the arrays should be visited and checked 15–20 times during the period from April to October. The best months of the year for finding most reptiles are April, May and September, although they may be found during all months between March and October. Effort should be concentrated on the best months (Gent & Gibson, 1998). To determine presence–absence, seven visits are recommended, again in suitable weather conditions at an appropriate time of year (Froglife, 1999).

The most suitable weather conditions for finding reptiles will vary depending on which species are present. In general, reptiles are not easily found during very hot, dry weather or during very cold, wet weather. The best conditions to find most species occur during warm days (11–19 °C) with intermittent sunshine following cool nights with little or no rain. The best time for surveying is between 09.00 and 11.00 hours, and 16.00 and 19.00.

When placing arrays to estimate population size, you should avoid choosing areas that look good for reptiles; this will give an upwardly biased result if you attempt to extrapolate results across a wider area. Ideally, array locations should be randomly or systematically located. However, sampling in areas that are obviously unsuitable (e.g. large expanses of closely grazed or mown grassland or the middle of dense conifer plantations) will be a waste of effort. Some form of stratification will usually be required at most sites (see Part I, Section 2.3.3).

The sheets should be well hidden in the vegetation but still exposed to the sun, and should be numbered and labelled. It is recommended that they be removed at the end of the survey and should not remain in one place for more than three seasons. Sheets should also be removed or relocated if it is suspected that they are being disturbed by people not involved in the survey work (Griffiths & Inns, 1998). A summary of the field equipment required for surveying and monitoring reptiles with artificial refugia is given in Appendix 6.

Data analysis and interpretation

Abundance and density can be calculated from counts made under refuge arrays. It is obviously important that survey methodology should be standardised so that counts can be compared between areas and sampling occasions.

Counts or densities from different years can, potentially, be analysed statistically by using standard tests (Part I, Section 2.6.4). It should be remembered that variations may be due to differences in weather conditions at the time of survey rather than to an actual change in reptile numbers. It is generally a good idea to record variables such as temperature and wind speed, so that any variation

that may be due to these factors can be identified and eliminated by only comparing results from surveys undertaken during similar conditions.

Care should be taken when extrapolating results across a wider area. It might be possible that the refuges attract reptiles in from the surrounding habitat, thus increasing counts in the survey area. This could occur in areas in which available natural cover for reptiles is limited.

23.2.2   Standard walk transects

Principles

Transects can be used for reptiles that commonly bask during sunny periods. They are effective for all reptile species except Slow-worms. A transect is selected and walked, and all reptiles seen are identified and recorded. Transects can be combined with other survey methods (particularly artificial refugia; see Section 23.2.1) and are generally the most effective way of surveying Grass Snake, Common Lizard and Sand Lizard, which are found less often under refugia.

Transects can be simply walked, or they can be more intensively searched by examining cover within a specified distance of the transect line, which will increase the number of individuals found.

This method requires a degree of competence and experience, and it is advisable that surveyors visit the site with an experienced herpetologist before starting surveys.

Field methods

Reptile transects are conducted in a similar manner to amphibian transects (Section 22.2.5). They can also be conducted as part of a survey involving a refuge array (Section 23.2.1).

Reptiles are not easy to spot; you should walk slowly, with your back to the sun, concentrating on likely basking spots outside the area of shadow and as far ahead as possible. Most reptiles are easily disturbed and will flee if you approach to within a few metres but will often return to their basking spot (or nearby) within a few minutes if you retreat and remain still. Close focusing binoculars are useful.

Searching should concentrate on suitable features; lizards will bask on log piles, stumps, the base of dry-stone walls, discrete open patches of ground among heather, fence posts, etc. and these should be examined carefully. Snakes are often seen on habitat edges or shaded from direct sunlight under bushes or shrubs.

Reptiles need to spend a lot of time basking when the sun is out but the air temperature is low. April, May and September are suggested as the key months, with April and May having the advantage of being the breeding season when reptiles are more active and less wary. The best weather conditions for surveying are temperatures between 10 °C and 17 °C with intermittent or hazy sunshine and little or no wind (Griffiths & Inns, 1998). Surveys should be timed to coincide with this temperature window, which will typically occur between 09.00 and 11.00 hours and between 16.00 and 19.00 hours.

Common Lizards can usually be found when the temperature exceeds 9 °C and the sun is out, and will bask in temperatures of up to 18 °C. Monitoring should start at the beginning of March. Pregnant females will bask during June and July; August and September are good times to look for hatchlings.

Slow-worms are rarely seen in the open, although they do bask and have timings and temperature tolerances similar to those of the Common Lizard. Sand Lizards are more elusive than are Common Lizards and should be surveyed starting in April and finishing with a hatchling search in September.

Adders emerge relatively early from hibernation, and will often bask together near their hibernation site. Surveying can start at the beginning of March. Adders bask in temperatures between 8 °C and 16 °C, and are less tolerant of higher temperatures than are other reptiles. Appendix 6 outlines the field equipment necessary for surveying and monitoring reptiles by standard transects.

Data analysis and interpretation

Measuring the amount of time spent can be used to estimate abundance, expressed as sightings per hour. This can be used to compare sites, and estimates from different years can be analysed statistically by using standard tests provided appropriate

standardisation and sampling is used (Part I, Section 2.6.4). A rule of thumb suggests that only one fifth to one third of the total population will be observed on a transect even during optimum conditions (Gent, 1994).

Transect walks may be used for censusing adult and juvenile populations. Recording the number of individuals provides a comparison for breeding success between years.

23.2.3   Trapping

Principles

Reptiles can be trapped on land by using pitfall traps and drift fencing. Reptiles encountering drift fencing will follow the fence line and fall into a pitfall trap. This method works best for small reptiles such as lizards. Traps, with or without fences, can be used to determine presence. Fences are useful for excluding animals from an area, but are probably not worth the effort for surveying reptile populations. Traps are a less suitable method than transects or refuges as the daytime activity of reptiles leaves them vulnerable to predation and extremes of heat.

Field methods

Pitfall (and fence) construction is covered in detail in Section 22.2.4.

Traps for reptiles should generally be placed in warm, open areas, but covered (i.e. with a raised lid on legs) to provide shade to reduce stress to trapped animals. They should be repeatedly checked during the day. Cover should also be provided in the traps to lessen the risk of any animals being predated or suffering from exposure. Animals should not be left in the traps overnight, and the traps should be fitted with lids when not in use.

Traps should be placed in grids similar to those for artificial refugia (Section 23.2.1) or placed along habitat edges. The requirements for surveying and monitoring reptiles by using trapping techniques in the field are outlined in Appendix 6.

Data analysis and interpretation

Trapping data are best used in conjunction with a mark–recapture study (Section 23.2.4); this allows more precise estimates of abundance to be made, as well as estimates of other population parameters. Otherwise, straight comparisons can potentially be made between trapping data from different occasions by using statistical tests (Part I, Section 2.6.3). However, because reptile densities are often low, the inherent variability of the data may make the identification of trends problematic. Trapping effort should be standardised to allow comparisons to be made, and traps should be sited in representative areas of habitat.

23.2.4   Mark–recapture

Principles

The principles of mark–recapture theory are discussed in Section 10.11. Essentially, animals are trapped by using one of the trapping methods described above, marked in some way so that recaptures can be identified, and then released. Subsequent trapping will reveal the ratio of recaptures to new captures, which is used to estimate total population size.

Mark–recapture studies will generally give the most precise estimates of population size, and also (providing a suitable model is used) allow the estimation of other population parameters such as births, deaths, immigration and emigration.

The type of mark chosen will depend upon the type of mark–recapture analysis that is to be used. Some methods require individual recognition, whereas others only need batch marking (i.e. all animals caught on one occasion are given the same mark). Again, see Sections 10.11 and 22.2.9 for details.

Field methods
Capture

Reptiles can be caught for marking with traps (Section 23.2.3) or by hand during tinning (Section 23.2.1) or transect (Section 23.2.2) surveys. Catching reptiles by hand requires experience and training, particularly for Adders, and is therefore not recommended unless it is absolutely necessary for a monitoring programme. Handling of reptiles, particularly Adders, should only be undertaken by trained personnel, and advice from an appropriate agency specialist should be sought before reptile handling is undertaken.

When catching reptiles by hand, take care to avoid damaging the animals. Slow-worms should be held firmly but not tightly between the head and body. Common Lizards should be caught by holding the whole of the head and body and supporting it in the hand. All lizards will drop their tails if badly handled, especially on warm days. This is damaging, particularly for Slow Worms, which do not fully regrow their tails once lost. Lizards should therefore never be caught by their tails. If it is necessary to catch and handle Adders, particular care and caution should be exercised. Guidance on recommended methods for the capture of Adders (including safety equipment) and other reptiles is provided by Griffiths & Langton (1998).

Reptiles are not easy to handle and are very prone to damage. On first capture, reptiles will writhe about, and snakes and Slow-worms may also defaecate. Adders should not be handled unless absolutely necessary. For lizards, it is very important that the surveyor does not panic and attempts to calm the animal by supporting it in the hand. Surveyors should also work in pairs in case of Adder bites, which, although rarely fatal, can potentially be very serious.

Marking

Marking methods are similar to those recommended for amphibians (Section 22.2.7); PIT tags can be used. Reptiles can also be marked with paint (e.g. nail polish); this causes no damage, although the marks are only temporary and may make animals more at risk of predation.

Reptile markings can be used to identify individuals without the need for external or invasive marks. Features that have been used include chin spots for the Slow-worm and markings around the cloaca for the Common Lizard. Markings on the head can be used for all snake species. In all cases, markings can be drawn onto pre-prepared blank sketches or photographed as the individual is held in a transparent container similar to that used for Great Crested Newts (Section 22.2.7). Non-invasive mark–recapture methods such as these should be adopted in preference to others if possible to avoid any adverse effects on reptile populations. The field equipment needed for surveying and monitoring reptiles by using mark–recapture techniques is listed in Appendix 6.

Data analysis and interpretation

Details on the analysis of mark–recapture data are provided in Sections 10.11 and 22.2.9.

23.3   REPTILE CONSERVATION EVALUATION CRITERIA

Key evaluation considerations

As outlined in Part I of this *Handbook*, the status of the species at the local and national scale is an important consideration when evaluating the conservation value of a site or population. The national status of reptile species is briefly outlined here, and is reflected in the legal protection afforded to each species.

Information about the local status of a species can sometimes be obtained from the County Recorder or Biological Information Centre (or BRC) or the local amphibian and reptile group. Other sources of data are local Red Data books and Local Biodiversity Action Plans.

Protection status in the UK and EU

Of the six reptile species resident in the UK, two (Smooth Snake and Sand Lizard) are fully protected on Schedule 5 of the Wildlife & Countryside Act 1981 (as amended), which affords them protection under Section 9. This makes it an offence to:

- intentionally (or recklessly, in Scotland) kill, injure, take or possess these animals;
- intentionally or recklessly damage, destroy, obstruct access to any structure or place used by a scheduled animal for shelter or protection, or disturb any animal occupying such a structure or place;
- sell, offer for sale, possess or transport for the purpose of sale (live or dead animal, part or derivative) or advertise for buying or selling these animals.

One species (Common Lizard) is fully protected on Schedules 5 and 7 of the Wildlife (Northern Ireland) Order 1985.

Smooth Snake and Sand Lizard are Schedule 2 species protected under Regulation 39 of the Conservation (Natural Habitats & c.) Regulations 1994 (as amended). As such, in addition to the above offences, the Conservation Regulations make it an offence to damage or destroy a breeding site or resting place of these species (not just intentionally, deliberately or recklessly). Smooth Snake and Sand Lizard are also listed on Annex IV of the EU Habitats Directive, and Sand Lizards are a UK Biodiversity Action Plan Species. Slow-worm, Adder, Grass Snake and Common Lizard are all afforded protection against killing, injuring or sale under Schedule 5 of the Wildlife & Countryside Act 1981.

All species of reptile may be Local BAP species, depending on their regional status.

Conservation status in the UK

The assessment of population status in the UK for each reptile species is based on tables available on the DEFRA website (www.defra.gov.uk/environment/statistics/wildlife/index.htm, assessed in 2004).

Within the UK, Common Lizards are considered common, and it is the most widespread reptile (Beebee & Griffiths, 2000). Sand Lizards are restricted to sites in Dorset, Merseyside and Surrey, with recent reintroductions to an area in Scotland, West Sussex and Wales (Beebee & Griffiths, 2000), and are regarded as rare. The Smooth Snake has the most restricted distribution of the UK reptiles, being confined to Dorset, Hampshire and Surrey in England (Beebee & Griffiths, 2000), and is considered rare. Slow-worms are widespread across Britain, but absent from Northern Ireland, and are locally common. Grass Snakes are widespread and locally common in the south of England and parts of Wales, but are uncommon in the north of England and largely absent form Scotland (Beebee & Griffiths, 2000).

Table 23.2. *Population size class assessment for different reptile species*

Species	Count for low population	Count for good population	Count for exceptional population
Adder	<5	5–10	>10
Grass Snake	<5	5–10	>10
Common Lizard	<5	5–20	>20
Slow-worm	<5	5–20	>20

Source: Froglife (1999).

Adders have a widespread but patchy distribution in Britain, and are absent from Northern Ireland (Beebee & Griffiths, 2000). They are considered rare.

Site designation criteria

Sites of international importance for their reptile fauna (i.e. candidate SACs) can be assessed by using the approach described in chapter 3 of this *Handbook* (based on IEEM 2002 guidelines); it would be difficult to give more precise selection criteria.

Sites may be designated as SSSIs on the basis of their reptile fauna (NCC, 1989). All established populations of Smooth Snake or Sand Lizard qualify for consideration, with the exception of those in Dorset, where the colonies have to be important and established. Areas that contain at least three of the other species of reptile may be considered.

A similar framework to that developed by the NCC (1989) for amphibian site assessment has been created by Froglife for 'Key Reptile' Sites, based on the scoring system outlined in Table 23.2. A site should be considered if it supports three or more reptile species or two snake species, supports an 'exceptional' population of a single species of reptile, or scores 4 or more points for its species assemblage (Table 23.2). In addition, consideration should be taken of the local ecology, and sites designated if they support a species particularly scarce in the region.

At the county level, site assessment should take local abundance and distribution into account. A site is considered to be of County importance if it contains a regularly occurring locally significant population of a Local Biodiversity Action Plan species, or species listed in the County Red Data Book.

For levels of importance below this, please refer to Part I of this *Handbook*.

Birds are highly mobile; although they are relatively conspicuous and easily identified, their populations are often difficult to estimate effectively. They are, none the less, the most intensively studied species group, and a large amount of data are available on the distribution, ecology and estimated population sizes of most species. A substantial network of experienced volunteers is involved in countrywide bird monitoring programmes such as the Breeding Bird Survey and the Wetland Birds Survey, organised by the British Trust for Ornithology (BTO) in the UK (the latter in association with the Wildfowl & Wetlands Trust, WWT). In some instances it may be possible to incorporate the information provided by these programmes into a site-based monitoring scheme.

The objectives of bird population assessment need to be clearly identified at the outset. Migratory birds may be winter or summer residents, or may only appear on passage between wintering and breeding grounds. Other species are resident all year round but may show seasonal variation in numbers owing to an influx of birds from other areas during the summer or winter. Autumn populations will also include birds that have fledged in that year (many of which will not survive over winter). It is important, therefore, to be able to separate natural population cycles from underlying trends in population size. Population estimates from similar times in each year should be compared, and it may be necessary to calculate 5 or 10 year means to remove 'noise' from the data.

For EIA studies the most critical factors are usually population size relative to other sites, based on evaluation criteria, and the spatial distribution of birds relative to the proposed location of the development footprint. More sophisticated approaches may involve relating bird numbers to food supply and distribution in relation, for example, to habitat loss or disturbance.

24.1 ATTRIBUTES FOR ASSESSING CONDITION

24.1.1 Population size

Estimates of population size for most common species, particularly the songbirds, are best made during the breeding season, when male birds are most territorial and vocal. Although females tend to be under-recorded, it may generally be assumed that the number of males and females is broadly equal. In other cases, the number of male 'territories' may be adopted as the unit of measurement. Many species have a non-monogamous breeding system so the assumption of parity in the sexes is often a common flaw. In the winter, songbirds tend to be more elusive and their distribution more clustered, making sample surveys difficult to carry out. Winter counts are conducted principally for species that breed at low density in remote areas but concentrate in a few easily counted, discrete areas (e.g. wildfowl and waders roosting at high tide on estuaries, or raptors at communal roost sites).

24.1.2 Breeding success and productivity

Methods of estimating breeding success vary depending on the ease with which nests can be found. It is important to be sure that nests that fail are no more or less difficult to find than nests that succeed. Observer impacts must also be avoided: there is evidence that observers can affect nesting success in a range of species. Breeding success is usually measured in terms of the number of independent young reared per nesting attempt. Clutch sizes and daily survival rates of eggs and chicks may also be calculated, providing an indication of the timing and possible causes of breeding failure.

24.1.3   Survival and mortality

Estimates of survival and mortality usually require that individuals be marked and recaptured, or resighted, over reasonably long time periods (Section 10.9). Birds may be ringed, wing tagged or dye marked. In each case, recoveries depend on the observer or a member of the public returning precise information on the location, date and identity of the bird. For some species, such as Whooper *Cygnus cygnus* and Bewick's Swans *C. columbianus*, facial markings have been used to identify individual birds and 'recoveries' made by simply observing birds passing through sites each year. In each case, the non-return of a bird to known sites implies mortality.

24.2   GENERAL METHODS

Table 24.1 outlines the general methods used for surveying and monitoring birds in the field.

24.2.1   Total counts

Principles
Direct counts are only practical for estimating the abundance of species when the whole population can be located with confidence. This can include species that breed in distinct colonies, e.g. seabirds, Herons *Ardea cinerea* and Rooks *Corvus frugilegus*, species that are large and conspicuous, e.g. swans and geese, and species that are 'charismatic' and confined to well-known fragments of habitat, e.g. Marsh Harriers *Circus cyaneus* breeding in reed beds or Slavonian Grebes *Podiceps auritus* breeding on lochs. Direct counts are also the most practical (although not entirely accurate) way to estimate populations of wintering waders or waterfowl on estuaries or other wetland habitats.

Field methods
If the target is a very common and widespread species or group of species, the method will inevitably require input from a large number of fieldworkers. The Wetland Birds Survey (WeBS) a partnership scheme of the BTO, WWT (Wildfowl & Wetlands Trust), RSPB (Royal Society for the Protection of Birds) and JNCC, uses a large volunteer base and conducts counts on predetermined dates between September and March at most key sites for waterfowl (e.g. estuaries, gravel pit complexes and reservoirs). Synchronising these counts helps to ensure that large movements of birds between sites does not cause birds to be missed or double-counted. The counts are also arranged to coincide with spring tides on most UK estuaries, when birds are generally concentrated into small areas and local movement is minimal. Observers record whether the accuracy of the count was influenced by weather or visibility and whether they believe that the counts were an underestimate of the true figure for other reasons.

Absolute counts are not confined to the winter, however; several schemes involve censusing breeding bird colonies, such as those of Grey Heron (Reynolds, 1979), and seabird species (e.g. Lloyd *et al.*, 1991).

Many single species counts are also undertaken as a means of tracking the population sizes of rarer species (for some of which further details are provided in Section 24.3).

For detailed information on carrying out seabird counts (and other seabird monitoring methods) see Walsh *et al.* (1995).

Data analysis and interpretation
It is best to be cautious when interpreting the reliability of direct count data. For example, attempts at counting all breeding upland waders on a site will usually result in many being missed. Extensive population studies either have to guarantee a uniform effort in all areas of the species distribution, or effort at each site needs to be measured and a note made of suitable breeding sites that are left out. Direct counts can be undertaken in sample plots, which will give a mean and range for

Table 24.1 *Methods for surveying and monitoring birds*

	Recommended species group	Population size data	Other attributes	Efficiency	Precision	Bias	Expertise required	Advantages	Disadvantages
Total counts	Conspicuous, colonial or flocking species	Presence Index Estimate	Flock or colony sizes	Good for recommended species group	Dependent on species involved	Underestimate	Visual identification of species	Simple methodology	May require a large amount of fieldwork and planning for large sites or colonies
Territory mapping	All distinctly territorial species	Presence Index Estimate (for appropriate species)	Behaviour Territory size	Low if surveying small area Highly costly per unit area compared with transects	Reasonable for its purposes	Underestimate	Identification of species, song and breeding behaviour	Enables interpretation of breeding distribution with habitat	Time-consuming at fieldwork and analytical stages; wasteful if only an index required
Line transects	Most species, especially widespread or common species in open habitats	Presence Index Estimate	Detectability Sex ratio Density	Generally good More efficient than registration mapping	Poor: improved by using distance bands	Potentially low	Visual, song and call identification	Versatile and efficient	Relies on skilled knowledge for reliable fieldwork and interpretation
Point counts	All species	Presence Index Estimate	Detectability Sex ratio Density	Reasonable for surveying dense habitats Not particularly good in open habitats	Poor: improved by using distance bands	Potentially low	Visual, song and call identification	Versatile and efficient	Relies on skilled knowledge for reliable fieldwork and interpretation
Trapping and ringing	All species	Presence Index	Age structure Sex ratio Breeding success Productivity	Low	Reasonable for its purposes	Dependent on attribute measured	Bird ringing licence	Best method of assessing mortality, productivity, etc.	Highly skilled and time-consuming

population size. With appropriate sampling, this can then be extrapolated to the whole area or to the area of habitat preferred by the species. The sampling of species populations is best carried out by using a standardised, quantitative method – territory mapping, line transects or point counts – as described later.

For the commonest species, long-term population trends can be derived from direct counts by simply comparing the total population counted each year. It should be remembered, however, that unless counts are known to be comprehensive and accurate, or effort has been carefully standardised, apparent short-term changes may prove to be artefacts. More often, the degree of inaccuracy inherent in direct count data is unknown. Regression analysis and log-linear models are among the tools used to establish whether there are long-term trends in counts.

24.2.2   Territory mapping

Principles

Territory mapping is used to estimate abundance and to examine the distribution of birds in relation to habitat or other environmental variables. The method relies on the fact that many bird species show conspicuous territorial behaviour when breeding. A series of mapped registrations for a particular species, gathered over several visits, will usually show signs of clustering, indicating the locations of territories. The number and distribution of territories can then be assessed across the whole site. The method works best for species that are extremely vocal, such as Wrens *Troglodytes troglodytes* and other songbirds, but does not work well for species that show little territorial behaviour or move long distances from their breeding sites, e.g. Grey Heron, Woodpigeon *Columba palumbus* and most corvids.

One form of territory mapping, the Common Bird Census (CBC), has been used for many years by the BTO as the principal method for monitoring farmland and woodland bird populations in the UK (Marchant *et al.*, 1990). The CBC was phased out as the main bird monitoring scheme, however, largely because of its complexity (which limits

participation by BTO members), the labour-intensive analytical methods it requires (registration maps are analysed by BTO staff) and its inability to provide measures of statistical confidence associated with each estimate. In 2001 the CBC scheme was replaced as the UK's principal bird monitoring scheme by the Breeding Bird Survey (BBS), begun in 1994. This utilises line transect methods, described below.

For most EIA studies, which require a site to be surveyed and assessed for its ornithological significance in respect of bird populations, the normal approach is to undertake a territory, or essentially, a registration mapping exercise. Most development related sites are reasonably small (<50ha) and so coverage in one day, repeated on five occasions during the breeding period, should be sufficient to provide reasonable data on (a) distribution, (b) relative abundance and (c) records of rarer species of most conservation interest.

However, some EIA studies require data to be collected on all manner of groups from farmland birds, estuary waders and wildfowl, overwintering ducks on large waterbodies, seaducks at sea, seabird colonies, geese flighting between roosts and feeding grounds, EU Annex I species on specially protected sites, etc. Specialist methods are available for surveying and monitoring these species or groups. This *Handbook* gives broad guidance for some of these, with more specific treatment of a number of high-profile species of conservation importance. The reader is referred to Bibby *et al.* (2000) for further details.

Field methods

Between five and ten field visits are usually made, during which the observer aims to cover the whole site evenly, to within 50 m of every point. Birds are usually recorded up to 50 m outside the boundary of the survey site in an attempt to ensure that territories that overlap with the boundary are included.

Between 50 and 100 ha can be covered in a 3–4 hour visit, the timing of which should coincide with the main singing period of the target species. All birds and their activities are recorded on a separate map (at least 1 : 2500 scale) for each visit, taking care to differentiate between individuals of the same species.

One of the most important points is to record instances in which two individuals are seen or heard singing simultaneously; this helps with the interpretation of clusters of records and hence assists in the definition of territory boundaries.

For further information and detailed field instructions see Marchant (1983). Appendix 6 outlines the equipment required for surveying birds by territory mapping.

Data analysis and interpretation

The method should exclude (where possible) counts of juveniles, plus unusually high counts resulting from the movement of non-breeding birds into the area. Data from field maps are transposed on to one map for each species, and clusters of registrations that indicate territories are identified. The minimum requirement for confirming a territory is that no more than one pair of birds is recorded at a certain location on at least two visits, 10 days apart. Counts of territories from different years can be analysed statistically by using standard tests (Part I, Section 2.6.4). Territory maps from different years can be compared to assess range contractions or expansions.

24.2.3   Line transects

Principles

Line transects are carried out by a surveyor, who walks along a line and either records the perpendicular distance from detected birds to the line (see Box 10.1) or places each individual within two or more distance bands (Section 10.6). These data can then be used to calculate densities. The method is generally used to estimate the populations of species that are either too common or too widespread to estimate by using direct counts, or too elusive for the whole population at any site to be reliably detected.

Line transects are best suited to open habitats, e.g. farmland and moorland, rather than enclosed habitats, such as woodland and scrub, especially where the habitat structure in the latter is fine-grained. Large conifer blocks, however, may be surveyed by transects (and point counts; see Section 24.2.4). Line transect methods are efficient as they enable the observer to cover large areas in a relatively short time on foot, or in a vehicle such as a boat or aeroplane. If exact distances to bird contacts are measured, results can be adjusted to take account of declines in detectability with distance from the observer (Section 10.6). Line transects can also be used to count indirect measures of bird populations or activity such as droppings.

Field methods

The method for collecting data will vary according to the aims of the survey and the species involved (see Section 10.6 for general principles). The observer may decide to record the age or sex of bird contacts, to record only one species, or to record many species. Birds in flight are usually recorded separately from those that are perched or swimming. This poses some problems for recording numbers of Swallows *Hirundo rustica*, Martins, Swifts *Apus apus*, Kestrels *Falco tinnunculus* and singing Skylarks *Alaunda arvensis*. A general rule may be to record some species when they are first observed 'using' the habitat on a transect. For example, a Kestrel may be recorded as a fly-over until it hovers in search of prey, when its location is marked and its distance from the line recorded. Similarly, Swallows may be recorded if they are noticed hawking over a piece of grassland near the transect. In all these cases, it is vitally important to ensure that birds are not double-counted as they move around the observer. The equipment recommended for surveying birds by line transects is listed in Appendix 6.

Data analysis and interpretation

The level of data analysis will depend on the aim of the survey and monitoring programme and the amount of information collected.

If the aim is to survey bird numbers, changes in the number of raw encounters can indicate change in abundance, so long as the method is fully standardised from year to year. However, this assumes that a species does not become proportionally more detectable as population density increases, or as a result of a change in its habitat preference (or a change in the habitat itself) over time. Differences between surveyors are also common causes of change in detection rates between years.

If there is any indication that detectability will affect the results of a study (this can be quickly ascertained on a pilot survey, or by reference to literature), then distance sampling may be more appropriate (Section 10.6). Although standardisation is still important, distance sampling has the advantage that each year's data can be corrected separately for incomplete detection. Analysis is carried out by using the computer program Distance (Section 10.6.4) and changes in abundance can usually be determined by using standard tests (Part I, Section 2.6.4).

For a fuller description of line transect methods and the use of the Distance computer program see Section 10.4.

24.2.4   Point counts

Principles
Point counts are similar in many respects to line transects: they are essentially a transect of zero length. They are, however, better suited to fine-grained or dense habitats, such as woodland and scrub, and are safer to use in steep or difficult terrain. They are also preferred if birds are likely to flee from the observer before they are detected. Point counts used for distance sampling require that greater care is taken over estimating the distance between the bird and the observer, and are less efficient than line transects in terms of the amount of data collected per unit time. Habitat and other environmental information, however, can be accurately applied to each point, so it can be a cost-effective method for collecting sample information from more structurally complex habitats. An example of a study that has used this approach is that of Hill *et al.* (1990).

Field methods
General field methods and equipment are the same as for the line transect method (Section 24.2.3). Point counts are also described in Section 10.8.

Data analysis and interpretation
The area sampled around each survey point is normally a circle, so methods used for analysing point count and transect data differ slightly. At the very least, the method gives a good indication of species presence–absence and of their association with habitat variables if these are recorded at each point. Relative abundance estimates for the commoner species (accounting for differential detectability) can also be obtained. Point counts can be used to estimate absolute abundance, by using the Distance software. Change between years where this is required can usually be determined by using standard tests (Part I, Section 2.6.4).

For a fuller description of point transect methods, the various levels of interpretation and using the Distance program, see Section 10.6.

24.2.5   Constant effort trapping and ringing

Principles
There are numerous methods used for catching and marking birds. The simplest of these is mist netting, although this is only really suitable for monitoring passerines. The BTO Constant Effort Site (CES) scheme began in 1983 and standardises mist netting at sites with an aim of assessing population trends, survival rates and the productivity of common passerines (Peach *et al.*, 1998). Trapping and ringing birds is a highly skilled activity and requires a licence (see Part I, Section 2.4.3). The BTO administers ringing licences on behalf of JNCC. If the surveyor can enlist the help of local ringing group members, who are prepared to carry out regular mist netting, CES methods may prove useful for site monitoring where data on productivity and survival are required.

Field methods
CES requires ringers to conduct mist netting at least once in each of 12 periods of 10–11 days from May to August. Visits should be conducted at least 3 days apart to minimise the problem of birds learning to avoid nets placed in standard locations. As well as net position, net length and timing is

also kept constant at each site. Mist netting usually takes place between dawn and a fixed time in late morning. Each capture is identified, aged and sexed where possible, and fitted with a uniquely numbered aluminium ring.

Data analysis and interpretation

Assuming there is no difference in the probability of capturing juveniles and adults, the ratio of juvenile to adult captures gives an estimate of productivity. However, birds may leave the trapping area or disperse into it from other sites. Individual marking allows the researcher to assess the significance of immigration and emigration as the change in the proportion of recaptured birds over time.

Survival rates can be assessed by using mark and recapture of individually marked birds. CES-type data may also be used to identify the number of adults and juveniles recaptured in successive years as an estimate of survival rates. This requires that the probability of recapture remains constant across years and that any correlation between age and survival is accounted for. One method of assessing survival rates is by using modelling software such as SURGE (Clobert *et al.*, 1987; Pradel *et al.*, 1990). Population change or the number of breeding pairs can also be estimated from recaptures of adult birds (e.g. individuals captured on two visits, at least 7 days apart) or females with brood patches. This has been shown to correlate well with data collected on the number of breeding territories by using territory mapping methods (Boddy, 1993).

24.3   SOME SPECIFIC METHODS USED IN SPECIALIST EIA STUDIES

The following methods are currently employed in a number of major EIA studies.

24.3.1   Collision mortality monitoring

Collision mortality surveys are adaptations of the line transect method described previously. The objective of such surveys is to identify the levels of bird mortality associated with various structures such as wind turbines and communications towers. When conducting such surveys a variety of factors must be considered to ensure the accuracy of the data collected. For instance, the frequency and timing (both day and seasonal) of surveys, search efficiency and scavenger activity can have a significant influence on the survey results, if not taken into account. It is important to include control sites (some distance from the study site) to establish a baseline of mortality and controlled carcass drops on the study site to assess search efficiency and levels of scavenger activity. The data collected during collision mortality monitoring surveys should include the location of carcasses, the number of birds and species involved, and the weather conditions preceding the search.

24.3.2   Flightline surveys

Flightline surveys are an adaptation of the point count method described earlier. These surveys are used to assess the potential impacts of developments such as airports and windfarms on bird behaviour, migration and local movements through the study area. The objective of such surveys is to identify important avian flight paths to and from sites used by birds for various activities (e.g. feeding, roosting). When conducting such surveys a number of factors should be considered. For instance, the frequency and timing (both day and seasonal) of surveys need to coincide with the avian activity being assessed. In addition, when selecting the survey viewpoint, it is important that the wider area being studied is clearly visible, while ensuring the surveyor(s) does not influence the birds' flight patterns and behaviour. The data collected in such surveys should include the altitude, direction, number of birds and species involved, and weather conditions during the survey. The length of survey period will be determined by the length of activity period of the birds. A series of scoping visits to record time of day of activity, spread of activity and approximate numbers of birds involved will enable the full survey to be fine-tuned.

24.3.3   Seabird surveys at sea

Surveys of seabirds at sea are primarily a variation on line transect methods. The objective of such surveys is to identify the potential impacts on resident and migratory marine birds of the construction of structures such as wind turbines in shallow productive waters during different periods of the birds' annual cycle. A recognised industry standard method for this type of survey has been developed by COWRIE (Collaborative Offshore Wind Research into the Environment). In summary, this involves trained, skilled offshore ornithologists, using a suitably specified vessel to steer a course at a specific speed (10 knots) along a series of transect lines (max. 300 m apart) in the study area. A number of surveyors record their observations (species, number, activity, direction of flight) of seabirds in distance bands (0–50 m, 50–100 m, 100–200 m, 200–300 m, 300+ m) from either side of the vessel. The survey is repeated a number of times to provide a statistically representative baseline evaluation of the avian presence in the study area. The start and end times and locations should be changed to ensure the time of day at which a particular area is surveyed is varied evenly across the survey area. This is to take account of seasonal, diurnal and tidal rhythms in the area. GPS can be used to fix locational information such as start and end points.

24.3.4   Radio tracking

Radio or satellite tracking is a technique involving the fitting of small lightweight transmitters to birds. Radio receivers or satellites can then track the birds' movements, which are then plotted on maps. These data provide additional detailed information, especially when used in conjunction with field observations. The data obtained from these studies provide greater understanding of foraging ranges, distribution, species interaction, habitats used and interactions with natural and man-made landscape features. It is particularly useful for species with large territories or ranges (e.g. large raptors) or secretive species (e.g. Bittern *Botaurus*

stellatus). Data obtained by satellite tracking can be downloaded remotely on a regular (e.g. daily) basis to a computer, making the actual data capture extremely cost-efficient.

24.3.5   Nocturnal surveys

All recognised standard generic bird surveys, i.e. breeding (BBS, registration mapping) and wintering (WeBs) bird surveys, and most species-specific surveys, are carried out during daylight hours. The nocturnal behaviour of birds is becoming increasingly important in assessing the impact of development proposals. For example, many large water bodies hold large populations of migratory waterfowl, yet it is apparent that their use may often be restricted to providing refuges rather than feeding habitat, with birds flighting out to surrounding land to feed under the cover of darkness. An understanding of this process is extremely important where site designations are concerned; protection afforded to refuge habitat may not safeguard the species if it needs feeding habitat in the vicinity which remains unprotected. Statutory bodies and NGOs are increasingly looking for studies to provide information on the impact of developments on nocturnal avian behaviour through the identification of important nocturnal habitats, e.g. Golden Plover *Pluvialis apricaria* feeding adjacent to roads; migratory birds' nocturnal flight paths near communications towers; and waterfowl feeding and roosting habitat around reservoirs.

Existing techniques involve surveyors equipped with night-sights observing and recording data by using standard line transect or point count methods. However, with increased image quality, infra-red (IR) cameras allow the development of cost effective techniques that avoid the need for surveyors to carry out night-time observations and hence reduce the potential reduction in data quality issues associated with survey or fatigue, etc. The IR techniques involve the setting up and appropriate siting of IR cameras, which then record the avian activity (e.g. flight path, feeding areas) to appropriate data storage media (videotape, CD). The images are then reviewed by using an appropriate interface. This technique is still in its infancy but has the potential to enhance the identification of important habitats that are used by birds at night, allow a better understanding of their nocturnal behaviour, and hence provide evidence as to how this behaviour may be affected by the developments being proposed.

24.4   SOME KEY SPECIES REGULARLY CONSIDERED IN EIA STUDIES

Barn Owl *Tyto alba*

Surveying for Barn Owls requires a Schedule 1 licence. A brief summary of the methods follows. For a detailed methodology, refer to Gilbert *et al.* (1998). The attributes indicating the status of this species and their interpretation are detailed in Box 24.1. A national monitoring programme for the Barn Owl is organised annually by the British Trust for Ornithology.

Population survey: breeding season

A minimum of two visits should be made, one between November and January and the second between the beginning of June and the middle of July. The winter visits may be carried out at any time of day; the summer visit should be carried out in late afternoon. The aim of the winter survey is to search all potential nest sites and to record signs (e.g. pellets, feathers, droppings) of Barn Owl presence. These signs are recorded on a map. The summer visit aims to revisit all the potential nest

---

Box 24.1   Attributes of Barn Owl

ATTRIBUTES INDICATING THE SPECIES' STATUS DURING THE BREEDING SEASON

- Number of active nest sites

INTERPRETATION
Number of occupied Barn Owl nest sites found = Number of breeding pairs of Barn Owl.

Box 24.2   Attributes of Nightjar

ATTRIBUTES INDICATING THE SPECIES' STATUS DURING THE BREEDING SEASON

- Number of individual churring birds;
- Number of territories

INTERPRETATION
Number of individual churring birds = number of territories = number of breeding pairs.

---

sites identified during the winter survey to look for signs of nesting activity; then to record the presence–absence of birds, their activity, sex, age, and map the location of nests.

Nightjar *Caprimulgus europaeus*

A brief summary of the methods follows. For a detailed methodology, refer to Gilbert *et al.* (1998). The attributes indicating the status of this species and their interpretation are detailed in Box 24.2.

Population survey: breeding season

A minimum of two visits should be made between the beginning of June and the middle of July, either at dusk or an hour before dawn. Surveys must not be undertaken during windy and wet conditions. Two surveyors work together to locate the position of churring birds, which can be difficult to pinpoint from one location. This may be achieved by positioning the surveyors 50–100 m apart and triangulating the direction of the churring bird and hence its location. As with territory mapping techniques, the location of churring birds is plotted on a map. At the end of the study all locations of churring birds are transferred to a single master map; those records believed to be from the same bird are enclosed in a territory boundary. The total number of separate churring males can be used to determine the number of territories and hence the number of breeding pairs.

Woodlark *Lullula arborea*

A brief summary of the methods follows. For a detailed methodology, refer to Gilbert *et al.* (1998). The attributes indicating the status of this species and their interpretation are detailed in Box 24.3.

Population survey: breeding season

Breeding population surveys require that three separate visits be made to the survey area. As

---

Box 24.3   Attributes of Woodlark

ATTRIBUTES INDICATING THE SPECIES' STATUS DURING THE BREEDING SEASON

- Number of separate singing males
- Number of territories

INTERPRETATION

Number of separate singing males = number of territories = number of breeding pairs.

Woodlarks start to show signs of territoriality early in the year the first visit is carried out between 15 February and 21 March, second between 22 March and 25 April, and the final visit between 26 April and 1 June. Visits should be made before midday. All observations of birds and their behaviour are plotted on a visit map by using standard BTO codes. After the final visit all records are transferred to a single master map; those records believed to be from the same pair are enclosed in a territorial boundary. Most territories will be determined through the presence of separate singing males. Simultaneous singing males, foraging pairs and flight directions help to identify territory boundaries, which establish the number of breeding pairs.

Black Redstart *Phoenicurus phoenicurus*

A brief summary of the methods follows. For a detailed methodology, refer to Gilbert *et al.* (1998). The attributes indicating the status of this species and their interpretation are detailed in Box 24.4.

Box 24.4   Attributes of Black Redstart

ATTRIBUTES INDICATING THE SPECIES' STATUS DURING THE BREEDING SEASON

- Number of confirmed breeding pairs
- Number of probable breeding pairs
- Number of possible breeding pairs
- Minimum number of breeding pairs

INTERPRETATION

The number of nests containing eggs or young, or the number of recently used nests, or the number of sites where adults are seen carrying food for young, or the number of sites where recently fledged young are seen = the number of confirmed breeding pairs.
the number of pairs of Black Redstart seen in ideal breeding habitat in the breeding season, or the number of males heard singing at the same place on two or more occasions, or the number of episodes of courtship or display behaviour observed, or the number of sites where birds are seen visiting a possible nest site, or the number of sites where adults show agitated behaviour (e.g. anxiety calls), or the number of nests observed being built = the number of probable breeding pairs.
The number of sites where a Black Redstart is seen in non-ideal nesting habitat during the breeding season, or the number of singing males heard once during the breeding season, or the number of birds seen in possible nesting habitat during the breeding season = the number of possible breeding pairs.
The number of confirmed pairs = the minimum number of breeding pairs.
The number of confirmed + probable + possible breeding pairs = the maximum number of breeding pairs.

Population survey: breeding season

At least five visits should be made between mid April and the end of June. These should occur either in the early morning (within an hour of sunrise) or in the evening leading up to sunset. Surveying in cold, wet and windy conditions may yield poor results and is not recommended. A survey route should be marked on a map and followed each visit. Singing birds are listened for and each visual or audible encounter recorded. The location and behaviour of the record is plotted on a visit map with standard BTO codes. After the final visit, transfer all records to a single master map. The data are used to assess the number of breeding Black Redstart present by using the interpretation criteria described in Box 24.4.

Dartford Warbler *Sylvia undata*

A brief summary of the methods follows. For a detailed methodology, refer to Gilbert *et al.* (1998). The attributes indicating the status of this species and their interpretation are detailed in Box 24.5.

Population survey: breeding season

Three visits should be made, the first between April and mid-May, one between mid- and late May and the last one in June. Surveys can be carried out from an hour after dawn onwards through the day. Dry, calm conditions are most favourable for Dartford Warbler surveys. On a visit map record all Dartford Warbler encounters. After the final visit transfer all records to a single master map; circle those records believed to be from the same pair.

Mapping of simultaneous registrations (eg. singing birds) is particularly important in analysis of maps to determine numbers. A territory is likely to be occupied if a singing male, territorial dispute or breeding activity is observed.

24.5   BIRD CONSERVATION EVALUATION CRITERIA

Key evaluation considerations

Bird populations, particularly in the UK, are generally more regularly and thoroughly surveyed and monitored than is any other group of taxa. This has led to a long history of bird monitoring in the UK, with an effective network of many highly skilled amateur and professional ornithologists involved in collecting data. Many of the long-term national monitoring schemes are run by partnerships between non-government conservation organisations (e.g. the British Trust for Ornithology, the RSPB and the Wildfowl & Wetlands Trust) and the UK statutory conservation agencies.

As a result the population sizes, range distributions, population and range trends, migratory movements and many key aspects of breeding success and survival are relatively reliably known and documented for many bird species. Outside the UK it has also been possible to define and quantify flyway populations, identify key migratory staging posts and assess the conservation status of birds at a European level.

Box 24.5   Attributes of Dartford Warbler

ATTRIBUTES INDICATING THE SPECIES' STATUS DURING THE BREEDING SEASON

- Number of separate singing males
- Number of separate territorial disputes
- Number of observed episodes of breeding activity

INTERPRETATION

- Number of occupied territories = number of separate singing Dartford Warbler + number of separate territorial disputes + number of observed episodes of breeding activity.

N.B. When reporting total number of occupied territories, include a separate note of the number of singing males only.

This has allowed the development of relatively sophisticated and largely quantitative criteria for the assessment of species and their conservation priorities. Most site evaluations for birds may be carried out by reference to quantitative assessment criteria provided that reasonable quantitative data are available for the site in question. There are various sources of reliable information relating to species distribution and abundance in the UK. These include Gibbons *et al.* (1993), Lack (1986), Lloyd *et al.* (1991), Stone *et al.* (1997), WeBS data (see www.bto.org) and annual summaries of the BBS (e.g. Raven *et al.*, 2003). A site's existing designation status and details can be obtained online from English Nature or the Joint Nature Conservation Committee (see www.english-nature.org.uk or www.jncc.gov.uk) for protected sites.

There are some significant complications with assessing the value of sites for migratory birds. The application of quantitative criteria such as the 1% threshold needs to take into account the turnover of birds using a site rather than simply peak numbers present (often numbers passing through over a migratory season may be considerably greater than numbers seen at any one time). This is often overlooked owing to the difficulties of measuring turnover rates.

Account also needs to be taken of local movements and the full range of requirements for a species. For instance, it is not enough to protect the nesting habitat of a species if its only feeding area, which may be some distance from its breeding site, is destroyed. Site requirements for birds therefore need to assess nesting habitats, feeding habitats, roosting areas and possible display areas (e.g. for lekking species), and to take into account diurnal, nocturnal, tidal and seasonal variation in the use of these.

Another key pitfall with site evaluations for migratory birds (including nomadic or partly migratory birds) is that intermittently important sites are overlooked. For example, periods of severe winter weather may result in some displacement of birds to milder regions that they would not normally visit. Such hard-weather movements have been documented in several species of wildfowl and indicate the importance of British west coast estuaries for birds displaced from eastern Britain and continental Europe (Ridgill & Fox, 1990). Without the protection of such sites, whole populations of birds may be put at risk during severe weather events. Site selection and evaluation assessments therefore need to take into account such possible occasional but critical uses. SPA and SSSI selection criteria therefore include the capacity to select sites that are only used under infrequent conditions.

In the evaluation of the avian conservation value of a study area that has been surveyed or is being monitored the criteria that need to be considered include international, national, regional, county and local levels of conservation importance.

Where a site is potentially of international importance, reference should be made to the criteria relating to the selection of SSSIs, SPAs, Ramsar sites and IBAs summarised in Table 24.2.

A useful method for assessing the avian conservation interest of a site at national, regional and local levels is based on bird species population size, diversity and rarity as described in Fuller (1980). This method is particularly useful for evaluating sites that do not have significant amounts of historical data and are therefore reliant on data obtained from specific avian studies.

An alternative method for assessing the avian conservation interest of a site at national, regional and local levels is provided by the guidelines for selection of SSSIs (NCC, 1989). These offer a scoring system for various habitats based on the presence of certain key characteristic species, and give a threshold value for SSSI selection. By using this system, bird community data obtained during site surveys can be compared both directly with other surveyed sites and with the standard of the SSSI network, providing a measure of its relative importance nationally, regionally and locally.

The evaluation of a site's historical avian conservation importance can also be assessed through comparison with data available from biological record centres, local bird recorders (for contact details see www.britishbirds.co.uk), county avifaunas (e.g. James, 1996) and bird reports (see Ballance, 2004).

Table 24.2. *Summary of avian conservation evaluation criteria*

Evaluation criteria	Regional context	Legal context	Thresholds
Threatened Birds of the World	Global	None	IUCN Version 3.1 criteria (IUCN, 2001)
Bonn Convention	Global	Legal obligations on contracting parties	Endangered migratory species listed in Appendix I of the Convention and by concluding multilateral agreements for the conservation and management of migratory species listed in Appendix II.
Bern Convention	Global	Legal obligations on contracting parties	Species listed on Appendices II and III. It is not normally necessary to take special account of requirements for birds listed under the Bern Convention as these are adequately covered by UK and European statutory instruments.
Ramsar Convention	Global	Legal obligations on contracting parties	Criterion 5: supports 20 000 or more waterbirds. Criterion 6: supports 1% of the individuals in a population of one species or subspecies of waterbird
Important Bird Areas	Global	None	See Table 24.3.
EU Birds Directive	European	EU Law	Stage 1: identification of areas likely to qualify for SPA status 1. An area is used regularly by 1% or more of the Great Britain (or in Northern Ireland, the all-Ireland) population of a species listed in Annex I of the Birds Directive (79/409/EEC) in any season. 2. An area is used regularly by 1% or more of the biogeographical population of a regularly occurring migratory species (other than those listed in Annex I) in any season. 3. An area is used regularly by over 20 000 waterfowl (waterfowl as defined by the Ramsar Convention) or 20 000 seabirds in any season. 4. An area that meets the requirements of one or more of the Stage 2 guidelines in any season, where the application of Stage 1 guidelines 1, 2 or 3 for a species does not identify an adequate suite of most suitable sites for the conservation of that species. This allows consideration, using the Stage 2 judgements, to be given to cases where a species' population status, ecology or movement patterns may mean that an adequate number of areas cannot be identified from Stage 1 criteria 1–3 alone. Stage 2: selection of most suitable areas in number and size for SPA classification. 1. Population size and density. Areas holding or supporting more birds than others and/or holding or supporting birds at higher concentrations are favoured for selection.

2. Species range. Areas selected for a given species provide as wide a geographic coverage across the species' range as possible.
3. Breeding success. Areas of higher breeding success than others are favoured for selection.
4. History of occupancy. Areas known to have a longer history of occupation or use by the relevant species are favoured for selection.
5. Multi-species areas. Areas holding or supporting the larger number of qualifying species under Article 4 of the Directive are favoured for selection.
6. Naturalness. Areas comprising natural or semi-natural habitats are favoured for selection over those which do not.
7. Severe weather refuges. Areas used at least once a decade by significant proportions of the biogeographical population of a species in periods of severe weather in any season, and which are vital to the survival of a viable population, are favoured for selection.
8. Stage 2 judgements were particularly important for selecting and determining the boundaries of SPAs for thinly dispersed and wide-ranging species.

Species of European Conservation Concern	European	None

SPEC 1: Species occurring in Europe which are of global conservation concern because their status on a world-wide basis is classified as Globally Threatened, Conservation Dependent or Data Deficient.
SPEC 2: Species whose global populations are concentrated in Europe and which have an Unfavourable Conservation Status in Europe.
SPEC 3: Species whose global populations are not concentrated in Europe, but which have an Unfavourable Conservation Status in Europe.

Wildlife & Countryside Act	National	UK Law

Species listed on Schedule 1 Part I comprise 79 rare, endangered, declining or vulnerable species. Schedule 1 Part II lists three wildfowl species that are specially protected only during the breeding season.

UK Birds of Conservation Concern	National	None

Red List species are those that are globally threatened, whose population or range has declined rapidly in recent years (i.e. by more than 50% in 25 years), or which have declined historically and not recovered. Amber list species are those whose population or range has declined moderately in recent years (by more than 25% but less than 50% in 25 years), those whose population has declined historically but recovered recently, rare breeders (fewer than 300 pairs), those with internationally important populations in the UK, those with localised populations, and those with an unfavourable conservation status in Europe.
Species that meet none of these criteria are green-listed.
Birds of Conservation Concern are those that are either Red or Amber listed.

Table 24.2 (*cont.*)

Evaluation criteria	Regional context	Legal context	Thresholds
UK BAP list of priority bird species	National		A list of 26 Species of Conservation Concern (SoCC) has been produced as part of the UK Biodiversity Action Plan programme (UKBG, 1998a).
SSSI selection criteria	National	UK Law	• Breeding aggregations and localities of very rare species. Localities that normally contain 1% or more of the total British breeding population of any native species and seabird colonies of over 10 000 breeding pairs are eligible for selection. In practice this guideline covers mainly colonial and rare species. • Small isolated colonies of seabirds and other birds and other breeding sites. • Localities regularly used by non-breeding birds. Localities that regularly contain 1% or more of the total British non-breeding population of any species are eligible for selection. In practice this guideline covers mainly wintering populations, but it can be applied at other seasons where adequate data are available. • Localities used by birds in particular conditions, e.g. sites used during severe weather. • Rich assemblages of breeding species. Localities are eligible which support an especially good range of bird species characteristic of the habitat, as defined by a 'BTO Index' given in the SSSI guidelines. • High densities of waders on upland habitats (including blanket bogs). • A high variety of species and semi-natural habitats. i.e. >70 breeding species, >90 wintering species or >150 species recorded on passage in recent years. • Particularly important rare species or features.
Other	Regional, County, Local	None	Population size, species richness, breeding community quality, rarity (Fuller, 1980)

24.6   PROTECTION STATUS IN THE UK AND EU

24.6.1   BirdLife list of Threatened Birds of the World

BirdLife International is the official Red Listing Authority supplying information on globally threatened birds for IUCN Red Lists. The most recent global overview, entitled *Threatened Birds of the World* (BirdLife International, 2000) used the IUCN 1994 version 2.3 criteria (IUCN, 1994). Information from this BirdLife assessment was supplied to IUCN for the 2000 IUCN Red List (Hilton-Taylor, 2000). In 2002, BirdLife updated this information for 25 species for the 2002 IUCN Red List (see www.redlist.org).

Up-to-date and complete lists of globally threatened or near threatened birds can be obtained from Birdlife at www.birdlife.org, together with accounts for globally threatened species.

Currently (2004), only two bird species that regularly occur in the UK are considered to be globally threatened, both of which are classed as Vulnerable: Corncrake *Crex crex* and Aquatic Warbler *Acrocephalus paludicola* (BirdLife International, 2000). White-tailed Eagle *Haliaeetus albicilla* is considered to be Near Threatened and Scottish Crossbill *Loxia scotica* Data Deficient (primarily because its taxonomic status is unclear).

Bonn Convention Annex 1

The Bonn Convention aims to conserve terrestrial, marine and avian migratory species throughout their range by providing strict protection for the endangered migratory species listed in Appendix I of the Convention and by multilateral agreements for the conservation and management of migratory species listed in Appendix II.

The only bird species listed under Appendix 1 that regularly occurs within the UK is White-tailed Eagle.

The only Bonn Agreement of direct relevance to birds in the UK at the moment is the African-Eurasian Migratory Waterbird Agreement (AEWA). The agreement covers 235 species of bird (listed in Annex II of the agreement) that are ecologically dependent on wetlands for at least part of their annual cycle, including many species that are common breeding or wintering wetland birds in the UK.

AEWA aims to conserve migratory waterbirds, giving special attention to endangered species and those with an unfavourable conservation status.

See the AEWA website at http://www.unep-aewa.org for details on requirements.

Bern Convention Annex 1

Birds listed under Appendices II and III of the Bern Convention are covered by UK and European instruments (Wildlife & Countryside Act, the CROW Act and the Habitats Regulations comprising the EU Birds and Habitat Directives). Appendix II is a long list of strictly protected fauna species which includes a high proportion of European birds. Appendix III lists other protected fauna species, which covers almost all birds not covered in Appendix II.

See http://www.nature.coe.int/english/cadres/bern.htm for more information on the Bern Convention and lists of species on the various Appendices.

Wild Birds Directive

The EU Birds Directive (79/409/EEC) provides for the protection, management and control of naturally occurring wild birds within the European Union.

The Directive lists, under Annex I, species that are considered to be in danger of extinction, vulnerable to specific changes in their habitat, rare, or requiring particular attention for reason of the specific nature of their habitat. The species mentioned in Annex I are subject to special conservation measures concerning their habitat in order to ensure their survival and reproduction in their area of distribution. This includes the designation of Special Protection Areas (SPAs) as conservation measures for Annex I listed species, particularly for certain rare or vulnerable species and for regularly occurring migratory species of bird not listed on Annex I, and pays particular attention to the protection of wetlands of international importance. In the UK this is implemented through the

Wildlife & Countryside Act 1981, where all SPAs have first to be notified as Sites of Special Scientific Interest (SSSIs), apart from marine SPAs.

Within SPAs Member States 'shall take appropriate steps to avoid pollution or deterioration of habitats or any disturbances affecting the birds'. The Directive requires the maintenance of the favourable conservation status of all wild bird species across their distributional range with the encouragement of various activities to that end. There is also a requirement for the establishment of a general scheme of protection for all wild birds, which is adequately addressed in the UK by the Wildlife & Countryside Act.

The Birds Directive and Annexes can be obtained from the European Commission nature conservation website at europa.eu.int/comm/environment/nature/legis.htm.

Further details of the application of the SPA criteria and the selected SPAs can be found in Stroud *et al.* (2001) and on the JNCC website at www.jncc.gov.uk/UKSPA/default.htm.

The Convention on Wetlands (Ramsar Convention)

Sites may be designated as Ramsar Sites (Wetlands of International Importance) under The Convention on Wetlands of International Importance especially as Waterfowl Habitat, more popularly known as the Ramsar Convention.

The Ramsar Strategic Framework and Guidelines note that wetlands identified as being of international importance under Criterion 5 should form an ecological unit, and may thus be made up of one big area or a group of smaller wetlands. A wetland is said to 'regularly' support a population of a given size if:

- the requisite number of birds is known to have occurred in two thirds of the seasons for which adequate data are available, the total number of seasons being not less than three; or
- the mean of the maxima of those seasons in which the site is internationally important, taken over at least five years, amounts to the required level (means based on three or four years may be quoted in provisional assessments only).

Criterion 6 requires a definition of each species' and subspecies' flyway populations and a quantitative estimate. These have been defined and estimated by Wetlands International and published and updated every three years. To ensure international comparability, Criterion 6 should therefore be judged against these international population estimates and 1% thresholds (the most recent being Wetlands International, 2002). Conventionally, assessments against the 1% threshold are based on a five-year mean.

Consideration may be given when assessing bird populations of a site to the turnover of waterbirds at migration periods. Further information on the application of the 1% criterion can be found on the Ramsar website at www.ramsar.org.

Species of European Conservation Concern

BirdLife International contributed to establishing European-wide conservation priorities by assessing the conservation status of all birds in Europe in 1994 (Tucker & Heath, 1994, BirdLife International, 2004) and identified Species of European Conservation Concern (SPECs).

Species are considered to be concentrated in Europe if more than 50% of their global breeding or wintering population occurs in Europe. Species are considered to have an Unfavourable Conservation Status if their European populations are small and non-marginal, or are substantially declining, or are highly localised.

The SPEC list has been widely used throughout Europe. BirdLife has used the SPEC categories to help identify priority habitat conservation measures (Tucker & Evans, 1997) and in their current criteria for Important Bird Areas in Europe (Heath & Evans, 2000). In the UK it has been used in the assessment of bird species of conservation concern, which has been co-developed with and recognised by the UK statutory agencies. The SPEC categories and threat status assessment also provide a useful means of incorporating European scale conservation priorities into general site evaluations for management planning and EIA purposes.

Important Bird Areas

One of BirdLife International's main activities is the identification of Important Bird Areas (IBAs) (see Heath & Evans (2000) for the European set of IBAs), which BirdLife recommend should receive appropriate statutory protection. IBAs were initially identified in Europe in 1989 for congregatory and migratory species, globally threatened species, species and subspecies that are threatened throughout all or large parts of Europe, and species with relatively small world ranges that have important populations in Europe (Grimmett & Jones, 1989). This initiated the IBA programme, and the subsequent production of a number of national IBA inventories in Europe, including one for the UK (Pritchard et al., 1992). The UK inventory identified 295 IBAs. These sites cover more than 31 000 km^2, representing over 12% of the UK surface area.

The criteria for identifying IBAs have since been updated and expanded globally. IBAs are now sites that are important for threatened species, congregatory species, assemblages of restricted-range species and assemblages of biome-restricted bird species. Sites qualify as IBAs if they meet any of the standard global criteria or regionally specific criteria. Twenty criteria have been developed for the selection of IBAs in Europe (Heath & Evans, 2000), which may categorize sites at three distinct levels, as follows.

- Global (Class 'A' criteria)
- European (Class 'B' criteria)
- European Union (Class 'C' criteria)

These criteria are summarised in Table 24.3. As with the Ramsar criteria, 1% thresholds for flyway or biogeographical populations of waterbirds should be based on Wetlands International estimates (Rose and Scott, 1997; Wetlands International, 2002). Thresholds for other European populations are largely taken from Tucker & Heath (1994), BirdLife International (2000) and BirdLife International (2004).

Wildlife & Countryside Act

In the UK all wild birds, their nests and eggs are protected under the Wildlife & Countryside Act 1981 (as amended), and by the Wildlife (Northern Ireland) Order 1985.

However, the protection afforded to individual species varies depending on their listing under various Schedules of the Wildlife & Countryside Act (as amended). Those on Schedule 1 receive special protection and cannot be intentionally (or, in England, Scotland or Wales, 'recklessly') disturbed when nesting. Schedule 1 Part I lists 79 rare, endangered, declining or vulnerable species. Schedule 1 Part II lists three wildfowl species that are specially protected only during the breeding season. In Scotland, the nests of certain bird species (in Schedule A1) are also protected, even when not in use, and certain species (in Schedule 1A) are protected from intentional or reckless harassment.

UK list of Species of Conservation Concern

This is a joint NGO and statutory agency assessment of the status of birds in the UK and a list of Species of Conservation Concern (Gregory et al., 2002). The following seven quantitative criteria are used to assess each species.

- Global population status
- Recent population decline
- Historical decline in breeding population
- European conservation status
- Breeding rarity
- Localised breeding and non-breeding species
- International importance during the breeding or non-breeding season

The criteria are then used to assess each species according to one of three categories: Red, Amber or Green. The red list reflects only the extent to which a species is threatened, whereas the amber list reflects both threat status and the UK's responsibility for bird populations. Full details of the application of these criteria, the datasets used to test them and the list of Species of Conservation Concern are provided in Gregory et al. (2002).

UK BAP list

Up-to-date lists of bird SoCCs can be obtained from www.ukbap.org.uk/ Library together with Species Action Plans for Priority Species.

Table 24.3. *Summary of the 20 criteria used in Europe to identify Important Bird Areas*

Category	Criterion
A. GLOBAL	
A1. Species of global conservation concern	The site regularly holds significant numbers of globally threatened species, or other species of global conservation concern.
A2. Restricted-range species	The site is known or thought to hold a significant component of the restricted-range species whose breeding distributions define an Endemic Bird Area or Secondary Area.
A3. Biome-restricted species	The site is known or thought to hold a significant component of the group of species whose distributions are largely or wholly confined to one biome.
A4. Congregations	i. The site is known or thought to hold, on a regular basis, at least 1% of a biogeographic population of a congregatory waterbird species.
	ii. The site is known or thought to hold, on a regular basis, at least 1% of the global population of a seabird or terrestrial species.
	iii. The site is known or thought to hold, on a regular basis, over 20 000 waterbirds or 10 000 pairs of seabirds of one or more species.
	iv. The site is known or thought to be a 'bottleneck' site where at least 20 000 storks, raptors, or cranes pass during spring or autumn migration.
B. EUROPEAN	
B1. Congregations	i. The site is known or thought to hold at least 1% of a flyway or other distinct population of a waterbird species.
	ii. The site is known or thought to hold at least 1% of a distinct population of a seabird species.
	iii. The site is known or thought to hold over 1% of a biogeographic population of a flyway or other distinct population of other congregatory species.
	iv. The site is a 'bottleneck' site where over 5000 storks, or over 3000 raptors or cranes regularly pass on spring or autumn migration.
B2. Species with an unfavourable conservation status in Europe	The site is one of the '*n*' most important in the country for a species with an unfavourable conservation status in Europe (SPEC 2 or 3) and for which the site-protection approach is thought to be appropriate.
B3. Species with a favourable conservation status in Europe	The site is one of the '*n*' most important in the country for a species with a favourable conservation status in Europe but concentrated in Europe (SPEC 4) and for which the site-protection approach is thought to be appropriate.

C. EUROPEAN UNION

C1. Species of global conservation concern	The site regularly holds significant numbers of globally threatened species, or other species of global conservation concern.
C2. Concentrations of a species threatened at the EU level	The site is known to regularly hold at least 1% of a flyway population or of the EU population of a species threatened at the EU level (i.e. listed on Annex I and referred to in Article 4.1 of the Birds Directive).
C3. Congregations of migratory species not threatened at the EU level	The site is known to regularly hold at least 1% of a flyway population of a migratory species not considered threatened at the EU level (as referred to in Article 4.2 of the Birds Directive, and not listed on Annex I).
C4. Congregatory: large congregations	The site is known to regularly hold at least 20 000 migratory waterbirds or 10 000 pairs of migratory seabirds of one or more species.
C5. Congregatory: bottleneck sites	The site is a 'bottleneck' where at least 5000 storks and/or at least 3000 raptors and/or 3000 cranes regularly pass on spring or autumn migration.
C6. Species threatened at the EU level	The site is one of the five most important in the European region (NUTS region) in question for a species or subspecies considered threatened in the EU (i.e. listed on Annex I of the Birds Directive).
C7. Other ornithological criteria	The site has been designated as a SPA or selected as a candidate SPA based on ornithological criteria (similar to but not equal to C1–C6) in recognised use for identifying SPAs.

Source: Based on Heath & Evans (2000).

Sites of Special Scientific Interest

Details are summarised in Table 24.2. Full details of the SSSI ornithological criteria and their applica-tion can be found in NCC (1989), but care should be taken in assessing some thresholds as many of the references used in the SSSI guidelines have been superseded.

25 • Bats

Bats are nocturnal, highly mobile animals that are adapted to foraging for insects in a variety of habitats. Generally during the day they roost in a variety of structures, commonly tree cavities, barns and buildings. In winter, they hibernate in built structures and underground places such as caves and mines.

Most information about bats has been obtained by making emergence counts from roosts, from activity surveys with bat detectors and from monitoring bat boxes, with some records from a variety of other sources. There is scope for gathering good-quality information by the use of novices with minimal training, while skilled enthusiasts, especially helped by modern technology, can produce valid results from a wide spectrum of habitats. The network of bat groups (supported by the Bat Conservation Trust in the UK) provides specialist training of new recruits, although expertise is patchily distributed.

Survey methods (Tables 25.1 and 25.2) include finding roosts by direct observation and locating dispersal routes and feeding habitats, often aided by equipment such as bat detectors (ultrasound detectors), as detailed below:

- Day searches: structures (e.g. buildings, walls, bridges, trees, mines and caves), finding signs and/or bats
- Dusk observations: emergence counts from roosts, dispersal commuting routes, flight paths from roosts, foraging habitats
- Dawn observations: aerial 'swarming' at roosts allows location of new roosts

Because of the difficulties inherent in recording bats, and because surveys often produce 'sample' rather than absolute results, it is best to encourage keen individuals to undertake projects in which the same methods and dates are used and the same search or time effort is expended, so as to reduce bias. Although unlicensed people can do much good work in monitoring roosts (externally) as well as work in the field, only trained and licensed people may disturb bats at roost, or catch or handle them.

25.1 ATTRIBUTES FOR ASSESSING CONDITION

25.1.1 Number of roosts

In the summer, female bats gather together in warm sheltered locations to give birth. These maternity or nursery colonies are critical indicators of population status and key targets for protection. Bats require warm, dry, undisturbed locations, sheltered from predators, in which to form maternity colonies, preferably with suitable foraging habitat nearby. If such places are not available, the reproductive success of the species, and consequently the population size, will decline.

The number of known roosts of a species is one attribute that is used to define status, i.e. common, rare, widespread or of limited distribution. One colony may roost at several separate sites during the breeding season and they are often faithful to roost sites for many years. Therefore, it is important to monitor roosts with evidence of bats, even if

Table 25.1. *Methods for surveying and monitoring bats*

	Recommended species group	Population size data	Other attributes	Efficiency	Precision	Bias	Expertise required	Advantages	Disadvantages
Exit counts at roosts	All bats	Estimate		Good	Variable	Little for large colonies	Identification	Direct assessment of cluster size	Requires seasonal visits per year. Bats use more than one roost site and some species are highly mobile, so roost counts can be unreliable. May disturb bats
Winter hibernation counts	All bats	Index		Poor	Good if site is easily searched, otherwise very poor	Favours species that hibernate in buildings, caves and mine workings	Licence required. Identification of hibernating bats	Straightforward methodology	Most sites are not easily searched. Only produces index. May disturb bats
Swarming counts	All bats	Not applicable	—	Good	Variable	Favours species that may swarm more often or prolifically (e.g. *Myotis*)	Identification useful, but not necessary	Straightforward methodology. May make roost and hibernation sites easier to find	Difficult to tell how many bats actually enter the roost; further investigations required
Bat box counts	All bats	Index	—	Requires visits to each box	Very high	May miss species that use boxes less often, e.g. Horseshoes and Serotines	Licence required. Identification	Allows positive identification of bat species. Can reveal presence of species that may be too quiet to be	Disturbs bats

Transects	All bats	Presence/possible absence	Index of activity	Poor	Low	Some species/bats not recorded	Identification of calls	heard on bat detector Simple method Fair method of establishing presence of some species in an area Identification of key foraging areas and commuting routes	Results cannot estimate population size
Indirect assessments of presence, e.g. droppings	All bats	Presence/possible absence	—	Variable quality	Variable	—	Knowledge of signs indicating bat presence	Can be used all year round	Hibernating bats leave little or no evidence of occupation
Radiotracking	All bats	—	—	High	Very high	—	High level of expertise required Specific licence required	Best way of finding new roosts Reveals more information about foraging requirements	Expensive equipment required High level of expertise needed

Table 25.2. *Conservation status of British bats*

Species	IUCN designation[a]	UK conservation status[b]	UK distribution[c]	Estimated UK population size[d]
Barbastelle	Vulnerable	Rare	Widespread throughout England (although more records from the southern half of the country) and Wales	Unknown
Bechstein's	Vulnerable	Rare	Restricted to south England and south Wales	May be around 1500 but very uncertain
Lesser Horseshoe	Vulnerable	Endangered	Mainly confined to south-west England and Wales	17 000 (7000 in England and 10 000 in Wales)
Greater Horseshoe	Lower risk, near threatened (close to qualifying for Vulnerable)	Endangered	Mainly confined to south-west England and south Wales	4 000–6 000
Leisler's	Lower risk, near threatened (close to qualifying for Vulnerable)	Vulnerable	Sparse records throughout England, no records for Wales, common in Northern Ireland	5 000–15 000
Whiskered	Lower risk, least concern	Endangered	Throughout England and Wales, south Scotland and Northern Ireland	40 000
Brandt's	Lower risk, least concern	Endangered	Throughout England and Wales	30 000
Nathusius' Pipistrelle	Lower risk, least concern	Rare	Throughout the UK	Unknown (only recently found breeding in the UK)
Grey Long-eared	Lower risk, least concern	Rare	South coast of England and Isle of Wight	Uncertain, may be around 1000
Serotine	Lower risk, least concern	Vulnerable	Southern England and occasionally in Wales. Absent from Northern Ireland	15 000

Noctule	Lower risk, least concern	Vulnerable	Throughout England and Wales and south-west Scotland. Absent from Northern Ireland	30 000–50 000
Natterer's	Lower risk, least concern	Not Threatened	Throughout the UK, apart from northern Scotland	10 0000
Brown Long-eared	Lower risk, least concern	Not Threatened	Throughout the UK	150 000–200 000
Daubenton's	Lower risk, least concern	Not Threatened	Throughout the UK	90 000–160 000
Common Pipistrelle	Lower risk, least concern	Not Threatened	Throughout the UK	Estimated 2 million Common and Soprano
Soprano Pipistrelle	Lower risk, least concern	Not Threatened	Throughout the UK	Estimated 2 million Common and Soprano

[a] IUCN (2003)

[b] Bat Conservation Trust website: www.bct.org.uk

[c] Richardson (2000); Altringham (2003)

[d] Altringham (2003); Macdonald & Tattersall (2001)

no bats are present at the time of discovery, as they may become occupied at a later date.

25.1.2   Roost size

The sizes of roosts may be used to indicate the status of the species in the area. However, roost size as an indicator of species condition should be interpreted with caution, and is best used on a small scale to monitor the condition of a particular site for bats, rather than for assessing the population of bats in the wider area.

Bats found in a roost can be a small part of a larger colony, or they may constitute the entire colony. A study in Switzerland showed that during one summer a group of Daubenton's bats *Myotis daubentoni* used over 100 trees in an area of woodland less than one hectare in size (P. Richardson, pers. comm.). Each visit to the roost only provides a 'snapshot' of the colony at that time; in most cases, it will not be possible to locate all the roost sites used by the colony.

Regular (perhaps once per month during the summer, and over at least five years) monitoring of roost sizes within a site could provide a useful indication of the status of the species *within that particular site*. Roost monitoring surveys will be most informative when combined with investigative surveys to look for new roosts on the site, as reduced colony sizes could mean fewer bats on the site but could also mean that the bats have found somewhere else on site to roost.

The Joint Nature Conservation Committee have produced a formula for assessing population changes in a roost monitored annually over a number of years (JNCC Common Standards Monitoring Guidance for Mammals website):

[(Population mean for reporting period – population estimate at designation) × 100]/Population mean for reporting period.

The population estimate at designation is the first count made at the site (the 'baseline' population).

25.1.3   Hibernacula

All bats hibernate in winter, with most hiding in unknown locations. Known sites should be protected and monitored. The number of bats counted at the same time each year in a hibernation site can be used as an index, allowing changes to be detected over a number of years.

25.2   GENERAL METHODS

Table 25.1 outlines the general methods available for surveying and monitoring bats.

25.2.1   Exit counts at roost sites

Principles

Direct counts of bats emerging from roosts can be used to obtain comparable, quantitative results in spring, summer and autumn when bats are active. In summer, female bats aggregate in clusters to give birth and nurture their young. They may, however, alternate between roost sites, and may also split into smaller groups depending on the weather, food availability and colony size.

A number of national bat monitoring schemes are already in place involving roost counts, such as the ongoing annual National Bat Colony Survey (since 1978) for all species and the National Bat Monitoring Programme (established in 1996) for eight species. Details of these schemes in the UK can be obtained from the Bat Conservation Trust (BCT) (15 Cloisters House, 8 Battersea Park Road, London SW8 4BG, tel. 0207 627 2629).

Field methods
Counting techniques

The simplest method of counting bats is to wait outside the roost site and count the bats as they leave. Observers must not approach too closely, as this would cause disturbance to the bats, or obstruct their flight path as they emerge.

The time of emergence will vary depending on weather and recent foraging success, but surveyors should be in place outside the roost or potential roost at least 15 min before sunset (Walsh *et al.*, 2001).

It is recommended that surveyors have a bat detector with them, as this may allow identification of the species emerging. More than one species may occupy a roost and a bat detector should enable counts of each species. If it is not known which species are present inside the roost, it is recommended that the detector is set at 30 kHz, as this frequency should pick up the echolocation calls of all species resident in Britain, except for the Horseshoe bat species (see Section 25.2.5 for more details on the use of bat detectors). However, it is important to note that bats may not echolocate as they emerge, or they may do so more quietly than usual, so the surveyor should not rely on the detector alone to warn of emerging bats.

For large colonies, it is advisable to have a hand-held counter. Never shine a torch directly on the exit holes, as this may deter the bats from leaving the roost. Observers should keep as quiet as possible. If there is only one exit, this can be covered by one observer. If the bats emerge from more than one exit, there should be an observer stationed at each one. Bats may fly in and out of the roost during the count period, so it is possible to overestimate numbers if bats are counted more than once. Count both out and in and subtract the 'ins'.

Some judgement is required as to when to stop the emergence counts. According to the NBMP (2001) the survey should end when there is no further bat activity for 10 minutes (but the '10 minute' rule should not be applied until the main departure of bats has begun). If more than one species of bat is roosting in the structure, it is important to remember that some species emerge much earlier than others, and the decision to stop the survey should take this into account. Once it is completely dark, it is usually best to stop counting because it will no longer be possible to count bats accurately if they cannot be seen as they emerge. If the weather deteriorates, particularly if it starts to rain heavily, the count should be abandoned. If bats start swarming around the emergence point and it becomes too difficult to determine how many bats are leaving and returning to the roost, the count should stop.

More sophisticated methods of counting bats can be constructed by using infrared light beams positioned across the exit, connected to a datalogger, which counts the number of times the beam is broken. No off-the-shelf systems are available, but many different systems have been used in the past. If two adjacent beams are used, it is possible to distinguish between bats entering and leaving the roost sites, enabling more accurate counts. Bats returning to roosts cannot be reliably counted but automation allows counts to be recorded continuously through the night. It may be possible to compare entry and exit counts to establish whether bats are moving between roosts. A large volume of results can be obtained throughout the year. An advantage of automation is that the system records over many nights, although check counts by people are necessary for calibration. Spurious counts may be caused by other species such as birds or moths or even by raindrops. These systems can be expensive to construct and maintain (thousands of pounds) if produced by a commercial company, and great care must be taken when installing them. If the exit is disturbed too much, the bats may vacate the roost.

Emergent bats may be recorded on video, from which accurate counts can be made. Suitable cameras can be expensive, but they have the advantage of creating a permanent record, which can be analysed in detail.

Survey times

To obtain a reasonably accurate estimate of the number of bats using a roost, it is necessary to make several counts including the birth period but before flight of juveniles. Juvenile bats emerge over a 3 week period, although the precise dates will vary depending upon weather conditions and also weather patterns earlier in the year. A generally accepted methodology is to make three counts, five days to a week apart, in June (e.g. National Bat Colony Survey, Countryside Council for Wales (CCW) Lesser Horseshoe Bat Monitoring Programme). It is pointless attempting counts in periods of bad weather, when bats may not emerge at all. Counts are best done on warm, windless nights.

Observers should be aware of the risks of working at night, especially in remote areas, and should preferably work in pairs and carry mobile phones (if reception is possible) or two-way radios. Appendix 6 lists the field equipment required for surveying bats by exit counts.

Data analysis and interpretation

Analysis of counts is straightforward. The maximum count can be used to obtain an estimate of the number of bats using a roost for comparison with the following year. If surveys (either manual or automated) have been undertaken regularly, numbers can be plotted against time to give an indication of changes in use by bats. Care should be taken when interpreting variation of counts in one season; numbers may fluctuate on account of many factors such as weather, food, roost availability and disturbance. Therefore, if trends are to be detected, several counts are needed per site and many sites should be covered simultaneously over a wide area. This method may not be appropriate for some highly mobile species (e.g. Natterer's Bat *Myotis nattereri*).

If only one roost site is known and monitored for a particular colony, care should be taken when identifying possible trends. Bats often move between roosts; it is feasible that not all the bats from a colony might use a monitored roost site in one year. This could be interpreted as a population crash, whereas the colony might simply have moved to another unknown site. In Scotland there is a tendency for nursery clusters to be more faithful to one roost than is the case in lowland England.

However, comparisons of roost counts are the only quantitative method of obtaining estimates of population size and thus monitoring population trends; as such they form a part of most bat monitoring programmes.

25.2.2   Swarming counts

Principles

Bats (sometimes of several species) will swarm together, often in large numbers, around the entrance to roosts and hibernation sites. Bats will swarm outside hibernation sites as early as August, and this behaviour can be observed through to November. Swarming usually starts during the hour before sunrise. Late summer to autumn is the bat mating period, and it is thought that swarming activity at this time of year may be related to mating behaviour.

Surveying at dawn can be useful for species such as Natterer's Bat, which leave the roost after dark, and often quietly, meaning that it can be possible to miss them on emergence surveys. Dawn surveys may also be useful for detecting tree roosts, as it may be difficult to tell from which tree bats are emerging as it becomes dark; swarming bats returning to a roost are more visible.

Field methods

Walking through potentially suitable bat habitat, for example along rides in woodland, one hour before dawn with a bat detector can locate bats swarming outside a roost entrance. Swarming activity is thought to occur throughout the summer, with the peak in swarming around hibernation sites occurring in September.

During the day, walk through the site and identify potential roosts, by looking for trees with suitable cavities and holes, or buildings with access points. Plan a transect route that is safe to walk just before sunrise. Start the transect one hour before sunrise and walk slowly around the transect route with a bat detector set at 30 kHz. As with evening emergence, different species return to their roosts at different times. Long-eared bats return earliest and noctules latest. If bats are found swarming, note the location of the structure (a GPS handset may be useful for recording a grid reference).

Appendix 6 summarises the necessary field equipment.

Data analysis and interpretation

Dawn swarming surveys are useful primarily for locating roosts and hibernacula and would be useful at the start of a monitoring programme to try to maximise the number of known sites.

25.2.3   Hibernation counts

Principles

Bats require different roosts seasonally; they may hibernate in sites that are not used in summer. If bats are to be adequately protected and monitored, it is necessary to know the locations of hibernation sites as well as of nursery and other roosts. However, hibernation sites are frequently difficult to locate and survey adequately because of the underground nature of many suitable sites and because of the preference of many bats for hibernating in small crevices.

Because relatively few hibernating bats are found each year, hibernation counts do not generally provide a reliable index of bat abundance in an area, but monitoring surveys are valuable for gaining or retaining the protection of sites and for research into the winter requirements of bats. Long-term monitoring may be useful as a general indicator of how local populations of bats are faring, but is more reliably used for checking that a site remains suitable for the bats that do use it.

The exception to this is the Horseshoe bats: more hibernation sites for these two species (*Rhinopholus ferremequinem* and *R. hipposiderus*) are known, relative to the overall estimated population size, and therefore monitoring of Horseshoe bat hibernacula contributes greatly to information about the overall status of these species.

The National Bat Monitoring Programme produces standard survey forms for hibernation counts. These can be obtained from the BCT (see Section 25.2.1 for contact details).

A licence is required to enter known bat roosts.

Field methods

Hibernation sites should be surveyed no more than once per month, and no more than three times per winter. More frequent disturbance risks awakening bats too often, which causes excessive energy loss and reduces survival. The key months for hibernation surveys are December, January and February.

Identification skills are particularly important when surveying hibernacula, especially when only part of one bat is visible. Several species may be hibernating in one site. Torchlight should not be shone directly on to bats, particularly from close range. All crevices and cracks should be examined, as bats will often hibernate in these. Total numbers per species should be recorded, with notes on the previous month's weather (a week or two of very cold weather results in many bats seeking caves and mines). It is generally a good idea to record temperature both inside and outside the site; it can also be useful to record humidity inside the hibernacula, as this is an important factor influencing the suitability of hibernation sites.

Survey methodology should give due regard to the size and safety of the site being monitored. Small, safe sites can reasonably be surveyed by a single worker. Potentially dangerous sites such as large abandoned mines should be surveyed by a team of people experienced in underground work and with appropriate safety equipment (see British Caving Council guidelines).

Bats may move between hibernation sites depending principally on temperature. Counts per site should be on the same date and involve the same method and search effort each winter for monitoring purposes. One person should be the leader for individual sites. The field equipment required for surveying and monitoring bats by hibernation counts is listed in Appendix 6.

For EIA studies, a single season of fieldwork is usually feasible, recording presence and distribution of species across the site.

Data analysis and interpretation

Caution should be made when identifying trends: the number of bats using a particular site will vary according to seasonal temperature, type of site, etc. A low count in a mild winter does not necessarily mean a reduction in the number of bats, but may indicate that they do not use that roost when the external temperature is high.

In some sites without cracks where bats may hide, it is possible to make accurate counts of all bats hibernating at the time of the survey. If there are cracks, the accuracy of the count will be considerably affected. As few as 3–8% of bats actually present may be counted (Stebbings, 1992).

For the Horseshoe bats, which hang out when roosting and hibernating, it is easier to make more accurate counts of total number of species than it is for those such as the *Myotis* bats, which often hibernate tucked away in crevices.

25.2.4   Counts in bat boxes

Principles

Bat roost boxes are usually fixed to trees to increase the roost resource in an area, especially in plantation forestry. They can form part of a regular monitoring programme if schemes are maintained for long periods and bats are counted at regular intervals. They are seldom used in EIA studies. This method will not yield quantitative evidence on species abundance in an area, but will provide a qualitative index of abundance per species per site.

They can be very useful for revealing the presence of 'quiet' species not usually heard on the bat detector, particularly Bechstein's Bat *Myotis bechsteinii*, and also species that are under-recorded because they may be confused with other species, such as Barbastelles *Barbastella barbastellus*.

If there are no bat boxes *in situ*, they can be installed as part of a long-term monitoring programme. See Stebbings & Walsh (1991) for details of construction and siting of bat boxes.

Bat boxes need regular maintenance. If meaningful results are to be gathered, monitoring of bat boxes must be a long-term undertaking (at least 15–20 years). In order to ensure that results are not biased, boxes should be maintained or replaced in a staggered rotation, rather than replacing all boxes in any one year.

Because bat boxes are known roost sites, a licence is needed to disturb them once occupancy has been confirmed, although the Bat Conservation Trust recommends that for large projects in public places, a licence should be obtained before inspection.

Field methods

Bat boxes are best visited in the day. Two visits per year are recommended: the first in May and the second in September. Boxes should not be disturbed from June to late August while births and weaning occur. The timing of visits per site should be consistent from year to year. A ladder will be necessary to gain access to each box. For safety purposes, surveyors should work in pairs.

When inspecting boxes, they must be opened cautiously because bats may be hanging on the lid or door. If practicable, check whether bats are present by using a torch to look through the entrance slit. In hot weather, bats may be highly active and often fly out of the entrance slit unless a hand or cloth is placed over the opening. In most cases, the species and numbers of bats should be recorded, with age assessment, especially in an autumn survey.

Bats can be taken out of boxes and placed in a cloth bag to calm the bat while the surveyor climbs down off the ladder. The lid should be replaced and, after identification, active bats must be released to fly off. If the animals are torpid, they should be placed carefully at the entrance slit and allowed to crawl up into the box. This prevents the possibility of legs or wings becoming trapped, which may cause the accidental death of some bats. The field equipment required for surveying and monitoring bats in bat boxes is summarised in Appendix 6.

Data analysis and interpretation

The number of bats in bat boxes may vary considerably from day to day. When bats are mating (late August–October), male bats often hold territories related to specific boxes. At other seasons, numbers will fluctuate depending on temperature and foraging needs. Bat box schemes can not only provide results on which species are present in the area, but will show changes due to season and stage of forest cropping. An index of population size will be gained as well as relative change with time.

Because colonies occupy territories measured in many square kilometres, information from one scheme should be aggregated.

25.2.5   Transects

Principles

Transects can be used to obtain a qualitative indication of bat species living, commuting or foraging in specific habitats. It is not possible to estimate abundance with any certainty because some bats may be recorded several times and others not detected at all.

Regular transect surveys with a bat detector can:

- provide an index of relative foraging activity;
- estimate minimum species diversity in an area;
- identify key habitats for commuting and foraging;
- indicate where roosts are located.

The principles of standard transect methods are considered in Sections 10.4.–10.5. Transects for bat surveys will not necessarily conform to the ideal theoretical transect: considerations of safety and ease of access to sites when working after dark often have to take precedence over scientific rigour. In any case, it is usually desirable to plan the transect route along specific habitats in the survey area. This should increase the number of species detected and enable identification of key habitats for bats. The National Bat Monitoring Programme (co-ordinated by the BCT) has a standard survey sheet and methodology for several bat species designed to produce unbiased results that can be pooled from surveys taken throughout the country. These can be obtained from the BCT (see Section 25.2.1 for contact details) but may not be the most preferable way of conducting a bat transect survey for monitoring or evaluating particular sites. This section aims to describe how to carry out a survey designed to maximise the number of species detected and identify and monitor the most important habitats present.

Field methods

A transect can be set up anywhere. It may be desirable to set up transect lines through known bat foraging areas. Alternatively, if the area has not been surveyed for bats before, a walk along a fixed route around the site can be used. Whatever method is used to select locations, transects should be standardised between visits in the same year, and between years. It is generally common practice to use permanent transects rather than temporary ones; the results obtained are usually so variable that introducing other sources of variation would be undesirable. For EIA studies, a series of transects through a site should be established, the number being dependent on site size and habitat composition.

Bat detectors translate the ultrasonic echolocation calls of bats into frequencies that humans can hear. Different species have recognisable peak frequencies at which the call is loudest. For Greater Horseshoe Bats the peak is at around 82 kHz and for Lesser Horseshoes around 102 kHz, whereas for the three Pipistrelle species the peak frequencies

are 39, 45 and 55 kHz. Natterer's Bat may extend as high as 105 kHz, although the peak frequency is around 50 kHz. Tuning the detector through different frequencies until the call is at its loudest is the principle behind finding the bat's peak frequency. Russ (1999) provides a useful introduction to the principles of echolocation and the characteristics of the calls of British bats. With some practice at call recognition, bat detectors can be very useful tools for bat identification at night. There are several different kinds of detector, varying greatly in price. Heterodyne detectors are the simplest, e.g. the Batbox III (Stag Electronics). Some bat detectors such as the Pettersson have, in addition to a standard heterodyne detector, a time-expansion function, which records calls and plays them back at a much slower speed. Most bat detectors have sockets for recording devices to enable calls to be recorded for later comparison with pre-recorded bat calls (e.g. Bat Detective, by Briggs & King, available from Stag Electronics) or (if time-expanded calls are recorded) sonograms can be produced by using computer software (e.g. BatSound) which enable detailed analysis of the call structure. The BCT maintain a database on bat detector equipment.

Walking a transect with a bat detector and recording contacts (e.g. passes or feeding buzzes) will provide an index of bat commuting or foraging activity. It is not possible to make accurate counts, especially if several bats are flying together, because it is not possible to distinguish calls from different bats of the same species. Heterodyne detectors translate only one frequency at a time, so that only some bats can be detected at one time. Time-expansion detectors scan on all frequencies at once. For general surveys, not targeted at any particular species, the optimum frequency at which to set the detector is 30 kHz, as this should pick up the calls of most of the bats found in Britain. For surveys targeted at specific species, the frequency should be tuned accordingly.

Prior to commencing the survey, notes should be taken about the weather. Temperature and percentage cloud cover should be noted, along with information about the wind speed and rain. The phase of the moon is also useful to record.

Surveys should commence at sunset. The route should be walked at a slow walking pace, kept as constant throughout the survey as possible.

When a bat is heard, the following information should be recorded.

- The species of bat.
- If a time-expansion detector is being used, all passes should be recorded, for post-survey analysis.
- The location of the surveyors when the bat was heard.
- If the bat was observed, the direction of its flight should be noted.
- The time the bat was heard.
- If feeding activity or social calls are heard, these should be noted.
- Any other relevant information, in particular whether the bat sounded distant; any information about the habitat that could alter the bat's echolocation should also be recorded to inform the species analysis.

The transect survey may be interrupted to monitor bat activity along potential flightlines such as mature hedgerows and watercourses. These can be important habitat features for bats, both as foraging habitat and as a sheltered commuting route. It may be best to stand next to the habitat at sunset and count the number of bat passes along it, where possible noting the direction of flight.

Whichever transect method is used, surveyors should be aware of the dangers of working at night, and, preferably, should work in pairs with mobile phones or two-way radios. The field equipment required for surveying and monitoring bats by using transects is outlined in Appendix 6.

Data analysis and interpretation

Results obtained by using transects are usually too variable to be analysed to give quantitative estimates of abundance.

Transects enable determination of species presence and can show the relative amount of bat activity for a particular transect during the course of one season. Plotting numbers of bats against date will give an indication of how foraging patterns vary within one year, which may be correlated to environmental variables such as temperature or insect abundance in different habitats throughout the season.

High bat activity in an area around sunset may suggest that roost sites are nearby. Observations of the direction of bats can be used to make estimates regarding where they may be roosting. Using a map of the wider area could pinpoint potential roost sites, which could then be investigated further.

Standing next to linear habitat features and counting bats can provide a very useful contribution to building a picture of how bats are using the site.

25.2.6   Torch counts

For this method, a powerful hand-held light is used to illuminate a transect line, and the number of bat passes through the beam is recorded, usually with a hand-held counter. The observer in this case can be static, rather than actively walking along the transect line. This method works best for surveying over large areas of open water.

Daubenton's Bat is often surveyed by shining a torch at low level across water and recording passes. In this case, the mode of flight (very close to the water surface) should be sufficient to allow identification by experienced observers (note: several species feed low over water on occasions). Otherwise, a bat detector should be used to aid identification of species.

25.2.7   Assessing bats by field signs

Principles

Fieldcraft techniques can establish that a site is being, or has been, used by bats, even if there are no bats present or visible at the time of survey. Although it is not possible to gain a precise quantitative estimate of abundance from these methods, they are useful for identifying roosts and judging their importance. They can also be used to build up a picture of patterns of bat distribution over an area and judge their importance, and to obtain insights into historic occupancy where bats are no longer present. It takes experience to be able to assess accurately the use of a site by bats from field signs alone. However, it is possible to recognise some signs such as bat droppings with only a brief period of training. Recognising field signs can be very important when looking for bats in buildings and other artificial structures, and can be carried out in all seasons. Because bat roosts are protected, even when bats are absent, indirect methods for determining whether bats are using a site can be very important. For further information refer to *The Batworkers' Manual* (Mitchell-Jones & McLeish, 1999).

Field methods
Droppings and remains

The presence of bat droppings shows that a site has been used by bats. Large numbers of droppings are a good indicator of a sizeable colony. Skilled observers can identify species and assess colony size. Remains of dead bats allow critical identification.

Lofts should be examined, particularly beneath the apex, for bat droppings. If surveying caves, bats tend to favour domes in the cave roof; look on the ground underneath these for droppings. Use a torch to examine cracks and crevices for droppings. It is always worthwhile examining cobwebs if any are present, since these will trap droppings, often in more easily visible locations.

Urine and oil stains

Staining from bat urine can often be seen on walls. Again this is an indication of presence or visits by bats. Similarly, oils from bat fur will stain walls and rocks in places that bats have frequently roosted in or crawled over.

Scratch marks

In some caves where large bat populations were once present, large areas of rock have been worn away on the cave roof where generations of bats have roosted. Scratches from their claws can sometimes be seen in other places where they have been roosting. Experienced and skilled observers are necessary both to identify and to interpret the signs. Appendix 6 lists the field equipment necessary for surveying and monitoring bats by using field signs.

Buildings can be surveyed at any time of the year to determine whether they are bat roosts. In most cases the status of the roost with respect to species and abundance can also be determined, but further surveys may be required at a different time of the year to do this properly.

The exterior of the building should be examined first for places that would give bats access into the roof space and also for features of the building that would provide bats with a suitable place to roost. These should be noted on a sketch of the building. Binoculars, torch and a ladder should be used to facilitate this. The interior of the building should then be searched. The extent of the search will depend on the type of building, but if there is an accessible and safe roof space this should be checked. The building should be searched for bats and evidence of bats (droppings and feeding remains). Angled mirrors and/or an endoscope are useful for searching in crevices. They are particularly useful for surveys of timber-framed barns, where the mortise joints can be difficult to look into. Pay attention to areas around the possible access points observed from the outside. If the building has a chimney, search around it in the roof space and also look on the floor below the ridge beam for droppings.

Data analysis and interpretation

Results from surveys such as these are usually only valid for establishing presence–absence and relative colony size.

If dead bats are found, these can be identified and their age and condition assessed. This may enable inferences to be drawn concerning bat use of the site. For example, finding a dead baby bat can be taken as reasonable proof that the site was used as a nursery roost.

Droppings can often be identified to species; with practice, the age of droppings can be estimated to give an indication of when the site was last used, or for how long it has been used. With experience it is possible to estimate the numbers of bats using a roost from the quantity of droppings.

25.2.8   Radiotracking

Principles
Radiotracking is one of the best ways to find new bat roosts and learn more about foraging

requirements. Bats from a known roost can be tracked to determine how far they go to forage and what route they take, and this can lead to the discovery of other roosts used by the tagged bat. Foraging bats away from roosts can be caught and tagged and followed back to their roost to discover new roosting areas. However, specialist training and expensive equipment is required.

Field methods

Field methods for radiotracking are not discussed in detail here because of the specialist training and licence required. Bats are caught near a known roost and a radio transmitter is attached to each bat. They are then tracked by a team of surveyors and the bats' movements are recorded on a map.

Data analysis and interpretation

This type of survey can produce information about the area of habitat that bats utilise for roosting and foraging. Following a bat during the course of an evening can reveal how the landscape influences (or not) their flight paths and perhaps how they respond to changes in the weather during an evening. When the maximum life of the radio tag is utilised (usually 7–10 days) it may be possible to investigate how often bats are switching roosts. Tagging female bats can be more useful as they may lead researchers to maternity roosts (although there are serious issues with avoiding tagging bats that are lactating, and this is another reason why this should only be carried out with well-trained researchers).

25.3   BAT CONSERVATION EVALUATION CRITERIA

25.3.1   Key evaluation considerations

There are currently sixteen species of bat confirmed as resident in the UK. These exhibit a range of roosting preferences, diets and foraging and social behaviours. Our knowledge of the different species varies greatly. For example, the range and foraging and roosting preferences of Greater Horseshoe Bats are relatively well understood, but in the case of the Barbastelle Bat, although it is believed to be one of the UK's rarest bats, recent

advances in technology have meant that more roosts are being found, and more Barbastelles are being identified from bat detector recordings, leading researchers to believe that it is more common than previously thought. Its UK population size is still unknown and relatively few roosts are known. Other species, notoriously those belonging to the *Myotis* genus, can be very difficult to distinguish from each other, with Whiskered *M. mystacinus* and Brandt's Bats *M. brandtii* very difficult to tell apart, even in the hand.

In 2001, a female Greater Mouse-eared Bat *Myotis myotis* was found, and in 2002 a young male Greater Mouse-eared Bat was discovered in Sussex. The species was previously thought to be extinct in the UK; further surveys are being conducted to determine whether or not there may still be a small population in the UK.

Given the huge variation in our knowledge of different species, and also the current lack of understanding as to how bats form colonies, how colonies divide into different roost sites, when and why bats change roosts and where bats hibernate, it can be very difficult to evaluate sites for their importance for bats.

The SSSI designation guidelines can be useful for assessing the national importance of the site, but these relate to roosts and hibernacula, and deciding how important a site is as foraging or commuting habitat is especially difficult. A knowledge of the status of bats in the area local to the site is currently one of the best ways to evaluate how important the site is on a local or regional level. Local BAPs are also worth consulting.

25.3.2   Protection status in the UK and EU

All British bats are included on Annex IV of the EU Habitats Directive, with some rarer species also listed in Annex II. All British bats are listed on Schedule 2 of the Habitats Regulations as European Protected Species. All British bats are also listed on Appendix II of the Bern Convention, except the Common Pipistrelle which is on Appendix III. The Bern Convention has been translated into domestic legislation through the Wildlife & Countryside Act 1981.

All British bat species are fully protected under Schedule 5 of the Wildlife & Countryside Act 1981 (as amended) and the Conservation (Natural Habitats & c.) Regulations 1994 (as amended). Taken together, these make it an offence to:

- intentionally (or recklessly, in Scotland) kill, injure, take or possess these animals;
- intentionally or recklessly damage, destroy, obstruct access to any structure or place used by a scheduled animal for shelter or protection, or disturb any animal occupying such a structure or place;
- sell, offer for sale, possess or transport for the purpose of sale (live or dead animal, part or derivative) or advertise for buying or selling these animals.

The Wildlife & Countryside Act does not extend to Northern Ireland, the Channel Islands or the Isle of Man. All bat species are fully protected on Schedule 5 and 7 of the Wildlife (Northern Ireland) Order 1985.

In addition, Greater Horseshoe, Lesser Horseshoe, Barbastelle and Bechstein's Bats are also listed on Annex II of the EU Habitats Directive, which effectively requires that the best of these species' known roosting and foraging sites be designated as Special Areas of Conservation (SACs).

From the Convention on the Conservation of Migratory Species of Wild Animals (Bonn Convention) came the Agreement on the Conservation of Bats in Europe, in 1994. The Agreement recognises that endangered migratory species can be properly protected only if activities are carried out over the entire migratory range of the species. Its main provisions are to: restrict the killing or capture of bats; protect key bat habitats; co-ordinate relevant research; and increase public awareness of bat conservation. The Eurobats secretariat was set up to address some of these provisions and each year it produces national reports on the implementation of the Agreement on the Conservation of Bats in Europe. These are downloadable from the Eurobats website.

The following species of bat are UK BAP Priority species.

- Barbastelle (*Barbastella barbastellus*)
- Bechstein's (*Myotis bechsteinii*)
- Common Pipistrelle (*Pipistrellus pipistrellus*)
- Soprano Pipistrelle (*Pipistrellus pygmaeus*)
- Greater Horseshoe (*Rhinolophus ferrumequinum*)
- Lesser Horseshoe (*Rhinolophus hipposideros*)
- Greater Mouse-eared (*Myotis myotis*)

The current action plan objectives and targets for Barbastelle and Bechstein's are:

- Maintain the known range
- Maintain the size of the known populations
- Increase the total population sizes of the species in the UK

The current action plan objectives and targets for Common Pipistrelle and Soprano Pipistrelle are:

- Maintain the existing population size
- Maintain the existing geographical range
- Restore population sizes to pre-1970 numbers

The current action plan objectives and targets for Greater Horseshoes are:

- Maintain all existing maternity roosts and associated hibernation sites
- Increase current population by 25% by 2010

The current action plan objectives and targets for Lesser Horseshoes are:

- Maintain the current range
- Maintain the size of current populations
- Expand current geographical range of the population

The current action plan objectives and targets for Greater Mouse-eared Bat are:

- Maintain any extant populations discovered in the UK
- Enhance any extant populations discovered in the UK

25.3.3 Conservation status in the UK

All British bats have been evaluated according to the IUCN Red List Categories and Criteria (IUCN, 2003). The Bat Conservation Trust has produced a UK Conservation Status for all bats in Britain. These have been summarised in Table 25.2 along with current understanding of the species' distribution and estimated population size.

25.3.4   Site designation criteria

National evaluation

Selection criteria for nationally important sites for bats are listed in the NCC *Guidelines* (1989, revised 1995):

- Greater Horseshoe: all main breeding roosts and all winter roosts containing 50 or more adult bats or 20% of local small 'edge' sub-populations.
- Lesser Horseshoe: all breeding roosts containing 100 or more adult bats and all winter roosts containing 50 or more bats should be considered for selection.
- Barbastelle, Bechstein's and Grey Long-eared Bats: all traditional breeding roosts should be considered for selection if found. Traditional roosts are those which have been used by bats over a number of years. The precise number of years of roost occupation required varies and is judged on a case-by-case basis.
- Natterer's, Daubenton's, Whiskered, Brandt's, Serotine, Noctule and Leisler's: exceptionally large colonies with a long history of use at a particular site may trigger the notification of a site for these species, but in most cases a roost will not result in SSSI designation and protection should rely on Section 9 of the Wildlife & Countryside Act, 1981.
- Pipistrelle and Brown Long-eared: protection should rely on Section 9 of the Wildlife & Countryside Act, 1981.
- Mixed hibernation assemblages of all bat species: all hibernacula containing (a) four or more species and 50 or more individuals, (b) three species and 100 or more individuals or (c) two species and 150 or more individuals should be selected. In some parts of Britain large sites are unknown, so in these areas one hibernaculum per Area of Search containing 30 or more bats of two or more species may be considered for selection.

Other than the SSSI designations for some species of bat, there is no standard methodology for evaluating areas for their importance for bats.

County/regional evaluation

It may be possible to evaluate the species diversity of a site by comparing the minimum number of species recorded on the site to the total number of species recorded for the county. Most counties have a bat group who collate bat records for the county. The *Bat Group Contacts* list is available from the Bat Conservation Trust (2001).

Another source of information for current knowledge regarding species distribution is the *Distribution Atlas* by Richardson (2000). Reference to this document, as well as county bat group records, can inform site evaluation for bats because the presence of a species of bat previously unrecorded in the county or where records are scarce in the area should increase the value given to the site.

Local BAPs are also important when trying to understand the importance of the site for bats. For example, the Serotine is a local BAP species in Kent, because this county is thought to be a stronghold for the species in the UK; therefore, although Serotines are not rare in Kent, their presence on a site in Kent is important.

Local evaluation

When evaluating a site for its importance for bats, consideration of specific habitats is important. Areas that are well-used by bats for foraging, particularly if more than two or three species are recorded, may be considered important for local populations of bats, especially if the habitat type is scarce in the area.

Linear habitats used for navigation, sheltered commuting and foraging that have been recorded as being well-used by bats may be incorporated in some local plans as 'wildlife corridors'. Small maternity roosts and hibernation sites that do not qualify for SSSI designation may be locally important.

Knowledge of the status of bats in the local area is very important, as is experience. Factors to consider when evaluating a site are:

- Number of species recorded
- Levels of bat activity

- The nature of the survey records (for example: roost, flightline, foraging area) and their relative availability in the surrounding area
- The overall 'picture' of the site obtained from the surveys; the way different bat habitats link together across the site may influence their perceived importance. For example, hedgerows linking roost sites to foraging areas are a key habitat for the bats in the roost

The Joint Nature Conservation Committee have produced Common Standards Monitoring Guidance for Mammals (available online) which gives guidance on assessing and monitoring the condition of designated sites. Sites that support bats are well covered in this document, which describes targets for conditions of maternity roosts and hibernation sites and methods for how to assess the condition of the sites.

Other mammals

There is a wide variety of methods for surveying and monitoring mammal species. Given that mammal species range in size from mice to whales, the techniques will vary considerably from one species to the next. Methods can be divided into indirect methods (Sections 26.3.1–26.3.5), which involve counting signs of presence rather than the animals themselves, and direct methods (Sections 26.4.1–26.4.4).

26.1 ATTRIBUTES FOR ASSESSING CONDITION

26.1.1 Population size

Many mammal species are secretive and make effective use of cover; this makes direct counts, even of small sample populations, impossible. However, larger mammals, such as Red Deer *Cervus elaphus* occupying open ranges, can be effectively counted by direct counts. Estimates of population size for the majority of small and medium-sized mammals depend on indirect methods, such as indices of evidence left by mammals or trapping. Population reconstructions can be made from knowledge of the age at death of animals dying naturally or being culled, if a large proportion of the dead animals are available.

26.1.2 Breeding success and condition

Breeding success is particularly time-consuming to evaluate in mammals as it requires location of a sample of breeding sites and direct observation of young at these sites. Observer bias is also an important issue here as disturbance around a breeding site may attract predators.

Alternatively, breeding status can be evaluated by examining trapped females. In most mammals, from large to small, lactation is easily diagnosed and breeding condition can be established from examining the vulva, or taking vaginal smears for signs of oestrus. Although this technique does not give direct data on breeding success, it can provide an assessment of the health of a population.

If dead animals are available (e.g. from deer or Fox *Vulpes vulpes* culls), then post-mortem examination can provide sound data on reproductive condition, including counts of corpora lutea in the ovary, foetuses, and evidence of milk in the mammary glands. Breeding success can be established in populations that are regularly culled, if the cull is standardised between years and the majority of animals are recovered. Kills can be aged to produce, over a number of years, a minimum number of animals born in each year.

26.1.3 Survival and mortality

Estimates of survival and mortality can be made from mortality data related to the age of individuals (see below), or by mark–recapture studies. The survival of individually marked animals from one trapping occasion to the next can be estimated. Unless dead animals are found, it is not usually possible to distinguish between mortality and emigration. Similarly, immigration and births can be easily confused, unless it is certain that the population is isolated (i.e. 'closed').

26.2 GENERAL METHODS

Table 26.1 summarises all the methods available for surveying and monitoring mammals.

Table 26.1. *Methods for surveying and monitoring mammals*

	Recommended species group	Population size data	Other attributes	Efficiency	Precision	Bias	Expertise required	Advantages	Disadvantages
Counting breeding sites or nests	Carnivores Rodents Lagomorphs	Presence Index Estimate	Presence of young from food signs	Can be time-consuming if large areas are searched	Low	Underestimate	Identification	Relatively good for species with obvious sites	Surveys may increase predation pressure through signs of disturbance near sites
Faecal pellet counts	Carnivores Ungulates Lagomorphs Rodents	Presence Index Estimate	Distribution	Can be used to provide a reliable population estimate for some species (e.g. deer, Rabbits)	Reasonable	Can attribute confidence limits to estimates	Identification	A useful method for elusive species Can identify individuals to investigate population structure through DNA analysis	Related species may have similar or indistinguishable droppings
Feeding signs	Carnivores, Ungulates Rodents Lagomorphs Insectivores	Presence Index	Distribution	Can provide a quick and easy measurement, but only gives a relative index	Low	Level of food plant damage depends on abundance of other foods Activity is related to season	Identification of signs and food species	Simple methodology	Does not estimate numbers

Table 26.1 (*cont.*)

	Recommended species group	Population size data	Other attributes	Efficiency	Precision	Bias	Expertise required	Advantages	Disadvantages
Bait marking	Carnivores	Presence	Distribution	Can be used to establish territory boundaries and home ranges	Reasonable	Territory marking is dependent on season	Identification of latrines	Simple methodology	Only establishes territory boundaries or home ranges Labour-intensive
Tracks	Carnivores Ungulates Rodents Lagomorphs Insectivores	Presence Index	Distribution	Can provide a quick and easy measurement but only gives a relative index	Low	Activity is related to season	Identification of signs	Simple methodology Good for elusive species	Does not estimate numbers Difficult to distinguish some species
Hair tubes/ catchers	Carnivores Rodents Insectivores	Presence	Activity within a site	Requires low collection effort, but identification may be time-consuming	Low	Some species leave more hair than others and are more mobile	Hair analysis, identification	Simple methodology Less invasive than trapping Can be used to examine population structure through DNA analysis	Cannot be used to estimate numbers Closely related species may be difficult to distinguish
Road kills	Carnivores Insectivores Rodents Lagomorphs	Presence	Age structure Health Sex ratio	Low	Low	Some species more prone to traffic accidents	Identification	Data can be gained on health, age and physiology	High frequency of surveys is required

Method	Taxa	Type	Information	Good for	Reasonable	Underestimate	Skills	Advantages	Disadvantages
Timed searches	Ungulates	Presence; Index; Estimate; Can provide accurate counts of ungulates over small areas	Information on distribution and sex and age ratio	Good for conspicuous species in large areas	Reasonable	Underestimate and errors relating to inaccurate mapping of sites	Identification	Aerial counts can be carried out quickly; provides a count of all individuals, enabling coverage of a large area	Aerial counts are often expensive; not effective in forested areas
Transects	Ungulates; Lagomorphs; Sometimes rodents and carnivores	Presence; Index; Estimate	Sex ratio	Can be time-consuming; Good for conspicuous species	Low	Under-estimate, may be unrepresentative of habitat	Identification	Easiest method for surveying areas of less than 1000 km^2	Individuals likely to be missed at high densities or in thick vegetation
Point counts	Rodents; Ungulates; Lagomorphs	Presence; Index; Estimate	Sex ratio	Good for conspicuous species	Low	Detectability declines with distance from the observer	Identification	Efficient and require less effort than transect counts	Counts of small areas may be unrepresentative; vegetation cover affects detectability
Live trapping	Rodents; Lagomorphs; Insectivores; Carnivores; Ungulates	Presence; Index; Estimate	Sex ratio; Population structure; Age ratio	Labour-intensive: traps must be checked a minimum of every 4 hours for insectivores, especially shrews	Good (if traps are in place long enough)	Some individuals or species are more 'trap-happy' than others; weather conditions also affect trappability	Identification; Handling; Construction	A variety of data can be collected from captured individuals	Traps can be expensive, particularly for larger animals, and time-consuming when animals occur at low densities

Table 26.1 (cont.)

	Recommended species group	Population size data	Other attributes	Efficiency	Precision	Bias	Expertise required	Advantages	Disadvantages
Mark–recapture	Rodents Lagomorphs Insectivores Carnivores Ungulates	Estimate	Survival Emigration Immigration Recruitment Population structure	Requires several trapping occasions and data analysis can be time-consuming	Good if assumptions are met and trapping effort is sufficient	Low if correct model is applied	Identification Handling Construction Data analysis	Provides most accurate, unbiased results	Requires several trapping occasions Analysis can be complex Not appropriate if species have large home ranges or are strongly territorial
Mortality data methods (e.g. game bag records)	Lagomorphs Ungulates Carnivores	Estimate	Age ratio Sex ratio Population structure	Quality of information varies between species and sites	Variable, depending upon methods and available data	Under-estimate, especially when dependent on natural mortality searches	Identification Data analysis	Low costs; data are readily available	Numbers vary owing to changes in land use, activity of gamekeepers and fluctuations in the population, so assumptions are often violated

26.3   INDIRECT METHODS

26.3.1   Counting breeding sites

Principles

Counts of breeding sites are useful for species with obvious nests or burrows such as Badger *Meles meles*, Rabbit *Oryctolagus cuniculus*, Fox, and squirrels. Artificial nest boxes have also been used to survey the presence and monitor the distribution of Red Squirrel *Sciurus vulgaris* and Dormouse *Muscardinus avellanarius*. Small mammal burrows can be examined for activity. However, other survey methods (discussed below) are more reliable.

Breeding site counts can be used to give an indication of population size by calibrating against the number of individuals present, although this requires the additional use of a direct monitoring method as outlined below.

Field methods

An area must be searched systematically for all nest sites. It is necessary to record the activity of a breeding site, as some may be disused. If the average number of individuals using each breeding site can be determined independently then this can be converted into a density estimate, provided that it is possible to estimate the total range of the population. Otherwise, counts of breeding sites can only provide a measure of presence–absence. If counts from different sites are to be compared, survey methodology must be standardised to ensure that the same area is searched at each location with the same search effort.

Trained dogs can be used to aid location of nest sites for some species, such as mustelids. Care must be taken not to disturb individuals at a site or inadvertently increase predation levels by leaving unnecessary tracks or disturbed vegetation. Outside the breeding season, burrows and nests can still be recorded for some species, although activity may be reduced, making accurate identification more difficult. Rabbit burrows, for instance, can be counted in late winter; 1 km line transects are recommended (Macdonald *et al.*, 1998). The number of burrows in use is linearly related to the number of Rabbits. This method can also be used in conjunction with faecal counts.

A standardised search for Badger setts, such as that outlined in the national survey undertaken by Cresswell *et al.* (1990), is the methodology most commonly used for surveying Badgers and can provide a good indication of Badger density (see also Section 26.5).

Foxes are known to commonly use more than one den at a time, making estimates of population size impossible from earth counts.

Nests of some mammal species, such as those of squirrels and Hedgehog *Erinaceus europaeus* can be used to monitor species presence. Hedgehog nests are often difficult to find but are most easily recorded in late winter at ground level in sheltered cavities. Great care is necessary not to disturb the insulation of hibernation sites, and it is perhaps safest to leave this work until the weather conditions suggest the end of hibernation. At present, records for these two species can only provide presence–absence estimates.

Nest boxes set up in sites known to hold Red Squirrel populations or Dormice can be used under a standardised monitoring scheme and in association with a mark–recapture methodology to estimate population abundance. However, such a scheme is time-consuming and would require a licence, as it is an offence to disturb Red Squirrel or Dormouse breeding sites under Schedule 5 of the 1981 Wildlife & Countryside Act and the Wildlife (Northern Ireland) Order 1985 (for Red Squirrels only). Alternatively, simple transect counts of food remains (e.g. cones and nuts) can be useful in providing indices of abundance, and at the very least can give some indication of their distribution within a site, or direct counts can also be undertaken (see Sections 26.3.2 and 26.4.1). The field equipment required for surveying and monitoring mammals by using counts of breeding sites is listed in Appendix 6.

Data analysis and interpretation

Breeding sites of some species can be difficult to distinguish, and inclusion of abandoned sites may result in an overestimate of population size. Breeding sites may be counted to give an index of population size if the average number of individuals using a breeding site can be determined.

Counts can then be compared annually and the trends analysed by using the appropriate tests. Analysis between sites would need to take into account habitat differences; this can be assessed by plotting number of nest sites with each habitat factor, such as sward height, and fitting regression lines.

It is important to standardise the survey between both visits and counts to reduce bias caused by an uneven distribution of sampling effort. Be aware also that counts may not be comparable within or between sites if there are significant differences in the topography or vegetation, as this may affect the ability to detect sites.

Analysis of mark–recapture data in association with artificial nest box monitoring is dealt with in Section 10.11.

26.3.2   Faecal pellet counts

Principles

Faecal pellets can be used for identifying many mammal species. However, Western Polecat *Mustela putorius*, feral Ferret *M. furo* and Mink *M. vison* scats can be easily confused, and different ungulate and lagomorph species can also be easily misidentified in this way. This is especially so if there are a number of similar species occupying the same area.

Many species, particularly carnivores, use their droppings to communicate with other individuals, for instance in territory marking. Faecal pellets are therefore not distributed at random, particularly during the breeding season. Carnivores and insectivores also defecate at lower rates than herbivores. Because of these constraints, faecal counts for carnivores and insectivores can usually only be used to provide information on presence–absence and data for distribution mapping.

Herbivores produce relatively large amounts of faeces and many appear to defecate at random within particular types of habitat. These factors enable estimates of population size and habitat use to be made for these species. Faecal pellet counts are one of the most commonly used methods for assessing abundance of deer populations (Staines & Ratcliffe, 1987; Ratcliffe & Mayle, 1993).

Field methods

Direct counting of faecal groups with a standardised transect or quadrat methodology is the easiest method to apply. Faecal counts can only be used to provide population estimates if animals can be assumed to be defecating at random within the survey area. In many deer species, animals use their home range differentially, but do appear to defecate at random within certain strata. These strata need to be defined and mapped as a preliminary to fieldwork and usually relate to easily detected vegetation types. Faecal counts can then be undertaken within each stratum to provide estimates of density (such as deer days of occupancy). Subsequently, estimates for each stratum can be added to provide an overall estimate. It is possible to analyse such data statistically to provide standard errors and confidence limits (Ratcliffe & Mayle, 1993).

Circular, square or rectangular plots, transects and nearest-neighbour (plotless) methods can be used to estimate faecal density. In addition, there is a choice between measurement of the standing crop from a single visit or the assessment of the rate of accumulation of faeces by clearing faeces from plots and counting faecal accumulation after a period of time.

These choices are to some degree arbitrary and dependent upon user experience, habitat type and personal preference, especially when considering plot shape. However, all methods have benefits and difficulties. The benefits can be maximised and the difficulties minimised by using transects to detect and measure low population densities (c. 1–3 deer per 100 ha), standing crop for plots with medium densities (c. 4–25 deer per 100 ha) and clearance plots for high densities (more than c. 25 deer per 100 ha). The clearance method is more labour-intensive and is only worth while if the faecal density is known to be high.

Standing crop

Standing crop methods use nearest-neighbour techniques or quadrats to estimate faecal density and rely on the assumption that there is a stable relationship between the number of pellets present and the number of animals. To estimate population size both defecation and decay rates are taken into account. Only a single visit to the site is necessary. For a full account of this method see Ratcliffe & Mayle (1993).

Assessment of the rate of accumulation or clearance plot methods

Clearance plot methods use a standardised quadrat methodology but the plots are cleared between successive surveys. Because the time interval between clearance and assessment can be chosen, it is possible to ensure that decay is not occurring during the interval. This eliminates the need to measure decay rates. An optimum time interval can be calculated from site-specific decay rates. The method is time-consuming, requiring the marking of permanent plots and repeat visits.

Genetic markers are now being used to identify individuals of some species from their faeces. However, analysis is time-consuming and expensive and can therefore only be recommended for use in research studies of small populations. The field equipment needed to survey and monitor mammals by using faecal pellet counts is summarized in Appendix 6.

Although Weil's disease, caused by infection with *Leptospira*, is rare, it can be caught by coming into contact with the urine of some mammals, particularly rats. Care should be taken to avoid unnecessary handling of faeces, and if you think you may be at risk refer to the appropriate government health and safety guidance.

Data analysis and interpretation

Standardised faecal counts can provide a useful measure of relative densities of a species between sites or over time by comparing changes in the counts. An index of abundance of some species (Strachan & Jefferies, 1993) can be calculated if the time spent searching is standardised to reduce bias that may occur because of an uneven distribution of effort.

Droppings of some species are often highly aggregated and have been shown to fit a negative binomial distribution (Stormer *et al.*, 1977). The advantage of the negative binomial distribution is that it allows the interpretation of changes in density and decay rate, which may reflect change in habitat use. The fit of the data can be tested by using χ^2 goodness-of-fit tests.

Simple statistical models can be used to estimate population size in herbivores, which produce large amounts of faeces, by using standing crop or plot clearance methods (Box 26.1). Although there are many potential sources of error in these estimates,

---

Box 26.1 Estimates of population size from faecal pellet counts

Population density can be estimated from faecal pellet counts using either clearance plots or standing crop methods.

(A) CLEARANCE PLOT METHODS

$$p = \frac{\left(\frac{m}{d}\right)\left(\frac{a}{s}\right)}{t},$$

where p = population size
m = mean number of pellet groups per plot

d = defecation rate
a = area of the site
s = plot size
t = time interval between surveys (minutes).

(B) STANDING CROP METHODS

$$p = \frac{mr}{d},$$

where p = population site
m = mean number of pellet groups per hectare
d = defecation rate
r = mean decay rate (number per day).

careful application can minimise them. Defecation rate does not appear to be strongly influenced by diet, although volume might be. Decay rates do vary, particularly in relation to soil acidity, vegetation, invertebrate activity and weather. For this reason greater accuracy can be achieved if local decay rates are determined.

26.3.3   Feeding signs

Principles
Many species leave conspicuous markings on food sources or remains and these can be useful for providing information on the presence and distribution of a species, usually in conjunction with other indirect methods. Also, assuming the relationship between the number of feeding signs and population size is constant spatially and between years, some indication of population trends can be gained. Signs of some species are indistinguishable from others, but signs can be used to detect squirrels, Wood Mouse *Apodemus sylvaticus*, Bank Vole *Clethrionomys glareolus*, Field Vole *Microtus agrestis*, Badger, Water Vole *Arvicola terrestris*, Dormouse, deer and Mountain Hare *Lepus timidus*.

Field methods
Systematic searching for signs along transects or within quadrats will provide an indicator of presence and distribution. For some target species, it may be appropriate to clear these transects of all debris prior to starting the study, allowing the remains to be found easily, and allowing a count of feeding remains over time. The specific methodology used will depend upon the species being surveyed and the habitat type. For example, if surveying for signs of Water Vole, standardised transect sampling along linear aquatic features would be most appropriate. Searching for signs in this way is a simple and fairly non-invasive method, which allows the survey of large areas. To aid identification of the species being surveyed, comparisons can sometimes be made between the feeding remains of other species that utilise the same food source. For example, gnawed Hazel *Corylus avellana* nuts may indicate the presence of Wood Mouse, Dormouse, Bank Vole or squirrel

(Sargent & Morris, 1997). The field equipment required for surveying and monitoring mammals by using feeding signs is outlined in Appendix 6.

Data analysis and interpretation
The presence of feeding signs depends on the availability of different food types, which may vary seasonally, making this method an unreliable measure of population changes. Analysis should therefore be restricted to using presence–absence data to compare sites within and between years, but even when using this approach it is important to relate estimates to seasonality of food availability. Count data will rarely be normally distributed, so non-parametric tests such as the Kruskal–Wallis test (Part I, Section 2.6.4) should be used to analyse these kinds of data.

26.3.4   Bait marking

Principles
Bait marking is used to establish territory size and boundaries for species that use latrines to mark their home-ranges (e.g. Badgers). By adding coloured indigestible markers to suitable bait, it is possible to pick out territory boundaries. By using different coloured markers, it is possible to determine the number of social groups using an area.

Field methods
This survey can only be done after an initial survey to locate all burrow entrances and latrines has been completed. The optimal time for bait marking is when the animals are at their most territorial (for Badgers, between February and April) and should not be attempted in mid-summer or mid-winter, as territorial activity is at its lowest during these periods. Bait marking surveys should run for a minimum of five successive days.

The inert marker should be mixed with a suitable sticky bait, so that the animal cannot selectively avoid ingesting the marker. The mix should be placed in a suitable location where the target species and individuals have access. This can be difficult, as in practice non-target species may also take the bait. However, with ingenuity, the target species can be favoured by the bait placement (e.g. covering the bait with a heavy stone will restrict access to the larger mammals such as Badgers).

Data analysis and interpretation

The resulting data should be mapped either into a suitable mapping program (e.g. a GIS package) or onto fair maps, showing the location of all setts and bait stations, and all latrines and recovered markers.

26.3.5   Tracks

Principles

Track counts can be used to identify a variety of species, but are usually used in conjunction with other methods such as counts of feeding signs and droppings. Tracks can be used to identify species such as deer, Rabbit, Hare *Lepus europaeus*, Fox, Badger, Water Vole, American Mink and Otter *Lutra lutra*. Small mammals cannot usually be identified to species, and the quality and quantity of prints is dependent on a number of factors such as soil, snow type, environmental conditions, activity, time of day and season.

Field methods

Systematic searching for signs along transects or within quadrats will provide an indication of presence and activity. However, the type of substrate is of crucial importance when recording tracks as some media are more effective than others. Soft mud and snow are ideal natural media but neither is permanently or uniformly distributed across sampling sites to allow for comparisons.

Tracking stations

A more reliable approach is to provide your own media such as trays of dry fine sand or an ink pad and blotter. Numerous designs for tracking stations have been created; for more details see Macdonald *et al.* (1998). Stations should be placed at intervals according to the sampling strategy, e.g. along transects or known runways. The station could be baited, but if using the data to calculate abundance this is not recommended as it may encourage individuals to use the site that would

not normally do so. Transects should be spaced far enough apart to reduce the chance of the same individual frequenting more than one set. If the population fluctuates annually, tracking stations are best used when the species is at its highest density. Scent stations work in a similar way to tracking stations but attract species by using a particular scent; as for baiting, this may introduce bias into the survey. Appendix 6 summarises the field equipment required for surveying and monitoring mammals by their tracks.

Data analysis and interpretation

Anecdotal records of tracks cannot be analysed but are an important source for mammal recorders and contribute to mapping the national distribution of species. Track data from tracking stations are inexpensive to collect, but interpretation of the results may be difficult. Estimates of relative density have been calculated for some species, although not in Britain, but the assumptions required are easily violated so tracks are most commonly used as a presence–absence measure. Activity may vary both spatially and temporally; it is almost impossible to distinguish individuals, and the stations themselves may attract or deter individuals and so will not be visited at random.

26.3.6   Hair tubes or catchers

Principles

Hair tubes are lengths of plastic piping, with a diameter similar to that of burrows or holes used by the target species. The inside top and sides are lined with double-sided sticky tape to trap hair of mammals passing through the tube. Hair tubes are most commonly used to detect the presence of Red and Grey Squirrels *Sciurus carolinensis* and (using smaller tube sizes) voles and shrews.

Field methods

The recommended size of tube for squirrels is a diameter of 65 mm, approximately 150 mm in length, and for small mammals a diameter of 25–40 mm and 100 mm in length, depending on the target species (Sargent & Morris, 1997).

Hair traps can be set up from spring onwards when individuals are more active.

Larger species such as Fox and Badger often leave telltale clumps of hair on barbed wire fences as they squeeze underneath. This can provide useful distribution data. A more systematic extension of this approach is to use loops of multi-stranded strong wire inserted into the ground across runways so animals will squeeze underneath. Clumps of finer wire are inserted within the strands to catch the hairs. Appendix 6 lists the field equipment required for surveying and monitoring mammals by using hair tubes or catchers.

Data analysis and interpretation

Although this method is relatively simple and unobtrusive, data analysis for this type of survey is restricted. This method cannot be used to distinguish numbers of individuals and it can be difficult and time-consuming to identify different species. Results can be used to construct distribution maps and if surveys are conducted annually changes in site use can be identified.

26.4   DIRECT METHODS

26.4.1   Transects (including point counts and spotlight searches)

Principles

Transects and point counts are useful for estimating numbers, particularly in low-density populations and in open habitats. The number of individuals counted along a transect under predefined conditions can be used to give an index of relative abundance. Transects can only be used for conspicuous species such as Rabbit, squirrels, Hare and deer. Lagomorphs and deer are less easily startled at night and so spotlight counts can also prove a reliable method (Barnes & Tapper, 1985).

Field methods

Line transects involve recording all individuals detected on and to each side of the transect line, following a suitable methodology (for more details see Sections 10.6 and 10.7). All transects must be surveyed with consistent effort. Observer training is important to reduce the chance of overlooking individuals, although this is less important if a distance sampling method is used (Section 10.6).

Point counts (Section 10.8) are similar to transect counts but the observer undertakes a timed count of all individuals detected from a single vantage point. If distance methods are employed, as for transect counts (Section 10.6), then estimates of abundance can also be made. Vantage point counts reduce disturbance and allow larger areas to be covered in less time. Point counts from vantage points are commonly used for deer species, but are limited to use in hilly country (Ratcliffe, 1987). Point counts reduce the chance of overlooking individuals, which may occur while walking, and can be set up to be more representative than transect counts would allow if the habitat is patchy. Both these types of survey should be carried out during periods when the target species is likely to be most active.

Spotlight counts are useful for species that are active and/or less easily alarmed at night. Individuals can be detected by the light reflecting in the pupils (known as eyeshine). Observation distances vary with weather conditions and habitat, so the length of the spotlight beam should be checked at the beginning and the end of each survey. Surveys should also be limited to times of year when the vegetation cover is low. Spotlight counts can be undertaken by using either transects or point counts, and are usually undertaken in conjunction with daytime counts for comparison.

Brown Hares are best surveyed by using these methods, between October and mid-January. Mountain Hares are more easily seen in late spring after snowmelt but before they lose their winter coat. Transects are best located along contour lines 20–100 m apart from the top of the hill, as individuals usually run uphill if disturbed (Flux, 1970).

Deer that occupy open range are regularly counted by direct counts by teams of observers equipped with binoculars, telescopes and two-way radios. Counts are usually conducted in the spring when daylength is increasing but when snow cover persists on high ground, restricting the deer to low ground. Relatively high levels of precision are often achieved (see Staines & Ratcliffe, 1987). Most other deer populations occupy woodland habitats and population estimates are usually done by vantage point or faecal counts (Section 26.3.2). The field equipment required for surveying and monitoring mammals by using transects is detailed in Appendix 6.

Data analysis and interpretation

Transect data can be converted into a density estimate either by estimating the perpendicular distance of each individual from the line or by counting the number of individuals within a set distance, which will depend on the type of habitat being surveyed. Analysis of transect data is covered in more detail in Sections 10.6 and 10.7. For further information on models used for estimating population density from Hare data, consult Hutchings & Harris (1996).

It is best to be cautious when interpreting the reliability of direct count data as population studies should guarantee a uniform effort in all areas of the species distribution and this can be difficult to maintain between different habitats.

Long-term population trends cannot be derived from direct counts by simply comparing the sample population each year. It is unlikely that short-term changes can be relied upon: the degree of inaccuracy inherent in direct count data is unknown.

26.4.2   Trapping

Principles

Live trapping of mammals is generally restricted to rodents and insectivores, although large species can also be trapped. Trapping can be used to provide information on species presence and distribution, and also provides more detailed information about the population such as age, sex and health of those individuals trapped. Despite this, trapping is labour-intensive, can be expensive and is stressful to individuals. Results are also easily biased by weather conditions, sex, age and trap odour.

Field methods

The type of trap to use will depend on the target species. Small mammals are most easily trapped; the most commonly used trap for these species in Britain is the Longworth trap, which is effective, but bulky. In the UK these traps are available from Penlon Ltd, Radley Road, Abingdon, Oxfordshire OX1 3PH, tel. 01235 554222. They are composed of an entrance tunnel with a trip mechanism and trap door and a detachable holding box, in which bait and bedding can be placed. Cheaper alternatives are widely available from pet shops.

Traps for larger species are also available. The most commonly used are Sherman traps, which are made in the USA. These are similar to Longworth traps without the entrance tunnel, and are available in a range of sizes. They are also collapsible for easy transport. For species of Rabbit size or greater, wire cage traps are the most effective but provide no cover or insulation for captured animals. The Clover trap is a design with a sliding drop-down door of flexible nylon netting at each end, which can be placed on deer runs without baiting. Deer can also be enticed into large corrals by providing food, but this is time-consuming and expensive.

Stoats *Mustela erminus* and Weasels *M. nivalis* can be very effectively trapped live by using wooden tunnel traps with a centrally pivoted 'see-saw' floor. If such traps are built into drystone walls they will often catch without bait. Smearing Rabbit guts on the inside of the cage will improve the number of captures. Handling these small mustelids is difficult and it is usually better to anaesthetise them, especially if they are to be marked or examined.

The layout of traps within a survey area is important in order to ensure that all individuals have an equal opportunity of being caught. Trapping webs can be used (see Section 10.9), but trap layout will depend on the target species. For small mammals a spacing of 10–15 m is sufficient; as a general rule, if 60% or more traps are filled on one visit, more traps are required. Traps should be positioned flush with the ground for ground-dwelling species, preferably in areas of cover. Placing traps in a location known to be used by a species, such as along runs or by a latrine site, will increase the success rate. Trap locations should be marked so they can be found easily later.

Traps for many species need to be baited to encourage use and to prevent animal deaths.

For small mammals, seeds and grain can be used but 'casts' (blowfly pupae) must also be included for insectivores such as shrews. They can consume 80–90% of their body mass per day (more if lactating) so a suitable amount of casts must be provided (i.e a handful). Bedding should also be provided, and traps laid to ensure that this will not become waterlogged should it rain. As high mortality rates for shrews can occur when trap checking is infrequent and insufficient food is provided, a licence must be obtained to deliberately trap shrews, and any protected species. If a trapping programme is planned, consult the licensing section within the relevant government department to check whether licences are needed.

Traps should be checked at least every 12 hours or more frequently depending on the species. Shrews are particularly susceptible to stress, starvation and cold so traps should be checked every 3–4 hours if there is a likelihood that they may be caught. Otherwise, the best time to check traps is morning and evening. Some species are neophobic (frightened of new objects), so a short period of pre-baiting may be required to allow individuals time to familiarise themselves with the traps. This is when the trap is baited but not set so individuals are free to enter and leave the traps. For small mammals, except Field Voles, this is not necessary. The minimum length of a trapping programme, excluding pre-baiting, should be 3 consecutive days or nights, longer if individuals are reluctant to enter the traps. The location of traps should be carefully noted, and possibly marked with canes. Traps should never be left out or lost. For further information on small mammal trapping, consult Gurnell & Flowerdew (1995).

Handling any animal can be difficult without practice; gauntlets are required for larger species. A 'dog-catcher' (a rope or wire noose, which is threaded through a long metal tube or pipe) allows Foxes and Badgers to be handled at arm's length and held prior to examination. A cotton or hessian sack is useful for handling squirrels and Rabbits; a large polythene bag is better for small mammals. The contents of a sprung trap can be gently tipped into the sack to stop the animal escaping. This reduces stress to the animal and enables one to manoeuvre the animal into a suitable position for handling. Small mammals can be gently held by the scruff of the neck.

It is best to obtain some specific advice before starting a trapping programme, and practical experience is needed of the techniques used prior to commencing a trapping survey. The equipment required for surveying and monitoring mammals by trapping in the field is listed in Appendix 6.

Data analysis and interpretation

If mammals are being caught as part of a mark–recapture study, refer to Sections 10.11 and 26.4.3. If not, a simple calculation of mean number of individuals caught per trapping occasion can be used to compare numbers between years. This method will only provide a population index as it is unlikely that all individuals in the population will be caught. Depending on the methods used, standard statistical tests may be applicable (Part I, Section 2.6.4).

26.4.3   Trapping and mark–recapture

Principles

Mark–recapture studies can be used to establish the ratio of recaptures to newly captured individuals, which can be used to estimate population size (Section 10.11). It will also provide further demographic information such as immigration and dispersal rates.

Mark–recapture studies will generally provide the most precise estimates of population size but such studies are labour-intensive and costly and are usually only used in research and not for EIA work.

Field methods

Mark–recapture studies follow the same basic methods as do simple trapping programmes (see Section 26.4.2). However, traps should generally be laid out on a grid (or along watercourses for semi-aquatic species) to standardise the survey. The success of the study will also depend on the accuracy of the marking strategy. Some mammals can be identified by distinctive markings, such as the throat markings of Mink. Species that cannot be recognised in this way require some permanent marking.

Short-term studies can employ the use of fur clipping, in which each individual has a small patch of guard hairs clipped at a particular site on its body. For example, three sites from foreleg, flank and hind leg on each side, three down the centre of the back and one on the head provides ten individual marks. Doubling up of these can add to the number of available combinations. However this is only useful for up to 4–6 weeks before the fur grows back. Semi-permanent vegetable dyes are also very effective.

Larger mammals such as Rabbits and deer can be ear-tagged. However, large coloured ear tags, which are visible at a distance, are frequently chewed off by other animals. Only the relatively obscure metal tags are more permanent, but these are not easy to see from a distance. Smaller tags have been used on small mammals with limited success; small mammal ears appear too fragile to hold a tag. Individually numbered Monel tags for use on laboratory rats (National Band and Tag Co., Newport, Kentucky, USA) can be used, or individually labelled medical metal sutures can also be used as ear tags. Plastic or leather collars with different coloured patches on them provide a very useful means of individually marking medium to large species (Foxes, Badgers, deer). Radio transmitters can also be attached to these to provide information on range use and activity (Biotrack, Wareham, is the only company in Britain making and supplying radio collars and receivers). With larger species, which can be easily observed in the wild, the recapture phase is often replaced by observation.

A more recent method involves inserting PIT (passive integrated transponder) tags just under the skin. These tags have a unique number, which can be read with a scanner upon recapture. This method is permanent and effective but is expensive and not suitable for mammals smaller than Rabbits without their being generally anaesthetised first. Invasive methods such as this require a Home Office licence under the Animals (Scientific Procedure) Act 1986. PIT tags cost £3–£5 each, and scanners cost between £300 and £1000. They are available from Trovan, UK ID Systems Ltd, Riverside Industrial Park, Preston, Lancashire PR3 0HP; Fish Eagle Co., Lechlade, Gloucestershire GL7 3QQ; and Labtrac Ltd., Holroyd Suite, Oak Hall, Sheffield Park, Uckfield, East Sussex TN22 3QY. Different systems are not compatible. The field equipment for surveying and monitoring mammals by trapping and mark–recapture is summarized in Appendix 6.

Data analysis and interpretation

There is a considerable amount of literature devoted to the analysis of mark–recapture data. This has been briefly reviewed in Section 10.11. It is important that the assumptions of the model chosen are met in order to provide an accurate population estimate. If using a trapping web (see Section 10.9), edge effects must be taken into account. Relatively more animals will be trapped on the edges of the web because individuals outside the web will be attracted in. These effects are not usually accounted for in the analysis and so you should be aware that the catchment area is underestimated and so the population density will be overestimated.

26.4.4   Mortality data methods

Principles

Mortality data primarily come from game bag or culling records. Records can be used to determine trends in population size, and distribution (Hutchings & Harris, 1996). There are a number of methods of using mortality data to estimate various population parameters. Population size can be estimated from the changes in sex ratio during a hunting season, or by using the age and sex of all individuals that die, if this information is known for every year. These methods can be used for all species with bag records. However, species that have been regularly culled at the same site for numerous years will provide more reliable information.

Field methods

Data are already available from many hunting estates. However, the quality of information varies between them; the rate of kill is rarely standardised between years and depends on the number and activity of gamekeepers, changes in land use and weather conditions. In addition, carcasses from natural deaths are not always found and recorded.

Data analysis and interpretation

Bag density is calculated as the number of animals killed per square kilometre per year per estate. These data can be used to provide an index of abundance from the number killed per hectare per year and can be compared between years and sites.

Population size can be determined from the observed change in the sex ratio before and after a hunt. The number of each sex culled is recorded and the population size that is consistent with the changes in the sex ratio is determined. This method is susceptible to observational bias, but if the bias remains constant between years, it can provide a reliable estimate.

Retrospective estimates of population size can be gained from cohort analysis. This is based on recovering most animals that die (as can be achieved for some deer populations). The age of each animal recovered is determined and thereby related to the year of birth. As information is accumulated over a period of years, particular cohorts can be reconstructed to provide counts of the minimum number of animals born in a particular year. This can then be related by birth rates, fecundity measures, etc. to give a population estimate (Ratcliffe, 1987; Staines & Ratcliffe, 1987; Ratcliffe & Mayle, 1993). This method is sometimes used to assess the accuracy of population estimates calculated by other methods, such as faecal counts.

26.5   REQUIREMENTS FOR SPECIES OF PARTICULAR CONSERVATION IMPORTANCE

This section includes the UK Biodiversity Action Plan species (Water Vole, Otter, Red Squirrel, Brown Hare and Dormouse) and Badger, included owing to its particular status in UK law (in respect of welfare issues) and its importance in EIA studies.

26.5.1   Water Vole

The prime method of surveying for Water Voles is to survey for field signs such as latrines and grazed 'lawns'. Latrines are characterised by accumulations of droppings in a particular site, often with the older droppings stamped flat. Territories are marked by latrines, so the densities of these can be taken as an indication of Water Vole population size.

A Water Vole survey should be confined to the optimal period of finding breeding territories, which are marked by latrines. This period is from late April to July. However, signs can be recorded up until the end of September. Water Voles cannot be accurately surveyed between October and March, as their activity is significantly reduced during this time, consequently leaving little sign of their presence.

All areas of potential Water Vole habitat on a site and any in the near vicinity beyond the site boundary (e.g. a drainage ditch that links with habitat within the site boundary) should be included in the survey. In a linear habitat (i.e. river or canal) the site can be divided into 500 m sections of bank (i.e. 250 m upstream and 250 m downstream of a mid-point grid reference); a more three-dimensional habitat (e.g. a series of drainage ditches on a grazing marsh) can be surveyed by each ditch, the length of which should be measured accurately. Where possible banks should be inspected from the river or ditch rather than from the bank top as this increases the probability of detecting signs. Approximately 45–60 minutes is required to survey each 500 m section of bank.

Basic survey methods follow those given in Strachan (1998). A list of essential equipment is shown in Appendix 6. All signs of Water Voles are recorded from both banks of the river, stream or ditch, including:

- visual sightings or sounds of voles entering the water;
- latrines;
- tunnel entrances;
- 'lawns' around tunnel entrances;
- feeding remains of chopped vegetation;
- paths and runs at waters edge or in vegetation;
- footprints in mud.

The number of vole latrines counted at a site gives an indication of the density of the Water Vole colony. Larger and more robust populations show greater densities of closely packed latrines. When vole populations are small and fragmented, there are fewer maintained latrines. In this situation feeding signs and burrows are often the most useful indicators of their presence.

To estimate numbers of adult and juvenile Water Voles from the numbers of latrines found in the survey, the regression to use (from Morris et al., 1998) is:

$$y = 1.48 + 0.683x,$$

where y is the number of Water Voles and x the number of latrines.

This equation may not be applicable to all habitat types and situations where Water Voles occur.

The number of Water Vole field signs in each discrete survey section should be ranked as abundant, frequent, scarce or none. This is done primarily by the number of latrines, or by feeding signs or burrows in more fragmented populations.

26.5.2   European Otter

As Otters are protected species, surveying requires a licence, which can be obtained from the relevant government department. Surveying only for Otter faeces (spraints) does not require a licence.

Field signs such as feeding remains, faecal deposits, tracks and holts can be searched for following a standardised transect methodology. Counts of spraints provide the most reliable measure of species distribution. Spraints are usually deposited on promontories, outside holts and at entry and exit sites from the water. They have a characteristic sweet smell (similar to that of jasmine tea) when compared with the rather pungent smell of some other carnivore scats. This allows them to be easily distinguished from scats such as those deposited by Mink. They often contain fish scales, amphibian bones and sometimes feathers and fur. Fresh spraints are usually dark green, black or grey in colour depending on the contents. Sprainting occurs throughout the year so there is no optimal monitoring time, although peaks have been recorded in winter and early spring (Macdonald & Mason, 1987).

Although spraint surveys are the most effective method for monitoring Otter populations, they do not provide a good indication of population density

and can only be used for assessing presence–absence and for mapping distributions (Jenkins & Burrows, 1980; Kruuk et al., 1986). CEH have developed a model for Shetland, which links population density to the number of holts. It should be borne in mind that in transient or low-density populations sprainting levels are known to greatly underestimate the activity or distribution of the species. It is particularly important that surveyors are experienced, as signs are easy to overlook, and this can also result in an underestimate of species distribution.

Other survey methods have been tried and tested and have been generally unsuccessful. Trapping is difficult and time-consuming, making mark–recapture studies unreliable. However, if a captive population is being reintroduced transponders can be fitted so that the activities of individuals can be studied by using radio tracking.

Research has been undertaken on DNA fingerprinting of Otters from spraints to identify individuals. This has been successfully used; although it is expensive, it has the advantage that it can often yield a better estimate of the numbers of individual animals and local population turnover.

Information on Otter distribution and status can be gained from road kills, as this allows information to be gathered on an individual's age, sex and health. This can also give an indication of areas that could be targeted for more detailed surveys.

26.5.3   Badger

Badgers are fully protected under the Wildlife (Northern Ireland) Order 1985; therefore any survey which may interfere with the animals or their places of shelter must by licensed by the appropriate agency.

The optimal method of survey for Badgers is to search the target area and the area around it for field signs of the species. Grassland areas should be surveyed for footprints, dung pits, snuffle holes and distinctive runways through the vegetation. Boundary hedges, walls and fences should be searched for latrines indicating a territory boundary. Runways under boundary fences and hedges should be searched for stray hairs. Hedgerows, earth banks, woodland and scrub habitats should be searched for signs of sett building activity, including dung pits and hairs close to sett entrances, discarded bedding, and spoil heaps from recent digging. Sett entrances are large holes (larger than Rabbit burrows) which can often be confirmed as Badger holes by the presence of characteristic guard hairs or footprints.

Setts found should be examined to establish their level of usage. Each hole should be classified under one of the following categories defining use.

- Well used: An entrance free of leaf litter and showing recent signs of excavation.
- Partly used: An entrance with some leaf litter and debris around the hole but also showing some signs of recent digging.
- Disused: An entrance with debris and leaf litter partially obscuring the hole with no recent signs of digging; or a hole that exhibits the characteristics of a Badger hole (with a large, D-shaped entrance and old spoil piles at the entrance), but shows no other signs of Badger activity.

The optimal time for survey is February to April when territories are most actively marked. Surveys can be undertaken at other times of year but signs of activity will be fewer, particularly over winter when Badgers may stay underground for days at a time if temperatures are low.

In addition, bait marking surveys are a very useful method of determining badger clan territories, and establishing whether different setts are used by the same group, or by two different social groups. The protocol is as in Section 26.3.4 above. To prepare the bait and marker mix, add around half a litre of inert marker (2 mm pellets of the raw material for plastic injection moulding) to around 7 litres of peanuts and/or cereal in a large bucket. Once they are well mixed, gently pour 1 litre of syrup over the mix and leave overnight for the syrup to seep through. Place the bait in small scrapes covered by a stone or log (to keep rain and other animals from the bait) near the sett entrances, around 20–30 scrapes per sett to allow all sett members access to bait. Where two or more setts are being marked, use different coloured markers for each sett. Carefully check each latrine for

coloured markers in the faeces; it may be necessary to smear these out with a stick to locate the markers. Should two colours turn up at one latrine, it is important to determine whether this came from one dropping (and hence from a single individual with access to different bait points) or from different droppings (different individuals using the same latrine). Continue searching for new latrines during the survey period.

26.5.4   Dormouse

Dormice are fully protected under Schedule 5 of the Wildlife & Countryside Act 1981, as updated by the Countryside and Rights of Way Act 2000. Dormice are also included on Schedule 2 of the Conservation (Natural Habitats etc.) Regulations 1994 as a European protected species.

Potential Dormouse habitat comprises:

- Woodland with a dense understorey;
- Coppice woodland;
- Overgrown hedgerows;
- Conifer plantations (less likely);
- Reed beds (less likely).

The presence of Dormice can be recognised from field signs. Gnawed Hazel nuts can provide positive confirmation of Dormouse presence; the hole in the nut shell will have a smoothed edge, unlike shells opened by mice and voles, which have transverse tooth marks across the cut edge of the shell.

Obviously, this is only possible if fruiting Hazel trees are present; even if extensive searches are made for nuts eaten by Dormice, the presence of Dormice cannot be ruled out if none are found. This survey methodology is not described in detail, but see Section 26.3.3. To obtain more detailed survey information on distribution and numbers, a survey using nest boxes or nest tubes is required.

Wooden nest boxes can be obtained from local mammal groups or the Wildlife Trusts. The entrance is at the back of the box, facing the tree, with spacing bars above and below the hole. The hole should be approximately 35 mm in diameter but the dimensions of the box itself are not critical. They should be approximately 120 mm wide × 120 mm deep × 200 mm high. The top should slide off, rather than being hinged to the box, to make it easier to check inside without the animals escaping.

Nest tubes are available from The Mammal Society. These consist of a wooden tray and a plastic tube. The wooden tray fits inside the tube and seals one end.

A minimum of 20 boxes or tubes should be put out, and they should ideally be placed approximately 20 m apart throughout all potentially suitable habitat on the site. They can be attached to trees of any species, but those well-linked to the understorey are most suitable. All boxes and tubes should be numbered.

Both boxes and tubes should be attached to trees with plastic-coated bell wire. Tubes should be attached to horizontal branches, or branches leaning downwards slightly, so that water does not accumulate at the end.

The height of boxes and tubes on the tree is not important, other than to ensure that they are easy for the surveyor to check. Boxes and tubes should be sited away from footpaths and where possible should not be visible to the public.

Boxes should be put out by March of the year in which the surveys will commence. Tubes should be put up by July of the year in which the surveys will commence. Tubes can be put out later in the year than boxes because tubes are primarily used by dispersing juveniles, born in that season. These individuals typically do not leave the maternal nest until late summer or early autumn.

Boxes need to be checked once per month from May through to October (inclusive). They should not be checked any less frequently as temporal changes in Dormouse behaviour could result in Dormice being missed if they use the box for a short time and do not make a nest. They should not be checked any more frequently as this could cause unnecessary stress to the animals; when they are woken from torpor they use up valuable fat reserves.

Tubes should be checked once per month from the month they are put out, through to October (and also early November if the weather is mild).

Nest boxes and tubes must not be checked when the weather is both cold and raining. Surveys should be re-arranged because disturbing Dormice

in these conditions can jeopardise their survival; their fur is not waterproof so they can become chilled, leading to critical losses of fat reserves. In light rain, or cold but dry weather, the surveyor should make a judgement with regards to whether or not to carry out the survey. In these situations, reducing handling and disturbance can lessen adverse effects on the animals.

When initial inspection of the box or tube leads the surveyor to suspect that Dormice may be inside, the hole in the box or front of the tube should be blocked with a plastic bag and the box or tube should be taken down and placed in a large plastic cement bag on the ground. Note: only one carrier bag 'stuffer' should be taken on the survey to avoid confusion about whether boxes or tubes have been put back with the hole blocked by a bag. The lid of the box or tray of the tube should be carefully and slowly removed.

If the surveyor is unsure whether the box is inhabited by Dormice or other small mammals, a stick should be used to gently move the nest or leaves in the box. Wood Mice and Yellow-necked Mice *Apodemus flavicollis* may bite, but Dormice very rarely do.

Careful note should be taken of the behaviour of the Dormouse inside the box in the breeding season (typically July to September, but varies according to the weather) because nests with babies should not be disturbed; furless young are vulnerable to the cold and new mothers can become distressed if handled. If the Dormouse sits still in the box when the lid is removed and slight disturbance to the nest is made, the box should be put back and a note of a likely breeding nest made.

Once Dormice have been counted, the lid should then be put back on the box and the 'stuffer' removed. Dormice should then be carefully caught and encouraged to re-enter the box through the hole. With tubes, the 'stuffer' should be removed from the front of the tube and Dormice caught and encouraged to re-enter. The hole or front is then re-blocked while the box or tube is placed back on the tree. Any notes should be made and all equipment packed away before the 'stuffer' is removed and the surveyors leave the vicinity of the box or tube quietly.

For the purposes of determining presence – absence and distribution it is not necessary to weigh and sex individuals, but a count of individuals in each box is useful. The nest (if present) should be carefully examined and lifted out of the box or tube to enable a count. If translocation of Dormice is a possibility, it may be beneficial to obtain information about their body mass and population dynamics through weighing and sexing individuals. This information can be valuable for research into Dormouse behaviour and population dynamics. For weighing, Dormice must be transferred to a plastic sandwich bag and weighed on a portable spring scale (max. 50 is sufficient).

Positive confirmation of Dormouse presence can be obtained from nests only. This is because Dormouse nests are distinctive and, although they could possibly be confused with Harvest mouse *Micromys minutus* nests, Harvest mice are very unlikely to be present in Dormouse habitat. Dormouse nests can be distinguished by a centre woven from grass or strips of Honeysuckle *Lonicera periclymenum* bark. The outer layer can be made of green leaves, but this is not always the case as nests have been found with dead leaves on the outer layer.

The location of boxes and tubes should be marked on a map of the site, with boxes or tubes with evidence of Dormice highlighted. If additional data on numbers, body mass and sex are recorded, these should be displayed in a table. See Bright *et al.* (1996) for further details.

26.5.5   Red Squirrel

Red Squirrels are fully protected under the Wildlife & Countryside Act 1981 and the Wildlife (Northern Ireland) Order 1985; any survey that may interfere with the animals or their places of shelter must therefore be licensed by the appropriate agency.

A variety of non-intrusive methods to survey for squirrels are available; however, some of these cannot be used to differentiate between Red and Grey Squirrels. Good sources of further information are the references by Gurnell *et al.* (2001, 2004).

Direct survey methods that can be used are transect counts and spot counts, the principles of which are outlined in the methods section above.

Spring and autumn are the times of year when the squirrels are most active and visible, and therefore the optimal times for survey. Surveys should be done in the early morning and late afternoon, and not be undertaken in periods of rain, strong wind or cold weather. A standardised method of survey is in use in areas of Scotland. This consists of a mix of transect counts and point counts; a transect of 10 m is walked slowly, taking around 5 minutes, followed by a point count of 3 minutes, etc. A kilometre of woodland can be walked in 1 hour and 20 minutes (Ayrshire Red Squirrel Group, 2004).

Monthly transect counts of Red Squirrels can provide a reliable index of population size, but this regular monitoring requires a dedicated team of volunteers. For details of this contact the UK Red Squirrel survey co-ordinator (Northumbria Wildlife Trust; tel. 0191 2846884).

Hair tube surveys can also be done, and will also distinguish between Red and Grey Squirrels (Gurnell *et al.*, 2001). The hair tubes should be approximately 6.5 cm in diameter and around 30 cm in length, and contain a detachable block with double-sided sticky tape attached to either end of the interior of the tube. The recommended density for red squirrels is 20 at 100 m intervals. These tubes should be placed along the upper side of a branch and baited with sunflower seeds, peanuts or corn. The tubes should be checked every 7–14 days (Gurnell *et al.* 2001). Hairs can then be identified through cross-reference with identified samples or from keys, using a reflected light microscope. Only guard hairs (the outermost longest hairs) can be used for identification. Ninety-five percent of guard hairs with a groove running the length of the transverse section can be confirmed as Red Squirrel. This can be observed by using reflective light and a dilute ink solution and a suitably powered microscope. Unfortunately, hair colour cannot be relied upon.

Other non-intrusive methods that cannot reliably separate Red from Grey Squirrels include drey counts and feeding transects. Drey counts consist of systematically surveying woodlands for intact dreys. Where it can be certain that these belong to Red Squirrels (i.e. where Grey Squirrels are absent) the number of Red Squirrels can be calculated by using the following equation (calculated for data collected in winter):

Number of Red Squirrels per ha = number of dreys per ha × 0.26. Feeding transects should be cleared prior to survey: a recommended size is 50 m × 1 m. These should be visited at regular intervals. The presence of stripped cones indicates the presence of squirrels (cannot differentiate between Red and Grey). The data can be used to estimate squirrel density (if only one species is present) by calculating the amount of energy being consumed by squirrels in the woodland over time, and dividing that by the average energy consumption of squirrels. A full description of the method can be found in Gurnell *et al.* (2001), with average figures for squirrel energy consumption and seed energy content. This method can only derive approximate density figures.

Trapping should use single catch traps, placed in a suitable sheltered location. These should be checked regularly; as this is a method requiring handling skills and causing some distress to a protected species, further information should be sought from the relevant agency and from Red Squirrel groups (e.g. Northumbria Wildlife Trust, Red Alert (http://www.redsquirrel.org.uk/)). A licence is also required. It is illegal to re-release any Grey Squirrels accidentally caught as part of the trapping effort.

26.5.6   Brown Hare

Large-scale monitoring and survey for Brown Hares can gain very useful data from game bag records, where these are available. As highlighted above, there are limitations to these, and they are only available where gamekeepers are active.

One method is to use night surveys. These can be driven transects (see for example, Preston *et al.*, 2002b) or spot counts from parked cars (Tapper, 2001). For the driven transects, a 4-wheel drive vehicle with a viewing deck is used, allowing one person to stand upright, scanning the surrounding area for hares with a powerful torch, while the vehicle is moving. The vehicle is driven at approximately 15 km h^{-1}. The point count uses a similar technique, but surveyed while the vehicle is stationary, at a position chosen for its vantage point over surrounding hare habitat. These surveys should be done from dusk onwards.

Walked transects in daylight hours are undertaken for the national Hare survey. The most appropriate survey technique is to use line transect sampling. On average transects in the national Hare survey are three kilometres long around a one-kilometre square. Each transect is walked three times, once a month between mid-October and mid-January. The survey is stratified by using the Institute of Terrestrial Ecology's (now CEH's) four land class groups.

26.6   MAMMAL CONSERVATION EVALUATION CRITERIA

Key evaluation considerations

The recently formed 'Tracking Mammals Partnership' aims to monitor the population of mammal species in the UK; certain programmes are already under way (e.g. the national Otter surveys). Further details can be found at http://www.jncc.gov.uk/species/mammals/trackingmammals/default.htm.

Protection status in the UK and EU

Many of the mammals in Great Britain are afforded legal protection under the Wildlife & Countryside Act, replaced in Northern Ireland by the Wildlife (Northern Ireland) Order 1985, the Nature Conservation and Amenity Lands (Northern Ireland) Order 1985 and the Conservation (Natural Habitats & c.) Regulations 1994. Legal protection is also afforded by the Bern Convention, the Convention on International Trade of Endangered Species of Wild Fauna and Flora (CITES) and the EU Habitats Directive.

The degree of protection afforded varies considerably, but is a function of the animal's rarity, status (native or introduced), and use by people. Restrictions on planning and development that may affect protected species are conducted through DEFRA's Planning Policy Guidance on Nature Conservation (PPG9) in Great Britain.

Table 26.2. *Summary of applicable conservation legislation and status of mammals in the UK*

Name	Scientific Name	EU Annex[a]	Bern App.	UK Act Schedule[a]	NI Order Schedule	BAP Priority	Conservation Status[b]
Water Vole	*Arvicola terrestris*			4a, 4b		P[c]	Major long term decline
Wild Cat	*Felis sylvestris*	IVa	II	5			Once found throughout mainland Britain, now confined to parts of Scotland
Grey Seal	*Halichoerus grypha*				5		
European Otter	*Lutra lutra*	IIa, IVa	II	5	5	P	Widespread in 1950s, twenty years later had disappeared from most of England and Wales; population slowly increasing
Pine Marten	*Martes martes*			5	5		Once found within 30 miles of London, now largely confined to remote areas in Scotland
Badger	*Meles meles*				5		Protection of Badgers Act (1992)
Dormouse	*Muscardinus avellanarius*	IVa		5		P	Has disappeared from half the range it occupied during the nineteenth century
Walrus	*Odobenus rosmarus*	IIa	II	5			
Common Seal	*Phoca vitulina*	IIa			5		Population has declined since the 1988 outbreak of phocine distemper
Red Squirrel	*Sciurus vulgaris*			5	5	P	Extinct over most of England and Wales
Brown Hare	*Lepus europaeus*					P	Showing signs of a general decline associated with intensification in farming
Polecat	*Mustela putorius*						Once widespread but now extinct in Scotland and most of England
Mountain Hare	*Lepus timidus*						Locally vulnerable, especially the isolated, small (and only) English population in the Peak District

[a] Full protection except Water Vole.
[b] Source: Mammal website factsheets of UK endangered mammals (www.abdn.ac.uk/mammal/endanger.htm).
[c] P, Priority BAP species.

Species-specific regulation to be aware of is the Badgers Act (1992). Certain animals are UK Biodiversity Action Plan species and/or Local Biodiversity Action Plan Species. The Species Action Plans for Northern Ireland are in the process of being completed.

At the time of writing, up to date species lists for these pieces of legislation can be obtained from the following websites:

- www.cites.org/eng/resources/species.html. Species protected from international trade through CITES.
- europa.eu.int/comm/environment/nature/habdir. htm. The EU Habitats Directive, with links to the different Annexes.
- www.nature.coe.int/english/cadres/bern.htm. The website for the Bern Convention.
- www.ukbap.org.uk/. Lists the local and UK Biodiversity Action Plan species.
- www.hmso.gov.uk. Contains the UK and Northern Ireland legislation.
- www.ehsni.gov.uk/natural/legs/legs.shtml. Contains links to the wildlife-related legislation of Northern Ireland.

Table 26.2 provides a summary of the applicable legislation and conservation status of selected mammals in the UK.

Conservation status in the UK

The status of UK mammals ranges from rare (e.g. Pine Marten *Martes martes*) to introduced pest species (e.g. Brown Rat). The species of most conservation concern are subject to Species Biodiversity Action Plans and/or protected by UK or EU legislation. Guides for Britain include Harris *et al.* (1995), Macdonald & Tattersall (2001) and JNCC (1994); for Ireland (including Northern Ireland) the Irish Red Data Book 2: Vertebrates (Whilde, 1993).

Site designation criteria

Areas may be considered of international importance if they contain a nationally important population of Otters, as this is a European Protected species.

The selection criteria for nationally important sites for mammals (other than bats or marine mammals) are the guidelines for the selection of SSSIs (NCC, 1989). For the Otter, in England and Wales, breeding holts and their surroundings may be considered of national importance. As other mammal species are so widely dispersed, the occurrence of Pine Marten, Wild Cat *Felis sylvestris*, Polecat *Mustela putorius*, Red Squirrel, Common Dormouse, Yellow-necked Mouse, Orkney Vole *Microtus arvalis* or Scilly Shrew *Crocidura suaveolens* are all considered as elements that enhance the value of a site on the national scale.

At the county level, any locally significant population of a mammal species that is listed in a County or Metropolitan Red Data Book or Local or National Biodiversity Action Plan species on account of its regional rarity or localisation is considered of county importance.

At levels lower than this, the approach described in Chapter 3 of this *Handbook* (based on IEEM 2002 guidelines) should be referred to.

Appendix 1
Monitoring and reporting obligations under international conservation agreements

Adapted from Shaw & Wind (1997).

Global

Agreement	Main aim	Site-based?	Requirement to monitor	Terms	Purpose of monitoring	Reporting to:	Frequency
The Ramsar Convention, 1971	To promote wise use of all wetlands and to provide protection for wetlands of international importance	Yes	Implied	'arrange to be informed', 'research' and 'the exchange of data'	To detect a change in ecological character	The Ramsar Bureau (IUCN)	≤ 3 years
Man and the Biosphere Programme, 1971	To improve links between people and the biosphere through the preservation of ecological and genetic diversity with consideration of the local economy, and of research, monitoring and training activities	Yes	Confirmed	'inventory' and 'monitoring'	To assess change within a network of baseline and monitoring stations in representative undisturbed biome areas	Man and the Biosphere Programme (UNESCO)	≤ 10 years
The World Heritage Convention, 1972	To identify formations of outstanding aesthetic, conservation or scientific importance, and to develop methods to counteract dangers to cultural or natural heritage	Yes	Confirmed	'systematic monitoring and reporting' conditions of the site to be recorded every year	Improved site management, advanced planning, reduction of emergency and ad hoc interventions, and reduction of costs through preventative conservation	UNESCO World Heritage Centre	5 years
CITES, 1973	To regulate international trade in endangered species	No	Implied	'review progress ... undertake scientific & technical studies'	To assess trade levels and changes in species' status	The Secretariat (UNEP)	≤ 2 years

The Bonn Convention, 1979	To ensure strict protection of migratory species in danger of extinction throughout all or a significant portion of their range	No	Confirmed[a]	present 'evidence' of status; 'monitor' measures taken	To determine the status of species and the effectiveness of measures taken	Bonn Convention Secretariat (UNEP)	≤ 3 years
The Convention on Biological Diversity, 1992	To identify important components of and processes affecting the sustainable use of biological diversity; their monitoring; ecosystem management; and the regulation of biological resources	Yes[b]	Confirmed	'Monitor, through sampling … biological diversity'	To determine levels of biodiversity and identify processes having significant adverse impact	Conference of Parties (UNEP)	To be determined
European							
European Diploma, 1965	To encourage the effective protection of certain landscapes, reserves and natural features of European interest	Yes	Implied	'on-the-spot appraisal'	To detect danger of a serious threat … serious deterioration and the effectiveness of existing precautions	Council of Europe	Annual (self-assessment); 5 yearly (independent assessment)
Biogenetic Reserves, 1975	To establish a European network of reserves that guarantee the biological balance, genetic diversity and representativeness of habitats considered typical, unique, rare or	Yes	Implied	'biological research' and 'maintain and … enhance target features'	To determine whether long-term measures have maintained or enhanced the potential and the diversity of the protected features	Council of Europe	Not specified

Table (*cont.*)

Agreement	Main aim	Site-based?	Requirement to monitor	Terms	Purpose of monitoring	Reporting to:	Frequency
	endangered, for biological research, training and education						
Birds Directive, 1979	To maintain bird populations at levels corresponding to ecological requirements and to regulate trade, hunting, exploitation and methods of capture and killing	Yes	Implied	'Trends and variations' '... taken into account'	To determine whether bird populations are maintained at levels corresponding to ecological requirements	The European Commission	3 years
Bern Convention, 1982	To conserve wild flora and fauna and their natural habitats, giving particular emphasis to endangered and vulnerable migratory birds	No[c]	Implied	Not specified	To determine whether species have attained satisfactory population levels; whether habitats have deteriorated; and the effects of derogations	The Standing Committee (Council of Europe)	2 years
Habitats Directive, 1992	To contribute towards ensuring biodiversity through the conservation of natural habitats and wild flora and fauna	Yes	Confirmed	'surveillance' of habitats and species; 'monitor' incidental capture and killing	Determine the conservation status of priority habitats and species; monitor incidental capture and killing and its effects; and report on derogations	The European Commission	2 years (derogations); 6 years (measures taken and status of habitats and species)

| EECONET, 1993 | To develop a coherent European network of habitats in which the full range of habitats is represented, the most important areas of the different habitat types are included and appropriate linkages to facilitate the dispersal and migration of species are incorporated | (Yes)[d] | Unclear | Several references to data collection, amounting to an inventory on which selection of core areas will be based | No indication of 'monitoring' or 'surveillance' requirements | Council of Europe | Not specified |

[a] An explicit reference to monitoring is made, but applies to measures taken, rather than to the target species themselves.

[b] The Convention on biological diversity proposes a variety of measures to safeguard or assess biodiversity, among them the need to 'establish a system of protected areas or areas where special measures need to be taken to conserve biological diversity'.

[c] The Bern Convention requires each contracting party to protect 'areas that are of importance for ... migratory species'. However, such areas are not formally designated under the convention.

[d] Requires the selection of 'core areas' and of corridors which link them into a habitat network.

Appendix 2
Relationship between BAP Priority Habitat and Broad Habitat categories and Habitats Directive nomenclature

BAP Priority Habitat	Annex I code	Habitats Directive[a] Annex I type	Comment
Upland oakwood	91A0	Old Sessile Oak (*Quercus petraea*) woods with *Ilex* and *Blechnum* in the British Isles	—
Lowland Beech and Yew woodland	91J0	*Taxus baccata* woods of the British Isles*	—
Lowland Beech and Yew woodland	9120	Atlantic acidophilous Beech forests with *Ilex* and sometimes also *Taxus* in the shrub layer (Quercion robori-petraeae or Ilici-Fagenion)	—
Lowland Beech and Yew woodland	9130	Asperulo-Fagetum Beech forests	—
Lowland mixed deciduous woodland	9160	Sub-Atlantic and medio-European Oak or Oak–Hornbeam forests of the Carpinion betuli	—
Upland mixed ashwoods	9180	Tilio-Acerion forests of slopes, screes and ravines*	—
Upland mixed ashwoods	91J0	*Taxus baccata* woods of the British Isles*	—
Upland mixed ashwoods	8240	Limestone pavements*	—
Wet woodland	91E0	Alluvial forest with *Alnus glutinosa* and *Fraxinus excelsior* (Alno-Padion, Alnion incanae, Salicion albae)*	—
Wet woodland	91D0	Bog woodland*	—
Lowland wood-pasture and parkland	9160	Sub-Atlantic and medio-European oak or oak–hornbeam forests of the Carpinion betuli	—
Upland birchwoods	—	—	—
Native pine woodlands	91C0	Caledonian forest*	—

BAP Priority Habitat	Annex I code	Habitats Directive[a] Annex I type	Comment
Native pine woodlands	91D0	Bog woodland*	—
Ancient and/or species-rich hedgerows	—	—	—
Cereal field margins	—	—	—
Coastal and floodplain grazing marsh	6510	Lowland hay meadows (*Alopecurus pratensis, Sanguisorba officinalis*)	—
Lowland meadows	6510	Lowland hay meadows (*Alopecurus pratensis, Sanguisorba officinalis*)	—
Upland hay meadows	6520	Mountain hay meadows	—
Lowland calcareous grassland	6210	Semi-natural dry grasslands and scrubland facies on calcareous substrates (Festuco-Brometalia) (*important orchid sites)	—
Upland calcareous grassland	6210	Semi-natural dry grasslands and scrubland facies on calcareous substrates (Festuco-Brometalia) (*important orchid sites)	—
Upland calcareous grassland	6230	Species-rich *Nardus* grassland on siliceous substrates in mountain areas (and submountain areas in continental Europe)*	—
Upland calcareous grassland	6170	Alpine and subalpine calcareous grasslands	—
Lowland dry acid grassland	2330	Inland dunes with open *Corynephorus* and *Agrostis* grasslands	—
Lowland heathland	4030	European dry heaths	—
Lowland heathland	4040	Dry Atlantic coastal heaths with *Erica vagans**	—
Lowland heathland	4010	Northern Atlantic wet heaths with *Erica tetralix*	—
Lowland heathland	4020	Temperate Atlantic wet heaths with *Erica ciliaris* and *Erica tetralix**	—
Lowland heathland	7150	Depressions on peat substrates of the Rhynchosporion	This 'micro-habitat' can occur within a range of mire and heath types

BAP Priority Habitat	Annex I code	Habitats Directive[a] Annex I type	Comment
Upland heathland	4030	European dry heaths	—
Upland heathland	4010	Northern Atlantic wet heaths with *Erica tetralix*	—
Upland heathland	4060	Alpine and Boreal heaths	Heath types restricted to the montane zone are not included in Upland heathland
Purple moor grass and rush pastures (*Molinia–Juncus*)	6410	Molinia meadows on calcareous, peaty or clayey-silt-laden soils (Molinion caeruleae)	—
Fens	7230	Alkaline fens	Lowland examples only
Fens	7210	Calcareous fens with *Cladium mariscus* and species of the Caricion davallianae*	—
Fens	7220	Petrifying springs with tufa formations (Cratoneurion)*	Lowland examples only
Fens	7140	Transition mires and quaking bogs	Lowland examples only
Fens	7150	Depressions on peat substrates of the Rhynchosporion	This 'micro-habitat' can occur within a range of mire and heath types
Reedbeds	—	—	—
Lowland raised bog	3160	Natural dystrophic lakes and ponds	Only bog pools within lowland raised bog systems are included
Lowland raised bog	7110	Active raised bogs*	—
Lowland raised bog	7120	Degraded raised bogs still capable of regeneration	—
Lowland raised bog	7150	Depressions on peat substrates of the Rhynchosporion	This 'micro-habitat' can occur within a range of mire and heath types
Blanket bog	3160	Natural dystrophic lakes and ponds	Only bog pools within blanket bog systems are included
Blanket bog	7130	Blanket bogs (*if active bog)	—
Blanket bog	7140	Transition mires and quaking bogs	Ladder fens are included with blanket bog

BAP Priority Habitat	Annex I code	Habitats Directive[a] Annex I type	Comment
Blanket bog	7150	Depressions on peat substrates of the Rhynchosporion	This 'micro-habitat' can occur within a range of mire and heath types
Mesotrophic lakes	3130	Oligotrophic to mesotrophic standing waters with vegetation of the Littorelletea uniflorae and/or of the Isoeto-Nanojuncetea	—
Mesotrophic lakes	3140	Hard oligo-mesotrophic waters with benthic vegetation of *Chara* spp.	—
Eutrophic standing waters	3150	Natural eutrophic lakes with Magnopotamion or Hydrocharition-type vegetation	—
Aquifer-fed naturally fluctuating water bodies	3150	Natural eutrophic lakes with Magnopotamion or Hydrocharition-type vegetation	Breckland meres
Aquifer-fed naturally fluctuating water bodies	3180	Turloughs*	—
Chalk rivers	3260	Water courses of plain to montane levels with the Ranunculion fluitantis and Callitricho-Batrachion vegetation	—
Limestone pavements	8240	Limestone pavements*	—
Maritime cliff and slopes	1230	Vegetated sea cliffs of the Atlantic and Baltic coasts	—
Coastal vegetated shingle	1210	Annual vegetation of drift lines	—
Coastal vegetated shingle	1220	Perennial vegetation of stony banks	—
Machair	21A0	Machairs	—
Coastal sand dunes	2110	Embryonic shifting dunes	—
Coastal sand dunes	2120	Shifting dunes along the shoreline with *Ammophila arenaria* (white dunes)	—
Coastal sand dunes	2130	Fixed dunes with herbaceous vegetation (grey dunes)*	—

BAP Priority Habitat	Annex I code	Habitats Directive[a] Annex I type	Comment
Coastal sand dunes	2140	Decalcified fixed dunes with *Empetrum nigrum**	—
Coastal sand dunes	2150	Atlantic decalcified fixed dunes (Calluno-Ulicetea)*	—
Coastal sand dunes	2160	Dunes with *Hippophae rhamnoides*	—
Coastal sand dunes	2170	Dunes with *Salix repens* ssp. *argentea* (Salicion arenariae)	—
Coastal sand dunes	2190	Humid dune slacks	—
Coastal sand dunes	2250	Coastal dunes with *Juniperus* spp.*	—
Coastal saltmarsh	1310	Salicornia and other annuals colonising mud and sand	—
Coastal saltmarsh	1320	*Spartina* swards (Spartinion maritimae)	—
Coastal saltmarsh	1330	Atlantic salt meadows (Glauco-Puccinellietalia maritimae)	—
Coastal saltmarsh	1420	Mediterranean and thermo-Atlantic halophilous scrubs (Sarcocornetea fruticosi)	—
Coastal saltmarsh	1130	Estuaries	—
Saline lagoons	1150	Coastal lagoons*	—
Seagrass beds	1140	Mudflats and sandflats not covered by sea water at low tide	—
Seagrass beds	1110	Sandbanks that are slightly covered by sea water all the time	—
Seagrass beds	1130	Estuaries	—
Seagrass beds	1160	Large shallow inlets and bays	—
Mudflats	1140	Mudflats and sandflats not covered by sea water at low tide	—
Mudflats	1130	Estuaries	—
Mudflats	1160	Large shallow inlets and bays	—
Sheltered muddy gravels	1160	Large shallow inlets and bays	—
Sheltered muddy gravels	1140	Mudflats and sandflats not covered by sea water at low tide	—
Littoral and sublittoral chalk	8330	Submerged or partly submerged sea caves	—

BAP Priority Habitat	Annex I code	Habitats Directive[a] Annex I type	Comment
Littoral and sublittoral chalk	1170	Reefs	—
Maerl beds	1110	Sandbanks that are slightly covered by sea water all the time	—
Maerl beds	1160	Large shallow inlets and bays	—
Mud habitats in deep water	—	—	—
Sabellaria alveolata reefs	1170	Reefs	—
Tidal rapids	1170	Reefs	—
Tidal rapids	1160	Large shallow inlets and bays	—
Modiolus modiolus beds	1170	Reefs	—
Modiolus modiolus beds	1160	Large shallow inlets and bays	—
Serpulid reefs	1170	Reefs	—
Lophelia pertusa reefs	1170	Reefs	—
Sabellaria spinulosa reefs	1170	Reefs	—
Sabellaria spinulosa reefs	1160	Large shallow inlets and bays	—
Sublittoral sands and gravels	1110	Sandbanks that are slightly covered by sea water all the time	—
Sublittoral sands and gravels	1160	Large shallow inlets and bays	—
Sublittoral sands and gravels	1130	Estuaries	—

BAP Broad Habitat	Annex I code	Habitats Directive[a] Annex I type	Comment
Broadleaved, mixed and yew woodland	9120	Beech forests with *Ilex* and *Taxus*, rich in epiphytes (Ilici-Fagion) (41.12)	—
Broadleaved, mixed and yew woodland	9130	Asperulo-fagetum beech forests (41.13)	—
Broadleaved, mixed and yew woodland	9160	Stellario-Carpinetum oak–hornbeam forests (41.24)	—
Broadleaved, mixed and yew woodland	9180	*Tilio-Acerion ravine forests (41.4)	—
Broadleaved, mixed and yew woodland	9190	Old acidophilous oak woods with *Ilex* and *Blechnum* in the British Isles (41.53)	—
Broadleaved, mixed and yew woodland	91A0	Old oak woods with *Ilex* and *Blechnum* in the British Isles (41.53)	—
Broadleaved, mixed and yew woodland	91E0	Residual alluvial forests (Alnion glutinoso-incanae) (44.3)	—
Broadleaved, mixed and yew woodland	91J0	*Taxus baccata* woods (42.A71 to 42.A73)	—
Broadleaved, mixed and yew woodland	91D0	*Bog woodland (44.A1 to 44.A4) p.p.	Bog woodland in the New Forest consisting of birch, willow and alder
Broadleaved, mixed and yew woodland	5110	Stable *Buxus sempervirens* formations on calcareous rock slopes (Berberidion p.) (31.82)	—
Broadleaved, mixed and yew woodland	5130	*Juniperus communis* formations on heaths or calcareous grasslands (31.88) p.p.	Juniper formations on calcareous grassland
Coniferous woodland	91C0	*Caledonian forest (42.51)	—
Coniferous woodland	91D0	*Bog woodland (44.A1 to 44.A4) p.p.	Bog woodland of Scots pine
Coniferous woodland	5130	*Juniperus communis* formations on heaths or calcareous grasslands (31.88) p.p.	Juniper formations on heath

BAP Broad Habitat	Annex I code	Habitats Directive[a] Annex I type	Comment
Boundary and linear features	—	—	—
Arable and horticultural	—	—	—
Improved grassland	—	—	—
Neutral grassland	6510	Lowland hay meadows (*Alopecurus pratensis*, *Sanguisorba officinalis*) (38.2)	—
Neutral grassland	6520	Mountain hay meadows (British types with *Geranium sylvaticum*) (38.3)	—
Calcareous grassland	6170	Alpine calcareous grasslands (36.41 to 36.45)	—
Calcareous grassland	6120	Semi-natural dry grasslands and scrubland facies on calcareous substrates (Festuco-Brometalia) (34.31 to 34.34)	—
Calcareous grassland	6210	Semi-natural dry grasslands and scrubland facies on calcareous substrates (Festuco-Brometalia) (*important orchid sites) (34.31 to 34.34)	—
Calcareous grassland	6230	*Species-rich *Nardus* grassland, on siliceous substrates in mountain areas (and submountain areas, in continental Europe) (35.1)	—
Acid grassland	2330	Open grassland with *Corynephorus* and *Agrostis* of continental dunes (64.1 × 35.2)	—
Bracken	—	—	—
Dwarf shrub heath	4010	Northern Atlantic wet heaths with *Erica tetralix* (31.11)	—
Dwarf shrub heath	4020	*Southern Atlantic wet heaths with *Erica ciliaris* and *Erica tetralix* (31.12)	—
Dwarf shrub heath	4030	Dry heaths (all subtypes) (31.2)	—
Dwarf shrub heath	4040	*Dry coastal heaths with *Erica vagans* and *Ulex maritimus* (31.234)	—

BAP Broad Habitat	Annex I code	Habitats Directive[a] Annex I type	Comment
Dwarf shrub heath	4060	Alpine and subalpine heaths (31.4) p.p.	Heaths that are mostly confined to the alpine zone, namely the NVC communities H13, H14, H15, H17, H19, H20 and H22, are included in the 'Montane habitats' broad habitat type
Fen, marsh and swamp	6410	*Molinia* meadows on chalk and clay (Eu-Molinion) (37.31)	—
Fen, marsh and swamp	7140	Transition mires and quaking bogs (54.5)	—
Fen, marsh and swamp	7210	Calcareous fens with *Cladium mariscus* and *Carex davalliana* (53.3)	—
Fen, marsh and swamp	7220	*Petrifying springs with tufa formation (Cratoneurion) (54.12)	—
Fen, marsh and swamp	7230	Alkaline fens (54.2)	—
Fen, marsh and swamp	7240	*Alpine pioneer formations of Caricion bicoloris-atrofuscae (54.3)	—
Fen, marsh and swamp	7250	Depressions on peat substrates (Rhynchosporion) (54.6)	—
Bogs	7110	*Active raised bogs (51.1)	—
Bogs	7120	Degraded raised bogs still capable of natural regeneration (51.2)	—
Bogs	7130	Blanket bog (*active only) (52.1 and 52.2)	—
Standing open water and canals	3110	Oligotrophic waters containing very few minerals of Atlantic sandy plains with amphibious vegetation: *Lobelia, Littorella* and *Isoetes* (22.11 × 22.31)	—
Standing open water and canals	3130	Oligotrophic waters in medio-European and perialpine areas with amphibious vegetation: *Littorella* and *Isoetes* or annual vegetation on exposed banks (Nanocyperetalia) (22.12) + (22.31 & 22.31)	—

BAP Broad Habitat	Annex I code	Habitats Directive[a] Annex I type	Comment
Standing open water and canals	3140	Hard oligo-mesotrophic waters with benthic vegetation of *Chara* formations (22.12 & 22.44)	—
Standing open water and canals	3150	Natural eutrophic lakes with Magnopotamion or Hydrocharition-type vegetation (22.13)	—
Standing open water and canals	3160	Dystrophic lakes (22.14)	—
Standing open water and canals	3170	*Mediterranean temporary ponds (22.34)	—
Rivers and streams	3260	Floating vegetation of *Ranunculus* of plain and sub-mountainous rivers (24.2)	—
Montane habitats	4060	Alpine and subalpine heaths (31.4) p.p.	Heaths that are mostly confined to the alpine zone, namely the NVC communities H13, H14, H15, H17, H19, H20 and H22, are included in the 'Montane habitats' broad habitat type
Montane habitats	4080	Sub-Arctic willow scrub (31.622)	—
Montane habitats	6150	Siliceous alpine and boreal grassland (36.32)	—
Inland rock	6130	Calaminarian grasslands (34.2)	—
Inland rock	6430	Eutrophic tall herbs (37.7 and 37.8)	—
Inland rock	8110	Siliceous scree (61.1)	—
Inland rock	8120	Eutric scree (61.2)	—
Inland rock	8210	Chasmophytic vegetation on rocky slopes: Calcareous sub-types (62.1 and 62.1A)	—
Inland rock	8220	Chasmophytic vegetation on rocky slopes: Silicicolous sub-types (62.2)	—
Inland rock	8240	*Limestone pavements (62.4)	—
Built-up areas and gardens	—	—	—

BAP Broad Habitat	Annex I code	Habitats Directive[a] Annex I type	Comment
Supralittoral rock	1230	Vegetated sea cliffs of the Atlantic and Baltic coasts (18.21)	—
Supralittoral sediment	1210	Annual vegetation of drift lines (17.2)	—
Supralittoral sediment	1220	Perennial vegetation of stony banks (17.3)	—
Supralittoral sediment	2110	Embryonic shifting dunes (16.211)	—
Supralittoral sediment	2120	Shifting dunes along the shoreline with *Ammophila arenaria* (white dunes) (16.212)	—
Supralittoral sediment	2130	*Fixed dunes with herbaceous vegetation (grey dunes) (16.221 to 16.227)	—
Supralittoral sediment	2140	*Decalcified fixed dunes with *Empetrum nigrum* (16.23)	—
Supralittoral sediment	2150	*Eu-Atlantic decalcified fixed dunes (Calluno-Ulicetea) (16.24)	—
Supralittoral sediment	2160	Dunes with *Salix arenaria* (16.26)	—
Supralittoral sediment	2170	Humid dune slacks (16.31 to 16.35)	—
Supralittoral sediment	21A0	Machair (1.A)	—
Supralittoral sediment	2250	*Dune juniper thickets (*Juniperus* spp.)	—
Littoral rock	8330	Submerged or slightly submerged sea caves p.p.	—
Littoral sediment	1140	Mudflats and sandflats not covered by sea water at low tide (14)	—
Littoral sediment	1160	Large shallow inlets and bays (12)	—
Littoral sediment	1310	*Salicornia* and other annuals colonising mud and sand (15.11)	—
Littoral sediment	1320	*Spartina* swards (Spartinion) (15.12)	—
Littoral sediment	1330	Atlantic salt meadows (Glauco-Puccinellietalia) (15.13)	—
Littoral sediment	1340	*Continental salt meadows (*Puccinellietalia distantis*) (15.14)	—
Littoral sediment	1410	Mediterranean salt meadows (*Juncetalia maritimi*) (15.15)	—

BAP Broad Habitat	Annex I code	Habitats Directive[a] Annex I type	Comment
Littoral sediment	1420	Mediterranean and thermo-Atlantic halophilous scrubs (*Arthocnememtalia fructicosae*) (15.16)	—
Inshore sublittoral rock	1170	Reefs (11.24)	—
Inshore sublittoral rock	8330	Submerged or slightly submerged sea caves p.p.	—
Inshore sublittoral sediment	1110	Sandbanks that are slightly covered by sea water all the time (11.25)	—
Offshore shelf rock	—	—	—
Offshore shelf sediment	—	—	—
Continental shelf slope	—	—	—
Oceanic seas	—	—	—

[a] Asterisks indicate Annex I Priority Habitat types.

Appendix 3
Annotated list of key references for plant identification

LICHENS

Broad, K. (1989) *Lichens in Southern Woodlands*. Forestry Commission Handbook No. 4. London: Her Majesty's Stationery Office.
Contains photographs of 24 species that grow on trees with a reproduction of a wall chart on lichens and pollution zones.

Coppins, B. J. (2002) *Checklist of Lichens of Great Britain and Ireland*. London: British Lichen Society.

Dobson, F. S. (2000) *Lichens. An Illustrated Guide to the British and Irish species*, 4th edn. Richmond: The Richmond Publishing Company.
General, with lots of photographs, descriptions, maps, keys.

Hodgetts, N. G. (1992) *Cladonia: A Field Guide*. Peterborough: Joint Nature Conservation Committee.
A small, cheap, simple, very useful field guide to this genus.

Jahn, H. M. (1981) *Collins Guide to Ferns Mosses and Lichens*. London: Collins.
General; contains lots of photographs, but no keys; now out-dated but still generally good.

Orange, A. (1994) *Lichens on Trees. A Guide to some of the Commonest Species*. British Plant Life No. 3. Cardiff: National Museum of Wales.
Contains 39 species, illustrated, although the photographs are a bit small.

Purvis, O. W., Coppins, B. J., Hawksworth, D. L., James, P. J. & Moore, D. M. (1992) *The Lichen Flora of Great Britain and Ireland*. London: Natural History Museum Publications/ British Lichen Society.
The standard work, but highly technical. The checklist by Coppins (2002) (see above) should be used for the up-to-date names of lichens.

Purvis, O. W., Coppins, B. J. & James, P. W. (1993) Checklist of lichens of Great Britain and Ireland. *British Lichen Society Bulletin*, **72** (Supplement).
An updated checklist with new names and more species added to the 1992 flora.

Seaward, M. R. D. (ed.) (1995 *et seq.*) *Lichen Atlas of the British Isles*. London: Lichen Society.
Contains A4 maps with ring binders, with comments on distribution, ecology, status and identification.

BRYOPHYTES

Blockeel, T. L. & Long, D. G. (1998) *A Check-list and Census Catalogue of British and Irish Bryophytes*. Cardiff: British Bryological Society.

Daniels, R. E. & Eddy, A. (1990) *Handbook of European Sphagna*. London: Her Majesty's Stationery Office.
Each species fully described and illustrated, but difficult for beginners.

Hill, M. O. (1992) *Sphagnum: A Field Guide*, Peterborough: The Joint Nature Conservation Committee.
A very useful field guide for non-specialists wanting to identify *Sphagnum* in the field.

Hill, M. O., Preston, C. D. & Smith, A. J. E. (eds) (1991, 1992, 1994) *Atlas of the Bryophytes of Britain and Ireland*. Volumes 1, 2 & 3. Colchester: Harley Books.
Essential information on distribution and habitats of British bryophytes.

Jahns, H. M. (1981) *Collins Guide to Ferns, Mosses and Lichens*. London: Collins.
Lots of photographs; general, but useful.

Paton, J. A. (1999) *The Liverwort Flora of the British Isles*. Colchester, Essex: Harley Books.
Now the definitive liverwort flora, essential for full identification.

Smith, A. J. E. (1978) *The Moss Flora of Britain and Ireland*. Cambridge: Cambridge University Press.
Full keys, rather limited illustrations. The definitive work on mosses to date, essential for full identification,

although some of the species and/genus names are now out of date and there have been species splits. The various individual keys for groups and the checklist by Blockeel & Long (1998) (see above) need to be consulted. The key to genera was updated by Smith (1991) in *Bulletin of the British Bryological Society*, **57**, 41–62. An updated edition of Smith's *Flora* is due to be published in 2004.

Smith, A. J. E. (1990) *The Liverworts of Britain and Ireland*. Cambridge: Cambridge University Press.
Full keys, many illustrations, now replaced by Paton (1999) (see above).

Watson, E. V. (1981) *British Mosses and Liverworts*, 3rd edn. Cambridge: Cambridge University Press.
Covers most species with keys, illustrations, and helpful ecological comments. Very useful and quicker to use, especially to genera, than the definitive works of Smith and Paton (see above). Some identification characters are erroneous, however (e.g. *Aloina*), the taxonomy is very out of date, and the species covered in detail are not always the commonest members of their genus (for example, *Plagiothecium denticulatum* is much less common than *P. nemorale* or *P. succulentum*).

CHAROPHYTES

Moore, J. A. (1986) *Charophytes of Great Britain and Ireland*. London: Botanical Society of the British Isles.
Covers identification (keys, descriptions, drawings) and distribution of all British and Irish species.

Stewart, N. F. & Church, J. M. (1992) *Red Data Books of Britain and Ireland: Stoneworts*. Peterborough: Joint Nature Conservation Committee.
Contains a key to identification.

FERNS

Hutchinson, G. & Thomas, B. A. (1997) *Welsh Ferns*, 7th edn. Cardiff: The National Museum of Wales.

Jermy, C. & Camus, J. (1991) *The Illustrated Field Guide to Ferns and Allied Plants of the British Isles*. London: Her Majesty's Stationery Office and Botanical Society of the British Isles.

Page, C. N. (1997) *The Ferns of Britain and Ireland*, 2nd edn. Cambridge: Cambridge University Press.
One of the best of several standard texts on fern identification, with descriptions, keys, ecological notes and small maps.

VASCULAR PLANTS

Blamey, M., Fitter, R. & Fitter, A. (2003) *Wild Flowers of Britain and Ireland*. London: A. & C. Black.

Clapham, A. R., Tutin, T. G. & Moore, D. M. (1987) *Flora of the British Isles*, 3rd edn, reprinted with corrections 1989. Cambridge: Cambridge University Press.
The 3rd edition of the once classic flora in standard use in Britain from 1951 to 1991, now largely superseded by Stace (1997) (see below). Still very useful as it contains more comprehensive descriptions of plants and their distributions.

Dudman, A. A. & Richards, A. J. (1997) *Dandelions of Great Britain and Ireland*, BSBI Handbook No. 9. London: Botanical Society of the British Isles.

Graham, G. G. & Primavesi, A. L. (1993) *Roses of Great Britain and Ireland*, BSBI Handbook No. 7. London: Botanical Society of the British Isles.

Haslam, S., Sinker, C. & Wolseley, P. (1987) *British Water Plants* (revised). Shrewsbury: Field Studies Council.

Hubbard, C. E. (1984) *Grasses*, 3rd edn (revised by J. C. E. Hubbard). London: Penguin Books.

Jermy, A. C., Chater, A. O. & David, R. W. (1982) *Sedges of the British Isles*, 2nd edn BSBI Handbook No. 1. London: Botanical Society of the British Isles.

Lousley, J. E. & Kent, D. H. (1981) *Docks and Knotweeds of the British Isles*, BSBI Handbook No. 3. London: Botanical Society of the British Isles.

Meikle, R. D. (1984) *Willows and Poplars of Great Britain and Ireland*, BSBI Handbook No. 4. London: Botanical Society of the British Isles.

Preston, C. D. (1995) *Pondweeds of Great Britain and Ireland*, BSBI Handbook No. 8. London: Botanical Society of the British Isles.

Rich, T. C. G. (1991) *Crucifers of Great Britain and Ireland*, BSBI Handbook No. 6. London: Botanical Society of the British Isles.

Rich, T. C. G. & Jermy, A. C. (eds) (1998) *Plant Crib 1998*. London: Botanical Society of the British Isles.
Hints on identification of numerous difficult genera.

Rose, F. (1981) *The Wild Flower Key*. London: Frederick Warne.
Contains the only vegetative keys available to various habitats (these are also sold separately), and numerous field jizz characteristics.

Rose, F. (1989) *Colour Identification Guide to the Grasses, Sedges, Rushes and Ferns of the British Isles and North-western Europe*. Middlesex: Viking. Keys and colour illustrations.

Sell, P. D. & Murrell, G. (1996) *Flora of Great Britain and Ireland*, Volume 5: *Butomacaeae – Orchidaceae*. Cambridge: Cambridge University Press.

Stace, C. A. (1997) *New Flora of the British Isles*, 2nd edn. Cambridge: Cambridge University Press. The current definitive flora with keys, drawings and diagnostic descriptions.

Stace, C. A. (1999) *Field Flora of the British Isles*. Cambridge: Cambridge University Press. A condensed version of Stace (1997).

Tutin, T. G. (1980) *Umbellifers of the British Isles*, BSBI Handbook No. 2. London: Botanical Society of the British Isles.

Appendix 4
Determining appropriate quadrat size for vegetation sampling

The size of a quadrat affects the measured values of frequency, density, and cover, etc. (see Figure A4.1 below). It is therefore important to decide in advance which values are to be measured. Experience has shown that different vegetation types and different measurement types require different quadrat sizes. In Part II, quadrat methods for habitat monitoring are described in Sections 6.4.2 (frame quadrats for cover and density estimates); 6.4.3 (random mini-quadrats for frequency estimates); 6.4.4 (FIBS analysis); and 6.4.5 (point quadrats). Quadrat size is also considered in the section on NVC mapping (Section 6.1.6). In Part III, the chapters on species groups and Chapter 10 also contain discussions of quadrat methods, where appropriate to the species group concerned.

This appendix deals with the selection of the appropriate quadrat size. Methods for calculating the number of quadrats required are given in Part I, Section 2.3.4. Frequency estimates are given the most attention, because quadrat size affects frequency measures more than others (see Figure A4.1). However, the lists of optimum quadrat size for different vegetation types can generally be applied to all quadrat sampling methods (with the obvious exception of point quadrats).

Techniques for determining optimum quadrat size for frequency measures are subjective, and a quadrat of any size will sample some species more adequately than others. The quadrat size chosen will therefore depend upon the type of vegetation being sampled. The use of random mini-quadrats for estimating frequency is described in Part II, Section 6.4.3.

Frequencies greater than 95% and less than 5% can result in heavily skewed distributions. The quadrat size should therefore ideally be such that mean frequencies of all species fall within this range. If a quadrat is one or two times larger than the mean area per individual of the most common species, randomly distributed species will have mean frequencies of 63% and 86% for these quadrat sizes (Bonham, 1989). However, selection of a single quadrat size is obviously not appropriate for measuring all the species in a community. This problem can be overcome by using a series of quadrat sizes at each sample point in a 'nested' design (see Part II, Section 6.4.4) that gives frequencies between 5% and 95% for the maximum number of species.

There will be no need to use nested quadrats if the type of community to be sampled is known in advance; there is little point in using quadrats of 1 m^2 if you are measuring the density of pine trees in a forest.

The type of measurement being made will also affect the optimal quadrat size; for example, cover estimates are most accurate in small quadrats. However, as a minor consideration with smaller quadrats, there is a proportionally increased error associated with the boundary of the quadrat because the edge : area ratio is higher (boundary errors are observer errors, such as including an individual near to the boundary when in fact it is outside the quadrat, or not including individuals that are inside the quadrat).

Vegetation with smaller plants, greater density or greater species diversity require smaller quadrats in order to reduce the complexity of the sampling unit to a manageable level. However, if specific species surveys are required, larger quadrats are needed for species that are small but rare.

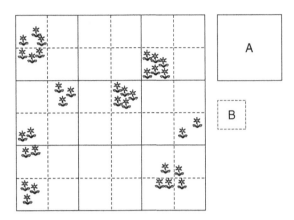

Figure A4.1. The effects of quadrat size on the measurements of biomass, cover, density and frequency. Quadrat A is four times the size of quadrat B. A single quadrat of size A will be more likely to 'hit' an individual of a species than a single quadrat of size B. If several quadrats are laid out (for simplicity the whole area is covered by quadrats in this example), the estimates of biomass, cover and density will be the same using quadrats A or B. However, there will be more between-quadrat variation for the B quadrats, and the different quadrat sizes give different estimates of frequency. This occurs for any distribution pattern of a species or habitat type. In this example with a clumped distribution, B quadrats give a frequency estimate of 13/36 = 0.36 and A quadrats give an estimate of 7/9 = 0.78. For frequency measures it is useful to choose a size that avoids extreme values. Source: Greenwood (1996).

There is much more that could be said about choosing optimal quadrat size; see Bonham (1989) for a more rigorous analysis. However, there is no simple rule for calculating optimal size. It is therefore probably more straightforward to use a rule of thumb based upon the community being sampled, such as that given below. Nevertheless, you should bear in mind the considerations outlined above, particularly for frequency data, rather than employing a certain quadrat size without thinking about it. One advantage of using nested quadrats of different sizes (Part II, Section 6.4.4) is that the most appropriate size for analysis of each species can be chosen once all the data have been collected.

The sizes most often used for different vegetation types are:

- 0.01–0.25 m^2 in bryophyte, lichen and algal communities
- 0.25–16.0 m^2 in grassland, tall herb, short scrub or aquatic macrophyte communities
- 25–100 m^2 for tall shrub communities
- 400–2500 m^2 for trees in woods and forests

However, other optimal quadrat sizes have been suggested. The following optimal quadrat sizes have been suggested for frequency estimates:

- 0.01–0.1 m^2 for the moss layer
- 1–2 m^2 for the herb layer
- 4 m^2 for tall herbs and low shrubs
- 10 m^2 for tall shrubs and low trees
- 100 m^2 for trees

NVC mapping (Part II, Section 6.1.6) uses standardised quadrat sizes for different vegetation types. These are summarised in Box 6.12.

There is also a consideration of cost and time to be made when deciding what size of quadrat to use; larger quadrats will obviously be more time-consuming (and therefore more costly) to record than will smaller ones. Finally, if you are repeating a previous monitoring survey, the same size of quadrat as was used in the previous survey should be employed to enable valid comparisons to be made between the different data sets.

Appendix 5
The relocation of permanent plots

Various techniques (e.g. quadrats and transects) have been used to mark permanent plots; these are described briefly below. A general point to consider is that the more techniques used, the quicker it will normally be to find plots again.

MAPPING

Measurements to nearby features have been widely used to map locations of plots and are relatively foolproof, provided that mapping is accurate (use a backsighting compass for bearings and measure distances correctly) and that the features chosen are fixed and permanent. This is particularly important for long-term monitoring studies; features such as fence posts may be damaged or lost over time. However, the method is often difficult to apply in large homogeneous habitats, such as grasslands, where obvious permanent features are lacking. It is also time-consuming when a large number of plots need to be relocated.

MARKER POSTS

Wooden or metal posts are widely used and can be quick to re-find in relatively small sites. However, small markers can be hidden by vegetation. Large markers can cause significant damage to habitats, tend to be unsightly and attract the attention of people. Animals too may scratch against large markers, thereby causing disproportionate disturbance to vegetation, resulting in bias in the sampling. Unless markers are strong and well secured they may be broken by livestock or removed by vandals, etc. Posts may also be lost over time through rotting or corrosion and even frost heave.

PAINT

Paint has been used to mark plots, especially where rocks, walls or posts are available nearby. It can often be used discreetly, but tends to fade and disappear with time. Timber dye is better for marking wood than is ordinary paint (N. A. Robinson, personal communication).

BURIED METAL MARKERS

Buried metal markers (aluminium plates, wire mesh, iron bars, etc.), which can be re-found by using metal detectors, can be used for marking plots. Transponders can also be used, which are re-found by using a hand-held scanning device. Transponders give off a unique signal, so there is no confusion about the identity of relocated markers.

As these are hidden they are not unsightly and do not attract the unwanted attention of people or livestock. However, burying the markers causes disturbance to the habitat, and the metal may corrode or cause localised toxicity; in addition, the widespread use of metal detectors by treasure hunters may result in their being dug up. It is difficult to bury markers on very shallow soils, and frost heaving of soil in the uplands may result in movement or exposure of the markers. Unless accompanied by measurements or photographs, the precise positions of markers can be very time-consuming to find.

PHOTOGRAPHS

Photographs can speed positioning of plots, but in most cases are unlikely to allow precise relocation of individual quadrats.

TOTAL STATIONS

Total Stations are essentially surveying instruments that combine theodolites and laser range finders to allow the highly accurate measurements of bearings, distances and ground level. These allow the fast and accurate relocation of plots as well as providing additional data if required (such as topography maps). Current models are now waterproof and relatively portable (pack size approximately the size of a suitcase, mass c. 11 kg) and are now much more suited to ecological fieldwork. Cranfield University, for example, has very successfully used them for relocating permanent transects as part of long-term studies of plant water requirements (D. Gowing, personal communication).

Plots are located by placing the Total Station over a fixed permanent base marker (e.g. a bolt drilled into a fixed object) and directing an assistant with a laser-reflecting prism on a staff to a location pre-recorded according to its bearing and distance. A radio is required to communicate between the station operator and the assistant holding the staff. Current Total Stations operate up to a distance of c. 1 km and have an accuracy of 2 in 1 million, and thus can relocate plots to within a couple of millimetres if required. In practice, this level of accuracy is tricky and time-consuming to obtain. However, an accuracy to 1–2 cm can easily be achieved. Quadrats can be relocated by recording two diagonal points of each plot, whereas for transects only the start and end points need to be recorded.

The main advantage of Total Stations is that they allow very rapid relocation of plots. They are also accurate enough to negate the need for marking the plot at all, thereby avoiding the damage caused by animals and other disadvantages of using posts, etc. They can also help enormously with accurate mapping of vegetation, topography and other physical features if required. Although new models cost about £4000 (£2000–£3000 for older versions)

they can be very cost-effective when the potential reduction in survey time is taken into account. They may also be hired for approximately £100 per week.

Their disadvantages are that they are not cost-effective or time-efficient when only a small number of plots need to be relocated. Two operators are also required. It is also problematical to use them on very large sites because they are cumbersome to move around and require about 25 minutes to set up at each fixed point. They cannot be used in enclosed habitats such as woodland or scrubland or on very uneven sites, unless the Station can be set up on a high point.

GLOBAL POSITIONING SYSTEMS (GPS)

Recent technological advances, together with the removal of signal degradation through 'selective availability', have led to considerable increases in the accuracy of handheld GPS. These are now capable of locating and relocating positions to an accuracy of 10 to 20 m or better, depending on atmospheric conditions. Hand-held GPS units can currently be purchased for about £200–£300.

If sub-metre accuracy is required, differential GPS (DGPS) can be used. DGPS units receive GPS signals and combine them with error correction signals from fixed stations, whose precise locations are known. DGPS can be more time-consuming to use and the equipment is much more expensive and bulky than hand-held units. Both of these systems are limited by a requirement to have a clear view of the sky, and do not function well in dense tree cover, for example.

Although by itself GPS is still insufficient for exact relocation of plots for most monitoring purposes, it can be very useful when combined with other techniques, particularly on very large sites. For example, GPS can be used on moorland sites to direct the surveyor to a search zone within which a small unobtrusive marker can be used to locate the exact plot.

Appendix 6
Equipment required for undertaking different types of survey

	Aerial photography	Fixed-point photography	Phase 1 habitat surveying	NVC mapping	Grapnel sampling of aquatic vegetation	Stock mapping	Permanent plots	Temporary plots	Plotless sampling	Dead wood survey and monitoring	Surveying fungi	Surveying fungi by using quadrats	Surveying fungi by using transects	Surveying fungi by using fixed-point photography
Good-quality overlapping aerial photographs	*		*											
Stereoscope/stereo-analyst software	*													
Photogrammetric plotting machine (used to create maps – optional)	*													
Sketchmaster for transfer of interpretation to base map (optional)	*													
Digitising hardware and software (optional)	*		*	*		*								
Light table (optional)	*													
35 mm single-lens reflex camera		*												*
28–35 mm lens for normal shots and 50 mm for detail		*												*
Slide films or digital memory				*			*	*	*					
Sturdy tripod with easily adjustable legs and central column and a ball and socket head. If the fixed-angle method is to be used (see text) then an additional Linhof Propan pan and tilt head (Model II) is recommended		*												*
Standard 2 m ranging pole (and ranging-pole support for rocky sites) if the centre pole system is to be used		*												
Cable release		*												*
Spare batteries for camera		*												*
Large-scale site map with pencils and ball-point pens		*												
Map of the site at a useable scale, e.g. 1 : 5000			*											
OS map or sketch map to mark location of the photograph						*								

Surveying lichens by using quadrats	Surveying lichens using fixed-point photography	Surveying lichens by fixed-point photography	Surveying bryophytes	Surveying bryophytes by visual estimation	Surveying bryophytes using transects	Surveying bryophytes using quadrats	Surveying bryophytes by using quadrats	Surveying bryophytes using fixed-point photography	Surveying aquatic vegetation by quadrats and transects	Surveying vascular plants	Surveying vascular plants by fixed-point photography	Vascular plant demography	Surveying dragonflies and damselflies by exuviae	Surveying dragonflies and damselflies by transect/timed count	Surveying butterflies by using timed larval/egg counts	Surveying butterflies by using quadrats and transects	Surveying butterflies by using larval/egg counts: quadrats and transects
	*						*			*	*						
	*									*							
							*		*							*	
	*									*							
	*									*							
	*									*	*						
									*		*						
										*	*						

	Aerial photography	Fixed-point photography	Phase I habitat surveying	NVC mapping	Grapnel sampling of aquatic vegetation	Stock mapping	Permanent plots	Temporary plots	Plotless sampling	Dead wood survey and monitoring	Surveying fungi	Surveying fungi by using quadrats	Surveying fungi by using transects	Surveying fungi by using fixed-point photography
Safety equipment as necessary		*	*	*	*	*	*	*	*	*	*	*	*	*
Copies of 1 : 10 000 or 1 : 25 000 field maps			*			*								
1 : 50 000 Ordnance Survey maps			*											
Binoculars/telescope			*											
Pen for annotating prints														
Clipboard coloured pencils, lead pencils, rubber, pens, notebook, waterproof paper, plastic bags or weather writer (for protection of notebook in wet weather)		*	*	*	*	*	*	*	*	*	*	*	*	*
Botanical field guides and × 10 hand lens			*	*							*	*	*	*
GPS			*	*	*									
Berol Verithin coloured pencils, Rotring drawing pens (0.35 mm, 0.5 mm)			*											
T-squares, set-squares, rulers			*											
Calculators			*											
Romer dot grids (for measuring areas and determining grid references)			*	*										
Line-hatching apparatus (optional)			*	*										
Planimeter (optional)			*	*										
Handbook for Phase I Survey Field Manual			*											
Quadrats, which for most circumstances can simply be made out of string or washing line (which does not tangle as easily as string) with a tent peg at each corner, and/or a 50 m tape measure with a tent peg at one end for convenience					*		*	*		*		*		
Summaries of NVC communities or copies of tables alone, or appropriate NVC volumes if summaries are not available				*										

Surveying lichens by using quadrats	Surveying lichens using fixed-point photography	Surveying bryophytes	Surveying bryophytes by visual estimation	Surveying bryophytes using transects	Surveying bryophytes by using quadrats	Surveying bryophytes using fixed-point photography	Surveying aquatic vegetation by quadrats and transects	Surveying vascular plants	Surveying vascular plants by fixed-point photography	Vascular plant demography	Surveying dragonflies and damselflies by exuviae	Surveying dragonflies and damselflies by transect/timed count	Surveying butterflies by using timed larval/egg counts	Surveying butterflies by using larval/egg counts: quadrats and transects
*	*	*	*	*	*	*	*	*	*	*	*	*	*	*
*							*		*	*				
						*								
*	*	*	*	*	*	*	*	*	*	*	*	*	*	*
*	*	*	*	*	*	*	*	*	*	*				
					*									
*					*		*	*						*

	Aerial photography	Fixed-point photography	Phase 1 habitat surveying	NVC mapping	Grapnel sampling of aquatic vegetation	Stock mapping	Permanent plots	Temporary plots	Plotless sampling	Dead wood survey and monitoring	Surveying fungi	Surveying fungi by using quadrats	Surveying fungi by using transects	Surveying fungi by using fixed-point photography
Coloured pencils/fine liner pens for mapping habitat extent				*										
Snorkelling/diving equipment (if required)														
Clipboard/weather writer, NVC recording sheets (or paper), waterproof paper				*										
Hand lens, plant identification guides and plastic bags with waterproof labels for samples; a plant press may be useful if away for long periods of survey for higher plants, and bryophyte packets or nylon mesh bags for samples				*							*	*	*	*
Grapnel (7 cm) and/or underwater viewer					*									
Graduated cord					*									
Standard recording equipment or data logger					*									
Boat (for most water bodies)					*									
Vertical aerial photographs						*								
Compass		*	*		*	*	*	*	*	*				*
Sighting compass														
Ranging poles						*	*	*	*	*				*
Increment borer (optional)						*								
Tape measure(s)						*				*				*
Cartographical equipment						*								
Equipment for analysis of maps once created						*								
30–50 m tapes, preferably bright yellow or white, to lay out plots, and provide axes for co-ordinates							*	*	*					
Galvanised angle-irons or posts, up to 1.3 m long, to be permanent markers							*							

Surveying lichens by using quadrats	Surveying lichens using fixed-point photography	Surveying bryophytes	Surveying bryophytes by visual estimation	Surveying bryophytes using transects	Surveying bryophytes by using quadrats	Surveying bryophytes using fixed-point photography	Surveying aquatic vegetation by quadrats and transects	Surveying vascular plants by fixed-point photography	Surveying vascular plants	Vascular plant demography	Surveying dragonflies and damselflies by exuviae	Surveying dragonflies and damselflies by transect/ timed count	Surveying butterflies by using timed larval/egg counts	Surveying butterflies by using larval/egg counts: quadrats and transects
							*							
*	*	*	*	*	*	*	*	*		*				
							*							
								*						
			*			*								
*		*	*	*	*	*	*			*				*
								*						

	Aerial photography	Fixed-point photography	Phase 1 habitat surveying	NVC mapping	Grapnel sampling of aquatic vegetation	Stock mapping	Permanent plots	Temporary plots	Plotless sampling	Dead wood survey and monitoring	Surveying fungi	Surveying fungi by using quadrats	Surveying fungi by using transects	Surveying fungi by using fixed-point photography
Girth tapes, short and long							*	*	*	*				
Paper, preferably squared (or datalogger for recording directly into a computer)							*	*	*					
Hypsometer or Abney level (optional)							*	*	*	*				
Relascope (optional)										*				
Quadrats or transect markers painted a bright light colour										*				
Pegs or hooks for attaching string to grid markers														
String							*	*	*	*			*	
Stopwatch (if searches are timed)											*			
Collecting materials: small containers, waxed paper, tubes, jars, plastic bags, etc. as appropriate											*	*	*	
Hand lens											*	*	*	
Transect, e.g. poles, measuring tape													*	
Permanent markers for quadrat corners (if required)							*					*		
Tape or rope to split larger quadrats				*			*	*		*		*		
Knife (with fixed blade) and bags for collecting				*							*	*	*	*
Transponders and metal detector							*							
KOH and bleach solution (used in identification)														
Hooked stick for collecting plants														
Plastic bag to keep the dry-wipe board dry														
Marker pen for the dry-wipe board														

Surveying lichens by using quadrats	Surveying lichens using fixed-point photography	Surveying bryophytes	Surveying bryophytes by visual estimation	Surveying bryophytes using transects	Surveying bryophytes by using quadrats	Surveying bryophytes using fixed-point photography	Surveying aquatic vegetation by quadrats and transects	Surveying vascular plants	Surveying vascular plants by fixed-point photography	Vascular plant demography	Surveying dragonflies and damselflies by exuviae	Surveying dragonflies and damselflies by transect/ timed count	Surveying butterflies by using timed larval/egg counts	Surveying butterflies by using larval/egg counts: quadrats and transects
*		*	*		*		*	*						
								*						
				*				*			*	*		
			*	*	*					*				
*			*		*			*					*	*
*			*	*	*		*	*						
*				*	*		*	*		*				
*			*	*	*		*	*						
*	*	*	*	*	*	*	*	*	*	*				
*					*			*						
*														
							*							
												*		
												*		

	Aerial photography	Fixed-point photography	Phase 1 habitat surveying	NVC mapping	Grapnel sampling of aquatic vegetation	Stock mapping	Permanent plots	Temporary plots	Plotless sampling	Dead wood survey and monitoring	Surveying fungi	Surveying fungi by using quadrats	Surveying fungi by using transects	Surveying fungi by using fixed-point photography
Dry-wipe board (or clipboard in a plastic bag) annotated with sample point location, etc. (included in the photograph to assist identification during later analysis)														
Pond net														
Butterfly net														
Sticks to place in water for emergent Odonata (if required)														

Surveying butterflies by using larval/egg counts: quadrats and transects	Surveying butterflies by using timed larval/egg counts	Surveying dragonflies and damselflies by transect/timed count	Surveying dragonflies and damselflies by exuviae	Vascular plant demography	Surveying vascular plants by fixed-point photography	Surveying vascular plants	Surveying aquatic vegetation by quadrats and transects	Surveying bryophytes using fixed-point photography	Surveying bryophytes by using quadrats	Surveying bryophytes using transects	Surveying bryophytes by visual estimation	Surveying bryophytes	Surveying lichens using fixed-point photography	Surveying lichens by using quadrats
					*									
			*											
		*												
			*											

	Surveying adult butterflies by using transects	Surveying macromoths by using light traps	Surveying macromoths by using pheromone traps	Surveying adult and larval invertebrates	Surveying invertebrates by using timed searches	Surveying invertebrates by using quadrats	Surveying invertebrates by using pitfall traps	Surveying invertebrates by using suction sampling	Surveying invertebrates by using window traps	Surveying invertebrates by using artificial refugia	Surveying aquatic invertebrates by vegetation	Surveying aquatic invertebrates by sweep netting	Surveying aquatic invertebrates by kick sampling	Surveying aquatic invertebrates by cylinder sampling	Surveying fish by direct counting
Safety equipment as necessary	*	*	*	*	*	*	*	*	*	*	*	*	*	*	*
Copies of 1:10,000 or 1:25,000 field maps	*	*				*	*			*	*				
1:50,000 Ordnance Survey maps															
Binoculars/telescope	*														*
Snorkelling/diving equipment (if required)															*
Boat (for most water bodies)															
Ranging Roles	*														
Tape measure(s)						*				*					
Fieldnote recording equipment	*	*	*	*	*	*	*	*	*	*	*	*	*	*	*
Quadrats or transect markers painted a bright light colour															
Pegs or hooks for attaching string to grid markers															
String									*						
Stopwatch (if searches are timed)					*										
Collecting materials – small containers, waxed paper, tubes, jars, plastic bags, etc. as appropriate								*							
Hand lens				*	*										
Quadrats or transects	*				*	*									
Permanent markers for quadrat corners															
Tape/rope to split larger quadrats															
Pond net											*	*			
Butterfly net	*														
Torch		*													
Pheromone trap	*				*										

Survey type	R1	R2	R3	R4	R5	R6	R7	R8	R9	...	Rx	Ry
Surveying fish by trapping	*					*			*			
Surveying fish by seine netting	*					*			*			
Surveying fish by trawl netting	*					*			*			
Surveying fish by push, throw and lift netting	*					*			*			
Surveying fish by electrofishing	*					*			*			
Surveying amphibians by torch counts	*								*			*
Surveying amphibians by bottle traps	*								*			*
Surveying amphibians by sweep netting	*								*			
Surveying amphibians by pitfall trapping	*							*	*			
Surveying amphibians by terrestrial transect searches	*	*							*		*	*
Surveying amphibians by egg searching	*								*			
Surveying amphibians by mark-recapture	*								*			
Surveying reptiles by using artificial refugia	*	*						*	*			
Surveying reptiles by using transects	*	*							*		*	
Surveying reptiles by using transects	*								*			
Surveying reptiles by using trapping techniques	*			*					*			
Surveying reptiles by using mark-recapture	*								*			
Surveying birds by using territory mapping	*	*		*					*			
Surveying birds by using line transects	*	*	*	*					*			

	Surveying adult butterflies by using transects	Surveying macromoths by using light traps	Surveying macromoths by using pheromone traps	Surveying adult and larval invertebrates	Surveying invertebrates by using timed searches	Surveying invertebrates by using quadrats	Surveying invertebrates by using pitfall traps	Surveying invertebrates by using suction sampling	Surveying invertebrates by using window traps	Surveying invertebrates by using artificial refugia	Surveying aquatic invertebrates by vegetation	Surveying aquatic invertebrates by sweep netting	Surveying aquatic invertebrates by kick sampling	Surveying aquatic invertebrates by cylinder sampling	Surveying fish by direct counting
Pheromones	*														
Pooter/aspirator				*	*	*				*					
Sampling equipment as required (e.g. secateurs, knife, trowel). Sample bags for vegetation or soil				*	*	*									
Clippers and bags for plant material						*									
Sieves and photographic trays for sorting						*									
Sieve and filters							*		*						
Pitfall traps (e.g. large yogurt pots) and lids							*								
Pieces of wire mesh (for covering trap) and staples							*								
Trowel, soil corer on first visit							*								
Ethylene glycol or other preservative							*				*	*	*	*	
Watertight collecting jars							*								
Funnel and container for removing trap fluid							*								
Suction sampler, nets and fuel								*							
Killing agent (ethyl acetate) and cotton wool								*							
Steel ring – 0.25 m²								*							
Wooden stake, mallet, platform, brackets, screws									*						
Perspex sheeting									*						
Trays of various colours, water, detergent									*						

Surveying fish by trapping	Surveying fish by seine netting	Surveying fish by trawl netting	Surveying fish by push, throw and lift netting	Surveying fish by electrofishing	Surveying amphibians by torch counts	Surveying amphibians by bottle traps	Surveying amphibians by sweep netting	Surveying amphibians by pitfall trapping	Surveying amphibians by terrestrial transect searches	Surveying amphibians by egg searching	Surveying amphibians by mark-recapture	Surveying reptiles by using artificial refugia	Surveying reptiles by using transects	Surveying reptiles by using trapping techniques	Surveying reptiles by using mark-recapture	Surveying birds by using territory mapping	Surveying birds by using line transects
								*								*	

	Surveying adult butterflies by using transects	Surveying macromoths by using light traps	Surveying macromoths by using pheromone traps	Surveying adult and larval invertebrates	Surveying invertebrates by using timed searches	Surveying invertebrates by using quadrats	Surveying invertebrates by using pitfall traps	Surveying invertebrates by using suction sampling	Surveying invertebrates by using window traps	Surveying invertebrates by using artificial refugia	Surveying aquatic invertebrates by vegetation	Surveying aquatic invertebrates by sweep netting	Surveying aquatic invertebrates by kick sampling	Surveying aquatic invertebrates by cylinder sampling	Surveying fish by direct counting
Interlocking Perspex sheets									*						
Ethanol/glycerol solution									*						
Collecting jars		*	*	*	*	*	*	*	*	*	*	*	*	*	
Cardboard/slate/ceramic/wooden tiles										*					
Collecting buckets or bottles and/or net											*	*	*	*	
White plastic tray for sorting captures											*	*	*		
Marker, waterproof labels											*	*	*		
Plastic specimen tubes											*	*	*	*	
Kick net or Surber sampler													*		
Cylinder sampler														*	
Polarised glasses															*
Fish counters and data loggers															*
Video camera (optional)															*
Traps (baskets, cages, pots, fykes or intercepts)															
Floats, rope (for marking traps)															
Seine net and haul ropes															
Dip net															
Measuring board, scale envelopes, etc.															
Trawl net															
Lines															
Nets															
Generator															
Electrofishing equipment															

Surveying fish by trapping	Surveying fish by seine netting	Surveying fish by trawl netting	Surveying fish by push, throw and lift netting	Surveying fish by electrofishing	Surveying amphibians by torch counts	Surveying amphibians by bottle traps	Surveying amphibians by sweep netting	Surveying amphibians by pitfall trapping	Surveying amphibians by terrestrial transect searches	Surveying amphibians by egg searching	Surveying amphibians by mark-recapture	Surveying reptiles by using artificial refugia	Surveying reptiles by using transects	Surveying reptiles by using trapping techniques	Surveying reptiles by using mark-recapture	Surveying birds by using mark-recapture	Surveying birds by using territory mapping	Surveying birds by using line transects
															*			
	*																	
	*																	
	*																	
		*																
		*																
			*								*				*			
				*														
				*														

	Surveying adult butterflies by using transects	Surveying macromoths by using light traps	Surveying macromoths by using pheromone traps	Surveying adult and larval invertebrates	Surveying invertebrates by using timed searches	Surveying invertebrates by using quadrats	Surveying invertebrates by using pitfall traps	Surveying invertebrates by using suction sampling	Surveying invertebrates by using window traps	Surveying invertebrates by using artificial refugia	Surveying aquatic invertebrates by vegetation	Surveying aquatic invertebrates by sweep netting	Surveying aquatic invertebrates by kick sampling	Surveying aquatic invertebrates by cylinder sampling	Surveying fish by direct counting
Bottle traps															
Tank to keep trapped animals (if they are to be photographed before release)															
Sweep net															
Holding tank															
10 litre buckets with lids															
Black plastic polythene sheeting (1000 gauge), 750 mm wide															
Staple gun, staples															
Spades, trowels, mallet															
Panjet ink gun (if required)															
PIT tags and scanner (if required)															
Camera and photobooth (clear perspex box and sponge) for photography (if required)															
76×65 cm galvanised corrugated steel sheets															
Gloves and gaiters (where adders are likely to occur).															
Laser range-finder for medium to long distance measurements where exact distance estimates are required															
Killing jar		*													
Moth trap		*													

Surveying fish by trapping	Surveying fish by seine netting	Surveying fish by trawl netting	Surveying fish by push, throw and lift netting	Surveying fish by electrofishing	Surveying amphibians by torch counts	Surveying amphibians by bottle traps	Surveying amphibians by sweep netting	Surveying amphibians by pitfall trapping	Surveying amphibians by terrestrial transect searches	Surveying amphibians by egg searching	Surveying amphibians by mark-recapture	Surveying reptiles by using artificial refugia	Surveying reptiles by using transects	Surveying reptiles by using trapping techniques	Surveying reptiles by using mark-recapture	Surveying birds by using territory mapping	Surveying birds by using line transects
						*					*						
						*											
							*	*			*			*	*		
								*			*						
								*			*						
								*			*						
								*			*						
											*						
											*			*			
											*			*			
												*					
												*	*	*	*		
																	*

	Surveying bats by exit counts	Surveying bats by swarming counts	Surveying bats by hibernation counts	Surveying bats by using bat boxes	Surveying bats by using transects	Surveying bats by using field signs	Surveying bats by using counts of breeding sites	Surveying mammals by using faecal pellet counts	Surveying mammals by using feeding signs	Surveying mammals by using tracks	Surveying mammals by using hair tubes or catches	Surveying mammals by using transects	Surveying mammals by trapping	Surveying mammals by using mark–recapture	Surveying Water Voles
Large-scale site map with pencils and ball-point pens															*
Map of the site at a useable scale, e.g. 1:5000	*	*	*	*	*	*	*	*	*	*	*	*	*	*	*
Safety equipment as necessary	*		*	*	*		*	*	*	*			*	*	*
Copies of 1:10 000 or 1:25 000 field maps															
1:50 000 Ordnance Survey maps															
Binoculars/ telescope															
GPS		*													*
Ranging poles														*	
Tape measure(s)														*	
Fieldnote recording equipment	*	*	*	*	*	*	*	*	*	*	*	*	*	*	*
Quadrats or transects							*	*	*	*		*			
Wellington boots/waders							*	*	*	*			*	*	
Torch	*	*	*	*	*	*									
Collecting jars						*									
Video camera (optional)	*														
Moth trap															
Hand-held counter	*														

	Surveying bats by exit counts	Surveying bats by swarming counts	Surveying bats by hibernation counts	Surveying bats by using bat boxes	Surveying bats by using transects	Surveying bats by using field signs	Surveying bats by using counts of breeding sites	Surveying mammals by using faecal pellet counts	Surveying mammals by using feeding signs	Surveying mammals by using tracks	Surveying mammals by using hair tubes or catches	Surveying mammals by using transects	Surveying mammals by trapping	Surveying mammals by using mark–recapture	Surveying Water Voles
Image intensifier	*														
Automatic counting device	*														
Bat detector	*	*			*										
Thermometer		*	*												
Monocular can be useful for sites with high ceilings			*												
Humidity gauge			*												
Ladder				*		*									
Cloth bag				*											
Bat boxes				*											
Tape recorder					*										
Angled mirrors						*									
Endoscope (if available)						*									
Fine sand in shallow trays with a simple canopy, or inkpads and blotter, depending on the chosen method										*					
Lengths of plastic drainpipe tubing, size and number depending on methodology											*				
Lengths of malleable wire to attach tubes to trees, if placed above ground											*				

	Surveying bats by exit counts	Surveying bats by swarming counts	Surveying bats by hibernation counts	Surveying bats by using bat boxes	Surveying bats by using transects	Surveying bats by using field signs	Surveying bats by using counts of breeding sites	Surveying mammals by using faecal pellet counts	Surveying mammals by using feeding signs	Surveying mammals by using tracks	Surveying mammals by using hair tubes or catches	Surveying mammals by using transects	Surveying mammals by trapping	Surveying mammals by using mark–recapture	Surveying Water Voles
Lengths of multi-stranded strong wire											*				
Shorter lengths of fine wire											*				
Bait: peanuts, sunflowers and other seeds											*				
Pliers											*				
Sticky tape											*				
Reflective tape												*			
100 W spotlight (or more powerful if car mounted)												*			
10 to 20 appropriate traps													*	*	
Suitable bait for your target species													*	*	
Absorbent bedding, such as hay													*	*	
Bags in which to empty traps													*		
Canes to mark trap locations													*		
Markers to indicate the location of each trap														*	
Ear tags, hair clippers, or PIT tags and scanner depending on species and methodology														*	

Recommended sources of further information

HABITAT REQUIREMENTS (CHAPTER 5)

See the following references:

Andrews (1995)
Bell (1996)
Boon & Howell (1997)
Boon & Raven (1998)
Boon et al. (1992)
Boon et al. (1996a)
Brookes (1991)
Calow & Petts (1992, 1994)
Environment Agency (2003)
Farmer (1990)
Gardiner & Dackombe (1983)
Golterman et al. (1978)
Harper et al. (1995)
Hellawell (1978, 1986)
Holmes (1983)
Holmes et al. (1998, 1999a)
Hynes (1970)
Klapper (1991)
Mackereth et al. (1978)
Mainstone et al. (1993)
Mason (1991)
Metcalfe-Smith (1994)
Moss (1998)
NRA (1992, 1994a,b)
Palmer (1989)
Palmer et al. (1992)
Parr (1994)
Petts (1983)
Raven et al. (1997, 1998a,b)
RSPB/NRA/RSNC (1994)
Stirling (1985)
Vollenweider (1968)
Whitton et al. (1991)
Wright et al. (1981, 1994)
Wright, J. F. et al. (1997)

SURVEY METHODS (CHAPTER 6)

See the following references:

Allen (1989)
Archibald (1981)
Barr et al. (1993)
Bignal (1978)
Bonham (1989)
Bragg et al. (1994)
Brassington (1988)
Bullock (1996)
Byrne (1991)
Cottam & Curtis (1956)
Dargie (1992)
Dawkins & Field (1978)
Environment Agency (2003)
FAO (1977)
Ferris-Kaan & Patterson (1992)
Fuller et al. (1994)
Gilbert & Gibbons (1996)
Gilman (1994)
Goldsmith (1991)
Grant et al. (1997)
Greenwood (1996)
Haines-Young et al. (2000)
Hamilton (1975)
Hodgson et al. (1995)
Hope-Jones (1994a,b)
Horsfall & Kirby (1985)
Huntings Surveys and Consultants Limited (1986)
Institute of Terrestrial Ecology (1986)
Jones & Reynolds (1996)
Kirby, K. J. (1992, 1988)
Koop (1989)
Langdale-Brown et al. (1980)
Lillesand & Kiefer (1994)
Lindsay & Ross (1994)
Lunetta & Elvidge (1999)
Mackey et al. (1998)
MLURI (1993)
Moodie (1991)
Mountford & Peterken (1998)
NCC (1987)
NCC (1990a,b, 1991)
Pakeman et al. (2000)
Peterken (1980, 1981, 1996)
Peterken & Backmeroff (1988)
Pooley & Jones (1996)
Raven et al. (1997, 1998a)
Reid & Quarmby (2000)
Robertson (1999)
RSPB/EN/ITE (1997)
Shaw & Wheeler (1995)
Sheldrick (1997)
Sykes (1981)
Thomson et al. (1993)
Wadsworth & Treweek (1999)
Ward & Robinson (1990)
Warren & Olsen (1964)

METHODS FOR SPECIES ASSESSMENT (CHAPTER 10)

See the following references:

Anderson et al. (1983)
Bibby et al. (2000)

Buckland *et al.* (2001)
Burnham & Overton (1978, 1979)
Greenwood (1996)
Otis *et al.* (1978)
Pollock *et al.* (1990)
Seber (1982)
White *et al.* (1982)

See also:

Borchers, D. L., Buckland, S. T. & Zucchini, W. (2002) *Estimating Animal Abundance: Closed Populations.* Berlin: Springer-Verlag.
Caughley, G. (1977) *Analysis of Vertebrate Populations.* London: John Wiley & Sons.
Jolly, G. M. (1965) Explicit estimates from capture–recapture data with both death and immigration – stochastic model. *Biometrika,* **52**, 225–47.

FUNGI (CHAPTER 11)

See the following references:

Fleming *et al.* (1998)
Hodgetts (1992)
JNCC (2004)
Lange (1982, 1984, 1991, 1993)
Newton *et al.* (2002, 2003)
Orton (1986)
Watling (1995)

See also:

Buczacki, S. I. & Wilkinson, J. (1992) *Mushrooms and Toadstools of Britain and Europe.* London: HarperCollins.
Coppins, B. J. & Watling, R. (1997) *Action Plans for Lower Plants in Scotland Project: Larger Fungi – Boletopsis leucomelaena. Species Dossier.* Edinburgh: Scottish Natural Heritage.
Droege, S. (1999) The variability of counts of mushrooms and truffles

(monitoring website). http://www.im.nbs.gov/mushroom/mushpow.html
Humphrey, J. W., Newton, A. C., Peace, A. J. & Holden, E. (2000) The importance of conifer plantations in northern Britain as a habitat for fungi. *Biological Conservation,* **96** (2), 241–53.
Kirk, P. M., Cannon, P. F., David, J. C. & Stalpers, J. A. (2001) *Ainsworth & Bisby's Dictionary of the Fungi,* 8th edn. Wallingford, UK: CAB International.
Nantel, P. & Neumann, P. (1992) Ecology of ectomycorrhizal Basidiomycete communities on a local gradient. *Ecology,* **73**, 99–117.
Newton, A. C. & Haigh, J. M. (1998) Diversity of ectomycorrhizal fungi in the UK: a test of the species area relationship and role of host preference. *New Phytologist,* **138**, 619–27.
Northern Ireland Fungus Group (undated) *Fungal News.* Northern Ireland Fungus Group website. http://www.nifg.org.uk/news.htm
Wilkins, W. H., Ellis, E. M. & Harley, J. C. (1937) The ecology of larger fungi. I. Constancy and frequency of fungal species in relation to vegetational communities, particularly oak and beech. *Annals of Applied Biology,* **24**, 703–52.
(1938) The ecology of larger fungi. II. The distribution of the larger fungi in part of Charlton Forest, Sussex. *Annals of Applied Biology,* **25**, 472–89.
Wilkins, W. H. & Patrick, S. H. M. (1939) The ecology of larger fungi. III. Constancy and frequency of grassland species with special reference to soil types. *Annals of Applied Biology,* **26**, 25–46.

LICHENS (CHAPTER 12)

See the following references:

Church *et al.* (1996)
Hodgetts (1992)
IUCN (2001)
Perkins & Miller (1987a, b)
Woods & Coppins (2003)

See also:

Broad, K. (1989) *Lichens in Southern Woodlands.* Forestry Commission Handbook No. 4. London: HMSO.
Coppins, A. M. & Coppins, B. J. (2002) *Indices of Ecological Continuity for Woodland Epiphytic Lichen Habitats in the British Isles.* London: British Lichen Society.
Coppins, B. J. (2002) *Checklist of the Lichens of Great Britain and Ireland.* London: British Lichen Society.
Dobson, F. S. (1979; 3rd edn 1992; 4th colour edn 2000) *Lichens: An Illustrated Guide to the British and Irish Species.* Richmond Survey: Richmond Publishing Co.
During, H. J. (1992) Ecological classification of bryophytes and lichens. In *Bryophytes and Lichens in a Changing Environment* (ed. E. W. Bates & A. M. Farmer), pp. 1–31. Oxford: Clarendon Press.
Ferry, B. W., Baddely, M. S. & Hawksworth, D. L. (1973) *Air Pollution and Lichens.* London: Athlone Press.
Gilbert, O. L. (2000) *Lichens.* London: HarperCollins.
Hodgetts, N. G. (1992) *Cladonia: A Field Guide.* Peterborough: Joint Nature Conservation Committee.
Jahn, H. M. (1981) *Collins Guide to Ferns, Mosses and Lichens.* London: Collins.
Orange, A. (1994) *Lichens on Trees. A Guide to Some of the Commonest Species,*

British Plant Life No. 3. Cardiff: National Museum of Wales.

Purvis, O. W., Coppins, B. J., Hawksworth, D. L., James, P. J. & Moore, D. M. (1992) *The Lichen Flora of Great Britain and Ireland*. London: Natural History Museum Publications/British Lichen Society.

Purvis, O. W., Coppins, B. J. & James, P. W. (1993) *Checklist of Lichens of Great Britain and Ireland*. British Lichen Society Bulletin 72 (Supplement). London: British Lichen Society.

Seaward, M. R. D. (ed.) (1995 et seq.) *Lichen Atlas of the British Isles*. London: British Lichen Society.

The Bulletin of the British Lichen Society, a journal published by the British Lichen Society, London.

The Lichenologist, a journal published by the British Lichen Society, London.

Watson, W. (1953) *Census Catalogue of British Lichens*. London: Cambridge University Press.

BRYOPHYTES (CHAPTER 13)

See the following references:

Blockeel & Long (1998)
Church *et al.* (2001)
During (1992)
Hodgetts (1992)
Porley (2000)

See also:

Blockeel, T. L. (2000) The identification of *Drepanocladus revolvens* and *D. cossonii*, and their distribution in Britain and Ireland. *Bulletin of the British Bryological Society*, **75**, 32–40. [This mentions the problems of mis-identifying *D. cossonii* as *Hamatocaulis vernicosus*.]

Daniels, R. E. & Eddy, A. (1990) *Handbook of European Sphagna*. London: HMSO.

Hill, M. O. (1992) *Sphagnum: A Field Guide*. Peterborough: Joint Nature Conservation Committee.

Jahns, H. M. (1981) *Collins Guide to Ferns, Mosses and Lichens*. London: Collins.

Joint Nature Conservation Committee (JNCC) (2004) *Plant Diversity Challenge: The UK's Response to the Global Strategy for Plant Conservation*. Peterborough: JNCC.

Murray, B. M. (1988) The genus Andreaea in Britain and Ireland. *Journal of Bryology*, **15**, 17–82.

Paton, J. A. (1999) *The Liverwort Flora of the British Isles*. Colchester: Harley Books.

Smith, A. J. E. (1978) *The Moss Flora of Britain and Ireland*. Cambridge: Cambridge University Press. [The key to genera was updated by Smith (1991) in *Bulletin of the British Bryological Society*, **57**, 41–62.]

(1990) *The Liverworts of Britain and Ireland*. Cambridge: Cambridge University Press.

Watson, E. V. (1981) *British Mosses and Liverworts*, 3rd edn. Cambridge: Cambridge University Press.

AQUATIC MACROPHYTES AND ALGAE (CHAPTER 14)

See the following references:

Bailey-Watts & Kirika (1981)
Bullock (1996)
Flower (1985)
HMSO (1984)
Hodgetts (1992)
Stace, C. A. (1997)
Stewart & Church (1992)

See also:

Bailey-Watts, A. E. (1994) *Loch Leven NNR: Water Quality 1992 and 1993 with Special Reference to Nutrients and Phytoplankton, and an Assessment of Phosphorous Levels in the Loch Sediments.*

Research Survey and Monitoring Report No. 29. Perth: Scottish Natural Heritage.

Belcher, H. (1979) *An Illustrated Guide to River Phytoplankton*. London: HMSO.

Boon, P. J., Lassiere, O. L. & Duncan, W. M. (1998) The use of a remotely operated vehicle (ROV) for surveying submerged aquatic plant communities in standing waters. *Verhandlungen der Internationalen Vereinigung für theoretische und angewandte Limnologie*, **26**, 2353–7.

Canter-Lund, H. & Lund, J. W. G. (1995) *Freshwater Algae – Their Microscopic World Explored*. Bristol: Biopress.

Church, J. M., Hodgetts, N. G., Preston, C. D. & Stewart, N. F. (2001). *British Red Data Books: Mosses and Liverworts*. Peterborough: Joint Nature Conservation Committee.

Cobham Resource Consultants (1996) *Techniques for Monitoring of Freshwater Macrophytes for Nature Conservation*, report to the Joint Nature Conservation Committee, Peterborough.

Holmes, N. T. H., Boon, P. J. & Rowell, T. A. (1998) A revised classification system for British rivers based on their aquatic plant communities. *Aquatic Conservation: Marine and Freshwater Ecosystems*, **8**, 555–78.

Joint Nature Conservation Committee (JNCC) (2004) *Plant Diversity Challenge: The UK's Response to the Global Strategy for Plant Conservation*. Peterborough: JNCC.

Jones, R. A. (1998) *Sample Survey of Submerged Macrophytes at Llyn Gynon (Elenydd SSSI), Cardiganshire*. Unpublished report to Countryside Council for Wales, Bangor.

Lomas, E., Teearu, T. & Rowlands, A. (1998) *Survey to Determine the Status of* Luronium natans *(L.) Raf. in a Sample of Six mid-Wales Lakes.* Unpublished report to Countryside Council for Wales, Bangor.

Moore, J. A. (1996). *Charophytes of Great Britain and Ireland.* BSBI Handbook No. 5. London: Botanical Society of the British Isles.

Preston, C. D. (1995) *Pondweeds of Great Britain and Ireland.* BSBI Handbook No. 8. London: Botanical Society of the British Isles.

Reynolds, C. S. (1984) *The Ecology of Freshwater Phytoplankton.* Cambridge: Cambridge University Press.

Rich, T. C. G., Graham, G. G., Wigginton, M. J. & Jermy, A. C. (eds) (1998) *Plant Crib 1998.* London: Botanical Society of the British Isles.

Rose, F. (1981) *The Wild Flower Key.* London: Frederick Warne.

VASCULAR PLANTS (CHAPTER 15)

See the following references.

Bonham (1989)
Bullock (1996)
Byrne (1991)
Dalby & Rich (1994)
Farrell (1991)
Greenwood (1996)
Hodgson *et al.* (1995)
Hutchings (1987a,b)
Kent & Coker (1992)
Kirby (1988)
Peterken (1981)
Preston *et al.* (2002)
Rich (2001)
Rich *et al.* (1999)
Rich & Jermy (1998)
Rich & Smith (1996)
Rich & Woodruff (1990)
Robertson (1999)
Sanger & Waite (1998)
Sheldrick (1997)
Shimwell (1971)
Stace (1997)
Watkinson (1986)
Wells Willems (1991)

See also:

Cowie, N. R. & Sydes, C. (1995) *Status, Distribution, Ecology and Management of String Sedge,* Carex chordorrhiza, Scottish Natural Heritage Review No. 41. Perth: Scottish Natural Heritage.

Hutchings, M. J. (1990) The role of demographic techniques in conservation: the case of *Ophrys sphegodes* in chalk grassland. In *Calcareous Grasslands: Ecology and Management* (ed. S. H. Hillier, D. W. H. Walton & D. A. Wells), pp.106–11. Bluntisham, Cambridgeshire: Bluntisham Books.

Joint Nature Conversion Committee (JNCC) (2004) *Plant Diversity Challenge: The UK's Response to the Global Strategy for Plant Conservation.* Peterborough: JNCC.

Olesen, J. M. & Warncke, E. (1990) The morphological, phenological and biochemical differentiation in relation to gene flow in a population of *Saxifraga hirculus. Sommerfeltia,* **II**, 159–73.

Page, C. N. (1997) *The Ferns of Britain and Ireland,* 2nd edn. Cambridge: Cambridge University Press.

Ratcliffe, D. A., Birks, H. J. B. & Birks, H. H. (1993) The ecology and conservation of the Killarney fern *Trichomanes speciosum* Willd. in Britain and Ireland. *Biological Conservation,* **66**, 231–47.

Rumsey, F. J., Jermy, A. C. & Sheffield, E. (1998) The independent gametophytic stage of *Trichomanes speciosum* Willd. (Hymenophyllaceae), the Killarney Fern, and its

distribution in the British Isles. *Watsonia,* **22**, 1–19.

Stace, C. A. (1999) *Field Flora of the British Isles,* Cambridge: Cambridge University Press.

Waite, S. & Farrell, L. (1998) Population biology of the rare military orchid (*Orchis militaris* L.) at an established site in Suffolk, England. *Botanical Journal of the Linnean Society,* **126**, 109–21.

Waite, S. & Hutchings, M. (1991) The effects of different management regimes on the population dynamics of *Ophrys sphegodes:* analysis and description using matrix models. In *Population Ecology of Terrestrial Orchids* (ed. T. C. E. Wells & J. H. Willems), pp. 161–75. The Hague: SPB Academic Publishing.

Wigginton, M. J. (ed.) 1999. *British Red Data Books. 1. Vascular plants,* 3rd edn. Peterborough: Joint Nature Conservation Committee.

DRAGONFLIES AND DAMSELFLIES (CHAPTER 16)

See the following references:

Askew (1988)
Ausden (1996)
Brooks (1993)
Merritt *et al.* (1996)
Moore & Corbet (1990)
RSPB/EN/ITE (1997)
Shirt (1987)
Southwood (2000)

See also:

Hammond, C. O. (1983) *The Dragonflies of Great Britain and Ireland,* 2nd edn (revised by R. Merritt). Colchester: Harley Books. [Note: the key to larvae is unreliable in some places.]

BUTTERFLIES (CHAPTER 17)

See the following references:

Butterfly Conservation (2001)
Emmet & Heath (1989)
Heath *et al.* (1984)
Pollard (1977, 1982, 1988)
Pollard & Lakhani (1985)
Pollard & Yates (1993)
Pollard *et al.* (1986)

See also:

Porter, J. (1997) *The Colour Identification Guide to Caterpillars of the British Isles.* London: Viking.

MOTHS (CHAPTER 18)

See the following references:

Ausden (1996)
Bradley *et al.* (1973, 1979)
De Freina & Witt (1997)
Ekkehard (1986)
Emmet & Heath (1989)
Fry & Waring (1996)
Pearce *et al.* (1996)
Skinner (1998)
Young (1979)

OTHER TERRESTRIAL INVERTEBRATES (CHAPTER 19)

See the following references:

Anon. (1995)
Ausden (1996)
Baars (1979)
Blackshaw (1994)
Buglife (2003)
Dennis *et al.* (1995, 1998)
Dietrick (1961)
Dietrick et al. (1959)
Disney (1986, 1987)
Duffey (1980)
Eyre *et al.* (1989)

Greenslade (1964)
Hawes (2003)
Honek (1988)
Key *et al.* (2000)
Luff & Rushton (1989)
Luff (1986)
Macleod *et al.* (1994)
McWilliam & Death (1998)
Morris (1991)
New (1998)
Oggier *et al.* (1998)
Okland (1996)
Prys-Jones & Corbet (1991)
Roberts (1996)
Samu *et al.* (1997)
Shirt (1987)
Southwood (2000)
Sparks *et al.* (1994)
Stewart & Wright (1995)
Strong *et al.* (1984)
Stubbs (1972)
Usher (1990)
Williamson *et al.* (1977)
Yarrow (1995)

See also:

Alexander, K. (1998) Non-marine molluscan conservation and the National Trust: policies and practices. *Journal of Conchology*, **S2**, 133–8.

Bratton, J. H. (ed.) (1991) *British Red Data Books: 3. Invertebrates other than Insects.* Peterborough: Joint Nature Conservation Committee.

Cameron, R. A. D. & Williamson, P. (1977) Estimating migration and the effects of distribution in mark-recapture studies on the snail *Cepaea nemoralis* L. *Journal of Animal Ecology*, **46**, 173–9.

Collingwood, C. A. (1979) The Formicidae (Hym.) of Fennoscandia and Denmark. *Fauna Entomologica Scandinavia*, **8**, 1–174.

Cooter, J. (1991) *A Coleopterist's Handbook.* London: Amateur Entomological Society.

Dennis, P. (1997) Impact of forest and woodland structure on insect abundance and diversity. In *Forests and Insects* (ed. A. D. Watt, N. E. Stork & M. D. Hunter), pp. 321–40. London: Chapman and Hall.

Desender, K. & Maelfait, J. P. (1986) Pitfall trapping within enclosures: a method for estimating the relationship between the abundances of coexisting carabid species (Coleoptera: Carabidae). *Holarctic Ecology*, **9**, 245–50.

Drake, C. M. (1991) *Provisional Atlas of larger Brachycera of Britain and Ireland.* Peterborough: Nature Conservancy Council.

Duffey, E. (1962) A population study of spiders in limestone grassland. Description of study area, sampling methods and population characteristics, *Journal of Animal Ecology*, **31**, 571–589.

Falk, S. (1991) *A Review of the Scarce and Threatened Flies of Great Britain.* Part 1, Research and Survey in Nature Conservation No. 39. Peterborough: Nature Conservancy Council.

Fowles, A. P. (1998) Implementing the Habitats Directive: *Vertigo angustior* Jeffreys in Wales. *Journal of Conchology*, **S2**, 179–89.

Fry, R. & Lonsdale, D. (1991) *Habitat Conservation for Insects – a Neglected Green Issue.* London: Amateur Entomological Society.

Gardenfors, U. (1987) *Impact of Airborne Pollution on the Terrestrial Invertebrates*, National Swedish Environment Protection Board Report.

Henderson, I. & Whittaker, T. (1976) The efficiency of an insect suction sampler in grassland. *Ecological Entomology*, **2** (1), 57–60.

Joy, N. H. (1932) *A Practical Handbook of British Beetles*, 2 vols. London: Witherby.

Kerney, M. P. & Cameron, R. A. D. (1979) *A Field Guide to the Land Snails of Britain and Northwest Europe*. London: Collins.

Kuno, E. (1991) Sampling and analysis of insect populations. *Annual Review of Entomology*, **36**, 285–304.

Kuscha, V., Lehmann, G. & Meyer, U. (1987) On working with ground traps. *Beitrage zur Entomologie*, **37**, 3–27.

Lindroth, C. H. (1986) *The Carabidae (Coleoptera) of Fenoscandia and Denmark. Fauna Entomologia Scandinavica*, Volume 15, Parts 1 & 2. Copenhagen: Brill/Scandinavian Science Press.

Luff, M. L. (1975) Some features influencing efficiency of pitfall traps. *Oecologia*, **19**, 345–57. (1998) *Provisional Atlas of the Ground Beetles (Col.: Carabidae) of Britain*. Monks Wood, Huntingdon: Biological Records Centre.

Morris, M. G. (1990) *Orthocerous Weevils*. Handbooks for the Identification of British Insects, 5 (16), London: Royal Entomological Society.

Puntilla, P. & Haila, Y. (1996) Colonisation of a burned forest by ants in the southern Finnish Boreal Forest. *Silva Fennica*, **30**, 421–35.

Stubbs, A. E. (1992) *Provisional Atlas of the Long Palped Craneflies (Dipt: Tipulidae) of Britain and Ireland*. Monks Wood, Huntingdon: Biological Records Centre.

Taylor, L. (1962) The efficiency of cylindrical sticky insect traps and suspended nets. *Annals of Applied Biology*, **50**, 681–5.

Topping, C. (1993) Behavioural responses of 3 linyphiid spiders to pitfall traps. *Entomologia Experimentalis et Applicata*, **68** (3), 287–93.

Topping, C. & Sunderland, K. (1992) Limitations to the use of pitfall traps in ecological studies exemplified by a study of spiders in a field of winter wheat. *Journal of Applied Ecology*, **29** (2), 485–91.

Watt, A. D, Stork, N. E. & Hunter, M. D. (1997) *Forests and Insects*. London: Chapman & Hall.

AQUATIC INVERTEBRATES (CHAPTER 20)

See the following references:

Bratton (1991)

See also:

Foster, G. N. & Eyre, M. D. (1992) *Classification and Ranking of Water Beetle Communities*. Peterborough: Joint Nature Conservation Committee.

Freshwater Biological Association Keys: Cladocera, Gastropoda, Plecoptera, Copepoda, Ephemeroptera, Tricladia, Dixidae, Crustacea Malacostraca, Megaloptera and Neuroptera, Chironomidae, Rotifera, Leeches, Caddis Larvae, Diatoms, Ephemeroptera, Culicidae, Hemiptera. Available from The Ferry House, Far Sawrey, Ambleside, Cumbria, LA22 0LP. [Note: this list of keys is not comprehensive.]

Friday, L. E. (1988) *A Key to the Adults of British Water Beetles*. Taunton, Somerset: Field Studies Council Publications.

Hyman, P. S. (1992, 1994) *A Review of the Scarce and Threatened Coleoptera of Great Britain*, 2 vols. Peterborough: Joint Nature Conservation Committee.

Hynes, H. B. N. (1984) *A Key to the Adults and Nymphs of the British Stoneflies*. Freshwater Biological Association Scientific Publication No. 17. Ambleside, Cumbria: Freshwater Biological Association.

Kirby, P. (1992) *A Review of the Scarce and Threatened Hemiptera of Great Britain*. Peterborough: Joint Nature Conservation Committee.

Wallace, J. D. (1991) *A Review of the Trichoptera of Great Britain*. Research and Survey in Nature Conservation No. 32. Peterborough: Nature Conservancy Council.

FISH (CHAPTER 21)

See the following references:

Buckley (1987)
Cowx (1990, 1996)
Cowx & Lamarque (1990)
Davies (2001)
Environment Agency (2004)
Mills (1989)
Perrow *et al.* (1996)
Puhr (1998)
Templeton (1995)

See also:

Bagenal, T. B. (1978) *Methods of Assessment of Fish Production in Freshwaters*. IBP Handbook No. 3. Oxford: Blackwell Scientific Publications.

Gardiner, R., Taylor, R. & Armstrong, J. (1995) *Habitat Assessment and Survey of Lamprey Populations Occurring in Areas of Conservation Interest*. Report to Scottish Natural Heritage, Edinburgh.

Harvey, J. & Cowx, I. (2003) Monitoring the River, Brook and Sea Lamprey, *Lampetra fuiviatilis, L. planieri* and *Petromyzon marinus.* Conserving Nature 2000 Rivers Monitoring Series no. 5. Peterborough: English Nature.

Jurvelius, J., Linden, T. & Louhimo, J. (1987) The number of fish in pelagic areas of Lake Pyhajarvi (Karelia), monitored by hydroacoustic methods. *Finnish Fisheries Research*, **8**, 48–52.

Kennedy, G. J. A & Crozier, W. W. (1991) Strategies for the rehabilitation of salmon rivers – post project appraisal, in *Strategies for the Rehabilitation of Salmon Rivers.* (ed. D. H. Mills), pp. 44–62. Pitlochry, Perthshire: Atlantic Salmon Trust/IFM/Linnean Society.

Maitland, P. S. & Campbell, R. N. (1992) *Freshwater Fishes of the British Isles.* London: HarperCollins.

Morris, K. H. & Maitland, P. S. (1987) A trap for catching adult lampreys (Petromyzonidae) in running water. *Journal of Fisheries Biology*, **31**, 513–16.

AMPHIBIANS (CHAPTER 22)

See the following references:

Baker & Gent (1998)
Beebee & Denton (1996)
Beebee & Griffiths (2000)
Buckley & Inns (1998)
Cooke (1995)
English Nature (2001)
Fasola *et al.* (1993)
Griffiths *et al.* (1996)
Griffiths & Inns (1998)
Griffiths & Raper (1994)
Halley *et al.* (1996)
Latham (1997)
Oldham (1994)

See also:

Arnold, E. N., Burton, J. A. & Ovenden, D. W. (1978) *A Field Guide to the Reptiles and Amphibians of Britain and Europe.* London: Collins.

Arnold, H. R. (1995) *Atlas of Amphibians and Reptiles in Britain.* Institute of Terrestrial Ecology Research Publication No. 10. London: HMSO.

Arntzen, J. W. & Teunis, S. F. M. (1993) A six year study on the population dynamics of the crested newt *Triturus cristatus* following the colonization of a newly created pond. *Herpetological Journal*, **3**, 99–111.

Banks, B. (1991) Identification – British newts. *British Wildlife*, **2**, 362–5.

Banks, B., Beebee, T. J. C. & Cooke, A. S. (1994) Conservation of the natterjack toad *Bufo calamitus* in Britain over the period 1970 to 1990 in relation to site protection and other factors. *Biological Conservation*, **67**, 111–18.

Clarke, R. D. (1972) The effect of toe-clipping on survival in Fowler's Toad (*Bufo woodhousei fowleri*). *Copeia*, 182–5.

Cooke, A. S. (1975) Spawn site selection and colony size of the frog (*Rana temporaria*) and the toad (*Bufo bufo*). *Journal of Zoology*, **175**, 29–38.

Denton, J. S. & Beebee, T. J. C. (1992) An evaluation of methods for studying natterjack toads outside the breeding season. *Amphibia–Reptilia*, **13**, 365–74.

Frazer, J. F. D. (1983) *Reptiles and Amphibians in Britain.* New Naturalist No. 69. London: Collins.

Gaywood, M. (1997) *The Ecology, Conservation and Management of the Great Crested Newt* (Triturus cristatus). SNH Information and Advisory Note No. 92. Perth: Scottish Natural Heritage.

Gent, A. & Bray, R. (eds) (1994) *Conservation and Management of Great Crested Newts.* Proceedings of a symposium held on 11 January at Kew Gardens, Richmond, Surrey. English Nature Science No. 20. Peterborough: English Nature.

Gent, A. H. & Gibson, S. D. (eds) (1998) *Herpetofauna Worker's Manual.* Peterborough: Joint Nature Conservation Committee.

Gibbs, J. P. (1996) Sampling requirements for detecting trends in amphibian populations. Presentation given at the Third Annual Meeting of the North American Amphibian Monitoring Program (NAAMP). http://www.im.nbs.gov/naamp3/naamp3.html

Halliday, T. R. (1996) Amphibians. In *Ecological Census Techniques* (ed. W. J. Sutherland), pp. 205–17. Cambridge: Cambridge University Press.

Heyer, R. W., Donnelly, M. A., McDiarmid, R. W., Hayek, L. C. & Foster, M. S. (eds) (1994) *Measuring and Monitoring Biodiversity: Standard Methods for Amphibians.* Washington, DC: Smithsonian Institution Press.

Joint Nature Conservation Committee (JNCC) (2004) Common Standards of Monitoring. http://www.jncc.gov.uk/csm/guidance/

Langton, T. E. S., Beckett, C. L. & Foster, J. P. (2001) *Great Crested Newt Conservation Handbook.* Halesworth: Froglife.

Swan, M. J. S. & Oldham, R. S. (1993) *National Amphibian Survey: Final Report.* English Nature Research Report No. 38, Volume 1. Peterborough: English Nature.

REPTILES (CHAPTER 23)

See the following references:

Beebee & Griffiths (2000)
Froglife (1999)
Gent (1994)
Gent & Gibson (1998)
Griffiths & Inns (1998)
Griffiths & Langton (1998)
Reading (1996)

See also:

Arnold, E. N. (2002) *A Field Guide to the Reptiles and Amphibians of Britain and Europe*. London: Collins.
Arnold, H. R. (1995) *Atlas of Amphibians and Reptiles in Britain*. Institute of Terrestrial Ecology Research Publication No. 10. London: HMSO.
Baker, J. & Gent, A. H. (1998) Marking and recognition of animals. In *Herpetofauna Worker's Manual* (eds A. H. Gent & S. D. Gibson). pp. 45–54. Peterborough: Joint Nature Conservation Committee.
Blomberg, S. & Shine, R. (1996) Reptiles. In *Ecological Census Techniques* (ed. W. J. Sutherland), pp. 218–26. Cambridge: Cambridge University Press.
Foster, J. & Gent, T. (eds) (1996) *Reptile Survey Methods*. Proceedings of a seminar held on 27 November 1995 at the Zoological Society of London's meeting rooms. English Nature Science No. 27. Peterborough: English Nature.
Frazer, J. F. D. (1983) *Reptiles and Amphibians in Britain*. New Naturalist No. 69. London: Collins.
International Union for the Conservation of Nature (IUCN) (2003) *2003 IUCN Red List of Threatened Species*. www.redlist.org. [Downloaded on 17 February 2004.]

Joint Nature Conservation Committee (JNCC) (2004) Common Standards of Monitoring. http://www.jncc.gov.uk/csm/guidance/
Riddell, A. (1996). Monitoring slow-worms and common lizards, with special reference to refugia materials, refugia occupancy and individual recognition. In *Reptile Survey Methods* (ed. T. Gent & J. Foster), English Nature Science No. 27, pp. 46–60. Peterborough: English Nature.
Stafford, P. (1989) *Lizards of the British Isles*. Natural History Series no. 46. Aylesbury: Shire Publications.
Swan, M. J. S. & Oldham, R. S. (1993) *National Reptile Survey: Final Report*, English Nature Research Report No. 38, Volume 2. Peterborough: English Nature.

BIRDS (CHAPTER 24)

See the following references:

Betten *et al.* (1990)
Bibby *et al.* (2000)
Birdlife International (2000)
Boddy (1993)
Clobert *et al.* (1987)
Gilbert *et al.* (1998)
Grimmett & Jones (1989)
Heath & Evans (2000)
Hill *et al.* (1990)
Hilton-Taylor *et al* (2000)
IUCN (1994, 2001)
JNCC (1996)
Lack (1986)
Lloyd *et al.* (1991)
Marchant (1983)
Marchant *et al.* (1990)
NCC (1989)
Peach *et al.* (1998)
Pradel *et al.* (1990)
Pritchard *et al.* (1992)
Reynolds (1979)

Rose & Scott (1997)
Stone *et al.* (1997)
Tucker & Evans (1997)
Tucker & Heath (1994)
UKBG (1998a)
Walsh *et al.* (1995)
Wetlands International (2002)

See also:

Anon. (1996) *The Annual Partridge Count Scheme: August Brood Count Recording Form and Instructions*. Fordingbridge, Hampshire: Game Conservancy Trust.
Bainbridge, I. P. (1995) *Sea Eagle Monitoring Procedures and Recording*. Unpublished report, Royal Society for the Protection of Birds, Edinburgh.
Bainbridge, I. P., Summers, R. W. & O'Toole, L. (1995) *Red Kite Monitoring In Scotland: Annual Red Kite Monitoring Procedures*. Unpublished report, Royal Society for the Protection of Birds, Edinburgh.
Beekman, J. H. (1997) International censuses of the north-west European Bewick's Swan population, January 1990 and 1995. *Swan Specialist Group Newsletter*, **6**, 7–9.
BirdLife International & European Bird Census Council (2000) *European Bird Populations: Estimates and Trends*. Cambridge: BirdLife International.
British Trust for Ornithology (BTO) (1991) *Guidelines and Site Record Form for the Fourth BTO Peregrine Survey 1991*, Thetford, Norfolk: British Trust for Ornithology.
Brown, A. F. & Shepherd, K. B. (1993) A method for censusing upland breeding waders. *Bird Study*, **40**, 189–95.
Browne, S. (1997) *BTO Survey of Breeding Skylarks: Instructions and Forms*.

Thetford, Norfolk: British Trust for Ornithology.

Buckland, S. T. & Summers, R. W. (1992) *Pinewoods Birds Project: Protocol for a Sample Survey of Conifer Woods*. Unpublished report, Royal Society for the Protection of Birds, Sandy, Bedfordshire.

Buckland, S. T., Anderson, D. R., Burnham, K. P. & Laake, J. L. (1993) *Distance Sampling. Estimating Abundance of Biological Populations*. London: Chapman & Hall.

Buckton, S. T. & Ormerod, S. J. (1997) Use of a new standardized habitat survey for assessing the habitat preferences and distribution of upland river birds. *Bird Study*, **44**, 327–37.

Cadbury, C. J. (1980) The status and habitats of the corncrake in Britain 1978–79. *Bird Study*, **27**, 203–18. (1981) Nightjar census methods. *Bird Study*, **28**, 1–4. (ed.) (1996) *RSPB Conservation Review*. Sandy, Bedfordshire: Royal Society for the Protection of Birds.

Campbell, L. H. & Mudge, G. P. (1989) Conservation of black-throated divers in Scotland. *RSPB Conservation Review*, **3**, 72–4.

Catt, D. C., Baines, D., Moss, K., Leckie, F. & Picozzi, N. (1994) *Abundance and Distribution of the Capercaillie in Scotland 1992–4: Final Report to SNH and RSPB*. Banchory: Institute of Terrestrial Ecology; Newtonmore, Inverness-shire: Game Conservancy Trust.

Clarke, R. & Watson, D. (1990) The hen harrier *Circus cyaneus* winter roost survey in Britain and Ireland. *Bird Study*, **37**, 84–100.

Cranswick, P. A., Bowler, J. M., Delany, S. N. *et al.* (1997) Numbers of whooper swans *Cygnus cygnus*

in Iceland, Ireland and Britain in January 1995: results of the international whooper swan census. *Wildfowl*, **47**, 17–30.

Crick, H. Q. P. & Ratcliffe, D. A. (1995) The peregrine *Falco peregrinus* breeding population of the United Kingdom in 1991. *Bird Study*, **42**, 1–19.

Crooke, C., Dennis, R., Harvey, M. & Summers, R. (1992) Population size and breeding success of Slavonian grebes in Scotland. In *Britain's Birds in 1990–1: the Conservation and Monitoring Review*, pp. 134–8. Thetford, Norfolk: British Trust for Ornithology.

Dennis, R. (1995) Ospreys *Pandion haliaetus* in Scotland – a study of recolonisation. *Vogelwelt*, **116**, 193–5.

Desante, D. F. (1981) A field test of the variable circular plot censusing technique in a California coastal scrub breeding community. *Studies in Avian Biology*, **6**, 177–85.

Etheridge, B. & Baines, D. (1995) *Instructions for the Black Grouse Survey 1995/6*. Unpublished document, RSPB/GCT/JNCC/SNH, Edinburgh.

Fair Isle Bird Observatory (1999) *Annual Report*. Fair Isle: Fair Isle Bird Observatory.

Fox, A. D. & Francis, I. S. (1996) *Report of the 1995/96 National Census of Greenland White-fronted Geese in Britain*. GWGS report to WWT, Kalø, Denmark, 16pp.

Galbraith, H., Murray, S., Rae, S., Whitfield, D. P. & Thompson, D. B. A. (1993) Numbers and distribution of dotterel *Charadrius morinellus* breeding in Great Britain. *Bird Study*, **40**, 161–9.

Gibbons, D. W., Bainbridge, I. & Mudge, G. (1995) *The 1994 Red-Throated Diver Gavia stellata Survey*.

Unpublished RSPB report to Scottish Natural Heritage.

Gillings, S. (1997) *BTO Wintering Skylark Survey: Instructions and Forms*. Thetford, Norfolk: British Trust for Ornithology.

Gomershall, C. H., Morton, J. S. & Wynde, R. M. (1984) Status of breeding red-throated divers in Shetland, 1983. *Bird Study*, **31**, 223–9.

Green, R. E. (1994) *Census of Corncrakes In Great Britain 1993*. Unpublished report, Royal Society for the Protection of Birds, Sandy, Bedfordshire. (1995) Decline of the corncrake *Crex crex* in Britain continues. *Bird Study*, **42**, 66–75. (1996) The status of the golden eagle in Britain in 1992. *Bird Study*, **43**, 20–7.

Gregory, R. D., Bashford, R. I., Balmer, D. B., Marchant, J. H., Wilson, A. M. & Bailie, S. R. (1997) *The Breeding Bird Survey 1995–1996*. Thetford, Norfolk: British Trust for Ornithology.

Grimmett, R. F. A. & Gammell, A. B. (1989) *Inventory of Important Bird Areas in the European Community*. Cambridge: International Council for Bird Preservation.

Gutzwiller, K. J. (1991) Estimating winter species richness with unlimited-distance point counts. *The Auk*, **108**, 853–62.

Hancock, M. (1991) *Common Scoter in the Flow Country, Results of the 1991 Survey: Comparison with Previous Years and Suggested Monitoring Method*. Unpublished report, Royal Society for the Protection of Birds, Sandy, Bedfordshire. (1994) *Black-throated Diver Newsletter*. Unpublished report, Royal Society for the Protection of Birds, Sandy, Bedfordshire.

Hudson, A. V., Stowe, T. J. & Aspinall, S. J. (1990) Status and distribution of corncrakes in Britain in 1988. *British Birds*, **83**, 173–87.

Hutto, R. L., Pletschet, S. M. & Hendricks, P. (1986) A fixed-radius point count method for breeding and non-breeding season use. *The Auk*, **103**, 593–602.

Jackson, D. & Hancock, M. (1994) *Black-throated Diver Survey Instructions*. Unpublished report, Royal Society for the Protection of Birds, Sandy, Bedfordshire.

Jonsson, L. (1992) *Birds of Europe with North Africa and the Middle East*. London: Christopher Helm.

Kirby, J. S., Rees, E. C., Merne, O. J. & Gardarsson, A. (1992) International census of whooper swans *Cygnus cygnus* in Britain, Ireland and Iceland: January 1991. *Wildfowl*, **43**, 20–6.

Komdeur, J., Bertelsen, J. & Cracknell, G. (1992) *Manual for Aeroplane and Ship Surveys of Waterfowl and Seabirds*. International Waterfowl and Wetlands Research Bureau (IWRB) Special Publication No. 19. Copenhagen: IWRB/JNCC/Ornis Consult A/S, Ministry of the Environment.

Lindén, H., Helle, E., Helle, P. & Wikman, M. (1996) Wildlife triangle scheme in Finland: methods and aims for monitoring wildlife populations. *Finnish Game Research*, **49**, 4–11.

Love, J. A. (1983) *The Return of the Sea Eagle*. Cambridge: Cambridge University Press.

Marquiss, M., Vickers, A. D. & Picozzi, N. (1997) *Baseline Survey of Pinewood Birds in Cairngorms Proposed Special Protection Area, Glenmore Forest SSSI and Ballochbuie Forest*. Institute of Terrestrial Ecology (Natural Environment Research Council) Report to SNH. Edinburgh: Scottish Natural Heritage.

Okill, J. D. & Wanless, S. (1990) Breeding success and chick growth of red-throated divers *Gavia stellata* in Shetland 1979–88. *Ringing and Migration*, **11**, 65–72.

Partridge, J. K., & Smith, K. W. (1992) Breeding wader populations in Northern Ireland, 1985–87. *Irish Birds*, **4**, 497–518.

Potts, G. R. (1986) *The Partridge: Pesticides, Predation and Conservation*. London: Collins.

Prater, A. J. (1989) Ringed plover *Charadrius hiaticula* breeding population in the United Kingdom in 1984. *Bird Study*, **36**, 154–9.

Rebecca, G. & Bainbridge, I. (1994) *Survey of Merlins in Great Britain 1993–1994: Survey Instructions*. Unpublished report, Royal Society for the Protection of Birds, Sandy, Bedfordshire.

(1995) *National Merlin Survey 1993–1995*, RSPB interim report to SNH, Scottish Natural Heritage, Edinburgh.

(1998) The breeding status of the Merlin *Falco columbarius* in Britain in 1993–1994. *Bird Study*, **45**, 172–87.

Redpath, S. M. (1994) Censusing tawny owls *Strix aluco* by the use of imitation calls. *Bird Study*, **41**, 192–8.

Reed, T. (1985) Estimates of British breeding wader populations. *Wader Study Group Bulletin*, **45**, 5.

Rees, E. C., Kirby, J. S. & Gilburn, A. (1997) Site selection by swans wintering in Britain and Ireland; the importance of geographical location and habitat. *Ibis*, **139**, 337–52.

Robertson, P. A., Woodburn, M. I. A., Tapper, S. C. & Stoate, C. (1989) *Estimating Game Densities in Britain from Land-use Maps*. Report to the Institute of Terrestrial Ecology.

Sage, B. L. & Whittington, P. A. (1985) The 1980 sample survey of rookeries. *Bird Study*, **32**, 77–81.

Sharrock, J. T. R. (1976) *The Atlas of Breeding Birds In Britain and Ireland*. Berkhamsted, Hertfordshire: Poyser.

Shewry, M. C., Buckland, S. T. & Shaw, P. (2001) *Distance Sampling and its Application to Monitoring Selected Species*. Scottish Natural Heritage Research, Survey and Monitoring Report No. 177. Perth: Scottish Natural Heritage.

Smith, K. (1994) Bird monitoring in the UK. *RSPB Conservation Review*, **8**, 19–23.

Stattersfield, A. J., Crosby, M. J., Long, A., & Wege, D. (1998) *Endemic Birds Areas of the World: Priorities for Biodiversity Conservation*. Cambridge: BirdLife International.

Stowe, T. J., Newton, A. V., Green, R. E. & Mayes, E. (1993) The decline of the corncrake *Crex crex* in Britain and Ireland in relation to habitat. *Journal of Applied Ecology*, **30**, 53–62.

Stroud, D. A., Mudge, G. P., & Pienkowski, M. W. (1990) *Protecting internationally important bird sites: a review of the EEC Special Protection Area network in Great Britain*. Peterborough: Nature Conservancy Council.

Taylor, K. (1982) *BTO Waterways Bird Survey Instructions*. Thetford, Norfolk: British Trust for Ornithology.

Taylor, K., Hudson, R. & Horne, G. (1988) Buzzard breeding distribution and abundance in Britain and Northern Ireland in 1983. *Bird Study*, **35**, 109–15.

Underhill-Day, J. C. (1990) *The Status and Breeding Biology of Marsh Harrier Circus aeruginosus and Montagu's*

Harrier Circus pygargus *in Britain since 1900*. Ph.D. thesis, Royal Society for the Protection of Birds and Institute of Terrestrial Ecology.

Waters, R., Cranswick, P., Smith, K. W. & Stroud, D. (1996) Wetland Bird Survey. *RSPB Conservation Review*, **10**, 32–8.

Whitfield, P. (1994) *Instructions to Montane Ecology Project Surveyors*. Unpublished report, Scottish Natural Heritage, Edinburgh.

BATS (CHAPTER 25)

See the following references:

Altringham (2003)
Bat Conservation Trust (2001)
Macdonald & Tattersall (2001)
Mitchell-Jones & McLeish (1999)
Richardson (2000)
Russ (1999)
Stebbings (1992)
Stebbings & Walsh (1991)

See also:

Ahlen, I. (1990) *Identification of Bats in Flight*. Sollentuna: The Swedish Society for Conservation of Nature; Stockholm: The Swedish Youth Association for Environmental Studies and Conservation.

Bat Conservation Trust website: www.bct.org.uk

Briggs, B. & King, D. *The Bat Detective: A field Guide for Bat Detection*. Steyning, UK: Batbox Ltd.

Catto, C. (1994) *Bat Detector Manual*, The Bat Conservation Trust, London.

Eurobats website: http://www.eurobats.org/

International Union for the Conservation of Nature (IUCN)

(2003) *2003 IUCN Red List of Threatened Species*. www.redlist.org

Joint Nature Conservation Committee (JNCC) (1989, revised 1995). *Guidelines for selection of biological SSSIs*. Peterborough: JNCC

(2004) *Common Standards Monitoring Guidance for Mammals*. http://www.jncc.gov.uk/communications/news/2004/csm.htm

Kapteyn, K. (ed.) (1993) *Proceedings of the First European Bat Detector Workshop*, Gorssel, The Netherlands, 1–5 July 1991. Amsterdam: The Netherlands Bat Research Foundation.

Stebbings, R. E. (1982) Radio tracking greater horseshoe bats with preliminary observations on flight patterns. In *Telemetric Studies of Vertebrates* (ed. C. L. Cheeseman & R. B. Mitson). Symposia of the Zoological Society of London No. 49, pp. 161–73. London: Academic Press.

(1985a) Radio-tracking bats. In *Animal Telemetry in the Next Decade*. pp. 20–2. Lowestoft, Suffolk: Ministry of Agriculture, Fisheries and Food.

(1985b) *Which Bat is it? A Guide to Bat Identification in Great Britain and Ireland*. London: The Mammal Society.

Vaughan, N., Jones, G. & Harris, S. (1997) Identification of British bat species by multivariant analysis of echolocation call parameters. *The International Journal of Animal Sound and its Recording*, **7**, 189–207.

Walsh, A. L. & Harris, S. (1996a) Foraging habitat preferences of vespertilionid bats in Britain I. *Journal of Applied Ecology*, **33**, 508–18.

(1996b) Determinants of vespertilionid bat abundance in Britain: geographic, land class and local habitat relationships II. *Journal of Applied Ecology*, **33**, 519–29.

OTHER MAMMALS (CHAPTER 26)

See the following references:

Ayrshire Red Squirrel Group (2004)
Barnes & Tapper (1985)
Cresswell *et al.* (1990)
Flux (1970)
Gurnell & Flowerdew (1995)
Harris *et al.* (1995)
Hutchings & Harris (1996)
Jenkins & Burrows (1980)
Kruuk *et al.* (1986)
Macdonald *et al.* (1998c)
Macdonald & Mason (1987)
Macdonald & Tattersall (2001)
NCC (1989)
Preston *et al.* (2002)
Ratcliffe (1987)
Ratcliffe & Mayle (1993)
Sargent & Morris (1997)
Staines & Ratcliffe (1987)
Stormer *et al.* (1977)
Strachan & Jefferies (1993)
Tapper (2001)
Whilde (1993)

See also:

Cooper, M. (1997) *Red Squirrels*. SNH Information and Advisory Note No. 70. Perth: Scottish Natural Heritage.

Corbet, G. B. & Harris, S. (1991) *The Handbook of British Mammals*. Oxford: Blackwell Scientific Publications.

Gurnell, J., Lurz, P., & Pepper, H. (2001) *Practical Techniques for Surveying and Monitoring Squirrels*. Practice Note, Forestry Commision, Edinburgh.

Sutherland, W. J. (1996) Mammals. In *Ecological Census Techniques* (ed. W. J. Sutherland), pp. 260–79.

References

Alcock, M. R. & Palmer, M. A. (1985) *A Standard Method for the Survey of Ditch Vegetation.* Unpublished Chief Scientist's Department Notes No. 37, Nature Conservancy Council, Peterborough.

Aldrich, R. C. (1979) *Remote Sensing of Wildland Resources: A State-of-the-art Review.* General Technical Report RM-71. Fort Collins, Colorado: Rocky Mountain Forest and Range Experiment Station, USDA Forest Service.

Alexander, K. N. A. (2003) *Provisional atlas of the Cantharoidea and Buprestoidea (Coleoptera) of Britain and Ireland.* Huntingdon: Biological Records Centre.

Alexander, G., Leaper, G., Francis, I. & Tulloch, M. (1997) *Biodiversity in North-east Scotland: a Preliminary Audit of Priority Habitats and Species.* Unpublished report by the North-east Scotland Local Biodiversity Action Plan Steering Group, RSPB, Aberdeen.

Allen, S. E. (1989) *Chemical Analysis of Ecological Materials*, 2nd edn. Oxford: Blackwell Scientific Publications.

Allen-Wardell, G., Bernhardt, P., Bitner, R. *et al.* (1998) The potential consequences of pollinator declines on the conservation of biodiversity and stability of food crop yields. *Conservation Biology*, **12**, 8–17.

Altringham (2003) *British Bats.* London: HarperCollins.

Anderson, D. R., Burnham, K. P., White, G. C. & Otis, D. L. (1983) Density estimation of small mammal populations using a trapping web and distance sampling methods. *Ecology*, **64**, 674–80.

Anderson, S. (2002) *Identifying Important Plant Areas. A site selection manual for Europe, and a basis for developing guidelines for other regions of the world.* London: Plantlife.

Ando, A., Camm, J., Polasky, S., & Solow, A. (1998) Species distributions, land values and efficient conservation. *Science*, **279**, 2126–8.

Andrews, J. (1995) Waterbodies. In *Managing Habitats for Conservation* (ed. W. J. Sutherland & D. A. Hill), pp. 121–48. Cambridge: Cambridge University Press.

Andrews, J. & Rebane, M. (1994) *Farming and Wildlife – A Practical Management Handbook.* Sandy, Bedfordshire: Royal Society for the Protection of Birds.

Anon. (1994) *Biodiversity: the UK Action Plan.* London: Her Majesty's Stationery Office.

(1995) *Biodiversity: The UK Steering Group Report*, Volumes 1 and 2. London: Her Majesty's Stationery Office.

Anselin, A., Meire, P. M., & Anselin, L. (1989) Multicriteria techniques in ecological evaluation: an example using the analytical hierarchy process. *Biological Conservation*, **49**, 215–31.

Archibald, J. F. (1981) *Management Control and Stand Structure Monitoring on Woodland Nature Reserves.* Unpublished report, Nature Conservancy Council, Peterborough.

Armitage, P. D., Machale, A. M. & Crisp, D. C. (1974) A survey of stream invertebrates in the Cow Green (Upper Teesdale) before inundation. *Freshwater Biology*, **4**, 368–98.

Askew, R. R. (1988) *The Dragonflies of Europe.* Colchester: Harley Books.

Atkinson, P. W., Austin, G. E., Burton, N. H. K., Musgrove, A. J., Pollitt, M. & Renfiscu, M. M. (2000) *WeBs Alerts 1998/ 99: Changes in the Numbers of Wintering Waterbirds in The United Kingdom at National, Country and Special Protection Area (SPA) Scales.* BTO Research Report no. 239. Thetford: British Trust for Ornithology.

Ausden, M. (1996) Invertebrates. In *Ecological Census Techniques* (ed. W. J. Sutherland), pp. 139–77. Cambridge: Cambridge University Press.

Ayrshire Red Squirrel Group (correct at 11/03/2004) *Walked Transect Surveys – Instructions for Surveyors.* www. e-ayrshire. co.uk/local/redsquirrel/walked_survey.asp.

Baars, M. A. (1979) Catches in pitfall traps in relation to mean densities of carabid beetles. *Oecologia*, **41**, 25–46.

Bailey, N. T. J. (1981) *Statistical Methods in Biology.* London: Hodder & Stoughton.

Bailey-Watts, A. E. & Kirika, A. (1981) An assessment of size variation in Loch Leven phytoplankton: methodology and some of its uses in the study of factors influencing size. *Journal of Plankton Research*, **3**, 281–2.

Baillie, J. & Groombridge, B. (eds) (1996) *1996 IUCN Red List of Threatened Animals*. Gland, Switzerland and Cambridge, UK: International Union for the Conservation of Nature.

Baillie, J. E. M., Hilton-Taylor, C. & Stuart, S. N. (2004) *2004 IUCN Red List of Threatened Species: a Global Species Assessment*. Cambridge, UK and Gland, Switzerland: IUCN.

Baker, J. & Gent, A. H. (1998) Marking and recognition of animals. In *Herpetofauna Worker's Manual* (ed. A. H. Gent & S. D. Gibson), pp. 45–54 Peterborough: Joint Nature Conservation Committee.

Ballance, D. K. (2004) County and local bird reports in Britain and Ireland. *British Birds*, **97**, 76–91.

Ball, S. G. & Morris, R. K. A. (2000) *Provisional Atlas of British Hoverflies (Diptera, Syrphidae)*. Huntingdon: Biological Records Centre.

Balmford, A. & Gaston, K. (1999) Why biodiversity surveys are good value. *Nature*, **398**, 204–5.

Bardgett, R. D. & Marsden, J. H. (1992) *Heather Condition and Management in England and Wales*. Peterborough: English Nature.

Barnes, R. F. W. & Tapper, S. C. (1985) A method for counting hares by spotlight. *Journal of Zoology (London)*, **206**, 273–76.

Barr, C. J., Britt, C. P. & Sparks, T. H. (1995) *Hedgerow Management and Wildlife: A Review of Research on the Effects of Hedgerow Management and Adjacent Land on Biodiversity*. May 1995. London: Ministry of Agriculture, Fisheries and Food.

Barr, C. J., Bunce, R. G. H, Clarke, R. T. *et al.* (1993) *Countryside Survey 1990: Main Report*. London: Department of the Environment.

Bat Conservation Trust (2001) *Bat Group Contacts List*. London: Bat Conservation Trust.

Batten, L. A., Bibby, C. J., Clement, P., Elliott, G. D., & Porter, R. F. (1990) *Red Data Birds in Britain*. London: T. & A. D. Poyser.

Beebee, T. J. C. & Denton, J. S. (1996) *Natterjack Toad: Conservation Handbook*. Peterborough: English Nature.

Beebee, T. and Griffiths, R. (2000) *Amphibians and Reptiles*. London: HarperCollins.

Beissinger, S. R. & Westphal, M. I. (1998) On the use of demographic models of population viability in endangered species management. *Journal of Wildlife Management*, **62**, 821–41.

Bell, S. (1996) *Techniques for Monitoring of Freshwater Macrophytes for Nature Conservation*. Cobham Resource Consultants, unpublished report to Scottish Natural Heritage.

Bennett, A. F. (1990) Habitat corridors and the conservation of small mammals in a fragmented forest environment. *Landscape Ecology*, **4**, 109–22.

Berk, K. N. & Carey, P. (2000) *Data Analysis with Microsoft Excel*. Pacific Grove CA: Duxbury.

Bibby, C. J. (1998) Selecting areas for conservation. In *Conservation science and Action* (ed. W. J. Sutherland), pp. 176–201. Oxford: Blackwell.

Bibby, C. J., Burgess, N. D., Hill, D. A. & Mustoe, S. (2000) *Bird Census Techniques,* 2nd edn. London: Academic Press.

Bignal, E. (1978) *The Fixed Angle Photographic Method used on Loch Lomond NNR*, Research and Technical Note No. 1, Nature Conservancy Council South West Region (Scotland) and Nature Conservancy Council, Peterborough.

BirdLife International (2000) *Threatened Birds of the World*. Barcelona and Cambridge: Lynx Edicions and BirdLife International.

BirdLife International (2004) *Birds in Europe: Population Estimates, Trends and Conservation Status*. Cambridge: BirdLife International.

Blackshaw, R. (1994) Sampling for leatherjackets in grassland. *Aspects of Applied Biology*, **37**, 95–102.

Blake, A. (1988) *The Vegetation Analysis Database. Version 3.0*. Nature Conservancy Council internal document.

Blockeel, T. L. & Long, D. G. (1998) *A check-list and census catalogue of British and Irish bryophytes*. Cardiff: British Bryological Society.

Boddy, M. (1993) Whitethroat *Sylvia communis* population studies during 1981–91 at a breeding site on the Lincolnshire coast. *Ringing and Migration*, **14**, 17–83.

Bonham, C. D. (1989) *Measurements for Terrestrial Vegetation*. New York: John Wiley and Sons.

Boon, P. J. Calow, P. & Petts, G. E. (eds) (1992) *River Conservation and Management*. Chichester: John Wiley and Sons.

Boon, P. J., Holmes, N. T. H., Maitland, P. S. & Rowell, T. A. (1996a) *SERCON: System for Evaluating Rivers for CONservation: Version 1 Manual*. Scottish Natural Heritage Research, Survey and Monitoring Report No. 61. Perth: Scottish Natural Heritage.

(1996b). A System for Evaluating Rivers for CONservation (SERCON): Development, structure and function.

In *Freshwater Quality: Defining the Indefinable?* (ed. P. J. Boon & D. L. Howell). Edinburgh: The Stationery Office.

Boon, P. J., Holmes, N. T. H., Maitland, P. S. & Fozzard, I. R. (2002) Developing a new version of SERCON (System for Evaluating Rivers for Conservation). *Aquatic Conservation: Marine and Freshwater Ecosystems*, **12**, 439–55.

Boon, P. J. & Howell, D. L. (1997) *Freshwater Quality: Defining the Indefinable?* Edinburgh: The Stationery Office.

Boon, P. J. & Raven, P. J. (eds) (1998) The application of classification and assessment methods to river management in the UK. *Aquatic Conservation: Marine and Freshwater Ecosystems*, **8** (special issue), 383–644.

Bradley, J. D., Tremewan, W. G. & Smith, A. (1973) *British Tortricoid Moths*, volume 1. London: Ray Society. (1979) *British Tortricoid Moths*, volume 2. London: Ray Society.

Bragg, O. M., Hulme, P. D., Ingram, H. A. P., Johnston, J. P. & Wilson, A. I. A. (1994) A maximum–minimum recorder for shallow water tables, developed for ecohydrological studies on mires. *Journal of Applied Ecology*, **31**, 589–92.

Brassington, R. (1988) *Field Hydrogeology*. Milton Keynes: Open University Press.

Bratton, J. H. (1991) *A Review of the Scarcer Ephemeroptera and Plecoptera of Great Britain*. Research and Survey in Nature Conservation No. 32. Peterborough: Nature Conservancy Council.

Bright, P., Morris, P. & Mitchell-Jones, A. (1996) *The Dormouse Conservation Handbook*. Peterborough: English Nature.

Brookes, A. (1991) Geomorphology. In *River Projects and Conservation: A Manual for Holistic Appraisal* (ed. J. L. Gardiner), pp. 57–66. Chichester: John Wiley and Sons.

Brooks, S. J. (1993) Review of a method to monitor adult dragonfly populations. *Journal of the British Dragonfly Society*, **9**, 1–4.

Brown, A. (1994) Setting management objectives for monitoring interest features. In *SSSI Features Monitoring System* (Anon.). Bangor: Countryside Council for Wales. (2000) *Habitat Monitoring for Conservation Management and Reporting. 3. Technical Guide*. Bangor: Countryside Council for Wales.

Buckland, S. T., Anderson, D. R., Burnham, K. P. *et al.* (2001) *Introduction to Distance Sampling*. Oxford: Oxford University Press.

Buckland, S. T., Anderson, D. R., Burnham, K. P. & Laake, J. L. (1993) *Distance Sampling: Estimating Abundance of Biological Populations*. London: Chapman & Hall.

Buckley, B. (1987) *Seine Netting*. Advisory Booklet from the Specialist Section – Management. Publications of the Institute of Fisheries Management, Birmingham.

Buckley, J. & Inns, H. (1998) Field identification, sexing and aging. In *Herpetofauna Worker's Manual* (ed. A. H. Gent & S. D. Gibson), pp. 15–32. Peterborough: Joint Nature Conservation Committee.

Buglife (2003) Conserving Invertebrates. http://www.buglife.org.uk/html/conserving_invert.htm.

Bullock, J. (1996) Plants. In *Ecological Census Techniques* (ed. W. J. Sutherland), pp. 111–38. Cambridge: Cambridge University Press.

Burd, F. (1989) *The Saltmarsh Survey of Great Britain. An Inventory of British Saltmarshes*. Research and Survey in Nature Conservation No. 17. Peterborough: Nature Conservancy Council.

Burnham, K. P. & Overton, W. S. (1978) Estimation of the size of a closed population when capture probabilities vary among animals. *Biometrika*, **65**, 625–33. (1979) Robust estimation of population size when capture probabilities vary amongst animals. *Ecology*, **60**, 927–36.

Butterfly Conservation (2001) *The Millennium Atlas of Butterflies in Britain and Ireland*. Oxford: Oxford University Press.

Byrne, S. (1991) *Botanical Monitoring Methods for Terrestrial Habitats*. England Field Unit Project No. 103. NCC internal report, English Nature, Peterborough.

Byron, H. J. (2000) *Biodiversity Impact. Biodiversity and Environmental Impact Assessment: a Good Practice Guide for Road Schemes*. Sandy: RSPB, WWF-UK, English Nature and the Wildlife Trusts.

Calow, P. & Petts, G. E. (1992) *The Rivers Handbook: Hydrological and Ecological Principles*, volume 1. Oxford: Blackwell Scientific Publications. (1994) *The Rivers Handbook: Hydrological and Ecological Principles*, volume 2. Oxford: Blackwell Scientific Publications.

Cassidy, K. M., Grue, C. E., Smith, M. R., *et al.* (2001) Using current protection status to assess conservation priorities. *Biological Conservation*, **97**, 1–20.

Causton, D. (1988) *Introduction to Vegetation Analysis*. London: Unwin.

Chadd, R. & Extence, C. (2004) The conservation of freshwater macroinvertebrate populations: a community-based classification scheme. *Aquatic Conservation: Marine and Freshwater Ecosystems*, **14**, 597–624.

Chatfield, C. (1996). *The Analysis of Time Series – an Introduction*, 5th edn. London: Chapman and Hall.

Cherrill, A. & McClean, C. (1999a) The reliability of 'Phase 1' habitat mapping in the UK: the extent and types of observer bias. *Landscape and Urban Planning*, **45**, 131–43.

(1999b) Between observer variation in the application of a standard method of habitat mapping by environmental consultants in the UK. *Journal of Applied Ecology*, **36**, 989–1008.

Church, J. M., Coppins, B. J., Gilbert, O. L., James, P. W., & Stewart, N. F. (1996) *Red Data Books of Britain and Ireland: Lichens*. Peterborough: Joint Nature Conservation Committee.

Church, J. M., Hodgetts, N. G., Preston, C. D. & Stewart, N. F. (2001) *British Red Data Books: Mosses and Liverworts*. Peterborough: Joint Nature Conservation Committee.

Clobert, J., Lebreton, J. D. & Allaine, D. (1987) A general approach to survival rate estimation by recaptures or resightings of marked birds. *Ardea*, **75**, 133–42.

Clymo, R. S. (1980) Preliminary survey of the peat-bog Hummell Knowe Moss using various numerical methods. *Vegetatio*, **42**, 129–48.

Cochran, W. G. (1977) *Sampling Techniques*, 3rd edn. Chichester: John Wiley & Sons.

Cooke, A. S. (1995) A comparison of survey methods for crested newts (*Triturus cristatus*) and night counts at a secure site 1983–1993. *Herpetological Journal*, **5**, 221–8.

Cooper, E. A. & Rodwell, J. S. (1995) *NVC Options for the Yorkshire Dales Natural Area*. Report to English Nature by the Unit of Vegetation Science, Lancaster University.

Coppins, A. M. & Coppins, B. J. (2002) *Indices of Ecological Continuity for Woodland Epiphytic Lichen Habitats in the British Isles*. London: British Lichen Society.

Cottam, G. & Curtis, J. T. (1956) The method of making rapid surveys of woods by means of pairs of randomly selected trees. *Ecology*, **30**, 101–4.

Countryside Commission (1991) *Landscape Change in the National Parks*. CCP 359. London: Countryside Commission.

Countryside Council for Wales (CCW) (1996) *A guide to the production of management plans for nature reserves and protected areas*. Bangor: Countryside Council for Wales.

Cowx, I. G. (ed.) (1990) *Developments in Electric Fishing*. Oxford: Fishing News Books.

(ed.) (1996) *Stock Assessments in Inland Fisheries*. Oxford: Fishing News Books.

Cowx, I. G. & Lamarque, P. (eds) (1990) *Fishing with Electricity*. Oxford: Fishing News Books.

Cressie, N. A. C. (1993) *Statistics for Spatial Data*. New York: John Wiley.

Cresswell, P., Harris, S. & Jefferies, D. J. (1990) *The History, Distribution, Status and Habitat Requirements of the Badger in Britain*. Peterborough: Joint Nature Conservation Committee.

Critchley, C. N. R. (1997) Monitoring methods. In *Grassland Management in Environmentally Sensitive Areas*, British Grassland Society Occasional Symposium No. 32, pp. 44–54.

Croft, P. S. (1986) A key to the major groups of British freshwater invertebrates. *Field Studies*, **6**, 531–79.

Crozier, R. H. (1992) Genetic diversity and the agony of choice. *Biological Conservation*, **61**, 11–15.

Currall, J. E. P. (1987) A transformation of the Domin scale. *Vegetatio*, **72**, 81–7.

Cushing, C. E., McIntire, C. D. & Sedell, J. R. (1980) Comparative study of physical-chemical variables of streams using multivariate analyses. *Archives of Hydrobiology*, **89** (3), 343–52.

Daily, C. G. (ed.) (1997) *Nature's Services: Societal Dependence on Natural Ecosystems*. Washington, DC: Island Press.

Dalby, D. & Rich, T. C. G (1994) *The History, Taxonomy, Distribution and Ecology of Mountain Scurvy Grass (Cochlearia micacea Marshall)*. Plantlife Back from the Brink Report No. 42. Unpublished report to Scottish Natural Heritage, Edinburgh.

Dargie, T. (1992) *Repeat Phase I Habitat Survey and the Detection of Vegetation Change*. English Nature Research Report No. 51. Peterborough: English Nature.

(1993) *Sand Dune Vegetation Survey of Great Britain: A National Inventory*. Part 2. *Scotland*. Peterborough: Joint Nature Conservation Committee.

Davies, C. (2001) *Database and Atlas of Freshwater Fishes (DAFF)*. National Federation for Biological Recording Newsletter 29. National Federation for Biological Recording website: www.nfbr.org.uk/html/newsletter_29.html#FreshwaterFish.

Davies, C. D., Shelley, J., Harding, P., McLean, I., Gardiner, R. & Peirson, G. (2003) *Freshwater Fishes in Britain: the Species and their Distribution*. Colchester: Harley Books.

Davies, J., Baxter, J., Bradley, M. *et al.* (eds) (2001) *Marine Monitoring Handbook: March 2001, UK Marine SACs Project*. Peterborough: Joint Nature Conservation Committee.

Davies, S. M. & Yost, L. (eds) (1998) *Conservation Objectives: Guidelines for Identifying the Attributes of Interest Features under the EC Habitats Directive and Wild Birds Directive*. JNCC working internal draft, Joint Nature Conservation Committee, Peterborough.

Dawkins, H. C. & Field, D. R. B. (1978) *A Long-term Surveillance System for British Woodland Vegetation.* CFI Occasional Papers No. 1. Oxford: Commonwealth Forestry Institute, Oxford University.

de Freina, J. J. & Witt, T. J. (1997) *Die Bobyces und Sphinges der Westpalaearktis (Insecta: Lepidoptera) – Sesiidae.* München: Forschung & Wissenschaft GmbH.

Dee, N., Barker, J., Drobuy, N., & Duke, K. (1973) An environmental evaluation system for water resources planning. *Water Resources Research,* **9**, 523.

Dennis, P., Usher, G. B. & Watt, A. D. (1995) Lowland woodland structure and pattern and the distribution of arboreal, phytophagous arthropods. *Biodiversity and Conservation,* **4**, 728–44.

Dennis, P., Young, M. R., & Gordon, I. J. (1998) Distribution and abundance of small insects and arachnids in relation to structural heterogeneity of grazed indigenous grasslands. *Ecological Entomology,* **22**, 253–64.

Department for the Environment, Food and Rural Affairs (DEFRA) (2002) *Working with the Grain of Nature. A Biodiversity Strategy for England.* London: Department for the Environment, Food and Rural Affairs.

Department for the Environment, Transport and the Regions (DETR) (1998) *A New Deal for Transport: Better for Everyone.* London: DETR.

Department for the Environment, Transport and the Regions (DETR) (2000) *Guidance on the methodology for multi-modal studies.* London: Department for the Environment, Transport and the Regions.

Department of the Environment (DoE) (1995a) *Land Use Change in England.* Statistical Bulletin No. 10. London: Department of the Environment.

(1995b) *Preparation of Environmental Statements for Projects which Require Environmental Assessment: a Good Practice Guide.* London: Her Majesty's Stationery Office.

Diamond, J. M. (1975) The island dilemma: lessons of modern geographic studies for the design of natural preserves. *Biological Conservation,* **7**, 129–46.

Dietrick, E. J. (1961) An improved backpack motor fan for suction sampling of insect populations. *Journal of Economic Entomology,* **54**, 394–5.

Dietrick, E. J., Schlinger, E. I. & van den Bosch, R. (1959) A new method for sampling arthropods using a suction collecting machine and modified Berlese funnel separator. *Journal of Economic Entomology,* **52**, 1085–91.

Dirkse, G. M. (1998) *The Validity of General Purpose Flora-based Classification of Vegetation.* IBN Scientific Contributions 14. Wageningen, The Netherlands: DLO Institute for Forestry and Nature Research (IBN–DLO).

Disney, R. H. L. (1986) Assessments using invertebrates: posing the problem. In *Wildlife Conservation Evaluation* (ed. M. B. Usher), pp. 271–93. London: Chapman & Hall.

(1987) Rapid surveys of arthropods and the ranking of sites in terms of conservation value. In *Biological Surveys of Estuaries and Coasts: Estuarine and Brackish-water Sciences Foundation Handbook* (ed. J. M. Baker & W. J. Wolff), pp. 73–5. Cambridge: Cambridge University Press.

Doody, J. P. (ed.) (1985) *Sand Dunes and their Management.* Peterborough: Chief Scientist Directorate, Nature Conservancy Council.

Drake, C. M. & Elliot, J. M. (1983) A new quantitative air-lift sampler for collecting macro-invertebrates on stony bottoms in deep rivers. *Freshwater Biology,* **13**, 545–59.

Duffey, E. (1980) The efficiency of the Dietrick vacuum sampler (D-Vac) for invertebrate population studies in different types of grassland. *Bulletin d'Ecologie,* **11(3–4)**, 421–431.

During, H. J. (1992) Ecological classification of bryophytes and lichens. In *Bryophytes and Lichens in a Changing Environment* (ed. E. W. Bates & A. M. Farmer), pp. 1–31. Oxford: Clarendon Press.

Dytham, C. (2003) *Choosing and Using Statistics: a Biologist's Guide,* 2nd edn. Oxford: Blackwell.

Eberhardt, L. L. (1976) Quantitative ecology and environmental impact assessment. *Journal of Environmental Management,* **4**, 27–70.

(2003) What should we do about hypothesis testing? *Journal of Wildlife Management,* **67**(2), 241–7.

Edwards, R. (ed.) (1997) *Provisional Atlas of the Aculeate Hymenoptera of Britain and Ireland, Part 1. Bees, Wasps and Ants Recording Society.* Huntingdon: Biological Records Centre.

Edwards, R. (ed.) (1998) *Provisional Atlas of the Aculeate Hymenoptera of Britain and Ireland, Part 2. Bees, Wasps and Ants Recording Society.* Huntingdon: Biological Records Centre.

Edwards, R. & Telfer, M. G. (eds) (2001) *Provisional Atlas of the Aculeate Hymenoptera of Britain and Ireland, Part 3. Bees Wasps and Ants Recording Society.* Huntingdon: Biological Records Centre.

Edwards, R. & Telfer, M. G. (eds) (2002) *Provisional Atlas of the Aculeate Hymenoptera of Britain and Ireland, Part 4. Bees*

Wasps and Ants Recording Society. Huntingdon: Biological Records Centre.

Ekkehard, F. (1986) *Breeding Butterflies and Moths – a Practical Handbook for British and European Species.* Colchester, Essex: Harley Books.

Elzinga, C. L., Salzer, D. W., Willoughby, J. W. & Gibbs, J. P. (2001) *Monitoring Plant and Animal Populations.* Oxford: Blackwell Science.

Emmet, A. M. & Health, J. (eds) (1989) *The Moths and Butterflies of great Britain and Ireland,* Volume 7, Part 1. Colchester, Essex: Harley Books.

English Nature (1993) *Air Pollution and Environmental Statements: Necessary Components for Assessing the Impact on Nature Conservation,* Peterborough: English Nature.

(1994) *Nature Conservation in Environmental Impact Assessment.* Peterborough: English Nature.

(1995) *The Grazing Index. Field Notes.* Peterborough: English Nature.

(2001) *Great Crested Newt Mitigation Guidelines.* Peterborough: English Nature.

Environment Agency (2003) *River Habitat Survey in Britain and Ireland. Field Survey Guidance manual: 2003 Version.* Warrington: Environment Agency.

Environment Agency (2004) *Freshwater Fish.* Environment Agency web pages: www.environment-agency.gov.uk/ yourenv/eff/wildlife/fish/161782/? version = 1&lang = _e.

Erwin, T. L. (1991) An evolutionary basis for conservation strategies. *Science,* **253**, 750–2.

European Commission (1999) *Interpretation Manual of European Union Habitats.* Version EUR 15/2. European Commission DG Environment.

(2000) *Managing Natura 2000 sites: the Provisions of Article 6 of the 'Habitats' Directive 92/43/EEC.* Luxembourg: Office for Official Publications of the European Communities.

European Commission DGXI (1995) Natura 2000 network. Council Directive 79/409/EEC on the conservation of wild birds and Council Directive 92/43/EEC on the conservation of natural habitats and of wild fauna and flora. Standard Data Form. EUR15 version. Brussels: European Commission DGXI.

Everitt, J., Hackett, R., & Sands, T. (2002) *Gaining Ground.* Newark: The Wildlife Trusts.

Eyre, M. D., Luff, M. L., Rushton, S. P. & Topping, C. J. (1989) Ground beetles and weevils (Carabidae and Curculionidae) as indicators of grassland management practice. *Journal of Applied Ecology,* **107**, 508–517.

Farmer, A. M. (1990) Effects of lake acidification on aquatic macrophytes – a review. *Environmental Pollution,* **65**, 219–40

Farrell, L. (1991) Population changes and management of *Orchis militaris* at two sites in England. In *Population Ecology of Terrestrial Orchids* (ed. T. C. E. Wells & J. H. Willems), pp. 63–8. The Hague: SPB Academic Publishing.

Fasola, M., Barbieri, F. & Canova, L. (1993) Test of an electronic individual tag for newts. *Herpetological Journal,* **3**, 455–70.

Ferris-Kaan, R. & Patterson, G. S. (1992) *Monitoring Vegetation Changes in Conservation Management of Forests.* Forestry Commission Bulletin 108. London: Her Majesty's Stationery Office.

Fewster, R. M., Buckland, S. T., Siriwardena, G. M., Baillie, S. R. & Wilson, J. D. (2000) Analysis of population trends for farmland birds using generalized additive models. *Ecology,* **81**, 1970–84.

Fitter, R. & Fitter, M. (eds) (1987) *The road to extinction: problems of categorizing the status of taxa threatened with extinction.* Gland, Switzerland: IUCN in collaboration with UNEP.

Fleming, L. V., Ing, B. & Scouller, C. E. K. (1998) Current status and phenology of fruiting in Scotland of the endangered fungus *Tulostoma niveum. Mycologist,* **12** (3), 126–31.

Flower, R. J. (1985) An improved epilithon sampler and its evaluation in two acid lakes, *British Phycological Journal,* **20**, 109–115.

Flux, J. E. C. (1970) Life history of the mountain hare (*Lepus timidus*) in north-east Scotland. *Journal of Zoology (London),* **161**, 75–123.

Food and Agriculture Organisation of the United Nations (FAO) (1977) *Guidelines for Soil Profile Description,* Rome: FAO.

Ford, J. B. (1962) The vertical distribution of larval Chironimidae (Dipt.) in the mud of a stream. *Hydrobiologia,* **19**, 262–72.

Fowler, J., Cohen, L. & Jarvis, P. (1998) *Practical Statistics for Field Biology,* 2nd edn. Chichester: John Wiley & Sons.

Froglife (1999) *Reptile Survey: an introduction to planning, conducting and interpreting surveys and lizards for conservation.* Advice Sheet 10. Halesworth, UK: Froglife.

Fry, R. & Waring, P. (1996) A guide to moth traps and their use. *The Amateur Entomologist,* **24**.

Fuller, R. J. (1980) A method of assessing the ornithological interest of sites for conservation. *Biological Conservation,* **17**, 229–39.

Fuller, R. J. (1982) *Bird Habitats in Britain*. Calton: Poyser.

Fuller, R. J., Stuttard, P. and Ray, C. M. (1989) The distribution of breeding songbirds within mixed coppiced woodland in Kent, England, in relation to vegetation age and structure. *Annales Zoologici Fennici*, **26**, 265–5.

Fuller, R. M, Groom, G. B. & Jones, A. R. (1994) The land cover map of Great Britain: an automated classification of LANDSAT Thematic Mapper data. *Photogrammetric Engineering and Remote Sensing*, **60**, 553–62.

Furse, M. T., Wright, J. F., Armitage, P. D. & Moss, D. (1981) An appraisal of pond-net samples for biological monitoring of lotic macro-invertebrates. *Water Research*, **15**, 679–89.

Gardiner, V. and Dackombe, R. (1983) *Geomorphological Field Manual*. London: Allen and Unwin.

Gardner, T. (2001) Declining amphibian populations: a global phenomenon in conservation biology. *Animal Biodiversity and Conservation*, **24**(2), 25.

Geddes, C. (1996) *Monitoring of Rare Montane Vascular Plants on Ben Lawers NNR and Caenlochan NNR*. Scottish Natural Heritage Review No. 44. Edinburgh: Scottish Natural Heritage.

Geissler, P. H. & Sauer, J. R. (1990) Topics in route-regression analysis. In *Survey Designs and Statistical Methods for the estimation of Avian Population Trends*, US Fish and Wildlife Service Biological Report 90 (1) (ed. J. R. Sauer & S. Droege), pp. 54–57. Washington, DC: US Fish and Wildlife Service.

Gent, A. (1994) *Survey and Monitoring of Reptiles. Species Conservation Handbook*. Peterborough: English Nature.

Gent, A. H. & Gibson, S. D. (eds) (1998) *Herpetofauna Worker's Manual*. Peterborough: Joint Nature Conservation Committee.

Gibbons, D. W., Avery, M. I., Baillie, S. R. *et al.* (1996) *Bird Species of Conservation Concern in the United Kingdom, Channel Islands and Isle of Man: Revising the Red Data List*. Sandy, Beds: RSPB.

Gibbons, D. W., Reid, J. B. & Chapman, R. A. (1993) *The New Atlas of Breeding Birds in Britain and Ireland: 1988–1991*. British Trust for Ornithology/Scottish Ornithologists' Club/Irish Wildbird Conservancy. London: T. & A. D. Poyser.

Gilbert, G. & Gibbons, W. (1996) *A Review of Habitat, Land Cover and Land-use Survey and Monitoring in the United Kingdom*. Sandy, Bedfordshire: Conservation Science Department, Royal Society for the Protection of Birds.

Gilbert, G., Gibbons, D. W. & Evans, J. (1998) *Bird Monitoring Methods: a Manual of Techniques for Key UK Species*. RSPB/BTO/JNCC/WWT/ITE/The Seabird Group. Sandy, Bedfordshire: Royal Society for the Protection of Birds/British Trust for Ornithology.

Gilman, K. (1994) *Hydrology and Wetland Conservation*. Chichester: John Wiley & Sons.

Gimingham, C. H. (1992) *The Lowland Heathland Management Handbook*. English Nature Science No. 8. Peterborough: English Nature.

Goldsmith, F. B. (ed.) (1991) *Monitoring for Conservation and Ecology*. London: Chapman & Hall.

Golterman, H. L., Clymo, R S. & Ohnstad, M A. M. (1978) *Methods for Physical and Chemical Analysis of Fresh Waters*, 2nd edn. Oxford: Blackwell Scientific Publications.

Goodall, D. W. (1952) Some considerations in the use of point quadrats for the analysis of vegetation. *Australian Journal of Scientific Research Series B*, **5**, 1–41.

(1953) Objective methods for the classification of vegetation. I. The use of positive interspecific correlation. *Australian Journal of Botany*, **1**, 39–63.

Gotmark, F., Ahlund, M., & Eriksson, M. (1986) Are indices reliable for assessing conservation value of natural areas. An avian case study. *Biological Conservation*, **38**, 55–73.

Grant, M., Tomlinson, R. W. & Harvey, J. (1997) *Hydrological Monitoring for Peatlands*. Advisory report from the Peatland Survey and Profiling Project 1997/8, for the Environment and Heritage Service, Department of the Environment for Northern Ireland, Belfast.

Green, R. E., Osborne, P. E. & Sears, E. J. (1994) The distribution of passerine birds in hedgerows during the breeding season in relation to characteristics of the hedgerow and adjacent farmland. *Journal of Applied Ecology*, **31**, 677–92.

Greenslade, P. J. M. (1964) Pitfall trapping as a method for studying Carabidae (Coleoptera). *Journal of Animal Ecology*, **33**, 301–10.

Greenwood, J. J. D. (1996) Basic techniques. In *Ecological Census Techniques* (ed. W. J. Sutherland), pp. 11–110. Cambridge: Cambridge University Press.

Gregory, R. D., Wilkinson, N. I., Noble, D. G. *et al.* (2002) The population status of birds in the United Kingdom, Channel Islands and Isle of Man: an analysis of conservation concern 2002–2007. *British Birds*, **95**, 410–48.

Greig-Smith, P. (1983) *Quantitative Plant Ecology*, 3rd edn. Oxford: Blackwell Scientific Publications.

Griffiths, R. A. & Inns, H. (1998) Surveying. In *Herpetofauna Worker's Manual* (ed. A. H. Gent & S. D. Gibson), pp. 1–14. Peterborough: Joint Nature Conservation Committee.

Griffiths, R. A. & Langton, T. (1998) Catching and handling. In *Herpetofauna Worker's Manual* (ed. A. H. Gent & S. D. Gibson), pp. 33–44. Peterborough: Joint Nature Conservation Committee.

Griffiths, R. A. & Raper, S. J. (1994) *A Review of Current Techniques for Sampling Amphibian Communities*. JNCC Report No. 210. Peterborough: Joint Nature Conservation Committee.

Griffiths, R. A, Raper, S. J. & Brady, L. D. (1996) *Evaluation of a Standard Method for Surveying Common Frogs* (Rana temporaria) *and Newts* (Triturus cristatus, T. helveticus and T. vulgaris). JNCC Report No. 259. Peterborough: Joint Nature Conservation Committee.

Grimmett, R. F. A. & Jones, T. A. (1989) *Important Bird Areas in Europe*. Cambridge: International Council for Bird Preservation.

Gurnell, J. & Flowerdrew, J. R. (1995) *Live Trapping Small Mammals: a Practical Guide*. Mammal Society Publication No. 3. London: Mammal Society.

Gurnell, J., Lurz, P. P. W. & Pepper, H. (2001) *Practical Techniques for Surveying and Monitoring Squirrels*. Forestry Commission Practice Note 11. Edinburgh: Forestry Commission.

Gurnell, J., Lurz, P. W. W., Shirley, M. D. F., Magris, L. & Steele, J. (2004) A critical look at methods for monitoring red and grey squirrels. *Mammal Review*, **34**, 51–74.

Hacker, J. E., Cowlishaw, G. & Williams, P. H. (1998) Patterns of African primate diversity and their evaluation for the selection of conservation areas. *Biodiversity and Conservation*, **84**, 251–62.

Haes, E. C. M. & Harding, P. T. (1997) *Atlas of Grasshoppers and Allied Insects in Britain and Ireland*. London: Her Majesty's Stationery Office.

Haines-Young, R. & Chopping, M. (1996) Quantifying landscape structure: A review of landscape indices and their application to forested landscapes. *Progress in Physical Geography*, **20** (4), 418–45.

Haines-Young, R. H., Barr, C. J., Black, H. I. J. *et al.* (2000) *Accounting for Nature: Assessing Habitats in the UK Countryside*. London: Department of the Environment, Transport and the Regions.

Halley, J. M., Oldham, R. S. & Arntgen, J. W. (1996) Predicting the persistence of amphibian populations with the help of a spatial model. *Journal of Applied Ecology*, **33**, 455–70.

Halsall, N. B. & Wratten, D. (1988) The efficiency of pitfall trapping for polyphagous predatory Carabidae. *Ecological Entomology*, **13**, 293–9.

Hamilton, G. J. (1975) *Forest Mensuration Handbook*. Forestry Commission Booklet No. 39. London: Her Majesty's Stationery Office.

Hariman, R. & Pugh, K. B. 1994. Water chemistry. In *The Fresh Waters of Scotland: A National Resource of International Significance* (ed. P. S. Maitland, P. J. Boon & D. S. McLusky), pp. 89–112. Chichester: John Wiley & Sons.

Harper, D. M., Smith, C., Barham, P. & Howell, R. (1995) The ecological basis for the management of the natural river environment. In *The Ecological Basis for River Management* (ed. D. M. Harper & A. J. D. Ferguson), pp. 219–38. Chichester: John Wiley & Sons.

Harper, J. L. (1977) *Population Biology of Plants*. London: Academic Press.

Harris, S., Morris, P., Wray S. and Yalden D. (1995) *A review of British Mammals: Population Estimates and Conservation Status of British Mammals other than Cetaceans*. Peterborough: Joint Nature Conservation Committee.

Harvey, P. R., Nellist, D. R. & Telfer, M. G. (eds) (2002) *Provisional Atlas of British Spiders (Arachnida, Araneae)* 2 vols. Huntingdon: Biological Records Centre.

Hawes, C. (2003) Stag Beetle News: Road Kill Survey 2003 – Monitoring Abundance. *White Admiral*, **56**. Suffolk Naturalists Society. http://www.boxvalley.co.uk/nature/sns/wad.htm.

Heath, J., Pollard, E. & Thomas, J. (1984) *Atlas of Butterflies in Britain and Ireland*. Harmondsworth: Viking.

Heath, M. F. & Evans, M. I. (2000) *Important Bird Areas in Europe: Priority Sites for Conservation*. Cambridge: BirdLife International.

Hellawell, J. M. (1978) *Biological Surveillance of Rivers: a Biological Monitoring Handbook*. Medmenham, Buckinghamshire: Water Research Centre.

(1986) *Biological Indicators of Freshwater Pollution and Environmental Management*. London: Elsevier Applied Science Publishers.

(1991) Development of a rationale for monitoring. In *Monitoring for Conservation and Ecology* (ed. F. B. Goldsmith), pp. 1–14. London: Chapman & Hall.

(1997) The contribution of biological and chemical techniques to the assessment of water quality. In *Freshwater Quality: Defining the Indefinable?* (ed. P. J. Boon & D. L. Howell), pp. 89–101. Edinburgh: The Stationery Office.

Her Majesty's Stationery Office (HMSO) (1978) *Methods of Biological Sampling: Handnet Sampling of Aquatic Benthic Macroinvertebrates*. London: HMSO.

(1980) *Quantitative Sampler for Benthic Macroinvertebrates in Shallow Flowing Waters*. London: HMSO.

(1983) *Methods of Biological Sampling: Sampling of Benthic Macroinvertebrates in Deep Rivers*. London: HMSO.

(1984) *Sampling of Non-planktonic Algae (Benthic Algae or Periphyton) 1982*. London: HMSO.

Hill, D. A., Taylor, S., Thaxton, R., Amphlet, A. & Horn, W. (1990). Breeding bird communities of native pine forest, Scotland. *Bird Study*, **37**, 133–41.

Hill, D. A., Andrews, J. Sotherton, N. and Hawkins, J. (1995) Farmland. In *Managing Habitats for Conservation* (ed. W. J. Sutherland and D. A. Hill), pp. 230–66. Cambridge: Cambridge University Press.

Hill, M. O., Preston, C. D. and Smith, A. J. E. (eds) (1991 et seq.). *Atlas of the Bryophytes of Britain and Ireland, volumes 1–3 (Liverworts)*. Colchester: Harley Books.

Hilton-Taylor, C. (ed.) (2000) *2000 IUCN Red List of Threatened Species*. Gland, Switzerland and Cambridge, UK: International Union for the Conservation of Nature, Species Survival Commission.

Hinton, G. C. F. (1989) *A Eutrophication Study on Bosherston Lakes, Dyfed, Wales*. Chief Scientist's Department Report No. 936. Peterborough: Nature Conservancy Council.

Hinton, G. C. F. (1997) Monitoring Lake SACs for Favourable Condition. Unpublished report to Scotish Natural Heritage.

Hirons, G., Goldsmith, B., & Thomas, G. (1995) Site management planning. In *Managing Habitats for Conservation* (ed. W. J. Sutherland & D. A. Hill), Cambridge: Cambridge University Press.

Hodgetts, N. G. (1992) *Guidelines for Selection of Biological SSSIs: Non-vascular Plants*. Peterborough: Joint Nature Conservation Committee.

Hodgson, J. G., Colasanti, R. & Sutton, F. (1995) *Monitoring Grasslands*. English Nature Research Report No. 156, 2 sections. Peterborough: English Nature.

Holmes, N. (1983) *Typing British Rivers according to their Flora*. Focus on Nature Conservation No. 4. Peterborough: Nature Conservancy Council.

Holmes, N. T. H., Boon, P. J. & Rowell, T. A. (1998) A revised classification system for British rivers based on their aquatic plant communities. *Aquatic Conservation: Marine and Freshwater Ecosystems*, **8**, 555–78.

(1999a) *Vegetation Communities of British Rivers: A Revised Classification*. Peterborough: Joint Nature Conservation Committee.

Holmes, N. T. S., Newman, J. R., Chadd, S., Rouen, K. J., Saint, L. & Dawson, F. H. (1999b) *Mean Trophic Rank: A Users Manual*. R&D Technical Report E38. Bristol: Environment Agency.

Honek, A. (1988) The effect of crop density and microclimate on pitfall trap catches of Carabidae, Staphylinidae (Coleoptera), and Lycosidae (Araneae) in cereal fields. *Pedobiologia*, **32**, 233–42.

Hooper, A. J. (1992) Field monitoring of environmental change in the Environmentally Sensitive Areas. In *Land Use Change: The Causes and Consequences* (ed. M. C. Whitby), Institute of Terrestrial Ecology Symposium No. 27, pp. 52–9. London: Her Majesty's Stationery Office.

Hope-Jones, P. (1994a) *Photomonitoring of Sites of Wildlife Interest in Wales*. CCW internal report, Countryside Council for Wales, Bangor.

(1994b) *Photomonitoring. A Procedural Manual*. CCW internal report, Countryside Council for Wales, Bangor.

Hope-Simpson, J. F. (1940) On the errors in the ordinary use of subjective frequency estimations in grassland. *Journal of Ecology*, **28**, 193–209.

Hopkins, J. J. & Buck, A. L. (1995) *The Habitats Directive Atlantic Biogeographical Region*. Report of Atlantic Biogeographical Workshop. Report No. 247. Edinburgh: Joint Nature Conservation Committee.

Hopkins, P., Evans, J., & Gregory, R. (2000) National-scale conservation measures at an appropriate resolution. *Diversity and Distributions*, **6**, 195–204.

Horsfall, A. S. & Kirby, K. J. (1985) *The Use of Permanent Quadrats to Record Changes in the Structure and Composition of Wytham Woods, Oxfordshire*. Research and Survey in Nature Conservation No. 1. Peterborough: Joint Nature Conservation Committee.

Howard, P., Davenport, T., & Kigenyi, F. (1997) Planning conservation areas in Uganda's natural forests. *Oryx*, **31**, 253–64.

Huntings Surveys and Consultants Limited (1986) *Monitoring Landscape Change*, volumes 1–10. London: Department of the Environment and the Countryside Commission.

Hurford, C., Jones, M. R. & Brown, A. (2000) *Habitat Monitoring for Conservation Management and Reporting. 2. Field Methods*. Bangor: Countryside Council for Wales.

Hurford, C. & Perry, K. (2000) *Habitat Monitoring for Conservation Management and Reporting. 1. Case Studies.* Bangor: Countryside Council for Wales.

Hutchings, M.J. (1987a) The population biology of the early spider orchid, *Ophrys sphegodes* Mill. I. A demographic study from 1975 to 1984. *Journal of Ecology*, **75**, 711–27.

(1987b) The population biology of the early spider orchid, *Ophrys sphegodes* Mill. II. Temporal patterns in behaviour. *Journal of Ecology*, **75**, 729–42.

Hutchings, M. R. & Harris, S. (1996) *The Current Status of the Brown Hare* (Lepus europaeus) *in Britain*. Peterborough: Joint Nature Conservation Committee.

Hynes, H. B. N. (1970) *The Ecology of Running Waters*. Toronto: University of Toronto Press.

Institute of Ecology and Environmental Management (IEEM) (2002) *Guidelines for Ecological Impact Assessment Amended Pilot November 2002*. Winchester: IEEM.

Institute of Terrestrial Ecology (ITE) (1986) *The Distribution of Sites of the Monitoring Landscape Change Project in Relation to Classes in the ITE Land Stratification*. London: Department of the Environment and the Countryside Commission.

International Union for the Conservation of Nature (IUCN) (1994) *IUCN Red Data List Categories*. Gland, Switzerland, and Cambridge, UK: IUCN Species Survival Commission.

(2001) *IUCN Red List Categories and Criteria: Version 3.1.* Gland, Switzerland, and Cambridge, UK: IUCN Species Survival Commission.

(2003) *Guidelines for the Application of IUCN Red List Criteria at Regional Levels*. Gland, Switzerland: IUCN Species Survival Commission.

Jackson, D. L. & McLeod, C. R. (eds) (2002) *Handbook on the UK status of EC Habitats Directive interest features: provisional data on the UK distribution and extent of Annex I habitats and the UK distribution and population size of Annex II species. Version 2.* JNCC Report, No. 312. Peterborough: Joint Nature Conservation Committee. Available online at www.jncc.gov.uk/publications/JNCC312/.

James, P. (1996) *Birds of Sussex*. Horsham: Sussex Ornithological Society.

James, P.W., Hawksworth, D. L. & Rose, F. (1977) Lichen communities in the British Isles: a preliminary conspectus. In *Lichen Ecology* (ed. M. R. D. Seaward), pp. 295–413. London: Academic Press.

Jenkins, D. & Burrows, G. O. (1980) Ecology of otters in northern Scotland. III. The use of faeces as indicators of otter (*Lutra lutra*) density and distribution. *Journal of Animal Ecology*, **49**, 755–74.

Jermy, A. C., Long, D., Sands, M. J. S., Stork, N. E. & Winser, S. (1996) *Biodiversity Assessment: a Guide to Good Practice*. London: Department of the Environment / Her Majesty's Stationery Office.

Joint Nature Conservation Committee (JNCC) (1993) *Handbook for Phase 1 Habitat Survey: A Technique for Environmental Audit*. Peterborough: JNCC.

(1994) *Guidelines for Selection of Biological SSSIs: Bogs.* Peterborough: JNCC.

(1996) *Birds of Conservation Importance*. Peterborough: JNCC.

(1997) *A Statement on Common Standards for Monitoring Designated Sites*. Paper to the Joint Nature Conservation Committee, JNCC 97 N9. Peterborough: JNCC.

(1998) *A Statement on Common Standards Monitoring*. Peterborough: JNCC.

(2004) *Plant Diversity Challenge: The UK's Response to the Global Strategy for Plant Conservation*. Peterborough: JNCC.

Jones, J. C. & Reynolds, J. D. (1996) Environmental variables. In *Ecological Census Techniques* (ed. W. J. Sutherland), pp. 281–316. Cambridge: Cambridge University Press.

Jongman, R. H. G., ter Braak, C. J. F. & van Tongeren, O. F. R. (eds) (1995) *Data Analysis in Community and Landscape Ecology*. Cambridge: Cambridge University Press.

Kennedy, C. E. J. & Southwood, T. R. E. (1984) The number of insects associated with British trees: a re-analysis. *Journal of Animal Ecology*, **53**, 455–78.

Kent, M. & Coker, P. (1992) *Vegetation Description and Analysis – a Practical Approach*. London: Belhaven Press.

Kerney, M. P. (1999) *Atlas of the Land and Freshwater Molluscs of Britain and Ireland*. Colchester: Harley Books.

Kershaw, K. A. & Looney, J. H. H. (1983) *Quantitative and Dynamic Plant Ecology*. London: Edward Arnold.

(1985) *Quantitative Plant Ecology*, Edward Arnold, London.

Key, R. S., Drake, C. M. & Sheppard, D. A. (2000) *Conservation of Invertebrates in England: a Review and Framework*. English Nature Science No. 35. Peterborough: English Nature.

King, M. (1995) *Fisheries Biology, Assessment and Management*. Oxford: Fishing News Books.

Kirby, K. J. (1988) *A Woodland Survey Handbook*. Research and Survey in Nature Conservation No. 11. Peterborough: Nature Conservancy Council.

(1992) Accumulation of dead wood – a missing ingredient in coppicing. In *Ecology and Management of Coppice*

Woodlands (ed. G. P. Buckley), pp. 99–112. London: Chapman & Hall.

(1994) *An Approach to a Woodland Monitoring Framework.* English Nature Research Report No. 98. Peterborough: English Nature.

Kirby, K. J., Nines, T., Burn, A., MacKintosh, J., Pitkin, P. & Smith, I. (1986) Seasonal and observer differences in vascular plant records from British woodlands. *Journal of Ecology*, **74**, 123–31.

Kirby, P. (1992) *Habitat Management for Invertebrates: A Practical Handbook.* Sandy, Bedfordshire: Royal Society for the Protection of Birds.

Klapper, H. (1991) *Control of Eutrophication in Inland Waters.* Chichester: Ellis Harwood.

Koop, H. (1989) *Forest Dynamics, SILVI-STAR: A Comprehensive Monitoring System.* Berlin: Springer.

Krebs, C. J. (1999) *Ecological Methodology*, 2nd edn. Menlo Park CA: Addison Wesley Longman.

Kruuk, H., Conroy, W. H., Glimmerveen, U. & Ouwerkerk, E. J. (1986) The use of spraints to survey populations of otters, *Lutra lutra. Biological Conservation*, **35**, 187–94.

Kupiec, J. (1997) *Guidance for Monitoring Woodlands.* Scottish Natural Heritage internal document.

Lack, P. (1986) *The Atlas of Wintering Birds in Britain and Ireland.* London: T. & A. D. Poyser.

Lack, P. C. (1987) The effect of severe hedge cutting on a breeding bird population. *Bird Studies*, **34**, 139–46.

Lamacraft, R. A. (1978) Observer errors in sampling ecological variables for range condition assessments. In *Proceedings of the 1st International Rangelands Congress* (ed. D. N. Hyder), pp. 514–16. Denver CO: Society for Rangeland Managment.

Lamers, L. P. M., Farhoush, C., Groenendael, J. M. V. & Roelofs, J. G. M. (1999) Calcareous groundwater raised bogs; the concept of ombotrophy revisited. *Journal of Ecology*, **87**, 639–648.

Langdale-Brown, I., Jennings, S., Crawford, C. L., Jolly, G. M. & Muscott, J. (1980) *Lowland Agricultural Habitats (Scotland): Air-photo Analysis of Change.* Unpublished Chief Scientist's Department Report No. 372, Nature Conservancy Council, Peterborough.

Lange, M. (1982) Fleshy fungi in grass fields. I. Dependence on fertilisation, grass species and age of field. *Nordic Journal of Botany*, **2**, 131–43.

(1984) Fleshy fungi in grass fields. II. Precipitation and fructification. *Nordic Journal of Botany*, **4**, 491–501.

(1991) Fleshy fungi in grass fields. III. Periodicity of fruiting. *Nordic Journal of Botany*, **11**, 359–69.

(1993) Macromycetes under twelve species in ten plantations of various soil types in Denmark. *Opera Botanica*, **120**, 1–53.

Latham, D. M. (1997) *The Terrestrial Habitat Selection and Utilisation by the Common Toad* (Bufo bufo L.) *in Agricultural Landscapes.* Ph.D. thesis, DeMontfort University, Leicester.

Leach, S. J. (1988) *The Rogate Plots.* Unpublished England Field Unit report, Nature Conservancy Council, Peterborough.

Leach, S. J., Cox, G. H. S., Blake, C. P., Byrne, S. A. & Porley, R. D. (1992) *Progress Reports on Monitoring of Grassland Transplant Sites: Brocks Farm, Devon, 1988–1992.* Unpublished report, English Nature, Peterborough.

Lee, P. M (1987) *Bayesian Statistics. An Introduction.* London: Arnold.

Legg, C. (2000) *Review of Published Work in relation to Monitoring of Trampling Impacts and Change in Montane Vegetation.* Scottish Natural Heritage Review Series No. 131. Perth: Scottish Natural Heritage.

Levy, E. B. & Madden, E. A. (1933) The point method for pasture analysis. *New Zealand Journal of Agriculture*, **46**, 267–79.

Lewis, J., Clements, D. K., Moore, L. & Rich, T. C. G. (1999) *Cardiff Hedgerow Survey 1998.* Cardiff: National Museums and Galleries of Wales.

Lillesand, T. M. & Kiefer, R. W. (1994) *Remote Sensing and Image Interpretation.* Chichester: John Wiley and Sons.

Lindsay, R. & Ross, S. (1994) Monitoring of peat bog systems. In *Proceedings of an IWRB International Workshop*, Linz, Austria, 1993 (ed. G. Aubrecht, G. Dick & C. Prentice), pp. 73–92. Slimbridge, Gloucestershire: International Waterfowl and Wetlands Research Bureau.

Lipsey, M. W. (1990) *Design Sensitivity: Statistical Power for Experimental Research.* Newbury Park, CA: Sage.

Llewellyn, P. J. & Shackley, S. E. (1996) The effects of mechanical beach-cleaning on invertebrate populations. *British Wildlife*, **7**, 147–56.

Lloyd, C., Mark, L. T. & Partridge, K. (1991) *The Status of Seabirds in Britain and Ireland.* London: T. & A. D. Poyser.

Lombard, A. T., Cowling, R. M., Pressey, R. L. & Mustart, P. J. (1997) Reserve selection in a species-rich and fragmented landscape on the Agulhas Plain. *South Africa. Conservation Biology*, **11**, 1101–16.

Luff, M. L. (1986) Aggregations of some Carabidae in pitfall traps. In *Carabid Beetles: Their Adaptations and Dynamics* (ed. P. J. den Boer, M. L. Luff, D. Mossakowski & F. Weber), pp. 386–97. Stuttgart: Gustav Fischer.

Luff, M. L. (1998) *Provisional Atlas of the Ground Beetles (Coleoptera: Carabidae) of Britain*. Huntingdon: Biological Records Centre.

Luff, M. L. & Rushton, S. P. (1989) The ground beetle and spider fauna of managed and improved upland pasture. *Agriculture, Ecosystems and Environment*, **25**, 195–205.

Lunetta, R. S. & Elvidge, C. D. (eds) (1999) *Remote Sensing Change Detection: Environmental Monitoring Methods and Applications*. London: Taylor and Francis.

MacArthur, R. H. & Wilson, E. O. (1967) *The Theory of Island Biogeography*. Princetown, NJ: Princetown University Press.

Macaulay Land Use Research Institute (MLURI) (1993) *The Land Cover of Scotland 1988. Final Report*. Aberdeen: MLURI.

MacDonald, A. & Armstrong, H. (1989) *Methods for Monitoring Heather Cover*. Research and Survey in Nature Conservation No. 27. Peterborough: Nature Conservancy Council.

MacDonald, A., Mayer, P., Armstrong, H., Immirzi, P. & Reynolds, P. (1998a) *A Guide to Upland Habitats. Surveying Land Management Impacts*, volume 1 (*Background Information and Guidance for Surveyors*). Perth: Scottish Natural Heritage.
(1998b) *A Guide to Upland Habitats. Surveying Land Management Impacts*, volume 2 (*The Field Guide*). Perth: Scottish Natural Heritage.

MacDonald, D. W. & Johnson, P. J. (1995) The relationship between bird distribution and the botanical and structural characteristics of hedges. *Journal of Applied Ecology*, **32**, 492–505.

Macdonald, D. W. & Tattersall, F. (2001) *Britain's Mammals: the Challenge for Conservation*. London: People's Trust for Endangered Species.

Macdonald, D. W., Mace, G. & Ruston, S. (1998c) *Proposals for Future Monitoring of British Mammals*. London: Department of the Environment, Transport and the Regions.

Macdonald, S. M. & Mason, C. S. (1987) Seasonal marking in an otter population. *Acta Theologica*, **32** (27), 449–62.

Mace, G. M. & Collar, N. J. (2002) Priority-setting in species conservation. In *Conserving Bird Biodiversity: General Principles and their Application* (ed. K. Norris & D. J. Pain), vol. 7, pp. 61–73. Cambridge: Cambridge University Press.

Mackereth, F. J. H., Heroc, J. & Talling, J. F. (1978) *Water Analysis: Some Revised Methods for Limnologists*. Ambleside, Cumbria: Freshwater Biological Association.

Mackey, E. C., Shewry, M. C. & Tudor, G. J. (1998) *Land Cover Change: Scotland from the 1940s to the 1980s*. Edinburgh: The Stationery Office.

Macleod, A. S., Wratten, S. D. & Harwood, R. W. J. (1994) The efficiency of a new lightweight suction sampler for sampling aphids and their predators in arable land. *Annals of Applied Biology*, **124**, 11–17.

Magurran, A. E. (1983) *Ecological Diversity and its Measurement*. London: Croom Helm.

Mainstone, C., Gulson, J. & Parr, W. (1993) *Phosphates in Freshwater: Standards for Nature Conservation*. English Nature Research Report No. 73. Peterborough: English Nature.

Manly, B. F. J. (1986) *Multivariate Statistical Methods – a Primer*. London, New York: Chapman and Hall.
(1997) *Randomisation, Bootstrapping and Monte-Carlo Methods in Biology*, 2nd edn. London: Chapman & Hall.

Marchant, J. H. (1983) *BTO Common Bird Census Instructions*. Tring, Hertfordshire: British Trust for Ornithology.

Marchant, J. H., Hudson, R., Carter, S. P. and Whittington, P. (1990) *Population Trends in British Breeding Birds*. Tring, Hertfordshire: British Trust for Ornithology.

Margules, C. & Usher, M. B. (1981) Criteria used in assessing wildlife conservation potential: a review. *Biological Conservation*, **21**, 79–109.

Margules, C. R. & Pressey, R. L. (2000) Systematic conservation planning. *Nature*, **405**, 243–53.

Marin, J. M., Diez, R. M. & Insua, D. R. (2003) Bayesian methods in plant conservation biology. *Biological Conservation*, **113**, 379–87.

Mason, C. F. (1991) *Biology of Freshwater Pollution*, 2nd edn. Harlow, Essex: Longman Scientific and Technical.

McCloskey, J. M. & Spalding, H. (1989) A reconnaissance-level inventory of the amount of wilderness remaining in the world. *Ambio*, **18**, 221–7.

McLeod, C., Yeo, M., Brown, A., Burn, A., Hopkins, J., & Way, S. (eds.) (2002) *The Habitats Directive: selection of Special Areas of Conservation in the UK*, 2nd edn. Peterborough: Joint Nature Conservation Committee.

McWilliam, H. A. & Death, R. G. (1998) Arboreal arthropod communities of remnant podocarp-hardwood rainforest in North Island, New Zealand. *New Zealand Journal of Zoology*, **25**, 157–69.

Mead, R., Curnow, R. N. & Hasted, A. M. (1993) *Statistical Methods in Agriculture and Experimental Biology*, 2nd edn. London: Chapman and Hall.

Menon, S., Pontius, R. G., Rose, J., Khan, M. L., & Bawa, K. S. (2001) Identifying conservation-priority areas in the tropics: a land-use change modelling approach. *Conservation Biology*, **15**, 501–512.

Merritt, R., Moore, N. W. & Eversham, B. C. (1996) *Atlas of the Dragonflies of Britain and Ireland*. Institute of Terrestrial Ecology Research Publication No. 9. London: Her Majesty's Stationery Office.

Metcalfe-Smith, J. L. (1994) Biological water-quality assessment of rivers: use of macroinvertebrate communities. In *The Rivers Handbook: Hydrological and Ecological Principles*, Volume 2 (ed. P. Calow & G. E. Petts), pp. 144–170. Oxford: Blackwell Scientific Publications.

(1996) Biological Water-quality Assessment of Rivers: Use of Macroinvertebrate Communities. In *River Restoration*, (ed. G. Petts & P. Calow) pp. 17–43. Oxford: Blackwell Science.

Mills, D. (1989) *Ecology and Management of Atlantic Salmon*. London: Chapman & Hall.

Mitchell-Jones, A. J. & McLeish, A. P. (1999) *The Batworkers' Manual*, 2nd edn. Peterborough: Joint Nature Conservation Committee.

Mitchley, J. & Malloch, A. J. C. (1991) *Sea Cliff Management Handbook for Great Britain*, University of Lancaster, Joint Nature Conservation Committee and National Trust, Lancaster.

Moodie, S. (1991) *Habitat Monitoring using Aerial Photographs in Restormel District, Cornwall*. Nature Conservancy Council (South-West Region) internal report, Nature Conservancy Council, Peterborough.

Moore, N.W. & Corbet, P.S. (1990) Guidelines for monitoring dragonfly populations. *Journal of the British Dragonfly Society*, **6**, 21–3.

Moore, P. D. & Chapman, S. B. (1986) *Methods in Plant Ecology*. Oxford: Blackwell.

Morris, M. G. (1991) *Weevils*. Naturalists Handbook 16. Slough, Berkshire: Richmond Publishing Co.

Morris, P. A., Morrris, M. J., MacPherson, D., Jefferies, D. J., Strachan, R. & Woodroffe, G. L. (1998) Estimating numbers of the water vole Arvicola terrestris: a correction to the published method. *Journal of Zoology*, **246**, 61–2.

Moss, B. (1998) *The Ecology of Fresh Waters*. Oxford: Blackwell Scientific Publications.

Mountford, E. P. & Peterken, G. F. (1998) *Monitoring Natural Stand Change in Monks Wood National Nature Reserve*. English Nature Research Report No. 270. Peterborough: English Nature.

Muller, K. E. & Benignus, V. A. (1992) Increasing scientific power with statistical power. *Neurotoxicology and Teratology*, **14**, 211–219.

National Rivers Authority (NRA) (1992) *River Corridor Surveys: Methods and Procedures*. Conservation Technical Handbook No. 1. Bristol: NRA.

(1994a) *Standard Methodologies for the Assessment of Freshwater Riverine Environments using Macrophytes*. Bristol: NRA.

(1994b) *Water Quality Objectives: Procedures used by the National Rivers Authority for the Purpose of the Surface Waters (River Ecosystem) (Classification) Regulations 1994*. Bristol: NRA.

National Water Council (1981) *River Quality. The 1980 Survey and Future Outlook*. London: National Water Council.

Nature Conservancy Council (NCC) (1987) *Report of the England Working Group on Photographic Monitoring*. Internal report, Nature Conservancy Council, Peterborough.

(1988) *Native Trees and Shrubs for Wildlife in the United Kingdom*. Peterborough: Nature Conservancy Council.

(1989) *Guidelines for the Selection of Biological SSSIs*. Peterborough: Nature Conservancy Council.

(1990a) *Handbook for Phase I Habitat Survey: a Technique for Environmental Audit*. Peterborough: England Field Unit, Nature Conservancy Council.

(1990b) *Handbook for Phase I Habitat Survey: a Technique for Environmental Audit. Field Manual*. Peterborough: England Field Unit, Nature Conservancy Council.

(1991) *A Review of Phase I Habitat Survey in England*. Peterborough: England Field Unit, Nature Conservancy Council.

Nee, S. & May, R. M. (1997) Extinction and the loss of evolutionary history. *Science*, **278**, 692–4.

New, T. R. (1998) *Invertebrate Surveys for Conservation*. Oxford: Oxford University Press.

Newton, A. C., Davy, L. M., Holden, E., Silverside, A., Watling, R., & Ward, S. D. (2003) Status, distribution and definition of mycologically important grasslands in Scotland. *Biological Conservation*, **111**, 11–23.

Newton, A. C., Watling, R., Davy, L. M., Holden, E. & Ward, S. D. (2002) Progress towards implementing the Biodiversity Action Plan for stipitate hydnoid fungi in Scotland. *Botanical Journal of Scotland*, **54**(1), 89–110.

Nilsson, S. G. & Nilsson, I. N. (1985) Are estimated species turnover rates on islands largely sampling error? *American Naturalist*, **121**, 595–7.

Oggier, P., Zschokke, S. & Baur, B. (1998) A comparison of three methods for assessing the gastropod community in dry grasslands. *Pedobiologia*, **42**, 348–57.

Okland, B. (1996) A comparison of three methods of trapping saproxylic beetles. *European Journal of Entomology*, **93**, 195–209.

Oldfield, S., Lusty, C., & MacKinven, A. (1998) *The World List of Threatened Trees*. Cambridge: World Conservation Press.

Oldham, R. S. (1994) Habitat assessment and population ecology. In *Conservation and Management of Great Crested Newts* (ed. A. Gent & R. Bray), English Nature Science No. 20, pp. 45–67. Peterborough: English Nature.

Ormerod, S. J. & Edwards, R. W. (1987) The ordination and classification of macroinvertebrate assemblages in the catchment of the River Wye in relation to environmental factors. *Freshwater Biology*, **17**, 533–46.

Orton, P. D. (1986) Fungi of northern pine and birch woods. *Bulletin of the British Mycological Society*, **20**, 130–44.

Otis, D. L., Burnham, K. P., White, G. C. & Anderson, D. R. (1978) Statistical inference from capture data on closed populations. *Wildlife Monographs*, **62**, 1–135.

Owens, I. P. F. & Bennett, P. M. (2000) Quantifying biodiversity: a phenotypic perspective. *Conservation Biology*, **14**, 1014–22.

Pakeman, R. J., Le Duc, M. G. & Marrs, R. H. (2000) Bracken distribution in Great Britain: strategies for its control and the sustainable management of marginal land. *Annals of Botany*, **85(b)**, 37–46.

Palmer, M. A. (1989) *A Botanical Classification of Standing Waters in Great Britain*. Research & Survey in Nature Conservation No. 19. Peterborough: Nature Conservancy Council.

(1992) *Trial of MATCH and TABLEFIT Computer Programs for Placing Survey Data with the NVC*. JNCC Report No. 20. Peterborough: Joint Nature Conservation Committee.

Palmer, M. A., Bell, S. L. & Butterfield, I. (1992) A botanical classification of standing waters in Britain: applications for conservation and monitoring. *Aquatic Conservation: Marine and Freshwater Systems*, **2**, 125–44.

Parish, T., Lakhani, K. H. & Sparks, T. H. (1994) Modelling the relationship between bird population variables and hedgerow and other field margin attributes. 1. Species richness of winter, summer and breeding birds. *Journal of Applied Ecology*, **31**, 764–75.

(1995) Modelling the relationship between bird population variables and hedgerow and other field margin attributes. 2. Abundance of individual species and of groups of similar species. *Journal of Applied Ecology*, **32**, 362–71.

Parker, K. W. & Savage, D. A. (1944) Reliability of the line interception method in measuring vegetation on the Southern Great Plains. *Journal of the American Society of Agronomics*, **36**, 97–110.

Parr, W. (1994) Water-quality monitoring. In *The Rivers Handbook: Hydrological and Ecological Principles*, volume 2 (ed. P. Calow & G. E. Petts), Oxford: Blackwell Scientific Publications. pp. 124–43.

Peach, W. J., Baillie, S. R. & Balmer, D. E. (1998) Long-term changes in the abundance of passerines in Britain and Ireland as measured by constant effort mist-netting. *Bird Study*, **45**, 257–75.

Pearce, I. S. K., Barbour, D. A., Bayfield, N. G., Young, M. R., Watt, A. & Holman, D. (1996) *Scottish Diurnal Lepidoptera Project: Sites, Protocols and Distribution*. SNH Research, Survey and Monitoring Report No. 81. Perth: Scottish Natural Heritage.

Perkins, D. F. & Miller, R. O. M. (1987a) Effects of air-borne fluoride emissions near an aluminium works in Wales. I. Corticolous lichens growing on broad-leaved trees. *Environmental Pollution*, **47**, 63–78.

(1987b) Effects of air-borne fluoride emissions near an aluminium works in Wales. II. Saxicolous lichens growing on rocks and walls. *Environmental Pollution*, **48**, 185–96.

Perrow, M. R., Cote, I. M. & Evans, M. (1996) Fish. In *Ecological Census Techniques* (ed. W. J. Sutherland), pp. 178–204. Cambridge: Cambridge University Press.

Peterken, G. F. (1980) *Classification of Stand Types in Semi-natural Woodland*. Chief Scientist's Department Note 23. Peterborough: Nature Conservancy Council.

(1981) *Woodland Conservation and Management*. London: Chapman & Hall.

(1996) *Methods for Estimating Dead Wood in British Woodlands*. Contract report to Forestry Commission (unpublished).

Peterken, G. F. & Backmeroff, C. (1988) *Long-term Monitoring in Unmanaged Woodland Nature Reserves*. Research and Survey in Nature Conservation No. 9. Peterborough: Nature Conservancy Council.

Peterman, R. M. (1990a) Statistical power analysis can improve fisheries research and management. *Canadian Journal of Fisheries and Aquatic Sciences*, **47**, 2–15.

(1990b) The importance of reporting statistical power: the forest decline and acidic deposition example. *Ecology*, **71**, 2024–7.

Petts, G. E. (1983) *Rivers*. London: Butterworths Publications.

Pollard, E. (1977) Methods of assessing the abundance of butterflies. *Biological Conservation*, **12**, 115–34.

(1982) Monitoring the abundance of butterflies in relation to the management of a nature reserve. *Biological Conservation*, **24**, 317–28.

(1988) Temperature, rainfall and butterfly numbers. *Journal of Applied Ecology*, **25**, 819–28.

Pollard, E., Hall, M. L. & Bibby, T. J. (1986) *Monitoring the Abundance of Butterflies 1976–1985*. Research and Survey in Nature Conservation No. 2. Peterborough: Nature Conservancy Council.

Pollard, E., Hooper, M. D., & Moore, N. W. (1974) *Hedges*. London: Collins.

Pollard, E. & Lakhani, K. H. (1985) *Butterfly Monitoring Scheme: Effects of Weather on Abundance*. ITE Annual Report for 1984, pp. 54–6. Monks Wood, Huntingdon: Institute of Terrestrial Ecology.

Pollard, E. & Yates, T. J. (1993) *Monitoring Butterflies for Ecology and Conservation*. London: Chapman & Hall.

Pollock, K. H., Nichols, J. D., Brownie, C. & Hines, J. E. (1990) Statistical inference for capture–recapture experiments. *Wildlife Monongraphs*, **107**, 1–97.

Pond Action (1999) *Conservation Assessment of Wetland Plants and Aquatic Macroinvertebrates*. Oxford: Pond Action.

Pooley, M. R. & Jones, M. M. (1996) *Application of Remote Sensing to Habitat Mapping and Monitoring*. Scottish Natural Heritage Review No. 57. Perth: Scottish Natural Heritage.

Porley, R. D. (2000) Bryophytes of arable fields: current state of knowledge and conservation. In *Fields of vision: a future for Britain's arable plants* (ed. P. Wilson & M. King), pp. 8–19. London: Plantlife.

Posey, D. A. (ed.) (2000) *Cultural and Spiritual Values of Biodiversity. A Complementary Contribution to the Global Biodiversity Assessment*. London: Intermediate Technology.

Pradel, R., Clobert, J. & Lebreton, J. D. (1990) Recent developments for the analysis of capture–recapture multiple data sets. *The Ring*, **13**, 193–210.

Prendergast, J. R., Quinn, R. M., & Lawton, J. H. (1999) The gaps between theory and practice in selecting nature reserves. *Conservation Biology*, **13**, 484–92.

Pressey, R. L., Johnson, I. R., & Wilson, P. D. (1994) Shades of irreplaceability: towards a measure of the contribution of sites to a reservation goal. *Biodiversity and Conservation*, **3**, 242–62.

Preston, C. D., Pearman, D. A. and Dines, T. D (eds) 2002. *New Atlas of the British and Irish Flora*. Oxford: Oxford University Press.

Preston, J., Prodöhl, P., Portig, A. & Montgomery, I. (2002b) *The Northern Ireland Irish Hare Lepus timidus hibernicus Survey*. Belfast: The Environment and Heritage Service, Northern Ireland.

Pritchard, D. E., Housden, S. D., Mudge, G. P., Galbraith, C. A., & Pienkowski, M. W. (1992) *Important Bird Areas in the United Kingdom including the Channel Islands and the Isle of Man*. Sandy, Bedfordshire: RSPB and JNCC.

Prys-Jones, O. E. & Corbet, S. A. (1991) *Bumblebees*. Naturalists Handbook 6. Slough, Berkshire: Richmond Publishing Co.

Puhr, C. B. (1998) *A Guide to the SFCC Electrofishing Protocol*. Version 1.1. Pitlochry, Perthshire: Scottish Fisheries Co-ordination Centre.

Pulliam, H. R. (1988) Sources, sinks and population regulation. *American Naturalist*, **132**, 652–61.

Purvis, A. & Hector, A. (2000) Getting the measure of biodiversity. *Nature*, **405**, 212–19.

Rabinowitz, D. (1981) Seven forms of rarity. In *The Biological Aspects of Rare Plant Conservation* (ed. H. Synge), pp. 205–17. Chichester: Wiley.

Ramsar Bureau (2002) *New Guidelines for Management Planning for Ramsar Sites and Other Wetlands*. Gland, Switzerland: Ramsar Bureau.

Randall, R. E. (1989) Shingle habitats in the British Isles. *Botanical Journal of the Linnean Society*, **101**, 3–18.

Ranwell, D. S. (1972) *Ecology of Salt Marshes and Sand Dunes*. London: Chapman & Hall.

Ratcliffe, D. A. (ed.) (1977) *A Nature Conservation Review*. Cambridge: Cambridge University Press.

Ratcliffe, P. R. (1987) *The Management of Red Deer in Upland Forests*. Forestry Commission Bulletin 71. London: HMSO.

Ratcliffe, P. R. & Mayle, B. A. (1993) *The Biology and Management of Roe Deer*. Forestry Commission Bulletin. No. 105. London: HMSO.

Raven, P. J., Boon, P. J., Dawson, F. H. & Ferguson, A. J. D. (1998a) Towards an integrated approach to classifying and evaluating rivers in the UK. In *The Application of Classification and Assessment Methods to River Management in the UK* (ed. P. J. Boon & P. J Raven), pp. 383–94. Chichester: John Wiley.

Raven, P. J., Fox, P., Everard, M., Holmes, N. T. H. & Dawson, F. H. (1997) River habitat survey: a new system for classifying rivers according to their habitat quality. In *Freshwater Quality: Defining the Indefinable?* (ed. P. J. Boon & D. L. Howell), pp. 215–34. Edinburgh: The Stationery Office.

Raven, P. J., Holmes, N. T. H., Dawson, F. H., Fox, P. J. A., Everard, M., Fozzard, I. R. & Rouen, K. J. (1998b) *River Habitat Quality: The Physical Character of Rivers and Streams in the UK and Isle of Man*. Bristol: Environment Agency.

Raven, P. J., Noble, D. G. & Baillie, S. R. (2003) *The Breeding Bird Survey 2002*. BTO Research Report 334. Thetford: British Trust for Ornithology.

Reading, C. J. (1996) *Evaluation of Reptile Survey Methodologies*. English Nature Research Report No. 200. Peterborough: English Nature.

Reid, E. & Quarmby, N. A. (2000) Determining the composition of the blanket bogs of Scotland using LANDSAT Thematic Mapper. In *Vegetation Mapping* (ed. R. Alexander & A. C. Millington), pp. 159–76. Chichester: Wiley.

Reynolds, C. M. (1979) The heronries census: 1972–1977 population changes and a review. *Bird Study*, **26**, 7–12.

Rich, T. C. G. (2001) *Flowering plants*. In *The Changing Wildlife of Great Britain and Ireland*. The Systematics Association special volume series 62. (ed. D. L. Hawksworth), pp. 23–49. London: Taylor & Francis.

Rich, T. C. G., Clements, D. A., Lewis, J. & Moore, L. (2000) A comparison of four methods used to survey hedges: The Cardiff Hedgerow Survey 1998. *Journal of Environmental Management*, **60**, 91–100.

Rich, T. C. G., Hutchinson, G., Randall, R. D. & Ellis, R. G. (1999) List of plants endemic to the British Isles. *BSBI News*, **80**, 23–7.

Rich, T. C. G. & Jermy, A. C. (1998) *Plant Crib 1998*. London: Botanical Society of the British Isles.

Rich, T. C. G. & Matcham, H. W. (1995) A quadrat for recording vertical surfaces. *Bulletin of the British Bryological Society*, **65**, 67–8.

Rich, T. C. G., Rodwell, J. S. & Malloch, A. J. C. (1991) *Effects of Air Pollution and Climate Change on British Calcicolous Ecosystems*. Interim first year report to the Department of the Environment, PECD Ref. No. 7/12/22. Lancaster: Unit of Vegetation Science, University of Lancaster.

(1992) *Effects of Air Pollution and Climate Change on British Calcicolous Ecosystems*. Interim second year report to the Department of the Environment, PECD Ref. No. 7/12/22. Lancaster: Unit of Vegetation Science, University of Lancaster.

Rich, T. C. G. & Smith, P. A. (1996) Botanical recording, distribution maps and species frequency. *Watsonia*, **21**, 155–67.

Rich, T. C. G. & Woodruff, E. R. (1990) *BSBI Monitoring Scheme 1987–1988*. Unpublished report to the Nature Conservancy Council, Peterborough.

Richardson, M. J. (1970) Studies on *Russula emetica* and other agarics in a Scots pine plantation. *Transactions of the British Mycological Society*, **55**, 217–29.

Richardson, P. (2000) *Distribution Atlas of Bats in Britain and Ireland*. London: Bat Conservation Trust.

Ridgill, S. C. & Fox, A. D. (1990) *Cold Weather Movements of Wildfowl in Western Europe*. IWRB Special Publication 12. Slimbridge: Wildfowl & Wetlands Trust and International Wetlands Research Bureau.

Roberts, K. A. (1991) Field monitoring: confessions of an addict. In *Monitoring for Conservation and Ecology* (ed. F. B. Goldsmith), pp. 179–211. London: Chapman & Hall.

Roberts, M. J. (1996) *Spiders of Britain and Northern Europe*. London: Collins.

Robertson, H. (1999) Grassland monitoring. In *Lowland Grassland Management Handbook,* 2nd edn (ed. A. Crofts & R. Jefferson), pp. 15.1–15.21. Peterborough: English Nature.

Rodwell, J. S. (ed.) (1991 *et seq.*) *British Plant Communities*, volume 1 (*Woodlands and Scrub* (1991)); volume 2 (*Heaths and Mires* (1991)); volume 3 (*Grasslands and Montane Communities* (1992)); volume 4 (*Aquatic Communities, Swamps and Tall-herb Fens* (1995)); volume 5, (*Maritime and Weed Communities and Vegetation of Open Habitats* (2000)). Cambridge: Cambridge University Press.

Rodwell, J. S. (1997) *The National Vegetation Classification and Monitoring*. Unit of Vegetation Science, Lancaster University, report to Countryside Council for Wales.

Roem, W. J. & Berendse, F. (2000) Soil acidity and nutrient supply ratio as possible factors determining changes in plant species diversity in grassland and heathland communities. *Biological Conservation*, **92**, 151–61.

Rose, F. (1981) *The Wild Flower Key*. London: Frederick Warne.

Rose, P. M. & Scott, D. A. (1997) *Waterfowl Population Estimates.* Report No. 44. Wageningen: Wetlands International.

Rosenzweig, M. L. (1995) *Species Diversity in Space and Time*. Cambridge: Cambridge University Press.

Rotenberry, J. T. & Wiens, J. A. (1985) Statistical power analysis and community-wide patterns. *American Naturalist*, **125**, 164–8.

Rowell, T. A. (1988) *The Peatland Management Handbook*. Peterborough: Nature Conservancy Council.

(1993) *Common Standards for Monitoring SSSIs*. Unpublished report to Joint Nature Conservation Committee, Peterborough.

(1994) *Ecological Indicators for Nature Conservation Monitoring*. JNCC Report No. 196. Peterborough: Joint Nature Conservation Committee.

(1997) *Common Standards Framework for Monitoring SSSIs*. Unpublished report of a designated sites monitoring workshop, Joint Nature Conservation Committee, Peterborough.

Royal Society for the Protection of Birds, English Nature, and Institute of Terrestrial Ecology (RSPB/EN/ITE) (1997) *The Wet Grassland Guide*. Sandy, Bedfordshire: RSPB.

Royal Society for the Protection of Birds, National Rivers Authority, and Royal Society for Nature Conservation (RSPB/NRA/RSNC) (1994) *The New Rivers and Wildlife Handbook*. Sandy, Bedfordshire: RSPB.

Russ, J. (1999) *The Bats of Britain and Ireland, Echolocation calls, sound analysis and species identification*. London: Alana Ecology Ltd.

Salmon, T. (2001) *First Report by the United Kingdom under Article 17 on Implementation of Directive 92/43/EEL from June 1994 to December 2000*. Bristol: DEFRA.

Samu, F., Nemeth, J. & Kiss, B. (1997) Assessment of the efficiency of a hand held suction device for sampling spiders: improved density estimation or over-sampling? *Annals of Applied Biology*, **130**, 371–8.

Sanger, N. P. & Waite, S. (1998) The phenology of *Ophrys sphegodes* (the early spider orchid): what annual censuses can miss. *Botanical Journal of the Linnean Society*, **126**, 75–81.

Sargent, G. & Morris, P. (1997) *How to Find and Identify Mammals*. London: The Mammal Society.

Schaeffer, R. L., Mendenhall, W. & Ott, L. (1990) *Elementary Survey Sampling*, 4th edn. Boston: PWS-Kent Publishing Company.

Scott, J., M., Davis, F., Csuti, B. *et al.* (1993) Gap Analysis: a geographic approach to protection of biological diversity. *Wildlife Monographs*, **123**, 1–41.

Scottish Natural Heritage (SNH) (1998) *Guidance on Site Condition Monitoring*. Perth: SNH.

(2000) *Site Condition Monitoring Guidance Folder*. Edinburgh: SNH.

Seber, G. A. F. (1982) *The Estimation of Animal Abundance and Related Parameters*. London: Charles Griffin.

Shaw, P. & Wind, P. (1997) *Monitoring the Condition and Biodiversity Status of European Conservation Sites*. Unpublished report to the European Environment Agency on behalf of the European Topic Centre on Nature Conservation, Paris.

Shaw, S. C. & Wheeler, B. D. (1995) *Monitoring Rehabilitation Work on Lowland Peatlands*. Report to English Nature by Environmental Consultancy, University of Sheffield, Sheffield.

Sheldrick, R. D. (ed.) (1997) *Grassland Management in Environmentally Sensitive Areas*. British Grassland Society

(BGC) Occasional Symposium no. 32. Reading: British Grassland Society.

Shimwell, D. W. (1971) *The Description and Classification of Vegetation*. London: Sidgwick & Jackson.

Shirt, D. B. (1987) *British Red Data Books. 2. Insects*. Peterborough: Nature Conservancy Council.

Simberloff, D. (1972) Properties of the rarefaction diversity measurements. *American Naturalist*, **106**, 414–418.

Simberloff, D. & Cox, J. (1987) Consequences and costs of conservation corridors. *Conservation Biology*, **1**, 63–71.

Skinner, B. (1998) *The Colour Identification Guide to Moths of the British Isles*. London: Viking.

Smartt, P. F. M. & Grainger, J. E. A. (1974) Sampling for vegetation survey: some aspects of the behaviour of unrestricted, restricted and stratified techniques. *Journal of Biogeography*, **1**, 193–206.

Smith, A. D. (1944) A study of the reliability of range vegetation estimates. *Ecology*, **25**, 441–8.

Smith, C. D., Harper, D. M., & Barham, P. J. (1991) *Physical Environment for River Invertebrate Communities*. Leicester: University of Leicester.

Smith, P. G. R. & Theberge, J. B. (1986) A review of criteria for evaluating natural areas. *Environmental Management*, **10**, 715–734.

Sneddon, P. & Ranwell, R. E. (1993) *Coastal Vegetated Shingle Structures of Great Britain, Main Report*. Peterborough: Joint Nature Conservation Committee.

(1994) *The Vegetated Shingle Structures of Great Britain. Appendix 2 – Scotland*. Peterborough: Joint Nature Conservation Committee.

Sokal, R. R. & Rohlf, F. J. (1996) *Biometry*, 3rd edn. New York: W. H. Freeman & Co.

Soulé, M. E. (1987) *Viable Populations for Conservation*. Cambridge: Cambridge University Press.

Southwood, T. R. E. (1978) *Ecological Methods*, 2nd edn. London: Chapman & Hall.

Southwood, T. R. E. (2000) *Ecological Methods*, 3rd edn. Oxford: Blackwell.

Sparks, T. H., Porter, K. Greatorex-Davies, J. N., Hall, M. L. & Marrs, R. H. (1994) The choice of oviposition sites in woodland by the Duke of Burgundy butterfly *Hameris lucina* in England. *Biological Conservation*, **70**, 257–64.

Spellerberg, I. F. (1991) *Monitoring Ecological Change*. Cambridge: Cambridge University Press.

Spellerberg, I. F. & Hardes, S. R. (1992) *Biological Conservation*. Cambridge: Cambridge University Press.

Stace, C. (1997) *New Flora of the British Isles,* 2nd edn. Cambridge: Cambridge University Press.

Staines, B. W. & Ratcliffe, P. R. (1987) Estimating abundance of red deer (*Cervus elaphus* L.) and roe deer (*Capreolus capreolus* L.) and their current status in Great Britain. *Symposia of the Zoological Society of London,* **58**, 131–52.

Standing Committee of Analysts (1987) *Methods for the use of Macrophytes for Assessing Water Quality 1985–1986.* London: Her Majesty's Stationery Office.

Stebbings, R. E. (1992) *The Greywell Tunnel: an Internationally Important Haven for Bats.* Peterborough: English Nature.

Stebbings, R. E. & Walsh, S. T. (1991) *Bat Boxes. A Guide to the History, Function, Construction and Use in the Conservation of Bats.* London: Bat Conservation Trust.

Steven, G. (1990) *A Botanical Survey of Unimproved Neutral Grasslands in East Sussex.* Unpublished report to English Nature.

Stewart, A., Pearman, D. A. & Preston, C. D. (eds) 1994. *Scarce Plants in Britain.* Peterborough: Joint Nature Conservation Committee.

Stewart, A. & Wright, A. (1995) A new inexpensive suction apparatus for sampling arthropods in grassland. *Ecological Entomology,* **20** (1), 98–102.

Stewart, N. F. & Church, J. M. (1992) *Red Data Books of Britain and Ireland: Stoneworts.* Peterborough: Joint Nature Conservation Committee.

Stirling, H. P. (ed.) (1985) *Chemical and Biological Methods of Water Quality Analysis for Aquaculturalists.* Stirling: University of Stirling.

Stone, B. H., Sears, J., Cranswick, P. A. *et al.* (1997) Population estimates of birds in Britain and in the United Kingdom. *British Birds,* **90**, 1–22.

Stone, D. (1997) *Guidance for Monitoring Complex Sites: Outcomes of the Buxton Workshop.* Unpublished report, English Nature, Peterborough.

Stoneman, R. & Brooks, S. (1997) *Conserving Bogs – the Management Handbook.* Edinburgh: The Stationery Office.

Stormer, F. A., Honkstra, T. W., White, C. M. & Kirkpatrick, C. M. (1977) Frequency distribution of deer pellet groups in Southern Indiana. *Journal of Wildlife Management,* **41**, 779–82.

Strachan, R. (1998) *The Walter Vole Conservation Handbook.* Oxford: English Nature, Environment Agency and the Wildlife Conservation Research Unit.

Strachan, R. & Jefferies, D. J. (1993) *The Water Vole* (Arvicola terrestris) *in Britain 1989–1990: its Distribution and Changing Status.* London: The Vincent Wildlife Trust.

Strong, D. R., Lawton, J. H. & Southwood, T. R. E. (1984) *Insects on Plants. Community Patterns and Mechanisms.* Oxford: Blackwell Scientific Publications.

Stroud, D. A., Chambers, D., Cook, S. *et al.* (eds) (2001) *The UK SPA Network: Its Scope And Contents* (3 volumes). Peterborough: Joint Nature Conservation Committee.

Stubbs, A. E. (1972) Introduction to craneflies. *Amateur Entomological Society Bulletin,* **31**, 46–54.

Sutherland, W. J. (ed.) (1996) *Ecological Census Techniques. A Handbook.* Cambridge: Cambridge University Press. (2000) *The Conservation Handbook: Research, Management and Policy.* Oxford: Blackwell Science.

Sykes, J. M. (1981) Monitoring in woodlands. In *Forest and Woodland Ecology* (ed. F. T. Last & A. S. Grainger), pp. 32–40. Cambridge: Institute of Terrestrial Ecology.

Sykes, J. M., Horrill, A. D. & Mountford, M. D. (1983) Use of visual cover estimates as quantitative estimators of some British woodland taxa. *Journal of Ecology,* **71**, 437–50.

Sykes, J. M., Marrs, R. H., & Mitchell, B. (1985) *The Impact of Red Deer* (Cervus elaphus *L.) on the Vegetation of Native Scottish Pinewoods: Selection of Sites for Further Studies using the Faecal Accumulation Method, and Recommendations for Sampling Vegetation.* Institute of Terrestrial Ecology contract report, Nature Conservancy Council, Peterborough.

Tapper, S. (2001) *Technical Annex VII: Brown Hare.* In *Ecological Evaluation of the Arable Stewardship Pilot Scheme, 1998–2000,* ADAS, University of Newcastle, University of Oxford, GCT, Report to Ministry of Agriculture, Fisheries and Food, London, UK.

Tausch, R. J., Charlet, D. A., Weixelman, D. A. & Zamudio, D. C. (1995) Patterns of ordination and classification instability resulting from changes in input data order. *Journal of Vegetation Science,* **6**, 897–902.

Taylor, B. L. & Gerrodette, T. (1993) The uses of statistical power in conservation biology: the Vaquita and Northern Spotted Owl. *Conservation Biology,* **7**, 489–500.

Templeton, R. G. (ed.) (1995) *Freshwater Fisheries Management.* Oxford: Fishing News Books.

ter Braak, C. J. F. & Smilauer, P. (1998) *CANOCO Reference Manual and User's Guide* (Version 4). New York: Microcomputer Power.

The Wildlife Trusts (1997) *The Wildlife Sites Handbook,* 2nd edn. Lincoln: The Wildlife Trusts.

Thomas, L. & Juanes, F. (1996) The importance of statistical power analysis: an example from animal behaviour. *Animal Behaviour,* **52**, 856–9.

Thomas, L. & Krebs, J. K. (1997) A review of statistical power analysis software. *Bulletin of the Ecological Society of America*, **78**, 128–39.

Thompson, S. K. & Seber, G. A. F. (1996) *Adaptive Sampling*. New York: Wiley.

Thomson, A. G., Fuller, R. M. & Wyatt, B. K. (1993) *Potential Integration of Remote Sensing and Vegetation Surveys*. CCW/ NERC Contract FC 73-01-56, final report to Countryside Council for Wales.

Treweek, J. (1999) *Ecological Impact Assessment*. Oxford: Blackwell Scientific Publications.

Tucker, G. M. & Evans, M. (1997) *Habitats for Birds in Europe: a Conservation Strategy for the Wider Environment*. Cambridge: BirdLife International.

Tucker, G. M. & Heath, M. F. (1994) *Birds in Europe: their Conservation Status*. Cambridge: BirdLife International.

Turpie, J. K. (1995) Prioritising South African estuaries for conservation: a practical example using waterbirds. *Biological Conservation*, **74**, 175–85.

Twinn, P. F. G & Harding, P. T. (1998) *Provisional Atlas of Longhorn Beetles (Coleoptera: Cerambycidae) of Britain*. Huntingdon: Biological Records Centre.

United Kingdom Biodiversity Group (UKBG) (1998a) *Tranche 2 Action Plans*, volume I (*Vertebrates and Vascular Plants*). Peterborough: English Nature.

(1998b) *Tranche 2 Action plans*, volume II (*Terrestrial and Freshwater Habitats*). Peterborough: English Nature.

(1998c) *Tranche 2 Action plans*, volume III (*Plants and Fungi*). Peterborough: English Nature.

(1999a) *Tranche 2 Action plans*, volume IV (*Invertebrates*). Peterborough: English Nature.

(1999b) *Tranche 2 Action plans*, volume V (*Maritime Species and Habitats*). Peterborough: English Nature.

(1999c) *Tranche 2 Action plans*, volume VI (*Terrestrial and Freshwater Species and Habitats*). Peterborough: English Nature.

United Kingdom Steering Group (UKSG) (1995a) *Biodiversity: The UK Steering Group Report*, Volume 1. *Meeting the Rio Challenge*. London: HMSO.

(1995b) *Biodiversity: The UK Action Plan*, Volume 2. *Action Plans*. London: HMSO.

United States Fish & Wildlife Service (USFWS) (1980) *Habitat Evaluation Procedures (HEP)*. Report No. 102. Washington, DC: Division of Ecological Services, Department of the Interior.

Usher, M. B. (ed.) (1986) *Wildlife Conservation Evaluation*. London: Chapman & Hall.

Usher, M. B. (1990) Assessment of conservation values: the use of water traps to assess the arthropod communities of heather moorland. *Biological Conservation*, **53**, 191–8.

van der Ploeg, S. & Vlijm, L. (1978) Ecological evaluation, nature conservation and land use planning with particular reference to methods used in the Netherlands. *Biological Conservation*, **14**, 197–221.

Vane-Wright, R. I., Humphries, C. J., & Williams, P. H. (1991) What to protect – systematics and the agony of choice. *Biological Conservation*, **55**, 235–54.

Vollenweider, R. A. (1968) *Scientific Fundamentals of the Eutrophication of Lakes and Flowing Water, with Particular Reference to Nitrogen and Phosphorous Factors in Eutrophication*. Paris: OECD Water Management Group.

Wadsworth, R. & Treweek, J. (1999) *GIS for Ecology: An Introduction*. London: Taylor and Francis.

Wallace, I. D. (1991) *A Review of the Trichoptera of Great Britain*. Research & Survey in Nature Conservation, No. 32, Peterborough: Joint Nature Conservation Committee.

Walsh, A., Catto, C., Hutson, T. *et al.* (2001) *The UK's National Bat Monitoring Programme Final Report 2001*. London: Bat Conservation Trust.

Walsh, P. M., Halley, D. J., Harris, M. P., del Nevo, A., Sim, I. M. W. & Tasker, M. L. (1995) *Seabird Monitoring Handbook for Britain and Ireland*. Peterborough: JNCC/ RSPB/ITE/Seabird Group, Joint Nature Conservation Committee.

Walter, K. S. & Gillett, H. J. (eds) (1998) *1997 IUCN Red List of Threatened Plants*. Cambridge, UK, and Gland, Switzerland: World Conservation Monitoring Centre and IUCN – The World Conservation Union.

Ward, R. C. & Robinson, M. (1990) *Principles of Hydrology*. London: McGraw-Hill.

Ward, S. D. & Evans, D. F. (1975) *A Botanical Survey and Conservation Assessment of British Limestone Pavements*. Unpublished Institute of Terrestrial Ecology report to the Nature Conservancy Council.

Ward, S. D. & Evans, D. F. (1976) Conservation assessment of British limestone pavements based on floristic criteria. *Biological Conservation*, **9**, 217–33.

Warren, W. G. & Olsen, P. F. (1964) A line transect technique for assessing logging waste. *Forest Science*, **10**, 267–76.

Warren-Wilson, J. (1960) Inclined point quadrats. *New Phytologist*, **59**, 1–8.

Watkinson, A. R. (1986) Plant population dynamics. In *Plant Ecology* (ed. M. J. Crawley), pp. 137–84. Oxford: Blackwell Scientific Publications.

Watling, R. (1995) Assessment of fungal diversity: macromycetes, the problems. *Canadian Journal of Botany*, **73** (suppl. 1), S15–S24.

Watt, T. A. (1997) *Introductory Statistics for Biology Students,* 2nd edn. London: Chapman & Hall.

Webster, R. & Oliver, M. A. (2001) *Geostatistics for Environmental Scientists*. Chichester: Wiley.

Wells, T. C. E. & Willems, J. H. (eds) (1991) *Population Ecology of Terrestrial Orchids*. The Hague: SPB Academic Publishing.

West, N. E. & Hatton, T. J. (1990) Relative influence of observer error and plot randomization on detection of vegetation change. *Coenoses*, **5**, 45–9.

Westman, W. E. (1985) *Ecology, Impact Assessment and Environmental Planning*. New York: John Wiley & Sons.

Wetlands International (2002). *Waterbird population estimates*, 3rd edn, Rep. No. 12. Wageningen, The Netherlands: Wetlands International.

Wheeler, B. D. (1989) Species-richness, species rarity and conservation evaluation of rich-fen vegetation in lowland England and Wales. *Journal of Applied Ecology*, **25**, 331–52.

Whilde, A. (1993) *Irish Red Data Book 2: Vertebrates*. Ireland: The Stationery Office Books.

White, G. C., Anderson, D. R., Burnham, K. P. & Otis, D. L. (1982) *Capture–recapture and Removal Methods for Sampling Closed Populations*. Los Alamos, NM: Los Alamos Nat. Lab. Publications.

White, J. (1979) The plant as a meta-population. *Annual Review of Ecology and Systematics*, **10**, 109–45.

Whitton, B. A., Kelly, M. G., Harding, J. P. C. & Say, P. J. (1991) *Use of Plants to Monitor Heavy Metals in Freshwaters: Methods for the Examination of Waters and Associated Materials*. London: Her Majesty's Stationery Office.

Wigginton, M. J. (ed.) (1999) *British Red Data Books. 1. Vascular Plants*, 3rd edn. Peterborongh: Joint Nature Conservation Committee.

Williams, P., Gibbons, D., Margules, C., Rebelo, A., Humphries, C. & Pressey, R. (1996) A comparison of richness hotspots, rarity hotspots and complementary areas for conserving diversity of British birds. *Conservation Biology*, **10**, 155–74.

Williams, P. H. (1998) Key sites for conservation: area-selection methods for biodiversity. In *Conservation in a Changing World* (ed. G. M. Mace, A. Balmford & J. A. Ginsberg), pp. 211–49. Cambridge: Cambridge University Press.

Williams, P. J., Biggs, J., Barr, C. J. *et al.* (1998) *Lowland Ponds Survey 1996*. London: Department of the Environment, Transport and the Regions.

Williamson, P., Cameron, R. A. D. & Carter, M. A. (1977) Population dynamics of the landsnail *Cepaea nemoralis* L.: a six year study. *Journal of Animal Ecology*, **46**, 181–94.

Wilmott, A. (1980) The woody species of hedges with special reference to age in Church Broughton parish, Derbyshire. *Journal of Ecology*, **68**, 269–85.

Wisniewski, P. J., Paull, L. M., Merry, D. G. & Slater, F. M. (1980) Studies on the breeding migration and intramigratory movements of the common toad (*Bufo bufo*) using Panjet dye-marking techniques. *British Journal of Herpetology*, **6** (3), 71–4.

Wisniewski, P. J., Paull, L. M. & Slater, F. M. (1981) The effects of temperature on the breeding migration and spawning of the common toad (*Bufo bufo*). *British Journal of Herpetology*, **6** (4), 119–21.

Witting, L., Tomiuk, J., & Loeschcke, V. (2000) Modelling the optimal conservation of interacting species. *Ecological Modelling*, **125**, 123–43.

Woods, R. G. & Coppins, B. J. (2003) *A Conservation Evaluation of British Lichens*. London: British Lichen Society.

Wright, G. G. & Birnie, R. V. (1986) Detection of surface soil variation using high resolution satellite data: results from the UK SPOT-Simulation investigation. *International Journal of Remote Sensing*, **7**, 757–66.

Wright, G. G. & Morris, J. G. (1997) LANDSAT TM spectral information to enhance the Land Cover of Scotland 1988 dataset. *International Journal of Remote Sensing*, **18**, 3811–34.

Wright, G. G., Allison, J. S. & Sibbald, A. R. (1997) Integration of satellite spectral analysis into a heather grazing management model (HGMM): the case of Moidach More, northeast Scotland, UK. *International Journal of Remote Sensing*, **18**, 2319–36.

Wright, J. F., Furse, M. T. & Armitage, P. D. (1994) Use of macroinvertebrate communities to detect environmental stress in running waters. In *Water Quality and Stress Indicators in Marine and Freshwater Ecosystems: Linking Levels of Organisation (Individuals, Populations and Communities)* (ed. D. W. Sutcliffe), pp. 15–34. Ambleside, Cumbria: Freshwater Biological Association.

Wright, J. F., Hiley, P. D., Ham, S. F. & Berrie, A. D. (1981) Comparison of three mapping procedures developed for river macrophytes. *Freshwater Biology*, **11**, 369–79.

Wright, J. F., Moss, D., Clarke, R. T. and Furse, M. T. (1997) Biological assessment of river quality using the new version of RIVPACS (RIVPACS III). In *Freshwater Quality: Defining the Indefinable?* (ed. P. J. Boon & D. L. Howell), pp. 102–8. Edinburgh: The Stationery Office.

Yarrow, Y. H. H. (1995) The British ants allied to *Formica rufa* L. (Hym., Formicidae). *Transactions of the Society of British Entomology*, **12**, 1–48.

Yates, F. (1981). *Sampling Methods for Censuses and Surveys*, 4th edn. London: Charles Griffin and Co.

Young, L. J. & Young, J. H. (1998) *Statistical Ecology: a Population Perspective*. London: Kluwer Academic Publishers.

Young, M. (1979) *The Natural History of Moths*. London: Poyser.

Young, M. R. (1995) *Survey and Monitoring of Freshwater Pearl Mussel in Scotland*. Scottish Natural Heritage Contract Report SNH/071/95 H&S. Edinburgh: Scottish Natural Heritage.

Zar, J. H. (1984) *Biostatistical Analysis*. Englewood Cliffs, NJ: Prentice-Hall.

Glossary

MONITORING TERMS AND ACRONYMS

Attributes   Characteristics, qualities or properties of a **feature** that are inherent in, and inseparable from, that feature (CCW, 1996). For species these may include population size, structure, habitat requirements, distribution and other parameters. Attributes of habitats may include key species, composition, structure, supporting processes and other parameters.

BAP   Biodiversity Action Plan.

Birds Directive   Council Directive 79/409/EEC (1979) on the Conservation of Wild Birds.

CCW   Countryside Council for Wales.

CMS   Countryside Management System.

Common Standards Monitoring   The common standards agreed by the UK statutory conservation agencies and the **JNCC** for monitoring the condition of **SSSIs**, **Natura 2000** and **Ramsar sites** consistently (JNCC, 1997). The term originates in the Environmental Protection Act 1990, which specifies 'special functions' to be discharged through the JNCC, including the establishment *of common standards throughout Great Britain for the monitoring of nature conservation . . . and for the analysis of the resulting information* (Environmental Protection Act 1990, Article 133).

Condition   The term used to describe a range of states through which the **feature** of interest may fluctuate naturally within a particular site, and within which it is likely to maintain or improve its status in the long term. Acceptable condition is defined by the **objective** set for the feature in question.

EIA   Environmental Impact Assessment.

Feature   A habitat, habitat matrix, species or species assemblage occurring on a site.

Formulated standard   A baseline state or objective position; an absolute value or acceptable range.

GIS   Geographical Information System.

GPS   Global Positioning System (Appendix 5).

Habitats Directive   Council Directive 92/43/EEC (1992) on the Conservation of Natural Habitats and of Wild Flora and Fauna.

Heterogeneous   Describes an area that comprises blocks of different habitat types (e.g. a mosaic of heathland and scrub).

Homogeneous   Describes an area that is uniform (e.g. an expanse of blanket bog).

Interest feature   See **feature**.

JNCC   Joint Nature Conservation Committee.

Limits   Threshold levels set with the intention of triggering management action. In the context of site monitoring, they are judgements on the range of fluctuations in condition that an interest feature is likely to exhibit at a particular site. These limits are intended to account for any normal cyclic change, which an interest feature might exhibit but which should not normally give cause for concern.

Monitoring   Surveillance undertaken to determine the extent of compliance with a predetermined standard or the degree of deviation from an expected norm (after Hellawell, 1991).

Monitoring unit   Part of one **feature**; features may be separated into monitoring units on the basis of variation in tenure, management measures or topography. Each monitoring unit should be part of only *one* feature.

Natura 2000   The Natura 2000 network is a series of protected areas established under the EU Birds Directive or the EU Habitats Directive. (See **SPAs** and **SACs**.)

NVC   National Vegetation Classification.

Objective   A statement of the nature conservation aspirations for the **features** of interest on a site, expressed in terms of the **condition** that we wish to obtain for each interest feature.

Ramsar sites Protected areas designated under the 1971 Ramsar Convention. The Convention seeks to promote the wise use of all wetlands, and to provide special protection for wetlands of international importance. Many Ramsar sites are also **SPAs**, classified under the Birds Directive.

RHS River Habitat Survey.

SACs *See* **Special Areas of Conservation**.

SCM See **Site Condition Monitoring**.

SEPA Scottish Environment Protection Agency.

SERCON System for Evaluating Rivers for Conservation.

Sessile Fixed in one position.

Site Condition Monitoring An interpretation of **Common Standards Monitoring**. It replaces what was formerly known as Site Integrity Monitoring (SIM), Site Quality Monitoring (SQM) and Loss and Damage Monitoring.

Sites of Special Scientific Interest (SSSIs) Sites notified under the Wildlife Countryside Act 1981, providing statutory protection for flora, fauna, or for geological or physiographical features. As well as underpinning other national designations (such as National Nature Reserves), the series provides statutory protection for terrestrial and coastal sites that are important within Europe (Natura 2000 sites) and globally (such as Ramsar Sites). SSSIs are the main nature conservation designation in Great Britain.

SPAs *See* **Special Protection Areas**.

Special Areas of Conservation (SACs) Protected areas designated under the EU Habitats Directive (92/43/EEC). The Directive requires the establishment of a European network of sites that will make a significant contribution to conserving habitats and species (excluding birds) considered to be most in need of conservation at a European level.

Special Protection Areas (SPAs) Strictly protected sites classified in accordance with the EU Directive on the conservation of wild birds (79/409/EEC), also known as the Birds Directive. They are classified for rare and vulnerable birds, and for regularly occurring migratory species.

SSSIs *See* **Sites of Special Scientific Interest**.

Standard See **Formulated Standard**.

Surveillance An extended programme of **surveys** systematically undertaken to provide a series of observations to ascertain the variability that might be encountered over time (but without preconceptions of what these might be).

Survey A set of observations using a standardised procedure and within a restricted period of time, without any preconception of what the findings might be.

Target A target specifies the range of states that an attribute of a **feature** should attain if the feature is to be considered in acceptable condition, i.e. if the feature is to maintain or improve its status on that site in the long term.

STATISTICAL TERMS

Accuracy The closeness of an estimated value to the true value.

Analysis of variance (ANOVA) A class of parametric methods for testing differences between two or more groups of samples. Tests compare the variability of the data within the groups and between the groups. If the variability within groups is similar to the variability between them, the groups could be drawn from the same population. If not, there are likely to be differences between the populations. See also **Tukey test**.

Average See **Mean**.

Bootstrapping A method for deriving estimates and confidence intervals that does not make parametric assumptions about the distribution of the data. It is a **resampling** method with new samples drawn repeatedly from the dataset, with replacement. For each of these samples a new estimate is calculated, generating information about the distribution of the attribute being measured. If many resamples are drawn and a 95% confidence interval is required, the resampled estimates are ordered from smallest to largest and the interval limits are such that 5% of estimates fall outwith the limits.

Chi-squared test (χ^2) A statistical test that can be used for homogeneity, randomness or goodness of fit. The test compares observed frequencies with expected frequencies derived from the **null hypothesis**. If observed frequencies differ significantly from those expected, the null hypothesis is rejected. The chi-squared test can be used for testing for significant changes in plant frequency data over time and for testing whether a dataset is distributed according to a probability distribution (e.g. normal, Poisson), i.e. as a **goodness-of-fit test**.

Cochran's test of linear trend   The standard **chi-squared test** gives the same result regardless of the order of the rows and columns. Cochran's test of linear trend (or Q-test) is more suitable for detecting trends across an ordered set of categories (e.g. years).

Coefficient of variation   The **standard deviation** divided by the **mean** (often multiplied by 100 and expressed as a percentage). This is useful for comparing variability between samples from populations with different means or units.

Confidence intervals   When a measurement, such as percentage cover of a species, is estimated from a sample, the confidence interval is a range of values within which we have some confidence the measurement for the whole population lies. A 95% confidence interval is such that if many samples were taken then we would expect 95% of the confidence intervals calculated from these to contain the population measurement. 95% is by far the most common level of confidence used.

Correlation   If two variables are correlated then one is related to the other. For example, soil moisture is correlated with soil organic matter content: a soil with a high organic matter content will also tend to have a high moisture content, and vice versa. Correlation can be positive or negative. Correlated variables are not **independent.** See also **correlation coefficient**.

Correlation coefficient   An index of the degree to which two variables are related, which can be tested for statistical significance. It varies between -1 (complete negative correlation) and $+1$ (complete positive correlation).

Degrees of freedom   A number used in many statistical tests that is based on the number of observations (n) in a sample and the number of estimated parameters. For example, if we are told that a sample has 5 observations and a mean of 50 and are asked to invent values for the observations, we can pick any four numbers, but the fifth number is fixed by the choice of the first four. The number of degrees of freedom is therefore $n - 1$, in this case 4. If the formula for estimating a parameter itself contains an estimate, a degree of freedom is lost. For

example, to estimate the population standard deviation, we first need an estimate of the mean, so the degrees of freedom are therefore $n - 1$.

Descriptive statistics   A numerical summary that concisely describes the properties of the observed frequency distribution (e.g. **mean** and **standard deviation**).

Distribution   The spread of observations of a variable over the range of measurement. Distributions are generally expressed in terms of the **probability** of a variable taking each value in its range or of being less than that value.

Errors, Type I and II   In statistical testing, a Type I error is the rejection of a **null hypothesis** when it is true. A Type II error is the acceptance of a null hypothesis when it is false.

Fisher's exact test   A useful alternative to the **chi-squared test** for assessing independence in 2×2 tables that have small expected values. The test calculates the exact probability that the observed table, or one showing a more extreme departure from independence, would arise by chance. An example would be presence–absence data collected on two occasions. Testing whether the proportion of presences has changed is equivalent to testing independence between time and the number of presences.

Friedman test   A **non-parametric test** that compares three or more paired samples.

Goodness-of-fit tests   Tests of hypotheses about frequency or probability distributions. An example is the **chi-squared test**, which examines the goodness of fit of our observed frequency distribution to the expected frequency according to our hypothesis. Goodness-of-fit tests can be used to test for randomness, or for conformation to a theoretical probability distribution. These tests can be used for continuous variables: in this case it is necessary to group classes together as a histogram, thus making a frequency distribution.

G-test   An alternative test to the **chi-squared test**, also known as the likelihood ratio test. The G-test supposedly has theoretical advantages over the chi-squared test. However, the chi-squared test is more commonly used.

Independent observations   Observations in which the value of one observation is not inherently affected by that of another.

Independent variables   Variables for which the value of one variable is not inherently affected by the value of another variable.

Kruskal–Wallis test   A **non-parametric test** for comparing the distributions of more than two unpaired samples.

Likelihood ratio test   See *G*-test.

Mann–Whitney test   A **non-parametric test** used to compare the distributions of two unpaired samples.

McNemar's test   A **chi-squared test** of symmetry used for paired samples in which the measurements are ordinal. A significant result indicates a greater change in one direction than in the other.

Mean   A measure of central tendency or of a typical value, calculated as the sum of a set of observations divided by the number of observations.

Median   The middle observation in a set of observations that have been ranked in magnitude. An alternative measure of central tendency.

Mode   The most common value in a set of observations. Another measure of central tendency, though rarely used.

Nominal variable   A measurement comprising a set of categories whose ordering is arbitrary. For example, habitat classifications are usually nominal as they have no natural ordering.

Non-parametric tests   Usually refers to tests based on ranks. Non-parametric tests are 'distribution-free', i.e. they do not require the same assumptions as **parametric tests**. They are usually less powerful than parametric tests, i.e. less likely to detect a real departure from the **null hypothesis**.

Null hypothesis   The basic starting hypothesis for a statistical test. For example, the null hypothesis may be that there is no difference between the populations from which samples have been drawn. This is rejected if the test produces a significant result.

Observation   A record (e.g. measurement of height, count of numbers) taken from a sample unit.

One-sided/two-sided test   A one-sided test tests whether a statistic is specifically larger or smaller than that given in the null hypothesis. A two-sided test merely tests whether the statistic is different from that given in the null hypothesis. In most cases a two-sided test is required, unless a one-sided hypothesis has been specified in advance of the survey.

Ordinal variable   A measurement comprising a set of ordered categories. For example, abundance of a species might be recorded as 'rare', 'occasional', 'frequent', etc.

Parametric tests   Statistical tests that involve the assumption that the data follow a particular distribution, usually normal. See also **non-parametric tests**.

Percentage relative precision   The difference between the **mean** of a sample and its 95% **confidence intervals**, expressed as a percentage of the estimate.

Percentiles   The values that divide a set of measurements into 100 equal parts. Thus the 25th percentile will be the value that 25% of measurements fall below. The 25th percentile is also known as the first **quartile**.

Population   Any collection of individual items or units that is the subject of investigation. The population is the total number of units, from which we usually take **samples**.

Precision   The closeness of the sample measurements to each other. An estimate is more precise if it has a smaller **standard deviation**.

Probability   A measurement of the likelihood of a certain outcome of an event taking place, measured on a scale from 0 (impossible) to 1 (inevitable). The sum of the individual probabilities for all possible outcomes of an event is equal to 1.

Probability distribution   A breakdown of the individual probabilities of all possible outcomes. Can be generated empirically (by measurement) or by a mathematical model (e.g. normal, binomial). If it can be shown that data agree well with a predicted probability distribution, we can make generalisations and predictions about the data. On the other hand, if collected data do not agree with a predicted distribution, we may have cause for rethinking our initial hypothesis.

Q-test   See **Cochran's test of linear trend**.

Quartiles   The values that divide a set of measurments into four equal parts. A quarter of measurments will be below the first quartile and three-quarters are below the third quartile. *see also* **Percentiles**.

Regression   Regression analysis produces an equation that links two (or more) variables, which can be used for predictions (i.e. for a given value of x, predict the value of y) or to examine the relationship between variables. If one variable is time, regression can be used to test for trends. Regression can be linear (a straight-line relationship) or non-linear (a relationship between two or more variables of a more complex form).

Sample   A subset of the units in a **population** that represents the population as a whole. If a sample is to be truly representative, the sample must be drawn randomly from the population.

Sample unit   An individual unit from a **sample**. A set of these forms a sample.

Standard deviation   A measure of the variability of data in terms of the difference of observations from the **mean** of the population (or sample) from which they are taken.

Standard error   The **standard deviation** of the sample **mean**. Calculated as the standard deviation divided by the square root of the sample size.

Statistical significance   Arbitrary thresholds of significance are set for the outcomes of statistical tests. A significance level of 5% means that the result is taken to be significant if there is only a 5% probability that the result occurred when the null hypothesis is true. This is commonly written as $P < 0.05$. See also **errors, Type I and II**.

t-test   A parametric statistical test used to compare the means of two samples; can be adapted for paired or unpaired data. Larger samples give results similar to those of the **z-test**.

Time-series analysis   A group of techniques for analysing fairly long time series. Can be used to examine cyclical patterns and correlation over time, and for predictive modelling.

Transformation   Transforming data by a mathematical function, for example to make a data set approximate a normal distribution more closely.

Tukey test   Test performed with **analysis of variance (ANOVA),** which, in the event of a significant result, establishes which samples are significantly different from each other.

Two-sided test   See **one-sided/two-sided test**.

Type I error, Type II error   See **errors, Type I and II**.

Variable   A characteristic of a population that differs from individual to individual (e.g. length, mass, height, cover, etc.).

Variance   The square of the **standard deviation**. Another measure of the variability of the data.

Wilcoxon signed rank test   A **non-parametric test** for comparing two samples of paired data.

z-test   A **parametric** test for comparing means of two large samples.

Index